War of Words, War of Stones

War of Words, War of Stones

Racial Thought and Violence in Colonial Zanzibar

Jonathon Glassman

Indiana University Press
Bloomington and Indianapolis

This book is a publication of

Indiana University Press
601 North Morton Street
Bloomington, Indiana 47404-3797 USA

iupress.indiana.edu

Telephone orders	800-842-6796
Fax orders	812-855-7931
Orders by e-mail	iuporder@indiana.edu

Portions of chapters 1, 3, and 4 have previously appeared in "Slower than a Massacre: The Multiple Sources of Racial Thought in Colonial Africa," *American Historical Review* 109, no. 3 (2004): 720–754, and "Sorting out the Tribes: The Creation of Racial Identities in Colonial Zanzibar's Newspaper Wars," *Journal of African History* 41, no. 3 (2000): 395–428.

Portions of chapter 7 have appeared in Derek Peterson, ed., *Abolitionism and Imperialism in Britain, Africa, and the Atlantic* (Ohio University Press, 2010).

⊖ The paper used in this publication meets the minimum requirements of the American National Standard for Information Sciences—Permanence of Paper for Printed Library Materials, ANSI Z39.48-1992.

Manufactured in the United States of America

Library of Congress Cataloging-in-Publication Data

Glassman, Jonathon.
    War of words, war of stones : racial thought and violence in colonial Zanzibar / Jonathon Glassman.
        p. cm.
    Includes bibliographical references and index.
    ISBN 978-0-253-35585-0 (cloth : alk. paper) — ISBN 978-0-253-22280-0 (pbk. : alk. paper) 1. Zanzibar—History—20th century. 2. Zanzibar—Ethnic relations—History. 3. Zanzibar—Race relations—History. 4. Violence—Tanzania—Zanzibar—History. I. Title.
    DT449.Z28.G53 2011
    305.8009678′1—dc22
                                                            2010034170

2 3 4 5   16 15 14 13 12

For James Kern

> *Papageno.* Mein Kind, was werden wir nun sprechen?
> *Pamina.* Die Wahrheit! Die Wahrheit,
> Wär' sie auch Verbrechen.

Swahili Psychology:

Hate: Hate is rarely violent; as a general rule the native is not capable of a deep enough feeling to enable him to hate thoroughly. He is very easy going and tolerant. Dislike is frequent, but I have never heard a native express hate for anyone.

W. H. Ingrams, *Zanzibar: Its History and Its People* (1931)

We liked to think of ourselves as a moderate and mild people. . . . Civilized, that's what we were. We liked to be described like that, and we described ourselves like that.

Abdulrazak Gurnah, *Admiring Silence* (1996)

Contents

Preface and Acknowledgments · ix

Note on Usage · xiii

PART 1. INTRODUCTION

1 Rethinking Race in the Colonial World · 3

2 The Creation of a Racial State · 23

PART 2. WAR OF WORDS

3 A Secular Intelligentsia and the Origins of Exclusionary
   Ethnic Nationalism · 75

4 Subaltern Intellectuals and the Rise of Racial Nationalism · 105

5 Politics and Civil Society during the Newspaper Wars · 147

PART 3. WAR OF STONES

6 Rumor, Race, and Crime · 179

7 Violence as Racial Discourse · 230

8 "June" as Chosen Trauma · 264

Conclusion and Epilogue: Remaking Race · 282

Glossary · 303

Notes · 305

List of References · 381

Index · 391

Preface and Acknowledgments

This book tells a story in which Africans' efforts to imagine a postcolonial political community resulted in racial violence and dehumanizing racial thought. Although the drama has a colonial setting and British rulers and educators play important supporting roles, its main protagonists are Africans, none of whom subscribed to the ideology of white supremacy. Thus it provides an opportunity to extend the comparative study of race beyond the Western world.

In telling this tale I court peculiar dangers, above all the risk of implying that things had to turn out as they did. All historians are familiar with the danger of hindsight. But in this instance the stakes are heightened by centuries-old intellectual traditions about how the world thinks about Africa, most prominently the myth that Africans have never created stable civil orders and are fated to suffer endless rounds of primal strife. For decades historians have striven to lay that myth to rest. Still, the danger remains that an exploration like this, especially when read in light of the unremittingly bleak coverage Africa receives in the Western media, might be misunderstood as suggesting the futility of all the continent's nation-building projects. The risks are particularly significant in my case, inasmuch as the bloodshed with which Zanzibar entered the postcolonial era has figured prominently in latter-day depictions of Africa as the heart of darkness. V. S. Naipaul opened his Conradian novel *A Bend in the River* by depicting the pogroms of Zanzibar's 1964 revolution as inevitable, a repetition of "the oldest law of the land." The widely screened "shockumentary" *Africa Addio* (also released under the title *Africa Blood and Guts*) used footage of Zanzibar's agony to illustrate much the same point, if with less subtlety. Like more recent commentators, the filmmakers chastised the colonial powers for abandoning Africa prematurely, before their wards had learned to repress their violent adolescent urges.[1]

The persistence of such myths has lent urgency to scholars' efforts to denaturalize African ethnic strife and restore it to the realm of history. The result, however, is a literature that can sometimes seem overly determined, exaggerating the role of colonial policy and of African elites' instrumental espousal of Western ideologies. In contrast, this book argues that the sources of racial thought must be sought in the continent's own intellectual histories. To the extent that imported concepts were significant, Africans' encounter with them took the form not of an embrace but of an entanglement, in which locally generated ideas were inextricably entwined. To explore this possibility—to look at the full range of influences from which African thinkers elaborated new and at times poisonous rhetorics of belonging—cannot be taken to imply a return to the old myths.

Nor do scholars' aversions to those myths and our rejection of colonialism's civilizing claims absolve us of the responsibility of considering the extent to which the continent's recurrent political difficulties have been shaped by the choices made by African political actors, including the nationalists who inherited power from colonial rulers. Over two decades ago, Crawford Young urged his colleagues not to overlook the possibility that African nationalisms are no less capable than their Western counterparts of generating "bestial elements" that might yield chauvinism and aggression.[2] Yet despite much excellent scholarship since then, and despite the withering critiques that African public intellectuals have aimed at postcolonial political culture, many in the academy are still reluctant to take up such subjects.[3] Foreign historians have shown particular reluctance to write critically of the political and intellectual movement that led the way in asserting Africans' humanity during the colonial era. That attitude was perhaps once understandable. But is such defensiveness still necessary or useful a half-century after colonialism's end?

Foreign scholars' avoidance of such themes takes added significance when it affects how they treat a story, like this one, that remains alive in African politics. In ways sketched out in the concluding chapter, political speakers in Zanzibar today constantly raise analogies to the colonial past to justify themselves or vilify their rivals. Of course, the historical narratives they propagate are tendentious in the extreme. They are invariably told as melodramas, with heroes, villains, and victims. In contrast, the story I tell is one of tragedy: of missed opportunities, wrong turns, constrained choices. Because I regard none of the actors as flawless champions or simple villains, many politically engaged Zanzibaris will find much to offend them. That is a peril I must face. To paraphrase one of my teachers, writing on a different part of the continent, the alternative would be to allow myself to underwrite the new myths that have burgeoned as part of postcolonial Zanzibar's ongoing political battles.[4]

The polarization of Zanzibaris' historical memories explains why I have chosen to rely on written sources. It has become almost an unthinking fashion for historians of colonial Africa to privilege oral sources and to question any account that omits them. We must remember, however, that oral accounts are *understandings* of the past, not records of them; even personal memories are tidied up to fit the narrator's latter-day perceptions of himself and the community to which he presently feels attached, or, as the novelist Abdulrazak Gurnah puts it, to craft a history closer to the narrator's own choice than the one he has been lumbered with.[5] The notorious difficulties of using oral history are especially acute where memories have been shaped by impassioned politics. I have found it useful, then, to set aside ex post facto oral accounts and concentrate instead on the words of Zanzibari historical actors as they were recorded at the time, including in their own writings. That was the surest way, I felt, to get around the orthodoxies that this study is devoted to challenging. It is also why the substantive part of this book ends on the eve of the 1964 revolution, for that is when the rich vein of literary and archival sources runs out. Including the revolution might have added immeasurably to Part 3's analysis of racial violence. But it would have involved an additional and substantially different research project, which I leave to others.

Despite this basis in written sources, I have benefitted much from years of conversations with Zanzibari interlocutors, who were crucial in challenging my assumptions, multiplying my perspectives, and shaping the questions I asked. My gratitude for their patience and forbearance is only deepened by my awareness that few if any will agree with all I have written. That awareness prompts me to place particular stress on the standard caveat against holding any of them responsible for my views. I cannot name them all, but particular thanks must go to Abdurahman Ali, Abdurahman M. Juma, Aisha Darwish, Ali Juma Mwinyi, Ali Omar Juma "Lumumba," Haji Gura, Mariamu Hamdani, Maalim Idris Muhammad, Kasid bin Chum, Mahmoud Hemed Jabir, Othman Bapa Mzee Mkadam, Salum Said, Salum Mzee, Silima Hassan, Suleiman Ali Nassor al-Kindy, and Tatu Pazi Mwinyi. I incurred an inordinate debt to the late Said Baes, who not only taught me much about history but also demonstrated how a spirit animated by ideals of humane social democracy can survive repeated defeat without yielding to chauvinism or despair.

Ali Abdalla and Khamis S. Khamis rendered invaluable assistance at crucial stages of the research. I am grateful to Jan-Georg Deutsch and Pier Larson, who read and commented on the full draft. Thanks also to Frederick Cooper, John Lonsdale, and Thomas Spear for their constructive critiques of substantial portions of this work. Like all historians of Zanzibar, I have benefited enormously from the learning and generosity of Professor Abdul Sheriff. Kate Babbitt edited the manuscript with tremendous care and skill. Others who have given much-appreciated guidance, encouragement, and criticism over the years include Ralph Austen, Sandra Barnes, Nicola Beisel, Florence Bernault, Paul Bjerk, James R. Brennan, G. Thomas Burgess, Cati Coe, Clifton Crais, Laura Fair, Steven Feierman, Jane Guyer, Bernard Haykel, Laura Hein, Allen Howard, John Hunwick, Neil Kodesh, Michael Lofchie, Nancy Maclean, Greg Mann, Juli McGruder, R. S. O'Fahey, Susan Pederson, Don Petterson, Philip Sadgrove, Heike Schmidt, David Schoenbrun, Kearsley Stewart, James Sweet, Farouk Topan, and Luise White. Chieko Maene helped with the maps. Portions of this study received bracing critiques from participants in the Johns Hopkins University History Seminar, the University of Chicago African Studies Workshop, the African history seminar of the School of Oriental and African Studies, Emory University's Seminar in African History and Culture, and the Wisconsin-Northwestern joint workshop on African history.

Research and writing were made possible by a Fulbright Senior Research Grant and fellowships from the Social Science Research Council and American Council of Learned Societies, the Institute for Advanced Study, and the John Simon Guggenheim Memorial Foundation. Teaching release was provided by Northwestern University's Alice Kaplan Institute for the Humanities. Thanks also to Hamad H. Omar and the staff of the Zanzibar National Archives and to David Easterbrook and the staff of Northwestern's Melville J. Herskovits Africana Library.

Figures 4.2 and 5.1 are photographs from F. D. Ommanney, *Isle of Cloves.* The photograph of Darajani by C. S. DeJoux, figure 2.3, is reproduced courtesy of the Melville J. Herskovits Library of African Studies, Northwestern University. All other photographs are from the Winterton Collection of East African Photographs, courtesy of the Melville J. Herskovits Library of African Studies, Northwestern University.

This book would have been unimaginable without the friendship and generosity of Ali Aboud Mzee and Khadija binti Issa, who made me part of their family. The caveat mentioned above, against associating my views of history with theirs, cannot be stressed enough. Yet to them must be attributed a central truth that I learned in Zanzibar: that faith in God and the Holy Koran can be a path toward a rigorous understanding of the oneness of humankind. My mother, Vera L. Glassman, was a constant source of support. James M. Kern contributed to virtually every page of this book and his love and humor sustained me throughout its long gestation. My greatest debt, in labor and in life, is to him.

Note on Usage

In this book, Swahili nouns that refer to classes of people (ethnic or occupational) will retain their singular *m-* and plural *wa-* prefixes: thus, *Mmanga,* a Manga person; *Wamanga,* Manga persons. "Unguja" is used to denote the island sometimes called "Zanzibar"; the latter is used only to denote the polity as a whole.

Swahili-speakers conventionally address one another by their "first" names, not the patronym, respect being indicated by use of a title: Bi Khadija, Shaykh Ali, Profesa Jonathon. But historical narrative presents peculiar difficulties, especially when an individual became well known by a patronym (Muhsin, Karume) or preferred to sign letters and official documents using the clan name (M. A. el-Haj). I have been flexible in choosing which form to use, informing my choice by my feeling for how a particular individual was commonly known or preferred to be known.

Translations are my own, except where noted.

PART 1

Introduction

Mvunja nchi mwana nchi.
The destroyer of the country is the child of the country.
—SWAHILI PROVERB

1

Rethinking Race in the Colonial World

The Sultanate of Zanzibar, a pair of islands twenty miles off the coast of East Africa, has captured the attention of the Western world at two moments in the modern era, both times as an emblem of the battle between civilization and barbarism. The first was in the third quarter of the nineteenth century, when David Livingstone and other ideologues of missionary Christianity made it famous as the seat of what they called the "Arab slave trade" that was then disrupting many parts of the continental mainland. Their crusade to end the slave trade and replace it with civilization and "legitimate commerce" culminated in colonial conquest at the century's end, undertaken in the name of advancing moral and social progress. The second moment, far briefer, seemed at the time a coda to the story of abolition. On the night of 11–12 January 1964, one month after Zanzibar had gained its independence from British rule, the Arab sultan and his elected constitutional government were overthrown by forces claiming to represent the islands' African racial majority and to be fighting to redress the centuries-old injustice of Arab rule. The coup was accompanied by pogroms that took the lives of thousands of the islands' Arab minority.

Contemporary observers regarded the latter events as a grave setback to the orderly processes of the preceding decade, in which British administrators and Zanzibari politicians had sought to nurture a civic nationalism that would take the place of colonial rule. Similar setbacks would occur elsewhere in the former colonial world, including in Nigeria, Rwanda, Sudan, and South Asia. In the language of social scientists, nationalists had aimed to build a "civil order" in which "the gross actualities of blood, race, language, locality, religion, or tradition" would be subordinated. But those "primordial sentiments" proved difficult to avoid, rooted as they were in the region's deepest histories.[1] In the case of Zanzibar, observers across the political and ideological spectrum agreed that the violence was the product of over two millennia of tension created by Arab racial domination. The African-American *Chicago Defender,* a venerable champion of African nationalism, explained that the revolution was an "Arab-African explosion which had its beginning in more than 25 centuries [of] Arab influence and unresolved racial conflicts," including the never-forgotten experience of the "Arab slave trade."[2] Mainstream pundits and policy makers, including those less sympathetic to African nationalism, issued similar pronouncements.[3] The widespread and apparently spontaneous pogroms in Zanzibar seemed powerful evidence of such primordialist interpretations.

These were not simply the views of foreigners. Only three years earlier, spokesmen for the party that would take power after the 1964 revolution, the Afro-Shirazi Party (ASP), had apologized for a similar outbreak of racial violence in much the same way: as a "spontaneous" outburst of popular anger that had sprung from centuries of racial oppression. The ASP was a party of explicit racial nationalism, and the elite Arabs who led its main rival, the multiracial Zanzibar National Party (ZNP), did not accept its narrative of Arab oppression. Nevertheless, until quite late the ZNP leaders had shared a similar historical vision of the deep-seated nature of Zanzibar's racial divisions. Indeed, the far-fetched idea that Arabs had been living in East Africa as a distinct racial elite for over two millennia had long been propagated by the Arab nationalists themselves. In short, primordialist explanations of Zanzibar's racial divisions had been ubiquitous among the islands' political thinkers.

Yet this model of deeply rooted divisions between Arab and African—boundaries that were clear cut, fixed, and slow to change—sat poorly with the most common representations of this part of East Africa. Zanzibar is part of the Swahili coast, a name given to the language and culture practiced along almost 2,000 miles of the Indian Ocean littoral. Although the language belongs to the Bantu linguistic family, it contains many Arabic loanwords and the culture is often represented as a synthesis of African and Middle Eastern elements. More pertinently, Swahili society has often been portrayed—by Western scholars, colonial administrators, and Swahili intellectuals themselves—

as the epitome of ethnic fluidity and racial indeterminacy. Swahili-speakers simultaneously perceive themselves as Arab, Persian, and/or Indian as well as African; the specific emphasis an individual gives to his or her racial identity can shift according to situation and generation. In the 1950s, the anthropologist A. H. J. Prins wrote that Swahili-speakers rarely thought of themselves as belonging exclusively to any one racial category (a person was "never Swahili and nothing else") and observed that individuals constantly crossed and straddled boundaries.[4] More recently, the literary scholars Alamin Mazrui and Ibrahim Noor Shariff have described Swahili "identity paradigms" as "assimilative and flexible," based on "a concept of belonging that is truly liberal." Such identity paradigms were quintessentially African, they write, and stand in contrast to the fixed, rigid identity paradigms characteristic of Western thought.[5] Throughout the colonial era, in fact, indigenous and British elites represented Zanzibar as islands of racial harmony. To a large extent this representation was a myth, informed by overlapping sets of paternalist ideals and belied by many instances of tension that punctuated the sultanate's public life. Yet it contained a kernel of truth, for Zanzibaris had not, as a rule, organized themselves into ethnically discrete communities, and, despite occasional tension, few thought of ethnic divisions with the kind of exclusionary rigidity that informed the pogroms of the early 1960s.

So primordialist explanations of Zanzibar's racial divisions are easily discounted—and, indeed, although simple primordialism is still commonplace among journalists, few serious scholars accept it anymore. But that leaves the puzzle of explaining how ethnic identities had become so polarized by midcentury. Within weeks of the 1964 revolution, the leaders of the ASP, in a sudden change of their primordialist views, began offering an answer that would soon become standard among scholars and political thinkers in many parts of the continent. In a speech in March, Abeid Amani Karume, the founding president of the Revolutionary Government, announced the prohibition of ethnic associations (*klabu za ukabila*). Imperialists had created such associations "in order to divide people," he explained, and to thus strengthen the rule of their puppets in the old Arab regime. Later that year Karume returned to the theme, telling audiences that ethnic divisions, in particular those between Arabs and Africans, had been introduced by British colonialism.[6]

In the second of these speeches, Karume went on to focus on the British use of history as a tool to divide their colonial subjects; this was one of his earliest salvos in a campaign that culminated in a ban on teaching history in the islands' schools.[7] Karume shrewdly understood that forgetting history would be useful not only for holding together a society so recently torn apart by racial violence but also for obscuring his own role in fostering those tensions: throughout the 1950s and early 1960s, he and his party propagated fiery rhetoric, including inflammatory historical narratives that urged people to identify their loyalties and enmities on the basis of ancestry and skin color. Indeed, Karume owed his political prominence to his longtime leadership of one of the ethnic associations, the African Association, that supposedly had been invented by the British.

Similar contradictions can be found in the utterances of the elite ZNP nationalists from whom Karume seized power. This intelligentsia had long advocated a civil order based on what they thought of as the islands' distinctive Arab-centered history, a history they portrayed as civilized, multiracial, and inclusive. Their vision was deeply chauvinist, however: throughout the 1950s and 1960s, they repeatedly warned that Zanzibari civilization was endangered by the barbarism of the mainland immigrants and their descendants who allegedly formed the bulk of Karume's party. Yet at the same time they blamed all divisive language solely on the ASP, which they claimed had been mentored and even created by the colonial authorities. They ridiculed ASP loyalists as British lackeys and *wamisheni*: people of the missionaries, from whose abolitionism they had supposedly imbibed their anti-Arab sentiments. (In fact, virtually all Zanzibaris were Muslim.) In his 1997 memoirs, Ali Muhsin al-Barwani, the de facto leader of the government that was overthrown in January 1964, reproduces the comforting illusion that Zanzibar was once an oasis of multiracialism in which most people were "mixtures of mixtures." "The only snag was the deliberate infusion of alien notions calculated to cause confusion and hatred." And yet, for most of his life Muhsin had never allowed for any "mixture" in his own proud self-identity as an Arab. The very memoirs from which this passage is quoted, to say nothing of Muhsin's previous six decades of political journalism, are imbued with an overt disdain for mainland Africans.[8]

For many readers, such disingenuousness will be remarkable only as a particularly bold example of Ernest Renan's famous statement about the need for nation-builders to get their history wrong.[9] But it takes on added significance for students of the colonial and postcolonial world, insofar as the opportunistic perspectives of such politicians have substantially shaped the analysis of many professional scholars. This book will argue that the rise of racial thought in colonial Zanzibar was largely the work of indigenous intellectuals, including those at the forefront of mainstream nationalism, who in their debates and disputations created a locally hegemonic discourse of racial difference. Rather than obstacles standing in the way of nationalists' efforts to build a civil order, in other words, the attachments of blood and tradition had been created in part by the nationalists' own efforts. Yet much of the literature on the colonial world assumes, in contrast, that ethnic conflict arose more or less automatically from social structures that had been bolstered or even created outright by colonial rule: its emphasis is not on indigenous thinkers but on European policy makers who defined and divided their subjects by race and ethnicity.[10] Historians who are cognizant of indigenous racial thinkers usually portray them as marginal figures, the tools of colonial mentors. The result is that such thinkers— especially those who incited dehumanizing racial violence—are treated as aberrations, as "subnationalist" demagogues isolated from the mainstream of anticolonial nationalist thought.

Such interpretations obviously have been shaped by the nationalist paradigm that has achieved hegemony in the postcolonial world in the past generation, an aspect of the literature to which I will return.[11] But there are, I believe, deeper reasons for such an emphasis, reasons that transcend the postcolonial moment and pertain to the broader study of race, ethnicity, and nationalism. Leaving aside questions of historical method—including an ingrained propensity in African studies to privilege oral sources for their "authenticity," thus allowing nationalists to shape the historical record with their own post facto self-representations—the central analytic flaw of many of these studies consists of what Ann Stoler has called the "scholarly quest for origins," the quest for the moment of "original sin" when "the die of race was cast." Such quests assume what Stoler's colleague Loïc Wacquant describes as "the logic of the trial," in which investigators seek to name "victims and culprits" rather than understand complex historical processes.[12] In the Zanzibar case the figures made to stand trial are typically the racial nationalists of the ASP. This is understandable, given that their virulent race-baiting informed most of the pogroms, which victimized Arabs and were perpetrated by ASP loyalists. But the racial thinking from which ASP demagoguery emerged and that made so many islanders susceptible to its seductions was fairly pervasive and as such is unlikely to be traced to a single source.

A pointed illustration of the perils of searching for a single origin of racial thought can be found in the literature on Rwanda, a case that parallels Zanzibar's in many ways.[13] In a recent synthesis, Mahmood Mamdani has observed that notions of Hutu and Tutsi became racialized during the colonial era. This concept of *racialization* is indispensable to an historical understanding of race, for it prompts us to ask how diverse forms of ethnic and national thought can become invested with racial meanings.[14] Yet like many authors, Mamdani traces the racialization process back to a single source, the actions of the colonial state. The result is a view of Rwandan intellectual history in which Europeans are the only actors, inventing and imposing identities as prompted by administrative needs.[15]

The literature on the colonial world, and especially on Africa, is rife with such interpretations. To understand why, we must confront a cluster of misapprehensions about the nature of race and associated forms of ethnic and national thought, some specific to the study of Africa, others more general. Only then can we craft a strategy that does not underestimate the role African thinkers played in the construction of race.

II

The first of these misapprehensions is a lingering tendency toward what Robert Miles calls the "conceptual inflation" of race into an element of social structure; as we shall see, this is especially pronounced in studies of the colonial world. Many sociologists now reject that tendency, preferring instead to understand race as a mode of thought—in constant interplay with social structures and political processes, to be sure, but best approached as a topic of intellectual history. This understanding stresses that the history of race has involved the "production and reproduction of meanings"—specifically, meanings concerning particular ways of categorizing humanity.[16] The history of race, then, like the history of ethnicity and nationhood (below I will consider the lack of clear distinctions among them), is a story of how particular ways of categorizing humanity became important modes of organizing social and political action at particular times and places—and, as Rogers Brubaker emphasizes, how they declined in importance at others.[17]

However, most studies of the history of racial thought limit themselves by regarding their subject only as a specific corpus of ideas: a "doctrine" that categorizes and ranks humanity in terms of biology. Racial thought is thus usually approached as a school of Western science ("raciology," as it once was called) that realized its classic distillations in nineteenth-century Europe.[18] To be sure, some authors have recognized the limits of such a view, since even at the height of raciology's academic respectability, few *pogromschiki* or lynch mob members would have been conversant with the writings of Gobineau or Houston Stewart Chamberlain.[19] More pointedly, over the past twenty years a substantial literature has emphasized the postscientific forms that have flourished in the wake of raciology's postwar academic demise. These "new racisms" demonstrate that racial thought need not be manifested in a scientific idiom or even entail a ranking of racial categories. There is now a "racism without races," writes Etienne Balibar, "a racism whose dominant theme is not biological heredity but the insurmountability of cultural differences."[20]

Yet even this literature on the "new racism" portrays it as a holdover from classic raciology or, more precisely, as a deteriorated version of that ideology, which once existed in a pristine, originary state.[21] Such literature is mistaken in its depiction of the supposed newness of culturalist racial thought. It is also mistaken in its depiction of the older forms, which in fact were neither invariably hierarchical[22] nor invariably built around a core of biological theory. Past social practices that are universally accepted as classic examples of "racism," including colonial racisms, were informed by a wide variety of ideologies, many of which had little to do with racial science. Far more influential than raciology, for example, was the anthropological concept of clearly bounded "cultural monads," a concept directly connected with contemporary culturalist thought. As Balibar recognizes, the idea of "racism without races" is far from revolutionary; there is little new about the "new racism."[23]

In succumbing to the search for origins, scholars overlook a central theme of the historical literature on racial science, which charts the latter's own varied and multiple sources, including many that were neither "racial" (in the conventional sense) nor scientific. Perhaps most significant of these sources was the concept of "barbarism" and its foil, "civilization," from which modern race thinkers inherited the project of comparing all humanity according to a single, universal standard.[24] It should be axiomatic that the history of a phenomenon cannot be found solely by looking for its earliest manifestations as it is defined a priori; to paraphrase Nietzsche, in defining a phenomenon we deny it a history.[25] Many scholars nevertheless insist on an absolute divide between racial thought and the concepts that contributed to it and search doggedly for the precise moment that race emerged from (for example) the discourse of barbarism. As Stoler archly observes, they come up with widely divergent dates.[26]

One of the implications for the study of the colonial world should be clear. If "race" is assumed to arise solely from scientific doctrines, then its presence in the non-Western world must be traced solely to the West. And that, in fact, has become a standard narrative. Building on a set of functionalist assumptions often associated with Immanuel Wallerstein, authors describe how Western expansion called racial thought into being as a way of structuring the worldwide division of labor between the subservient "periphery" and the ruling "core."

In tying race so mechanistically to the structures of global capitalism, such analyses remove it from the realm of intellectual history. The result is the kind of conceptual inflation Miles warns against; several authors, in fact, explicitly insist that race can be defined only in terms of the "inequalities . . . inherent in a social structure" of Western conquest.[27] Again, such explanations are undermined by a historical literature on the multiple sources of Western racial thought, sources that included, for example, seminal debates about *European* difference.[28] Still, despite disagreements concerning the precise relationship between imperial expansion and the rise of racial thought, there is wide consensus that race was invented in the West and carried to the rest of the world in the toolbox of colonial rulers.

A better approach to the comparative history of race would abandon the fixation on scientific doctrines and instead recognize racial thought as a shifting field of discourse: a general set of assumptions that humankind is divided among constituent categories, each of which is distinguished by inherited traits and characteristics. Such a move brings several advantages. For one, it becomes clear that *racism*, a belief that racial qualities can be ranked according to moral status and other criteria, is but one possible form of *racial thought*.[29] Few of my readers are likely to endorse racist ideas, either in the form of an absolute ranking of the qualities of different racial groups or even in the seemingly more benign form of recognizing a greater moral obligation to members of one's "own" race over others.[30] Yet we all are accustomed to distinguishing between racial groups, even if the more critical among us are aware that science has decisively rejected any biological basis for racial boundaries. These general habits of thought are historical products no less than are more precise ideologies of white supremacy or racial separatism. In contrast, studies that conflate racial thought and racism and concentrate only on the genesis of the latter will tend to ignore the ways that racial thought itself was historically constructed. Such studies will thus imply that racial categories are natural givens.

The approach advocated here, then, begins with the recognition that raciology and other Western racisms are historically specific manifestations of a much broader trend in Western thought—and in human thought generally. Relatively few of the intellectual currents that contributed to raciology were peculiar to the West: drawing boundaries between peoples or ethnicities and even ranking them according to universalizing registers of inferiority and superiority have been far from unusual in world-historical terms. Concepts convergent with the ideal of civilization,[31] ostensibly inclusive yet contributing to hierarchical beliefs and practices that look uncomfortably like "racism," have occurred in many non-Western intellectual traditions, including those of the Swahili coast.[32] Indeed, Igor Kopytoff has argued that discourses of civilization and barbarism—including tropes marking barbarians as physically different—have been so common in sub-Saharan oral traditions that one might almost speak of them of as part of a continent-wide political culture.[33]

Still, there's a common assumption throughout the literature that race can be fundamentally distinguished from other ways of categorizing difference, such as ethnicity or xenophobia, by the central conceit that cultural identities (and hence cultural boundaries) are fixed in the body or the "blood." (A narrower understanding of "race" as a form of thought that categorizes humanity according to objectively existing somatic traits such as skin color is historically and conceptually untenable.)[34] The ubiquity of this distinction is surprising, since it is of recent vintage: it came into its own only after World War II, as social scientists strove to isolate raciology, recently discredited by the Nazis, from more general concepts of ethnic and national difference. "Ethnicity," in fact, was something of a neologism.[35] Yet the distinction is misleading, for it obscures the fact that all these modes of thought build on the same two core elements. First is the assumption that humanity consists of a discontinuous series of authentic cultural wholes, each internally homogeneous, the creation and property of a distinct "people." Brubaker, with admirable directness, calls this assumption "groupness."[36] Second is the metaphor of descent; that is, the general idea that the peoples who are the guardians of these discrete cultures are somehow linked by consanguinity. Such "blood ties" are imagined with greater or lesser degrees of vagueness. Language we call "race" places more explicit emphasis on the metaphor of descent—or, indeed, on the conviction that the "blood relationship" is more than mere metaphor[37]—than does language we call "ethnicity." The distinction between "race" and "ethnicity," then, is one of degree, not kind, and rather than regard them as qualitatively distinct, it is more useful to recognize them as modes of thought that fall toward opposing ends of a single continuum, the "aura of descent" hovering around them all.[38]

I do not mean to deny the usefulness in historical analysis of distinguishing *descriptively* between doctrines or political ideologies that are based on explicitly racial concepts and those based on other kinds of ethnic criteria. (So, for example, contrary to the claims of neoconservative critics, one must acknowledge the historical specificity of white supremacy and the unique forms of oppression it has produced.)[39] But it should be recognized that at any particular historical juncture all such doctrines are part of a common discourse of difference that categorizes humanity via metaphors of descent. The "family resemblance"[40] among them must be grasped if we are to understand how virtually any form of ethnic thought carries implications that can be elaborated in terms of qualities fixed in the "blood." Such elaboration—the process of racialization—is rarely the work of a unified cadre inspired by a single coherent doctrine. Rather, it emerges from the debates of a diverse range of intellectuals drawing on multiple and overlapping sources, united only by the general assumptions of racial/ethnic discourse.

Nationalism has proven no less susceptible to racialization than any other form of ethnic thought—despite the assumptions of an earlier generation of social scientists who saw an inherent difference between the civic character of the nation and the primordial character of other group attachments. We might define nationalism as any political philosophy based on the assumption that each of the mutually exclusive ethnic groups into which humanity is presumably divided ought "naturally" to control its own state.[41] By the mid-twentieth century, the politics of the nation-state had become a global "categorical order," a set of concepts taken for granted by leading political thinkers throughout the colonial world and a central element of what was commonly accepted as the norms of civilized "modernity."[42] This is not to say that national thought was taken for granted automatically or at all levels of colonial society.[43] Nor did a common discourse of nationalism necessarily lead to unity. Nations have never been defined by any single set of criteria,[44] and conflicts have always been rife among nationalist ideologues over who, precisely, belongs to the national community. It has become a truism that nations are defined as much by exclusion as inclusion; that is, in terms of who does *not* belong. When such exclusionary rhetoric is considered alongside the genealogical metaphors that underlie all ethnic discourse, one can understand how virtually any form of national thought—including, as we shall see, thought based on an ostensibly inclusive, universalizing language of civilization—might be interpreted in ways that denigrate certain categories of people by dint of their descent.[45]

III

The misconceptions I have been highlighting are especially common in the literature on Africa, much of which continues to approach ethnicity, race, and nation as analytically distinct. There is a tendency to regard only the last of these as the product of ideologies consciously crafted by African thinkers. This tendency is compounded by a pair of narrow a priori definitions of nationalism, which in turn further accentuate the illusion that nationalism was conceptually distinct from other ways of imagining political communities. The first of these defines nationalism as necessarily accepting the boundaries of the colonial state as circumscribing an inviolable national unit: "nation-statism," Basil Davidson calls it. The second defines nationalism as a political philosophy that stands in necessary and unwavering opposition to colonial rule.[46] The uncritical acceptance of such definitions produces narratives of nationalism that elide political thinkers who were willing to accommodate themselves to the colonial regime and/or who imagined political units that were larger or smaller than the colonial state.[47] The latter, of course, are castigated as "tribalists" or "subnationalists," as enemies of "true" nationalism and by that very fact allies of the colonial rulers. All of this encourages the illusion that a firm boundary exists between nationalism—defined as anticolonial nation-statism, elaborated by civic-minded, forward-thinking patriots—and all other forms of ethnicity or "groupness."

To be sure, students of African nationalism commonly recognize the important role played by propagators of pan-Africanist racial thought. In East Africa, as throughout what came to be defined as the African diaspora, pan-Africanism had been a major force in advancing a discourse of racial solidarity.[48] In this regard, the pan-Africanist project was aided by colonial administrators and educators, for whom racial identification was a form of "modernity" to be encouraged among colonial subjects.[49] But like other kinds of nationalists, the region's leading pan-Africanists eventually convinced themselves that the racial community they were doing so much to imagine into existence was in fact immanent in the order of things; that their intellectual labors (and those of their forebears) had not created it but had simply revealed its existence for the edification of their less educated compatriots. By the close of the colonial era, this perspective had become commonplace among scholars as well as among political actors. And so pan-Africanism is now generally assumed to have built on racial solidarities that themselves had arisen automatically: either from the natural givens of continentally defined racial distinctions or as the inevitable outgrowth of the distinctions enforced by colonial racial dictatorships. In either case (usually both are involved), pan-Africanists, like successful nationalists of any stripe, succeeded in covering their tracks and the role that pan-Africanism played in fostering racial solidarities in the first place was elided. As a result, the notion of an African racial category is often taken as a given for which no historical explanation (or, at most, only an explanation of the most rudimentary kind) is needed.

But if unifying sentiments of racial identity are sometimes presented as the product of heroic national romance and self-discovery,[50] that is by no means the case with group identities that are seen to fragment the nation-state. Such forms of ethnicity are often inflated into "sociological facts," nowadays usually explained instrumentally. Some scholars, as we have seen, dismiss ethnic thought as little more than a European invention, a form of false consciousness accepted by Africans in order to secure access to resources controlled by missionaries and the colonial state.[51] Mazrui and Shariff are among those who advance such a view: the desire to divide and rule prompted British rulers and missionaries to supplant Swahili-speakers' older, supple identity paradigms with fetishized notions of racial purity. The culmination of this "colonially induced" process, they write, were the pogroms of 1960s Zanzibar.[52] Other scholars, more persuasively, emphasize the role of African intellectuals, who cast ethnic appeals in ways calculated to resonate with concerns that had been shaped by labor migration, clientelism, and other processes associated with the construction of the colonial political economy. Yet even these authors assume that ethnic rhetoric can be traced to European origins. Hence, as Leroy Vail argues in an often-cited overview, African intellectuals should be seen as "brokers." More fundamentally, these authors stress that the power of ethnic appeals can be explained only in terms of material need. In downplaying all other factors, which Vail dismisses as "non-rational" and therefore irrelevant, they minimize the impact of the content of ethnic thought, even while focusing on the intellectuals themselves.[53]

Despite their shortcomings, these softer versions of instrumentalism (many of its adherents prefer the label "constructivism") marked a signal advance in African ethnic studies, insofar as they historicized modes of thought commonly assumed to be fixed and timeless.[54] In part, the widespread embrace of instrumentalism constituted a response to the old canard, usually associated with Hegel, that Africans were immune to history, trapped in "gyrations" of unchanging behavior, irrational and rooted in tradition; the epitome of such behaviors was a supposedly ageless tribalism.[55] Given the prevalence of such ideas, it is understandable that students of African politics and history—especially those sympathetic to Africans' efforts to build strong nation-states capable of escaping colonial and neocolonial domination—would automatically shy away from anything that smacked of old-style primordialism, almost as if their position were an article of faith.

But in positioning themselves in steadfast opposition to any interpretation that focuses on the "non-rational" power of ethnic ideologies, the constructivists unnecessarily limit the power of their analysis. In contrast, there is a growing social science literature that focuses *precisely* on the "primordial" nature of ethnonational discourses: that focuses, that is, on those elements that encourage people to regard ethnic bonds as fixed, primordial, and "beyond reason."[56] Many of these scholars are anthropologists or social psychologists who are interested chiefly in how the rhetoric of primordialism works to enhance the power of ethnic appeals, including how it resonates with everyday habitus. Yet despite the caricature of their views sometimes advanced by their constructivist critics, few of these "neo-primordialist" scholars (indeed, few of the old-school primordialists) would deny the historicity of such discourses.[57] On the contrary, their concerns suggest useful lines of inquiry for historians: How were such modes of thought created over time, and by whom? What locally inherited intellectual sources did they draw on that made these discourses so powerfully evocative to ordinary people? And what were the specific processes by which these discourses came to be accepted by significant numbers of people in particular times and places? In short, the neo-primordialists raise questions that are ideally suited for constructivist historical analysis; the two positions "need not be mutually exclusive."[58]

The failure of many of the self-described instrumentalists or constructivists to consider such matters derives in part, ironically enough, from what they hold in common with the more conventional old-school primordialists: an unexamined acceptance of the categorical divide between nationalism and ethnicity. What instrumentalists and conventional primordialists alike seek to explain are the forces that divide the civic nation-state, as if the emergence of the latter, as the natural order of historical progress, requires no explanation at all.[59] And all this is part of a more general failure to break fully with the nationalist paradigm that has shaped African historical studies for the past forty years. Literatures on ethnonational politics in other parts of the world have examined how intellectuals crafted locally compelling languages of belonging and exclusion whose affective power often had little to do with the utilitarian logics that Vail and his colleagues describe as "rational." In contrast, the Africa literature has largely treated political thinkers "empirically," describing their roles in creating and leading parties and associations but reducing the content of their thought to the formulae of a nationalist calculus: "nationalism" as inherently inclusive and liberating, "ethnicity" as the divisive legacy of colonialism. The result is a history written from the perspective of the nationalists who took control of the state from the departing colonial powers.[60]

Many of these shortcomings have been addressed over the past two decades in a literature that engages seriously with the thought of African intellectuals who debated the public good in ethnically specific discourses that were

once dismissed as "tribalism" or "sub-nationalism."[61] Rather than force ethnic thought onto a procrustean bed of utilitarian "rationality," these authors
reconstruct alternative rationalities that did not necessarily rest on logics of
straightforward material advantage. By tracing the deep histories of these discourses, they demonstrate the limits of colonial-era "invention."[62] They also
demonstrate that ethnic thought had multiple sources, not just the material demands created by the colonial state as interpreted by instrumentally minded
political entrepreneurs, let alone the ideological constructs imposed by colonial rulers. Thus they avoid what Nancy Hunt calls the cliché of the colonial
encounter, the nationalist paradigm that interprets all aspects of modern African history in terms of a transcendent tension between colonizer and colo-
nized.[63]

But studies of the racialization of African ethnonationalist thought, and
especially of the exterminationist violence it has at times engendered in places
such as Rwanda, Sudan, and Zanzibar, have proven stubbornly resistant to
this kind of analysis. There are two reasons for this, I believe. One is the common assumption that race is a Western doctrine. Most studies of African ethnic politics deal with vertical or regional divisions that were once commonly
described as tribes: ethnic categories that are imagined to exist side by side,
each an "incipient whole society." But genocide and other forms of exterminationist violence tend to be accompanied by rhetoric in which ethnic categories are imagined as hierarchical strata, linked to one another in relationships that structure the entire society; the violence itself is prompted either
by the subordinate group's attempt to throw off those it sees as its oppressors
or the dominant group's attempt to preempt such a revolt.[64] Such situations of
"ranked" ethnic stratification parallel the Western experience of race; in fact,
there is a sociological literature that distinguishes "race" from "ethnicity" precisely by the presence of such ranking.[65] A recognition of those parallels is
what has prompted several authors to write of "race" when describing clashes
like those in Rwanda or Zanzibar. But combined with the persistent assumption of an originary distinction between "race" and "ethnicity" as well as the
assumption that race is a Western invention, the parallels have also prompted
many of the same authors to assume that racialization arose mostly from colonial indoctrination.

As a result, relatively little attention has been paid to African initiatives in
the racialization of "ranked" ethnic thought.[66] Undoubtedly this has much to
do with the same nationalist triumphalism that prompts many of the cruder instrumentalists to downplay the significance of African intellectuals in the gen-

eration of tribal thought. But in addition, one suspects that many authors are immobilized by a set of political scruples born of the assumption that all racial thought originates in white supremacy; in short, they don't want to appear to be blaming the victim.[67] That assumption and those scruples seem confirmed by the undoubted influence that Western teachings had on African racial thinkers as well as by the fact that the antagonists in some of these conflicts, including the "Arabs" and "Africans" who fought for political advantage in Zanzibar, defined themselves in terms that converged with major categories of Western racial thought.

These characteristics are amply displayed in the Zanzibar literature, much of which portrays race as a peculiarly Western disease that was introduced to the islands by the effects of colonial rule and even the deliberate machinations of European officials and educators.[68] Authors vary in their identification of the malady's local vectors. Many focus on immigrants from the African mainland, reputedly the ASP's most militant loyalists. Mainlanders presumably were more susceptible to European influences, including the anti-Arab propaganda of abolitionist mission education, than were people rooted in the islands' Islamic communities, who in contrast continued to nurture more flexible local concepts of belonging. Other authors blame the ruling "Arabs," who championed British policies that propped them up as a racial elite.[69] Both variants reflect the political scruples already mentioned, born of postcolonial politics. In their cruder forms they constitute rival nationalist orthodoxies—one supportive of the revolutionary government, the other of the opposition—in which politicians who before independence took the lead in fomenting racial politics absolve themselves of all responsibility by simply blaming the colonial state and its stooges.[70] Whether crude or scholarly, such interpretations depict African intellectuals as having either too little autonomy or too much: either dupes whose thinking was easily molded by British mentors or steadfast anti-imperialists who clung to an authentic subaltern consciousness. Neither circle spoke to the other, and the anti-imperialists avoided all contamination from colonial thought.

The following chapters, especially those in Part 2 of this book, will illustrate how such assumptions might be subverted by reconstructing the precise conversations and debates from which racial thought emerged, a task that requires us to abandon images of authentic indigenous discourses and imported infections and the "logic of the trial" that goes with them. Such a reconstruction reveals that indigenous intellectuals spoke to one another more than they addressed the colonial state or responded to its demands and that their impact on the emergence of racial thought was arguably greater, and certainly more direct, than that of colonial educators. (As Anthony Appiah has remarked, the colonizers were never as fully in control of intellectual life as the nationalist elite subsequently made them appear.)[71] This is not to deny that colonial educators and administrators were significant interlocutors in such conversations. But they were only one set among a variety of influences on East African intellectuals, and latecomers at that. The national and ethnic thought of twentieth-century Zanzibar drew on a wide range of sources that were global in scope, including many inherited from centuries of historical experience within East Africa itself. Moreover, intellectual influences went both ways: local intellectuals had at least as much influence on British perceptions of Zanzibar as colonial educators had on islanders. To understand the etiology of racial thought, then, we must abandon the cliché of colonial encounter. It is just as misleading to speak of two discrete spheres of discourse—one colonial, the other indigenous—as it is to speak of the colonial state's domination of its subjects' consciousness.

It is equally misleading to assume that popular discourse existed in isolation from that of the elite intelligentsia. To be sure, the most learned and active of the ethnonationalist intellectuals belonged to the upper social strata, and, not surprisingly, they were often the most influential in introducing new forms of discourse, in particular the international model of the nation-state. But, as we will see, their concepts were quickly taken up by subaltern intellectuals: persons of low social standing (and, usually, of low levels of schooling) who nevertheless were recognized in the communities of the poor for their leadership in imagining and enunciating new ways of understanding society.[72] These subaltern intellectuals challenged the elite intelligentsia on many issues, and the constant arguments and debates between them were central to the mechanisms by which racial meanings were reproduced in the daily activities of ordinary people.

IV

As I have indicated, the assumption that racial thought originates in Western doctrine is but one of two reasons that studies of African ethnonationalist violence have stalled relative to studies of other forms of ethnic tension. The other, plainly, is that in order to explain the dehumanizing and dehumanized violence of pogroms and attempted genocide it is necessary to navigate through territory that Africa scholars, understandably, have long preferred to avoid. That territory, of course, is the "heart of darkness," the most disparaging variant of the old Hegelian canard. For a while, Africa scholars were able to take grim satisfaction in a century's worth of European genocide and ethnic cleansing, which had disabused laypersons (or so we had hoped)[73] of the illusion that such behavior is the specialty of any one part of the world. But that satisfaction was dampened by the renewed horrors that emerged in Central and West Africa in the decades around the new century's turn.

Among responsible authors the most common reaction to such discomfort has been to focus on instrumentalist explanations, in which entrepreneurs of ethnic violence mobilize their dependents and clientele to make war on their rivals.[74] In societies undergoing political and economic collapse, such as in certain West African countries following the end of the Cold War, such patronage networks often are all that the most vulnerable have to turn to for security, resulting in a level of desperation that induces many to acquiesce to the entrepreneurs' demands. Elsewhere, where lives have been profoundly disrupted by the pressures of long-distance labor migration, ethnonationalists hold out hope that the communities described in their historical narratives—communities of moral certainty and unchallenged gender authority—might be reestablished in the here and now. Like religion in Marx's famous dictum, the imagined ethnonationalist community serves as the heart of a heartless world, and the anxieties that feed those illusions render people willing to shed blood in its defense.[75]

Although such analyses are indispensable for understanding the tensions that shape ethnic violence, on their own they are incapable of explaining the violence itself. Ethnic tension is common enough in the modern world, even ubiquitous. But in historical terms, ethnic violence is only sporadic and momentary. So it cannot be explained simply by the presence of ethnic competition or any other kind of tension; there is nothing inevitable about social tension culminating in violence.[76] Moreover, by its very nature the violence of a pogrom or ethnic riot defies instrumentalist interpretations: it is typically ritualized and theatrical, as if intentionally transgressive of a multitude of commonly accepted norms. Disembowelments, massive sexual assault, the mutilation of corpses: such acts are evidently meant to do far more than simply kill an enemy in order to seize political or material advantage. To use a term commonly attributed to Primo Levi, they are all, from an instrumentalist perspective, "senseless violence."

A rich literature on ethnic (or "communal") violence in contemporary South Asia and other parts of the world provides an explanation of these phenomena that at first glance seems relatively straightforward. This literature focuses on the social and cultural "construction of fear"; it focuses, that is, on "the rhetorical processes, symbolic resources, and representational forms through which a demonized, dehumanized, or otherwise threatening ethnically defined 'other' has been constructed." Key to these fears are accounts of outrages that ethnic enemies have perpetrated in the past and are plotting to repeat in the near future. Thus, ordinarily nonviolent people are made to sense that a preemptive strike is vital to their own safety. The spectacular nature of those strikes is meant as revenge and as warning. Such vivid fears and the passions they arouse are in fact anything but "senseless." To the contrary, they make enormous sense when read in light of the historical narratives of violence and victimization that have been elaborated by the ethnonationalist intellectuals.[77]

On closer consideration, however, such explanations are far from straightforward. The fears that produce pogroms and race riots are not like those that make us squirm at a ghost story or a horror film. Rather, they are deeply *personal* fears: fears of immediate bodily harm based on memories of having been victimized by the ethnic other in the past. They are fears, that is, that stem from the *personal subjectivity* of each member of the ethnic crowd, from a sense of self based on a particular awareness of lived experience, real or imagined. To observe that ethnonationalist entrepreneurs provoke violence by manipulating popular fears does little to explain how this sense of self came into existence. To explain why the entrepreneurs' manipulations evoke the responses they do, we must understand a peculiar transmutation by which ethnonationalist historical narratives—narratives of events understood to have befallen the ancestors of the ethnic group—are reinscribed as part of the personal experiences of significant numbers of ordinary people. In other words, we must try to understand how "historical memories," as they are often but somewhat misleadingly described, become transformed into *remembered* memories.

Such inquiries return us to the heart of the old primordialist concerns: to the fears and memories of countless generations of ancestors that seem inscribed in the consciousness of their descendants. Yet despite the reservations of constructivist critics, it is possible to investigate such matters without abandoning a historical perspective; possible, in other words, to investigate how the inscription of such fears and memories occurred over time. To do so, however, requires moving beyond the cadre of ethnonational intellectuals and asking how their rhetoric of exclusion and dehumanization resonated with preexisting or parallel concepts of popular discourse. Not coincidentally, the most convincing analyses of these processes have come from social psychologists and cultural anthropologists who have been able to conduct in-depth interviews with perpetrators and victims soon after the events in question, before memories have been overly obscured by subsequent layers of political ideology.[78] Lacking such sources, in Part 3 of this book I will use conventional historical records to arrive at some tentative understandings of the processes by which historical memories of racial violence were transmuted into remembered memories at the close of the colonial period. The focal point of all three chapters will be the race riots of June 1961, known in Zanzibar as the War of Stones, which were later recognized as a kind of dress rehearsal for the revolution itself.

The most relevant nonpolitical discourses in this regard concerned crime and criminal violence, discourses that had shaped how people categorized those who should and should not be protected as members of the moral community long before the nationalist intellectuals introduced their own recondite languages of exclusion. Chapter 6 will look at the history of those discourses. Many of the specific fears that sparked acts of violence during the closing years of the sultanate were couched in the language of crime. Political propagandists were well aware of the power of that language and made ample use of it. But, as we shall see, subjective fears of racialized criminal violence were shaped far more by rumor than by any overtly political channel of communication. This concern with rumor continues in the following two chapters.

The 1961 riots and their aftermath are documented in historical records that are more detailed and transparent than those for the revolution itself. They therefore provide an excellent opportunity to explore some of the specific processes by which ethnonationalist historical memory was transmuted into violent group subjectivities. That exploration, undertaken in chapters 7 and 8, reveals a paradox. It is commonplace to describe episodes of ethnic violence as the culmination of growing sentiments of hatred and fear. But we shall see that in many cases a violent group subjectivity—that is, the widespread personal conviction that one's social position is determined by membership in a group (in this case ethnic or racial) defined by its experience of violence as victim and/or as perpetrator—did not precede the outbreak of racial violence but was in many ways the product of that violence. Violent racial hatred, in other words, was as much produced by the riots as it was productive of them.

This observation implies that without subsequent spirals of sustained discursive vituperation and retaliatory violence, violent group subjectivities are evanescent, not deep-seated. Such spirals, lasting several decades, are what explain the intractability of tensions in places such as Burundi, Rwanda, and parts of South Asia.[79] Zanzibar's experience of such spirals, in contrast, was brief. Chapter 8 examines the sultanate's final thirty months, focusing on the circulation of rumors that were inflected by the fears and anxieties aroused by the June riots. In this regard, the War of Stones constituted a transformative moment that profoundly shaped how many islanders perceived their personal experiences of racial division. Memories of those experiences (both real and constructed) played a significant role in shaping their responses to the January 1964 coup and in mobilizing the militants who perpetrated another, far deadlier round of pogroms in its wake. The regime that took power after the revolution had no interest in perpetuating this violence, however, especially after it merged with the government of Tanganyika in April 1964. The pogroms thus ended quickly, and racial tensions, although never entirely disappearing, subsided in the decades that followed.

But in recent years, with the reopening of political debate after decades of closure, worrying signs have emerged that some political speakers are prepared not only to revive racialized group identities but also to increase their emotive force by investing them with historical "memories" of racial violence, including narratives of the early 1960s pogroms. This apparent persistence of racial identities, despite the radical changes in the postcolonial political economy that have eradicated the material bases of Arab supremacy and African resentment, poses a challenge to simple instrumentalist interpretations. And, indeed, explanations of today's ethnicized political tactics often depict them as voicing loyalties that have continued, repressed but unchanged, throughout the past half-century. Both views are at odds with the interpretation advanced in the chapters below. As we shall see in a brief Epilogue, contemporary Zanzibar's communal identities are neither wholly inherited nor wholly invented. Rather, like all such ways of thinking about the collective self and the collective other, they have been refashioned from generation to generation, in part from old discursive materials, in part from others newly imagined.

2

The Creation of a Racial State

Nothing in the preceding pages was meant to minimize the significance of structural factors or the literature that focuses on them. On the contrary, the instrumentalist literature has been central to demolishing the fallacy that ethnic identities are primal and inborn. In the present case, several scholars have demonstrated how processes related to the construction of institutions of economic and political power, many quite recent, were important in shaping the context in which discourses of race became pertinent to Zanzibaris' everyday lives. This scholarship is an essential starting point for tracing the racialization of ethnic thought in colonial Zanzibar, provided we not overlook the limitations of its ability to explain phenomena such as the transgressive violence that plagued the sultanate's final years.

We must also correct for the instrumentalist literature's overemphasis on European rule. Contrary to the impression given by some authors, the construction of a racial state began not with British conquest in 1890 but with the actions of Omani Arabs who conquered Zanzibar and the adjacent coast during the preceding century. And the Omanis, in turn, built on a much older political culture of Arabocentrism that for centuries had accorded status and prestige to those who claimed connections to the Islamic Middle East.

Arabocentrism and Omani Conquest

Peoples of the East African coast had been in contact with the wider Indian Ocean world since early in the Common Era. By the middle of the first millennium these peoples included speakers of an ancestral form of Swahili, one of the Bantu family of African languages, who at that time lived in small settlements on the northern coast of present-day Kenya. These early Swahili-speakers were farmers, ironworkers, and fisherfolk who also traded with visiting merchants from the Persian Gulf. But by the eighth century many of the settlements had begun to specialize in commerce, some growing into large, densely populated towns. During the following few centuries, Swahili-speakers established communities along nearly 2,000 miles of coast and on islands as far offshore as the Comoros in a process whose rapidity bespeaks their maritime skills. This period coincided with an increase of international commerce throughout the western Indian Ocean that was attendant on the rise of the Abbasid Caliphate, and it is likely that the expansion of the Swahili communities was linked to the pursuit of coasting trade. After ca. 1000 CE the pace of international commerce rose dramatically, resulting in a complex web of interlocking trade networks that linked the whole arc of the northern Indian Ocean littoral and contributed to the growth of many of the Swahili settlements into powerful city-states. At the peak of their prosperity, roughly from the thirteenth through fifteenth centuries, cities such as Kilwa and Mombasa mediated a rich trade between the Red Sea, the Persian Gulf, and northwestern India on the one hand and the African interior on the other. This was the city-states' classic age, when Arab geographers described them as oases of civilization in the land of "Zanj"; that is, the land of the blacks.[1]

These early overseas contacts had the most lasting impact in the form of Islam, which reached the coast by the eighth century. Though at first restricted to foreign visitors and a handful of local converts, Islam spread quickly and by the fourteenth century was central to the civic life of all the towns. Merchants and rulers probably led the way in propagating the faith, welcoming Muslims from foreign lands as honored guests, especially if they were religious scholars. As in other premodern global trade systems, the security of transactions across the Indian Ocean had been maintained by trust, which, in turn, rested on links of common faith. The benefits derived from being part of the community of the faithful thus were material as well as intellectual and spiritual.[2]

By the time of the city-states' classic age, Islam was central to how the coast people defined themselves, both in relation to their pagan neighbors and in relation to one another. More than their shared language or their shared urban and maritime orientation, the Swahili-speakers' shared faith induced a sense that they differed crucially from the people of the coastal hinterland. (Islam did not penetrate beyond the coastal fringe until the nineteenth century.) This

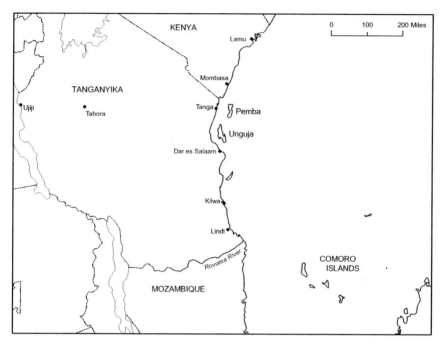

MAP 2.1. The Swahili Coast and East Africa, showing colonial boundaries.

should not be mistaken for an overarching sense of "Swahili" ethnic identity. Before modern times, that ethnic label, which is derived from an Arabic word for "coast," existed only as an epithet of reference, used mainly by foreign visitors; local people themselves identified primarily with their clan or village or with the ruler of the city-state to which they owed political allegiance. Still, the townspeople's devotion to Islam helped cement a notion among them that they lived in a world apart, connected more with their trade partners and coreligionists overseas than with their cultural cousins of the near interior.

Islam and commerce, then, combined on the Swahili coast to foster a world view that assigned prestige to all things connected to the distant Islamic heartland. Those values were expressed most strikingly in the practice of the coast's leading families of claiming ancestral origins in various parts of the Islamic Middle East. In the central portion of the coast, including Zanzibar, such claims often referred to the Persian town of Shiraz. Legends of Shirazi origin were connected to traditions that told of Persian immigrants who had supposedly introduced Islam to the coast and established the major towns. It is unclear when these tales originated; the earliest known version was recorded by a Portuguese visitor in the sixteenth century, though some scholars speculate that they may have accompanied the first pulse of Islamic expansion along the coast early in the second millennium.[3]

Yet whatever the precise source of the Shirazi myths, the custom of basing authority in claims of exotic origins predates even the long history of coastal Islam. Part of the cultural legacy of the townspeoples' Bantu-speaking forebears was a political tradition, widespread throughout Central, Southern, and East Africa, that marked rulers as the descendants of exogenous conqueror-heroes who had introduced their indigenous subjects to the traits deemed central to local values of civilized life, such as smithing, cattle-keeping, or state-building. Islam's powerful language of civilization and barbarism thus reinforced pre-existing rhetorical practices in the description of political authority.[4] In the modern era, European visitors found that the myths of Shirazi state-building meshed perfectly with their own racial preconceptions about Africans' innate inability to build urban civilizations. Colonial scholars later developed these themes by observing that the ruins of the classic city-states did not extend beyond the coastal fringe. In the myths and ruins, as in the common political culture shared by the peoples of Zanzibar and the adjacent mainland coast, Europeans believed they detected the vestiges of a Persian "Zanj Empire" that had once encompassed the coast and islands.[5]

So, long before formal conquest by Europeans or Omani Arabs, local and imported discourses had converged to give rise to the widespread belief that the ancient Swahili city-states were alien creations planted on an otherwise benighted shore. This belief is still common, within East Africa as well as abroad. As proof, its proponents usually point to the heavy component of Arabic loanwords in modern Swahili. In fact, there is no evidence to support it.[6] Although several of the cultural traits that distinguished Swahili-speakers from their neighbors had indeed been introduced from the Middle East (most notably Islam and literacy), historical linguistics demonstrates that pronounced foreign hegemony—Arab, not Persian—dates to a period well after the classic city-states had begun their decline.

That decline was largely induced by the intrusion of the Portuguese into the Indian Ocean trade system after 1498 and their attempts to subjugate it to monopolistic control. Though they never succeeded, they sowed much turmoil in the attempt. Over the course of the sixteenth century they sacked Mombasa three times and subjected most of the other towns to similar fates; Kilwa, the most powerful of the city-states at the start of the century, was a backwater at its close. The towns' rulers formed shifting alliances with the newcomers, using them against local rivals. Yet those alliances rarely lasted long. The Portuguese usually managed to evince resentments even among their allies because of their unorthodox mercantilist policies and because of their methods, which were shaped by an unusually hostile attitude toward Islam.[7]

It is no wonder, then, that when another maritime power appeared on the horizon, many townspeople welcomed it as a potential counterbalance. In the seventeenth century, the new Yarubi dynasty in Oman ousted the Portuguese from that Persian Gulf sultanate and undertook measures to supplant them as the dominant power in the western Indian Ocean. (At the same time, Portugal was being challenged by the Dutch at the eastern end of its Indian Ocean empire.) The rulers of the Swahili towns attempted to play the imperial rivals against one another, continuing the previous century's pattern of political jockeying. But the general trend ran against Portugal. By the end of the century local people had enlisted the Omanis to help drive the Portuguese from their two main strongholds, Mombasa and Pemba; the Swahili ruler of the latter island, who had secured his dominion through Portuguese backing, was also expelled. In 1729, after the Portuguese were also driven from the neighboring island of Unguja—or Zanzibar,[8] as foreigners called it (from the term "Zanj")—the most powerful of the Shirazi[9] rulers there, the *mwinyi mkuu,* prudently switched his allegiance to the Omanis.

Omani intervention in coastal affairs escalated throughout the eighteenth century, and it is in this late period of its history, and no earlier, that the Swahili language first reflected the marked impact of Arabic.[10] The Omanis, no less than the Portuguese, aimed at conquest and control. But in their dealings with local people they were more politic than their predecessors, and as Muslims they were less odious as allies and overlords to townspeople who had long imagined themselves exemplars of Islamic civilization. Furthermore, as longtime participants in the old noncentralized Indian Ocean trade networks, the Omanis did not seek to impose the kind of mercantilist monopolies that had proven self-defeating to the Portuguese. The most successful of the Omani intruders were merchant princes skilled at blending trade interests with the politics of force, adventurers who saw East Africa as a field that remained open to their ambitions even when political intrigues limited them at home.

In the second half of the eighteenth century Omani intrusion entered a new phase, in part the result of political instability in Oman. The Yarubi dynasty fell in 1749 and was replaced by rulers from the rival Busaid clan. But the new dynasts were not immediately recognized by the Omanis who held power on the East African coast, many of whom had begun to marry locally and es-

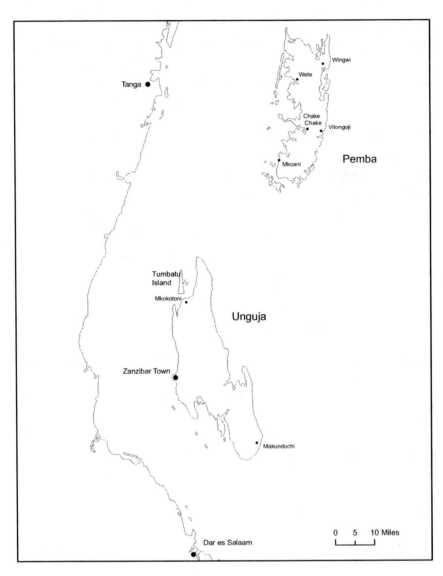

MAP 2.2. Zanzibar (Unguja and Pemba).

tablish themselves as a fully naturalized elite, virtually independent of Oman.
The Busaids' main antagonists belonged to the Mazrui clan, whom the Yarubi
had installed as governors of Mombasa and Pemba, its dependency (and bread-
basket). But the Busaids managed to secure an early toehold in Unguja, renew-
ing an arrangement their Yarubi predecessors had made with the *mwinyi mkuu,*
by which the latter pledged loyalty in exchange for an annual subvention and

the right to continue ruling his indigenous subjects. Unguja subsequently became the center of the Busaids' aggressive campaigns to dominate the entire coast. They established headquarters on the island's western shore, on a spit of land near the fishing village of Shangani, where the Portuguese had once maintained a trading factory. By 1776, some 300 Omanis had settled at or near this site, a number that soon would multiply.

In the nineteenth century the settlement near Shangani blossomed into the metropolis of Zanzibar Town, capital of an Arab-ruled state that encompassed the whole Swahili coast and financial center of a vast commercial empire. The merchant prince remembered as the founder of the new polity was Said bin Sultan al-Busaid, first *seyyid* (prince or ruler) of the Busaidi Sultanate of Zanzibar. Said was a minor when his father, the reigning sultan of Oman, died in 1804; two years later, at the age of fifteen, he murdered his cousin, the prince regent, and seized the throne.[11] Such violent succession disputes were common in Omani politics, and they continued during Seyyid Said's reign, encouraging the young prince to take a keener interest in opportunities overseas. Those interests were further encouraged by the newest and mightiest naval power in the Indian Ocean, British India, whose consuls regarded Said as a useful counterbalance to France. With his domestic power debilitated by continuing dynastic conflicts, Said shifted virtually all his attention to Zanzibar, locating his court there in the 1830s.

During his long reign (he died in 1856), Seyyid Said succeeded in exerting his authority along most of the Swahili coast, placing Omani governors and military garrisons at each of the major towns. His success lay in no small part in coupling muscular political policies with commercial reforms that benefited many of the towns' merchant elite. He encouraged financiers from Gujarat, who had long played a dominant role in Oman's commercial life and had been active in East Africa as well, to settle at Zanzibar Town, granting the most important of them leases to collect export duties at the port towns. He also signed treaties with major trading nations (beginning with the United States) and enacted other measures that established Zanzibar as East Africa's central emporium of international commerce. Indian capital and Busaid political patronage thus combined to underwrite Arab and African entrepreneurs in a remarkable expansion of coastal and caravan trade, the latter reaching ever deeper into the continental interior as the century progressed. The foreign merchants sought a wide array of raw materials, chiefly ivory; local people purchased an equally wide array of goods manufactured by Western and Indian industry, particularly cotton cloth.[12]

Seyyid Said also encouraged his Omani followers to settle on Unguja and establish estates on lands expropriated or otherwise acquired from the islanders. Though the settlers experimented with several crops, Said is remembered for having required each to plant coconut and especially clove trees, thus laying the foundations of Zanzibar's modern economy. Cloves were an entirely new crop, and they thrived in Unguja's fertile northwestern quadrant. The estates were worked by slaves imported from the mainland, long a source of labor in the Persian Gulf.[13] Slavery and the slave trade thus underpinned Zanzibar's prosperity as much as did trade in nonhuman commodities. But even more significant: by investing commercial profits in land and slaves, Omanis established a manorial lifestyle that became central to their self-perception as a landed gentry and to the sultanate's political culture of racial paternalism.[14] The importance of these factors was out of all proportion to the actual wealth produced on the estates, as the islands' subsequent political history would reveal.

The commercial and political power of the sultanate continued to grow under Said's successors, helped in no small part by their growing reliance on British patrons. Though initially Britain was drawn to the Busaids by a desire to secure the sea-lanes in the Arabian Sea and to protect Indian trade interests, from midcentury Anglo-Zanzibar relations became dominated by the rising tide of British abolitionism. In return for steadfast political and military support, some of it pressed on them by aggressive British diplomats and naval officers, the sultans agreed to a series of treaties that restricted and, in 1873, outlawed the seaborne trade in slaves. By this time, slave exports were of little importance to Zanzibar's economy, and the sultanate's own domestic demand continued to be supplied by slaves brought legally from the interior by caravan and then smuggled across the Zanzibar Channel, easily evading British cruisers.

As the reach of the sultanate expanded, so did perceptions of Arab power. Omani governors consolidated their political control over the towns of the mainland coast, using force to marginalize indigenous rulers who proved refractory and patronage to co-opt the rest. Such patronage proved especially flattering to elites who were already proud of their own Arab or "Shirazi" ancestry, and even when it produced tensions, Omani rule only further strengthened local concepts of Arabocentrism. Zanzibari commercial and political influence along the trade routes also contributed to the uneven spread of Arabocentrism and Islam into the continental interior. Still, the resultant prestige was never as overwhelming as Zanzibaris liked to think. Zanzibari intellectuals are still fond of quoting an adage of the time: "When the pipes play at Zanzibar, they dance at the lakes." But this was more an expression of Zanzibaris' self-perception than an actual description of their ability to determine fashion or political events.[15] In later years that perception, with its chauvinism vis-à-vis peoples of the interior, would have troubling reverberations.

The political and social categories generated by the rise of the Busaid sultanate—Arabs, Indians, indigenous islanders, and slaves—laid the foundations of modern Zanzibar's major ethnic divisions; as has often been the case, race-making was connected to state-building. In many ways the sultanate was a colonial state that had been built on conquest, its political authority derived from the status of belonging to a foreign and supposedly superior racial caste. Early in the twentieth century, before the ascendance of anticolonial sentiment, intellectuals with ties to the sultanate's ruling families were unapologetic about the colonial nature of Omani rule. Like their British mentors, however, they often papered over the violence inherent in Omani colonialism, a violence that was central to the governing practices by which the Busaid state sought to define and divide its subjects.[16]

That violence was most apparent on Unguja, where Omani domination was more complete than elsewhere. By the mid-nineteenth century most of the island's indigenous population—that is, those who were neither slaves nor immigrants from overseas—were known as Hadimu.[17] This label, derived from an Arabic word for servant, originally referred to the population's subjection to the *mwinyi mkuu*. The *mwinyi mkuu* had once shared power with several other "Shirazi" potentates, but the Busaids helped him extend his authority over the entire island, with the exception of its northwest fringe and the adjacent islet of Tumbatu. This policy reached its peak under Seyyid Said, whose support of the incumbent *mwinyi mkuu*, Muhammad bin Ahmed, came with the stipulation that the latter collect taxes and corvée labor from his subjects. Most of the labor was expended on the sultan's clove estates, but the *mwinyi mkuu* was allowed to keep half the tax revenues for himself, in lieu of the annual subvention he had received from Seyyid Said's predecessors.

Muhammad bin Ahmed commanded considerable respect and authority, and for a time his relationship with the Omani sultans resembled a "dual monarchy."[18] Yet by the end of his reign he found his power seriously undermined, and repeated clashes with the Omanis eventually compelled him to abandon his holdings in Zanzibar Town and take refuge in a fortified palace in the center of the island, at the edge of the clove-producing zone. He died in 1865. His ineffective successor as *mwinyi mkuu*, who outlived him by only a few years, was the last to hold the title; he died under the rule of the most powerful of the sultans,

Barghash bin Said (r. 1870–1888). This marked the end of the Wahadimu's relative political autonomy. Meanwhile, the expansion of Arab-dominated clove production had driven the Wahadimu into the island's rocky eastern and southern regions, where plantation production was impossible.[19] The Busaids had anyhow always forbidden Unguja's indigenous populace from planting cloves.

By the end of the century, the term "Hadimu" had begun to change from a political status into a quasi-ethnic one that conveyed many of the connotations it would retain into the twentieth century: indigenes native to specific regions in the east and south that lay outside the urban and plantation zones of the island, distinct both from the Arabs who dominated the latter zones and the slaves who labored in them.[20] Those who accepted the label took pride in being descended from the clients of a Shirazi nobleman, as distinct from most other low-status islanders (that is, slaves). Over time, this identity with their former Shirazi ruler became transmuted into memories of actual Shirazi descent, mixed inconsistently with preexisting traditions of diverse mainland origins. By early in the twentieth century the term "Hadimu" had lost its pejorative connotations and villagers circulated fanciful folk etymologies that masked its otherwise well-known servile derivation. The fisherfolk who lived on Tumbatu and the adjacent coast of northwest Unguja preserved similar memories of mixed mainland and Shirazi ancestry and of having preceded the island's Omani and slave inhabitants. But since the Watumbatu (as they were called) had never been fully subject to the Mwinyi Mkuu, they did not share the Wahadimu's overarching historical identity.

On Pemba, divisions between islanders and Omani settlers were far less pronounced. This difference stemmed partly from geography. Though Unguja is the larger of the two islands, fertile, well-watered lands are located only in its western and northern third, the areas closest to Zanzibar Town. Once those lands had been seized by Omani settlers, all that was left for the Wahadimu and Watumbatu were the so-called coral lands, where arable soil occurs in small, ill-watered patches and clove cultivation is impossible.[21] Pemba, on the other hand, is evenly covered with fertile soil. Cloves were introduced there late, after a freak hurricane in 1872 destroyed most of Unguja's trees. But Pemba proved so much better suited for the crop that by the time Unguja's production had recovered in the late 1880s, the smaller island was already producing twice as many cloves, a position it still holds.[22] As it happened, the introduction of cloves to Pemba coincided with the abolition of the sea-going slave trade. Though slaves were smuggled from the mainland to feed Pemba's post-hurricane clove boom, an overall labor shortage nevertheless induced Omani

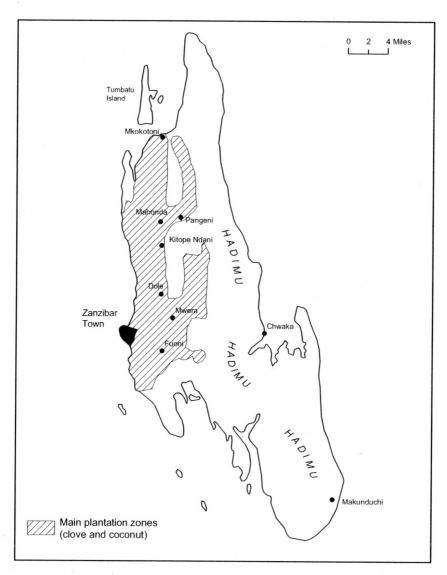

MAP 2.3. Unguja.

settlers to share the opportunities of clove cultivation with the local populace. Pembans who assisted the settlers in clearing land and planting trees were granted half the estates they had helped to lay.[23]

Omani domination on the two islands thus differed decidedly. Whereas on Unguja most islanders had been dispossessed and forbidden to plant cloves, on Pemba indigenous people were fully involved in clove production from the beginning. Moreover, never having experienced the kind of unified political rule that marked off the subjects of the *mwinyi mkuu*, Pembans mediated their relations with the Busaid state through local-level networks of kinship and patronage. Because of all these factors, islanders and settlers interacted on a more intimate level on Pemba than on Unguja—living together in the same locales, planting cloves together, intermarrying—and although Pemba's Omanis dominated ownership of the island's largest estates, they found it impossible to maintain unambiguous social boundaries between themselves and the local people. Indigenous Pembans therefore never developed the kind of discrete, overarching sense of ethnopolitical identity that characterized the Wahadimu, except insofar as they distinguished themselves from Arab and slave newcomers as *Wapemba wa asili*, the original inhabitants of Pemba.[24] In short, the rise of the Busaid state did less in Pemba than in Unguja to inhibit islanders from continuing to claim elevated status as "Shirazi" and "Arabs." To be sure, the practice continued on both islands (as we shall see). But in Unguja, the vagaries of dispossession, as well as the proximity of the Busaid court and the other central institutions of the Arab state, restricted upward mobility and made it relatively more difficult for ambitious islanders to make viable claims to Arab status. By contrast, many locally born Pembans described themselves as Arabs.[25]

Violence of course was also central to the distinction between slaves and masters, a distinction that assumed greater economic and cultural significance with the expansion of plantation agriculture in Busaid-ruled Zanzibar, although, as we shall see in later chapters, the precise nature of that violence has been obscured by the claims and counterclaims of latter-day political propagandists. As in all systems of slavery, the root acts of violence were those by which people were torn from their natal homes and brought into the slave society as quintessential aliens, shorn of all social ties save those to their master.[26] In coastal East Africa, slavery had long been governed by Islamic doctrines that justified such violence on the grounds that it rescued pagans from spiritual death (pagans were the only category of persons permissibly enslaved) and brought them into the realm of belief and civilization, where masters were enjoined to convert them. Conversion did not relieve slaves of their bondage, although Islam did encourage masters to free worthy slaves (if only in their wills), a teaching that contributed to the high rates of manumission in Islamic slave societies.

Slaves, then—and especially first-generation slaves, who had been born in the pagan interior—were ever-present emblems of the *ushenzi* (barbarism or unbelief) that supposedly distinguished the coast and the islands from their inland neighbors. Masters, in contrast, were exemplars of civilization, or *uung-wana*, a word derived from an expression meaning "the children of God."[27] The word also denoted nobility, and its personal noun form, *mwungwana* (pl. *waungwana*), is often interpreted to mean simply a free person as opposed to a slave. But the contrast between slave and nonslave was practically coterminous with that between barbarian and civilized. Acculturated slaves, or slaves born in coastal society (*wazalia*, or "born slaves"), occupied a particularly anomalous position. They were Muslims, but because of their inheritance of *ushenzi*— the same quality that justified their continued bondage—they were routinely assumed to be less Muslim than *waungwana*. At issue was not the content of a slave's beliefs but his or her descent from barbarians of the continental interior, the seat of *ushenzi*. Concepts of slavery thus meshed with Arabocentrism to give rise to ethnicized notions that imputed inborn barbarism to mainland descent. That such prejudices could coexist with Islamic universalism should come as no surprise to anyone familiar with similar contradictions in the history of Western slavery.

The preceding paragraphs describe only the ideals cherished by the *waungwana*, who liked to think that the main forces holding their slaves in bondage were the gratitude and respect slaves felt for having been exposed to Islamic civilization and the promise, no matter how vague, of manumission. The literary iteration of these ideals (and Islam's well-known prescriptions for the humane treatment of slaves) have sometimes encouraged the perception that slavery in Islamic societies was always benign compared to Western forms. But Muslim slave-owners were no less prone than their Christian counterparts to be tempted away from the teachings of their faith. Masters who from opportunity and by temperament were more intent on exploiting their slaves for economic gain were also more likely to use violence to exert their will. Hence slavery was probably harsher in the plantation sector of the Busaid economy than had been the norm in the smaller-scale enterprises that characterized the coast before the rule of Seyyid Said. Still, the levels of violence were far from uniform. As we have seen, many planters valued their estates as much for the manorial lifestyle they afforded as for the wealth they produced. A large retinue of loyal slaves added to the prestige and honor a master commanded in coastal society, be he Arab or indigenous. And a master's prestige was all the greater if his slaves were perceived as elevated above the rank of common serviles.[28]

Slaves themselves made use of these ideals, manipulating them in struggles to shape their lives. Not content with hegemonic notions that defined them as socially inert, ambitious slaves pushed masters to allow them to carve relatively

autonomous positions for themselves within society. They did so through behavior that typically involved going to town: to sell surplus foodstuffs from the
garden plots they were customarily allotted among the clove trees, to practice
a skilled craft, or to sign up as caravan porters (who traded independently on
the side). Such slaves paid their masters a regular tribute, but no less important
than the amount of such payments was the satisfaction masters derived from
knowing they commanded the loyalty of "civilized slaves," to say nothing of
a sense of pious magnanimity. To be sure, slaves often forced their masters to
accept such situations, and most masters, especially the larger planters, probably resisted. But the masters' own paternalism left them little room to object
when the most determined *wazalia* sought to divert their resources to establish
autonomous households or to invest in the ritual expenditures by which they
claimed the attributes of *uungwana* and Islamic piety that marked full membership in the coastal communities.[29]

The acculturated slaves who made such claims (as well as other low-status
newcomers from the continental interior) were the first to use "Swahili" as a
label of self-identity, a euphemism by which they might mask their pagan origins. Slaves thus adopted Islamic urban culture and became Swahili in processes that might be taken as an index of the degree to which coastal slavery
retained the element of "absorption" often said to have been characteristic of
slavery throughout the continent—not, however, as a predisposition somehow
intrinsic to Africa, but as an outcome of the slaves' own strategies of inclusion.[30] To the extent that such absorption took place in nineteenth-century
Zanzibar, plantation slavery there differed from the race slavery more familiar
in the West, where racial categories posed stiff obstacles to social advancement even for manumitted slaves. Still, as we have seen, the masters' notions of
Arabocentrism and *ushenzi* ensured that the practice of slavery gave rise to assumptions of ethnic difference, no matter how much the slaves contested such
notions. Pemba again provides a useful contrast with Unguja. The smaller island's clove boom in the last quarter of the century meant that slaves continued
to be smuggled there even after British conquest in 1890. Hence at the time of
abolition in 1897, it probably had a relatively high proportion of unaccultur-
ated first-generation slaves. Such slaves were less likely than *wazalia* to make
effective claims that they belonged to island communities. Furthermore, the
broad participation of *Wapemba wa asili* in clove production, if even on a small
scale, generated a keener interest in maintaining slaves' social exclusion than
was typical of their Hadimu counterparts at Unguja. So although on Pemba
the boundaries between Omanis and islanders were more relaxed than on Un-

guja, the same could not be said about relations there between slaves and those who were freeborn.[31]

The above discussion suggests how something like a geography of ethnic difference had begun to emerge by the last quarter of the nineteenth century. Each island's particular experience of Omani rule and economic development had led to different practices of ethnic identification. And Unguja's landscape, in particular, was already marked by the broad divisions that would take on political significance at the close of the colonial era. People who identified themselves as indigenous to Unguja (Watumbatu and Wahadimu) were concentrated in the island's northwest and southeast fringes, while Omani settlers and their mainlander slaves prevailed in the north-central plantation sector. Zanzibar Town was further subdivided. The ambitious slaves and other low-status newcomers who were drawn to the city congregated in a fast-growing suburb on the eastern side of the tidal inlet that separated the old town from the rest of the island—an area still known as Ng'ambo ("The Other Side"), although the inlet has long since been filled in. The typical housing in Ng'ambo was built of wattle and thatch, in contrast to the massive stone buildings that characterized the seaward side of the inlet. The latter quarter, now known as Stone Town, was the seat of the Zanzibar elite and the state and financial institutions that Omanis and Indians controlled.[32]

But such an ethnic geography, like any schematic description, risks overstating the consistency and salience of Zanzibar's ethnic boundaries. While no account of the changing practices of ethnic identification can ignore their rough correlations with economic activity, there is little to justify the common contention that ethnic boundaries mirrored the interests of class.[33] Nor is it accurate to describe Zanzibar as a classic "plural society," in which "each racial group possessed a separate social and economic sub-culture, and most social relations"—save those in the marketplace—"were carried on within ethnic boundaries."[34] Such social endogamy was true to a limited extent only of the islands' small Indian[35] minority, who tended to engage in urban pursuits, marry among themselves (often bringing their spouses from India), and otherwise maintain relatively firm boundaries around their varied communities. This had something to do with doctrinal divisions: in contrast to islanders, who were overwhelmingly Sunni Muslims, over two-thirds of Zanzibar's Indians belonged to Shia denominations, and of the rest all but a handful were Hindu.[36] Furthermore, as British subjects, Indians were forbidden by the British consuls general from owning slaves, which meant that even the wealthiest were unlikely to partake of the manorial lifestyle of Zanzibar's landholding elite.

Nevertheless, Indians interacted with their non-Indian neighbors more than is commonly acknowledged. Contrary to popular images of Indians as financiers and wealthy shopkeepers, many in fact were impoverished laborers and tradespeople, often living in squalid tenements on the fringes of Stone Town.[37]

The boundaries between the islands' other ethnic categories were even more fluid and situational. Newcomers of mainland origin, including manumitted slaves, constantly jockeyed for positions that would enable them to make plausible claims of acceptance as indigenous islanders, even Shirazi. Members of long-established island families, for their part, felt that their preeminence in the attributes of Islamic civilization was threatened by the growing power and prestige of the Omani elite. Busaid rule thus accelerated the cultural process of Arabization that had long characterized the coast, and many islanders took to calling themselves "Arabs," especially when having any kind of interaction with mainlanders. As a result, the boundaries between mainlanders, islanders, and Arabs remained highly permeable. Paradoxically, that permeability ensured the persistence of an ethnic hierarchy that privileged Middle Eastern descent and disadvantaged those who could not shed the taint of pagan (that is, upcountry) descent. Far from constituting a "plural society," then, with discrete, ethnically specific registers of status, nineteenth-century Zanzibaris subscribed to a single register, most accepting some form of Arabocentric cultural hegemony. A telling mark of the mounting impact of Arab prestige in the final decades of the century was the eclipse of the old Bantu-derived term for civilization, *uungwana*, by a new word derived from Arabic, *ustaarabu*. The very word implied the etymology of its Arabic cognate, which had meant, literally, the act of becoming an Arab.[38]

Despite this permeability, elite Omanis preserved their character as a ruling caste through their domination of landholding and the state as well as through adherence to their own small sect of Islam, the Ibadi rite, which most islanders found forbiddingly ascetic. Nevertheless, though powerful individuals who belonged to specific Omani clans were indisputably Arabs, the broad concept of "Arab" was not the clearly bound racial category that many islanders would later imagine it. Not all landlords and slaveholders were Omanis—although possessing a large estate and numerous slaves was the best way for an indigenous islander to cement his claim to Arab status. Much of the Omanis' authority was based on the cultivation of indigenous clientele, aristocrats whose amour propre was flattered by the patronage of powerful Arabs whom they liked to regard as their peers in *ustaarabu*. Paradoxically, as the power of the Busaid state grew, so too did the blurring of the boundaries around the Omani

elite, largely because of their intimate ties to local people. The processes of cre-
olization that had transformed the Omani families who preceded the Busaids
continued among those who had accompanied Seyyid Said. Arab men who settled on the coast often took local wives, and since descent was reckoned patri-
lineally, the children of such unions were usually considered Arabs. Many of
the Omani elite had African mothers, and most spoke Swahili as their first and,
in many cases, only language. Many who were not directly involved with the
Busaid court even left the Ibadi sect to worship with the Sunni majority.

The very breadth of Arab hegemony meant that the term "Arab" (Mwa-
arabu; pl. Waarabu) was loosely applied. Unmarked, it referred to a Muslim
aristocrat, a person who commanded all the attributes of *ustaarabu*. Although
Middle Eastern ancestry was implied, the individual in question was also assumed to be a Swahili-speaker, that is, someone who was removed from actual
Arab settlers by at least a generation. *Waarabu* who wanted to indicate their origins more specifically did so by appending an Arabic clan name, the most prestigious of which were those of Omani clans whose members had come with
Seyyid Said or earlier, such as al-Mazrui, al-Harthi, or al-Busaid itself. (Social
climbers who could make no such claims might use a vague clan name such as
"al-Shirazii.")[39] But actual Arabic-speaking immigrants were described with
other terms. Most common was the epithet "Manga." The word had once referred simply to any Arab from overseas, especially from the region of Muscat, in Oman. But by the close of the century, when the creolized Omani elite
had become firmly established, the term had become almost purely pejorative,
calling up images of the unruly dhow crews whose annual visits during the
northern monsoon caused much-resented disruption. Immigrants from Yemen
were usually called "Shihiri"; like the Wamanga, most pursued humble occupations, although some garnered respect as Sufi religious scholars. As we shall
see in later chapters, these labels picked up much opprobrium, and it was Wamanga and Washihiri, rather than landowning Waarabu, who would bear the
brunt of anti-Arab violence at the end of the colonial era. ↘ *the immigrant Arabs
rather than the long esp.... Arabs.*

British Rule

Like Omani rule, British rule was founded on conquest, which was justified during its initial, most violent phase by a paternalist ideology that claimed
to be saving all Zanzibaris, masters and slaves, from the brutalizing effects of
the slave trade. But, as throughout the continent, this initial phase soon gave
way to one in which colonial violence was masked by an administrative apparatus that relied on forms of indirect rule via local intermediaries. At Zanzibar

this transition played out more fully than elsewhere, in ways that marked the sultanate as something of an anomaly among Britain's African colonies.

During the imperial scramble of the 1880s, Britain and Germany divided the sultanate's mainland possessions between themselves. But the Busaids managed to preserve their sovereignty over the islands by accepting British "protection." In 1890, then, Zanzibar became not a colony but a "protected Arab state." No governor was appointed; rather, the highest British official occupied the old diplomatic post of agent and consul general; his official role was to advise the sultan and the sultan's cabinet. This arrangement, of course, was a thinly veiled legal fiction: during a decade of tension (punctuated in 1896 by a naval bombardment to ensure the succession of Britain's choice as sovereign), the sultans lost most of their effective power to the British agent, who presided over a rising number of Britons staffing the highest echelons of the "Arab state." In 1913 the agent, who after that date was called the resident, was instructed to report not to the Foreign Office but to the Colonial Office, as would any conventional colonial governor.

Yet the legal fiction had real consequences. Other African territories were also classified as "protectorates," their administrative policies conceived as a form of supervised "native rule" in which local potentates were granted limited powers while being trained to assume full sovereignty in the distant future. Such paternalist policies became especially prevalent after World War I, when the League of Nations mandated Britain to administer the former German colonies while paying strict attention to "the paramountcy of native interests." But as an official report observed in 1932, the Zanzibar situation was different. "Zanzibar is a Protectorate proper with a ruling Sovereign," it noted. "This Ruler is not an African but an Arab, and any scheme of devolution . . . must be one which aims at supporting the Sultan's Government."[40] The result was a peculiar form of indirect rule in which administrative thinking was informed by a double set of racial assumptions: dual colonialism (as a similar arrangement in Rwanda was called by its Hutu opponents) or, as Anthony Clayton has described it, "Arab sub-imperialism." More specifically, most British administrators shared a governing vision aptly described by J. E. Flint: "The population was labeled by race, and race denoted function; Arabs were landowners and clove-planters [and, Flint might have added, political administrators], Indians were traders and financiers, and Africans were labourers."[41]

Scholars working in the instrumentalist tradition often observe that such policies were responsible for the entrenchment of communal boundaries; some assert that that was their aim. But such interpretations are of limited validity:

boundaries continued to be porous and situational, and, as we shall see, political division was rarely if ever the intended outcome of policy. Frederick Cooper usefully writes of the "circularity" of processes by which Zanzibaris crafted their identities partly in response to administrative incentives and pressures and partly in defiance of them. British assumptions that ethnic boundaries followed social function thus became self-fulfilling. Yet, as Cooper acknowledges, even this more limited instrumentalist approach cannot stand on its own; the shifting effects of African political mobilization, as I shall discuss in subsequent chapters, must also be taken into account.[42]

Colonial rule was most effective in entrenching boundaries around the two ethnic categories that already had been most discrete before British conquest, Indians and Omani Arabs. Yet even in those cases, the choices administrators faced cannot be disentangled from the political pressures brought to bear by Indian and Omani elites who mobilized support along ethnic lines. In 1909 some prominent Indian businessmen formed a committee to defend their interests as creditors, merchants, and urban landlords and to protest policies they feared would reduce Indians to the status of ordinary Zanzibaris.[43] In the interwar years this organization, by then known as the Indian National Association, focused on the concerns of the main clove exporters, who at that time were enmeshed in a prolonged conflict with the leading estate owners. The planters dominated the Arab Association, founded in 1911 by some of the islands' most prominent Omanis.[44] British policy makers, who had encouraged Indian immigration as a way to further the islands' commercial and financial development, sometimes felt torn between the demands of these two pillars of the colonial economy. But in the end the protectorate's official designation as an "Arab state" as well as the British officers' aristocratic prejudices against merchants had palpable consequences in shaping policy decisions.

Those consequences were most straightforward in the political realm. Almost from the start, the British entrusted much day-to-day administration to Omani aristocrats.[45] Official thinking on such matters fluctuated over time, but the number of British officials was never large, and the general trend, especially from the mid-1920s, was to use local people to staff all but the highest bureaucratic posts. This trend was accelerated during the Depression by London's fixation on cutting costs, a fixation that entailed, in this instance, doing something about the disproportionately large salaries paid to European civil servants. The preference for employing the sons of prominent Arab families can be explained to some extent by the Arabs' predominance among those with a Western education. But had that been the sole explanation, one would expect the administration to have been dominated even more by Indians (as indeed it was during the protectorate's first decades), who had responded more readily to the opportunities to learn the clerical and professional skills that British administrators valued. However, Arabs were the ones envisioned as the islands' governing caste, and British educators crafted preferential policies that aimed to prepare young Arabs for positions of administrative responsibility.

By thus recruiting Arabs into government, the British ensured that the bureaucratization central to all colonial state-building also contributed, in Zanzibar, to race-making. Whereas before 1890 the Arab regime had been a loose affair that relied on patrimonial networks between the sultan's court and a variety of Arab, Indian, and Shirazi vassals, under British rule it grew into a substantial bureaucracy of administrators and government-employed professionals whose qualifications were defined as much by their race as their professional attainments.[46] The most powerful state authority with whom ordinary Zanzibaris were likely to come in contact were local-level officers called mudirs, who by policy were educated elite Arabs. Indeed, the Provincial Administration (the equivalent of what in other British territories was called the Native Administration) defined all its lower-level officers by race. The "Arab mudirs" presided over a cadre of African *masheha* (sing. *sheha*), who were expected to serve as the mudir's eyes and ears in the villages. (A slightly different arrangement obtained in town.) Unlike the mudirs, who exercised considerable leverage in issuing judgments and collecting taxes, *masheha* had no administrative power and served essentially as the messengers of their supervising mudir.[47]

In their everyday lives, then, most Zanzibaris experienced colonial rule as a routinized form of Arab supremacy. British administrators recognized that despite the vaunted language of "trusteeship" and "native interests" that informed ideologies of indirect rule throughout the empire, Zanzibar differed radically from the standard model. In mainland territories such as Tanganyika, "native authorities" were chosen specifically because they were "members of the tribe over which they were placed"; hence they were expected to maintain the trust of the local populace at the same time as they fulfilled the commands of their British supervisors. But Zanzibar's mudirs had no such conflicts. Having been drawn not from among their constituents but from "the ruling race," their position was more akin to that of British district officers in mainland administrations.[48] In fact, by the 1950s, as the British "Zanzibarized" the Provincial Administration, the mudirs' own supervisors, the three district commissioners, were themselves usually Arabs.

The British rulers' ultimate vision was to transform Zanzibar into a constitutional monarchy with a parliamentary government. But, as Michael Lofchie has noted, their policies regarding representative government plainly revealed their vision of Zanzibar as "constitutionally an Arab state."[49] In 1926 they established a Legislative Council (or Legco) and gave it advisory and limited lawmaking powers. Representation was allocated by race. Like similar bodies in Britain's mainland territories, the Legco's key historical significance between the wars lay in "helping to create political races."[50] On the mainland, those races were Indians and Europeans, who, as "non-natives," were not entitled to the special protection of the paternalist state; they were offered the Legco as a forum in which their appointed representatives might defend their interests (though always within the hegemonic discourse of paternalism). The Africans themselves, who were considered not yet advanced enough to be capable of participation, were represented by European officials. Zanzibar's Legco differed in that the dominant voices there belonged to representatives of a third "political race," the Arabs. Before direct elections were instituted in 1957, British policy was to appoint more Arab members than from any other racial category. Arab interests were also articulated formally by the sultan, who presided over a separate Executive Council, and informally by the elite Arabs with whom British policy makers frequently conferred. Africans, on the other hand, were totally excluded from the Legco until 1946, their interests supposedly articulated by the district commissioners, who were members ex-officio.

The net result of such arrangements was to entrench a conviction among leading Arabs that they had been born to rule over the islands' other inhabitants. Unlike Indians and Europeans, the "political races" of the mainland territories, no one (yet) considered Arabs to be aliens. On the contrary, though the Arabs' Middle Eastern ancestry was central to how they were perceived by themselves and others, British policy was nevertheless built on the assumption that Arabs were the islands' indigenous ruling race. The general attitude, Arab and European alike, was enunciated by the administrator W. H. Ingrams. Although the British ideal was to teach Zanzibaris to govern themselves through "an organisation partly Arab and partly African," he wrote, that organization would remain stratified by race. "The principal posts will no doubt usually be held by the Arabs," who have long been in power and thus "have wider capacities" for governing than the islands' Africans; the latter, he claimed, understood and accepted Arab control.[51] Such expectations proved self-fulfilling. Still, British policy was not a strict supremacist one like the policy that colored Belgian support of Tutsi rule in Rwanda. By the 1930s most administrators were liberal on racial issues, meaning that although they thought in racial terms, they did not subscribe to notions of innate biological superiority. Though "there can be no suggestion" of teaching the sultan's African subjects to govern themselves without the apparatus of the Arab state, reported a 1932 committee, Africans must nevertheless have room for advancement.[52] British officials sincerely believed that the Arabs' historical role was to enlighten and uplift their non-Arab brethren, and after the war they promoted a handful of educated non-Arabs to responsible posts.

Official efforts to preserve Omani political dominance were matched by efforts to bolster Arabs' economic dominance as a landholding caste. But because the policy makers' command of social and economic structures was more tenuous than their command of the political apparatus, the results were decidedly ambiguous. In fact, few officials recognized the fatal weakness of the islands' monoculture economy, in which cloves accounted for 70 percent of export earnings (coconut products made up virtually all the rest) and, in the form of duties, half the state budget. Already the world's leading clove producer, Zanzibar was cursed with steadily rising clove prices throughout the first quarter of the twentieth century, a situation that convinced the British of the rightness of policies that encouraged further expansion. By the 1920s Zanzibar was growing almost 90 percent of the world's supply.[53] But the time clove trees took to mature left producers little room to shift investments to other crops should clove prices collapse—as prices inevitably did, several years ahead of the Depression. The following decades saw similar cycles of boom, when planters were urged to plant ever more trees, and bust, when they became mired ever more deeply in debt.

The officials' failure to appreciate these dangers was largely a function of their governing vision, which committed them to maintaining Zanzibar as the spice islands and Zanzibar's Arabs as a dominant planter class, contrary to what might have seemed self-evident economic logic.[54] Rather than deal with the structural causes of the planters' chronic indebtedness, causes common to plantation economies, officials preferred to blame the middlemen who sold the crop (and who held most of the notes on the overmortgaged estates) and, to a lesser extent, the laborers who produced it. This diagnosis originated in large part with the planters who dominated the Arab Association, whom the director of agriculture had consulted in a series of meetings in the mid-1920s. As an outgrowth of these meetings, the director invited the association in 1927 to form a new government-sponsored Clove Growers' Association (CGA), in which the larger planters cooperated to take a few steps toward holding down wages and securing greater control of the market. When the Depression rendered the indebtedness problem acute, administrators were jolted into taking stronger actions. In 1934 they enacted a spate of new laws, almost all directed against what the British and their Omani clients regarded as the excessive exactions of merchants and creditors. (Wage pressures continued to be a concern, but, as we shall see in chapter 3, they did not become a political issue until the war, when measures to contain them sparked effective resistance by clove pickers.) A moratorium was declared on all debts, and the CGA, which had become moribund, was transformed into a quasi-official marketing board that was dominated by the large planters and had near-monopsonistic purchasing powers.

Within a few years these actions led to the defining political crisis of the interwar period. Indian merchants correctly believed that the debt reduction schemes targeted them; one of the new laws, in fact, explicitly outlawed the alienation of land to Indians. That officials framed economic policies in racial terms is a logical consequence of their overall habits of thought: Zanzibar's economic woes, most believed, stemmed from the improvidence of an Arab plantocracy that was innately unsuited to commercial pursuits and the rapaciousness of an Indian merchant caste that was suited all too well to them. But whereas the Britons were officially committed to helping the planters overcome their shortcomings—the goal of economic policy, one observed, should be "the preservation of the Arab against himself"—their attitudes toward the merchants were less indulgent. The thinking of many betrayed the influence of classic European anti-Semitism: Indians as a class were usurers and parasites, like the Jews of Russia and Egypt, who fattened themselves on "the people of the soil."[55]

These metropolitan discourses, however, were complemented by well-established local prejudices. So when the Indian National Association protested the new laws by organizing a boycott of all clove exporting in late 1937, they elicited a bitter response that plunged the islands into a crisis "border[ing] on hysteria and racial violence."[56] For the first time in its 25-year history, the Arab Association turned to mass mobilization, warning islanders that Indian moneylenders threatened their shared history of Islamic civilization and urging them to support a counter-boycott of all Indian-owned businesses. Arab toughs roamed the countryside to enforce compliance and intimidate Indian shopkeepers. Although this crisis was short lived (in mid-1938 the government brokered a compromise that left the merchants in control of clove exports but preserved the CGA's central marketing role), it left a lasting impact on Arab-led nationalism. More generally, its drama reinforced popular images of Arab planters and Indian financiers.

The debt-reduction schemes and the formation of the CGA had the effect of further excluding Indians from agricultural production; that is, of bringing socioeconomic realities more closely in line with the image of Indians as a mercantile caste (although, as we have seen, that process had already been under way before British conquest). The planters, on the other hand, continued to suffer chronic indebtedness, and that in turn rendered the image of Arabs as a planter elite less accurate than it had been. Many met their debts by selling off parcels of the estates. Arab estates thus became fragmented, and non-Arab islanders—including some of recent mainland descent, the ambiguously labeled "Swahili"—came into possession of greater proportions of the islands' clove trees. All this contributed to the further erosion of a major economic component of the boundary that separated Arab elites from the other islanders, even as British policy makers strove to shore up the political components. To be sure, Omani families continued to dominate ownership of the largest estates, especially on Unguja. (Distribution on Pemba was less skewed, for reasons already discussed.) But the increasing economic fragility of their position meant that the Arabs were becoming ever more dependent on the state for their domination of Zanzibar society.

As in many parts of Africa, the colonial abolition of slavery posed a key problem for the would-be economic reformers, and it was in this realm that the aims of policy bore the least resemblance to outcome. Officials hoped to reshape the relationship between planters and estate laborers according to what they regarded as rationalized models of capitalist production. Theirs was a vision born of nineteenth-century abolitionism, which had always foretold that with the expansion of market economies and good government, former slaves would acquire a taste for commodities and thus learn the value of disciplined wage labor. In the earliest decades of British rule, officials were confident that a wide range of corollary benefits would ensue. J. T. Last, the administrator in charge of Unguja, predicted in 1906 that the very "idea of slavery would gradually vanish and be forgotten."

> The caste line of slaves and freeman would be lost and in due course all would commingle on [a footing of] equality. . . . In due course, the old idea of what is slave's work and what is suitable for freemen would be removed, for all being free, each could engage in whatever calling he might choose without any fear of losing his social status.[57]

But this vision failed to reckon with the varied aspirations of the planters and former slaves themselves. Officials frequently expressed frustration with planters who preferred to regard their former dependents not simply as units of labor but as clients, part of the prestigious accoutrement of estate ownership. Planters who had entrepreneurial aspirations were often too strapped for cash to be able to afford the capital outlays that would render their estates profitable enough to afford attractive wages. Most crucially, as Cooper has shown, the Britons failed to properly gauge the extent of the former slaves' reluctance to become agricultural proletarians.[58]

That reluctance took the form of chronic labor shortages. Seasonal shortages of harvest labor were nothing new (the clove bud must be picked at just the right moment or its value is lost), though planters had always managed by hiring additional labor. But in the closing decades of the nineteenth century the estates also suffered shortages of the day-to-day labor that had been done by slaves alone, especially the regular weeding necessary for the trees' health. Most observers attributed these shortages to the strangling of slave imports that had resulted from the British-imposed treaties and, from the mid-1880s, the European conquest of the mainland. After abolition in 1897, the shortages became acute. Many slaves left the plantations altogether and went to town, where, together with the autonomous slaves who had already taken up residence there, they formed the core of an urban labor force that found employment in road-building and other colonial projects as well as seasonal clove-picking.[59]

Those who remained on the plantations used their newfound autonomy to renegotiate the terms of their service. Instead of the relations between capitalists and wage-laborers that policy makers had envisioned, planters and their former slaves settled on arrangements whereby the latter remained on the estates as labor tenants (or "squatters," as they later came to be known). The details varied and were never spelled out in law, but labor tenants were usually obliged to perform regular weeding labor and participate in the clove harvest at the going wage rate. In exchange they were allowed to grow annual crops among the clove trees, an opportunity that many used to raise surpluses to market in town. Although they were expressly forbidden to grow cloves, some insisted on planting other tree crops.[60]

These patterns were in fact adaptations of a common element of the master-slave relationship, and they continued to be understood within languages of patron and client that were a legacy of slavery. Thus, contrary to Last's prediction, abolition did not disrupt the ethnic thinking that had been built on relations between slave and master but rather recast it. At the same time, former slaves seized the opportunities opened by abolition to accelerate the pace at which they engaged in activities by which they might shed the taint of enslavement, specifically by constructing networks of kin and community that were autonomous of their former masters. As we have seen, such behavior was not new. But the new conditions made it easier for a large proportion of former slaves and their descendants to successfully identify themselves as "Swahili" and for many even to become accepted as members of indigenous Hadimu, Tumbatu, or Shirazi communities. Among the most successful were those who managed to gain outright ownership of their own small farms, thus escaping the obligation to perform servile labor on an Arab estate.[61] But that labor itself, particularly weeding, continued to be denigrated as "slave's work" (to use Last's expression), and the labor tenants who performed it continued to be associated with the inheritance of *ushenzi*, or barbarism.

Cultural and economic factors thus combined to make most Zanzibaris reluctant to undertake labor on the estates except for relatively well-paid seasonal work as clove-pickers. (Another factor was the ability of indigenous islanders to meet their cash needs through the growing international demand for copra and other coconut products.) In 1902 the director of agriculture, R. N. Lyne, inaugurated a policy of recruiting contract labor from the mainland to weed clove plantations and perform other labor, such as road work, which islanders also avoided. By 1909 Lyne could report that mainlanders "have become an established feature in Zanzibar plantation life"; they were prized for weeding "better and more cheaply than Zanzibar laborers." Labor immigration became more substantial after World War I, when restrictions from what had been German East Africa, now the British territory of Tanganyika, were removed. At this time many immigrants began to stay in the islands past the expiration of their government contracts and encouraged their friends and relations to join them. Some gravitated to Ng'ambo, the popular neighborhood of Zanzibar Town, where they became part of the urban work force. But most settled in Unguja's plantation zone. From the beginning the immigrants had been allowed to cultivate subsistence gardens on the clove estates, but as they became better established they aggressively seized the opportunity to raise large surpluses of market crops.[62]

Over time, then, mainland immigrants became the most prominent component of the population living on the estates. A constant refrain among officials was that the former slave population was "dying out"; probably this perception was a function of the processes by which people of slave descent were leaving the estates and becoming absorbed into local communities as "Swahili," or indigenous islanders. Meanwhile, the net rate of voluntary immigration from the mainland rose or remained steady throughout most of the period following World War I.[63] Many of the immigrants never returned home; they established families and became a permanent presence in Unguja's plantation zone. Among planters and officials alike they developed a reputation for their superior strength and work ethic, a reputation that no doubt had something to do with the process of self-selection by which the labor-exporting regions of the mainland territories—regions with limited opportunities for wage labor and cash cropping—sent out young males who possessed the vigor and determination to undergo the arduous life of the migrant laborer.

By the interwar years, then, plantation labor was performed by a complex assortment of workers. Weeding and other everyday tasks were left to labor tenants, a mix of immigrants and slave descendants, all of whom tended to be disdained by islanders for their origins (ancestral or actual) on the mainland, the heart of *ushenzi*. Labor tenants also assisted in the clove harvest, but seasonal harvest labor was also hired among the mixed urban population and among indigenous villagers. The abolitionists' dream of an ethnically undifferentiated wage labor force, with all respecting the dignity of wage labor, went unfulfilled, as the general pattern of power in the plantation sector, as in the realm of the state, remained one between patrons and landlords who regarded themselves as "Arabs" (and therefore gentlemen) and clients and laborers whose service implied servility.

Shifting Ethnic Identities in Colonial Zanzibar

British rule, then, like Busaid rule before it, contributed to reproducing racial categories and their salience in Zanzibaris' everyday lives, though by no means can it be said to have invented them. Nor, despite governing assumptions, did colonial reforms have the effect of crystallizing ethnic and racial boundaries along the lines of economic function, let alone "freezing" them in place.[64] Few colonial officials were so wedded to the racial or tribal paradigm as to fail to recognize the fluidity of ethnic identity in the Protectorate. In fact, Zanzibaris' penchant for holding multiple and shifting ethnic identities repeatedly frustrated census takers who were charged with surveying the islands' ethnic and racial makeup.

Though these census data are not without flaws, several authors have made effective use of them to chart the broad shifts in how Zanzibaris imagined ethnic boundaries.[65] These authors generally emphasize two points. First, the shifts demonstrate the contingent, situational nature of ethnic identity; that is, they demonstrate that ethnicity is not part of nature but is created historically. One should beware, however, of accepting a common corollary to this view: that the impermanence of ethnic identities somehow attests to their "fictional" quality and to their marginal significance. On the contrary, the story I will tell in the following chapters shows that Zanzibaris' efforts to redefine their ethnic identities—their efforts to reimagine their place in communities bonded by ties of common descent—were central to how they debated issues of power in the second half of the colonial era.

Second, in common with much of the literature on African ethnicity, authors often use census data to emphasize the material factors that induced Zanzibaris to shift their identities in one way or another. The implication of insincerity is sometimes made explicit, as such explanations are offered as further evidence of the supposedly fictional quality of ethnic attachments.[66] Common explanations suggest that redefining oneself ethnically was a ploy to gain access to resources controlled by the colonial state, though others argue, more convincingly, that ethnic discourse arose from the patrimonial and kinship networks that people constructed to help cope with the trying circumstances of colonial and postcolonial society.[67] While material incentives did indeed play a role (as we shall see), identity shifts had a multiplicity of motivations, including, especially in the postwar years, the effects of political mobilization.

Among the most visible trends was the steady increase of those who claimed to be Arabs, from less than 8 percent of the total population in the 1924 census to 17 percent in 1948.[68] Of course, given the long history of Arabocentrism, it is not surprising to find that Zanzibaris continued the old fashion of "becoming Arab," despite British administrators' desire to demarcate a restricted ruling caste. Indeed, the state's efforts to bolster Arab rule no doubt added to the allure of Arab status. But there is little justification for explaining the increase in Arab identity as the result of an intensification of state-sponsored "inducements for laying claim to such an identity."[69] The political perks that came with Arab rule were distributed within personal networks dominated by highborn families as well as through voluntary organizations controlled by wealthy Arabs, such as the Arab Association and the Clove Growers' Association. Simply claiming Arab descent would not bring them, unless those claims were recognized by one's would-be peers. (Unlike South Africa or Rwanda, Zanzibar had no formal system of ethnic registry.)

One possible exception involved the brief imposition of forced clove-picking labor in Pemba in the early decades of the century. Arabs were customarily exempt from these exactions (not in law, but according to the ad hoc discretion of local officials), a consideration that apparently contributed to the

Table 2.1. Ethnic Identification in Zanzibar, 1924–1948

	1924		1931		1948	
	N	%	N	%	N	%
Africans "native to Zanzibar"[1]	116,400	53.5	119,500	51	143,100	54
"Swahili"	33,900		2,000		insignificant	
"Shirazi"	26,400[2]		40,900[2]		unrecorded	
Africans, mainlanders	64,800	30	68,300	29	58,000	22
born in islands	unknown		33,700		40,000	
born mainland	unknown		34,600		18,000	
Arabs	16,500	7.5	30,600	13	45,000	17
born overseas	unknown		6,400		6,000	
Indians	unknown		14,000	6	15,900	6
born in India	unknown		7,000			
Others, including Comorians	unknown		3,000	1	3,000	1
Total population	216,800		235,400		265,000	

1. In addition to Swahili and Shirazi, this category includes Pemba, Hadimu, and Tumbatu.

2. In 1924, the total number of "Shirazi" were divided more or less equally between Unguja and Pemba (although Pemba's overall population was lower). In 1931 the number of Unguja residents who declared themselves "Shirazi" had dropped by 36%, while those in Pemba had increased by over 150%.

Sources: Edward Batson, Report on Proposals for a Social Survey of Zanzibar (Zanzibar, 1946); Edward Batson, "The Social Survey of Zanzibar," 1958, BA 28, ZNA. Revised with reference to published sources, chiefly Lofchie, Zanzibar; Clayton, The 1948 General Strike; Cooper, From Slaves to Squatters; and Fair, Pastimes and Politics. The figures in these sources are internally and comparatively inconsistent and this table represents only a rough estimate.

attempts by some Pemba Shirazi to claim that they, too, were Arabs. But such claims were never accepted, and the incentives that sparked them did not long outlive World War I.[70] Pembans nevertheless continued to claim Arab identity at a higher rate than people in Unguja, but for reasons that are unlikely to have had anything to do with formal government incentives. We have seen that Wapemba were more likely than Wahadimu to have owned clove estates and (in the precolonial period) slaves; people who enjoyed such privileges were those most prone to claim Arab status.[71] Similarly, Pemba's more relaxed boundaries between Arabs and Shirazi no doubt allowed for a greater degree of hypergamous marriage between Shirazi women and Arab men, and the children of such marriages were normally accepted as Arabs.

The continued prestige of Arab status in colonial Zanzibar was part of the overall political culture of the Protectorate, where the British devoted much of their legendary skill in such matters to public ceremonies that sacralized the sultan's position as head of state. Colonial citizenship decrees preserved the old paternalist language that had attached to the sultanate, in which being the sultan's "subject" (raia) marked a person as a member of the Islamic civilization of the coast. It was the lowest common denominator of civic status, available to all who accepted the sultan's sovereignty, no matter what their ethnic descent was.[72] The hegemony of Arab rule can perhaps best be read in the behavior of marginal Zanzibaris who, even in the midst of open rebellion, nonetheless pinned their hopes on the myth of the just monarch who would redress their grievances if only he could be made to hear them.[73] Such attitudes toward the sultan of course varied with the incumbent.[74] But for most of the colonial era the throne was held by a genuinely popular figure, Khalifa bin Haroub, during whose long reign (1911–1960) antimonarchical sentiment was rarely encountered.[75] Yet the Arabocentrism that undergirded the sultanate rarely prompted simple emulation of the Arab aristocracy. Given the difficulties individuals faced in making viable claims that they belonged to the Arab elite, it is not surprising that islanders more commonly claimed Shirazi identity or one of the other indigenous identities imbued with Arabocentric pretensions: Hadimu, Tumbatu, or Wapemba wa asili. (Census takers and respondents alike understood that these categories were by no means mutually exclusive.) In contrast to the ambiguous label "Swahili," an individual's identification with any of these communities implied an assertion of his or her status according to the prevailing ideals of ustaarabu and Arabocentrism.[76]

An interpretation that has gained currency since the revolution explains colonial-era claims of Shirazi identity as a ploy by which islanders sought the material advantages that colonial racism supposedly accorded "non-natives": if islanders could convince administrators they were Shirazi, goes the argument, they would be accepted as "Arabs."[77] Apart from the implication of bad faith, this arch-instrumentalist interpretation suffers from two problems of evidence. The first is that officials never accepted Shirazis as Arabs. Though the twentieth-century surge in specifically Shirazi identity (as opposed to Hadimu, Tumbatu, or Pemba) began in Pemba in the 1920s, those claims did nothing to win exemptions from forced labor, as we have seen. The most commonly cited material incentive to becoming Shirazi was the ability to secure "Asiatic" rations during the war, particularly rice, which administrators deemed vital for Arab and Indian lifestyles but not for the lifestyles of Africans. Attempts to secure "Asiatic" rations were briefly promoted by the Shirazi Association, which was founded in Pemba in 1940. But rationing was a short-lived grievance, having been introduced quite late in the war, in 1943, well after the surge in Shirazi identity in Pemba that had led to the founding of the Shirazi Association there. It is true that claims to specifically Shirazi identity rose in Unguja at about the same time as rationing, but, as we shall see in the next chapter, this involved other factors. And claims to Shirazi identity continued to rise throughout the war and postwar years, even though Shirazis never were recognized as "Asiatics."[78]

A more fundamental problem is that Shirazis themselves never claimed to be Arabs or any other kind of "non-native." (In fact the legal distinction between "native" and "non-native" was irrelevant: it had been abolished in 1925, and Arabs had never been legally classified as "non-natives" anyway.)[79] Far from demanding enhanced wartime rations as Arab "non-natives," Shirazi Association spokesmen voiced resentment that Arabs were being granted such privileges while native-born islanders like themselves went without; the issue even prompted them to make a joint representation with their archrivals in the African Association, which was dominated by mainlanders and pan-Africanists.[80] If the interwar turn to Shirazi identity was in any way affected by colonial racial discourse, it was not through an acceptance of colonial racism and its implications of "non-native" privilege but, on the contrary, through the influence of the paternalist rhetoric of "native rights." In the immediate postwar years the Shirazi Association continued to denounce Arab privilege as the denial of "native rights" in favor of "alien races."[81]

But Shirazi nativism was not directed solely against Arabs. In fact, the Shirazi Association was established primarily in hostile reaction to what its founders regarded as the alien mainlanders who dominated the African Association.

The latter organization had been founded in Unguja in 1934 as a branch of the Tanganyika African Association; its leading members at that time were immigrants, townsmen, and mostly Christian. The following year a branch was established in Pemba, but its efforts to recruit members among the island's indigenous population aroused resentment among Pembans who did not like the implication that mainlanders were their equals. The "persons of note" who founded the Shirazi Association in Wete in 1940 were motivated by a sense that "the African Association does not represent the natives of this Island."[82] Anti-mainlander nativism remained a hallmark of Shirazi Association rhetoric throughout its history, as did its rivalry with the African Association. Paradoxically, this was a nativism based on concepts of *ustaarabu* that valued foreign heritage; mainlanders were disdained in large part because of their non-Muslim ancestry.[83]

Much about the rivalry between the Shirazi and African Associations can indeed be explained in terms of the effects of state policies, along the lines suggested by the best of the instrumentalist literature. But the relevant policies were more political than economic, and the rewards were as much honorary as material. For instance, the founders of the Shirazi Association resented that when administrators sought "native opinion" regarding who should serve on various advisory bodies (in particular, committees overseeing wartime volunteer activities), they accepted the recommendations of the African Association. This does not mean that the administration had created the ethnic associations to serve its own needs, as is claimed by authors who write within the nationalist paradigm. On the contrary, the evidence shows unambiguously that the British made do, often unwillingly, with the communal associations they found at hand. A corollary of the nationalist position is that the British favored communal organizations as part of a policy of "divide and rule"; the promotion of Shirazi consciousness supposedly prevented the non-Arab population from uniting among itself. In fact, officials had misgivings about the existence of two organizations to represent Pemba's non-Arabs and tried to persuade them to unite. But, recognizing that their own influence was minimal, the officials went along, hoping and expecting that one of the associations would "die a natural death."[84]

So although the colonial state may have created the conditions to which Zanzibaris responded by crafting exclusionary ethnic politics, the particular content of those politics was created by islanders themselves, in part from ideological components that had long been present. There was nothing new about the rhetoric of *ustaarabu* that informed twentieth-century Shirazi nativism; it certainly did not stem from colonial notions of "non-native" supremacy. Nor, for that matter, was there any significant increase in the number of islanders who perceived themselves as indigenous non-Arabs; that number remained surprisingly constant, at just over 50 percent. What was new was islanders' growing tendency to claim Shirazi identity to the exclusion of, or in primacy over, other forms of political identity. We have seen that speaking of one's Shirazi ancestry had long been a common rhetorical device with which islanders of varied backgrounds claimed distinction from slaves and other low-status newcomers. But such rhetoric was not necessarily the same as declaring "Shirazi" as one's sole or primary community of shared descent. During the colonial period, in other words, islanders' perceptions of the differences between them and the two main categories of "others" from which they distinguished themselves, Arabs and mainlanders, became increasingly polarized.

The clearest indication of this polarization was the virtual disappearance of the ambiguous label "Swahili" as a term of self-identity. Early in the century, calling oneself "Swahili" was still part of the strategy by which former slaves and other newcomers of non-Muslim mainland descent signaled their rootedness in local society. By mid-century, however, this strategy had been all but abandoned and very few "Swahili" were to be found. Edward Batson, a sociologist employed by the government to survey census data, noted that the drop in the numbers of those claiming to be Swahili accounted almost exactly for the increase of those identifying themselves as Shirazi, Hadimu, Tumbatu, and Wapemba. In other words, most of the erstwhile "Swahili," rather than continue to accept a label that conveyed thinly veiled connotations of pagan ancestry, now asserted unambiguous claims of belonging to Arabocentric island society.

To some extent this shift was an effect of the end of slavery. Use of the label "Swahili" had always been but the first step up a ladder of social mobility that might eventually lead to one's acceptance (or the acceptance of one's descendants) as Hadimu, Tumbatu, or Shirazi. Yet while such mobility kept people constantly moving out of the ranks of "Swahili," those ranks had been replenished just as constantly by the slave trade and the workings of the broader commercial system that lured other mainlanders to the islands. With the end of the slave trade, however, the ranks of those content to identify themselves as Swahili thinned and eventually disappeared altogether. As we have seen, the abolition of slavery itself also contributed to this process, by giving former slaves a stronger position from which to negotiate the terms of their integration into local society. The decline of Swahili identity was paralleled, though less dramatically, by a partial decline of the number of those who identified themselves as members of the particular mainland ethnic groups that had been associated with slavery, especially Yao and Nyasa. The latter trend can be understood partly as a result of the passing away of first-generation slaves who had been raised in the interior; their islands-born children were less likely to identify with mainland cultures.

So although the absorption of those who once called themselves "Swahili" into Shirazi and other indigenous ethnic categories marked something of a demographic watershed, it did not mark a new way of thinking. But the abolition of slavery did not put an end to the arrival of newcomers from the mainland, and most of these voluntary immigrants—including those who settled more or less permanently in Ng'ambo or as labor tenants in the plantation districts—chose neither to call themselves "Swahili" (no matter what they were called by others[85]) nor, by and large, to otherwise identify with the islands' Arabocentric culture. Instead, they clung to mainland ethnic identities.

This was a genuinely new departure in Zanzibar's cultural history, one that was to have enormous political repercussions. To be sure, the overall proportion of Zanzibaris who claimed mainland origins declined steadily between 1924 and 1948, which is hardly surprising, given the continued taint of mainland *ushenzi* and the expanding ability of most slave descendants to identify themselves as indigenous islanders. Yet the actual number rose in the 1920s, no doubt as a result of labor migration, and, after dropping precipitously as the war interrupted labor flows, it spiked again during the economic boom of the 1950s. In any case, simple numbers are of less significance than the fact that so many residents of mainland background persisted in identifying themselves as such. And most telling of all is the increase of those who, *though born in the islands,* nevertheless identified themselves as mainlanders.[86]

Not all of these self-identified mainlanders were the children of labor migrants; a minority were slave descendants who failed to follow the common pattern of identifying with local ethnic categories.[87] Research has yet to determine why some slave descendants continued to identify with the mainland ethnic categories of their forebears. Early in the century they no doubt included first-generation slaves and slaves who had failed to secure manumission in the bureaucratic schemes introduced upon abolition in 1897; their children and grandchildren might have subsequently encountered greater difficulties than others in shedding the taint of mainland ancestry. It is probably significant that in 1924 women predominated among the mainlander ethnic categories most associated with slavery,[88] since former female slaves would have been generally disadvantaged in their access to the assets (particularly land and ties of kinship to established communities) that made it easier to craft plausible claims of local descent.

Labor migrants had less ambiguous attitudes toward coastal culture than did slave descendants. Though most immigrants were Muslims (contrary to stereotypes that would become politically prominent in the 1950s),[89] the mystique of *ustaarabu* had less allure for them than it had for subalterns with deeper roots in the islands. Most came to the coast as single men, hoping eventually to return upcountry to marry, and, although many ended up staying in the islands and raising families there, their initial aspirations no doubt colored how they perceived their position in local society. Among the most significant local ties were those by which they sought kin and countrymen from similar mainland regions who would introduce them to employment opportunities in the plantation zones; consequently, communities of labor-tenants tended to be marked by ethnic affiliations based on common region of origin. So although ties of network and clientele with non-immigrant neighbors and landlords were of some significance to them, most retained a strong sense of identity with their mainland relatives even as they struggled to carve places for themselves in island society.[90]

A major factor that contributed to the accentuation of mainland identities was the growing prevalence of pan-Africanist nationalism between the wars. Its leading proponents were members of the African Association, who espoused an explicit identity of interests with subjects of the mainland colonies, particularly Tanganyika. Like their rivals of the Shirazi Association, they championed what they called "native rights," but they defined "native" status in terms that closely matched Western concepts of race. Concepts of *ustaarabu* and Arab paternalism took a back seat to the almost mystical component of racial pride that linked "native" identities to the soil of the African continent. As we will see in Chapter 4, these nativists encouraged immigrants to take pride in their mainland ethnic cultures. But pan-Africanist nativism was not restricted to mainlanders. As prominent members of the urban workforce and as estate laborers, the immigrants came into sustained contact with island-born people, especially Hadimu and slave descendants who had been pushed into marginal positions on Arab estates and in town. The impact of pan-Africanist ideas on the urban poor was forcefully demonstrated in a series of high-profile labor actions in the immediate postwar years. The leaders of these strikes identified themselves as mainlanders and used explicit pan-Africanist rhetoric to secure broad popular support. Clayton emphasizes the strikes' significance as the first concerted political acts in which Zanzibaris defined themselves as "Africans."[91]

As we will see in later chapters, such tensions made urban workers more receptive to pan-Africanist rhetoric in which the bonds of patron and client that had shaped many aspects of labor relations were reinterpreted as the fault lines of a racial conflict. Similar trends accompanied tensions between landlords and estate laborers. During and after the war, booming urban demands induced many labor tenants to intensify production of food crops. Many cultivated plots on several estates at once, even commuting to them from a home base in Ng'ambo. Landlords regarded such enterprise as a dereliction of the obligations of clientage, a form of disloyalty that left the clove trees overgrown with weeds and even threatened with destruction. Moving away from the language of personal dependency, spokesmen for the largest planters agitated for government to authorize stricter controls on labor tenants, whom they portrayed as undisciplined, lazy, and inveterate criminals. Their protests increased in pitch in 1950s, when, in a sign of how the old patron-client bonds were being frayed, the English word "squatters" first became common in elite discourse. It had been imported from Kenya, where European settlers used it to impugn the legitimacy of their tenants' occupancy rights. But in Zanzibar before the 1950s, even the harshest Arab Association rhetoric invariably used neutral terms such as "cultivator" or "food-grower."[92]

Such shreds of decorum were abandoned during the political crisis that gripped Zanzibar after 1957. Politicians affiliated with the Arab Association and the planter-dominated ZNP, invoking the old language of *ustaarabu*, inveighed against the squatters as aliens whose inheritance of mainland barbarism rendered them unfit for inclusion in the national community. A rash of politically motivated evictions ensued. This ongoing assault, economic and rhetorical, only confirmed most squatters in their reluctance to couch their aspirations in terms of the overarching status register of *ustaarabu*. But the squatters did not ignore the dominant discourse of Arab civilization. On the contrary, they made historical memories of Arab settlement central to their own self-definition. Under the influence of pan-Africanist nativism, however, they reversed the dominant version's moral coordinates, remembering *ustaarabu* not as patronage and enlightenment but as bondage and racial victimization.

The Politicization of Racial Identities

Squatter-landlord relations entered a crisis when they became enmeshed in the politics of nationalist mobilization that occurred after World War II, es-

pecially the hotly contested electoral campaigns of 1957–1963, years now remembered as the Zama za Siasa, or Time of Politics. Before that time, ethnic identities, though part of people's everyday subjectivities, rarely interfered
with more general notions of community and common humanity. Indeed, ethnic markers had often delineated the contours of the patron-client bonds that
tied society together, between landlord and tenant, employer and employee,
teacher and pupil. In contrast, by the eve of independence in December 1963,
ethnic identities had come to mark instead the boundaries between imagined
racial communities. The result was an acute degree of mutual dehumanization,
including widespread racial violence.

Why did political competition during the Time of Politics result in racial
polarization? The instrumentalist consensus places the onus of explanation on
British policies of communal political representation. But this interpretation is
often overdrawn, especially when it asserts that ordinary Zanzibaris were allowed to express their political views only via officially sanctioned communal
associations narrowly defined by ethnicity.[93] The colonial record in fact shows
that when British officials wanted to solicit popular opinion, their methods
were fairly haphazard.[94] To be sure, for the most part they were content to
rely on what they were told by the mudirs and by the Arab representatives appointed to the Legislative Council. That fact does indeed speak to the colonial
state's role in bolstering a broad racial divide between Africans and an Arab
elite, but it does nothing to support the contention that British policy was behind the ethnic subdivisions among Hadimu, Shirazi, and mainlanders that
became particularly acrimonious in the postwar years. Moreover, the impetus
for preserving and extending Arab racial privilege came more often from the
Arab community itself than from the administration. As late as 1945, when the
concept of African nationalism was sweeping the continent and even many
British rulers were starting to move away from the ideal of racial paternalism,
spokesmen for the Arab Association openly protested against being treated
equally with "uncivilized Africans."[95]

We have already seen that British officials disapproved of the creation of
two separate associations for the representation of "African" interests, one for
Shirazi and one for mainlanders. Yet such tensions bedeviled the appointment
of the Legco's first African members, in 1946. The African Association protested that Shirazis, as "Asiatics," were not qualified to occupy the two Legco
seats reserved for Africans. (Such nativist baiting is the apparent origin of the
erroneous latter-day contention that Shirazis themselves claimed to be "non-
natives.") British officials firmly rejected such reasoning—"the policy of Gov-

ernment was to make no distinction in dealing with these two groups of the African population"—although they did nothing to lessen the rivalry when they awarded both seats to Shirazi Association leaders Ameri Tajo and Ali Sharif Musa. The latter immediately indulged in nativism of their own. Ali Sharif stated publicly that any additional African seats should be restricted to people who could prove ancestral roots in the islands at least five generations in depth, and Ameri Tajo vilified the urban labor unionists as troublesome mainlanders.[96]

The most obvious shortcoming of a focus on colonial policies of communal representation lies in its inability to explain why ethnic tensions became most acute after such policies were abandoned in the mid-1950s. Neither the policy change nor the nationalists' response to it came smoothly. In early 1954, the resident, John Rankine, proposed constitutional changes that would enhance popular representation in the Legco (Africans and Arabs were to have an equal number of seats) but still adhere to the principle of appointing members by race. Tajo and the African Association endorsed the proposal. But it produced bitter divisions among Zanzibar's most self-conscious nationalists, the elite intellectuals of the Arab Association. While the older men who controlled the Arab Association's executive committee voted to support the Rankine constitution, they were opposed by younger, more educated members, who had been deeply influenced by the militant anticolonialism emanating from Cairo. Among these was Ahmed Lemke, editor of the association's weekly paper Al-Falaq. Lemke's editorials demanded that Legco members be elected directly from a noncommunal voters' roll; he couched these demands in aggressive anticolonial rhetoric that was meant to embarrass the moderates who supposedly published his paper. In June 1954 his editorials prompted the British to arrest him and all of the executive committee on charges of sedition.[97]

This ham-handedness had the effect of delivering the entire Arab Association over to Lemke's position. Protesting the arrests and, at last, endorsing Al-Falaq's demand for direct, noncommunal Legco elections, the association proclaimed a boycott of all government advisory bodies and its members withdrew from the Legco. The sole holdout was Ali Sultan Mugheiry, a member of the association's executive committee who, by apologizing to Rankine, was spared arrest. In November 1955, less than a week after taking his seat in the Legco, Mugheiry was knifed to death. His assassination would have repercussions for years to come.

Ironically, at this very moment the British were preparing to partially abandon communal representation and announce direct Legco elections from a common (that is, noncommunal) electoral roll. Triumphalist narratives portray this turnabout as an example of how the divisive policies of colonialism were overcome by nationalist pressures for an ethnically undifferentiated standard of citizenship. But such narratives are undermined by the internecine violence that climaxed the Legco boycott. In fact, not all colonial officials were opposed to direct, common-roll elections, nor were Zanzibar's nationalists united in demanding them.[98] When the administration announced in 1956 that such elections would be held the following year, the Arab Association lifted its boycott. But African Association spokesmen continued to press for appointed, communally defined members, even threatening to boycott the elections. Their reluctance to contest the vote was based partly on a calculation of their unpreparedness to compete with the Zanzibar National Party (ZNP), formed in 1955 by Arab Association liberals in an effort to appeal to a non-Arab constituency. In contrast to the Arab community, the mainlanders who dominated the African Association had few intellectual and material resources to draw on. Their ability to engage in political organizing had been further hampered by a 1953 decree that forbade civil servants from any political involvement: unlike the independently wealthy aristocrats who headed the Arab Association and the ZNP, the African Association's handful of educated members mostly earned their livings as government clerks and lower-level functionaries.

But at their heart, all the African Association's misgivings were built on a fundamental conception of the nation as a racially exclusive entity that was threatened by internal aliens of Middle Eastern descent. Their brand of nationalism, in other words, did not transcend the ethnic divisions that had grown out of the previous centuries of Omani and British rule; rather, it embraced and reinforced them with new ideological influences. As we will see, the same might be said of the nationalism of the Arab elite. This state of affairs contradicts what is commonly assumed about the inherently integrative function of nationalism in colonial Africa. Michael Lofchie recognized the anomaly forty years ago in his classic study of Zanzibar politics.[99] Yet authors still write as if the mounting pace of racial tensions in late colonial Zanzibar was an automatic outgrowth of divisions introduced by colonial policy. In fact, it was a product of ideas introduced by nationalist thinkers, whose influence reached a peak during the Time of Politics.

Part 2 of this book will examine the precise pathways by which these nationalist thinkers effected the racialization of ethnic thought. As elsewhere on the continent, the pioneers of nationalism were Western-educated intellectuals who came of age between the wars. But Zanzibar's early nationalists were unusual, not only in their pronounced level of self-consciousness as a cohesive intelligentsia but also in their sense of constituting part of a *racial* elite. Most were the scions of prominent Arab families with connections to the Arab Association. In their writings and teachings they expressed a sense of the historic role their Arab forebears had played in supposedly civilizing the East African coast and building its classic city-states, of which Zanzibar was said to have been the paragon. Their main strategy for rallying the broader populace to form an independent nation was a call to restore the precolonial sultanate to its former glory, a beacon of *ustaarabu* to all East Africa.

As the initiators of nationalism in Zanzibar, this elite intelligentsia had an impact on the thinking even of the subaltern intellectuals who later challenged them. But the subalterns refracted elite nationalism through the prism of their own preoccupations. We have seen that already by the 1940s, many of the popular resentments that had built up against the structures of Arab sub-imperialism had come to be crystallized, for many, in nativist identities as "African" or "mainlander." Many who harbored such identities came to regard the Arab state not as an example of precolonial independence but as a symbol of their history of subjugation to foreigners. Indeed, most African Association propagandists wedded their nativism to a defense of British rule for having liberated Africans from Arab enslavement. Yet although the elite and subaltern intellectuals propounded rival visions of the nation—one rooted in the rhetoric of civilization, the other in race—both visions shared the same starting assumptions. For all their emphasis on the transcendent values of Islam and *ustaarabu*, the intelligentsia's historical narratives reproduced the fundamental racial divide between Arabs and Africans. And for all their dismissal of Arabs as racial aliens, the subalterns built their vision of the nation on the same Arabocentric narratives.

Such rhetoric of history and belonging had far more power to evoke emotional responses than did any rhetoric that might have been built around instrumental issues of economic or administrative policy—issues on which the nationalists differed little, in any case.[100] This explains why the polemicists of the rival political parties relied so much on historical rhetoric when they competed for the support of the islands' voters. Competition was most acute for the loyalties of the majority of islanders who regarded themselves neither as Arabs nor as mainlanders. The intelligentsia stressed the lessons of coastal exceptionalism, which supposedly bound Arabs and islanders together in a shared historical experience of *ustaarabu* that rendered them superior to the benighted peoples of the African interior. Islam and the sultan were the unifying symbols of this *ustaarabu*, though the most skilled of the ZNP propagandists took care to steer attention away from the Arab hegemony those symbols implied. The subaltern intellectuals reacted by highlighting the chauvinism implicit (and often explicit) in the intelligentsia's vision. In early 1957, prodded by the respected Tanganyikan nationalist Julius Nyerere, the African Association negotiated a fragile electoral coalition with members of the Shirazi Association. In announcing the new Afro-Shirazi Union—later the Afro-Shirazi Party (ASP)—its leaders urged islanders to unite against Arabs on the basis of race.

Building on the ambiguity inherent in Shirazi identity, which was simultaneously Arabocentric and expressive of anxieties vis-à-vis the Omani elite, both sides made appeals based on the exclusion of a racial "other." For the intelligentsia, that "other" was the mainland African, whose inheritance of *ushenzi* rendered him unfit for full membership in the national community. For the subalterns of the African Association/ASP, he was the Arab, the worst of the various "white people" (*watu weupe*) who had invaded the islands over the centuries, certainly far more noxious than the Britons who, they argued, had liberated Africans from the cruelties of Arab enslavers. Not surprisingly, the most prominent Shirazi figures in the ASP coalition were from Unguja, where, as we have seen, Shirazi and Hadimu identities had long contained a strong undercurrent of anti-Arab sentiment. Pemba, in contrast, showed a greater resistance to pan-Africanist racial nationalism and a greater openness to Arabocentric coastal chauvinism. These divergent responses were shaped by the two islands' disparate experiences of Omani settlement. But the nativist nationalisms embraced in both places were in no manner determined by those experiences; they were constructed by twentieth-century intellectuals and political actors.

The British intended the elections of 1957–1963 to produce a representative government on which they might devolve limited self-rule and, ultimately, independence. But the close succession of four elections and their narrow outcomes kept the campaign rhetoric on a constant high boil. Within a year of the first election, political rivalries were shaping virtually every aspect of civil society: where people shopped, what buses they rode, and whom they employed or worked for were all decisions that became tied up in party loyalties. And because the electoral rhetoric on both sides was increasingly racialized, that led to mounting racial tensions throughout society. Violence became endemic, and for several days following the penultimate election, in June 1961, Unguja was engulfed by race riots. In that election, a ZNP-led alliance managed to form a parliamentary majority despite narrowly losing the popular vote. ASP stalwarts felt robbed, and although both sides were aggressors in the riots, virtually all the deaths were the result of anti-Arab pogroms.

The final Legco election, in July 1963, had similar results (though a tougher police presence prevented further riots), and in December Zanzibar became independent as a constitutional monarchy, under a ZNP-led government. But the celebrations of *uhuru* (freedom, independence) were muted, with many ASP loyalists saying it was *uhuru* for Arabs only, just another act of dispossession. Barely one month later, the sultanate and government were overthrown by an armed coup led by the ASP Youth League and former policemen whom the ZNP government had dismissed because they were mainlanders. By April, the revolutionary government had negotiated a union with Tanganyika (which had attained independence two years earlier) to form the United Republic of Tanzania.

The precise causes and progress of the 1964 revolution are still hotly debated, and the following pages are not intended to provide an explanation. They should, however, cast some light on the pogroms that accompanied the revolution, pogroms that resembled those of June 1961, although many times deadlier. The emergence of racial thinking in colonial Zanzibar and its reproduction within discourses of nationalism—the subject of the next three chapters—is of obvious significance for understanding such violence. Yet no matter how virulent such discourses became in the sultanate's final years and no matter how many ordinary Zanzibaris were exposed to them, we must still account for the processes by which they became transformed into an impulse to kill. That question will be taken up in this book's closing chapters, where I will ask how the relatively recondite teachings of the racial nationalists became transformed into popular conceptions that induced significant numbers of Zanzibaris to transgress, however momentarily, long-held notions of common humanity.

FIGURE 2.1. An elite quarter in Stone Town, ca. 1900. Turbans and umbrellas had long been markers of status in male attire.

FIGURE 2.2. Zanzibar Town, with the creek and Ng'ambo
in the distance. In the 1880s, when this picture was taken,
many of the houses in the eastern edge of what is today
Stone Town were still roofed in coconut thatch.

FIGURE 2.3. Darajani ("At the Bridge"), the commercial district linking Stone Town and Ng'ambo, ca. 1890. The bridge is visible as the open section of road in the middle distance.

FIGURE 2.4. Near the market on Stone Town's eastern edge, ca. 1900.

FIGURE 2.5. Ng'ambo, ca. 1900.

FIGURE 2.6. Hamed bin Muhammad el-Murjebi, also known as Tippu Tip, one of the most powerful Zanzibari Arabs of the later nineteenth century.

FIGURE 2.7. Sultan Khalifa bin Haroub, ca. 1912.

FIGURE 2.8. "Bringing in bananas," 1908. On their days off from plantation labor, squatters and former slaves often clogged the roads into town as they carried produce to market.

PART 2

—•—

War of Words

Ulimi ni mkali kuliko meno.
The tongue is sharper than the teeth.
—SWAHILI PROVERB

3

A Secular Intelligentsia and the Origins of Exclusionary Ethnic Nationalism

> Educated Africans are continually agitating to be given more responsibility, but I submit to you . . . that you will be unable to take that part unless and until you have inculcated in your own people a PRIDE OF RACE. Without this, education is useless.
>
> —A. W. Norris, in *Mazungumzo ya Walimu*, 1930

> Soap and education are not as sudden as a massacre, but they are more deadly in the long run.
>
> —Mark Twain, quoted in *Mazungumzo ya Walimu*, 1957

The above passages appeared in *Mazungumzo ya Walimu* (Teachers' Conversations), a magazine written and edited by schoolteachers employed by the colonial Department of Education, most of whom were recruited from Zanzibar's elite Arab families. While both quotes are unusual for having been written in English rather than Swahili and by Westerners rather than Zanzibaris, they nevertheless reflect the schoolteachers' overall faith in the power of education to advance the goals of nation-building and moral improvement. But they are also significant in other ways. The passage by Norris, which had originally been directed toward teachers from the majority Akan ethnolinguistic category in Gold Coast, indicates the ubiquity of racial thought—not of raciological doctrine but of the commonplace understanding that race, ethnicity, and nationality were overlapping if not identical phenomena. The aphorism by Twain, appearing as it did in the opening year of the Time of Politics, conveys a significance that, in hindsight, seems chilling. Its intended irony was surely lost on *Mazungumzo*'s editors, who, unlike Twain, believed implicitly in the value of everything that conventionally passed for civilization. Yet despite the schoolteachers' conviction that their 30-year project of uplift and nation-building had been as salutary as the teaching of modern hygiene, their rhetoric in fact can be shown to have helped shape the atmosphere of racial hatred that would culminate in massacres.

Zanzibar's schoolteachers typify the elite intelligentsia who dominated mainstream nationalism in Zanzibar and throughout Africa in the middle decades of the century. Indeed, a striking number of *Mazungumzo*'s editors and contributors became major figures in the islands' pioneer nationalist organizations, the Arab Association and the ZNP. Yet they are not the type of figure that is usually cited as the source of racial politics, nor is theirs the type of rhetoric usually linked to such politics. A more obvious place to start would be the poorly educated ideologues of the African Association and ASP, whose crude anti-Arab polemics informed most of the later pogroms. ASP racial populism came late to the political scene, as did the migrant workers and urban poor who constituted the core of the ASP's constituency. In contrast, the intelligentsia who spearheaded the ZNP had long advocated an inclusive vision of the nation, both in the classroom and on the public stage, in which all divisions of race and class would be transcended by loyalty to the sultan and to the values of Islamic civilization that he supposedly represented. This unifying message gained support throughout the 1940s and 1950s (according to the standard account), only to run aground on the racial fears whipped up by the ASP during the Time of Politics.[1]

It is undeniable that ASP racial demagoguery lay behind much of the violence of the Time of Politics. But that demagoguery did not arise in a vacuum; rather, it emerged within the context of ethnonationalist political debates whose general terms had been set largely by the elite intelligentsia. The intelligentsia's influence took two forms. Most generally, they can be credited for the fact that by the end of World War II, significant numbers of Zanzibaris had come to think of politics in terms of a national categorical order. Even those most bitterly opposed to the intelligentsia's project of civilizational nationalism (mostly activists affiliated with the African Association) agreed that politics ought to be about the rights of national groups. What divided them—ultimately to the point of violence—was the question of how those groups should be defined.

Yet the intelligentsia's role in the racialization of political thought went further than simply introducing the broad language of ethnic nationalism. Many of the specifics of ASP racial thought were derived from a corpus of historical narratives and sociological "facts" that had become common intellectual currency by the end of the war, thanks to the teachings and writings of the elite intelligentsia. Most significantly, the intelligentsia had devoted decades to reflecting on the history of the Islamic civilization of the Swahili coast, of which they considered Zanzibar the paragon. It was this distinctive *ustaarabu,* they argued, that formed the core of Zanzibar's national identity. The intelligentsia liked to think of this national vision as liberal, inclusive, and ecumenically tolerant. But, as has often been the case with civilizational nationalisms, the cultural criteria they used to mark their national vision privileged one racially defined stratum of society—the town-dwelling, land-owning Arab elite—which they made the archetype of all that was elevated and "civilized" about national life. The implications of such rhetoric were eventually noticed by less cultured political thinkers, who accused the intelligentsia of seeking to exclude anyone who did not fully identify with urban high culture, especially squatters and the urban poor who traced their roots to the African mainland. By the early postwar years, subaltern intellectuals were crafting their own versions of the intelligentsia's historical narratives. As we shall see in subsequent chapters, the subaltern versions retained many of the fundamental assumptions that informed the originals, including assumptions of originary African barbarism. But where the intelligentsia invoked an Arab-driven history of Zanzibari civilization, propagandists affiliated with the African and Shirazi associations countered with narratives of Arab conquest and enslavement and with a definition of the nation based on race rather than *ustaarabu.*

Thus, any attempt to recount the history of Zanzibari racial nationalism must begin, paradoxically, with the intelligentsia's liberal discourse of history and civilization. In focusing on the formative influence of the interwar intelligentsia, we are avoiding the common assumption that all that was divisive in colonial political discourse was introduced directly by colonial rulers and educators. Of course, it would be misguided to neglect the impact of Western thought, including general Western concepts of ethnicity and nation. But as we shall see, such concepts were almost always introduced indirectly, and only after much reworking. (As Partha Chatterjee has remarked, the fact that nationalism's intellectual pedigree is rooted in the West does not mean that nationalists in the colonial world had nothing left to imagine.)[2] The key actors were local intellectuals, the only ones capable of innovating versions of national thought that were locally compelling in ways that pallid imitations of Western discourse could not be. And for these intellectuals, Western thought was but one of many influences.

To treat Western influence as a form of indoctrination would be a serious misrepresentation of the intellectual community from which Zanzibar's nationalist intelligentsia was drawn, a vibrant and self-conscious community that long predated British rule. The most prestigious intellectual circles were dominated by members of town-based elite families who considered themselves Arab. Their main idiom of discourse was religious, although, as we shall see, a new cadre of secular intelligentsia began to emerge early in the twentieth century, often from the same families that dominated the ranks of the *ulamaa* (religious scholars). The most learned knew Arabic, with which they read not only religious texts but also Cairo newspapers that championed Islamic modernism and Arab nationalism. Families were especially proud if they could send their children to study in Cairo. Intellectual accomplishment was an important component of family pride, and given the kind of learning that was most valued, it is not surprising that such accomplishment was closely connected to a family's ability to claim Arab status.[3]

Zanzibar's intelligentsia, then, were keenly cosmopolitan—more so, in many ways, than their British rulers and sometime teachers—and, though hardly isolated from colonial discourse, they had ample intellectual resources to be able to engage with the ideas of nationalism without merely parroting Western ideas. Influence in fact flowed in more than one direction: Zanzibari intellectuals had a marked impact on the thinking of British educators and administrators. Colonial historians acknowledged the influence of their local informants far more readily than is consistent with the image of a discrete and overpowering colonial discourse.[4] As we have seen, the lower echelons of the Provincial Administration were staffed almost entirely by members of elite Arab families. These men were routinely commissioned to write reports on local customs and history, which were then circulated throughout the colonial bureaucracy.[5]

After the war, representatives of Zanzibar's secular, Western-educated intelligentsia became even more prominent in government service. And yet members of these same intellectual circles—young men who had experienced sustained, direct interaction with British educators and administrators and who in many cases were responsible for maintaining the colonial state from day to day—were also those who developed the earliest and most determined anticolonial consciousness. This state of affairs was not unusual for the colonial world (although Zanzibar's "dual colonialism" was matched in only a handful of other African colonies); a growing literature has documented how such colonial "middles" became colonialism's "intimate enemies."[6] My purpose in noting it here is simply to emphasize that the following narrative cannot be under-

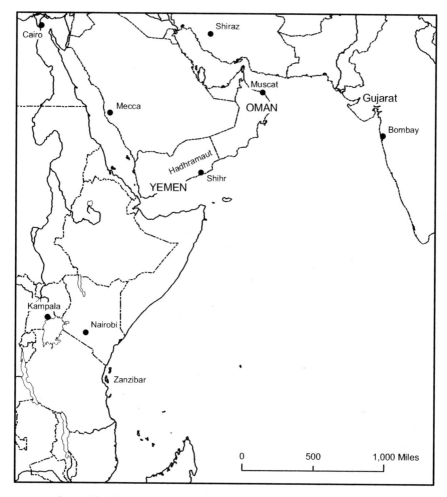

MAP 3.1. The worlds of the Zanzibar intelligentsia.

stood if one imposes false dichotomies between discrete realms of discourse, one colonial and Western, the other anticolonial and indigenous.

Another misleading dichotomy is that between popular discourse and the discourse of the intelligentsia. The subalterns who later would support the ASP were not as lacking in political awareness in the interwar years as the standard sources assume;[7] they were listening to and arguing about many of the same issues that propelled the urban intelligentsia. Like any change in political culture, new ways of thinking about ethnic difference emerged from circuits of discourse in which diverse intellectuals spoke to one another—elite and popular, European and African—and in which their ideas were interpreted and debated by the population at large. Thus, any history of the popular racial nationalism of the 1950s and 1960s must take account of the elite intellectual discourse of a generation before.

Civilization and Nation-Building

It is not unusual to find that schoolteachers formed a disproportionate share of the secular intellectuals who forged a nationalist discourse between the wars. From its beginnings, modern nationalism had been understood as an educational project in which intellectuals had the duty of making citizens out of their less enlightened countrymen.[8] The link between teaching and nationalism was especially strong in colonial Africa, where schoolteachers were more numerous than other figures (say, journalists) defined by the institutions and discourse of national "modernity." Teachers were also more ubiquitous: most were posted to village communities, where they were in an excellent position to forge versions of nationalist ideology couched in local cultural idioms.[9] But Zanzibar's schoolteachers were unusual in their belief that they were destined to lead not only by dint of their mastery of Western education but also by dint of intellectual attributes they considered part of their distinct racial inheritance.

This situation was the outcome of several convergent trends. From its inception early in the century, Zanzibar's system of secular education was geared toward training an administrative cadre who could serve as the functionaries of a modern state. (Unlike in other British colonies, where mission schools prevailed, in Zanzibar virtually all secular education was state run.) Following general governing principles, that cadre was drawn principally from Arab families.[10] But persistent Arab preponderance in government schools, especially in the higher grades, cannot be understood simply as the result of British policy. The racial vision was never pursued with the rigor that marked, say, Catholic education in colonial Rwanda. In fact, throughout the 1920s and 1930s the government made repeated efforts to expand education for rural non-elites— efforts that foundered, as we shall see, on villagers' keen distrust of secular education. The urban gentry, in contrast, quickly overcame such suspicions, no doubt influenced by modernist ideas emanating from the Middle East that stressed the benefits of a secular, government-sponsored education.[11]

In 1923 the Education Department opened its first postprimary institution, the Teachers Training School. Twelve years later, in accord with empire-wide educational reforms inspired in part by the theories of Booker T. Washington, the school was closed and the bulk of its teacher-training functions shifted to the Rural Middle School at Dole.[12] Teachers chosen to receive advanced training were sent to the new Government Secondary School in town, from which the most promising were to be sent up to Makerere College in Kampala. None of these schools, however, were intended merely to train teachers. Rather, classroom teaching was to serve as a forcing-bed for the cultivation of an administrative elite. That policy was endorsed by the islands' leading families, who, speaking via the Arab Association, had been demanding that government provide opportunities for sons who were being marginalized by the foundering of the plantation sector.[13] For the next thirty-five years, the Teachers Training School and its successor institutions trained a disproportionate share of the islands' administrative staff, many of whom began their careers in the classroom and finished them as prominent nationalists.

By 1930 these young schoolteachers had begun to cohere as a self-aware intelligentsia, imbued with a responsibility for building the "modern civilization" upon which a nation could be based. Their cohesion was mediated in large part by the Education Department, in particular by the remarkable L. W. Hollingsworth, first director of both the Teachers Training School and the prestigious Government Secondary School, whom many of Zanzibar's leading intellectuals later remembered as a formative influence.[14] In 1927 Hollingsworth launched the teachers' journal *Mazungumzo ya Walimu*, intending it as a forum in which teachers might continue the debates on pedagogical and social topics that he encouraged in the schools and in the process improve their writing skills in English and Swahili. From the start he edited the magazine in close collaboration with his Zanzibari staff, and in 1937 he placed it in the charge of an editorial committee consisting of some of its most frequent contributors.[15] Despite his supervision, then, *Mazungumzo* was written and edited largely by Zanzibaris. Many of postwar Zanzibar's most prominent intellectuals and politicians first published there in the 1920s and 1930s.[16] The magazine thus served as the center of an inordinately influential circle of intellectuals, who no doubt propagated many of their ideas in the classroom before becoming directly involved in politics.[17]

From its earliest numbers, *Mazungumzo* reveals the schoolteachers' confidence that they constituted a cultural elite: masters of the skills of modernity as well as of what they considered proper Islam, aloof from the rustic "natives"[18] whose children they were charged to teach but at the same time conscious of their obligations to exemplify Arab civilization in the villages where most were posted. Hollingsworth and his Zanzibari colleagues encouraged this self-image, urging teachers to take seriously their obligation to exert a salutary influence on village life. Their thinking on these matters reflected a convergence of influences. British educators saw it as their long-term job to help lay the foundations of a modern nation (albeit one that would not assume self-government until well into the future), making their charges "better Africans" rather than a species of European. Their main strategy, encouraged by the Tuskegeeist principles associated with Booker T. Washington and his disciples, involved cultivating schoolteachers as the core of an indigenous elite that would lead local communities in the building of modernity.[19]

British pedagogues, however, were not the schoolteachers' only mentors. Many had older relatives active in the Arab Association, which since its founding had been immersed in the currents of pan-Arab nationalism. Many, too, were related to the islands' leading *ulamaa,* who since before the turn of the century had been reading and debating Islamic modernism.[20] From those intertwined intellectual movements, perhaps more than from British teachers, the schoolteachers learned of their unique responsibility to lead in building a "modern civilization." Nineteenth-century intellectuals in Cairo and Damascus had originally borrowed the latter concept from Europe (though one should not ignore the rich intellectual legacy inherited from Arab thinkers such as Ibn Khaldun), but by the interwar years it had been elaborated to include elements intended to challenge Western pretensions to represent the moral if not technological epitome of "civilization." Arabs must learn the history of their own civilization, argued the pan-Arabists, and in this crucial nation-building task schoolteachers were to play the leading role. The central figures in spreading this message were pedagogues based in Baghdad, but their influence was felt among educators throughout the Arab world, and it is no doubt significant that many of the first generation of instructors in Zanzibar government schools—that is, the new intelligentsia's own teachers—were recruited from Cairo, another center of interwar pan-Arabism.[21]

These convergent pedagogies, then, all encouraged schoolteachers to think of themselves as a cultural and political elite. But none, at least in their original forms, can be credited as having prompted the schoolteachers' conviction that they were *ethnically* distinct from the communities they were to lead.[22] That distinction, of course, was in accord with Britain's unusual form of indirect rule over the "Arab sultanate." But it did not originate with the British; rather, like the policy of "Arab rule" itself, it was an outgrowth of the concepts of *ustaarabu* and Arab hegemony that had marked paternalist social relations in Zanzibar long before the colonial era.

The continuity between precolonial notions of paternalism and the school-teachers' sense of cultural and educational superiority is illustrated in how *Mazungumzo*'s editors and contributors dealt with the recurring problem of teachers who disliked their rural assignments and expressed open contempt for the villagers they were meant to serve. In the early 1930s this contempt became a policy issue, since the Education Department believed it was one of the reasons that village schools had difficulty enrolling students. Conversely, hostility to government schools only exacerbated the teachers' discomfort and their disdain for village elders who did not understand the benefits of modern secular education.[23] During those years, *Mazungumzo* carried a string of essays admonishing schoolteachers not to let their sense of superiority yield to arrogance. Hollingsworth in particular was disturbed by reports of teachers who used abusive language toward their pupils, including the epithet *washenzi* (barbarians).[24]

One of the most explicit discussions of the problem was written in 1929 by Abdulla Ahmed Seif, assistant director of the Teachers Training School. Seif traced the teachers' arrogance to their class aspirations. But, significantly, when prescribing proper behavior, Seif, himself a planter, played on those same aspirations. The ill-mannered schoolteacher (he wrote) arrives in the village acting superior to everyone and as a consequence finds that he has no students, no friends, and no local influence. In contrast, the well-mannered schoolteacher acts humbly and solicits the villagers' trust and friendship. Villagers thus learn to seek his advice as an educated man; he attracts students and clients and soon becomes the local "big man" or "grandee" (*bwana mkubwa*). Seif highlighted the moral with a Swahili proverb: "Arrogance does not make a gentleman" (*kiburi si maungwana*). Hollingsworth made the same point a year later, when, while touring the village schools, he was alarmed to see young teachers loudly violating what should have been their sense of noblesse oblige.[25]

External intellectual currents were significant, then, largely in how they influenced the intelligentsia in their elaboration of inherited concepts. Perhaps the most significant examples involve imported teachings about history, many of which reinforced local distinctions of civilization and barbarism in ways that accentuated their implicit racial undertones. Pan-Arab nationalism, for instance, was no different from other forms of nationalism in its compatibility with the idea of race.[26] Reeva Simon writes that pan-Arabist historians themselves were inspired by Volkish philosophies of diffusionist universal history, in which the origins of civilization were traced to a "primeval ancestor nation" that carried it to other parts of the globe during wanderings from an original homeland. Adapting such theories to their own ends, the pan-Arabists focused on ancient Semites rather than Aryans and invoked the American anthropologist James Henry Breasted to describe how "Semitic waves" emanating from Arabia and the Fertile Crescent had spread civilization to the rest of the world. Despite differences concerning the precise identity of the earliest Semites, all agreed that their crowning achievements, the Arabic language and Islam, were the gifts of the Arabs.[27]

Hollingsworth and his colleagues also urged the teaching of history of much the same kind. Though the ideas of universal history pervade the entire colonialist historical literature, schoolteachers encountered them most readily in school texts, including several prepared by Hollingsworth himself. Most accessible was *Milango ya Historia* (Gateways of History), a world history primer Hollingsworth wrote in collaboration with Abdulla Ahmed Seif and other Zanzibari members of the *Mazungumzo* editorial board, which was used widely from its first appearance in the 1920s into the postcolonial period.[28] The primer's principal narrative, the progress from savagery to civilization, is painted in broad strokes, with an emphasis on how relatively small groups such as the Greeks and Hebrews were responsible for having spread civilization to the rest of the world. Accordingly, the first of the three slender volumes opens with a chapter on "cavemen" ("their appearance was absolutely barbarian," it states, assuming an easy link between physical appearance and level of civilization) and closes with four chapters on ancient Greece. The primer's definition of civilization must have seemed familiar to its adult readers: proper government (meaning obedience to a single monarch), literacy, and, implicitly, monotheism.[29]

The implication was clear: the attributes of civilization had been introduced to East Africa by outsiders. And to make it clearer still, whenever a foil was needed to highlight the accomplishments of (say) the Greeks, Hollingsworth drew his example from the foolish customs of pagan Africans. Aside from such stray comments, only one of *Milango*'s thirty-eight chapters concerns Africa; the text flatly explains that is because black Africans are barbarians who have never done anything of historical significance. But the primer allows a significant exception: peoples living along Africa's coasts are worthy of study because they had come under the influence of foreigners. To demonstrate, it relates how centuries of Arab presence had rendered East Africa's coastal population more civilized than their upcountry neighbors, a story elaborated in greater detail in Hollingsworth's other texts.[30]

Texts like Hollingsworth's thus flattered the schoolteachers by giving the imprimatur of colonial modernity to their inherited ideas of *ustaarabu* and coastal exceptionalism. It is hardly surprising, then, that such ideas were prominent in the many essays on local history the schoolteachers wrote for *Mazungumzo*. The editors solicited these essays as part of a nation-building project in which colonial, Arabist, and inherited themes played out in an ironic counterpoint. The project was launched in 1930, when Seif, who had been left in control of *Mazungumzo* while Hollingsworth was away on leave, came across an essay by the Gold Coast educator A. W. Norris and decided to reprint it in *Mazungumzo*. Norris's refrain was the need for teachers to cultivate "PRIDE OF RACE"; the phrase recurs throughout, always in capital letters. Such pride, Norris observed, has been necessary to the success of "every known empire and nation"; without it, no nation can "rule itself or others." [And the best strategy for cultivating national pride, he argued, was to cultivate historical memory,] which might be learned by listening humbly to the tales of the elders.[31]

Norris's essay impressed Seif not only for its emphasis on history and nation-building but also for its chastening of teachers who disdained non-educated villagers. But the message originally crafted for readers in Gold Coast had the opposite effect in Zanzibar. Norris had urged teachers to seek pride not in their modern education or in their position within the colonial order but in the history of their entire "race," by which he alluded specifically to "the Akan race" or the Akan "nation." He thus addressed a contradiction that beset most British colonies governed by the standard forms of indirect rule, where the discourse of modernity threatened to undermine the "traditional" authority of chiefs and elders on which colonial officials relied. By encouraging political traditions built around metaphors of seniority and common descent, Norris and other colonial officials hoped to cultivate "tribal" (or "racial") solidarity between chiefs and commoners, including the educated "youngmen" who resented chiefly prerogatives.[32] But Zanzibar's very different traditions of *ustaarabu* and Arab hegemony, and the unusual form of indirect rule that grew from them, ultimately rested on metaphors of *separate* descent. These traditions thus shaped the schoolteachers' historical narratives in ways that emphasized not unity but difference. Most of the narratives published in *Mazungumzo* concerned Arab or Persian figures whom local lore remembered as having built the city-states that made the coast distinct. (In this regard, they echoed narratives that pan-Arabists in Cairo and Damascus had urged their parents to write to preserve the history of world's Arab heroes.) The most prolific contributor of historical essays, M. Abdulrahman of the Dole Rural Middle School, wrote a series that depicted the nineteenth century as the story of Arab heroes who explored the mainland, where they contended with the depravity of African cannibals.[33]

The authors of such narratives plainly drew from colonial texts; Abdulrahman acknowledged as much. But Abdulrahman also relied on oral informants, and it is evident that colonial sources only reinforced distinctions between Arab civilization and African barbarism whose roots were multiple and
deep. Some of those roots were revealed in a 1938 exchange in which several of
Mazungumzo's most accomplished authors debated the origins and usage of
the word *ustaarabu* and its personal noun form, *mstaarabu* (civilized person).
All agreed that the words were derived from an Arabic source, *mustaariba*,
meaning those "who became Arabs by following Arab customs" rather than
by being born into an Arab tribe. At issue was whether it is valid to use the
Swahili cognate to denote a person who had been educated only in the ways
of Western civilization. Muhammad Othman, opening the debate, argued not:
given the word's etymology, "it is a mistake . . . to call someone '*mstaarabu*' who
follows neither the Arab religion nor Arab customs." So, for example, a West
African "who has received a European education and lives like a European"
might be described using the English word "civilized" but cannot be said to
be *mstaarabu*. (Othman presumably was referring to the missionary-educated
"creole" elite who dominated much African intellectual life throughout the
first decades of the twentieth century.) He argued that an alternative Swahili
term should be found.[34]

The most erudite response was by Ali Said al-Kharusy, a 22-year-old teacher
at the elite Government Secondary School and scion of a prominent family.
(He would leave teaching in 1942 and devote the rest of his career to civil service, the family businesses, and nationalist politics; in the 1950s he served as
secretary of the Arab Association.) Like most contributors to the debate, al-
Kharusy took issue with Othman's lexical proposals, noting the difficulties of
trying to make an Arabic etymology govern the usage of a standard Swahili
word. But his main purpose lay elsewhere. Most of his contribution consists
of a pre-Islamic and indeed pre-Abrahamic genealogical charter of the Arab
people, the complexity of which suggests the influence of the pan-Arabists and
their interest in Semitic prehistory. He demonstrates that the first of the *mustaariba* Arabs was none other than Ismail, who was regarded as the forefather
of the Quraysh—the tribe of the Prophet—and of all the Arabs. His argument
therefore reaffirms the absorptive nature of Arabocentric ethnic identity, which
encouraged people to become civilized by aspiring to become Arab. He notes
that the Arabic infix *sin-teh* (s-t), by which the Swahili root -*staarabu* is derived
from *Arabu* (Arab), indicates the process of becoming. Strictly speaking, then,

a Swahili-speaking *mstaarabu,* like a *mustaariba* Arab, implies someone who has become an Arab by "manners and upbringing" rather than by ancestry.[35]

Al-Kharusy's extended gloss on *ustaarabu* can be recognized as an early lesson in the liberal civilizational nationalism that would later dominate ZNP rhetoric. But the underlying assumption is that while the paths to civilization were supposedly open to anyone who wished to travel them—using al-Kharusy's definition, to anyone who "understood and followed good ways and abandoned barbarian ways"—those paths all led out of Africa. To be sure, al-Kharusy and his colleagues allowed for an alternative to the Arab path toward civilization, that of Western education. But none ever imagined an African model of civilization. Indeed, Zanzibaris were known to disdain as barbarians even mainlanders who had attained a Western education—an attitude that British educators, who put more stock in Eurocentric ideals than in Arabocentric ones, found amusing.[36] Abdullah Muhammad al-Hadhrami, perhaps the preeminent figure on *Mazungumzo's* editorial board and certainly one of the most erudite, evidently sensed such disdain in Othman's comments about West Africans and took pains to correct it. But he did so by pointing out that the ancient civilizations of Sudanic West Africa stemmed from a history of Arab contact longer even than Zanzibar's, thus reinforcing the common assumption that all "civilization" in Africa originated outside the continent.[37] No matter what the precise definition was, then, all agreed that the *mstaarabu* who completed the journey toward civilization could be recognized chiefly in contrast to another left behind.

That other, the African barbarian, was not, strictly speaking, defined racially; after all, an *mstaarabu,* in the word's original (Arabic) sense, was one who *became* Arab. (In the same vein, the Swahili word, like its Arabic counterpart, was related to a verb: *staarabika,* to become civilized.) But while the concepts of Arab civilization conveyed in both colonial and pan-Arabist texts focused on culture rather than blood, they also relied, to a greater or lesser extent, on the metaphor of descent. The same is true of locally inherited notions of *ustaarabu* and Arab and Shirazi identity.[38] So although *Mazungumzo's* historical narratives were *multi*racial, in that they portrayed civilization being shared by diverse peoples, they were not *non*racial; in their focus on waves of civilized peoples spreading to East Africa and elsewhere, sharing a common ancestry and identity which they kept intact over centuries or even millennia, they reproduced many of the core assumptions of racial thought. It is no surprise, then, that Muhammad Othman, having made the small leap from civilization to descent, made the further leap from descent to the body—an association not universal to racial thought but not unique to raciology, either.[39] After describing how the Arabs' introduction of Islam had prompted "the natives of the coast to regard them as their leaders and mimic them in every way," Othman added that as a mark of having become more civilized, coastal people's skin became clearer and brighter than that of "barbarians" (*washenzi*), "that is, the bush-people of the African interior."[40]

A discourse of racial chauvinism, then, was beginning to emerge from the intertwined discourses of civilization, modernity, and nation-building. The interconnections can be seen in *Mazungumzo*'s campaigns for the construction of a national culture, another instance in which the nation-building concerns of British educators converged with those of Zanzibari colleagues. These concerns were clearly evident in the linguistic project that the editors considered one of their core missions. In March 1931 Hollingsworth wrote in his typically patronizing tone that he had been saddened to discover that many teachers ignored the magazine's Swahili portions, preferring to read only in English. To combat such attitudes, he reprinted an article in which the educator and linguist G. W. Broomfield argued that "the development of the Swahili language" would be necessary to the task of building an "African Civilization" that would be more than merely an imitation of Europe.[41] Later that year Hollingsworth began publishing his monthly "editor's letter" in Swahili—in the hope, he said, that he might thereby help teachers perfect their Swahili prose. (His pretension in this regard is lessened by the likelihood that Seif or another of his assistants translated from his English original.) By this time the magazine was almost entirely in Swahili, and it carried many items about the improvement and standardization of Swahili as a literary language capable of bearing all the tasks of modern civilization.

The pan-Arabists based in the Middle East also promoted linguistic and literary nationalism. But whatever the main inspiration for such projects, it remained for Zanzibari intellectuals to invest them with local linguistic materials—materials, as it turned out, that were expressive of a particular kind of chauvinism. The form of Swahili spoken in urban Zanzibar had recently been proclaimed the standard lingua franca for all of East Africa by an interterritorial conference of educators, a proclamation that encouraged *Mazungumzo*'s contributors to belittle as "dialects" the forms spoken in rural districts. Those dialects marked their speakers as members of indigenous ethnic groups, such as Hadimu or Tumbatu, rather than Arabs.[42] Disdain for rural dialects, in fact, elicited one of Hollingsworth's most forceful columns on abusive teachers, in which he responded angrily to a submission from a teacher who had compared villagers' speech to the grunt of apes. In the same issue he published a letter from a correspondent in Pemba who complained that townspeople expressed contempt for countryfolk as soon as the latter opened their mouths.[43]

Yet such protests were in vain, for the project of building a national language necessarily involved denigrating and excluding alternative forms of speech. Many elites regarded Swahili itself as a vulgar language and a "symbol of ignorance," and the Arab Association conducted a sustained campaign criticizing the Education Department for emphasizing it in government schools at the expense of Arabic. (Arabic had long been moribund in the islands as a spoken language.) Such an emphasis, the association argued, threatened to debase islanders to the level of "Tanganyika natives."[44] Similar attitudes affected the thinking even of educators who were dedicated to the project of improving Swahili. The linguistic values they deemed worth preserving were those connected with the Arab-centered civilization peculiar to the coast towns, and those to be purged were connected not simply with the countryside per se but with the non-Muslim "barbarians" (*washenzi*) of the African mainland. Such thinking appears most elegantly in a leading essay from October 1937 by A. M. al-Hadhrami, that month's editor, in which he called on readers to participate in officially sponsored projects for turning Swahili into a modern literary language—a task, he noted, that only native speakers could accomplish. Al-Hadhrami called attention to the factors that made Swahili "more advanced" than all other Bantu languages, particularly the high degree of *"ustaarabu"* embodied in its many Arabic loanwords. In fact, he argued, Swahili's superior literary elegance was attributable entirely to Arabic (a language he spoke): "People often say that Swahili stripped of Arabic is no longer Swahili but the language of barbarians."[45]

Another nation-building project that appealed both to British educators and the nationalist intelligentsia was the reform of popular culture. In numerous condescending essays on village customs, especially dance rituals, one can catch echoes of a debate within the *Mazungumzo* circle between those who would simply dismiss such customs as incompatible with the values of modernity and civilization and those who would reform and preserve them as symbols of national pride and solidarity. That the latter position quickly won the argument in the pages of *Mazungumzo* is not surprising, given that it accorded with the Tuskegeeist position championed by dominant figures in the Education Department.[46] Still, the critiques of village customs were often harsh. Particularly biting were descriptions of Hadimu practices, including the calendrical rite of Mwaka Koga performed at Makunduchi, at the southern end of Unguja. (Since the early 1960s the Makunduchi Mwaka has become imbued with the politics of Shirazi nativism.)[47] Though *Mazungumzo's* readers were familiar with a muted version performed in town, Makunduchi's elaborate festival was ridiculed for its "foolishness" and lack of restraint. Other Hadimu dances were described even more scathingly as indecent and unhealthy; the headmaster at Makunduchi thrashed pupils he caught participating in them. A common adjective in these descriptions was *kishenzi* (barbaric). Such condemnations, and the attitudes they reflected, no doubt aroused deep resentments, since festive dance was central to the rites by which indigenous islanders defined their very communities and the lines of authority within them.[48]

Even more central was Islam, the rituals of which were fundamental to delineating the boundary between the civilized and the barbaric. Yet the intelligentsia made little effort to hide their contempt for villagers' religious practices. Indeed, some saw the critiques of village festive rites as part of a broader campaign for the reform of popular Islam. For well over a generation, Zanzibar's leading *ulamaa,* inspired by global currents of Islamic modernism, had been warning of the dangers of *bidaa,* or innovation, forms of worship sanctioned neither by God nor His prophets, and *shirk,* mixing worship of God with pagan idolatry.[49] They particularly disapproved of melding religious ceremonies such as funerals with the competitive feasting and dance that had long been an important component of community life. During the Depression and again after the onset of the war, these theological concerns meshed with British desires to discourage such festivities on the grounds that they were economically wasteful. The *ulamaa* supported the resulting government campaigns against "extravagant feasts," displaying a zeal and initiative that impressed their British partners.[50] In 1936 the senior qadi issued an unusually strong statement, warning that Islam forbade *all* festive dances, even those not combined with a religious rite. Although the secular intelligentsia rarely went that far, their general critiques conveyed the message that the villagers' Islam was tainted by barbarism and needed to be corrected by Arabs.[51]

Elite intellectuals, secular and religious, held particular scorn for village Koran schools, or *madarasa,* and once again their preoccupations, inspired by modernist Islam, converged with those of British educators. The latter regarded the *madarasa* as obstacles to the spread of secular education in the countryside. The town *ulamaa,* meanwhile, scorned the *madarasa's* pedagogical practices, particularly teaching children to recite Koranic verses in Arabic "like parrots," without understanding their meaning. In the mid-1920s, a commission consisting of four eminent qadis and the director of education recommended that both problems be tackled by integrating religion into the curriculum of the government schools, where selected verses would be taught in Swahili. But villagers clung to the *madarasa*, resenting any attempt to limit their children's ability to recite in the language of the Prophet.[52] These tensions were still simmering ten years later, when they were captured in a widely circulated report by Muhammad Abeid al-Haj, a mudir and former schoolteacher who would soon be among the most influential intellectuals in the colonial administration. Al-Haj described the *madarasa* teachers as ignorant and avaricious people who routinely mistreated their students and exploited them for personal gain. But, he asserted, such abuses were characteristic of "African teachers" only. Arab teachers, in contrast, were expert and conscientious.[53]

It is ironic that Islam, with its reputation for condemning all ethnic distinctions, should have provided some of the language with which the intelligentsia constructed their chauvinist rhetoric; it is also a powerful index of the breadth of sources on which racial thought can draw. Yet the irony is not unheard of: like all universalizing creeds (including Enlightenment ideals of civilization and progress), Islamic ideologies have often been used to express difference.[54] Locally inherited concepts of Arab hegemony were in fact compounded by the teachings of Cairo-based religious modernists who made an exception for Arab ethnic solidarity, arguing that it is the one form of ethnic identity sanctioned and even encouraged by Islam as necessary for the well-being of the faith.[55] In the Middle Eastern societies where such teachings originated, they gave religious support to calls for national unity. But in a place such as Zanzibar they were divisive. They told islanders that in order to be moral beings according to the religious ideals they themselves held dear, they had to accept the leadership of an ethnically distinct Arab elite.

Still, because the intelligentsia's interwar teachings on Arab hegemony stressed the lessons of coastal exceptionalism, their impact on indigenous islanders was ambivalent (as we will see below). But the message conveyed to mainlanders was straightforward: they were described unreflectively as *washenzi* and hence automatically excluded from any community built on the values of *ustaarabu*. The Arab Association and its weekly paper *Al-Falaq*, with which the *Mazungumzo* circle had close connections,[56] was particularly plainspoken on such matters. *Al-Falaq* frequently rhapsodized about Zanzibar's historical glories, describing not only the heroism of the Arabs who had shed their blood to build the "Great Arabic Empire" of precolonial Zanzibar (a favorite theme was their role in liberating the coast from the unenlightened rule of the

Portuguese)[57] but also the civilizing influence they had exerted on the islands' indigenous inhabitants. Centuries of such influence were said to have resulted in inherent differences between islanders and mainlanders: whereas islanders had become "sufficiently Arabianized" to have lost most of the qualities of African barbarism, mainlanders were still "primitive natives . . . whose culture and history are in process of formation only now."[58]

[Hovering around all the paternalist rhetoric about how islanders had been civilized by Arab tutelage was the specter of slavery, which would haunt some of the worst violence of the later years.]In accordance with local sensibilities, slavery was rarely mentioned openly before the 1950s, although in their historical essays the intelligentsia sometimes delicately alluded to the "help" slaves had given Arab settlers in building up Zanzibar's precolonial wealth.[59] Some also indulged in the kind of apology for "Arab slavery" that was common fare in pan-Arab and pan-Islamic journalism emanating from the Middle East. Echoes of the abolitionist zeal that had accompanied Europe's late-nineteenth-century imperial expansion were still to be heard in colonial descriptions of the Arabs' role in the sub-Saharan slave trade, descriptions the pan-Arabists resented as slurs on their national honor. Their response was to expose the hypocrisy of Europe's civilizing pretensions by contrasting the cruelties of Western slavery with the supposed benignity of its Arab or Islamic counterpart.[60]

In Zanzibar, the pioneer of such discourse, as of many other aspects of nationalist rhetoric, was Ali Muhsin al-Barwani, scion of one of Zanzibar's wealthiest families and for a time a teacher at Dole Rural Middle School, who later would be instrumental in forming the ZNP. In 1937, while still an undergraduate of eighteen, he published an essay on Zanzibar slavery in the *Makerere College Magazine*. Stressing a lesson in universal history he probably had learned from his former teacher Hollingsworth, Muhsin urged readers to remember that in the past slavery had been considered "one of the inexorable laws of nature." Yet at Zanzibar slavery was "entirely devoid of the cruelties that were its usual concomitants in the other parts of the world." Islamic injunctions to treat slaves well were carried out "almost to the letter," and "such was the happy state of slaves that they loathed freedom."[61] Muhsin's article provoked a heated response from a fellow student signing himself "Sceptic," who accused Muhsin of apologizing for the "monstrosities" of Zanzibar's "Arab" slave-masters. The entire debate was given local prominence in the pages of *Al-Falaq*, which portrayed Sceptic's critique as a slanderous attack on the entire Arab world.[62]

A few months after publicizing this exchange, *Al-Falaq* published an article that argued what had usually been merely implied; namely, that slavery was among the key institutions by which Arabs had civilized East Africans, by imposing the control necessary to channel their anarchic energy into productive labor. To be sure, the argument was made obliquely, as befitted a topic seldom raised in polite conversation. The occasion was a comment on a government study commissioned to determine the causes of "the indolence and lethargy inherent in Natives." The study had concluded that the "patent disinclination to do any hard work" was due to a vitamin-poor diet. *Al-Falaq* disagreed. The paper first noted that the storied wealth of precolonial Zanzibar had been built by "Native Labour" who enjoyed much the same diet as they did in the late 1930s. That today's "natives" were "loath to do any manual labour" could not be ascribed to lack of strength, the editorial reasoned, since they were "ever ready and enthusiastic to dance uninterruptedly for 24 hours at a stretch." In fact, the writer noted, one often saw "natives" working incredibly hard—during the clove harvest, for example, or on the wharfs; in other words, when they were under direct supervision. "Thus in our opinion the disinclination of [the] Native to work is not due to malnutrition but principally to his rooted habit of living from hand to mouth and [the] *absence of any control on his doings.*"[63] This essay was undoubtedly intended as part of *Al-Falaq*'s ongoing campaign to persuade the administration to enact some legal apparatus by which estate owners might more effectively control agricultural labor. Yet the implied historical lesson was clear: despite their present laziness, "natives" had once worked hard. But that had been in the precolonial past, when they had been firmly controlled—that is, when they had been slaves.

These debates on slavery, no matter how muted, reflect how the nationalist intelligentsia was working multiple intellectual strands into a densely woven discourse of difference. Bringing barbarians into the light of religion and civilization had once been the central justification of enslavement in Islamic doctrine. *Al-Falaq*'s rhetoric shows that doctrine lingering in post-emancipation Zanzibar, complemented by European concepts of labor discipline.[64] As we have seen, it also shows the influence of pan-Arabist apologies for "Arab slavery." Those apologies grew out of two separate historical misunderstandings, which in turn were rooted in both imported and local ways of thinking. First was the assumption that despite its long and varied history, an institution such as slavery could be characterized and labeled in fixed terms. In fact, although slavery in the Arab Middle East (and Islamic Africa) was indeed often "benign" compared to New World forms, the East African experience shows that such relaxed relations of bondage could become transformed over time.[65] So the label "Arab slavery" in fact corresponded to no single set of practices. Yet such labeling was central to nationalist understandings of history, in which institutions were held to reflect discrete national spirits. In this case, the intelligentsia used the history of Zanzibar slavery to demonstrate the humane paternalism of Arab civilization.

Second, whatever slavery looked like in Zanzibar at any given moment, there was nothing particularly "Arab" about it: contrary to conventional assumptions, many masters had been Africans. This misunderstanding stemmed not from imported nationalist philosophies but from local usages, in which the claim of Arab status connoted descent from the planter elite and the absence of slave ancestry. Memories of slavery, in other words, were central to local understandings of Arab identity, and that placed the intelligentsia in the uncomfortable position of having to apologize for the institution and, in the process, reproduce racialized understandings of it. Given the bitterness with which ASP nationalists would later accuse them of the inherited sin of slavery (the 1937 exchange between Muhsin and Sceptic was a good foretaste of those battles), it is ironic that the intelligentsia chose to use the history of slavery as a narrative tool in their construction of an Arabocentric civilizational nationalism. But the choice was virtually forced on them by past practices in the construction of ethnic difference.

Second-Class Civilization

The denigration of mainlanders implicit in the intelligentsia's civilizational rhetoric was to be potent fuel in the hands of racial nationalists after the war, especially for stoking the resentments of slave descendants, squatters, and others who preserved memories of mainland descent. But the majority who considered themselves indigenous to the islands responded to the intelligentsia's rhetoric with ambivalence. On the one hand, Arab intellectuals invited them to join the nation-building project on the basis of their shared history of *ustaarabu* and Islam. But on the other, the invitation was unmistakably condescending: [although the intelligentsia encouraged islanders to consider themselves superior to mainland barbarians, they also implied that Arabs alone were in full command of the civilizing arts] The latter message appeared frequently in *Al-Falaq*, whose writers took Arab leadership as the norm in all matters, civil and political; Zanzibar was, after all, "an African country ruled by Arabs."[66] The nationalist rhetoric deployed by the Arab Association during the 1937–

1938 clove-buying crisis aimed explicitly at recruiting support for a struggle led by Arab elites and fought to defend their interests. Commenting on one of the anti-Indian business cooperatives that had been formed during the tense years running up to the crisis, *Al-Falaq* asserted that unless Arabs were in charge, "any institution established . . . by Natives" was doomed to fail.[67]

Given such attitudes, it is easy to understand why acceptance of Arabo-centric notions of *ustaarabu* did not translate into simple consent for Arab leadership but on the contrary sometimes encouraged anti-Arab resentment— resentment that ASP propagandists later sought to racialize. This irony was dramatically revealed by a wartime surge of Shirazi ethnic nationalism in the Hadimu zones of southern and eastern Unguja, a development that not only provides necessary background for understanding why this area became so bitterly contested during the Time of Politics but also illustrates the potentially diverse sources of racial thought, which in this case included local discourses of community as well as historical narratives borrowed from the Arab intelligentsia itself.

We have seen that Arab domination had long bred greater bitterness among the Wahadimu than among the sultanate's other indigenous people, in large part because of how Wahadimu had been pushed out of the fertile portions of Unguja to the margins of the plantation economy. By World War II, Hadimu villages had become reserves of seasonal agricultural labor, in good years sending the majority of their male population to assist in the clove harvest. Severe shortages of arable land also sent many of the younger villagers, male and female, to seek longer-term opportunities in town and as squatters on the Arab-owned estates.[68]

Not surprisingly, the intelligentsia's historical narratives skirted the processes by which the expansion of the Arab-dominated plantation sector relegated the Hadimu to Unguja's rockiest fringes. The most common ploy was simply to deny that tensions had ever existed.[69] In a 1940 report on land tenure, M. A. al-Haj, whose disdain for village *madarasa* teachers we have already encountered, crafted an imaginative apology for Hadimu expropriation. Relying on stereotypes of inborn characteristics, he explained that although the Hadimu "are by nature very good cultivators," they are also "by nature very shy and extremely conservative." Thus they "felt very uneasy when living near an Arab," and when Arabs started settling on the western part of the island, the Hadimu moved away to the barren coral lands of the east and south. That these areas were unfit for cash crops did not bother them, wrote al-Haj, because unlike the Arabs, the typical Hadimu lacked foresight and did not appreciate the value of land. He was quite satisfied with the little he got and that was all. This tendency is prevalent to the present day. A native will show surprise at a man who thinks of tomorrow.

Such passages suggest that al-Haj shaped his language in accord with colonial myths about "native" backwardness that were standard among his fellow officers. But the details of his analysis showed plenty of originality. With an almost gratuitous contortion of reasoning, he added that the Hadimu actually preferred the aridity of the coral lands, since it kept them from having to bother too much with weeding.[70]

Elite assumptions about Hadimu fecklessness were further encouraged by the peculiar conditions of clove-picking labor. Cloves are a delicate crop that must be picked at the precise moment when the buds have fully ripened but have not yet begun to flower. Planters therefore preferred that harvesting be done by seasonal target workers, who, being paid piece rates for properly harvested buds, had an incentive to work quickly.[71] Hadimu villagers, for their part, who had stubbornly resisted proletarianization, sought harvest work as an opportunity to earn substantial amounts of cash in a short period of time. The cash might be needed to fill various gaps in their household economies, which were based on fishing and subsistence agriculture, but often the most pressing need was to accumulate bridewealth or other ceremonial funds. In the prestatory moral economy of the villages, countless rites of passage such as weddings and circumcisions required celebrants to host their neighbors at feasts where guests were lavished with food and commodities. A shorthand term for such festivities was *ngoma* (lit., drumming and dance); they were, in other words, the same rites that came under such scathing criticism by the reformers of *Mazungumzo ya Walimu*. The raucous and competitive nature of these public displays only furthered villagers' reputation for fecklessness among officials and more sober-minded elites.[72]

Both sets of incentives, the planters' and the pickers', gave rise to behavior that administrators deplored as abuses of the system of contract labor they had introduced for clove harvesting in 1920. The standard practice was to give pickers a substantial cash advance upon signing a contract. But pickers often signed several contracts at once, intending to honor only one (if any), and absconded with the advances. This was a particular problem during bumper harvests, when planters, fearing they would lack sufficient labor to get in the crop, tempted pickers to break contracts with their neighbors, offering larger advances, better food, or other incentives.[73] At the end of the season, aggrieved planters usually found it impossible to recover the advance from abrogated contracts.

During the war these tensions converged to produce a crisis that induced many in the Hadimu fringe to embrace Shirazi ethnic nationalism. Five years before that, however, *Mazungumzo* published a remarkable essay that engaged with these tensions and indicated how at least one member of the intelligentsia envisioned addressing them as part of the nationalist project of reforming popular culture. Entitled "Karafuu" (Cloves) and published at the height of the 1938 harvest, the essay is a condescending piece of faux naive literature that purports to be a first-person account of the life of a Hadimu harvest laborer. Its anonymous author uses studiously rustic idiom to affect the voice of a humble clove picker, and, in keeping with many other contributions to *Mazungumzo*, takes the opportunity to explain specialized language and rural folkways. He also describes some of the hardships of the clove picker's life. Yet in its idealized depiction of a paternalist relationship between picker and planter and in its tendency to blame the pickers' problems on their own shortcomings, "Karafuu" reflects a decidedly elite perspective.[74]

The fictional narrator opens by telling of his difficulties in finding harvest work in the current season, owing to the poor clove crop. He contrasts this with the preceding year, describing, in passages of bucolic idyll, the thoughtless pleasures of a bumper harvest. The description is filled with images of fecundity: buzzing bees, scampering children, pregnant women, and tree branches heavy with cloves. In a supreme act of wastefulness, which the narrator now regrets, laborers cut down branches so children and women might pick cloves while seated on the ground. (Such damage was one of the planters' main complaints about their laborers and a key theme stressed by the author of "Karafuu.") What bliss it was, he reminisces, to be in a plantation filled with people happily working, chatting, singing. Owners of neighboring estates came by to sweet-talk us into working for them, offering good pay and free food, he says. We ate side by side with the planters, whose wives had to cook for us as if they were our own personal servants.[75]

That bumper crop enabled us to hold weddings, dances, and feasts, the narrator recalls, none of which will be possible this year. In fact, he explains ruefully, our foolishness during last year's prosperity has contributed to this year's indebtedness. Anticipating good wages, some of us got "greedy" and took out loans from deceitful Indian moneylenders. But then we thoughtlessly spent all our wages, including our advances, on *ngoma* and other festivities.[76] The narrator expresses gratitude that he, for one, has a generous employer, who covered his debt to the Indian and has not pressed for repayment. Throughout the essay, the pickers' employers are called their *matajiri*; that is, their wealthy patrons. Planters are also referred to simply as Waarabu, "Arabs." In other words, the author casually describes the three-way economic relationship in racial terms, characterizing each party by a set of inherent qualities: the naive, dependent Hadimu clove picker; his sharp-dealing Indian creditor; and his magnanimous Arab patron.

Even the narrator of this idealized description admitted that not all *matajiri* were as forbearing as his; some had "their people" arrested for defaulting on advanced wages. In fact, planters were often reluctant to press charges against pickers who broke contracts, not so much from magnanimity as from a knowledge that they were unlikely to recover the legal costs of doing so and, perhaps, because many had connived at such behavior themselves.[77] Still, that connivance had been forced on them by pickers who took advantage of a tight labor market. By the late 1930s the Arab Association was demanding that government find ways to crack down on "clove pickers who take away our money and play tricks with their promises."[78] Administrators obliged when wartime economic concerns prompted them to impose new regulations to improve the efficiency of labor recruitment. Reforms enacted in 1943 and 1944 provided for more rigorous enforcement of clove-picking contracts, especially recovery of the cash advance.[79]

The new regulations altered the uneasy balance of power between picker and planter and produced immediate unrest. Pickers complained that the new contracts enabled planters to reduce their mobility and hence their wages.[80] Emboldened by their newly won power, employers demanded that pickers pay for the food they provided, and when the short rains came early in 1943, many refused to allow pickers to return home to tend their household gardens. Pickers also resented the government's more determined intervention in the recovery of advanced wages. In the second season of their operation the new regulations sparked a massive boycott of clove-picking contracts throughout the Hadimu region. At Makunduchi, where the boycott was concentrated and, apparently, coordinated, only three people had signed contracts by September 1944; the usual number was about 2,000.[81]

The tensions that produced the boycott crystallized anti-Arab sentiments in the area, especially once those sentiments were shaped by rhetoric provided by the Shirazi Association. The association's Unguja branch had been founded in 1941, and although its headquarters were in town, most of its founders were from the southern part of the island. Its leading intellectuals were decidedly different from the cosmopolitan sophisticates clustered around the Arab Association and *Mazungumzo ya Walimu*; their president, Ameri Tajo, was a *madarasa* teacher from Makunduchi who had little command of English.[82] More to the point, they did not consider themselves members of the Arab elite, and on most issues they were vociferously opposed by the Arab Association. Among those issues was their advocacy for indigenous islanders in the ethnically defined rationing schemes being discussed during the war, especially islanders' right to consume rice, a prestige staple and an essential component of any feast. *Al-Falaq* opposed the demand, insisting that rice was a customary food of Arabs only. The Shirazi Association had also proposed that a Hadimu be appointed mudir at Makunduchi; this, too, was opposed by the Arab Association.[83]

Yet despite this animosity, much of the Shirazi Association's rhetoric was derived from the Arab intelligentsia's own discourse, particularly historical narratives about Arab conquest. In 1944, as *Al-Falaq* thundered against the striking clove pickers for their laziness and disloyalty, Shirazi Association activists moved in and told the pickers that the cause of their troubles was not the labor reform per se but the whole history of Arab dispossession.[84] By August, word was going around the villages that contract labor was a new form of slavery. (Perhaps some of the oldest residents could remember the islands' first, short-lived experiment with labor contracts, which had been introduced at the turn of the century to regulate relationships between newly freed slaves and their former masters.)[85] At the end of that month one of *Al-Falaq*'s most prominent authors, who signed his articles "Mafveraky," attempted to address such rumors. "Clove picking contracts are a sort of slavery," he began. "Let us suppose that to be true." But if so (he continued), those being forced to work for nothing are not the pickers, who are robbing us blind; it is we planters.[86] To the planters' chagrin, this crude attempt at irony backfired. Shirazi Association activists circulated Mafveraky's article in the Hadimu villages, offering its opening line as proof that the planters were gloating over having used contracts to enslave the Hadimu.

Whether or not this misinterpretation was intentional (Mafveraky's broken English is opaque even to a native speaker), the Shirazi Association's deft use of its enemy's propaganda was a major coup in its campaign to recruit support for its project of cultural nationalism. Association activists reminded villagers of the servile origins of the ethnonym "Hadimu" and told them that clove-picking contracts were the latest move in a long history of Arab oppres-sion. By boycotting such contracts villagers refused enslavement, the associa-tion said, and in the same spirit they ought to stop calling themselves "Hadimu" and instead embrace "Shirazi" identity. Officials at Makunduchi noted that the rejection of Hadimu identity at this time was forceful and widespread.

Although one can readily comprehend why striking clove pickers were re-ceptive to the Shirazi Association's anti-Arab rhetoric, it is less easy to explain why entire villages in the Hadimu fringe responded so readily at this moment to the whole package of Shirazi ethnic nationalism. This kind of question be-devils many studies of ethnic or racial consciousness, insofar as the functional-ism still prevalent in the social sciences can more easily explain the emergence of class consciousness in such contexts.[87] To answer it, it is helpful to consider the broad terms in which villagers debated issues concerning the definition and constitution of community. In this instance, those terms included deeply rooted ideals of *ustaarabu*—ideals that differed in significant ways from the hegemonic versions of *ustaarabu* espoused by the intelligentsia affiliated with the Arab Association and the government bureaucracy. We have seen that the intelligentsia had long belittled the ability of village non-elites to become civi-lized without firm guidance and control and that practices that villagers re-garded as central to their own affirmation of *ustaarabu*, particularly those tied up with the moral economy of feasting and prestation, had been disdained by the elite reformers as feckless and quasi-pagan. A consideration of the tensions within Unguja's Hadimu communities suggests why villagers came to see the new labor regulations as part of this broader assault on their ability to construct civilized communities.

Within the Hadimu villages, the clove-picking conflict came at a time of acute anxieties about the cohesion of community institutions and dreams of their renewal. One year before the boycott, in 1943, an in-depth study of Hadimu customs was undertaken by R. H. W. Pakenham, a district commis-sioner with long experience in rural Zanzibar.[88] Although Pakenham's main re-search site was in the eastern portion of the island, much of what he found can reasonably be interpreted as pertaining to other parts of the Hadimu fringe, including Makunduchi.[89] Like most colonial administrator–anthropologists, Pakenham had been mandated to record a uniform code of customary practice (in this instance regarding land tenure); that is, a charter on which government might base its policies. Unlike most, however, he frankly acknowledged his in-ability to find it. He had no doubts that such a charter had once existed, but his informants left him unsure about the extent to which "the traditional Hadimu system" still operated. More significant was the tone of "embarrassment" with which his informants "admitted" that most traditional community institutions had ceased to function and the nostalgic haze that surrounded their memories of how those institutions had once guaranteed harmony and order. Villagers lamented that over the past generation they had allowed "greed, jealousy and self-interest" to erode their old communal solidarity. "The trouble with us Wahadimu," said one informant, is that we have "close[d] up our hearts against one another."[90]

"Tradition," of course, had never ensured communal solidarity; the golden age of the Hadimu communities was a myth with which Pakenham's informants tried to confront present uncertainties. The significance of these laments lay rather in their suggestion of what those informants longed to regain. Key was a complaint about the young, who had engaged in outmigration throughout the interwar period: if they return to the village at all, Pakenham was told, they do so ignorant of village traditions and disrespectful of their elders. But in fact the most disruptive elements were not young people who had permanently abandoned the village to live in town or as squatters on the estates; they were, rather, those who preferred temporary labor migration precisely because it allowed them to maintain a connection to village affairs and intrude more forcefully in them, using their wages to sponsor feasts and *ngoma* or to pay bridewealth. Although such young people may have irked Pakenham's senior informants as disrespectful, like those seniors they perceived their interests in terms of the "traditions" of the prestatory moral economy.[91]

Given these persistent generational tensions, observers were surprised by the solidarity displayed during the clove-picking boycott. Significantly, the regulations that aroused the most unified opposition were those providing for the recovery of advanced wages. Under the new contracts, recruiting agents posted in the villages were given authority to collect repayment upon the pickers' return home. In 1943, the first year of the new arrangement, many pickers were unable to make repayment, either for the typical reasons—they had already spent most of their wages or had taken advances from several employers at once—or because the new labor conditions made it necessary for pickers to work for longer periods than they had anticipated to earn the amount owed, thus tempting them to desert before completion of the contract. According to the mudir of Makunduchi, these pickers' fathers (and other senior male relatives) were then forced to redeem their sons' debts by selling off livestock and coconut trees. Angered by this experience, fathers refused to let their sons sign the new contracts a second year, insisting that they pick cloves only as free-lance workers.[92]

The elders probably did not so much forbid their children to perform con-tract labor as much as they joined them in opposing it. The protest over clove-picking contracts gave seniors and juniors an issue over which they might unite, not simply in defense of common economic interests but more specifically in defense of the ability to use cash earned in the plantation sector to invest in the prestatory moral economy. Elders who dreamed that revitalized village tra-ditions might bolster their crumbling authority were able to use the issue to recruit support from juniors. And the rhetoric of the Shirazi Association pro-vided an ideology that resonated with those dreams. In this crisis both migrant clove pickers and the villagers who stayed behind came to see their enemies as "Arabs": the "Arab" planters in whose interests the new labor regulations had been written and the "Arab" intellectuals who disdained their customs as un-civilized. To those Arabs they said, using language borrowed from the Shirazi Association: We are not slaves or servants, not "Hadimu," but civilized people, "Shirazi," with an inheritance of ustaarabu as deep as your own.

Conclusion

That activists in the Hadimu fringe adapted the Arabocentric rhetoric of ustaarabu to express resentments against Arabs themselves is an irony that well illustrates the degree to which the elite intelligentsia had set the basic terms of political discourse by the end of the war. To be sure, like the intelligentsia's own political language, the language of Shirazi ethnic revival arose from a variety of sources, some generated locally and others introduced by the subaltern intel-lectuals of the Shirazi Association. But the latter derived much of their rhetoric from their opponents and teachers among the elite intelligentsia, and the en-tire project of Shirazi ethnic nationalism rested on the fundamental distinc-tion between civilization and barbarism that the intelligentsia had elaborated so assiduously. And that meant, in turn, that the ethnic category most often excluded from Shirazi visions of the nation—the category most often used as a foil in comparison to which Shirazi ethnic nationalists defined themselves and their followers—was not Arab but mainlander. This was most apparent in Pemba, the birthplace of the Shirazi Association and its stronghold throughout the postwar years. Because ownership of clove estates was more evenly dis-tributed there than in Unguja, Pemba was not plagued by the economic ten-sions that plagued the Hadimu fringe. Hence, in Pemba, enmity toward Arabs never overtook the hostility to mainlanders that had prompted the creation of the Shirazi Association in the first place. This fundamental ambivalence in the rhetoric of Shirazi nationalism would continue to mark Zanzibar politics.

The nationalist political discourse advanced by the intelligentsia was not racial in the sense that is now conventional; it relied on the rhetoric of history, civilization, and barbarism more than on biological essence. (Although restricting the definition of race to biological concepts when writing of the prewar years would be an anachronism.) Nevertheless, the metaphor of descent played a recurrent role in the intelligentsia's teachings about the core achievements that defined the nation: the peoples who had first introduced the qualities of civilization, the peoples who had learned from them, and the peoples who had yet to become civilized, were all defined in ethnic terms. More to the point, the intellectual processes of racialization that would become so pervasive in the postwar decades all built on elements of the discourse the intelligentsia had introduced. Historical questions about civilization and Islam, especially the islands' role in mediating the relationship between the African continent and the "civilized" world, would continue to preoccupy political thinkers and actors—elite and subaltern, in party polemics and in street-corner brawls—as they debated who belonged to the nation and who should govern it.

I do not mean to suggest that the seeds of racialization were inherent in the intelligentsia's discourse; as we saw in chapter 1, the historian's logic is not the logic of the trial, and any search for the decisive moment when racial thought originated will only result in a quest after an ever-receding vanishing point. Scholars commonly locate the origins of racial thought in the teaching of colonial doctrines. Yet our reconstruction of the intellectual trajectory of the Zanzibar intelligentsia—who experienced the most direct and most sustained exposure to colonial ideologies of any Zanzibaris—has offered ample illustration of the limits of colonial indoctrination. As we shall see in the following chapters, the main actors in the elaboration of an explicitly racial politics came from entirely different quarters. Unlike the intelligentsia, the subaltern intellectuals clustered in the African and Shirazi associations had little education and virtually no experience within the colonial administrative bureaucracy. Whatever rhetoric they knew of colonial modernity they had learned at second or third hand, and the distinctive glosses they put on those lessons were the products of their own intellectual labor.

Nor can the origins of racial thought be found in searches inspired by "invention of ethnicity" models. Although this book's entire analysis stresses the active work performed by Zanzibari intellectuals, both elite and subaltern, nevertheless intellectuals could not "invent" ethnic or racial traditions simply as they wished. Cultural history and intellectual precedent placed limits on the kind of traditions they could create or, more exactly, on the kind of traditions they and their audience would find compelling. We cannot assume bad faith on their part; most of the intellectuals we are discussing worked sincerely to make sense of the world they had inherited and to convey that understanding to others. Widely shared historical memories placed limits on the abilities of even the most innovative of them to invent new political traditions. This appears with particular clarity in the dilemma faced by elite nationalists who felt they had to apologize for "Arab slavery."

In short, racial politics cannot be said to have originated in any one political or intellectual faction or in any one set of doctrines. Rather, it emerged from complex circuits of discussion and debate that had many and varied participants: the intelligentsia, the intelligentsia's British mentors and colleagues, and, increasingly, subaltern intellectuals who claimed to speak for the clove pickers, squatters, and urban poor who were left out of the intelligentsia's vision of the nation. The significance of the intelligentsia's discourse of civilization and nation was not that all political actors adopted their way of thinking but that it set the terms for an intense round of political argument that would grip the islands after the war.

4

Subaltern Intellectuals and the Rise of Racial Nationalism

Instructing a nation is the same as civilizing it. . . . Ignorance is the lot of the slave and the savage.

—Denis Diderot

When the fool becomes enlightened, the wise man is in trouble.

—Swahili proverb

The uses the subalterns made of the intelligentsia's high-minded teachings were not what the latter expected. So long as nation-building was understood as an act of uplift, the intelligentsia, as exemplars of all that was most enlightened and civilized, could expect to remain in control of the process. Like nationalists everywhere, they also understood nation-building as an exercise in uncovering histories and other truths previously hidden, a task that seemed tailor-made for them, the islands' leading educators.[1] But creating a nation is not an act of discovery. It is, rather, an exercise of the imagination, and by inviting ordinary Zanzibaris to participate, the intelligentsia invited them to exercise their own. As in the proverb about the wise man and the fool, the outcome augured trouble.

By the end of the war the thinking of subaltern nationalists had begun to diverge significantly from that of the nationalist intelligentsia. Spokesmen for the latter, building on themes many had first explored in essays written for *Mazungumzo ya Walimu*, voiced a belief in a multiracial nation in which all ethnic and racial divisions would be subsumed by an overarching loyalty to the sultan and the ancient values of civilization he supposedly represented. Subaltern intellectuals, in contrast, argued that issues of national belonging should be

reckoned through a strict calculus of racial descent. God and nature had fash-
ioned humankind into irreducibly separate races and nations, they reasoned.
Therefore to try to mix or combine them, as the elite nationalists wanted, was
an act of folly and even blasphemy. A contributor to *Afrika Kwetu*, the weekly
paper of the African Association, posed the question pithily in 1952. Inspired
perhaps by the Bible, he asked: "Who can straighten out mankind, whom God
has made a hunchback?"[2]

Yet despite these dramatic differences, the two visions had much in common. Although the subalterns' political imagination had been shaped by a variety of intellectual currents—among them pan-Africanism, European abolitionism, the colonial rhetoric of "development," and home-grown ideas arising
from their daily experiences as labor migrants, squatters, and the urban poor—
their racial propaganda nevertheless drew on the same narratives of history
and civilization that the intelligentsia had taught them. More fundamentally,
the intelligentsia had been largely responsible for introducing the subalterns to
the very idea of nationalism. (Indeed, some of the ASP's leading activists had
served political apprenticeships under Arab Association nationalists.)[3] And in
that respect, both sides were equally engaged in trying to straighten out hunch-
backed humanity. Central to all national projects are efforts to sort out the
muddle of multiple and overlapping identities and supplant them with categories whose boundaries are hard and clear. In Zanzibar the rival nationalists
differed mainly over what criteria should be privileged when redrawing those
boundaries—civilization or race.

Both nationalist visions, that is, were exclusionary. But the intelligentsia's
vision looked more supple and embracing—at least at first. More attuned than
their subaltern rivals to international trends critical of overt racial politics and
conscious too that they were generally perceived (and indeed perceived themselves) as members of a small racial minority, they castigated the African and
Shirazi associations for trying to divide the nation along the lines of racial distinctions. Although the idea of race was not alien to them and their rhetoric
often invoked vague metaphors of descent, by the postwar years the most liberal of them were urging that such distinctions be set aside because they had
served the interests only of foreign intruders, Indian and British. You must now
recognize, they exhorted, that "an Arab is not an Arab, a Shirazi is not a Shirazi, and an African is not an African." Rather, "you are all Zanzibaris."[4]

But calls to multiracial unity sat awkwardly with the intelligentsia's overall paternalism. The exhortation just quoted, from 1946, appeared in a series
of brief items in *Al-Falaq* that were among the first in the paper to address

such themes. (They apparently were prompted by continuing tensions between planters and their workers.)[5] Significantly, they were also the paper's first items to appear in Swahili; previously, *Al-Falaq* had published exclusively in English and Arabic, languages known only to a minority of islanders. But if *Al-Falaq*'s editors thus sought to include non-elites in the national project, they made the terms of that inclusion clear: "WARNING: By our publishing a few articles in Swahili our readers should not be misled in thinking that we invite Swahili correspondence for publication."[6] Readers who were literate only in Swahili would now be spoken to, but they were not to speak back. Though this warning was retracted a few weeks later, the tone of the Swahili items remained, literally, those in which "Father Zanzibar" lectured his "children." Or he lectured his wives: during the first year, at least, the Swahili items consisted disproportionately of advice on cooking, decorating, and child-rearing.

The clumsiness of these early attempts to argue for an inclusive nationalism is understandable. *Al-Falaq* had always directed its political appeals specifically toward Arabs, emphasizing that their status as such—as distinct from the unfortunate "Negroes" of mainland Africa—is what gave their nationalist demands particular credibility.[7] But by the war years some within the Arab Association were beginning to argue for a more broadly based national movement. The most cogent arguments could be heard in the pages of an independent weekly, *Mwongozi*, founded in 1942 by Ahmed Seif Kharusi and from 1948 edited by Ali Muhsin al-Barwani, both of whom were scions of prominent Omani families and former Hollingsworth students.[8] (Ali Muhsin was the young man who had been lionized in the pages of *Al-Falaq* a decade earlier for his defense of "Arab slavery.") Until its demise at the time of the revolution, [*Mwongozi* was Zanzibar's most influential political publication, its influence culminating in the mid-1950s when it spearheaded the founding of the ZNP.] It was also the most sophisticated. Composed in elegant Swahili and (often) equally elegant English, for most of its history it sustained a tone of high moral purpose, committed to antiracialism and ecumenical tolerance. Yet despite its contributors' considerable polemical skills, they never fully escaped the condescension inherent in their historical vision of coastal exceptionalism and Arabocentric civilization. Thus their writings often had the net effect of confirming African Association activists in their suspicion that the intelligentsia's rhetoric of inclusion was simply a ruse with which to paper over the continuing reality of Arab racial domination.

This chapter is the first of two that will examine the complex give-and-take between elite and subaltern intellectuals that led to the racialization of politics in postwar Zanzibar. These intellectual exchanges were close, even intimate; at times the intimacy bred a personal tone that was a major factor in the bitterness that eventually tore Zanzibar apart. Of more immediate significance, the intimacy was such that the speech of each faction had a profound impact on the speech and thought of its rivals. At first glance it would seem that the intellectuals of the African Association were at a distinct disadvantage in these exchanges. The editor and founder of their main weekly, Mtoro Reihan, was an immigrant from Tanganyika who had received only a few years' schooling and spoke little English.[9] *Afrika Kwetu* was a much cruder publication than *Mwongozi,* much of it preoccupied with responding defensively to debates launched by its more urbane rival. Nevertheless, the propagandists who contributed to *Afrika Kwetu* took the lead in convincing significant numbers of Zanzibaris to calculate their political interests in terms of explicit racial categories. Contrary to nationalist orthodoxies, this chapter will show that these ideas were not simply absorbed from colonial doctrine but were the products of the subalterns' own imaginative intellectual labor. And in the chapter that follows we shall see how the racial abuse that had first assumed prominence in the rhetoric of the African Association soon spread throughout political culture, infecting even the utterances of literati who in their youth had written high-minded essays on civilization and uplift.

The Emergence of Mainlander Political Identities

The role of pan-Africanism in shaping African political imaginations has often been obscured in the literature by nesting teleologies. One of these is the assumption, discussed in chapter 1, that any opposition to the effects of colonial rule (opposition to "what colonialism did") can be subsumed to a grand narrative of growing sentiment for the creation of nation-states. As Frederick Cooper reminds us, such assumptions lose sight of the possibility that political actions might have had entirely different motivations. The communities that political actors strove to create might have been narrower or broader than the nation-state or both of these at once. In Cooper's wide-ranging studies of African politics, a recurring example of such alternatives were efforts to imagine political communities in terms of the global interconnections of race that form the core of pan-Africanist visions.[10]

Other teleologies stem from dominant narratives of the pan-Africanist movement itself. When pan-Africanism emerged into full view on the continental stage in the 1950s, its African proponents positioned themselves as staunch opponents of colonial rule and of all the divisive loyalties of ethnicity and tribe that, they argued, had been tools of empire. The leading figures were nationalist politicians, such as Kwame Nkrumah and Julius Nyerere, who had been disciples of the radical pan-African intellectuals George Padmore, C. L. R. James, and W. E. B. Du Bois. But in Zanzibar pan-Africanism had rarely been so militant. Even in the 1950s, when Nkrumah and Nyerere were already mobilizing mass support for immediate independence, Zanzibar's main proponents of pan-Africanism assumed an attitude toward the British empire that was surprisingly apologetic—some might call it reactionary—and promoted tribal identities as paths for retracing one's racial inheritance as an African.

The intellectual currents that fed pan-Africanist racial politics were in fact multiple and protean and not always anticolonial. In East Africa between the wars, the accommodationist teachings of Booker T. Washington and his successors at Tuskegee were far more influential than Du Boisian radicalism. Ironically, given the prevalence of triumphalist anticolonial narratives, Tuskegeeist British educators might be said to have been among Zanzibar's leading pan-Africanists. Garveyite populism was also influential. Garvey's *Negro World* was read in many parts of the mainland, and the Garveyite paper *Kwetu* (Our Homeland), published in Dar es Salaam, was read more widely still. The latter was the creation of Uganda-born and mission-educated Erica Fiah, who had been a successful entrepreneur before turning to political journalism in 1937.[11] *Kwetu*'s correspondents and contributors included readers in the islands.

Few Africans, however, drew distinctions among these pan-Africanist currents. Rather, local thinkers combined them to create composite versions.[12] The most militant of these, including Fiah, combined combative calls for racial political unity with a discourse of commercial-industrial improvement and a faith in Western models of "civilization" whose exact derivation—Garvey, Washington, or colonial educators—would be impossible to disentangle. As a result of such efforts, "pan-Negroist" political rhetoric became common on the mainland between the wars, and from there it was introduced to the islands, no doubt by some for whom the experience of labor migration provided a potent object lesson in the relevance of pan-Africanist identity. The net impact in Zanzibar was the emergence of an explicit racial rhetoric that went beyond the anti-Arab nativism expressed during the Makunduchi clove-picking boycott. As we will see, this rhetoric encouraged island-born subalterns to identify themselves as part of the same racial community as immigrants from Tanganyika and Kenya. Thus it not only excluded Arabs as aliens, it also struck an attitude toward the discourses of Arab and Shirazi *ustaarabu* that ranged from ambivalence to outright hostility.

Explicit expressions of pan-Africanist racial rhetoric do not appear in the historical record until after 1948, when Mtoro established *Afrika Kwetu*, modeled in many ways on *Kwetu*. But there is ample evidence that such ideas were being discussed in the islands before then, especially within the diverse voluntary associations that drew their membership from the diasporas of migrant workers who shuttled between town, the plantations, and the mainland. The African Association was but one of these. Its early significance has been distorted by an accretion of nationalist myths meant to bolster the anticolonial credentials of some of the men who would later lead it, notably Abeid Amani Karume, who would become first president of the revolutionary government in 1964. Among those myths is the degree to which oppositional political awareness was fostered within the urban football clubs from which the association emerged. Such details must be treated with caution. There is no evidence that the football clubs or the African Association itself voiced militancy of any kind before the war. They certainly never played the kind of role of the informal networks of religious leaders and neighborhood toughs who led poor Ng'ambo residents, mainlanders and islanders, in a series of bitter rent strikes against Indian landlords in the 1920s (an example we will return to in chapter 6).[13]

Yet although never as politically charged as the official narratives claim, [the football clubs nevertheless played a significant role in fostering sentiments of communal solidarity and nurturing popular leadership within urban neighborhoods.] In her valuable history of sport and leisure, Laura Fair shows that such sentiments were reinforced not only among club members but also among the populace at large, men and women, who gathered at the soccer pitch to cheer their neighborhood teams and jeer their rivals. Those neighborhoods and the corresponding rivalries were often marked ethnically, but the most visible divide of this sort was the growing one between Stone Town, whose clubs were dominated by Arabs, and Ng'ambo, whose clubs reflected the mixed population of mainlanders and islanders who formed the bulk of the urban poor. In 1933, three Ng'ambo teams merged to form the African Sports Club, an attempt to maximize their players' talents and compete effectively against Arab-dominated teams and teams sponsored by government employers. The new club was short lived, but within a year its core members had shifted their interests to form the African Association.[14] Like the football club, the new association was a social rather than a political organization, formed, as Mtoro Reihan wrote in 1937, "for [the] purpose of upliftment of the children of the soil." That purpose, he added, meshed perfectly with the paternalist goals of the colonial administration.[15]

Still, the African Association's very name indicated a new form of cultural politics in the islands: by identifying their common interests as those of *Africans,* including immigrants from the mainland, the association's leaders defied the prevailing local fashions by which newcomers had long sought to distance themselves from their mainland origins. Indeed, they brandished their African ancestry as a claim of nativist status ("children of the soil") meant to trump the elites' emphasis on origins in the civilized Near East. They regarded their association in explicitly interterritorial terms as a branch of Tanganyika's African Association, which they themselves had been instrumental in founding some five years earlier. The latter organization, as John Iliffe has emphasized, embodied the ideal of the unity of all African people.[16] But the logic of race imposed limits on such universalism. We have seen the association's bitter protest when a Shirazi was appointed the first African representative to the Legco: because Shirazis' ancestral origins lay in Persia, the association asserted, they had no right to represent true Africans.[17] By the end of the war, then, African Association ideologues were already outspoken proponents of an explicit racial nativism.

At its founding the association's executive committee was dominated by mission-educated mainlanders, particularly *mateka* or their descendants: that is, captives who had been liberated from slaving vessels, usually as children. (Others had been educated at mission stations on the mainland before moving to Zanzibar.) Their Christianity and long exposure to mission abolitionism had alienated them from the values of *ustaarabu* by which most islanders envisioned their bonds to the Arab elite. This explains not only their conciliatory attitudes toward the British regime but also their notion of themselves as leaders of a community imagined in interterritorial and indeed racial terms. Its president, Augustine Ramadhani, had been a senior teacher at the Anglican Kiungani School, until the 1930s the main center for the training of African clergy and schoolteachers for the mainland stations run by the Universities' Mission to Central Africa. These men and women (the association had a women's branch from the start) had been trained to think of themselves as an intellectual and cultural elite, the modernizing vanguard of colonial society. Unlike the Arab intelligentsia, they also had a keen perception of themselves as outsiders and a historical sense of grievance against the landholding elite. Yet at the same time their educational qualifications and class aspirations (to be a member of the large Executive Committee one had to pay a monthly fee) set them apart from the migrant workers and descendants of plantation slaves who were their most logical constituents.[18]

The association's earliest leaders, then, were doubly unrepresentative of those whom they thought of as their followers. The popular organization was based in Ng'ambo and in 1937 claimed over 2,500 members, no more than a handful of whom were likely to have been Christian or educated. Indeed, within a few years the association's leadership was facing challenges from men who were Muslim and largely uneducated. Among the most prominent of the challengers were Mtoro Reihan and Abeid Amani Karume. Karume had been born in 1905 near Mwera, in the plantation zone of central Unguja. Both his parents had been born on the mainland. It is an indication of the pervasiveness of the *ustaarabu* ideal that even Karume, who was to become leader of a party that championed the rights of slave descendants, felt compelled throughout his political career to refute assertions that his parents had been slaves.[19] After completing only three or four years of schooling, Karume took work as a seaman. His many years of travel in the merchant marine and his skills as a boxer and footballer contributed to his popular charisma, and upon his permanent return to Zanzibar in the late 1930s or early 1940s he became a prominent figure in several social organizations in town, including sporting clubs and a boatmen's syndicate that coordinated the interests of the men who worked the harbor launches that ferried passengers between ship and shore.[20]

Signs of a rift between figures such as these and the African Association's middle-class Christian leadership emerged as early as October 1936, when Mtoro Reihan and other dissidents made the first of several requests that the district commissioner (DC) intervene to stop alleged fiscal mismanagement by the association's leaders. The DC and his superiors, who depicted the dissidents as representatives of the association's "Mohammedan element," refused to get involved, being especially wary of stepping into what they regarded as a conflict imbued with "religious feeling." They advised the dissidents to seek private legal counsel.[21] These tensions kept the association bitterly divided for well over a decade, as the faction led by Mtoro and Karume aggressively challenged the Christian old guard and the latter in turn charged them with stirring up religious divisions. The dissidents' endless lawsuits finally forced the DC to attempt to broker a power-sharing compromise in 1947. But that arrangement quickly degenerated into fresh lawsuits and further disarray. By this time the old guard was on the defensive. In 1948 they created a rival executive committee, whose supporters raided the association headquarters and made off with some office furniture.[22] But Karume was not able to take formal control until 1954, after a new law forced the president, Herbert Barnabas, to resign in order to keep his government job as a sanitary inspector.[23]

With the African Association crippled by such divisions into the early 1950s, other voluntary organizations were at least equally important in fostering a sense of racial solidarity among mainlanders. During the years that Karume and his allies were struggling for ascendancy within the association, they also devoted their energies to organizing an African Dancing Club. (In this regard, it is perhaps significant that Mtoro Reihan had originally immigrated as a musician.) They later changed the club's name to the African Youth Union, an organization that Karume, then well into his forties, apparently perceived as a youth wing of the African Association. The first clause of the new organization's membership rules stipulated that only Africans could apply.[24]

Also influential were voluntary associations with even fewer overt political aspirations. Among these were mutual aid societies formed by immigrants from particular mainland regions.[25] Such "tribal" associations are familiar in narratives of African political history, where they are often used to explain the obstacles that faced the growth of pan-Africanist nationalism. But they often had the opposite effect. In Zanzibar, this effect was enhanced by the peculiarities of dual colonialism and the taint of *ushenzi* shared by all mainlanders. As we will see below, in the 1950s racial nativists connected to the African Association and ASP encouraged pride in mainland tribal identities as a counterbalance to the elite nationalists' rhetoric of *ustaarabu* and coastal exceptionalism. They did not link such sentiments to antimonarchism until just before the revolution. But within the tribal associations the connection was being made well before the Time of Politics.

An early instance involved the so-called Manyema immigrants from eastern Congo. We saw in chapter 2 that in Zanzibari political culture the status of being the sultan's "subject" (*raia*) was basic to concepts of citizenship or belonging, regardless of ethnicity or descent. Yet between the wars a divide opened between Manyema who accepted that status and others who rejected it. Both sentiments were probably fed by memories of Zanzibar's nineteenth-century political presence in eastern Congo, where trading warlords from the coast established conquest states that were nominally subservient to the Busaid sultans. The political and mercantile activities of these "Arab" rulers enhanced the prestige of Arabocentric fashions, particularly among their caravan personnel and armed retainers, and in the new century, many immigrants from the region continued to value the connection. But by the end of World War I, a vocal minority was expressing overt resentment of Arab rule, perhaps drawing on memories of the depredations committed by the warlords' men. In a foretaste of the kind of geopolitical rhetoric that would become prominent during the Cold War, they proclaimed themselves subjects of Belgium rather than of the Busaids, using the Belgian flag as an emblem of their defiance. By the mid-1930s the growing numbers of these dissidents in Ng'ambo had formed a Belgian Congo Club, later renamed the Manyema Union, whose officers engaged in bitter contests with the officially recognized "tribal headmen" over the right to represent Manyema interests.[26] (The most acute conflicts centered on the disposition of the estates of immigrants who had died in Zanzibar.)[27] Their rivals among the "Arab Congos" derided them as *makafiri*, or infidels, although most in fact were Muslims.

The leaders of the Manyema Union had led checkered careers on the mainland and the islands as dockworkers, soldiers in the King's African Rifles, and manual laborers. Their president in the early 1930s had for many years been the elevator operator in Zanzibar's central government building. Calling himself "Chief of the Manyemas," he had an associate write to the Belgian consul in Nairobi to seek advice on the proper regalia for a Manyema headman. (He himself was illiterate.) British officials characterized these men's motives as fraudulent, and there may have been some truth to the accusation. Nevertheless, it is significant that they brazenly defied Arab and British authority (sometimes with threats of violence) and used racial rhetoric to do so. They expressed revulsion at being ruled by Arabs or associating with "any other tribes than the African." They demanded to be "segregated" from all non-Africans, "especially the Asiatics" (i.e., Arabs).[28]

Similar rhetoric was expressed in the years after World War II by dissidents within the Nyamwezi Association. "Nyamwezi" was a loose label that in the nineteenth century had been attached to porters and caravan traders who traveled to the coast from the west Tanganyikan plateau, first as autonomous entrepreneurs but as the century progressed finding themselves increasingly subordinated to the domination of coastal merchants. The label's figurative meaning is simply "from the west," and it referred to peoples who under the colonial system of indirect rule would come to be known as Nyamwezi, Sukuma, and Sumbwa. After European conquest, young men from the western plateau continued to seek their fortunes at the coast, where they quickly established themselves as the single most important source of labor migrants.[29] At Zanzibar they were particularly valued as agricultural laborers, performing jobs that coastal people deemed suitable only for slaves and other *washenzi*. But their fathers' and grandfathers' bitter struggles to preserve their autonomy in the caravan trade had left a legacy of ambivalence toward coastal pretensions of *ustaarabu*. At the coast the migrants may have been scorned as uncivilized, but (as one said in 1912) they prided themselves on performing labor that "coastal people, through their idleness," had refused. In a 1939 polemic, *Kwetu* praised Nyamwezi migrants to Zanzibar as an example of the heights of "civilization" that Africans were capable of attaining. This kind of civilization was different from the Arabocentric notions. Stressing the values of accumulation and modernity shared by Tuskegeeist educators and Garveyite populists, *Kwetu* hailed the migrants for investing their pay in herds and other improvements, thus bringing "civilization" and glory to their homeland.[30]

Like the Manyema, Nyamwezi immigrants established their association at least partly in response to the government's interwar policy of appointing a "tribal headman" to assist in settling the estates of immigrants who had died in the islands. In addition to serving as a liaison to the government, the Nyamwezi Association ran a guesthouse for new arrivals and helped immigrants find jobs, secure the proper permits, and arrange for transportation back to the mainland.[31] But during the war a DC noted that the Nyamwezi Association, like the Shirazi Association, had become "racially conscious"—more so, he noted, than the African Association itself.[32] This mounting sense of political activism and racial grievance was largely the work of younger men who chafed at the control exerted by the elders of the association's executive council, the Baraza Kuu. The dissidents were better educated than their elders and, as their rhetoric would reveal, more attuned to pan-Africanist ideological currents. They accused the Baraza Kuu of neglecting the interests of squatters and paying more attention to cronies who had established themselves in town. They also charged the Baraza Kuu with fiscal abuses, including the extortion of payments from migrants returning to the mainland.[33]

In 1949, frustrated by the government's official recognition of the Baraza Kuu, the dissidents formed a rival organization that they called the Agreement Wanyamwezi and Basukuma Union (Agreement Union for short).[34] The Agreement Union's relationships with the government and the Baraza Kuu were stormy. As had been the case of the Manyema Union, the most frequent clashes were over the administration of decedents' estates. Spokesmen for the Agreement Union charged that by hewing strictly to Islamic inheritance laws, the Baraza Kuu routinely disinherited non-Muslim heirs, especially those living on the mainland. Ramping up the rhetoric, they alleged that British and Arab government officials connived at this policy and in fact had created the Baraza Kuu themselves for the express purpose of appropriating immigrants' property. To stop those abuses they demanded the Baraza Kuu be abolished and a member of their own group be made a salaried tribal headman. The latter post had been eliminated the decade before, but the Agreement Union argued that Zanzibari officials were in no position to know or care about an immigrant's mainland heirs.

British officers found these demands outlandish. They also asserted that the Agreement Union represented the interests of only a handful of "malcontents," although they probably underestimated the level of support the union enjoyed.[35] But in any case, the dissidents are significant because they represented the more politically active members of the Nyamwezi community (they were in close contact with the African Association), and their utterances foreshadowed much of the rhetoric that would become familiar within a decade. [We will see how *Afrika Kwetu* would emphasize mainland tribal identities as a marker of pan-Africanist loyalties.] By proclaiming themselves a branch of Tanganyika's Sukuma Union (and maintaining correspondence with that organization's headquarters in Mwanza), Agreement Union spokesmen made clear their refusal to think of themselves as members of a national community that coincided with the boundaries of the sultan's dominions. Their *taifa*—a word now commonly glossed as "nation" but at that time used interchangeably with other words denoting ethnicity, tribe, and race—was that of "the Nyamwezi and Sukuma." Despite being as combative with British officials as with Arabs, their arguments drew explicitly on an interpretation of the logic of indirect rule then prevalent in Tanganyika. The British have taught us that we should be governed by tribal chiefs and according to our tribal laws, they noted. Why then should we be subject to the rule of the sultan? Invoking historical narratives, they asserted that the complicity of the Baraza Kuu and the sultan's government amounted to a restoration of the regime of slavery. "Henceforth we no longer want to be subject to the Seyyid's government," they declared, arguing it had swindled and insulted them.[36] Such open rejection of the sultan's authority would not be heard in mainstream African Association or ASP circles until the eve of the revolution.

Labor organizations were among the most significant settings for the early development of a sense of pan-Africanist racial solidarity, not least because unlike the tribal associations, they were not tied to any one ethnic subcategory. The key events in this regard were a series of labor actions in the late 1940s that culminated in a general strike led by workers at the docks and affiliated sectors that paralyzed Zanzibar Town for three weeks in 1948. These events—like the renewed pace of labor conflicts during the post-1957 Time of Politics—illustrate how the twin influences of working-class politics and pan-Africanism worked to racialize the patron-client relationships that had long defined ethnic categories. Indeed, Anthony Clayton has argued persuasively that the 1948 general strike "created for the first time a sense of unity" among mainlanders, a unity that was largely political rather than industrial, "the politics being those of mainland protest, African and anti-foreign—anti-British as much as anti-Arab."[37] This dimension has been obscured by authors who, writing in a vein once prevalent in the field of labor history, were determined to attribute the 1948 strike to the emergence of a pristine working-class consciousness.[38] Their approach contrasts with a newer literature that examines how African wage laborers imagined their place in communities broader than those defined by the parameters of the workplace.[39] But in following this last strategy, we need to guard against memories that would substitute a nationalist teleology for a class-based one: if the 1948 strike was not simply an effort to create and empower communities of full-time wage laborers, neither was it a straightforward effort to create a transcendent Zanzibari national solidarity.[40] It was in fact an event that both built on and reproduced tensions between islanders and mainlanders and between Stone Town and Ng'ambo.

According to a survey undertaken in the year of the general strike, the overwhelming majority of wage earners in manual labor were mainlanders; such employment was concentrated in Zanzibar Town, where mainlanders constituted about one-third of the population.[41] Yet few of these townspeople perceived their interests solely in terms of wage employment, let alone in terms of a single occupation. A high proportion were single men who were either unmarried or had left their wives on the mainland. Townsmen often shuttled between urban wage employment and a squatter plot in the countryside; if the man was married, his wife might maintain the farm. (Since wage employment was almost exclusively for men, women earned money in the informal sector.) In general, wage laborers valued their mobility: that is, their ability to shift between the wage sector and farming, to shift among occupations in town, and to return to the mainland to pursue opportunities there.[42]

In 1948 the government was the largest single employer of regularly paid wage labor in Zanzibar Town, with 1,800 workers employed on monthly terms; the privately owned African Wharfage Company was next largest, employing 335 dockworkers and stevedores.[43] But the earliest labor organizing was undertaken by workers in an occupation that straddled the boundary between wage employment and the informal sector. These were the carters or porters, known as *wachukuzi*, who hauled goods in heavy four-wheeled carts between the town's warehouses and to and from the port. They also specialized in packing agricultural commodities for export. In 1948 a government official estimated that 800 men were working as *wachukuzi*, but the number fluctuated according to need, sometimes reaching as high as 2,000.[44] Combined with the casual nature of their employment, such fluctuations meant that the boundaries between *wachukuzi* and other categories of worker were far from fixed. *Wachukuzi* worked in small, autonomous crews, each organized by a foreman, or *chepe*, who arranged contracts for individual jobs and rented the cart on daily terms from a small entrepreneur. After receiving payment for a particular job, the *chepe* paid what he owed for the rent of the cart, then divided what was left among himself and his crew. Because such work was casual, an *mchukuzi*'s best odds of getting consistent employment was to belong to a crew whose *chepe* maintained reliable networks of patronage among the town's merchants and shippers.[45]

In many ways these conditions were a direct continuation of nineteenth-century patterns, in which the same tasks had been performed by quasi-autonomous slaves whose obligations had been divided between their masters and the entrepreneurs for whom they worked. Such slaves had been known as *vibarua*, the same word used in the new century to describe the casual day laborers epitomized by *wachukuzi*. Townspeople raised within the prejudices of local culture would have understood *chukuzi* labor as slaves' work.[46] And indeed, like nineteenth-century slaves, *wachukuzi* were perceived as African mainlanders and identified themselves as such (although many had been born in the islands or had been resident there for years). Their patrons were Indians or Arabs, the latter including the Yemeni and Manga entrepreneurs from whom they rented the carts.[47] The patron-client relationships among these parties thus helped delineate and reproduce ethnic distinctions inherited from the previous century.

Yet despite such perceptions, the *wachukuzi* thought of themselves as a laboring elite and restricted membership in their crews. They were in fact among the best paid manual laborers in Zanzibar. They also commanded a peculiarly pronounced importance to Zanzibar's mercantile economy—certainly as pronounced as the regularly employed dockworkers of the African Wharfage Company, if not more so. As a legacy of its nineteenth-century commercial history, Zanzibar's import-export business was divided among numerous merchant houses, many of them locally based, whose warehouses were scattered throughout the town rather than concentrated at the waterfront. This fact of urban space enhanced the *wachukuzi*'s colorful and indeed intrusive presence. Being paid piece rates, they valued speed, and they took pride in their ability to rush perilously loaded carts through the town's winding alleys, shouting at passersby to clear the way.[48]

During World War II, when shipping became erratic, the wild fluctuations in demand for labor prompted *wachukuzi* to organize a mutual aid association. They were also aggrieved by new traffic regulations that limited the size of their loads and prohibited anything faster than a walking pace. Meanwhile, British administrators, concerned about the uncertainties of having to rely on casual labor supplies in such a crucial sector, were considering how properly supervised labor organizations might contribute to economic stability. Accordingly, they encouraged the *wachukuzi*'s efforts, which in 1945 resulted in Zanzibar's first trade union, formally called the Labourers (Wachukuzi) Association. In early 1946 the DC helped broker an agreement for higher pay rates between the union and the Indian Exporters Association. These developments gratified the DC's superior, Provincial Commissioner O'Brien, who was confident he could guide the union along the lines of "accepted labour principles." The *wachukuzi* "are a pleasant collection of people," he wrote, and "very reasonable."[49]

Yet by March they were engaged in their first strike, sparked when a clove shipper hired a dhow crew to replace a *chepe* and his *wachukuzi*. The union called on all *wachukuzi* to stop work "in sympathy with those who had been displaced by dhow crew labour." Because *chukuzi* labor was geographically and institutionally dispersed, the immediate effects of this strike were felt more broadly than if their work had been concentrated at the docks. Even food marketing was disrupted. As a result the entire range of the town's mercantile interests responded with hostility. The most bitter complaints came from Manga copra sellers, who helped the shippers and larger merchants coordinate efforts to break the strike. Those efforts quickly succeeded. (They were supported by O'Brien, who let the *wachukuzi* know of his displeasure.) They also very nearly destroyed the union: in the strike's aftermath, *wachukuzi* were hired only if they dropped their membership. Union leaders tried to deal with these setbacks by registering with the government under a 1941 Trade Union Decree, the first union to do so.[50] They also petitioned Ameri Tajo, the newly appointed African Legco member, but to no avail. Tajo would completely betray them two years later, as we will see.[51]

Although it was a failure, the 1946 strike had a marked impact on union organizing in Zanzibar, which can be said to have begun from this time.[52] It also no doubt had a broader impact on the political perceptions of the mainlanders who constituted the town's laboring poor. As we have seen, during the 1940s the Shirazi and Arab Associations pointedly excluded mainlanders from their demands that Zanzibaris have a voice in public affairs. So it must have made a dramatic contrast when, in the same year that Ali Sharif Musa demanded in the Legco the disenfranchisement of anyone of mainland ancestry (see chapter 2), workers who identified themselves as mainlanders led a movement that paralyzed Zanzibar's commercial life. As Wachukuzi Association activists rebuilt their organization the following year, they followed events in Mombasa and Dar es Salaam, where dockworkers instigated general strikes that shut down those ports in January and July, respectively. Undaunted by their experience in 1946, they agitated for a similar strike in Zanzibar.[53] In the event, the general strike that broke out in Zanzibar in August 1948 was begun not by *wachukuzi* but by dockworkers employed by the African Wharfage Company. But this was a closely allied form of labor (individuals often shifted between them), and the Wachukuzi Association played a major role in spreading the strike beyond the docks.

There are several ways to understand why virtually all the town's wage earners responded to the strike call in 1948. Clayton, as we have noted, emphasizes a growing sense of racial solidarity among people who thought of themselves as "Africans" rather than Arabs or Shirazi. Other authors minimize the role of race and instead emphasize socioeconomic class. But such a choice is misleading. Certainly one must take account of the general sentiments of solidarity among the town poor that had been growing in Ng'ambo at least since the rent strikes of the 1920s, including concerns over the steadily rising costs of living.[54] Yet one cannot infer from this that strikers were motivated by an unproblematized "working class solidarity." Such inferences lead Hadjivayanis and Ferguson to argue that a central cause of the dockworkers' action was their resistance to employers' attempts to render them casual day laborers.[55] In fact, the opposite was the case. Much to the bafflement of employers and government officials, the dockworkers went on strike shortly after the African Wharfage Company had announced significant wage increases, largely as a measure to prevent a repeat of the Mombasa and Dar es Salaam strikes. But those raises were to be contained in new six-month contracts, part of an overall effort to replace "casual" labor, which policy makers regarded as unreliable and difficult to control, with a more stabilized workforce. Significantly, when the dockworkers finally returned to work, their main achievement was a reversion to daily employment.[56] This achievement was important to workers who thought of their interests not chiefly in terms of permanent employment in urban wage labor but rather as having the ability to shift among occupations in town, countryside, and (for many) their natal villages on the mainland.

Like their demands for reduced costs of living, then, dockworkers' demands for casual labor terms were crafted to express the interests of a community of the poor defined in ways other than the conventional terms of class. This was certainly the case once the strike spread beyond the ranks of union members and formally employed wage earners, when it became clear that the town poor were mobilizing to defend their interests at least in part according to considerations of racial politics. As the strikers "claimed moral support from other Africans," wrote the DC at the time, Salim M. Barwani, "the whole trouble began to take the shape of a racial movement."[57] In fact, as it spread from the workplace into the streets of the town, the strike quickly assumed the form of a movement of Ng'ambo versus Stone Town. Strikers blocked food deliveries to the main market in Stone Town, diverting them to markets in Ng'ambo. Ng'ambo women picketed shops in their neighborhoods to prevent sales to customers who had come out from Stone Town. They also launched a boycott of all Indian-owned shops, in protest over the high prices charged for women's wrappers, or *khangas*.[58]

All this only enhanced the perception that the strike was a movement that mostly concerned mainlanders. ("As most of the strikers were African mainlanders," wrote Barwani, "the local inhabitants refrained from taking active part.") The strike remained restricted to town, although mainlanders in the squatter areas assisted the strikers with food supplies, apparently provided on credit.[59] The strikers themselves did not necessarily see matters in terms of mainlanders versus islanders: when they called on all "Africans" to cease work they directed their appeals to islanders as well as immigrants. But they made no effort to distance themselves from their mainland origins, leading some British officials to mistake them for "agitators" who had come from Tanganyika expressly to stir up trouble.[60] In fact, like those who led the *wachukuzi* strike two years earlier, most of the mainlanders who led the general strike were longtime island residents. The dockworkers' key organizer, Abbas Othman, though he had been born near Dar es Salaam and self-identified ethnically as Zaramo, had lived in Zanzibar for over a decade; he had one home in Ng'ambo and another near Mwera, where his wife and mother-in-law, probably as squatters, raised produce for town markets.[61] Abbas Othman operated under the alias "Jomo Kenyatta," taking the name of the Kenyan nationalist who had already achieved quasi-mythic status as a pan-Africanist icon. The real Jomo Kenyatta was also famous as an unapologetic champion of a pagan African culture, a reputation that could not have sat well with islanders who cherished the values of *ustaarabu*. Yet the nom de guerre proved alluring for Abbas Othman's constituents, investing him with much mystique. In the months following the strike, officials were repeatedly alarmed by rumors suggesting the appearance of a "new Kenyatta" bent on stirring up trouble.

This defiant pan-Africanism, used to shape calls to African racial solidarity, no doubt contributed to the hostility the strikers evinced from members of the Shirazi and Arab associations. In the Legco, Ameri Tajo, whose appointment had been opposed by the African Association on the grounds that as a Shirazi he was an "Asiatic," denounced the strikers as outsiders bent on harming islanders. Such a response was in keeping with the general atmosphere of the immediate postwar years, when nativists were alleging that mainlanders worsened urban overcrowding and stole jobs from indigenous islanders.[62] The development of racial nationalism among the strikers and their supporters was probably further strengthened by the fact that prominent among the officials who represented the face of the colonial government were elite Arabs such as Salim Barwani and Saud (or Soud) Busaidi. In the following decade both men would become known as backers of the Arab Association and the ZNP. Busaidi, the town mudir in 1948, played an especially high-profile role, drawing threats for carrying messages from the senior commissioner. He also helped arrange the recruitment of strikebreakers from the Tumbatu fringe in the north of Unguja; it was their rumored arrival at the port that set off some of the most heated confrontations between strikers and the police.[63] (Watumbatu would be notable for their antimainlander sentiments during the Time of Politics, when again they would be recruited in attempts to break ASP-affiliated unions.)

The emergence of aggressive worker protest, made more potent by its simultaneous investment with pan-Africanist political awareness, finally invigorated the floundering African Association. Although the association's conciliatory leader, Barnabas, had acted as a go-between during the strike, the episode made clear that the future of pan-Africanist organizing lay with more populist figures such as Karume. In the months following the strike, African Association activists attempted to coordinate renewed labor unrest. Some tried to connect with Abbas Othman, who had dropped from sight; others adopted the alias of "Jomo Kenyatta" for themselves.[64] (Labor unions would become a key tool of political mobilization in the late 1950s, when it would sometimes seem as if each leading member of the ASP held an official post in one.) It is perhaps not entirely coincidental that Mtoro Reihan registered his new weekly with the government on 11 October 1948, exactly one month after the end of the strike.[65] The strike had thrust the homegrown ideas of aggressive pan-Africanism onto the public stage in a way no Zanzibari could ignore. Henceforth those ideas would be elaborated and promoted in the pages of *Afrika Kwetu* and its offshoots, and, through them, would engage with ideas of a different kind of nationalism, rooted in the more genteel intellectual traditions of *ustaarabu.*

The Search for Nativist Authenticity in the Early ZNP

The conjoined discourses of democracy and "native rights" were gaining in respectability, even hegemony, in the colonial world of the immediate postwar years. That climate helps explain some of the ideological purchase enjoyed by pan-Africanism. But it also had an impact on the intelligentsia. Clearly, it was no longer politically tenable to argue that the Arab elite, because of their advanced levels of civilization, had special qualifications for self-government—particularly after the general strike had demonstrated the potential of a mass movement to defy the colonial government with no input from the elite. All of this strengthened the hand of the liberal nationalists within the Arab Association who had been arguing for a multiracial nationalism that embraced the mobilization of the protectorate's non-Arab majority.

The intelligentsia's first decisive moves toward a concept of territorial mass nationalism came in response to one of the constitutional reforms introduced by Britain as gestures toward the discourses of self-government in vogue after the war. In 1948 the administration proposed that Arab and Indian Legco representatives be popularly elected from separate electoral rolls. (African representatives would still be appointed.) This provoked a campaign by the Arab Association that Lofchie has described as the intelligentsia's first attempt to craft a broad theory of the sultanate as a national state. What particularly aroused their ire was the suggestion that the vote be given to residents who were Indian or Pakistani subjects, a category that included most of Zanzibar's "Indian" population. In arguing against the franchise for residents who did not embrace subject status to the sultan, Lofchie writes, the intelligentsia crafted their first cogent defense of the sovereignty of the national unit. Modern Zanzibari nationalism, in other words, was born in a campaign to limit the rights of those defined as aliens. Lofchie characterizes the campaign as "a virulent racial attack" on Indians, whom the nationalists described "as a 'political Trojan horse.'"[66]

This situation of course is not unusual; the process of imagining one's place in the categorical order of nations has frequently involved marking off internal aliens, a category of persons who although resident *on* the national soil are not "children *of* the soil." But Zanzibar's elite nationalists faced a particular dilemma. They had long imagined their place in the world not in terms of territorial indigenousness but as part of a diasporic community with roots in the Middle East. Some of the most prominent polemicists in the Indian franchise controversy, in fact, had themselves been born abroad; hence their insistence that Indians become "naturalized" Zanzibar nationals. Benedict Anderson has commented on the ironies of the latter term, which implies that a political process can produce a fact of nature. But that, of course, is exactly the challenge that confronted the nationalist intelligentsia, as it confronts all who construct nations: they needed to find a basis for claiming that the nation they imagined was rooted in the natural facts of the local soil. For the subaltern pan-Africanists (as will become clear) the solution was straightforward: racial identities were a primal fact of geography, each race rooted to its own continental land mass. But the intelligentsia's rhetoric of civilizational nationalism, tied up as it was with the concepts of *ustaarabu* and loyalty to an Arab monarch, did not lend itself easily to such reasoning. Their situation bore some resemblance to that of Latin America's creole nationalists, who in an earlier century had felt compelled to imagine ties to subalterns whom they otherwise disdained precisely for their indigeneity. As we will see, Zanzibar's elite intellectuals made the simple villager a national icon, masquerading behind him in an attempt to demonstrate their own native authenticity.[67]

The British soon compromised on the constitutional proposals (replacing them several years later with others that would prove even more controversial), and the Arab Association nationalists soon recognized that they faced little threat from Zanzibar's Indians, who had no interest in competing with them politically.[68] More serious were the threats posed by mobilized pan-Africanism and the more narrow nativism represented by the Shirazi Association, both of which expressed resentment of the Arab elite themselves. The nationalist intelligentsia responded to those challenges by arguing that the values of *ustaarabu* and respect for the monarchy united all true Zanzibaris regardless of skin color or ancestral origin. This multiracialism was so important to the young nationalists that it prompted them to face down their elders in the Arab Association during the second franchise controversy of the mid-1950s, which led to the boycott of the Legco and the formation of the ZNP in 1955. Yet these concepts did not lack their own exclusionary rhetoric, which the young nationalists were not shy about invoking. *Ustaarabu* and loyalty to the sultan were presented as a kind of birthright that marked the true Zanzibar national—a set of attributes, moreover, that were not the exclusive preserve of the cultured elite but were rooted in the very soil of the countryside, practiced by the humblest villager.

In making these arguments, the nationalist intelligentsia had much material to work with, since the discourses of *ustaarabu* and the just monarch were
indeed common in many parts of the countryside. But as we have seen, those
discourses were not necessarily incompatible with resentment against the Arab
elite. It was thus doubly important for the intelligentsia to avoid giving the impression that their nationalist political movement was simply another elite-
dominated institution. For this reason official narratives of the founding of the
ZNP stressed the role played by village organizers who were indigenous islanders (or "Zanzibar Africans") rather than members of the Arab Association. In
the early 1960s, Ali Muhsin and other ZNP activists told Michael Lofchie that
their party originated in a movement organized by the villagers of Kiembe Samaki, four miles south of town, that in 1951 culminated in disturbances that
came to be remembered as the Cattle Riot or Cattle War (Vita vya Ng'ombe).[69]
The story was an oversimplification at best, and the connection to the Cattle
Riot was probably an invention. Nevertheless, as it has colored virtually every
subsequent account of the ZNP's founding, it is important to take a moment
to examine its genesis.

Throughout the 1940s the villagers of Kiembe Samaki had undergone a
series of conflicts with the colonial state that contributed to a heightened distrust of the government and an unusual sense of community. The latter was expressed chiefly by the creation of communal religious institutions, particularly
a Koranic school that also served as a general meeting hall and headquarters
of a football club. Key sources of conflict were government demands that villagers sell large parcels of land so Zanzibar's airport could be enlarged. But the
proximate cause of the 1951 crisis was a succession of cattle diseases in the 1940s
that intensified villagers' anxieties and brought them into closer contact with
the state. This culminated in 1949 when the government made dipping for tick-
borne diseases compulsory and in June 1951, when, in response to an anthrax
outbreak, all owners of cattle were ordered to present their livestock for inoculation and possible quarantine. While the wealthier dairy farmers complied,
the area's many smallholders, owners of a head or two of nongrade cattle, believed the government-ordered measures would cause their livestock to die or
miscarry. Resistance to dipping and inoculation quickly spread, and eventually nineteen smallholders were charged with criminal violations.[70]

The arrests brought a coordinated response, which, like the resistance to
dipping and inoculation itself, was apparently led by the same men who had
been active in Kiembe Samaki's religious and other community institutions.[71]
Solidarity was maintained in part through public threats of ostracism and di-

vine punishment—traditional sanctions long used to enforce dominant village norms—against anyone who cooperated with government or veterinary officials. On 30 July the trial of the nineteen defendants drew a large crowd to town. Their conviction sparked an angry confrontation, first outside the High Court, where the crowd overpowered the police and forced the release of eleven men, and subsequently outside the main prison, where police fire killed five.

Just as the general strike had galvanized pan-Africanists to an awareness of the potential of mass organizing, the Cattle Riot seems to have had a similar impact on the progressive nationalists of the Arab Association. The Kiembe Samaki protesters had openly defied the colonial regime, both in their refusal to inoculate their cattle and in their confrontation with the police. None were recorded uttering anything that might be interpreted as a nationalist sentiment; the most audible expression of a mobilizing sense of community were the calls of "jihad" and "Allahu Akbar" heard outside the courthouse, echoed afterward when some of the rioters told police they had been motivated by religion.[72] Yet despite this lack of ideological clarity, the town nationalists could not but be impressed. Ali Muhsin and Mtoro Reihan were both seen mingling with the crowds outside the courthouse.

But a protest against veterinary science, expressed in a vague language of Islamic solidarity, was not the stuff of modern nationalism as the young intelligentsia envisioned it at the time. Not surprisingly, then, they took pains to distance themselves from the rioters, despite their fascination. None of the weeklies then flourishing in Zanzibar attempted to make the riot or the police shootings a political issue. *Afrika Kwetu,* perhaps predictably, struck a toadying position. But even *Al-Falaq* defended the police, as did other vocal nationalists.[73] And while Muhsin's paper *Mwongozi* questioned the government's use of live ammunition, it too chastised the protesters, whom it described as "ignorant" and "deluded." Their chief delusion, the paper opined, went beyond their ignorance of the dangers of anthrax and the futility of "mass defiance." Rather, it was their assumption that they could accomplish anything without the advice and leadership of people more sophisticated than they.[74]

Later, however, these same elite nationalists remade the Cattle Riot as the founding event of their party. They told Lofchie that in the years following the riot the simple villagers of Kiembe Samaki who had led that act of defiance formed a new organization, the monarchist Hizbu l'Watan l'Riaia Sultan, or National Party of the Sultan's Subjects (NPSS). When Muhsin and the other Arab Association liberals heard about it in December 1955, they quickly joined, and persuaded the founders to change its name to ZNP (although it continued to be known simply as Hizbu, the Party). The story in this form took a few years to gel. Its earliest versions, in fact, made no mention of either the Cattle Riot or Kiembe Samaki. In 1959 *Mwongozi* published a history of the ZNP written by Abdulrahman Babu, the party's general secretary and its main proponent of mass organizing. Babu mentioned the names of the NPSS founders but said nothing of their particulars; a pamphlet by Muhsin published in 1960 was similarly vague.[75] In later decades both men misrepresented the position of the Arab Association at the time of the riot, even changing the date of the event in attempts to make it appear more directly connected to the founding of the ZNP.[76] Babu, who in 1956 was still describing the Cattle Riot as a "stupid and . . . bloody caboodle" caused when Kiembe Samaki's villagers lost control of their emotions, later came to hail it as the "epoch making" event that "ushered in the era of 'party politics.'"[77]

I do not mean to suggest that the ZNP propagandists simply invented their connections to rural activists. More likely they subtly reshaped them, in efforts similar to those taken by nationalists elsewhere in the colonial world to make their politics appear to have sprung from the authentic impulses of peasant protest.[78] There is little reason to doubt that the NPSS had been organized independently of the intelligentsia and that the latter sought an alliance with it as they set out to establish their own party. But whatever role the peasant leaders of the NPSS subsequently played in the early days of the ZNP, including positions on the party's executive committee, the record is plain that they merely served as figureheads and were quickly pushed aside by Muhsin and his colleagues. Nor is it possible to substantiate the connection between the NPSS and Kiembe Samaki or between the NPSS and the anti-inoculation campaign. In any case, the earlier movement bore little resemblance to the NPSS, except, perhaps, in its stress on Islamic unity. The Cattle Rioters expressed no monarchist sentiments. They and the peasants who resisted dipping and inoculation included many who identified themselves by mainland tribal affiliations, yet the NPSS took care to exclude mainlanders.[79]

The NPSS was in fact the latest in a succession of short-lived nativist and monarchist organizations that had appeared in the countryside since the 1930s, in which members of the Arab landed gentry sought to forge alliances with villagers in efforts to counter the influence of the African and Shirazi associations. The particulars of these organizations are often mysterious.[80] Some may have had genuinely humble origins, but the influence of an elite patron—a landlord or one of the venerated religious scholars who belonged to the islands' aristocratic families (including Muhsin's father)—was rarely absent.[81] One of the earliest and most prominent instances was Itihad al-Watan, Arabic for National Union, which was founded in 1935 in Mkokotoni, located in the Tumbatu zone of northern Unguja. Itihad's leading figure was Muhsin's cousin and brother-in-law Badr Muhammad al-Barwani, an influential landlord who owned two estates in the area. (He would later collaborate with Muhsin in planning the ZNP.) Muhsin described Badr and his closest confidants admiringly as imperious men who prized their honor and were quick to defend it with violence. Like other movements formed around the time of the clove-buying crisis, Itihad was established specifically to drive Indians out of business. It began as a bus-owning syndicate: Indian owners were forbidden to join, and nativist rhetoric encouraged villagers to boycott buses that did not display Itihad's insignia. During its brief existence it also ran some rural cooperative shops that had similar aims.[82] The elite Arabs who organized Itihad, then, aimed to forge a populist alliance around a common hatred of Indians—"usurious moneylenders," as Muhsin called them, who sought to "squeeze the last drop of blood" from planter and villager alike. The likeness of such rhetoric to classic Western anti-Semitism, particularly the type then enjoying a renascence in Middle Europe, is startling, but it also nicely captures the work for which such rhetoric was used, in which the threat of the internal alien binds up the *Volk*.[83]

If we were to search for a single origin of the ZNP, it would be not among the peasants of Kiembe Samaki but among the nationalist intelligentsia who were in charge of the party from the beginning. In the 1940s, Muhsin tells us, members of his circle regularly fanned out through the countryside on weekends and holidays to read aloud from *Mwongozi* at rural coffee shops, thus forging networks among the village nationalists. Schoolteachers played leading roles in these reading groups, and one of them, Zam Ali Abbas, founded the islands' first explicitly nationalist party, the short-lived Zanzibar National Association. In 1953 his collaborator Ahmed Lemke, editor of *Al-Falaq*, established the Zanzibar National Union, which in structure and ideology, Lofchie writes, served as "the prototype of the ZNP."[84] Still, there is little reason to accept ASP charges that claims of popular participation in the party's founding are fraudulent. It would be more accurate to say that the nationalist intelligentsia, looking to enhance their nativist credentials, sought out peasant allies such as the NPSS and the village religious leaders. Such connections helped make the ZNP, despite its domination by the intelligentsia, a genuinely popular party—popular not simply in organizational terms (a quality enhanced in subsequent years by the grassroots organizing of leftists such as Babu), but also in how its propagandists shaped their rhetoric to resonate with village activists who had expressed themselves in the languages of nativism, monarchism, and Islamic regeneration. In the pages of *Mwongozi*—which was virtually a party organ after 1955—Muhsin's circle argued that their vision of a multiracial nation united by respect for the sultan and Islam was shared at all levels of society as part of the coast's unique culture of *ustaarabu*. The politics of racial and communal division propounded by the Shirazi and African associations, they asserted, were alien to Zanzibar.

Yet dangers inhered in basing claims of nativist authenticity on the values of *ustaarabu*. The intelligentsia, after all, had long championed those values as having originated with enlightened foreigners—their own forebears—and as best exemplified by the Arab elite. Such an emphasis, then, was likely to remind ordinary Zanzibaris of the supremacist pretensions that African Association ideologues accused Arabs of harboring. So, as is often the case with civilizational nationalism, ZNP ideologues frequently found it less expedient to emphasize the nation's positive attributes than to define it in negative terms—to focus attention not so much on the true nationals who best embodied *ustaarabu* but rather on the threat of false nationals living in Zanzibar who they alleged lacked a firm commitment to Islam, *ustaarabu*, and loyalty to the sultan.[85] As a result, although *Mwongozi*'s polemicists usually took pains to claim the moral high ground, few issues of the paper lacked some reference to the dangers posed by internal aliens. Unlike *Al-Falaq*, *Mwongozi* rarely targeted Indians, some of whom were among the ZNP's leading supporters.[86] More significant were its warnings that the rights of true "sons of the soil" (a ubiquitous cliché on all sides) were being trampled by uncivilized mainlanders. Before *Mwongozi* became engaged in heated polemics with the ASP after 1957, Muhsin usually tried to avoid the kind of overt chauvinism that we saw in *Al-Falaq* and some of the intelligentsia's other writings between the wars. But the insinuations were always there, and during the election campaigns they became explicit.

The paramount emphasis on monarchism, for example, signaled exclusion of mainlanders who shuttled between the sultanate and the mainland territories. The founders of the NPSS were said to have secured the personal endorsement of the sultan himself; the party thus was the sultan's own, and ZNP propagandists asserted that a person's refusal to join demonstrated that he was disloyal and an alien. In fact, virtually all political voices agreed on the monarchist concept of the citizen that was enshrined in law, specifically the concept of *raia*, or His Highness's subject. *Afrika Kwetu*'s writers constantly proclaimed their loyalty to the sultan and sometimes questioned that of their rivals. (They even offered a novel interpretation to demonstrate that Arabs were not true nationals: because Africans were the ones conquered and enslaved by the Busaids, they claimed, they alone were the sultan's true "subjects.")[87] Nevertheless, ZNP activists aggressively challenged mainlanders to demonstrate their subject status. Those challenges became especially pointed in the run-up to the first common roll elections in mid-1957.

Although Muhsin and his circle idealized the constitutional monarchy as a tool for unifying an inclusive multiracial state, the Arabocentric language of monarchy introduced contradictions they were unable to avoid. This became most marked in an assertively monarchist campaign to restore the Kenyan coastal strip to Zanzibar, which elicited some of the most explicit chauvinist rhetoric to appear in *Mwongozi* before the Time of Politics. Under the terms of colonial conquest set in the 1890s, the Kenya coast remained officially under the sovereignty of the sultan, who received a nominal yearly rent from the Kenyan government. In the early 1950s, alarm over the Kenya settlers' threats to declare unilateral independence prompted a movement among some residents of the coast to reclaim their status as the sultan's subjects. Although the sultan himself remained aloof, Zanzibar's nationalists joined the cause, which soon took the form of a campaign for the restoration of the sultan's "lost dominions." In 1953 Ali Muhsin introduced the demand in the Legco, where he was an appointed member. During the first public rallies of NPSS/ZNP in January 1956, speakers explained that the Kenya coast, the Mwambao, was an indissoluble part of the single nation united under the sultan.[88] *Mwongozi* argued that by divorcing the coast from the islands the British had destroyed East Africa's only "natural" geographical unit. At the core of this argument were themes that we have seen in the intelligentsia's interwar writings: that upcountry people's history (or rather their lack of it) had rendered them inherently less civilized than the Muslims of the coast and hence inherently less suited for self-rule.[89]

Similar contradictions attended *Mwongozi*'s emphasis on Islam. In many ways the paper was primarily a religious publication, especially before 1957, when more of its copy was given over to Islamic themes than to any other matter. These writings were always liberal and universalist; a common ploy was to cite the most humanist teachings of Islam and use the hypocrisy of Western Christianity as a foil. But Christianity in East Africa had been loudly abolitionist, and that put Muhsin and his contributors in a bind, for it made them feel compelled to engage in the kind of apologies for "Arab" and "Islamic" slavery that we have seen from the interwar years, now resumed with vigor and erudition.

We will see how such apologies raised the hackles of many islanders of slave descent. *Mwongozi's* historical polemics became especially heated during the Suez crisis, when, in a tone of assertive pan-Arab nationalism, the paper cast them as indignant ripostes to slanders about the entire Arab and Muslim world that it alleged were being spread as part of an imperialist conspiracy against Islam. The conspirators included not only missionaries and Zionists, *Mwongozi* hinted, but also their local hirelings, the supporters of Hizbu's rivals.[90] Such rhetoric contributed to an atmosphere in which Hizbu nationalists taunted all mainlanders as slaves and lackeys of the Europeans who had supposedly converted them to Christianity. (It mattered little that the majority of mainlanders, including most of those leading the African Association by this point, were in fact Muslims.) These attributes were united in the scornful epithet *wamishen*—people of the missions—which was used with the same force as epithets that referred to slave ancestry or black skin.[91]

So although Muhsin and his circle postured themselves as liberal and tolerant, the logic of their civilizational nationalism often led them to a nativism that targeted entire groups that were incapable of being true "sons of the soil." The ultimate result was rhetoric that criminalized and dehumanized mainlanders. Such rhetoric became most pronounced in the debates over immigration that contributed to the violence of the late 1950s and early 1960s that I will discuss in chapter 6. Immigration also figured in the intense debates that preceded the first common-roll elections in 1957, which the African Association opposed on the grounds that Africans were not yet developed enough to compete with the "Arab immigrant minority." *Mwongozi* and the ZNP replied that opposition to the elections came only from "foreign Africans" hostile to the nation's interests.[92]

The central contradiction of *Mwongozi's* position was that its claims of racial and ethnic inclusiveness rested on chauvinist assumptions. Its contributors claimed that the wise rule of the sultans and the unifying effects of Islam had produced a "happy state of affairs" where all true nationals had learned to live together "harmoniously"; such harmony was doubted only by foreigners.[93] During the 1957 election campaign, *Mwongozi* ran frequent alarms that the voter rolls were being swamped by "alien" Africans who spoke "a debased Swahili" and refused to accept Zanzibar's Islamic, monarchist national traditions. Their goal was to stir up racial hatred where it had never before existed, *Mwongozi* claimed, adding that British electoral officials, "engaged in a ruthless campaign of creating racial conflicts," were encouraging them as part of an "obvious and classical" policy of divide and rule.[94] The paper thus marked the

ZNP's rivals as aliens in a double sense: not only as foreign Africans but also as imperialist stooges. This second accusation of course is the nationalist orthodoxy, which has been replicated over the last fifty years by propagandists and scholars of many stripes who disagree only about which party were the British pawns.

Afrika Kwetu and Racial Essentialism

The ideologues of the African Association responded to *Mwongozi's* nationalist project by propounding an alternative definition of "sons of the soil" based on explicit concepts of race. Whereas Muhsin and his circle stressed Islam and acceptance of the sultan's overrule as the unifying attributes of the nation, their rivals argued instead for a pan-African identity fixed in nature and the blood. This was Zanzibar's first unambiguously racial nationalism, and, contrary to standard understandings of the etiology of such thought in the colonial world, it was not a simple product of Western indoctrination. Rather, it was the product of the subalterns' own creative intellectual labor, often undertaken in response to the polemics of the nationalist intelligentsia.

As evidence of their contention that pan-African identities were fixed in nature, *Afrika Kwetu's* writers pointed to the map. *Mwongozi's* campaign for a multiracial national identity, they observed, was based on the idea that islanders were inherently different from (and superior to) upcountry Africans. *Afrika Kwetu* rejected that idea as a malicious attempt to destroy the "family feeling" between mainlanders and islanders.[95] A mere glance at the map, *Afrika Kwetu* argued, reveals that the islands are part of the African continent. An article in 1954 bolstered the argument by asserting that the islands and mainland had once been connected by dry land. Apparently adapting material from Hollingsworth's school primer *Milango ya Historia,* the article claimed that "in olden times our ancestors walked from Pemba to Tanga." Unguja and Pemba, therefore, "are part of the land of Africa, and its owners are Africans."[96]

The idea of dividing humanity by continental categories was derived in part from colonial usage, which classified Arabs and Indians jointly as "Asiatics."[97] *Afrika Kwetu* thus used the word "Asians" (Waasia) as a euphemism for Arabs. Throughout the early and mid-1950s it attacked "Asian" racial privilege in education and in government service, using geography to argue not that racial privilege was wrong but that the wrong racial group was being privileged. Using the same phrase as *Mwongozi* to denote true or legitimate nationals but giving it a more literal interpretation, *Afrika Kwetu* asserted that only Africans had rights as "sons of the soil." In this and many other articles, *Afrika Kwetu* argued that each race should seek its political rights only on the continent God had apportioned to it. "God Almighty divided humankind by color," it argued in 1956, placing one on each continent.[98] Thus, to accusations that it was preaching racial division, *Afrika Kwetu* replied:

> We were divided from the day of our birth you see that we (Africans) have black skin and our hair is [kinky] and black too. We were given this continent to be our home. Other human being have either white or yellow skin with soft wooly hair on their heads, and where [sic] given other parts of continents to be their own sweet homes.

Although we believe in "live and let live," this polemic concluded, we will not share our home with the *Mwongozi* circle and their "so-called countrymen."[99]

Abeid Karume elaborated these themes in a widely reported speech given in February 1957 at a mass meeting held at Makunduchi to inaugurate the union of the African and Shirazi associations. After echoing the preceding speakers' calls for racial solidarity, Karume explained to the crowd that each continent had people of a particular color:

> There's Europe where white people live. There's Asia where people are colored this way and that: Indians, Arabs, Chinese and so on. And then there's Africa, here where we live, we people with big bad black skin [*gozi jeusi*], called Africans. God divided mankind among the various continents and into various colors so they may get to know one another and love one another. He said that if a European sees another European he will know right away that "this European is my brother," and similarly if an Indian sees his fellow Indian he'll know that "ah my brother is coming." Just so, if an African sees his fellow black man he knows that is my brother African even if he is surrounded by a million white people or red people. Well then, these things were brought to us so that people might love one another. Therefore it is our duty, we black people, to love one another and to join together.[100]

Karume was glossing *Afrika Kwetu*'s basic geography lesson with reference to a famous Koranic verse: "Oh mankind! We created you from a single pair of male and female, and made you into nations and tribes, that ye may know each other (not that you may despise each other)." But his interpretation that God intended these divisions to be fundamental to human behavior would have been regarded by most Islamic scholars, including those of *Mwongozi*, as tendentious.[101] When speaking of color, Karume's language is colloquial and untranslatable. Asians are "colored this way and that" (*watu wa rangi rangi*): they undoubtedly have some color to their skin, but (the contrast with the following phrase is implied) they aren't the shocking black of Africans. "Big bad black skin" is my inadequate translation of "*gozi jeusi*," a usage that would later become significant. *Gozi* is the amplicative form of the noun *ngozi*, "skin"; in Swahili the amplicative can convey derogatory connotations of excess. The word is thus an example of a pejorative racial epithet that its targets appropriated and turned into a badge of defiance and pride, much as African Americans revived "black" in the 1960s and 1970s and, more recently, some inner-city youths have reclaimed "nigger." ("*Gozi*" in fact parallels "nigger" more closely, since it continued to be deemed an insult if spoken by an Indian or Arab.)

Such rhetoric is recognizable as a particularly essentialized version of pan-African racial nationalism: an African is an African no matter where he lives: on the islands, the mainland, the Americas, or "up in the air." It is built around the central metaphor of ethnic and racial thought, the metaphor of origins, by which descent is imagined to be the primordial determinant of social identity. From this metaphor, *Afrika Kwetu*'s authors drew the logical corollary. All island peoples originated on continental mainlands, they argued, "because a human being is not a fungus that can just sprout up anywhere." And since true Zanzibaris have their origins on the African mainland, each must belong to an ancestral mainland tribe.[102]

The writers at *Afrika Kwetu*, then, extolled mainland tribal identity as an emblem of African origins. This no doubt explains why the paper's editor, who was born Mtoro Abdureihan Kingo, chose to list his name on the masthead as "M. A. Reihan Mzigua," the last word identifying his origins among the Zigua-speakers of northeastern Tanganyika. The custom of thus using one's "tribal" identity as a sort of surname, after the European fashion, was derived in part from colonial convention, in which official documents listed the person's given name and patronym and after that his "tribe" (Zigua). That convention converged with the customs (among highborn Arabs) of appending Arabic clan names and (among ambitious non-Arabs) of using Arabic-sounding labels such as "al-Shirazii." But sometime during the war years, Mtoro made a conscious, ideologically driven choice to call himself "Zigua." He thereby proclaimed his origins on the African mainland, bucking Arabocentric fashions that had prevailed at the coast for generations. A poem in the paper later hailed him with the praise epithet "Child of the Zigua."[103]

The value *Afrika Kwetu*'s authors placed on tribal identities prompted them to praise indirect rule in Britain's mainland territories for having recognized and preserved the structures of tribal authority. Yet in the islands, they charged, tribal order had been allowed to disappear. For this calamity they blamed the Arabs, who had destroyed tribal identity first by enslaving Africans and tearing them away from their homes in the interior and then by forcing them to abandon their mainland identities after they had reached the islands. This was a ploy to make us forget our Africanness, the paper argued, thus enabling Arabs to claim equal rights as "sons of the soil." Scrutinizing the ethnic labels then most common among those who claimed to be indigenous to the Protectorate, *Afrika Kwetu* noted that two, Tumbatu and Wapemba, merely referred to the islands of those names, and a third, Hadimu, merely denoted that group's subjugation to Arab conquerors. None referred to ancestors from whom the identity had been inherited.

In contrast, the paper claimed, true Africans never forget their ancestral tribal origins. Yet while *Afrika Kwetu* could be forgiving toward those who had been fooled into adopting identities such as Hadimu or Tumbatu, it was scathing in its denunciation of those who claimed the label "Shirazi." In part this was motivated by the African Association's pre-1957 rivalry with the Shirazi Association. But *Afrika Kwetu* couched its objections in terms of a more general philosophy against attempting to deny one's inborn racial identity. Those who claimed to be Shirazi did so in a futile attempt to be accepted as "Asiatic," the paper asserted. But because Africans' identity has been inscribed on their bodies, such attempts are futile; "their curly hair and their negroid skin betrays them."[104]

We have seen that ethnic identity in East Africa had always been flexible. *Afrika Kwetu* now railed against that flexibility, using racial concepts keyed to fixed somatic traits. In support of its argument, the paper vaguely invoked the modern wisdom of Europeans. But it also sought to hallow the racial paradigm with the wisdom of the ancestors. A piece published in 1955 began with the implausible claim that the fashion of changing one's ethnicity was a recent phenomenon, not twenty years old. By contrast, "people in centuries past liked to identify themselves by their tribe and their origins of birth." Although our ancestors possessed neither religion nor "true civilization" before Arabs and Europeans brought those things, the author claimed, at least they knew who they were; they were not so foolish as to deny their origins. Yet nowadays people flee from their inborn ethnicity "as if thorns were inside their bodies." Anyone with a little knowledge of Arabic pretends to be an Arab or, if he learns a little English, he wears a necktie and disdains "the people he was born with."[105]

Afrika Kwetu's campaign against Shirazi identity, then, is a concrete example of the processes by which African intellectuals argued for rigid identity paradigms—processes that, according to much of the literature, were undertaken in emulation of colonial thought. A pointed illustration is one of the many poems that appeared in *Afrika Kwetu*. Its author was Kesi Mtopa Salimini, who would later become the ASP's quasi-official poet.[106] This particular poem, from 1955, is a scathing attack on those who are cavalier about shifting their ethnic identity. The title, which is repeated in each verse as a refrain, can be translated, "He who denies his origins is truly unjust." The poet's choice of words is significant. The word *asili*, which I have translated as "origins," was widely used in *Afrika Kwetu* (and indeed in all the political writings of the day), especially in articles extolling African identity. In those articles the word was invested with several intertwined meanings. They are summed up by the *Standard Swahili-English Dictionary* of 1939, which defines *asili* not only as "origin, source, ancestry, family," but also as "nature, inborn temperament" and as "essence, fundamental principle." The word thus carried the full force of the ethnic or racial paradigm, in which descent is imagined to determine not only one's social identity but also one's behavioral characteristics and most essential qualities. Given this rich concatenation of meanings, one difficult to parallel in any English equivalent, it seems ill advised to baldly attribute the ethnic paradigm solely to European influence.[107]

Kesi gives several examples of the behavior he finds so appalling. An individual of Nyasa ancestry—the ethnonym is a catchall attribution shared by many from the general region of Lake Nyasa, often connoting slave descent—changes his simple Swahili name to something grander, suggesting that his ancestors have been coastal Muslims for several generations. Another takes to calling himself "al-Mauli," an aristocratic Arabic name. Yet in reality, "his grandfather was a Swahili / of the Pogoro tribe"—that is, a common townsman, possibly of slave descent, who had been born in an interior region that had exported many labor migrants in the years since the war. Kesi's explanation of such behavior focuses on pride and social climbing: people "purchase a new ethnicity with bags of money" so they might "play the lord." In the final verse he totally repudiates such behavior by proclaiming his own origins:

> Although I'm a Mahiwa—
>   yes, those are my origins—
> I'll never buy [a new] ethnicity
>   and leave my fellows.

Those [who do so] fool themselves with pride,
    they have no fear of God.
He who denies his origins
    is truly unjust.

Mahiwa, who were from southeast Tanganyika and northeast Mozambique and were often conflated with the closely related Makonde, were widely feared and reviled in the islands and were stereotyped as the epitome of the mainland barbarian: violent, thieving, barely human. (We will return to these stereotypes in chapter 6.) Kesi's proclamation of his Mahiwa origins was therefore doubly bold.

The core of Kesi's indictment comes in verses that describe the disastrous effects of changing one's ethnicity. In calling himself "al-Mauli," the grandson of the Pogoro immigrant harms his brothers, breaks with his benefactors, and tries the patience of his neighbors. And, unfortunately,

He is not the only one;
    many, many do the same,
Especially here in Unguja.
    Things are really very bad.
They jumble up the tribes;
    we cannot know one another.
He who denies his origins
    is cruel and ignorant.

The phrase about knowing one another is perhaps a reference to the same Koranic verse that Karume would invoke two years later. The word "tribes" is *kabila*, which *Afrika Kwetu*'s readers understood to stand for concepts of tribe, ethnicity, and race. "Jumble" is how I have translated the verb *-fuja*, meaning to stir up, make a mess of, disarrange; it also means to misuse something. (It is the root of the common noun *fujo*, disorder, mess, disturbance.) So the main implication of the poem is this: whereas God divided humankind into neat, orderly divisions—one race for each continent—these unjust hypocrites are making a mess of things by trying to deny our divinely ordained racial identities.

Blood and Marriage

The main thrust of *Afrika Kwetu*'s campaign against changing ethnicity was not to boost mainland tribal identities per se but to convince readers that their most significant identities were inborn, bequeathed by God and the ancestors. So it was not difficult for the paper to suddenly drop its anti-Shirazi campaign when in 1957 the African and Shirazi associations merged to fight the ZNP in the impending Legco elections. In something of an ideological compromise, African Association propagandists now accepted Shirazi as an indigenous African category. In turn, Shirazi Association leaders, led by Ameri Tajo and other activists from the Makunduchi area where anti-Arab sentiment had been so pronounced during the war, joined in proclaiming the racial solidarity of mainlanders and Shirazi, based on their common history of Arab oppression and their common blackness, which proved Afro-Shirazi unity to be God's plan.[108]

The propagandists at *Afrika Kwetu* invoked the concept of racial identities in order to challenge the efforts of Muhsin and his circle to forge a multiracial national identity. *Afrika Kwetu* disparaged those efforts as going against nature: people in the islands were either Africans or Arabs and "Zanzibari" was an unnatural category. A month before the ASP's inaugural rally at Makunduchi, one of *Afrika Kwetu*'s most prolific columnists, "Ng'weng'we," mocked ZNP's nationalist propaganda. (The title of the piece—"Why Are Africans Hated by Their Guests?"—concisely expressed the argument that Arabs deserved no citizenship rights in Zanzibar.) "All these efforts to get Africans to change into something else is hard work," Ng'weng'we wrote, "and the difficulty lies in erasing this bad black skin (*gozi jeusi*) that is stuck on us." This was not the first time Ng'weng'we used the provocative epithet "*gozi*"; in an earlier piece that probably influenced Karume's Makunduchi speech he wrote that "this *gozi jeusi* and this kinky hair constitute a precious gift, an identity card, which God Almighty has bestowed upon you."[109] ASP propaganda quickly became marked by strident racial rhetoric. When trying to persuade ZNP acquaintances to shift parties, the ASP propagandist Jamal Ramadhan Nasibu would point to their nose, hair, and skin and ask whose they resembled, his or Muhsin's. ASP activists mocked non-Arab ZNP members as "Muddy Hizbu," implying that they had committed racial betrayal by darkening the Arab party's otherwise all-white complexion and that the ZNP's chauvinist leaders refused to accept them as equals.[110]

Such language had disastrous effects, especially when used in debates over slavery, intermarriage, and "blood mixture." In many ways those debates were first raised by the nationalist pioneers at *Mwongozi*, who liked to argue that one of the fundamental factors that had created an overarching Zanzibari national identity was the "mixture of blood" that had occurred through many centuries of intermarriage under the benevolent antiracial influence of Islam.[111] At first, *Afrika Kwetu* vehemently disagreed, using language that starkly equated nationality, blood descent, and race:

> We're constantly told that there's a portion of foreign blood in our veins. But there's not a bit of truth to this. . . . People want us to think that we have the blood of other nationalities so that we would stop calling ourselves Africans and instead call ourselves Zanzibaris. . . . That way we would give foreigners the opportunity to make themselves citizens here in our islands.

Whatever *Mwongozi* and their ilk might say, this article continued, the only true citizen here is the "pure African."[112] Other articles protested that racial mixture was an affront to nature, like a rooster laying an egg. By early 1956, rhetoric excoriating *Mwongozi*'s idea of racial "admixture" had reached a nasty level, with *Afrika Kwetu* warning "the minority immigrant class" (that is, Arabs) "that in Zanzibar colours will never mix." This last statement was followed by a thinly veiled threat of expulsion.[113]

But this initial line on racial purity put *Afrika Kwetu* in a bind, for the paper could not easily deny that Arabs had always married locally.[114] Ultimately, debates over intermarriage would be not about whether it had occurred but about its nature. The issue was first raised to prominence by the Islamist nationalists of the Arab Association, who argued that Zanzibar's long history of intermarriage was a prime example of the ideal race relations Islam fostered. Thus, in 1941, *Al-Falaq* noted that "Arabs do not regard [Africans] as low human beings. . . . The Arabs marry their womenfolk, eat with them from one dish, and join in prayers with them shoulder to shoulder in mosques."[115] But it was left to the racial nationalists of the African Association and the ASP to highlight the basic assumption implicit in the passage just quoted: that although Arab men had often married African women, it rarely happened the other way around. And it was also left to the racial nationalists to point out the issue that lurked just below the surface of all discussions of intermarriage, an issue that was often left unspoken. That issue was slavery.

By the 1950s Muhsin had matured into a polemicist shrewd enough to avoid blunt statements about the "happy state of slaves" like those he had published as an undergraduate. Still, his writings on slavery continued to strike an apologetic tone, as did those of other authors in *Mwongozi* and *Al-Falaq*.[116] In some regards such a position was merely another indication of Muhsin's status as a pioneer of anticolonial nationalism. Abolitionism had been the ideology with which Britain justified its African conquests, and Zanzibar in particular was the epicenter of the old abolitionist movement, with its memories of David Livingstone and Bishop Steere. Throughout the continent nationalists felt compelled to take on that ideology, usually by comparing "African slavery" with its more brutal trans-Atlantic counterpart. But in most of West Africa, masters and slaves were remembered as simply that: masters and slaves. In Zanzibar, by contrast, historical memories of slavery were caught up inextricably in the complex discourses of race. Regardless of the historical reality, masters and slaves were remembered above all as Arabs and Africans. As a result, when elite Arabs such as Ali Muhsin published apologetic descriptions of Zanzibar slavery, it appeared to many not as a defense of national honor against the slurs of imperialist abolitionism but as an evasion of inherited racial guilt.

Afrika Kwetu, on the other hand, made no effort to finesse the implications of its position. In essay after essay on the history of slavery and the slave trade, the paper took a fiercely abolitionist stand. British heroes such as Livingstone and Kirk had cleansed East Africa of the "filth" of "Arab slavery." (The word "filth" [*uchafu*] often was used alone, as shorthand.) Many of these historical essays asked, rhetorically, why various "white people" (*watu weupe*) had come to Africa. Indians came simply to do business, such essays explained; if they haven't helped Africans much, they haven't harmed us, either. Arabs came to conquer and enslave. But Europeans came to spread light and progress, these authors continued, and many gave their lives to liberate us from slavery. Often these historical narratives were made more provocative by referring to the Omani conquerors and slave traders by the loaded word "Manga," usually used to describe the impoverished Omani immigrants who, as we shall see in a later chapter, had become stereotyped as violent criminals. Thus, these narratives tarred all Arabs with the brush of slaving, criminal violence, and filth.[117]

From Muhsin's first published contribution to the debate in the *Makerere College Magazine* and continuing thereafter, he and his colleagues used intermarriage between Arab masters and their African slaves as prime evidence of the benign nature of Zanzibar slavery. "It was a very ordinary thing for a rich Arab to marry his slave," wrote the young Muhsin, "so much so that the intermingling of blood between them has caused a friendly and brotherly feeling between Arabs and Africans, two ethnologically different peoples." Muhsin thus used the history of slavery to bolster his claim of the existence of a multiracial Zanzibar nation. His critics, however, used the same history to highlight the divisions between Arabs and Africans. Again, this began at Makerere, when Muhsin's fellow student, "Sceptic," responded that such marriages were in fact nothing more than "concubinage," "a cloak" used to conceal what was, in effect, rape. ("Sceptic" may have been Othman Sharif, who as an ASP politician would later use similar rhetoric.) Moreover, he added, "The blacks [i.e., black men] in no instance married Arab women; it was the most unspeakable derogation. This cannot be rightly termed 'inter-marriage.'"[118]

Arguments over intermarriage were unavoidably informed by broader debates about the Islamic legal principle of *kafa'a,* suitability or equality in marriage. A prevalent interpretation of *kafa'a* held that while a man might marry beneath his status, a woman could not; she must marry either within her status or above. In the first half of the century debates over *kafa'a*—prompted, no doubt, by the reluctance of many high-status women to so restrict their marriage choices[119]—simmered throughout the Indian Ocean world. They centered on a tension between the principle's emphasis on status hierarchies, which often were understood in terms of ethnicity and lineage, and Islamic teachings against drawing such distinctions.[120] In Zanzibar, *kafa'a* was commonly interpreted racially, especially by Arabs anxious to preserve their exclusivity; since descent was reckoned by patriline, men would be particularly concerned lest their daughters or sisters, by marrying down, would produce non-Arab offspring.[121]

But the crux of the dispute between Muhsin and Sceptic was the shared assumption that in a relationship of marriage the male partner is dominant, the female subordinate. Invoking the history of intermarriage therefore did little to strengthen Muhsin's argument that Arab and African had always lived in harmony: so long as intermarriage was understood to have involved Arab husbands and African wives, it could be interpreted as simply another example of Arabs lording it over Africans. Muhsin was eventually forced to recognize this dilemma, and one of his most visible efforts to come to terms with it makes suggestive reading. In January 1954, *Afrika Kwetu* responded to a speech that Ali Muhsin had broadcast on Voice of Mombasa and subsequently printed in *Mwongozi* in which he had proclaimed the egalitarian values of Islam. Readers have asked us (wrote *Afrika Kwetu*) whether Muhsin's claims are correct. *Afrika Kwetu*'s answer: "As for equality in Islam: there is and there isn't." Muslims of different colors do certain things together, such as pray in the same mosques and bury their dead in the same graveyards. "But other things are not done together. Which are they? We'll leave aside all but one: if all Muslims are brothers, why then is it so very difficult for a Muslim African man to marry a Muslim woman who is not an African?"[122]

This elicited a lengthy reply from Muhsin, as remarkable for its content as for the fact that the editors of *Afrika Kwetu* devoted space in two consecutive issues to publishing it. Quoting extensively from his friend and *Mwongozi* colleague Abdullah Saleh al-Farsy, one of East Africa's best known religious scholars, Muhsin defended Islam's record in fostering equality between African and Arab, both in Zanzibar and the world of the Prophet. Much of his essay concerned slavery and stressed how slaves often held positions of social and political power. Muhsin paid considerable attention to Zaid bin Harith, the Prophet's slave who at the same time was a prominent military commander in the defense of Islam; he stressed that some of the most distinguished of the Prophet's companions served under Zaid's command. In a section subtitled "Equality in Intermarriage," Muhsin offered an idiosyncratic commentary on Koranic verses concerning Zaid's marriage to a young kinswoman of the Prophet. Although the Prophet himself proposed the marriage (wrote Muhsin), the girl's family refused to let her marry a slave. The Prophet finally had to force the issue, his authority strengthened by a Koranic verse providentially revealed at that moment. "And the companions followed the Prophet's example," wrote Muhsin, "and arranged for their daughters and sisters to be married by their slaves." Knowing all this, Muhsin concluded, can anyone doubt that Islam enjoins strict equality among Muslims?[123]

One wonders how this disquisition by a prominent critic of the African Association was received by *Afrika Kwetu*'s regular readers. Mtoro Reihan no doubt chose to print it in part because it represented the views of al-Farsy, a popular figure on both sides of the political divide.[124] Yet probably Mtoro also found the piece attractive for its implicit acknowledgment of what the racial nationalists had been arguing all along: that slave masters and their descendants have always resisted allowing their daughters to marry African men. And there's a darker implication: the story of the Prophet compelling his kin to let their daughter marry a slave and of his companions subsequently following his example may well have provided some of *Afrika Kwetu*'s readers with a blueprint for behavior that Muhsin and Farsy would have abhorred. That behavior included the political use of sexual assault during the racial violence of 1961 and 1964 and the notorious "forced marriages" of 1970, when the revolutionary government forced young girls of Middle Eastern descent to marry senior ASP officials, ostensibly as a project of racial leveling.[125]

Such behavior was first publicly hinted at in thinly veiled threats published in 1959 by Jamal Ramadhan Nasibu, an ASP journalist who later would hold high posts in the revolutionary government. From the mid-1950s onward Jamal Ramadhan published a string of his own crude papers, each one successively banned, usually on charges of inflaming racial tension. The most successful of his papers was *Agozi,* launched in 1959 during a crisis sparked when Nyerere persuaded Karume to take the ASP into a short-lived alliance with the ZNP (the so-called Freedom Committee alliance). Jamal led the ASP hardliners who bitterly opposed the alliance, and he used his new paper to accuse Karume of racial betrayal in cooperating with the ZNP. Much of *Agozi*'s prose resembled the more colorful and racially inflammatory passages in the earlier years of *Afrika Kwetu.* Even the paper's title was provocative. Its rhetoric made prominent use of the epithet *gozi* to conjure up the image of the downtrodden African who was despised for his or her black skin. "*Agozi*" was plainly intended to suggest the standard plural, *magozi*: roughly, "blacks" or "niggers."[126]

In August 1959, Jamal Ramadhan published an explicit statement on the theme of blood and intermarriage that made startling use of the story of Zaid bin Harith. The piece was addressed to the Arab nationalists who had allegedly tricked Karume into joining the Freedom Committee by preaching that all Zanzibaris were brothers, regardless of race. If you really want brotherhood, argued Jamal, and not merely deception, you need follow one simple course: forge true "blood kinship" with Africans. Like all who wrote on this issue, Jamal assumed an exclusively male audience. "Africans have given you perfect opportunities to unite with them by blood," he wrote; you have married our daughters and sisters, they have borne your children. But these opportunities have been spoiled by "your overweening pride."

> Remember that when the Prophet Mohamed wanted to build bonds of
> love among various sorts of peoples, without regard to color or tribe, he
> gave the daughter of a kinsman in marriage to a young African whom
> he had raised, whose name was Zaydi bin Harith. Without regard to
> ideas of mistress and slave, white and black, wealth and poverty.

Jamal's assumption that Zaid was African flowed from his assumption that "slave" equals "African" and "master" equals "Arab," an assumption Muhsin's article fostered as well. The only way to build real political unity between us, Jamal continued, will be through true "blood kinship"—that is, to let us father your daughters' children. But if you refuse to allow such marriages, he warned, and instead cling "to the concepts of master and mistress," then tension and violence will escalate.[127]

We cannot be certain that Jamal Ramadhan first came across the story of Zaid bin Harith in Ali Muhsin's article, although the idiosyncrasies shared by both accounts make it likely. At any rate, the threats implied in these and other passages from *Agozi*,[128] threats later made terrifyingly real, were forged in the context of discourse over blood, marriage, and race that had been initiated by the civilizational nationalists of the ZNP.

Conclusion

Afrika Kwetu's critics, noting its extreme conservatism and the degree to which many of its fundamental arguments were drawn from abolitionism, often asserted that the paper was merely a mouthpiece for the British administration. That interpretation, though obviously motivated by a polemical impulse to paint ASP nationalism as inauthentic, continues to echo in the scholarly impulse to attribute racial thought to the impact of colonial indoctrination. But if *Afrika Kwetu* vaguely invoked Livingstone and Kirk when condemning the cruelties of "Arab" slavery, the intelligentsia who wrote for *Al-Falaq* and *Mwongozi* actually cited similar authorities, chapter and verse, on the benignity of "Arab" slavery and the enlightenment that Arab civilization had brought to the Dark Continent.[129] Colonial intellectual influence was hardly limited to any one circle or political faction, and it makes little sense to emphasize the role of colonial discourse in *Afrika Kwetu*'s racial nationalism but not in *Mwongozi*'s civilizational nationalism. It was the intelligentsia, after all, who were most directly exposed to British thought. Indeed, the vision of Zanzibar as a multiracial bastion of Arab-centered "civilization" informed British policy during most of the colonial period, and the ZNP's model of Zanzibari citizenship, based on loyalty to the sultan, was adapted directly from the colonial nationality decrees.

But if those interpretations underestimate the reach of colonial intellectual influence, at the same time they overestimate its force. In this and the preceding chapter we have seen that Zanzibar's intellectuals did not simply absorb British notions whole and repeat them unthinkingly. Rather, like intellectuals anywhere, they reflected upon new ideas and transformed them into something new, something their own. More crucially, it is misleading to assume that the British were the dominant intellectual forces in colonial Zanzibar. The elite intelligentsia had far greater impact, not only in propagating the general discourse of a national categorical order but also in providing many of the specific ideas that underlay the subalterns' vision. Even the most militantly pan-Africanist of *Afrika Kwetu*'s writers, who urged islanders to embrace their continental cultural heritage, accepted the intelligentsia's teachings that the nation must be built on values of civilization and modernity, that those values had been introduced to Africa from abroad, and that upcountry Africans had received them late, from Europeans rather than Arabs.[130] And like the intelligentsia, they understood the history of the coast in racial terms, as the story of Arab state-building and Arab rule. Of course, interpretations of that history differed markedly. The intelligentsia told a story of civilization, enlightenment, and "blood mixture" that had produced a multiracial nation whose traditions of racial harmony were thwarted only by colonial policies of divide and rule. The subalterns responded with a story of conquest and enslavement by Arab foreigners that tied Africans together in a history of shared victimhood. Guild historians will protest that both narratives are inaccurate, but our protests are beside the point. These narratives became powerful historical forces in themselves when they were used to mobilize people around rival understandings of the national community.

The rhetoric of racial solidarity appealed most directly to mainlanders, but with the introduction of electoral politics, African Association activists also used it in efforts to win support from indigenous islanders. The contest between the two rival visions of the nation—one based on *ustaarabu,* the other on race—was fought most hotly in the Hadimu fringe, owing to the intense ambivalence there of Shirazi identity. Two years after leading the Shirazi Association into the Afro-Shirazi alliance, Ameri Tajo bolted to form a splinter party, which he allied with the ZNP. In marked contrast to the speech he gave at the ASP's founding rally in 1957, Tajo and his new party now vilified mainlanders as barbarians and appeared on the hustings with members of the intelligentsia who used history lessons to persuade listeners that by origin and essence Shirazi were the same as Arabs. In the 1961 and 1963 elections, Tajo's party and the ASP battled fiercely and violently for Makunduchi's votes.[131]

The racialization of Zanzibari politics was the product of this kind of circular give-and-take among Zanzibari (and foreign) intellectuals. The polarization of political viewpoints during the Time of Politics obscures the fact that such give-and-take was becoming even more intense during those years. Yet there was nothing inevitable about these developments. Although the subaltern intellectuals of the African Association interpreted pan-Africanist themes in terms of racial exclusion, they might instead have followed the more inclusive models of Julius Nyerere or the "Africanists" of the South African ANC.

The intelligentsia of Muhsin's circle, rather than raise alarms about the threats posed by diseased and criminal pagans from the mainland (see chapter 6), might have followed any of the several more embracing intellectual traditions in which they were versed: the internationalist socialism of Babu, for example, or the ecumenical, resolutely universalist Islam of scholars such as Abdullah Saleh al-Farsy. To explain why those paths were not taken, we must look beyond the pronouncements of intellectuals and journalists and instead examine the processes by which daily life became imbued with the politics of racial exclusion.

5

Politics and Civil Society during the Newspaper Wars

Since the moment politics arrived . . .
Our hearts have been troubled
    And burdened with foreboding.

In February 1961, *Mwongozi* published a poem warning that the overall state of political discourse was bringing the country to ruin. Like most poetry in the Zanzibar newspapers, this was submitted by a reader, S. M. Khamis of Pemba. Unusually for a comment on politics, however, it was nonpartisan. The poet focused on the spread of *matusi*—a powerful word combining the concepts of insult, curses, abusive language, defamation, and dishonor—writing that such behavior is self-destructive, and, like all enmity among neighbors, contrary to God's will. Most poignant is the poet's lament for the change this represented from Zanzibar's old ways, a change he or she associated with the introduction of "politics" (*siasa*) since 1957.

Such things, what are they? . . .
Our old love for one another
    Now has disappeared.

In the past we loved one another,
    We elders and our children.
Nor did we discriminate against one another.

Matters now are "astonishing to contemplate," the poem continues.

Enmity has infiltrated [the land]
    And respect has vanished.

The child knows not his mother,
So low has he stooped.

God's creatures quarrel with one another
And exchange curses and abuse.[1]

Such laments were ubiquitous throughout the Time of Politics. As political activities heated up, with both parties holding public meetings weekly in town and countryside, officials noted with alarm the growing practice of shouting abuse at passersby.[2] The general tenor of political speech was later described by P. A. P. Robertson, who had been civil secretary at the time. Robertson emerges in the sources as an imperious man who resented anticolonial politics almost as a form of lese majesty. Nevertheless, his strongly worded description squares with what one reads elsewhere, including in much of the printed propaganda itself. The language at the political meetings, Robertson said, was "revolting, horrible."

> The most horrible things used to be said about individuals, about Britain, about anything they could think of, . . . over loudhailers which were turned up to really loud decibels, quite unacceptable to a Western ear. . . . Voices filled with hatred pour[ed] forth abuse and inflammatory material by the hour . . . [and] there was always a vociferous round of applause from a large crowd.[3]

During the political campaigns of 1957–1963, then, the language of exclusive ethnic nationalism could be heard everywhere. Much of that language was racialized, much was deeply personal, and its net effect was to arouse bitter resentments. The depth of its impact could be read in the appearance of sporadic but widespread acts of racial violence within a year of the introduction of electoral politics, culminating in the election riots of June 1961, which came to be remembered as the Vita vya Mawe, or War of Stones. Several months after the riots, a relatively impartial government commission conducted a careful inquiry into their causes. In a phrase first coined by its chairman, Sir Stafford Foster-Sutton, the commission concluded that the major cause of the riots were tensions aroused by "the 'bombardment of words,' both written and spoken, which the people of Zanzibar were subjected to, more or less continuously, after the first General Election in July, 1957."[4]

That conclusion raises two puzzles. One is to discern the processes by which racialized discourse led to popular racial violence. (As we will see in later chapters, the June riots were not planned by the political parties but were generated on the spot.) There was nothing inevitable about this. To be sure, propagandists on both sides of Zanzibar's political divide often dwelled on violence, either in imaginative historical evocations or in paranoid fantasies of behavior imputed to their rivals. But those were mere words, at times playful. How did that rhetoric take on sufficient force to persuade people to turn against their neighbors? How did a war of words become transformed into a war of stones?

We will turn to those questions in part 3 of this book. To answer them, however, we must first address a separate set of issues. The racialized discourse that provided the ammunition of the "bombardment of words" had arisen, as we have seen, from discussions and debates among Zanzibar's intellectuals, including activists and ideologues who specialized, full-time or part-time, in politics. Prior to the Time of Politics, those ideas were fairly recondite to the vast majority of Zanzibaris. Before we can examine their role in prompting popular violence, then, it is necessary to understand how they had become reproduced in the thinking of non-intellectuals. How had the novel rhetoric of racial politics come to shape the lived experiences of large numbers of ordinary Zanzibaris?

The general explanation of this second puzzle is to be found in the ways that everyday life in Zanzibar became politicized after 1957—which means, given the overall texture of politics then, the ways that everyday life became racialized. This was widely understood at the time. In S. M. Khamis's poetic lament, readers were reminded that in the past, before the Time of Politics, "We lived together with a common purpose. If a difficulty arose for Shaame or Ali / we all pitched in to help him. / There was no antagonism between African and Omani / European and Indian, Shirazi and Asiatic." The word translated here as "difficulty" is *shughuli,* which in Zanzibar is commonly used to refer to a social affair: a wedding, funeral, or other obligation in which a host is expected to feast his neighbors and kin. In many ways, these are the defining events of social life, sites where everyday relationships of friendship and patronage are negotiated and reaffirmed. But as this poem suggests, after 1957 such events became riven by the divisions of racial politics. So did more mundane kinds of social interaction. In this climate, any kind of civil conflict might become politicized, especially if it involved a hint of violence: a traffic accident, a commercial rivalry, an altercation between servant and mistress. In many cases it was impossible to ascertain whether the civil conflict fed into partisan politics or grew out of them—impossible not simply for the historian but often for the participants themselves.

Political Events and Political Rhetoric, 1957–1961

In the space of six years, from July 1957 to July 1963, Zanzibar underwent four hotly contested election campaigns. General elections were a novel form of political behavior, and they called forth novel forms of political speech shaped by the parties' needs to mobilize potential supporters to register and vote. The exigencies of practical politics thus brought to the fore explicit questions of belonging and exclusion.

The nationalist intellectuals did not address those questions only to one another, of course. More than ever before, the electoral campaigns compelled them to direct their words at a popular audience, who discussed and debated them on street corners and in the villages; those debates were then conveyed back again to be taken up by the journalists and politicians. Among the most significant media for these cross-fertilizing intellectual circuits were the numerous weekly newspapers—almost two dozen—that flooded the islands during the Time of Politics and that have preserved for the historical record much of what was discussed in the streets. Strictly speaking, these were not "newspapers" at all[5] but cheap, roughly printed periodical pamphlets, the roughest a single sheet folded to make four pages. As in Stuart England, the sudden appearance of this new mass medium during a time of political upheaval enabled large numbers of non-intellectuals to participate in a public debate that had hitherto been restricted to the literati.[6] The papers were avidly read and discussed, taken to the countryside, and passed from hand to hand. At the hangouts on city streets where vendors sold small cups of strong coffee and in the eating houses that catered mostly to young wage workers, the papers were read aloud. Thus, even the illiterate could participate in the arguments that ensued. Things reached such a state that *Afrika Kwetu* began a campaign to shame people into buying their own copies, regularly printing such fillers as "He who borrows another's newspaper [is a] HYENA."[7] "For one newspaper to be read by ten or twenty people," the paper chastised, "is not the behavior of those who desire Uhuru." (This item went on to link individual newspaper reading and newspaper purchasing to modernity as well as to nationhood.)[8] Nevertheless, much of its language and that of the other popular papers was crafted to be read aloud.[9]

As the election campaigns heated up, so did the papers' rhetoric: like the pamphleteers of early modern England, Zanzibar's political journalists engaged in personal insult and other forms of *matusi* that tested the limits of conventional discourse. The excesses one finds in print no doubt represent a toned-down version of what was said on the street corners and the hustings, because papers could be shut down on charges of sedition and libel.[10] The papers associated with Jamal Ramadhan Nasibu and the Afro-Shirazi Youth League faced such charges more often than most: whereas *Mwongozi* and some other ZNP-affiliated papers frequently offered reasoned political analysis, *Agozi* rarely offered anything other than vitriol. Still, neither side lacked for journalists willing to indulge in nasty personal assaults. Something of the flavor of the polemics is conveyed in a front-page article in *Mwongozi* that, while obviously biased and rhetorically over the top, is not entirely unjustified in its description of the ASP journalists' own race-baiting and name-calling. The ASP "traitors" call us "'bearded rice-eaters,' 'Arabs,' 'settlers,'" *Mwongozi* wrote.

> They dare to curse loyalty to our Sovereign by all sorts of methods: by barking like dogs on the hustings, by scratching on the pieces of paper they call newspapers, and by underhanded means of treachery and slander. . . . They'd slit their own grandparents' throats if they could benefit from it.[11]

In leveling such charges, of course, *Mwongozi* only further ramped up the vituperation. It also engaged in a tactic used in all the papers: by repeating and perhaps exaggerating their rivals' most offensive rhetoric, the journalists got a calculated rise out of their own loyal readers. A telling example comes from 1957, after *Mwongozi* published an item denouncing mainlanders as responsible for a host of the islands' ills, including crime, filth, and irresponsible journalism. An angry response in *Afrika Kwetu* repeated the charges almost verbatim.[12]

In the aftermath of the first election, political tensions became if anything more acute, with sporadic violence appearing by 1958. The ZNP had been routed in the 1957 election, its rhetoric of a multiracial national unity unable to overcome the implications of racial elitism contained in that rhetoric's emphasis on *ustaarabu* and coastal exceptionalism, implications that were highlighted by ASP race-baiting. Publicly, the party attributed its defeat to the votes of unqualified immigrants from the mainland who "had no real loyalty to the country."[13] Still, the challenge was clear to the party's leadership, some of whom began to think that further ASP victories were inevitable and to toy with the idea that their own political future might best be sought as civil servants in an ASP government.[14]

In late 1958, the two parties entered a fragile alliance brokered by representatives of the Pan-African Freedom Movement of East and Central Africa

(PAFMECA). The latter was a short-lived organization of African political leaders that had been founded that year in Tanganyika to discuss the progress of the region's nationalist politics; the standoff in Zanzibar quickly emerged as a major concern. Among the few substantive differences between the parties were their respective stands on the date of independence: ZNP demanded an early date, while the ASP, in contrast, argued for a delay, to 1963 or later, on the grounds that anything else was likely to preserve the structures of Arab dual colonialism. The Tanganyikans who dominated PAFMECA favored the ZNP's position and pressured the two parties to work together to achieve it. PAFMECA's second meeting was held at Zanzibar in April 1959; at a large joint rally held that month to celebrate the new alliance, Julius Nyerere admonished islanders to abandon their ubiquitous talk of "slave and master."[15]

This Freedom Committee alliance (as the PAFMECA alliance was called) led to a temporary abatement of tensions between Hizbu and the ASP. *Afrika Kwetu*, invoking Nyerere's authority, suddenly embraced the ZNP's argument that racial divisions had been imposed by imperialists to maintain their rule.[16] But within the ASP a significant faction opposed this volte-face. The dissidents were led by Jamal Ramadhan Nasibu, who started *Agozi* to battle the new party policy, and Othman Sharif Musa, a veterinary officer who was among the ASP's most skilled polemicists. They were joined by erstwhile Shirazi Association leaders who had never been comfortable with the leadership of Karume and others from the African Association. In Unguja, Ameri Tajo was the leading representative of this group, his anti-Arab nativism meshing neatly, in this instance, with his similar distrust of the mainlanders who dominated the party. In Pemba the key Shirazi dissidents were Othman Sharif's brother Ali Sharif and his in-law Muhammad Shamte, a former schoolteacher, who together had led resistance to the amalgamation of Pemba's Shirazi and African associations. Karume, Mtoro Reihan, and the other party leaders came down hard on the dissidents, vilifying them in the press, on the hustings, and in the rumor mill. Tajo was treated with particular harshness: his religion classes were boycotted and in a party meeting in mid-1959 he was publicly humiliated and drummed out of the party. Othman Sharif was brought to heel, but behind the scenes he continued to support the dissidents, perhaps contributing anonymous pieces to *Agozi*.[17]

Jamal Ramadhan, however, was not intimidated, and his furious polemics ensured that racial vituperation continued throughout the short life of the Freedom Committee alliance. *Agozi* denounced Karume's cooperation with the ZNP as an act of racial betrayal, arguing that Arabs and Africans were inveterate enemies who could never mix, owing to their inbred differences and 150 years of Arab oppression. "Hey GOZI, wake up!" the paper admonished. "There can be no alliance between CAT and RAT." (A vulgar joke in this piece illustrates Jamal Ramadhan's distinctive voice, which was at once engaging and inflammatory.)[18] Responding directly to *Afrika Kwetu*'s newfound embrace of the nationalist orthodoxy, *Agozi* retorted that the roots of racial tension lay not in British rule but in Arab discrimination. The paper charged that Karume had allowed himself to be seduced by the flattery of his Arab allies, who now addressed him as "Uncle." He and the others in the party leadership—*Agozi* singled out Mtoro Reihan and *Afrika Kwetu* for special scorn—had become nothing but "yes-men" (*akina naam-naam*). Jamal's position enjoyed considerable support; at the beginning of the crisis, even *Afrika Kwetu* felt compelled to report on public meetings convened by his allies at which audience members spoke out against cooperation with the ZNP.[19] The dissidents' humiliating personal attacks on Karume posed a potent threat to his leadership and opened lasting rifts in the party.

The crisis over the Freedom Committee alliance revealed the ASP leadership's growing inability to control the party's younger militants. The dissidents included educated men who ridiculed Karume's lack of qualifications—Othman Sharif in particular pressed this issue—as well as what British officials called the "hooligan element," young single men, mostly mainlanders, who worked as squatters and/or in casual urban employment.[20] But in many ways "youth" was less a personal description of the militants than a positional one. Both sides in the dispute used the time-honored rhetoric of seniority and youth to describe tensions between those in positions of authority and those who challenged that authority.[21] The dissidents based their activities in organizations that claimed to speak for the party's youth, while Karume and Mtoro, for their part, urged loyalists to trust the party's "elders."[22] Similar rhetoric and similar tensions beset the ZNP, where militants led by Abdulrahman Babu struggled to shape the party along the lines of left-wing national liberationist thought derived from China, Cuba, and the Non-Aligned Movement.[23] Babu's efforts included organizing the ZNP's youth wing, the Youth's Own Union (YOU), whose military-style parades and effective community-based organization placed enormous pressure on the more conservative Muhsin. Jamal Ramadhan's allies among the ASP militants followed suit, forming the Afro-Shirazi Youth League (ASYL) in May 1959, at the height of the Freedom Committee schism.

Karume's inability to control the Youth League would culminate in 1964, when its members played a leading role in the revolution against his judgment and without his knowledge.[24]

The Freedom Committee Alliance ended in 1960 with the announcement of new elections to be held in January of the following year. At that point, the ASP leadership quickly reverted to the race-baiting that Jamal Ramadhan had never abandoned and again came out in opposition to early independence. But the party remained divided. *Agozi* gloated over the reversal, mocking *Afrika Kwetu* for embracing positions for which it had only recently accused the dissidents of being "Quislings." The more serious split, however, occurred when the Shirazi leaders of the anti–Freedom Committee dissidents, Ali Sharif Musa, Muhammad Shamte, and the humiliated Ameri Tajo, formed a splinter party at the end of 1959, the Zanzibar and Pemba People's Party (ZPPP). The new party positioned itself as the champion of the islands' indigenous Shirazi majority. Its spokespeople urged Shirazis to leave the ASP, which they charged was dominated by foreigners, especially Tanganyikans. (Karume's reliance on Tanganyikan advisers and the latter's leading role in the PAFMECA alliance made such allegations all the more plausible.) Suddenly forgetting their recent opposition to the Freedom Committee, ZPPP speakers praised the ZNP, hinting at a possible alliance. They made ample use of the discourses of *ustaarabu*, castigating the ASP as inimical to Islam and a party of *wahuni*—hooligans, vagabonds, disreputable youth. The *wahuni* themselves, meanwhile, were deployed by ASP operatives to gather outside Tajo's home and chant abuse.[25]

All these divisions took a toll on the ASP in the January 1961 elections, in which it won only a bare plurality of the votes cast for the three parties. It suffered most in Pemba, where it came in third after the ZPPP with less than a quarter of the vote. Of the Protectorate's twenty-two constituencies, the ASP took ten and the ZNP nine. That left the ZPPP, with its three seats (all in Pemba), holding the balance of power. As Lofchie observed, the jockeying that resulted, in which both major parties courted the three ZPPP representatives to join them in a coalition government, crystallized the central issue that had divided self-identified Shirazis: should they align themselves according to the explicit racial appeals of the ASP or according to the appeals of monarchy, religion, and *ustaarabu* espoused by the ZNP? Shamte, deeply anti-mainlander, quickly agreed to an alliance with the ZNP, and, after bitter arguments bordering on violence, so did one of his colleagues. But the third ZPPP representative, Ali Sharif, decided instead to resign from the party and rejoin the ASP. The result was a stalemate, each side holding eleven seats. With no parliamentary majority to form a government, the British hastily called for a second election in June. A twenty-third constituency was added, in Pemba, to avoid another deadlock.

The election campaigns brought the politicians' battles into the streets and villages most palpably in the form of contests over voter registration. Registration for the 1961 elections were tumultuous affairs, not least because the potential electorate had been vastly enlarged since the 1957 election by the enfranchisement of women and the relaxation of property and literacy qualifications. Four years of steady party propaganda also had their effect, as had the general excitement over political participation associated with the "wind of change" that was ending colonialism across the continent. As a result Zanzibaris clamored to be registered, in contrast to the relatively restrained response in advance of the 1957 polls.[26]

Once successfully registered, anyone had the legal right to challenge subsequent applicants, and local party leaders made sure to be present at each registration point. The result, according to the official who oversaw registration for the January elections, was constant "bickering."[27] *Agozi* captured the spirit of both sides when it declared that the goals of registration ought to be "for Hizbu to prevent Afro [from registering], and Afro to prevent Hizbu. . . . An election is no time for Brotherhood, Friendship, [or] Impartiality."[28] Each side accused the other of trying to register foreign nationals, Arab or mainlander. There is some evidence that the ASP did indeed encourage migrant workers to try to register. The ZNP, for its part, insisted on the narrowest interpretation of the law, which stipulated that those not born in the islands could vote only after taking out formal citizenship papers. This stance not only served the ZNP practically, it also furthered its monarchist rhetoric. Citizenship was defined legally as being a "subject of the Sultan," and during the 1957 campaign Hizbu activists had spread rumors that only members of the sultan's party—that is, their own—would be allowed to vote.[29] They continued such propaganda during the subsequent campaigns. *Afrika Kwetu* complained that passersby, presumably those suspected of being mainlanders and/or ASP supporters, were assaulted by shouts of "You're not the sultan's subject!" In an act that would cause considerable bitterness, the ZNP even adopted the sultan's red flag as their party emblem, accusing anyone who refused to fly it of disloyalty.[30]

The ASP therefore harbored reservations about the naturalization requirement. This did not prevent them from making similar accusations that their rivals were registering foreign nationals. But in contrast to the legal definition, the ASP defined citizenship in strictly racial terms. Zanzibar was part of the

African continent and hence part of an African nation; Arabs should go back to their homes in the Arabian peninsula to vote. Party propaganda demanded to know why Africans from the mainland had to "purchase" citizenship (a reference to the fees charged for taking out naturalization papers) while the real foreigners did not.[31]

In fact, neither side was willing to accept naturalization or long-term residence as qualifications for registering an individual as a voter.[32] As a result, battles over registration rapidly advanced the racialization of national thought. This was obviously the case with the ASP. But it applied equally to ZNP activists, who regarded "every mainlander . . . as an enemy," no matter what his or her legal status was.[33] As a result, many who had lived virtually all their lives in the islands or who had even been born there but of immigrant parents found themselves targeted for disenfranchisement. The insinuation that mainlanders were aliens was imbued with the old language of slavery and as such aroused deep resentments. J. R. Naish, who served as deputy supervisor of the 1957 elections, later recalled the kind of tensions that ZNP objections could raise:

> I remember that when I was registering electors in 1957, a very old
> man . . . came forward to register his name and an objection was made.
> And I asked him where he was born. . . . And he said that he wasn't sure
> where he was born—this was a vital point because if you were not born
> in Zanzibar you were not entitled to vote. And I said, "Well, what are
> your earliest memories?" And he said that, as far as he knew, he'd been
> brought to Zanzibar by his mother who'd been brought to Zanzibar as
> a slave by the Arabs. This remark caused an electric atmosphere in the
> court. One could sense that—there was a murmur among the Africans.
> The memories of the slave trade and of the atrocities and injustices
> which were committed against the Africans was [sic] still very much
> alive, even in 1957.[34]

Naish was only partly right in thinking that memories of the atrocities of slavery were "still" alive in 1957; rather, such memories had been revived and reimagined in the preceding decade as a way of mobilizing support for African racial nationalism.

In a similar incident from 1957 that gained huge notoriety and still rankled four years later (indeed, it still echoes today), the ZNP brazenly attempted to disqualify Abeid Karume from voting and from running against Ali Muhsin for the Ng'ambo constituency by claiming he had been born in central Africa and carried to the islands as an infant by his enslaved mother. When the registration officer ruled in Karume's favor, the ZNP took the issue to court; Muhsin made a show of attending the sessions every day as the ZNP's lawyers labored to prove that Karume's mother had been a slave. The trial became a cause célèbre, and Karume became an overnight hero to less famous Zanzibaris who resented ZNP slave-baiting.[35] He easily trounced Muhsin for the Ng'ambo seat.

These concerted attempts to disenfranchise voters and political figures were reflected in the overall tenor of political discourse during the campaigns; each side charged that its rivals were aliens. ASP polemicists responded to the routine assertions of the ZNP and ZPPP that the ASP was a "party of foreigners" by shifting the frame of reference by which indigenousness and foreignness were calculated, contrasting their African ancestry to the ancestry of Hizbu "settlers."[36] ZNP and ZPPP campaigners warned of the threats that alien barbarians posed to the islands' culture and material well-being and demanded crackdowns on immigration from the mainland. They charged that the ASP had won the 1957 elections through the votes of foreigners who had sold the country's interests to its enemies. They painted the ASP as a party of traitors and imperialist stooges, created by British officials as part of a master plan to extend colonial rule through the promotion of racial tension.[37]

During the existence of the PAFMECA alliance, ZNP spokesmen had indulged in occasional pronouncements of pan-Africanist solidarity. But that now went by the wayside, and the party became more stridently anti-mainlander. Among the policy issues that divided it from the ASP was the latter's continued espousal of an East African federation to follow independence, in partnership with Kenya and Tanganyika. The ZNP heaped scorn on the proposal and on mainland politicians such as Nyerere who supported it, darkly warning that both were tools of "neocolonialism."[38] Even during the PAFMECA period, ZNP expressions of pan-Africanism had always taken a back seat to pan-Arabist loyalties. Muhsin, especially, spoke often of Zanzibar's place in the pan-Arab world and trumpeted his personal connections with Nasser.[39] That position of course was perfectly in line his party's championing of civilizational nationalism, in which Zanzibar national identity was defined by the values of *ustaarabu*. Accordingly, the party stressed the need for Arabic instruction in the schools and presented itself as the party of Islam. Muhsin was celebrated as a religious scholar. In contrast, the ASP and its leaders were castigated as barbarians. At public meetings and in the press, audiences were warned that if Karume and his henchmen had their way, Zanzibar's vaunted *ustaarabu* would be destroyed and islanders would be forced to clothe themselves in leaves and hides. After all, wrote one of *Mwongozi*'s correspondents, our "history and civilization certainly did not come from KATANGA, nor from RUFIJI." Rufiji was a region in southeastern Tanganyika, whence came immigrants who were widely perceived as quintessential mainland barbarians. Congo's secessionist Katanga Province was much in the news at the time, a symbol of violent disorder to polemicists on all sides.[40]

As we have seen, for years ASP partisans had been honing a rhetoric that painted the foreignness of Arab political leaders in stark racial terms. During the 1961 election campaigns the most inflammatory rhetoric of this kind emanated from the militant wing of the party associated with Jamal Ramadhan Nasibu and his allies in the ASYL and the Human Rights League. The latter was an independent group not formally affiliated with any party, although much of its membership overlapped with that of the ASYL. It had been founded in 1956 by Mmanga Said Kharusi, also known as Bamanga, a close colleague of Jamal Ramadhan in labor union activities. The league began as a multiracial organization that derived its ideals from the UN's Universal Declaration of Human Rights. Among its first actions was a protest to the UN over the invasion of Suez; otherwise it restricted itself, at first, to bland pronouncements about press freedoms, human rights, and the like. (In an early statement Bamanga named U.S. president Eisenhower as an inspiration.)[41] But subsequently Bamanga and his organization became known for their extreme rhetoric on a variety of issues; their positions shifted in displays of opportunism as reckless as Jamal Ramadhan's.[42] Despite its initial pan-Arabist and internationalist sympathies and despite being headed by a member of a prominent Arab clan, the league had become virulently anti-Arab by the time of the PAFMECA alliance, and most of its Arab members had abandoned it. The league and the ASYL were responsible for some of the most provocative activities during the election campaigns, and members of both groups would be implicated in the June 1961 pogroms.[43] In the weeks leading up to the June election, Karume and other party leaders became so alarmed by these groups' *matusi* that they ordered them to stop. Still, party leaders had actively wooed them and felt that they needed their support.

More significantly, for all their last-minute scruples about the ASYL and the Human Rights League, mainstream ASP advocates, including *Afrika Kwetu*, engaged in much the same kind of rhetoric throughout the election campaigns. Making use of one of the most powerful mobilizing tools of international pan-Africanism, they likened Zanzibar Arabs to Afrikaners (Makaburu; Boers) or Kenyan settlers (*masetla*). In the geopolitical climate of the time, this was a sure tactic for delegitimizing political rivals and even dehumanizing them. Like their Kenyan and South African counterparts, Zanzibar Arabs were members of "immigrant races" who could make no legitimate national claims outside the lands of their ancestral origins (*asili*) and who did so only as a strategy to continue their oppression of Africans. This alien status inhered to the Arab "settler" even if his family had been settled in Africa for ten generations or more.[44]

Such depictions of Arabs were bolstered by an emphasis on their historic role as slave masters. As I have shown, the rhetoric of slavery was not exclusive to any one side, and ASP propagandists in fact claimed that they were simply responding to Hizbu slave-baiting. ZNP's attempt to disqualify Karume from the 1957 elections was bitterly remembered. Similar slave-baiting continued to be directed at Karume, including by his erstwhile allies who were to form the ZPPP.[45] Besides arousing the resentments of low-status islanders for whom imputations of slave ancestry rankled as an assault on one's honor, such ill-judged polemics also provided a basis for the ASP's repeated assertions that ZNP multiracialism was a fraud and that Arab politicians had never abandoned their puffed-up attitudes as slave masters. Propagandists spread allegations that Ali Muhsin and other party leaders openly abused Hizbu's African members as uncivilized slaves, and the allegations were made all the more believable (and all the more inflammatory) because they named precise individuals and incidents. Under such conditions, any African who agreed to follow Arab political leaders had to be a servile lackey (*kibaraka*) suffering from a slave mentality. "A slave returns to the long-beards," commented *Agozi*, "when he remembers the rice they fed him."[46]

By reaching back to the mythologized histories of "Arab slavery," ASP polemicists invested nationalist politics with an apocalyptic quality. A vote for Hizbu, they proclaimed, was a vote for reenslavement. Lurid descriptions of slavery became a staple of their speeches. A common rhetorical strategy was to use the second-person plural, as if reminding audiences of outrages they themselves had suffered. Thus, speakers encouraged listeners to endow emotion-laden historical narratives with the power of personal memory.[47] On 1 May, Nyerere's Tanganyika African National Union (TANU) sent one of its most effective speakers, Bibi Titi Muhammad, to address a large ASP rally in Zanzibar Town. Her widely reported speech generated heated debates and mutual vituperation and was remembered long afterward. Bibi Titi's main theme was the shamelessness of "black people" who, by selling their votes to Arab "bloodsuckers," refused to throw off the yoke of slavery. At the core of her speech was an overheated description of the brutalities Arabs had supposedly inflicted on their African slaves. Female slaves were forced to sweep the floors with their breasts and males were castrated like cattle, she said. She told of Arab mistresses who, curious about what a human fetus looked like in the womb, persuaded their husbands to cut open the bellies of pregnant slaves. The latter anecdote was to have a particularly grim afterlife one month later.[48]

The success of Bibi Titi's speech indicated the Zanzibar public's broad fascination with violence. Violent rhetoric, emanating from all sides and aimed in all directions, endowed political speech with compelling drama. Some was shaped by memories of Mau Mau or, more precisely, by the sensationalized accounts of Mau Mau that had circulated widely in the preceding decade. All parties accused their enemies of Mau Mau tactics. During the PAFMECA crisis, *Agozi* vilified Karume and his allies with assertions that they had taken Mau Mau oaths to decapitate their internal party rivals and kill their children. But with typical abandon, *Agozi* embraced Mau Mau in other articles, hinting that Arab "settlers" and their lackeys (i.e., Karume himself) would soon face a homegrown version.[49] Overt threats of violence were rarely offered in print, for reasons that no doubt included awareness of sedition laws. But hints were there for the taking. Again, the clearest examples come from *Agozi*. One issue carried a thinly veiled threat of Arab expulsion and, treading dangerously close to outright treason, an obscure threat against the monarchy itself.[50]

More common in the published polemics, and potentially more incendiary, were accusations that rivals were plotting violence, a rhetorical ploy (as we will see in later chapters) that effectively dehumanized them and made them fair targets for preemptive or retaliatory violence. During the 1961 election campaigns, ASP propagandists alleged that the ZNP planned to kill Africans after taking power, starting with ZNP's own deluded African followers. A paper loyal to the ZNP described ASP members as "potential murder[er]s of women and children."[51] In her May 1st speech, Titi Muhammad asserted that Arab youths, who she said were more brutal even than their slave-owning fathers, intended "to kill Africans slowly and keep them in humiliation." The threats Africans faced were so great, she said, that friends had warned her not to travel to Zanzibar. "You'll be slaughtered, they told me. But I laughed and said, If my head falls, so will the heads of all the Manga Arabs living on our land."[52] One month later the despised Manga would be the prime targets of ASP pogroms.

Politicizing Everyday Life

As one campaign followed another, each fought more bitterly than the last, ordinary Zanzibaris found themselves forced to choose among racialized political identities in their daily lives. Decisions about where to shop or work, how to travel, whether to celebrate a kinsman's marriage or to attend his burial: all became assertions of political and racial loyalties.

In many ways, the ASP took the first decisive steps to inject electoral politics into everyday life when it established party-run cooperative shops. Inspired no doubt by Garveyite teachings, party activists encouraged their followers to patronize the ASP shops as a way to demonstrate loyalty to their own kind and to wrest alleged commercial dominance away from Arab shopkeepers. (Most Arab shopkeepers were Omani or Yemeni immigrants, the so-called Manga and Shihiri Arabs, respectively. ASP attitudes toward Indian businessmen— some of whom supported the party financially—were ambivalent.) The general idea grew from popular shop boycotts that had taken place during the previous two decades. Ironically, the Arab Association itself had championed commercial boycotts as a political tactic during the clove-buying crisis, using them to unite communities against Indian businesses. But shop boycotts were also a common tool of popular protest, having been used by villagers to enforce a moral economy against shopkeepers accused of cornering scarce markets in rice, for example, or to force businessmen to redistribute some of their profits to the community.[53] As we have seen, they were also used during the 1948 general strike. The first "African" boycotts of "Arab" businesses during the Time of Politics were sparked in early 1957 by the rank and file, not by party leaders; they involved three eating houses frequented by *wachukuzi*.[54]

Late in 1957, ASP leaders announced their plans to open two dozen general cooperative shops; by early the following year five were up and running, all in Ng'ambo, as well as numerous street stalls that served food and tea. The party also sponsored an open-air market in front of one of its Ng'ambo branch offices. Party activists linked use of the shops to boycotts of Arab businesses, and the Arab Association and the ZNP responded immediately with alarm. Some within the latter organizations spoke of militant action; others proposed setting up a fund to subsidize Arab shopkeepers so they might undersell the cooperatives. And indeed, early in 1958 Arab shopkeepers were offering African customers large lines of credit to coax them back. ASP activists warned their constituents not to accept. The cooperatives' fortunes waxed and waned according to the vagaries of political mobilization and never got a very firm footing. Business declined during the PAFMECA alliance, in part because Karume's faction within the party was urging an end to anti-Arab boycotts. And that decline, in turn, brought to the fore charges of mismanagement and corruption. The charges fueled some of the most bitter polemics between *Agozi* and *Afrika Kwetu* and contributed to the tensions that surrounded Ameri Tajo's expulsion from the party.[55]

Hizbu's response to the boycotts and cooperative shops revealed its much stronger position for engaging in commercial combat. Given its leaders' greater levels of wealth, education, and commercial experience, the party's own cooperative schemes were inevitably better financed and better organized than the ASP's. So, for example, Hizbu acquired estates (one donated by Ali Muhsin's wife) on which needy party members could cultivate so long as they agreed to sell their produce to the party cooperative.[56] A sympathetic British journalist praised the efficiency and depth of ZNP's street-level organization, which the ASP could not match. The ZNP claimed over 100 neighborhood branches throughout the islands, through which it provided a variety of welfare services and cooperative enterprises. Much of this activity was credited to Babu, who had taken a course in party organization with the Labour Party during his six years in London as a student and postal worker. The branches also offered evening classes for adults and children, and in early 1960 the party opened an independent school. The headmaster was Juma Aley, a former Hollingsworth student and contributor to *Mazungumzo,* and Ali Muhsin made use of his Cairo connections to recruit Egyptian teachers. In 1958 Muhsin had announced, with great fanfare, that he had secured several dozen scholarships for Zanzibari students to study in Cairo. He had even offered some to the ASP to distribute to its followers, but Karume had rejected the offer on the grounds that such training would expose Africans to ideological taint.[57]

In short, the ZNP was better equipped to deliver patronage to its supporters. It was also better equipped to withhold opportunities from those who supported its rivals. From the start of the Time of Politics, the party advertised that it was keeping lists of members seeking employment; ZNP speakers urged supporters to hire only from those lists and to refuse to hire "aliens" or "foreigners," by which they plainly meant mainlanders and ASP sympathizers.[58] Such tactics were soon supplemented by efforts to establish ZNP-affiliated labor organizations to rival those dominated by ASP pan-Africanists. (Eventually there were two trade union federations, each affiliated with one of the major parties.) Babu and a handful of like-minded colleagues hoped to base the new unions on principles of internationalist socialism. But the Marxists were a small minority, and the new unions quickly proved little more than vehicles for chauvinist partisan politics. Their main actions aimed at displacing mainlander labor, especially in the casual sector. As such they were part of what some in the party were calling "V2 bombs," retaliatory measures that were to be launched in revenge for ASP boycotts of Arab-owned businesses.[59]

A campaign of this sort that attained particular prominence targeted the largely mainlander *wachukuzi* who had been the backbone of the 1948 general strike. It began in August 1958, when ZNP activists, including some well-known toughs, stopped trucks bringing cloves and copra into the city produce market and pressured them not to hire the "foreigners" of the Wachukuzi Association but to hire instead their own teams of workers. The Hizbu workers, in fact, were not experienced *wachukuzi* at all but were instead Tumbatu villagers bused in from ZNP strongholds for the occasion. Tensions mounted in subsequent weeks as growers, shippers, and dealers (the latter mostly Manga and Shihiri) were pressed to demonstrate their patriotism by denying work to the *wachukuzi* crews whom they normally employed. The organizers of this campaign were candid in explaining their motivations: they wanted to deprive "aliens" and ASP supporters of a livelihood in revenge for the losses the ASP boycotts and cooperative stores had inflicted on their Arab "friends and relations."[60] They taunted the mainlanders with raw nativist language, including the epithet *washenzi*. Karume played a major role in averting violence, in part by appealing to racial unity among the rival workers.[61]

The most lasting resentments of this sort resulted from the eviction of hundreds of squatters who refused to take out ZNP membership cards. The evictions, which began in 1958 (as did the moves against the *wachukuzi*), were concentrated in Unguja's main plantation zone, north of town, and as we shall see in the next chapter they lay behind some of the worst of the June pogroms. They aroused particular bitterness because of how blatantly they violated the old norms of patronage. The Hizbu landlords no doubt regarded their tenants as equally neglectful of the loyalties expected of clients. But even they seemed to recognize that the sanction of eviction was unprecedented on such a scale, and they sometimes made half-hearted efforts to mask their political motives, especially when responding to official inquiries.[62]

Such campaigns only served to prompt fresh ASP actions, and very quickly the islands were caught in a spiral of retaliatory boycotts, counter-boycotts, evictions, and sackings. Inevitably, given the greater economic vulnerability of its members, the ASP came out the worse in such contests. Party propagandists protested that people with black skin and "kinky hair" were routinely refused employment, including at government offices, where "straight-haired people" gave preference to members of their own clans.[63] (ZNP sympathizers were in fact disproportionately represented among the largely Arab bureaucrats who staffed the lower and middle levels of the civil service.) In mid-1960 the ZNP called on its supporters to display party insignias on all businesses, shops, and transportation they owned. Party loyalists should patronize only those businesses and should fire known ASP sympathizers, ZNP leaders said. Intimidation was sometimes direct, as during an ASP boycott in Pemba, when young men belonging to the Human Rights League stood outside Arab shops writing down the names of Africans who entered.[64]

Bus boycotts proved to be a particularly powerful way to force people to identify themselves in terms of racial politics. (They had been used as such before, during the chauvinist anti-Indian campaigns of the 1930s.) This was because of how the microeconomics of public transport drew passengers into the fray alongside owners, drivers, and conductors. Buses in East Africa typically do not depart from their starting point until they are filled, and they stand at major stops en route until they gather enough passengers. A bus that was being boycotted, then, might stand for a long time waiting for passengers while those who had already boarded—whether out of sympathy for the bus owner's party or merely in an effort to ignore politics altogether—grew more and more impatient. Buses displayed party insignias, either the red party flag of the ZNP or baskets made of green coconut fronds (*mapakacha*) for the ASP. But the bus owners' political alignments were local knowledge anyhow. And it was difficult for owners and drivers to sit on the fence. If a person perceived as the supporter of one party (perhaps because of racial markers) got on a bus filled with passengers from the other side, the latter would get off, leading to disputes between passengers and driver. In one recorded incident, ASP bus personnel invoked racial loyalty in their attempts to force Africans off an Arab-owned vehicle and onto their own. The ensuing argument quickly drew a crowd.[65]

The most effective way the strikes and commercial boycotts were enforced was through another type of popular action that was also called "boycott" in the English-language sources. This was not a conventional boycott of shops and businesses—or more precisely, it was not *only* that. Rather, it was a kind of personal ostracism, in which a targeted individual would be shunned by the entire community. Similar practices in South Asia were sometimes called "social boycotts." In 1937, a British district commissioner gave them a more precise name, drawing on his own country's history, when he wrote that an individual in a village south of Zanzibar Town had been "sent to Coventry" for violating a bus boycott. "Shop owners will sell him nothing and other drivers refuse to accept him as a passenger; the only thing he is allowed is water which he must himself fetch from the well."[66] Such behavior was a well-established sanction against individuals who had offended community norms.[67] Like business boycotts, shunning might be seen as a form of enforced majoritarianism, as when four ASP supporters in a ZNP stronghold were refused any kind of social intercourse, including the ability to buy or sell anything in the village market.[68] Of course, majority consensus is never automatic. It must be created, and some voices in its creation are more powerful than others. But the prevalence of social boycotts during the Time of Politics signaled the existence, at least, of widespread habits of thinking about politics as a matter of community consensus. This observation does not negate the fact that such consensus was never total (ostracism itself, a form of intimidation, is the best evidence of that) or the fact that it often arose through bitter arguments about history, race, and nation.[69] Indeed, the assumption that politics must reflect consensus only made those arguments all the more bitter.

Boycotts of both types, then, were powerful mechanisms that forced people in their everyday actions to choose a community of belonging defined by the dominant politics of the day, and, as such, they played a central role in furthering the spirals of retaliation and recrimination that gripped civil society after 1957. *Zuia*, one of the Swahili verbs commonly used to indicate both a commercial and a personal boycott (its literal meaning is to prevent or obstruct), became a buzzword and rallying cry.[70] Such actions could divide what had once been a single community, making it difficult for people to draw water or attend a funeral without risking charges of political or racial betrayal or even physical intimidation.[71] But the boycotts' most damaging impact lay in how they dehumanized their victims by publicly excluding them from the everyday community. Thus they could lead to more forceful action against persons stigmatized as outsiders, as in the incidents of arson that became especially frequent in the years after the 1961 riots.[72]

Although the preceding comments apply especially to acts of shunning, the distinction between social and commercial boycotts was far from clear cut. Swahili-speakers used the same interchangeable verbs, *zuia* and *pinga,* to describe both kinds of boycotts; those words also were sometimes used to denote labor stoppages.[73] Ostracism, commercial boycotts, evictions, and strikes were all perceived as varieties of the same kind of activity, intended to "block" or "obstruct" the targeted individual's participation in the life of the community. They can have wholly discrete meanings only within a discursive framework in which commercial relationships—between retailers and customers, employers and employees, landlords and tenants—are perceived as conceptually distinct from affective relations among kin and friends. Such a distinction was weak in Zanzibar society. So too was a closely related distinction: that between "politics"—defined as electoral politics and other affairs linked directly to the state—and other spheres of social life. Tellingly in this regard, the "social boycotts" put *masheha* under particular pressure. Their superiors believed that as civil servants they had to remain insulated from local political alignments. But because the *sheha,* unlike the mudir and the district officer, lived fully within the community in which he served, his impartiality was constantly undermined by threats of being shunned "by his own cousins, etc."[74]

Here, then, is the key to the rapid and thorough politicization of civil society. Britain had introduced electoral politics on the working assumption that they would be kept separate from other aspects of social and economic life (just as Britain had hoped a transfer of state power would leave untouched the fundamental structures of colonial capitalism). But Zanzibaris, especially party activists, made no such assumptions, and the activists worked assiduously to ensure that the language of nationalist politics would permeate myriad realms of social interaction. In doing so, they in effect engaged in a hegemonizing project. Insofar as party leaders claimed to represent populations defined in terms of national communities, it was imperative that they get voters to think of those communities as pertinent to their daily lives. Thus they employed tactics such as the two kinds of boycott to pressure people to reimagine their ties to one another (and their differences) in terms of national communities of belonging and otherness.

Such pressures produced the most bitterness when they contributed to reshaping relationships between people of different ranks and status. As in many agrarian or recently agrarian societies, those relationships had often been idealized in a language of personal dependency, a language that in Zanzibar had been inflected with the idioms of racial or ethnic difference. But the polarizing rhetoric of the Time of Politics had contributed to a situation in which ties between patrons and clients became recast in terms of a fundamental racial divide: not as people joined by bonds of mutual obligation but as people separated by competing claims of national loyalty. Much of this situation was summed up in observations made before the Foster-Sutton commission by Mervyn Smithyman, an administrator with long East African experience. "The essence of the problem," he testified, "is that during the last few years there have been big changes in the relationships of people." Earlier, "people knew their respective places in society and were content to stay there. Lately it has not been quite the same." Before the 1950s, Arabs had been accepted as natural leaders, he explained; nowadays they must endure rude remarks when walking on the street.[75] Of course, Smithyman's rosy picture of the once-easygoing relations between Arabs and Africans is grossly overdrawn and reflects his own deeply conservative perspective. Paternalism, a form of domination, never precluded oppression or even brutality; slavery itself had been governed by norms of paternalism. As we shall see in the following chapter, landlords did not always treat their squatters with the care and kindness Smithyman implies. But if the myth of paternalism had enjoined subordinates to defer to their superiors, it had also enjoined the latter to at least make gestures of personal responsibility. That is one reason the evictions were so deeply resented.

The language of paternalism did not die easily during the Time of Politics. At times feelings of strained friendship prompted contending parties to seek compromises, making it all the more disappointing when those attempts foundered on the new solidarities of racial politics. In September 1958, as part of its campaign to displace ASP workers, Hizbu persuaded the owners of most of the town's slaughterhouses to take on new workers who were ZNP loyalists. Butchers were told to teach the newcomers their trade—so the butchers could be subsequently replaced, according to rumor. (Muhammad Abeid al-Haj, the investigating district commissioner and himself a ZNP sympathizer, found the rumors plausible.) The move prompted an immediate walkout by ASP butchers. One slaughterhouse owner, Muhammad Mahadi, failed to go along with the ZNP campaign, but his workers told him, with regret, that it had been decided that if any ASP butchers engaged in a work stoppage, then all must do so. At first, they agreed to his request to finish up the day's work before walking off, "because they are good friends," but they soon returned to Mahadi's office to tell him they "couldn't do him that favour" after all. We do not know whether this turnabout was prompted by a reconsideration of political principles, by intimidation from other ASP butchers, or by a combination of factors. In at least one case, ASP butchers told their employers they would not work alongside Hizbu co-workers because they feared the arguments that might ensue in a workplace filled with sharp knives.[76]

But the *personal* nature of the relationships between workers and employers, businessmen and customers, is precisely what made the strikes and boycotts so bitter, what invested them with a sense of personal affront, of ingratitude or disloyalty. Hence, Hizbu-affiliated employers and landlords reacted angrily when their workers or tenants refused to demonstrate the political deference and loyalty they considered their due. ASP polemicists, on the other hand, strove to expose paternalism as a myth that Arabs used to mask the realities of racial oppression. This is reflected in the epithets they coined. Arabs were "al-Harara"—the haughty ones, domineering, filled with scornful pride—who could only imagine Africans, even those among their own political followers, as servile laborers. (Why, asked *Agozi*, had Hizbu recruited only Africans to displace ASP *wachukuzi* in 1958? Weren't Arabs capable of such labor?)[77] Arabs were also "feudalists" (*makubeli*), and black people who accepted their leadership were guilty of slavish false consciousness and insufficient racial pride. The latter were like islanders who had once believed that prayers would reach the Almighty only if they were led by an Arab imam, claimed *Agozi*.[78] *Agozi* berated Karume for such obsequiousness during the PAFMECA alliance, alleging that he had been flattered to have connections to highborn Arabs.

To drive home the point, ASP propagandists circulated stories dramatizing the abuses that, they alleged, Arab patrons routinely inflicted on their personal retainers. This was not a new theme. For years *Afrika Kwetu* had inveighed against a common form of domestic service by which impoverished village parents placed a child with a wealthy family in town as a "houseboy" or "housegirl."[79] Ideally this was a kind of quasi-adoption, but *Afrika Kwetu*'s writers noted that the adopted children and the household's own children were treated far from equally: the former were given endless chores, were denied schooling and decent clothes, and were even forbidden to eat out of the same dishes as the other members of the household. The paper called on government to apply child labor laws to end the practice. But more significantly, it represented the relationship as a racial one—the servant children were depicted as Africans, their employers or foster parents as Arabs or Indians—and argued that only a slave mentality could account for Africans who allowed their children to be subjected to such indignities. Party propagandists revived these complaints during the election campaigns.[80]

Agozi took this theme one step further, offering up colorful tales of violent abuse that Arabs allegedly meted out to their African servants. Like many of their contemporaries, *Agozi*'s polemicists typically provided sufficient details to get the gossip mill in motion while remaining vague enough to avoid prosecution for libel. Thus, they told the story of "Mr. Opel," a wealthy Arab who lived in an opulent stone house. "Opel" was a reference to the car he drove, a common symbol of ill-gotten wealth in the pages of *Agozi*. Mr. Opel had an old family retainer, an African nursemaid who had reared his mother as well as him and had recently cared for the mother in her final illness. In May 1959, the nursemaid's hovel caught fire. Mr. and Mrs. Opel were relaxing on their terrace at the time, not ten feet away, yet they did nothing to save the old woman.

It was left to the "*gozi* neighbors" to pull her from the fire and take her to the hospital, badly burned. When hospital personnel asked who her people were, she said she belonged to the Opel family. But Mr. and Mrs. Opel disavowed her, and a few days later she died, in the care of an another impoverished "*gozi*" who had taken her in. The tale was told as a parable of the ingratitude of Arab patrons and the values of racial solidarity.[81]

Bearing her master's abuses less submissively was another "Mama Gozi," who served a powerful Arab family in Shangani, perhaps Stone Town's most elite quarter. This servant's mistress had taken a dislike to her because she was "GOZI, not HIZBU," and so, in a narrative detail that perhaps echoes the motifs of feminized envy that animate the myths of slave disembowelments, she complained to her husband, who promptly tied up the servant and gave her a brutal whipping. *Agozi* took care to replicate the master's words as he wielded the lash:

> You goat, you animal, you dare talk back to your mistress. . . . I'll teach you manners, slave! What kind of people are you Africans? Dogs are better than you people. You and your darky leaders are nothing but barbarians.

His wife urged him on, using similar language. By the time the unfortunate Mama Gozi reached the hospital, a phone call had been made, and the Arab staff nurse (or rather, the "Settler staff nurse") had been told simply to give the beaten servant an aspirin and send her home. When the Mama Gozi filed a legal complaint, the "settler" who beat her contacted the ASP leadership, who in turn tried to persuade her to accept a paltry monetary payoff and be proud that such a highborn Arab was begging her forgiveness. (The legal case was doomed to failure, *Agozi* noted, since both the police superintendent and the judge were also "settlers.") *Agozi* used the incident to condemn Karume's participation in the PAFMECA alliance as a manifestation of toadying.[82]

Spread through the circuits of rumor and gossip, such stories undermined the ideals of patron and client that may once have prompted subalterns to regard themselves and the ethnic other as members of the same community and encouraged them instead to think of the bonds of racial solidarity as more pertinent to their lives. When combined with the strikes and boycotts, the net result was to foster an atmosphere in which virtually every aspect of community life seemed infused with the tensions of racial politics.

This was especially evident in the performance of public dances and other festive rites. Such occasions had always been prone to the crystallization of social tensions; patrons and clients used them as forums in which to jockey for position and assert their privileges and obligations.[83] Makunduchi's boisterous Mwaka Koga festival, which for decades had drawn spectators from throughout Unguja (and critics, too, as we saw in chapter 3), suffered particularly rancorous political tensions—understandably, given how hotly the elections were contested there.[84] The village of Wingwi, near Wete in Pemba, was divided just as deeply, and it, too, had recurring disputes over the performance of public dances, or *ngoma*. In 1960 youth groups attached to the two electoral blocs made repeated attempts to stop one another's *ngoma* by force.[85] Those tensions resurfaced in October 1962, culminating in a riot occasioned by a ceremonial visit by the ZPPP chief minister, Muhammad Shamte. At issue was not the visit itself but which party's dancers would perform at it—or rather, as the ASP youth who disrupted the ceremony insisted, what form of musical performance was customary on such occasions.[86] Performative religious rites were no less marked by political rivalries, particularly the performance of *maulid*, the musical recital of a text on the birth of the Prophet. Sponsorship of *maulid* performances had long been a common way for patrons to compete for prestige and clientele. The practice was now put to political purposes; the ZNP, which liked to position itself as the party of Islam, was especially active in this regard. In the nervous months following the June riots, politically sponsored *maulids* caused officials particular worry. When the post-riot emergency measures were lifted in late 1962, special provisions were retained to continue tight control over *ngoma* and other public "fêtes and dances."[87] To no avail, however: on the eve of the revolution one year later, the islands were gripped by rumors of nighttime *ngoma* and Manga sword dances at which nefarious plots were being hatched.

More telling than the politicization of festive rites—which, after all, had long been sites for the public contestation of power, including at moments of political crisis—was the wide range of mundane incidents that took on political overtones. I have already mentioned several: business rivalries, bus rides, house fires, disputes between servants and employers. The picture might be completed by a brief catalog of others:

- *Marriage.* As we saw in chapter 4, polemicists had turned marriage into a central issue of racial politics as early as the mid-1950s. During the Time of Politics, in addition to partisan-inspired disputes over attending or being invited to wedding feasts (and similar disputes about funerals and other social affairs), there were reports of parents stopping a wedding altogether if they suspected their child was about to marry a member of the opposing political party.[88] In Pemba, there were rumors that "several ASP husbands . . . divorced their wives who voted for ZNP."[89]

- *Sex.* The newspapers associated with Jamal Ramadhan Nasibu and the ASYL were particularly shameless about printing gossip about sexual misconduct, although the particulars are usually too cryptic for a contemporary reader to decipher. Among other allegations, they wrote of Hizbu youth engaging in rampant fornication in back alleys and behind baobab trees and of married Hizbu leaders impregnating girls in the party's youth wing.[90] *Afrika Kwetu* accused ZNP of protecting Arab brothels that had been established in Ng'ambo.[91]

- *Death.* As in most Islamic cultures, in Zanzibar a premium is placed on quick burial of the dead, and it is customary for members of an entire neighborhood or community to cooperate in the matter. This cooperation was disrupted by the tensions of the Time of Politics. In one case a man murdered under mysterious circumstances was claimed by both sides as a martyr, and a tussle ensued over disposal of the body.[92]

- *Language.* *Mwongozi* protested that the "debased Swahili" used by some speakers on the Voice of Zanzibar was incomprehensible to true Zanzibaris and betrayed a bias in favor of mainlanders.[93] Letters published in *Agozi* made the opposite complaint: they said that radio announcers indulged in so much needless Arabizing that their language could not even be said to be Swahili. One correspondent held women announcers up for particular scorn: "They are so exceedingly pretentious that we cannot even understand what they're saying. There is a time for putting on airs and preening yourselves, but not while at work. Shut your mouths. . . . Who are you to be so pleased with yourselves?"[94] One cannot help but imagine that similar misogynist resentment helped shape the sexual assaults that would follow.

- *Water.* Some landlords refused squatters access to wells, in violation of Islamic injunctions.[95] Elsewhere, government projects to sink wells and build cisterns were frustrated by charges of racial and partisan favoritism. In at least one sharply divided community, officials tried to get around this obstacle by presenting each of the political factions with keys to a new water tank. But in a provocative move, the leader of the ASP faction surreptitiously removed the padlock and put a new one in its place, to which he alone had the key. "This annoyed the ZPPPs who regarded [themselves] as being stopped from getting water because, they argued, it was known to the Afro-Shirazis that due to political differences the ZPPPs would not mingle with them at drawing water." The ZPPP faction threatened to break the lock, the mudir and the district commissioner intervened, and the ASP leaders yielded but vowed not to use the water themselves.[96]

- *Traffic.* Accidents that occurred in public thoroughfares could quickly become politicized; collisions or near-misses introduced a hint of violence that could escalate. And when only one of the parties to the altercation was driving a motor vehicle, that introduced the element of class—or, as it was commonly perceived, of race. Stories were told of Arab drivers threatening or assaulting traffic police, virtually all of whom were mainlanders.[97] One Youth League paper, *Kipanga*, seemed to savor reporting on incidents in which rude and dangerous Hizbu drivers threatened *gozi* pedestrians. In February 1962 the paper devoted an entire issue to one such anecdote; the language reveals not only the invective typical throughout the Time of Politics but also how the June 1961 riots had escalated the tone of mutual recrimination. The incident involved a young *mchukuzi* who was pushing his cart through the narrow alleys of Mtendeni, a town neighborhood well known for its ZNP sympathies. As he neared the ZNP branch office, he was approached by a pickup truck whose driver "was undoubtedly a Hizbu member." The *mchukuzi* pressed himself up against a wall to allow the truck to pass. But the driver got out, overturned the cart, and began to curse the youth and his family. Soon a crowd of ZNP supporters had joined in, shouting, "Beat the barbarian!" The *mchukuzi* managed to escape to the police, but at the station he was told, "You all did a lot of beating in June, now it's your turn to be beaten." *Afrika Kwetu*, which reported on the same incident, emphasized that the young man had simply been trying to earn his daily bread, and it threatened to publish the Hizbu offender's name should he repeat such outrages.[98]

- *Crime.* As we shall see in the next chapter, criminal acts frequently took on political meanings. This was not only a question of victims and observers making racial assumptions about the identity of criminals and imputing political motives to them. In many cases, criminals themselves struck political poses. And conversely, disruptions in the social fabric that were occasioned by political tensions, such as those described above, were often imagined as criminal transgressions. So, for example, squatters and their political allies regarded eviction as an act of theft and reacted accordingly. More than any other discourse, shifting discourses about crime and victimhood signaled shifting ways of determining who belonged to the same moral community and who was likely to be targeted by the dehumanizing language of racial exclusion.

As incidents of politicized civil conflict proliferated, they had the net effect of reproducing the salience of racialized political categories in Zanzibaris' everyday lives. To be sure, much of the "experience" of such incidents was merely imagined: a traffic accident, a robbery, or a dispute between servant and mistress may have had no connection to racial thinking other than the meanings imputed to it by propagandists or rumormongers. But, as we shall see in the following chapters, those overlapping discursive circuits, especially rumor, were capable of transforming discourse into what many came to imagine as actual lived experience, which in turn shaped how they thought of themselves and others.

Conclusion: Force and Consent

Because both sides had confidently predicted landslide victories in the January 1961 elections, it was inevitable that the losing party would cry foul. The ASP forecasters fell victim to their own racial propaganda, which reasoned that because the ZNP was the party of Arabs and Africans constituted a clear majority, an ASP loss was arithmetically impossible. In fact, they predicted, the ASP's victory in 1961 would be even greater than in 1957, when many *magozi* had been disenfranchised by property and literacy qualifications. When the ASP nevertheless failed to win a majority, the conviction spread that the ZNP had used massive fraud.[99] In the following election on 1 June, then, ASP loyalists were determined not to let Hizbu again cheat them of victory. The riots in fact broke out when ASP crowds assaulted voters and poll watchers whom they accused of trying to rig the vote. When the poll results became known that evening—although narrowly losing the popular vote, the ZNP/ZPPP alliance managed to form a three-seat parliamentary majority—ASP fears and suspicions seemed fully confirmed.

The politicization of everyday life intensified during the sultanate's remaining two-and-a-half years. One last election was scheduled, for July 1963, with full independence to follow in December. In the meanwhile the protectorate was under a limited self-rule government dominated by Hizbu. (Although the ZPPP's Shamte was named chief minister, little effort was made to disguise the fact that Ali Muhsin was the leading figure in the governing alliance.) To those already susceptible to ASP racial rhetoric, the existence of that government, with its dubious mandate, served as a constant reminder of Arab domination. Its ministers pursued policies that favored estate owners, imposed barriers on the immigration and naturalization of mainlanders, and pushed what they called the "Zanzibarization" of employment, both in government and the private sector. The latter policy openly targeted mainlanders, whom Muhsin and his allies vilified as debased foreigners. Hizbu landlords and employers continued to rid themselves of workers and tenants because of their assumed or real ASP loyalties, and ZNP labor unions renewed their efforts to displace "foreign" workers.

A central feature of the turmoil of these years was incessant talk of violence, including memories of the June pogroms and the repeated rumors that retaliatory violence was being plotted. Much of the harshest language was connected to the widening divisions within both major parties, as leaders lost virtually all control over their militant "youth." The June riots themselves indicated Karume's weakness in this regard, and in the years that followed, members of the ASYL and the Human Rights League, many of whom had played significant roles in the pogroms, sharpened their challenges to his leadership. On the ZNP/ZPPP side, there was a growing chasm between the leftists, led by Babu, and the conservative nativists, led by Muhsin and Shamte. Conveniently for the latter, Babu was put out of the way in mid-1962 when the British imprisoned him on charges of sedition (Muhsin and the other government ministers seemed to acquiesce in the action). In his absence, Hizbu's right wing took decisive control of the party and Babu's allies began cultivating contacts with militants in the ASP's youth and labor organizations. After his release from jail in mid-1963, Babu formally split with the ZNP and formed his own party, Umma, enlisting the support of dissident ASP trade unionists who shared his Marxism.

During all this time, there was widespread talk of using force to overthrow the ZNP/ZPPP government, should it be reelected, from Youth League and other ASP dissidents. By mid-1963, roving gangs of young toughs from both major parties were intimidating ordinary voters as well as one another; the ASYL gangs were rumored to be "suicide squads" prepared to fight to the finish. The revolution, then, was far from a surprise. On the eve of independence, the resident, George Mooring, expressed concern not only about Karume's total loss of control over his party's "extreme elements" but also about the needless provocations of the Shamte-Muhsin government. Most alarming among the latter was the dismissal of the majority of the islands' police force because they were mainlanders, part of Muhsin's program of "Zanzibarization."[100]

As we have seen, the language of violence was not restricted to political threats; it permeated many aspects of civil life. Combined with more direct forms of intimidation, such language gave non-activists little choice but to participate in daily reenactments of the racialized rhetoric of the political parties. But in emphasizing the role of coercion, I do not mean to suggest that ordinary people necessarily acted against their "true" beliefs and convictions. It would be more accurate to suggest that when people got caught up in the strikes and boycotts, for whatever reasons, they became engaged in a set of social dynamics that fed back to shape their perceptions of the everyday world. The distinction between coercion and belief will be explored at greater length in chapter 7, but it would be useful to mention the problem here in order to convey the full significance of the various actions by which Zanzibaris were forced to choose sides. In a classic essay on the contentious role of social boycotts in Indian nationalism, Ranajit Guha observes that the "balance of force and consent" was a central concern to middle-class opponents of the practice. With his typical moral fastidiousness, Gandhi attempted to distinguish between "civil" or "political" boycotts, which aimed at spiritual persuasion, and "uncivil" or "social" boycotts, which aimed at physical coercion. As Guha notes, the distinction was impossible to pin down in practice, in part because of the devastating impact that any act of avoidance, even one so seemingly nonmaterial as avoidance of a wedding feast, could have on a person's reputation and hence on his ability to function in the day-to-day world.[101]

We might go one step further, however, and question the very distinction between coercion and persuasion, at least in this instance. The distinction assumes the existence of an authentic, fully autonomous inner self, a "self-originating, self-determining individual, who is at once a subject in his possession of sovereign consciousness . . . and an agent in his power of freedom."[102] For such an individual to yield to "external" pressures is to abandon his true conception of himself, to abandon his true subjectivities. But such an individual is a phantom, not one of flesh and blood whose daily existence consists of making choices rarely of his own creation. Such choices are what shape a person's subjectivities, and even if forced they can have a "persuading" effect. Of course, intimidation and violence can nevertheless force people to act in ways that violate deeply held personal convictions—a plain fact that is perhaps too obvious to need stating.

But there is a vast gray area, and the net impact of the strikes, social boycotts, and other pressures that were applied to everyday life was to induce people to play along with the political activists, thus turning their rhetoric into reality.

The ultimate acts of force occurred during the June riots. In many ways, however, the most significant forms of coercion were not those inflicted on the victims of the pogroms but those threatened against the bystanders and, especially, against the pogromists themselves. The latter were often ordinary persons intimidated into committing acts of dehumanizing violence against friends or neighbors whom only moments before they had considered members of the same moral community. Yet even in those instances, as we shall see in the following chapters, coercion could have the effect of reshaping a person's subjectivities in ways that made the world seem genuinely divided by racial boundaries.

PART 3

War of Stones

Mkuki kwa nguruwe; kwa mwanadamu mchungu.
A spear for a pig; for a human it's painful.
—SWAHILI PROVERB

6

Rumor, Race, and Crime

Whenever there is trouble in Zanzibar . . . there have been current
two rumours. One has been that the Manga Arabs would be coming
in with their swords to kill the Africans, and the other is that the
Makonde were making spears and bows and arrows to attack the Arabs.
Whenever there is any tension, those two rumours circulate with
unfailing regularity.

—Police Commissioner R. H. V. Biles, September 1961

In April 1962, concerned over the continuing threats of political violence
that had been simmering since the election riots of June 1961, a small group of
officials met "to consider measures to counteract rumours." Acting in accord
with empire-wide principles promulgated since the war, they agreed that the
best way to control rumors was to keep the public well informed—especially
about "such criminal activity as might give rise to rumour." The meeting led
to the creation of formal district intelligence committees, each charged with
collecting information on sensitive security issues, including crime.[1]

It is not difficult to understand why officials were worried about rumor
during this tense period: as more than one observed, the spread of rumors,
even when false, can have "a factual effect, i.e. where people [are] induced to
take some action as the result of hearing the rumour." Less explicable, at least
at first glance, is their preoccupation with crime. Why, for example, would the
intelligence committees consider an instance of common robbery an indicator
of the state of racial politics? And why, during the Time of Politics, did so much
police information on crime originate with the political parties?[2]

Part of the answer, as we saw in chapter 5, is that by the late 1950s the discourse on crime, as on practically every other matter, had become imbued with
the discourse of racial politics. At the most superficial level, propagandists ac-

cused their rivals of a wide range of illicit behavior, including assassination, embezzlement, and rape. But at a deeper level, such rhetoric resonated with popular discourse that had been developing for decades. It is no coincidence that the two groups mentioned by Police Commissioner Biles as those most often rumored to be plotting racial terror had accrued reputations for inherent criminality long before the Time of Politics. Immigrants from Yemen and the Persian Gulf, especially the "Manga" Arabs, had become stereotyped as sharp dealers and receivers of stolen goods; Wamakonde and other mainlanders had become stereotyped as inveterate thieves. Central to both stereotypes were motifs of violence, best encapsulated in the emblematic weapons supposedly favored by Wamakonde (spears, bows and arrows) and Wamanga (swords and daggers).[3]

One of this chapter's three tasks will be to reconstruct the double process by which particular communities at the margins of Zanzibar society first became stigmatized in the popular imagination as inherently criminal and then were made representative of broader racial categories: Wamakonde as the epitome of all mainlanders; Wamanga and Washihiri as the epitome of all Arabs, including those born locally. Like the intellectuals' discourse of race and nation, popular discourse about crime raised ideas of exclusion and dehumanization, focusing on who should and should not be granted the protection of the moral community. Tracing the convergence of how people talked about race and crime thus helps us understand the thinking that made possible the violence of a pogrom. It also accounts for officials' preoccupation with crime rumors in the wake of the June riots: they had learned from experience that rumor could construe any criminal act, no matter how apolitical, as an act of racial politics and that such rumors, thus invested with mythic power, could in turn prompt actual racial terror. Wamanga were imagined not simply as inherently criminal but also as inherently violent, with little regard for human life, especially that of Africans. They were also imagined as blindly loyal to the ZNP. So if a person heard of an incident that suggested Wamanga were sharpening their swords to attack Africans, he might feel justified in taking preemptive action against the entire category.

But the spectacle of crowds engaged in looting and assault prompts a second set of questions. How had ordinarily law-abiding people come to perceive a moral dimension to behavior that, in other times, they would have regarded as criminal? To understand such phenomena it is useful to distinguish between two types of crime and two types of criminal. One type of crime consists of acts that are generally agreed to be violations of moral codes. Acts of violence, such as robbery and murder, are the most obvious examples, and they figured prominently in the images that were invoked to demonstrate racial "otherness." The other consists of acts that the poor do not necessarily see as crimes, although the powerful (and the law) define them as such. Typical of such acts are appropriations of property that the poor may deem their customary right but that landlords or employers and their allies within the state deem theft.[4] The two types of criminal correspond roughly to the same distinction. The individual who habitually transgresses local mores is usually regarded as an outcast. But the individual who defies his landlord by engaging in customary appropriation—or even the daring individual who, for exceptional personal reasons, commits occasional acts of violence—might not be regarded by his neighbors as a habitual criminal. Despite his crimes in the eyes of the law and the landlord, he will be accepted as more or less a full member of the local community, if perhaps an extraordinary one.

This distinction is valuable insofar as it subverts the assumption that all members of a given society subscribe to a homogeneous view of matters of legitimacy and transgression, particularly in regard to property. Some of the literature based on this distinction, however, has been criticized for implying the existence of a coherent counterhegemonic ideology of property—and a constant state of conflict between it and the hegemonic ideology—that is just as idealized as the notion of a single overarching set of norms. The most persuasive interpretations recognize that the "social criminal" is as much an ideal type as is the antisocial criminal outcast whose behavior is motivated by an utter contempt for all social mores.[5] Although the hegemony of the law is often embattled and incomplete (perhaps nowhere more so than in colonial settings), it is nevertheless real; even the most purely "social" criminals, including peasants who poached their landlords' game or stole their coconuts, would have internalized, if only partially and inconsistently, the notion that such behavior was in some aspects immoral.

The distinction between "social crime" and "criminal crime" is most useful, in fact, for what it suggests about the conflicted or contradictory consciousness that lies behind most criminal acts. At times of rapid social transformation or political crisis, people who are engaged in "social crime" may be less prone to emphasize the distinctions that mark off their behavior from that of habitual or professional criminals and might even take the latter as models. And the professional criminals, sensing a collapse of the moral codes that had defined them as outcasts, may imagine an opportunity to reduce the chasm separating them from their more respectable neighbors.[6]

[Attention to the rough interface between crime and politics makes it possible to consider the impact that racial discourse had on the criminals themselves, our third theme.]Simple economic explanations of crime, in contrast, can take us only so far. Clayton, for example, argues that the rising crime rate of the late 1950s reflected deteriorating economic conditions among the poor.[7] Yet contemporary observers noted that there was more to it than that. Rising crime rates were to some extent a reflection of plantation owners' increased aggressiveness in the prosecution of crop theft. As we shall see, this implied the criminalization of behavior that tenants and employees had deemed customary. Officials also observed that the "criminal element" had become emboldened in the later years of the Time of Politics.[8] Such comments cannot be taken uncritically; many of those officials harbored ZNP sympathies and believed criminal gangs to be mere agents of the ASP. Yet evidence suggests that many criminal acts from these years can be interpreted as challenges to dominant understandings of property relations, challenges in which the thieves were encouraged by political rhetoric that depicted planters as alien expropriators. Other crimes appeared more wanton, particularly robberies accompanied by brutal violence. Yet, as we shall see, even those criminals heard political rhetoric in ways that sometimes induced them to imagine their crimes as acts of racial justice.

Images of Race and Crime between the Wars

The Mainlander as Criminal and Police

As in other instances, perceived outsiders—people living at the margins of established community structures—were frequently imagined to have an innate propensity for crime and other antisocial behavior. There was often a kernel of truth to such stereotypes, insofar as marginal individuals tend to be more vulnerable to the pressures of economic and social insecurity that drive some to crime and tend to share the fewest bonds of mutual obligation with their neighbors.

Prior to abolition in 1897, slaves were the most prominent category of marginal outsiders. As we have seen in chapter 2, islanders disdained slaves for their origins in the African interior, beyond the civilizing influences of Islam and coastal culture. Institutions of slavery served to incorporate slaves economically while keeping them at the margins of community institutions. With abolition, planters lost those instruments of control. They were replaced by ad hoc "squatting" relationships or labor tenancy, in which a work force consisting of slave descendants and newer, voluntary immigrants from the mainland performed tasks that had once been done by slaves. Although these were not the relations of agrarian capitalism that British policy makers and the better-capitalized entrepreneurs who led the Arab Association had hoped for, they nevertheless served to maintain the racial order valued by both.

Still, the planters never felt that their control of squatters was secure. British administrators shared those worries and worked to stabilize the new arrangements, especially during the first few decades after abolition. A fundamental problem, as they saw it, was the disorder posed by persons with "no regular employment" or other formal enforceable tie to an elite patron. This "floating population," they felt, displayed less respect for property and propriety than did their neighbors.[9] Frederick Cooper has described how the British concern with rural crime during these years was part of a broader "assault on the social complex of idleness." The initial targets of this assault were the former slaves whom abolition had rendered masterless—ironically, a condition that the British criminalized, through the imposition of vagrancy laws.[10] Over time, however, they were joined by the mainland immigrants who were to form the bulk of the squatter population and whose ties to established island communities were more tenuous than those of the slave descendants.

But members of this "floating population" were not arrested solely for vagrancy: officials in the rural areas frequently noted that they were responsible for most crimes of property. Their explanations often resembled the colonial cliché of the "detribalized native" who, cut adrift from the moorings of tradition and no longer sharing the values of those around him, becomes dangerously asocial or antisocial. (By contrast, they wrote, crime was negligible in the culturally "homogeneous" Hadimu fringe outside of Unguja's plantation zone, because villagers there were restrained by the authority of custom.)[11] Such perceptions cannot be accepted at face value. Persons accused of leading vagabond lives did not consist solely of mainlanders. Seasonal harvest laborers from Hadimu villages, for example, were often blamed for theft and other forms of disorder as they roamed the countryside searching for work. Nor were "squatters" necessarily as transient as that term implies; many stayed for decades, building substantial homes and making other investments in property to which, however, they had only the most tenuous legal claims.[12]

Still, there were precise historical reasons why mainlanders came to be regarded as marginal by Zanzibaris and Britons alike. Despite the lengthy stays of many, they often thought of themselves as temporary sojourners, hoping eventually to rejoin their families on the mainland or return there to marry.

While in Zanzibar, they reproduced upcountry cultural practices, including pagan or Christian rites that drew a particularly sharp line between them and locally born Muslims.[13] Perceptions of common place of origin played a role in the networks through which immigrants sought work in the islands: a newcomer from Tabora, for example, asking at the wharf where he could find others from his part of the world, might be directed to one of the visible Nyamwezi communities in the west-central parts of Unguja. This process helped foster local concentrations of squatters from particular parts of the mainland, which in turn intensified their consciousness of belonging to communities of immigrants.[14]

Hence, the conditions of immigration and settlement encouraged squatters to think of themselves as living apart from other islanders, despite their reliance on ties of patronage to a local landlord. These conditions differed markedly from those of the slavery era. Yet Zanzibaris' perceptions of the mainlanders continued to be colored by the legacy of slavery. The tasks performed by squatters had been associated with slave labor; indeed, islanders' reluctance to perform them was prompted in part by a desire to avoid the imputation of slave ancestry. (Actual slave descendants had particularly pointed anxieties in that regard.)[15] From the islanders' perspective, and particularly from the perspective of elite Arabs, the immigrants possessed the same quality of *ushenzi* as had slaves. As we have seen, even if the immigrants were believers, their Islam was regarded as less pure and less historically rooted than that of the islands.

By the 1930s, simply being from the mainland was sufficient to draw suspicion of criminal behavior, as when the *sheha* of Muyuni, in southern Unguja, searched the baskets of two men at a coffee shop on apparently no more pretext than that they were "strange mainlanders." (He found cannabis, which explains why this particular incident found its way into the archive.)[16] The image of the mainlander as a habitual lawbreaker had been in the making for years, both in the official mind and in the minds of many islanders. In the 1920s, as much as 40 percent of those convicted of serious property crimes were of mainland origin.[17] In the first decade of the century the most commonly prosecuted crime was public drunkenness, an offense already associated with mainlanders and one that underscored the stereotypical gulf separating them from good Muslims.[18]

The image of the disorderly savage was epitomized in stereotypes of Makonde immigrants from the coastal hinterland of southern Tanganyika and northern Mozambique. Even African Association poets acknowledged that Wamakonde had become an emblem of mainlander barbarism and as such a foil for the image of the urbane *mstaarabu*.[19] Although many were Muslims, they were nevertheless stereotyped as quintessential pagans. Their paganism was said to be marked by the distinctive facial scarifications some wore; thus, "the mere physiognomy of a Mmakonde makes a local person afraid." That quote comes from a remarkable analysis of anti-Makonde prejudices written in 1962 by Khamis Hassan Ameir, a district officer born in southern Unguja. Ameir was an unusually reliable observer, in part because of his ambiguous position in the Zanzibar administration; unlike all but a tiny handful of civil servants he identified himself as an African rather than an Arab and for that reason was suspected of ASP sympathies.[20] Yet even he confessed that

> local people, including myself, are afraid of Wamakonde, just because they are Wamakonde. . . . Many people believe that the Wamakonde are cannibals. . . . It is also known that the Wamakonde are as a tribe generally violent people and are not afraid to kill as evidenced by the various murder cases we have had.

They "hastily resort to violence," especially when drunk, and "stealing, especially foodstuffs, is their hobby."[21]

Although these sentiments were recorded at the height of the Time of Politics, there is ample evidence that they had been widespread for decades. In fact, apart from the motif of crop theft—which, as we will see, arose largely from tensions associated with changes in plantation production—many elements of this reputation can be traced to the nineteenth century. The people who came to call themselves Wamakonde originated as refugees of diverse backgrounds who, fleeing Ngoni and Yao slave raiders, sought protection in inaccessible highlands on either side of the Rovuma River. Like others who succeeded in keeping the slave trade at bay, Wamakonde cultivated a reputation for reclusiveness and ferocity (an alternate ethnonym, Mavia, meant "fierce"). Adapting to the climatic peculiarities of their highland refuge, they developed a system of shifting cultivation that resulted in a notoriously impenetrable overgrowth of dense thicket. Protected by this thicket, they also became known for their expertise in forest hunting and trapping, practices which for them became central markers of masculine identity.[22]

Thus, when they later came to the islands to take up positions previously occupied by slaves, Wamakonde brought with them an established reputation for behavior that marked them as emblematic barbarians. And once in the islands, some of their cultural preferences cemented the reputation. Between stints of employment on the estates, many squatted in forest reserves, where they thrived because of their skills in hunting and clearing heavy undergrowth. (This gave rise to complaints that they felled valuable timber without securing villagers' permission.) Their fondness for bushmeat ("they eat any animal they can get hold of," wrote Ameir, "snakes, pigs, monkeys, animals of cat family, etc.") constituted a colorful violation of Islamic dietary restrictions and accentuated their reputation for ritual impurity. They were commonly seen repairing and sharpening the tools needed for clearing and hunting, and fearful islanders often found them well armed with machetes, spears, or bows and arrows.

As early as the 1920s, Wamakonde's reputation for hardiness in the bush and expertise in the violent arts made them favored as night watchmen on remote estates.[23] Those qualities, like the others, were regarded as typical of mainlanders in general and contributed to the official assumption that mainlanders were as naturally suited for law enforcement as for crime. The police department explained its preference for recruiting mainlanders (both immigrants and those already resident in the islands) on the grounds of their supposedly superior physical stamina.[24] Such reasoning was part of a "martial races imperative," found throughout the British empire, by which racial categorization shaped calculations of who made the best soldiers or police. Colonial officers preferred to recruit among minorities or outsiders, particularly people who were different from those who dominated commerce and education in a given colony and who therefore would not have complicated loyalties. There was also a preference for people who were regarded as having been less "corrupted" by coastal town life.[25] In Zanzibar all these factors no doubt contributed to British calculations of why mainlanders made more attractive police recruits.

But although British officers may have arrived in East Africa predisposed to think in racial terms, their specific preferences were shaped by the realities they encountered on the ground. Police commanders in Zanzibar often lamented their inability to find suitable local recruits. Islanders seemed to disdain police work as much as they disdained the weeding and clearing that had been dominated by slaves in earlier times, and they left both to mainlanders. Hence the policeman's lot became a form of migrant labor. Pay and work conditions did nothing to attract anyone who had other options. Indeed, the police became figures of ridicule. They were poorly equipped, and when they were deployed to suppress public disorder their batons often proved no match for rioters' machetes or swords. In a culture where shoelessness had been associated with slave status, islanders scorned them as the "barefoot police." Their garb included a crudely sewn sack with holes cut for head and arms, which was also worn by the prisoners who could be seen doing forced labor such as road cleaning.[26]

In short, mainlanders' prevalence in the ranks of the police played as much of a role in fostering their unsavory image as did their reputation as criminals. Over time, British beliefs that mainlanders made better police proved self-fulfilling and contributed to islanders' perceptions that mainlanders were natural adepts in the use of violence, be it state sponsored or criminal. In a colonial setting, where the police enjoyed little more popular legitimacy than did criminal gangs, both forms of expertise seemed to confirm islanders' prejudices.

Customary Appropriation and Professional Crime

As we have seen, crop theft was considered a Makonde "hobby"; Ameir wrote that Makonde squatters harvested whatever they wanted from the landlord's plantation any time he was absent. In this, too, Wamakonde were believed to epitomize all mainlanders. By the 1930s, crop theft was the most common form of property crime.[27] It was usually attributed to squatters and it had become a major concern of officials and the larger planters who hoped to rationalize agricultural production along capitalist lines. British officials called it "praedial larceny," a term that specifies the theft of crops standing in the field. The obscurity of the term is useful insofar as it suggests that the act sometimes reflected disagreements over the proper ownership of the goods in question— that is, whether the act constituted "theft" at all. The more straightforward word "theft," on the other hand, reflects primarily the landlords' point of view. Squatters were at the forefront of conflicts engendered by the haphazard processes that were changing relations of property and labor in the countryside. Those processes often entailed the criminalization of behavior that once had been deemed customary.

In the opening decades of the century the planters' rights of freehold tenure were not universally accepted; indeed, tenants would still be challenging those rights on the eve of independence. Few, however, questioned the planter's ownership of trees and other permanent crops growing on his land.[28] Tensions stemmed rather from ambiguities over use rights in those trees. Squatters regarded it as legitimate to take whatever tree crops they wanted for their personal use. In addition, many planters, especially the smaller ones, paid their employees in produce. As a result squatters were often in possession, with the landlord's consent, of substantial surpluses of coconut or cloves that were theirs to market as they wished. Moreover, many planters turned a blind eye to their tenants' appropriation of still more crops, believing that indulgence in such matters made them more attractive as patrons and thus better provided with labor.[29] It is likely that by countenancing what they may have privately considered theft, landlords contributed over time to a situation in which their tenants came to regard such appropriations as accepted custom.

Officials sought to deal with the problem by restricting agricultural laborers' ability to trade in the major cash crops. The earliest measures in this regard, issued within the first decade after abolition, foundered over opposition from Indian merchants, who were suspected of dealing in stolen produce, and from the smaller landlords, who wanted to preserve their ability to pay workers in kind. But an Agricultural Produce Decree passed in 1915 and amended several times over the following decades imposed both a system of trading licenses as well as permits for transporting cloves or coconuts.[30]

As cash-crop production expanded between the wars, these measures became subjects of some debate. Theft of coconuts was particularly difficult to control because, unlike cloves, they had a wide range of everyday household uses; therefore someone seen hauling a gunnysack of coconuts could not reasonably be assumed to be engaged in a commercial or larcenous transaction. Yet as rising copra prices prompted increased theft in the mid-1930s, growers and copra curers demanded that measures be tightened. Thus, in 1937, the limit on the number of coconuts that could be carried without a permit was lowered from ten to four.[31] This effectively criminalized behavior as common as carrying a few coconuts home from market. The new regulations could not possibly have been enforced with any consistency. But they could be used to target individuals suspected of criminal behavior, like the "strange mainlanders" detained by the *sheha* of Muyuni. Such racial profiling mounted during the war years, and, as we shall see, during the Time of Politics mainlanders were routinely harassed with accusations of coconut theft.

Most who indulged in praedial larceny probably did so only occasionally, regarding it as a customary appropriation. But the practice depended on networks of well-organized professionals who specialized in processing and marketing stolen produce. Rural shopkeepers were best placed for such activities, particularly the Manga Arabs who, in addition to keeping *maduka* (small general shops; sing., *duka*), often leased small plantations in order to set up in the parallel business of harvesting and drying cloves or coconut. In the 1930s and 1940s officials described Manga shopkeepers as dominating the business of receiving stolen goods, using the lease of a handful of trees as a cover with which to disguise their source of contraband.[32]

Receipt of stolen goods was but one of several well-established criminal professions between the wars. In the early 1920s officials in the rural districts noted a marked increase in the activities of what they described as well-organized "dacoit" gangs that specialized in armed burglary and the ready use of violence. The police reported that these gangs preyed especially on Indian shopkeepers and Arab planters and that ordinary countrypeople were reluctant to cooperate in apprehending them. Nevertheless, from 1925 through 1927 the worst of them were arrested in successive sweeps and sentenced to uncommonly long prison terms. Most, the police observed, were mainlanders.[33]

The incarceration of these gangs at the Kilimani prison, located about two kilometers south of Zanzibar Town, gave rise to tensions that bring them into closer view in the historical record, revealing the porousness of the boundary between even these career criminals and the "straight" community of the town poor. Previously, most inmates had been only occasional lawbreakers, jailed for petty offenses such as crop theft. Officials considered them "hardly more dangerous" than "degenerate children." Prison conditions were accordingly lax, said these officials; criminals even dubbed it "Club Kilimani."[34] This is perhaps an exaggeration, as perhaps are officials' statements that the "hardening" of the inmate population in the second half of the 1920s was entirely due to the influence of the burglary gangs. In fact, penal practices themselves were harsh enough to help create a criminal subclass. Children as young as nine were flogged for a variety of offenses, including victimless crimes such as gambling, and they were also vulnerable to substantial sentences of "rigorous confinement." (One child had spent an aggregate of four years in prison by the time he was fifteen.) Lashings or imprisonment were meted out disproportionately to the poor; those with means often had the option of paying a fine instead. Not surprisingly, homeless children figured prominently in the ranks of offenders. Would-be reformers noted a pattern by which recurrent spells of imprisonment interspersed with life on the streets pushed many such children toward adult criminal careers.[35]

Nevertheless, officials noted a change in the "tone" of the prison after the arrest of the burglary rings, whose members eventually constituted about 20 percent of all inmates. The chief of police observed that the "prisoners coming in for long sentences for dacoity were treated as heroes"; some came to be regarded as "persons to be reckoned with," demanding respect even from the guards. Officials blamed them for stirring up a tide of discontent. The more proximate cause of unrest was a tightening of discipline introduced after 1926 by a new set of administrators who arrived at roughly the same time as the burglary gangs. These administrators disapproved of the prison's lax atmosphere, which they believed inappropriate for the hardened criminals who now dominated prison life. They were particularly bothered by the open flouting of rules against possession of "prohibited articles" such as cigarettes and outside food items. Inmates obtained such goods with the connivance of the guards while performing forced labor outside the prison. These loosely supervised work details—clearing fields, repairing roads—allowed inmates to interact more or less freely with the general populace. Such interaction, which the authorities found unwholesome, sheds valuable light on the inmates' relationship with the noncriminal population.[36]

The campaign against contraband aroused widespread resentment. Its main tools included canings and intensified personal searches. These methods appeared to produce immediate results: a year after their introduction in 1926, the possession of prohibited articles plummeted. But subsequent events suggest they had merely induced inmates to find ingenious ways to defy the regulations, such as devising well-hidden stashing places. It is also probable that the new regime prompted the creation of more elaborate and tightly protected networks for the transfer and hiding of contraband, which no doubt gave the experienced burglars an added lever for building up their patronage and power.

On 29 October 1928 these resentments culminated in a carefully organized riot and prison break. The riot broke out in the Old Offenders' Ward, where the burglar gangs dominated and the hardest cases were confined. Inmates there had stashed clubs in water barrels that had earlier been used as caches for contraband. After easily overcoming the warders, they released all of the sixty or seventy prisoners in the ward and kept the prison guards and police reinforcements at bay throughout the night. The next morning, the prisoners declared that if the senior commissioner or chief secretary refused to speak with them, they would break out of the prison altogether and take their grievances to the sultan. That afternoon they made good their threat. After breaking out with a tactical finesse that left their warders scrambling, they headed to the palace, passing through some of the most densely populated town neighborhoods, pursued by police who were barely better armed than they and just as ragtag.[37] The sultan agreed to interview two of their spokesmen. We do not know what was said, but afterward he instructed the prisoners to return to prison, upon which they meekly gave up their arms and marched quietly back to Kilimani.

This event no doubt contributed to the public impression, especially in town, of the existence of a class of inveterate criminals, a disproportionate number of them mainlanders,[38] who were adept in the use of violence and prepared to use it to defy the law. But there were signs, too, that these supposedly hardened outlaws did not exist wholly separate from the "respectable" community and that they did not reject all hegemonic forms of authority. That is certainly not the image the prisoners had of themselves, as can be seen in their insistence on taking their grievances to the sultan and in their subsequent submission to him. Indeed, at the heart of those grievances was their ability to secure "prohibited articles" through what authorities disapproved of as "easy intercourse with the public."[39]

Criminality and Popular Leadership among the Town Poor

None of this negates the likelihood that the poor regarded career criminals as marginal figures. On the contrary, as we will see, many islanders had come to imagine certain kinds of criminal behavior as the specialty of particular marginal groups. But it is evident that the line dividing criminal from noncriminal behavior was far more ambiguous in the popular imagination than it was in legal codes. The poor regarded certain property crimes, such as smuggling and some forms of praedial larceny, as within the bounds of propriety, and "thieves' slang" was in wide use in Ng'ambo neighborhoods in the 1920s.[40] The poor, then, were well acquainted with career criminals and had significant interaction with them. And as particular outcast groups became associated with particular illegal activities, islanders came to value them precisely for those skills—turning to a Manga shopkeeper, for example, when they wished to dispose of an odd lot of coconuts without having to face any uncomfortable questions.

Moreover, in unusually turbulent times, career criminals' expertise in the violent transgression of the law even made them seem especially well suited as community leaders.[41] The 1928 prison break occurred during just such a moment, when Zanzibar Town was gripped by popular protests led by figures who straddled the categories of criminal and community leader and who encouraged their followers to behave in ways virtually identical to those of the "old offenders" who breached the walls of Kilimani prison.

The protests were directed against the collection of ground rents in Ng'ambo. Before the colonial period, most land in Ng'ambo had belonged to the sultan and a handful of his closest courtiers, much of it held in waqf trusts for the benefit of former slaves and other clients who built houses there and lived rent free. (Waqf refers to property set aside in religiously sanctioned trusts.) But beginning in the 1890s, as part of its islands-wide effort to transform property relations, the British government sought to persuade landholders to charge ground rent, even when doing so would violate the terms of the waqf trusts. The first sultan to attempt this was condemned by religious leaders, and his sudden death in the midst of the ensuing uproar was widely interpreted as divine retribution; his immediate heir did not dare continue the policy. Protests against ground rents on rural Crown lands met with similar success in 1911, soon after the accession of Khalifa bin Haroub, and in the following year popular resistance persuaded the government to also stop its attempts to impose hut taxes. This succession of events encouraged the view that appeals to the sultan over issues related to land and taxation could yield results and gave an early boost to Khalifa's reputation as a just monarch.[42]

Yet despite these early successes, ground rents soon became firmly established in Ng'ambo. By the 1920s much of the land there had passed into the hands of a new class of commercial landlords, many of them Indian, or into the care of the Wakf Commission, a government entity that had been established as part of the British effort to commercialize waqf holdings. But, as Laura Fair has shown, Ng'ambo's residents continued to remember the older ties of patronage that had once governed interactions with their landlords, and they resented the transformations that had ended them. A spiral of rent increases beginning at the end of World War I exacerbated these resentments, which culminated in a series of rent strikes in the later 1920s.[43] The strikers often expressed their grievances as an anti-Indian movement. Such communal thinking was not simply a reflection of socioeconomic realities; as we saw in chapter 2, ethnicity and class did not coincide as neatly as racial rhetoric made them seem, and in fact the tenants who launched the first of the rent strikes were themselves Indians.[44] But it was encouraged by the strikes' leaders, who exhorted tenants "not to pay rent to the Indians." They also reviled British officials as "brothers of the Indians" who had bullied the sultan to cooperate.[45]

One of the rent strikes' two leading figures, Shaykh Zahor bin Muhammad al-Barawa, was an elderly cleric who had been deported from German East Africa in 1908. His authority was based in the Sufi orders that for decades had provided urban newcomers a platform from which to challenge the elitist focus of coastal Islam.[46] Manyema immigrants were among his core supporters. The other was Feraji Mpira, who lived in the Ng'ambo neighborhood of Raha Leo. Fair's elderly informants remembered Feraji as a "slave of the Arabs" (that is, a former slave or slave descendant) with a reputation "as a rapist and a thief." He was particularly renowned for his strength and his skills in the use of violence. Yet despite their very different sources of authority, Feraji and Shaykh Zahor worked in tandem. Feraji made speeches threatening that the Ahl Badr would be read against anyone who broke the strike. Ahl Badr was a religious rite, commonly used to enforce communal solidarity, that invoked divine sanctions against wrongdoers—although coming from a man of Feraji's reputation, the threat was probably understood as more than supernatural. The performance of the ritual was entrusted to Shaykh Zahor.[47]

Feraji Mpira was the most visible of these two figures; Shaykh Zahor preferred to stay in the background. But what makes Feraji particularly significant for our purposes was his reputation for criminal violence and how he used it to bolster his authority. In the circumstances, those qualities appeared especially valuable. In July 1928 the government affirmed the right of landlords to seize the houses of tenants who were in arrears. As most of those houses were of little commercial value, landlords usually demolished them and sold off the building materials, as a brutally efficient method of eviction. By August, Feraji was urging crowds to use force to resist these tactics, offering his own services for the toughest cases. "If any landlord comes to Ng'ambo to collect rent he must be assaulted," he told a crowd of several hundred, adding that if the government sends a soldier or policeman, "send word to me and I will . . . deal with him." He hinted that if the crowd returned with sticks and clubs, he would lead them on an armed mission.[48]

By September, the unrest had forced officials to begin discussing how to ease pressures on the poorest tenants. But their very talk made matters worse. Feraji soon was telling audiences that the pending reforms would abolish private land ownership altogether and that the sultan himself, having heard his subjects' protests, had endorsed the rent strike. In late September, a crowd forcibly spirited a rent striker out of court before he could begin serving a sentence for refusing to vacate. Two days later he turned himself in, but the Kilimani prison was immediately besieged by 400 protesters, led by Feraji. Although the police managed to hold them at bay, the authorities nevertheless were persuaded to remit the prisoner's sentence.[49]

The rent strikers' attempted breach of the prison walls anticipated the inmates who broke out exactly one month later. And in January 1929 the strikers seemed to follow the prisoners' example, when Feraji led several hundred to the sultan's palace.[50] They were met by two senior British officials, whom Feraji angrily defied as the crowd looked on. The officials tried to arrest him; he escaped in the ensuing melee but was soon recaptured. Later that day Feraji's supporters, learning that the sultan was at his seaside villa at Kibweni, several miles north of town, decided to march there to appeal for his release. Approximately 200 marchers armed with clubs and machetes, three-quarters of whom were women, were turned back by the police. Meanwhile, it was reported that armed gangs were forming to liberate Feraji and the other arrested "ringleaders" from the central police station.[51]

That a figure such as Feraji could reach such a leadership position suggests that for many among the town poor, the line between criminality and respectability was not defined with the concreteness of prison walls. Feraji's reputation for violent criminality may have placed him on the margins of the community of the poor, but it did not necessarily place him outside that community or at odds with it. On the contrary, in this instance he was able to turn his well-known antipathy toward the rule of private property into a quality that seemed useful to many. But this was possible only because certain property relations had become understood in communal terms. Once that had happened, theft might be imagined as an act of popular politics, as when armed gangs threatened to loot Indian shops in retaliation for the arrest of the leaders of the Kibweni Palace marchers.[52] It could even lead protesters to imagine that the sovereign would support them, even though he was the islands' largest land owner and the very emblem of the Arab establishment.

Wamanga and Washihiri as Violent Criminals

The most visible brokers between the criminal and respectable worlds were the low-status Arab immigrants who, as we have seen, were widely believed to dominate the profession of receivers of stolen goods. The so-called Wamanga and Washihiri were also stereotyped as skilled purveyors of the violent arts, entrepreneurs of violence who sold their services as hired thugs.

Their unsavory reputation stemmed in part from their peculiar cultural liminality: although linguistically and phenotypically they exemplified the Arab identity that was a mark of high social status, they had arrived in the islands as hewers of wood and haulers of water, often quite literally. Yet the pejorative images were shaped and reproduced by a series of precise historical experiences, some dramatic enough to figure prominently in both the archival record and in popular memory. One such event occurred in 1928, the same turbulent year when mainlander criminals had assumed prominence in the rent strikes and prison break. The so-called Manga-Shihiri riot in March of that year and a similar event in 1936 were remembered a generation later as illustrations of the supposedly violent nature of both groups. Both incidents helped crystallize the image of Wamanga and Washihiri as interstitial and dangerous figures who occupied positions between the criminal underworld, mainstream civil society, and the state. They also contributed to the process by which these criminalized outgroups came to represent, for many Zanzibaris, the entire racial category of "Arabs."

The development of these images can be traced to well before the British period. Throughout the nineteenth century, Zanzibar was troubled by unruly crews of vessels from the Persian Gulf, the Red Sea, and Yemen, who descended on Zanzibar with the northern monsoon at the end of each year and stayed until the winds shifted to the southwest in March. These "Northern Arabs"— so called to distinguish them from the elite of the coast itself—specialized in transporting high-bulk, low-cost items such as grain, dried shark, and mangrove poles. They also developed a reputation as slave traders who were not above kidnapping local children. Townspeople dreaded their annual sojourns, and the wealthier ones sent their children and young slaves to estates in the interior of the island for security. Sultans from Seyyid Said onward took futile measures to control the disorder they created.[53]

Such fears were vibrant well into the twentieth century, encouraged by parents who frightened disobedient children with the bogeyman of Manga kidnappers. During the dhow season of early 1939, an eleven-year-old Indian boy, evidently trying to create an alibi for his absence from school, caused a general scare when he told the police that Omani sailors had tried to drag him off in a sack. Coming in the aftermath of the 1938 clove-buying crisis, these allegations fed into the lingering tensions between Arabs and Indians.[54] Yet it was not only non-Arabs who promoted the stereotype. An essay in *Mazungumzo ya Walimu* in 1931 described the myths of Manga kidnapping associated with the famous "slave caves" of Mangapwani (that is, Manga Beach), located about twelve miles north of Zanzibar Town. The author was precise in his language: by attributing the terrors of the slave trade specifically to the "Wamanga," he was able to exonerate the "Waarabu," the local Arab elite, whom he described as the peaceful victims of Manga depredations.[55]

Thus most Zanzibaris regarded Wamanga as distinct from the islands' Waarabu elite. Although the term "Manga" generally referred only to immigrants from Oman, it was sometimes used to describe all low-status Arab immigrants, especially dhow crews.[56] The word is derived from the Arabic *munqaʿa* (the sea). The Arabic root, *naqaʿa*, also yields a verb meaning "to soak." Thus it is easy to imagine how the term came to be applied to Arab sailors or to any Arab who came from overseas. (That the same Arabic root can be used as a verb, "to shout, to raise the voice," perhaps further contributed to its use in describing rowdy sailors.)[57] Omanis were the most prominent of these sea-soaked Arabs in the nineteenth century, but by the century's end those Omani families who had become creolized were described simply as Waarabu, leaving the term Wamanga for the more humble newcomers. As we saw in chapter 4, racial nationalists tried to force a further shift in the 1950s and '60s, when they used the epithet "Manga" to depict all Arabs as violent, criminal slave raiders.

The other main category of low-status "Northern Arabs" were the Washihiri. Strictly speaking the term refers to immigrants from the coastal plains around the ports of Shihr and Mukalla, but in common usage it also designated immigrants from the Hadhramaut, Yemen's mountainous interior. Like Wamanga, Washihiri came to East Africa in a variety of humble occupations, but their social trajectory after arrival was somewhat different. Many Wamanga were able to claim kinship with local elite families, who took them on as guests or retainers; such immigrants took an interest in local affairs and considered Zanzibar a second home. The Shihiri immigrants, lacking such connections, almost always maintained an identity as strangers. Whereas Wamanga were often able to move comfortably into the countryside, where they set up as small-scale shopkeepers and copra producers, Washihiri tended to be more concentrated in town; they formed a disproportionate share of Ng'ambo's small shopkeepers, for example, and were the town's preeminent coffee sellers. Yet despite their sense of aloofness, or more likely as part of it, Washihiri often considered themselves defenders of Sunni orthodoxy in a land ruled by Ibadi heretics.[58] (Yemenis were among Zanzibar's most respected Shafi'i scholars.) For many this sense of religious and indeed racial exclusiveness was bolstered by a vigorously defended claim of direct descent from the Prophet.[59]

Both Washihiri and Wamanga, then, regarded themselves as members of diasporic communities, living more or less apart from their neighbors. Although they competed with some of the humblest members of Zanzibari society for economic opportunities, as Arabs they could claim superiority according to locally hegemonic registers of status. All these factors, plus their domination at the lower ends of the retail trade, help explain why they drew suspicions of sharp dealing and of legally marginal activities such as smuggling and reception of stolen goods. Their reputation for violence seemed confirmed by the pride they took in martial skills, which they displayed in public dances that often turned disruptive. Wamanga were especially renowned for the *raz'ha*, a dance marked by mock combats with swords and daggers. (The *jambia*, a curved dagger worn in an inlaid sheath, was an emblematic component of Omani male attire.) Washihiri had similar dances, which in the previous century had contributed to their reputation as mercenaries in the service of the sultans.[60]

The Washihiri's notoriety was bolstered by the activities of their communal association, the Shihiri Council, which combined religious politics with extortion. In 1926 control of the council was seized by a faction of Hadramis whom the police had charged with running an extortion racket throughout the decade.[61] Their central figure, Nasir bin Abdulla al-Kathiri, was a middle-aged man who had spent his entire adult life traveling between Zanzibar and the Hadhramaut; he maintained homes in both places and ran a business provisioning meat. Although illiterate, he spoke Swahili as well as Arabic and, "as he said, bad language . . . in every tongue." His cronies, however, included some educated men, including a religious scholar who claimed descent from the Prophet.[62] The targets of this circle's threats suggest that they were motivated at least in part by Sunni chauvinism. As early as 1923 they were accused of demanding protection money from the town's Shia and Hindu communities; in 1924 the Ismaili community paid 800 rupees after a Shihiri crowd ransacked their mosque. Subsequent events also point to anti-Ibadi sentiments.[63] Much of the rhetoric surrounding the 1928 riot, in fact, suggests that some Washihiri found their social and political marginalization particularly galling because they considered themselves better exemplars of Islamic civilization than Zanzibar's leading Omani and Indian citizens.

The events of March 1928 seemed to confirm stereotypes of the violent nature of both Wamanga and Washihiri. According to the police, the riots were the culmination of a "feud" that had begun in April 1927, when a Mshihiri was accused of picking a Mmanga's pocket at a public auction. The ensuing confrontation brought Wamanga in from the countryside to defend their compatriots. Resentments were still simmering in March of the following year, when, one night during Ramadhan, "a Manga retainer whilst lying on the verandah of a house was insulted by a Shihiri child." The offended Mmanga struck the child; in retaliation, one of Nasir bin Abdulla's closest confederates had his grown sons beat the Mmanga. This was all doubtlessly witnessed and talked about by the clusters of people who sat up late into the night during the Holy Month on the stone benches that line the narrow town streets. Anger spread rapidly throughout the Manga community, to the point that the Shihiri Council, meeting two days later, thought it prudent to issue a formal apology. But that same night Manga toughs began attacking Washihiri indiscriminately and looting their shops in Ng'ambo, setting off five days of running battles between Manga and Shihiri gangs that left six dead and scores wounded.[64]

High-ranking officials blamed the riots exclusively on the Washihiri, particularly Nasir bin Abdulla and his confederates, whom they deported; the Wamanga, they insisted, were passive victims. But this assessment was based less on the facts than on the anti-Shihiri biases of the Britons' Omani subordinates and colleagues, including the sultan and his courtiers. In fact the contrast between the Shihiri Council's rapid apology and the Wamanga's continued aggressiveness suggest that the latter felt they might with impunity exploit the Washihiri's relatively greater marginality. Officials at the highest level even reversed the standard stereotype about the Wamanga, describing them as congenitally "peaceful and law abiding" and hence easy prey for the violent Washihiri.[65]

This disproportionate response could only have confirmed popular impressions that the Wamanga were linked as kin and servants to the elite Waarabu who dominated the state. That image certainly informed the actions of the Shihiri gangs, who targeted not only Wamanga but also senior members of prominent ruling families; Nasir bin Abdulla even made open statements against the sultanate. Yet it would be a distortion to characterize Nasir as a principled political actor.[66] Rather, as is so often the case with "social" criminals, he found satisfaction, and perhaps a measure of self-respect, in invoking an oppositional rhetoric in order to make his extortion racket seem more than simply self-serving. The Shihiri Council extortionists imagined themselves as defenders of orthodox Islam against Shia and Ibadi heresy and Hindu paganism; they saw low-status Wamanga, their immediate rivals, as but surrogates for the Omani elite.

The Wamanga and Washihiri who battled over their wounded honor no doubt agreed that Africans were irrelevant to all these issues. Many details point to their disdain, and a decade later, Nasir bin Abdulla's central regret about the whole affair was the shame of having been beaten by Zanzibar's disreputable mainlander police.[67] Yet one wonders what onlookers made of the spectacle as gangs of toughs claiming to represent Arab civilization looted and brawled. It is unlikely that either the Washihiri or the Wamanga managed to convince many in Ng'ambo that they deserved collective respect by dint of their cultural attainments. But other messages probably did get through. Most relevant for our purposes was the message that Wamanga might serve as emblems of the Arab elite. That message was signaled not only by the Shihiri Council but also by the elites' defense of the Manga gangs, who were thus made to appear as their hired thugs. As we shall see, the Arab Association reinforced the connection during debates over immigration that took place in the 1940s.

Eight years later another riot dramatically enhanced the Wamanga's notoriety and connected it to the threat of Arab political domination. Because it was directed in part against Europeans, the one-day "Manga Riot" of February 1936 drew considerably more attention from officials and from subsequent nationalist ideologues than the multiple disturbances of 1928. As we saw in chapter 2, the mid-1930s was a moment of rising Arab political assertiveness.[68] In the midst of those tensions, Manga copra producers, a group with a particular reputation for criminal behavior, provoked a violent incident directed against the colonial state. Although the Arab elite had nothing to do with the riot, after the war they appropriated memories of it as an opening salvo in the Arab-led struggle for independence. Such propaganda provided further ammunition to the conservative rhetoric of the African Association, who portrayed their Arab rivals as dangerous figures willing to use violence to undermine all social order. A central image in that postwar rhetoric was that of the criminal Mmanga, whose innate violence they made a metonym for the dangers posed by Arab domination.

The 1936 riot was sparked by enforcement of a new Adulteration of Produce Decree, which imposed quality standards meant to make Zanzibar exports more competitive on world markets. The decree was part of a raft of legislation enacted in the mid-1930s to protect indebted Arab planters. These measures had the effect of disadvantaging small-scale entrepreneurs such as the Wamanga who produced and purchased small lots of cash crops. The revival of the Clove Growers' Association in 1934 had already excluded such entrepreneurs from dealing in cloves; the Adulteration Decree threatened to have a similar impact on Manga copra producers, most of whom had entered the trade with limited experience and capital. Moreover, according to the report of a government commission, Manga producers often cut costs by purchasing stolen coconuts, which tended to be picked prematurely, before they were ripe enough to produce high-quality copra. Wamanga therefore were more prone to fall afoul of the new standards than were large-scale producers and shippers. The latter, in fact, were effectively exempted from the compulsory inspections mandated by the decree.[69]

The Adulteration Decree was first applied to copra in the week preceding the riot, when independent traders bringing copra to the town market discovered that before they could approach a broker they had to have their produce approved by government inspectors. The commission reported that the minimally supervised inspecting staff were Shirazi and mainlanders who used the opportunity to lord it over the impoverished Manga copra sellers, demanding bribes and taunting them with "insolence and insulting behaviour." The Wamanga were particularly offended by one inspector who was of recognized slave descent. Most of the inspected copra was rejected; by the end of the week approximately 1,500 sacks had been impounded in the inspection sheds and according to rumor were to be dumped in the harbor.

The riot began in the Malindi quarter, between the wharves and Darajani, the latter a bustling place of business where Stone Town and Ng'ambo meet. On the morning of Friday, 7 February, a crowd of about forty or fifty Manga copra dealers, armed with swords, sticks, and knives, waited for their representative to come from a meeting in which he was presenting their grievances to the agricultural produce inspector. As the spokesman emerged, the crowd assaulted him for alleged betrayal. The produce inspector managed to escape, but the assistant DC, Ian Rolleston, who tried to calm the crowd, later died of his wounds. When the police got to the scene they found themselves badly out-armed and quickly retreated. The crowd then proceeded to Darajani, where they sacked the police station, and to the nearby market, where they hacked an Indian police inspector to death. Police reinforcements armed with rifles soon managed to disperse the crowds. By late afternoon, all police posted in the countryside had been summoned to town, where they imposed a blockade cutting off Stone Town from Ng'ambo and the rest of the island; a detachment of Tanganyika Police arrived later that evening. In addition to the two government fatalities, four rioters had been killed, all of them Wamanga.

The riot lasted no longer than six hours, but in their panic British officials effectively abandoned control of the entire island except for Stone Town. That they were so rattled by this limited disturbance[70] is not hard to understand: they were among its main targets along with the police (rioters attacked even traffic guards), and they had reason to fear it might signal the start of a full-scale Arab rising. (The Arab Association had in fact intervened on behalf of the Manga copra dealers just before the riot.) The riots made a similar impression on non-elite onlookers. The latter would also have noticed that in targeting the police, the Wamanga were attacking mainlanders who had succeeded in attaining a modicum of authority within the government hierarchy—much like the Agriculture Department employees who had affected such impertinence in the copra inspection sheds.

To be sure, as the riot proceeded many "Swahili" joined from the sidelines, particularly at the market. These participants were largely petty market vendors who during the previous weeks had been involved in a dispute that overlapped with that of the copra dealers insofar as it also involved government efforts to control produce marketing. They and the Manga peddlers and copra dealers occupied similar social positions and shared the same hardships. It is therefore possible that some of them regarded the stereotypes of Manga aggressiveness with the same ambiguity that colored the reputations of "social" criminals such as Feraji Mpira. Still, there is no doubt that for most onlookers the riot was a

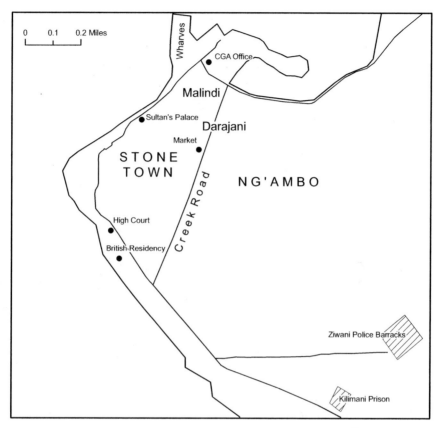

MAP 6.1. Zanzibar Town.

Manga affair, in particular one led by Wamanga from the countryside whose interests were linked to those of the planters, and that it came to be remembered as an instance of Manga violence and troublemaking.[71] In a moment we will see how the riot was remembered after the war. But already by 1939 the image of the "Manga Riot" figured powerfully in the local political imagination, particularly in rhetoric about the aspirations of the Arab elite.[72]

Immigration, Crime, and the Winds of Change

The Mmanga as Emblem after the War

Ethnicized images of innate criminality and criminal violence became more prominent in the debates over immigration that first emerged as a divisive issue just after World War II. As was so often the case, the terms of the de-

202 / *War of Stones*

bate were set by the elite intelligentsia, who protested immigration policies that, they charged, discriminated against Arabs and favored immigrants from the African mainland. This led to yet another instance of the elite's chauvinist rhetoric being turned against them by the racial nativists of the African Association.

With the onset of the war, the government took steps to restrict the flow of immigration. At first, the Arab Association expressed little concern; in fact, in marked contrast to the position it would take after the war, *Al-Falaq*'s main worry was that the flow of Nyamwezi agricultural workers not be impeded.[73] But those attitudes changed as wartime restrictions took firmer hold, particularly restrictions targeting Omanis and Yemenis. Beginning in 1943, food shortages focused authorities' attention on the "rice-eating" immigrants who arrived each year during the dhow season. The most pressing threat came from the Hadhramaut, where a killing famine was producing thousands of refugees desperate to use the generations-old economic strategy of migrating to East Africa.[74] At this moment, the Arab Association began a vigorous defense of Arab immigration, citing historical precedent to argue that a steady influx of Arabs had long been the sultanate's cultural and economic lifeblood and would be crucial to postwar reconstruction.[75]

This change in attitude can best be understood as part of a broader transformation in the political climate of the time, as the "winds of change" blowing over East Africa roused the Arab Association to an awareness of the political implications of immigration policies. The Atlantic Charter and the surge of anticolonial politics throughout Africa and the Indian Ocean world raised with pressing urgency the question of the shape postcolonial society would take. *Al-Falaq* responded by stressing the sultanate's "Arab" nature, which could be maintained only by continued Arab immigration. The paper expressed fears that Arabs' privileged social position would be threatened if majority rule were to coincide with the repression of immigration. Its justification of those anxieties resembled the statements of Kenya settlers who at the same time were arguing for the importance of maintaining Kenya as a "white man's land": in the coming era, argued *Al-Falaq*, the islands' undisciplined laboring strata would still need a steadying paternal hand. Unimpeded Arab immigration was therefore necessary if "historical progress" and the civilizing mission were to continue.[76]

This political transformation included the rehabilitation of Shihiri immigrants, whom the Arab elite had only recently reviled as congenital criminals. But Arab Association propagandists were mainly concerned with defending immigration from Oman. Their rhetorical strategy involved eliding the distinction between Manga immigrants and the ruling elite. Despite popular misconceptions, *Al-Falaq* insisted, the only differences between them were in minor matters of dress.[77] Thus, by culture and descent, the Wamanga were identical to the ruling families whose forebears had occupied the islands "by the right of conquest." Historical narratives of the Omanis' bloody sacrifices in wresting control of the coast from the Portuguese had been a prominent component of Arab Association polemics since the days of the clove-buying crisis. "Arabs had descended upon this part of the world with a sword in one hand and a dagger in the other," *Al-Falaq* wrote in 1939, adding that they had done so with the laudable object of using force to civilize the Africans "whom fate had placed under them." Fourteen years later, the paper was asserting that the Wamanga who came each year during the dhow season were part of the same liberating process. The culmination of the process, it said, the introduction of anticolonial nationalism, was heralded by the 1936 Manga riot.[78]

The Arab Association's own rhetoric thus not only tapped into the popular image of Wamanga as inherently martial and violent but also helped promote the notion that Wamanga might be taken as representative of the entire Arab racial category. When African Association propagandists entered the debate over immigration in the early 1950s, they made full use of the elision their rivals promoted, suggesting that all Arabs approximated the negative stereotype of the Mmanga. Anti-Manga sentiment had been simmering since the later war years, when Manga shopkeepers were boycotted for alleged rudeness to their African customers and for selling staples above the controlled prices.[79] The African Association now accused all Arab immigrants of cheating Africans. More pointedly, *Afrika Kwetu* built on memories of the Manga rioters of the interwar years to bolster their argument that immigration laws should be amended to prohibit those it repeatedly called "riotous immigrants."[80] By the mid-1950s, "immigrants" and "immigrant races" had become *Afrika Kwetu*'s shorthand for all Arabs, immigrant or otherwise. The paper warned that in the future they would not be accorded citizenship.

The degree to which ASP's anti-Arab rhetoric built on images of the Wamanga is remarkable. During the Time of Politics, party propagandists claimed that their rivals represented the interests of foreign Arabs from Oman and emphasized the need for Africans to rid themselves of "Manga rule."[81] In an exercise of blaming the victims, ASP spokesmen appearing before the Foster-Sutton Commission tried to deflect responsibility for the 1961 election riots by invoking the stereotype of Manga violence. Karume observed that Wamanga had always caused trouble. In 1928, he said, when Zanzibar was otherwise "so peaceful and quiet" (a remarkable comment given all the other turbulence of that year), Wamanga started a riot by coming in from the countryside to kill Washihiri. Shrewdly, Karume also reminded the commission that a European had been killed in the 1936 Manga riot. The ASP's lawyer attempted to get an uncooperative British witness to confirm this version of history. Is it not true, the lawyer asked, that Zanzibaris have "always been very peaceful," and that "when the peace has been broken it has mostly been due to one section, and only one section of the population?" When the witness demurred, the lawyer reminded him of the 1928 and 1936 riots. He even suggested that the famous bombardment of 1896, in which British gunboats ousted a sultan who was not suitably pliant, "was brought about by an Arab."[82] The image of the "riotous" Mmanga was thus made the premise for the ASP's racial syllogism: Wamanga are violent; Wamanga are Arabs; therefore all violence in Zanzibar has been caused by Arabs.

Crop Theft and Labor Control in the 1940s and 1950s

Afrika Kwetu's invective against Arab immigrants was partly a reaction to the vilification of African immigrants that had been emanating from the Arab and Shirazi associations. And that anti-mainlander rhetoric was closely connected to mounting concerns over the control of squatter labor. Responding to high wartime prices for foodstuffs, squatters were devoting more time to raising food crops for sale in town markets. *Al-Falaq* complained that squatters found such enterprise easier and more lucrative than weeding their landlords' clove and coconut trees. Indeed, many seemed to make a show of neglecting their obligations as tenants as they shuttled among garden plots on several different estates. Planters also complained that squatters endangered the trees by using fire to clear land for their expanded market gardens. *Al-Falaq* urged the government to intervene to force squatters to weed; otherwise, the paper warned, landlords would evict them. In voicing this demand, *Al-Falaq* spoke primarily for the larger, more "progressive" planters; few others could afford to rely entirely on the open market for labor. But *Al-Falaq*'s advocacy on this issue was a harbinger of the tensions that would divide landlords and tenants in the following decades.[83]

Rhetoric concerning undisciplined and uncontrolled squatter labor was complemented by a growing panic over crop theft. Officials noted divergent popular attitudes toward crop theft, depending on the type of crop stolen. Villagers were incensed over theft of foodstuffs, especially rice, the most valuable staple. But coconut theft—a growing problem driven by steadily rising copra prices throughout the 1940s—aroused little concern, and the police were unable to secure much cooperation in pursuing it. The crime's principal victims were the absentee planters and large brokers who had come to dominate the coconut trade, people for whom squatters and villagers felt little affinity. Officials therefore directed much of their attention to the Manga shopkeepers and copra dealers whom they suspected of dealing in stolen nuts. Most of the actual theft, however, was attributed to bandit gangs of a type not seen since the roundup of the burglary rings of the 1920s. They operated on a large scale, not merely taking coconuts that had already been picked and bagged, but organizing nighttime harvests of entire coconut groves, preferably those owned by absentees. If discovered at their work they readily turned violent. The gangs were most active in northwestern Unguja, areas of heavy mainlander presence that during the Time of Politics would witness some of the worst conflicts between landlords and squatters.[84]

As panic over coconut theft mounted in the second half of 1946, rural elites, including mudirs and others within the Provincial Administration, took the lead in organizing vigilante "night patrols."[85] The vigilantes further criminalized the "floating population," in particular those with neither a farm of their own nor a fixed relationship with a landlord, by targeting them as "potential thieves" and turning them over to the authorities for prosecution under wartime vagrancy laws.[86] At about the same time, *Al-Falaq* undertook a campaign calling attention to the "gangsters" terrorizing the countryside and warned that violence might spread as landlords organized to protect their legitimate interests. In June 1946 representatives of the leading planters founded the United Agriculturalists Organization (UAO) to pursue these issues. Despite the UAO's declarations that it would represent the interests of all in the agricultural sector, its propaganda scapegoated squatters as one of the two root causes of the sector's troubles (the other were "Indian moneylenders"), and it renewed calls for criminal sanctions to help landlords evict undesirable squatters. Timothy Welliver writes that although the Provincial Administration was sympathetic, it was not prepared to enact regulations that might be misinterpreted as abolishing squatting. It did, however, oblige the UAO by enacting decrees in 1949 that created several new offenses, including "loitering" on someone else's land and transporting produce at night.[87]

Although *Al-Falaq* undoubtedly exaggerated the battles between bandits and vigilantes in the 1940s, the formation of the UAO had a significant impact on the escalation of rural violence in the following decade. Sometime in the

1950s, probably soon after the onset of the Time of Politics, the UAO responded
to what it considered inadequate government measures against crop theft by
forming a private police force that coordinated the activities of the landlord-
dominated vigilante patrols.[88] The new force was called the Muzariin Rangers,
or Askari wa Muzarina, using the Arabic word for agriculture that figured in
the Arabic and Swahili forms of the UAO's name. In addition to apprehending
suspected crop thieves, the Rangers also aided planters in conflicts with squatters over the terms of tenancy. The police, fearing unrest, refused to evict unwanted squatters, telling landlords that such matters were subject to the civil
courts, so landlords turned to the Rangers.[89] The resulting evictions gave rise
to much of the resentment and violence that gripped the countryside of northwestern Unguja after 1958, and soon even the most sympathetic officials recognized that the Rangers were little more than a private gendarmerie with which
landlords, using the rhetoric of crime and law enforcement, attempted to impose their personal and political agendas.[90]

Squatter Evictions and Reciprocal Criminalization after 1957

The anti-squatter invective of the UAO and the Arab Association was always premised on the assumption that squatters were mainlanders.[91] Thus it
fed into and was further nourished by the general vilification of mainlanders
that was central to ZNP and ZPPP rhetoric after 1957. One effect of the rise
of electoral politics during those years was to lend questions of categorization and residence—Which people should be classified as immigrants or barbarians? In what neighborhoods do they or should they reside?—a political
dimension they had previously lacked. Such questions no longer simply addressed whether particular classes of people would enhance a particular lo-
cale's level of civilization or wealth or crime. Now, since party allegiances were
assumed to follow ethnic identities, they might determine the outcome of electoral politics. In all four elections, the ZNP and its allies accused their rivals of
bringing immigrants from the mainland to register and vote illegally. The ASP
made similar accusations concerning Wamanga, and both sides used stereotypes of innate criminality to justify their hostility to these respective immigrant groups.

Thus, in the aftermath of its 1957 electoral defeat, the ZNP issued a statement declaring mainland immigrants not simply a threat to democracy (their
illegal presence on the voter rolls, reads the statement, threw the election) but
also to public order. Mainlanders commit most of the islands' crime, the party
asserted, and are vectors for disease. A few months earlier a letter in *Mwongozi*

had blamed mainlanders for all of Zanzibar's ills, including the recently introduced crime of pickpocketing. The correspondent traced the problem to immigration policies that allowed such foreigners "to pour into our islands as if
this were a rubbish-heap for every type of filth"—or, as the editors themselves
put it in March 1961, policies that "left the door open to admit thieves, cannibals and naked people."[92] The vilification of mainlanders, Wamakonde in particular, was among the first tasks of the Shirazi Association politicians who in
1956 founded a short-lived precursor to the ZPPP.[93]

Such rhetoric was deployed in the strikes and boycotts of the Time of Politics. It had its greatest resonance in the conflicts engendered by the squatter
evictions, in which landlords and their political allies played off the ongoing
panic concerning crop theft. (The panic intensified after the June riots, when
many landlords abandoned the countryside out of fear, thus allowing the thieving gangs to go about their business relatively undisturbed.)[94] The pervasiveness of racial politics meant that planters, who already tended to perceive theft
in racial terms, also came to perceive it in political terms: that is, a consensus
arose among the planters and district officers who were largely sympathetic
to the ZNP that crop thieves were politically motivated. This perception may
have had some basis in fact, since, as we shall see, some thieves posed as the
instruments of racial vengeance.

More than the actions of the thieves themselves, however, it was the aggressive actions of the vigilante patrols, which targeted people according to
race, that generated the most serious tensions linked to crop theft. A telling
incident occurred at Fuoni, a settlement a few miles east of town that was the
site of some of the worst violence of the Time of Politics. Years before the onset
of electoral politics its mainlander population had gained a reputation for harboring criminal gangs and crop thieves, and by the early 1960s its Arab citizens
were known for their aggressive vigilantism.[95] In September 1962 two civilians
from prominent Arab families arrested a squatter for carrying ten unhusked
coconuts, six nuts above the legal limit, and took him to the local police post.
The offending squatter, George Cheusi, asserted that his landlord had given
him the nuts, but the landlord denied it. Still, the sergeant at the police post
decided there was insufficient evidence to prosecute, and he ordered Cheusi
released. Incongruously, he told the arresting Arabs that they should take the
coconuts, an act perhaps meant to placate them. But that only exacerbated
their suspicions of the sergeant, who, like Cheusi, was a Christian and a mainlander. They filed a complaint with the mudir, S. M. al-Mauly, who, in support,
forwarded it to the district commissioner.[96]

The crux of the arresting Arabs' complaint was that the police sergeant had refused to accept what to them seemed common sense: that for a mainlander to be carrying coconuts was sufficient grounds to suspect him of theft. In releasing Cheusi, the sergeant berated them for the excessive vigilantism plaguing Fuoni. This outraged the Arabs; as one of them asked, did a citizen have no right to make an arrest "when he sees another stealing"? The mudir, more level-headed, recognized the distinction between actually witnessing a crime and merely suspecting that one had occurred. But he, too, thought the citizens' arrest had been warranted by a "reasonable" presumption of Cheusi's guilt, and he pressed what to him was the central issue: the public's dissatisfaction with a police force that refused to act on such presumptions. The DC, Saud al-Busaidy, shared this concern. No doubt thinking back to the riots of the previous year, he warned that unless the police take "drastic action" in cases of crop theft, "members of the public will eventually take the law into their hands resulting [in] . . . mobs, riots and bloodshed."[97]

The family of one of the men who had arrested Cheusi had earlier been involved in a bitter dispute with a squatter whom they wanted to evict because he was "troublesome," a vague charge that undoubtedly masked their suspicion that, being Makonde, he belonged to the ASP.[98] Similar conflicts racked the Unguja countryside from 1958 onward, as ZNP landlords used the threat of eviction in attempts to make political loyalty one of the obligations of squatter clientage. Crop theft was a common accusation made against unwanted squatters. Landlords were most likely to level the accusation if the squatters in question were Wamakonde.[99] In fact, in October 1960 members of the UAO formally resolved to evict all Makonde squatters.[100] By that moment, the polarization of Zanzibar's racial politics had reached such a degree that for a squatter to be "troublesome" was sufficient to have him labeled a mainlander, no matter what his actual origins were. And to be a mainlander, landlords assumed, was to be an ASP supporter.[101]

Although the evictions were prompted mainly by politics, they also expressed tensions between the economic motives of squatters, particularly those who had been able to take advantage of markets in foodstuffs, and of planters, particularly the few who hoped to transform squatters into cash-paying tenants or wage laborers. But despite landlords' occasional protestations that the evictions were not political, it is unlikely that many were prompted by attempts to transform production; in 1958 hardly more planters were prepared to forego squatter labor than had been previously.[102] Still, it would be misleading to choose between purely political and purely economic explanations of the squatter crisis; landlords and squatters both were motivated by a multiplicity of goals. Most significant for our purposes is asking how the rhetoric of racial politics, including racialized accusations of criminality, shaped economic tensions that had been aroused by squatters who had become aggressive in ignoring the clientelist obligations their landlords expected of them. The complementarity of economic and political tensions added force to the propaganda of racial nationalists on both sides and helps explain why racial violence was concentrated in central and northern Unguja, where squatters had greatest access to town markets.

No matter what precise factors motivated a given squatter or landlord, the conflicts themselves were organized affairs in which the political parties were deeply implicated.[103] Nativist ZNP propaganda urged landlords to evict mainlanders, and the landlords typically enforced eviction by turning to the UAO Rangers. The squatters, for their part, often sparked conflicts by engaging in what amounted to coordinated land invasions in which they aggressively expanded their garden plots and invited newcomers from town to squat nearby. Although the invasions were not necessarily initiated by the ASP, party activists took up the squatters' cause and shaped their actions. One large-scale incident, for example, at Kitope in north-central Unguja was coordinated by a squatter who persuaded his neighbors to extend their gardens in defiance of the ruling of a qadi's court. In doing so he invoked an ASP cause célèbre in which a leading UAO and ZNP figure, Hilal Muhammad al-Barwani, had lost a court case involving his attempt to imprison a squatter for criminal trespass. ASP propaganda had trumpeted the ruling as a victory for "Africans" and had vilified Hilal Muhammad for allegedly racial motives. This rhetoric encouraged many squatters to defy landlords, sparking a renewed rash of evictions.[104]

The ZNP, in fact, blamed much of the crisis on a speech Karume had given in early 1958 at Chuini, an area about six miles north of town and a hotbed of landlord-squatter tensions. Karume was reported to have encouraged land invasions by promoting an ASP slogan that revived the old notion that planters owned only the trees planted on their property: "The trees are theirs, the land is ours." The slogan had appeared in *Afrika Kwetu* as early as 1955 in an essay that used crude racial terms to challenge the planters' rights of freehold. Africans had been forced to squat, the paper argued, because Arabs had taken all the fertile land from them. And should the squatter's market plot flourish, the Arab landlord used deceit, including accusations of theft, to get a share of the crop. *Afrika Kwetu* protested that all land properly belonged to the "Africans" or "natives"; Arabs owned only the trees they had planted. *Afrika Kwetu* thus responded to charges of squatter criminality by depicting Arab settlement itself as a massive act of theft.[105]

Both sides, then, used the rhetoric of dispossession to challenge the rights of the racial "other" to reside in the islands. It is significant that the bitterest disputes erupted over efforts to deprive squatters of the most basic essentials of existence, cassava and water. Landlords often attempted to force out unwanted squatters by denying them access to wells; this issue was said to have been behind much of the violence of June 1961.[106] Another widespread grievance concerned landlords who sent UAO Rangers to uproot squatters' cassava. Cassava was usually the first crop squatters planted when staking a claim to a garden plot. This was partly because of the ease with which a row of cassava can make a cultivator's presence visible: it is planted simply by laying in cuttings. Cassava is also the humblest of subsistence crops, one that the poorest islanders expect to be able to eat. (Many squatters, however, planted substantial surpluses to market in town.) Landlords who tore it out—like landlords who prevented squatters from drawing water and maimed their livestock—were perceived as assaulting squatters' fundamental ability to exist.[107]

The squatter crisis continued to smolder after 1958, directly contributing to the violence of June 1961. As we will see in the next chapter, that violence not only deprived its victims of life and limb but also served as a powerful rhetorical device that effected the reciprocal dehumanization of entire racial categories. Yet even before then, the basic terms of this rhetoric were present in the discourse surrounding the evictions, which each side used as evidence that the other was composed of criminal savages. For ZNP ideologues, the squatters' inherent disrespect for property and their refusal to honor their obligations as clients demonstrated a pervasive contempt for the values of civilization that were so central to the ZNP vision of the nation. On the other side, the evictions figured prominently in some of the ASP's fiercest racial rhetoric. Although the squatter crisis abated during the months of the Freedom Committee alliance, Jamal Ramadhan Nasibu sought to keep it alive as a way of demonstrating the futility of any political partnership with Arabs. "They are not human," insisted a typical article in *Agozi* in October 1959. To illustrate, it described "a SETTLER at Kitope" who "evicted people from his estate, and, since evicting them was not enough, also went and charged them in court." The case was heard by another Arab "settler," the rural DC, who jailed the squatters for fifty days on charges of coconut theft.

I ask you, my brothers, can any good come between us and such people? . . . People's livestock are being attacked with knives for no reason; at Fuoni the *Mahizbu* slashed a *GOZI's* donkey; people's crops were uprooted for no reason; they were arrested for no reason, falsely charged, of all things, with stealing coconuts! And why all this hatred? Why was he locked up? Imagine! Because he's a *Gozi* and doesn't want to take a Hizbu membership card!

All the jailed squatters, the author emphasized, were mainlanders.[108]

Agozi identified the treacherous planter as a kinsman of Ali Muhsin al-Barwani and in fact emphasized the kinship ties that linked all elite Arabs to the ZNP leadership. Such maneuvers were common in Jamal Ramadhan's polemics. They served not only to make his assaults more personal, they also underscored the metaphor of descent that lay at the heart of *Agozi's* racial logic. This is illustrated in the paper's continuing vilification of Abdullah Said al-Kharusi, the DC who jailed the Kitope squatters and whom *Agozi* denounced for routinely persecuting squatters. The charge may well have been justified.[109] Abdullah Said belonged to a prominent family of land owners and business-men; he and his brothers constituted some of the luminaries of the secular intelligentsia in government service and nationalist organizations. In vilify-ing him, *Agozi* stressed both those connections and his alleged kinship to Ali Muhsin. A polemic from 1961 addressed Muhsin directly, charging that "your Kharusi cousin, the DC," arrests Africans unjustly; that "your other Kharusi cousin," a police superintendent, bullies them; and so on with other alleged cousins in high positions. The author never named these miscreants but iden-tified them only by their Arab clan names, thus illustrating his argument that the Arab elite were tied together as kin and were therefore all the same.[110]

ASP propagandists further emphasized the descent metaphor by mocking the ZNP as nothing more than the "Barwani Association." In addition to chal-lenging Ali Muhsin's claims that his party had nothing to do with ethnic soli-darity, this epithet allowed polemicists to attribute to it every misdeed of the large and influential Barwani clan, including those of Hilal Muhammad, the ZNP figure notorious for his persecution of squatters. The ugliest accusation was constructed by telescoping synecdoches so that a single Barwani was made to stand for the entire clan, the clan for the entire party, and the party for an en-tire race. The syllogism was based on the fact that a Barwani was the assassin of Ali Sultan Mugheiry, who was killed in 1955 for having broken the Arab As-sociation's boycott of the Legislative Council. An article published only weeks before the 1961 riots used lurid language to remind readers how "the Barwanis" had "slaughtered" Mugheiry, thus proving that all members of the "Barwani Association" were violent, murderous, and—the emphasis is in the original—"**CRIMINAL**."[111]

Crime Rumors and Racial Violence

By the late 1950s many Zanzibaris had come to believe that racial categories were fundamental to the constitution of society and that the behavior of the racial "other" could be understood in terms of inherent criminality. As racialized political discourse permeated almost every aspect of everyday life, it complemented people's already racialized understandings of crime, prompting them to repeat and explain crime stories in terms of racial politics. In such an atmosphere, virtually any report of crime could be transformed into a rumor of racial terror.

Rumors about crime and criminal violence were therefore central to the discursive spirals of reciprocal dehumanization that culminated in bloodshed in June 1961 and during the revolution itself. Crime rumors typically contributed to these cycles in two phases. First, they confirmed general notions of the depraved criminality of the racial "others" and hence the conviction that they were not fully human. Second, specific reports of such behavior, either planned or under way, conveyed the message that true nationals were threatened by inhuman victimization, thus justifying preemptive actions that in other contexts would themselves be considered "criminal." The targets of such preemptive violence, in turn, would interpret it as evidence of the attackers' own bestial nature.

Rumors of Arab Criminal Violence

Agozi and other papers affiliated with the ASP Youth League were particularly forceful in their accusations of criminal behavior, describing their enemies with epithets such as "thug" and "robber." Although the slurs sometimes targeted the polemicists' rivals within the ASP, the most inflammatory passages were directed at the ZNP. Accusations stressed the racial nature of the alleged crimes, particularly the use of weapons emblematic of Manga and Shihiri violence: swords, scimitars, and the *jambia*, or curved dagger. ASP papers repeated rumors accusing members of the ZNP's youth wing of sexual misconduct, including rape. Such accusations may have resonated with the long-standing rhetoric that vilified Arab men for having forced themselves on their slave women.[112]

In May 1959, *Agozi* published a brief but telling item that neatly captures how rumors of criminal violence were shaped into evidence of racial depravity. The specific references are obscure. But chillingly clear is the author's use of criminalizing rhetoric to justify what appears to be a threat of extermination, likening Arab "gangsters" to vermin. Unlike most pieces in *Agozi*, this was written in English, perhaps in an effort to mimic the pulp novels then popular in East Africa. The reference to people "who have throughout history been notorious for causing trouble" is no doubt meant to evoke images of Manga rioters and criminals. The emblematic daggers and the list of Arab neighborhoods within and just outside Stone Town further enhance the tone of race-baiting.

Gossips Trifles
Tendency to Gangstarism

It is rumoured that some ring leaders of gangsters and certain people who have throughout history been notorious for causing trauble . . . in their lust for power and corrapted dignity are conspiring an attack in order to precipitate another horrible murder. The same dagger policy and dagger politics. . . . People are watching the move with greatest interest and if anything happens, Heaven alone knows what will be the result, the sun may never shine, and grass may never grow at least in some area. Of cause the ring leader are very well known. . . . The mast wicked ones are said to be those at Kisiwandui, Mkunazini, Sokomuhogo, and those living on the fringes of Mnazi Mmoja. So you better look out. You won't always get away with it chaps, there will be a real sweap this time and no prerogatives of mercy. No fear! So think before you leap. What will your sixteen children do if you go to the gallows and who knows, it may turn out to be mice trap—*Aaah! Mtego wa Panya Baba, basi tahadhari!* [Father, watch out! A mousetrap!][113]

The discourse of criminality shaped the actions of the election-day crowds that instigated the June riots. The ZNP poll watchers and suspected sympathizers who were pulled from voting queues were accused of trying to "steal votes" and treated like common thieves.[114] Among the first victims of this crowd justice was none other than Hilal Muhammad al-Barwani, who had appeared in a Ng'ambo ward on behalf of the ZNP. The police intervened to take him into protective custody, but the crowd dragged him from the police car and, shouting that being a thief he must walk, force-marched him to the police station, beating him and tearing his clothes as they went. This procedure is recognizable as the quasi-ritualized treatment commonly meted out to thieves in

East Africa, here being inflicted on an elite Arab who was notorious for falsely accusing his squatters of coconut theft. It was inflicted on other victims of the polling-place crowds as well.[115] The crowds apparently had some confidence in police justice, although typically they gave up their victims only at the station, bloodied and in some instances stripped of their clothing. They were so convinced that their victims were in the same category as common criminals that they expected that European police officers would approve of the beatings.[116]

The ASP's recurrent electoral frustrations made it seem to many that Arab perfidy was ensconced at the highest levels of the body politic and had to be excised by force. But, as is suggested in the item from *Agozi* on "gangstarism," attacks on Arabs were typically justified as preemptive strikes. ASP ideologues had been speaking for some time of ZNP plans to kill all "Africans" after taking power; ironically, the carnage of the June riots, in which most who lost their lives were Arabs, only accentuated ASP fears of Arab vengeance. Such fears, typically, were focused on Wamanga. Polemicists had blamed the Wamanga for the worst excesses of the squatter crisis, depicting them as the core of the UAO security forces that uprooted crops and razed squatter houses and as the main beneficiaries of the evictions themselves.[117] In the closing months of 1963 the image of the Wamanga as armed ZNP thugs was revived, as they were rumored to be preparing a wholesale massacre of mainlanders in retaliation for the 1961 killings. Meanwhile, ASP Youth League branches in Ng'ambo were forming vigilante patrols, ostensibly to protect their neighborhoods from criminal activities during the independence celebrations.[118] One can only assume that these patrols were among the Youth League paramilitaries that were preparing for the revolution, masking their preparations (and no doubt justifying them) as a defensive move against Arab criminals.

The June Riots as Mainlander Criminality

ZNP ideologues, and many within the Provincial Administration who sympathized with their views, regarded the June riots as a manifestation of mainlander depravity. The mudir of central Unguja, for example, reported that the ASP had encouraged criminal gangs to rob and kill, even ferrying them from town in an effort to intimidate voters.[119] To a certain extent this was a example of the familiar phenomenon in which elites portray any insurrectionary behavior as the work of criminal malcontents. Yet the prevalence of looting and armed robbery during the riots suggests that this view was not entirely without foundation.

Testifying before the Foster-Sutton Commission, W. Wright, the super-intendant of the Criminal Investigation Department, made a balanced assessment of the role of criminals and criminal motivations in the riots. Although Wright refused to racialize crime or lay blanket blame for looting on the ASP, he also acknowledged the difficulty of distinguishing between political and criminal motivations. There is no question, he said, that many townspeople took advantage of the disturbances to loot and rob for nonpolitical reasons. A number of "known criminals" were apprehended for doing so, but many normally law-abiding citizens also indulged. Criminal gangs were among the first to carry the violence to the countryside of central and northern Unguja in the days after the election, perpetrating some of the most wanton murders. Those gangs were comprised largely of "African" squatters, Wright stated, but among them were a handful of "Arabs." Each had leaders who could be seen "egging them on" as they robbed and looted. Some of these leaders were common "hooligans," but others were low-level political activists who exploited the racial tensions that had arisen from the squatter crisis.[120]

ZNP propaganda, however, did not share Wright's nuances. The party's construction of events was that the riots were the result of criminal lusts peculiar to mainlanders, unloosed and channeled by ASP and TANU operatives who hoped to turn them to political advantage. In the aftermath of the riots *Mwongozi* stressed the image of mainlanders as criminals and ratcheted up demands that their immigration be restricted. The ZNP's lawyer at the Foster-Sutton hearings, S. H. M. Kanji, labored to impress on the commission that mainlanders were responsible for a disproportionate share of the islands' crime and that the riots could have been prevented by stricter immigration controls. He encountered a bit of trouble on this point when cross-examining Police Commissioner Biles. "I have been carefully maintaining statistics on this very point," Biles insisted, "and they show over the past three years that for every mainlander convicted [of a crime] there are two Zanzibaris." Moreover, he added, most of the "mainlanders" among the recidivists "have been here for a very long time," some "for as much as 25 years."[121]

Rumors and reports that advanced the ZNP interpretation, including those from some sympathetic administrative staff, relied on the image of the criminal Mmakonde. Presumed experts in violence, Wamakonde were said to have provided the ASP the same security services as Wamanga supposedly provided the ZNP. Their mere appearance during the riots or the rumor of their appearance, "carrying arms like arrows and spears and bush-knives," was enough to spark a panic. Such fears could inflate a sighting of three Makonde forest squatters into a rumor of thirty who were preparing weapons for war.[122] Rumors of impending Makonde violence did not dissipate after the riots, and in the months before the revolution they merged with rumors of ASYL members meeting secretly in the bush to plot violence.[123]

Yet the myth of Makonde savagery transcended party propaganda; even the ASP promoted it when it suited their purposes. At the Foster-Sutton Commission hearings, ASP spokesmen invoked the stereotype of the Mmakonde's violent passions as a way to refute the allegation that the riots had been politically orchestrated. In his own cross-examination of Biles, the ASP lawyer, K. S. Talati, asked him to repeat his previous characterization of the Wamakonde.

> Biles. I said they were rather a primitive and uneducated people. . . .
> Talati. I do not think they would be capable of any political thought.
> Biles. I do not agree with that—well, perhaps they would be capable of
>   emotions but possibly not a great deal of thought.

Pointedly, Talati then asked Biles if the Wamakonde had any history similar to that of the Wamanga: that is, if they had ever been guilty of causing "trouble like rioting, violence, on a large scale."

> Biles. I do not recall it. There have been, to my memory, one or two
>   armed robberies committed by Makonde, but nothing on the scale of
>   riots or civil disturbances—this was pure, straightforward crime.
> Talati. You mean on account of their primitive nature they are likely to
>   have sudden loss of temper and less reasoning, is that not so?
> Biles. Yes, I think so.[124]

The willingness of even an ASP spokesman to invoke this particular stereotype speaks to its peculiar power. If ASP activists were indeed guilty of trying to spread rumors of impending violence, one can easily imagine them turning to the bogeyman of Makonde savages. Such were the fears Wamakonde evoked that Khamis Hassan Ameir, in the 1962 report discussed above, recommended they be expelled, despite his frank recognition that those fears were largely groundless. "However peaceful they may remain," he wrote, in times of trouble their actions will always be misconstrued by ZNP and ZPPP loyalists, just as Wamanga are always feared by ASP members. "Rumours will therefore be always spread that Wamakonde are doing this or that . . . and to get rid of them will minimize our security problem." This recommendation was all the more surprising given Ameir's ASP sympathies. Yet it stemmed from more than his own freely admitted distaste for Wamakonde. As a competent administrator whose memories of the 1961 riots were still fresh, he recognized that his job was made more difficult by a situation in which the sight of a single Mmakonde sharpening a spear could give rise to general panic.[125]

A series of events from mid-1963 illustrate how such motifs of popular thought shaped crime reports into rumors of political-racial terror. They occurred near Vitongoji, Pemba, an area of concentrated Makonde forest squatting. For several years Vitongoji had also been a center of Youth League activities, anti-Arab shop boycotts, and racial politics.[126] One evening in May 1963, a Manga shopkeeper, Said Muhammad al-Ruwehy, was murdered. The murder had no political connection but was the result of either a botched robbery or a personal quarrel. The following morning a human leg washed up on a nearby beach. Police believed the leg was that of a fisherman who had earlier been lost at sea, evidently severed by a shark. Yet although al-Ruwehy's body had been found intact, the rumor mill instantly linked the two events. Rumors circulated as far as Zanzibar Town that al-Ruwehy had been dismembered by Makonde terrorists, who had acted as part of an ASP campaign of racial terror.

The murder of the Vitongoji shopkeeper became one of a cluster of rumors that circulated just before and after the July 1963 elections that linked what were "no more than routine crimes" into a supposed campaign of anti-Arab intimidation. In fact there was no pattern to the crimes; victims and perpetrators were a random mix, politically and ethnically. But rumor transformed each crime into a drama of racial vengeance and retribution. The crime that most captured people's fears was murder, particularly since memories of the bloody aftermath of the previous elections were still fresh. Hence the DC for Pemba, Muhammad Abeid al-Haj, warned of "large scale retaliation if these isolated murders continue since it would be difficult to convince the general public that they are not political."[127]

ASP Crowds and Criminal Gangs

Despite the distortions created by propaganda and rumor, there was much in the actual behavior of the ASP crowds to encourage their enemies' view of them as little more than criminals. Most obvious was the prevalence of looting and theft during the June riots. As Superintendant Wright pointed out, many offenders were neither habitual criminals nor political activists. We can safely reject the explanations of ZNP ideologues that ascribed this behavior to a combination of innate barbarism and ASP manipulation. But there remains the question of what would lead normally law-abiding people to shed their inhibitions, whether those inhibitions were based on moral codes, fear of sanctions, or both. Clearly they were encouraged by political rhetoric that for some time had depicted Arabs as dispossessing aliens, rhetoric that implied alternative norms of community from which Arabs were excluded. Once the thieving had begun and individuals found themselves in crowds of neighbors who seemed to be acting on those alternative norms, actions that in ordinary times would have been regarded as transgressive took on the appearance of being necessary for the realization of the new Arab-free community.

As we have seen in earlier chapters, general models of such behavior had been suggested in the rhetoric of racial nationalism, which for years had implied that the demands of racial justice might countenance dispossession, rape, and even extermination. But for more specific and immediate models, ASP crowds turned to criminals—the common "hooligans" who according to Wright were often seen egging them on. This influence was revealed in the most common weapons ASP crowds used in June 1961, which have given the riots the name by which they are remembered, the War of Stones. Of course, stones often were simply the weapon most readily at hand when an argument turned into a brawl. But there is ample evidence that in many instances the use of stones was not only planned and organized—particular members of ASP crowds were assigned the task of carrying baskets of stones for others to use[128]—but was also intended as a discursive implement of racial terror.

The use of concerted stone-throwing was rooted in the practices of the rural criminal gangs that specialized in housebreaking and crop theft. Those gangs would commonly barrage a house with stones to determine whether the inhabitants were at home. An official reporting on the rash of bandit activity during the war noted that the practice had persisted unchanged since the 1920s. During the unrest of June 1961 it was revived by gangs bent solely on theft. But other crowds adapted it as a deliberate tool of racial terror, surrounding a house where they knew their victims were present and raining torrents of stones on the roof and windows before ransacking the house and slashing its Arab inhabitants to death. They also used the threat of stoning to intimidate people they did not intend to kill, such as servants or other dependents.[129]

The June 1961 massacres endowed the act of stone-throwing with the discursive power of racial myth, and in the years that followed, any sound of rocks hitting a roof or door could give rise to rumors that ASP thugs were on the rampage, hunting for Arabs. One evening in March 1962, a man near Chake Chake in central Pemba arrived at his lover's house and found her with another man. Enraged, he commenced kicking the door and threatening the couple inside.

Neighbors quickly spread the rumor that the enraged lover was an ASP loyalist who was stoning the house of a ZNP member, and within days this and
a similar incident gave rise to rumors throughout the islands that ASP gangs
at Chake Chake were stoning and assaulting ZNP-ZPPP loyalists. At Wete
shopkeepers started boarding up their shops, and the DC for Pemba stationed
there, M. A. al-Haj, was surprised by phone calls from Zanzibar Town inquir-
ing about riots at Chake Chake. Embarrassed to have been caught off guard,
al-Haj demanded an explanation from his subordinate at Chake Chake, K. H.
Ameir. Ameir replied testily (he apparently considered al-Haj's reprimand a
racial slight), telling al-Haj that if he reported every insubstantial rumor he,
al-Haj, would get no sleep. Ameir suspected that the latest rumors had been
spread by members of the ZNP, but, he wrote, given the widespread occurrence of stone-throwing during the 1961 riots, one could hardly blame people
for believing them. Indeed, a senior ZNP leader had confided to Ameir that
some irresponsible members of his own party's youth wing were in the habit of
throwing stones at houses, calculating "that the accusation will always be made
against the ASP . . . as stones were used at the Zanzibar riot." Ameir noted, however, that even those who had made the most recent allegations admitted that
"the stones were not thrown in a volley"—that is, not thrown as per the practice of the 1961 mobs or the burglary gangs—"but one at a time."[130]

The emulation of criminal behavior that manifested itself in actual volleys
of stone-throwing (as distinct from simply rumored ones) suggests an over-
lap between popular political leadership and the leadership of criminal gangs.
Known thugs served as local-level ASP activists, and John Okello, the shad-
owy leader of the armed groups that overthrew the sultanate in January 1964,
explicitly stated that he recruited members of his revolutionary vanguard from
among the jobless and destitute. Party officials, particularly within the Youth
League, did not seem to have any scruples about enlisting the support of known
criminals, as the ZNP charged.[131]

But it also appears that ASP and African Association rhetoric, by encouraging people to perceive issues of property and dispossession in racially collective terms, had set the stage for criminal gangs to imagine themselves as
agents of popular justice, independent of any party involvement. As we have
seen in the cases of Feraji Mpira and the Shihiri Council, such behavior was
not without precedent. Some of the armed gangs that preyed on north-central
Unguja in the 1940s posed as agents of social leveling, claiming to steal only
from the rich and giving themselves provocative names such as Tuwe Sawa (Let
Us Be Equal) and Pangusa (Sweep Clean).[132] The temptation to strike similar

poses must have been great in the aftermath of the June riots, when crowds of otherwise respectable citizens emulated criminal gangs in the name of racial justice and with the seeming approval of nationalist politicians. Although such poses may have been purely cynical, it is likely that at least some of the habitual criminals involved believed sincerely, if inconsistently, that their predations were morally justified.

In any case, the pose itself was enough to encourage the fears of many who were already predisposed to imagine any criminal act as an act of racial terror. This can be seen in rumors sparked in the second half of 1962 by the activities of a criminal gang that preyed on Arabs in central and northern Unguja, areas that had been hit hard by the racial violence of the year before. In September 1962 the newly constituted District Intelligence Committee expressed concern that a recent crime wave posed a threat to "racial relations" there. "There is a great deal of intimidation by gangs who visit places in lorries," the committee reported, "attacking isolated Arab shop-keepers."[133] Further amplifying this report, the senior district commissioner, Yahya Alawi, acknowledged that the object of the attacks plainly was theft, not racial intimidation. They typically involved a nighttime visit by a "gang" of a half-dozen men who appeared as if from nowhere and demanded cash, threatening its victims with death should they resist or subsequently go to the police. But, Alawi explained, the intelligence committee wished to "draw attention to the psychological effect of such attacks," exaggerated rumors of which "spread quickly and created fear among those who live in isolated areas."[134]

Police believed the extortion was the work of a single gang whose members lived near Kitope, the site of some particularly bitter disputes over squatter evictions. The gang gave itself a striking name, the Ghana Party, plainly meaning to signal an association between their predations and nationalist politics.[135] Throughout the 1950s, Ghana and Ghanaians had been prominently featured in the political press as the pacesetters of pan-Africanism, and by invoking Ghana the gang elicited the cachet of the international language of nationalism. More ominously, during the final years of the Time of Politics both sides believed that Nkrumah's and Nyerere's governments were providing moral and material support for the ASP's alleged plots to expropriate and evict Arabs. Automobiles were the most talked-about form of support that the ASP allegedly received from foreign sources. Activists supposedly used the cars in mysterious nighttime missions on remote estates to plot actions by squatters.[136] Significantly, the Ghana Party's alleged possession of a motor vehicle was central to its mystique, distinguishing it from ordinary criminal gangs and making it seem all the more powerful. The centrality of this element to the rumors is highlighted by specific reports in which the gang's victims did not actually see the vehicle in question. In one incident the gang absconded with a meager twelve shillings when they heard the sound of a car approaching; they told their victim that the car was theirs. In another, an Arab shopkeeper was aroused by the sound of "a car reversing near his house, followed by knocks at his window."[137]

Such images figured in Yahya Alawi's summary of the complex cycles of fear and rumor set off by criminal gangs such as the Ghana Party. "Probably a good deal of such reports is pure imagination," he wrote, "but [they] reveal a very important factor—that a knock in the middle of the night by a thief [or by an enraged lover, he might have added, or by any other unexpected visitor]— brings fear of 'a gang' and the owner of the house begins to see 'things' following the pattern of what he had heard the previous day, such as the sound of a car, the sound of many feet, etc."[138] Such was the power of rumor that many Zanzibaris were convinced, even during a lull in the actual killing, that violence was being plotted and quasi-political criminal gangs were already on the prowl.

Conclusion

This chapter has raised two intertwined sets of questions. One concerns perception: that is, how images of criminals and criminal behavior became central motifs in racial thought, complementing other motifs we have examined in previous chapters. As we have seen, images of innate criminality had long commanded a place in popular discourse as emblematic of the "otherness" of certain marginal subgroups and their supposedly transgressive nature. Images of criminal *violence* were especially prominent in this regard, for unlike many forms of property crime, they constituted unambiguous transgressions of valued moral codes. During the Time of Politics, those images became incorporated into racialized political discourse as propagandists and rumormongers made stigmatized subgroups such as the Makonde squatters or the Manga copra dealers stand as synecdoches for entire racial categories.

The second set of questions is in many ways more difficult. Why did so many crowds on both sides of the political divide act in ways that seemed calculated to confirm those images in their enemies' eyes? How are we to understand the motives of ordinarily law-abiding citizens who during the Time of Politics looted, robbed, and engaged in seemingly senseless violence, taking as their models and perhaps even their leaders not nationalist politicians but professional criminals? How do we distinguish between acts prompted by the

FIGURE 4.1. Manyema ritual with spectators, Zanzibar Town, 1906.

FIGURE 4.2. Wachukuzi, 1950s.

FIGURE 5.1. Street scene in Funguni, a largely Shihiri section of Stone Town, 1950s.

FIGURE 6.1. Young man with spear and ceremonial attire, probably indicative of a mainland ritual, Zanzibar Town, 1912–1913.

FIGURE 6.2. Manga traders with sacks of spices, ca. 1906.

FIGURE 6.3. Prisoners on work detail, ca. 1900.

FIGURE 6.4. "Party of Wahadimu just returned from a pig drive," 1909.

passions of racial politics and those that Police Commissioner Biles called "pure, straightforward crime"?

I would suggest that this distinction can be misleading. Ultimately it is based on our readings of motive, and it would be foolhardy to expect the motives lying behind violent transgressions to be consistent or "pure." In some instances we might be content to label a theft prompted by material desperation, linked perhaps with cupidity, as a simple crime. The thief himself knows that such actions, especially if habitual, exclude him from "respectable" society, and he often seeks refuge in the alternative community of a criminal subculture. But what if this thief (whose motives, in fact, are rarely "straightforward") should come under the influence of political rhetoric that encourages him to perceive himself as oppressed by unjust relations of property and power? He may absorb such rhetoric incompletely and unreflectively and his prime motive may still be self-centered. But the rhetoric provides him with language that may reduce the feelings of alienation that separate him from his neighbors; he may persuade himself that his crimes are really for the greater good. Such a sense of self-justification will be all the more powerful if he is suddenly surrounded by crowds of respectable citizens engaged in what look like similar pursuits. Such actions can no longer be described as "straightforward crime." But few observers would wish to describe them as straightforward politics either, for they are not prompted by a consideration of how they will affect the distribution of power. Insofar as they are prompted by social consciousness at all, it is one of simple communal subjectivity: that is, the individual imagines that his personal interests are synonymous with those of one communal group vis-à-vis another. This explains why the kind of political thought with which "social" criminals have often been justified by their admirers or themselves has been communal or racial, in which political questions are simplified to questions of personal identity.[139]

Stated so simply, however, there is a danger that this argument might be interpreted in terms of a Hobbesian assumption that the urge to inflict violence on a racial or tribal "other" is part of the natural condition of humanity (if not simply of particular savage races), needing only a chance opportunity to be unleashed. That of course has been the conventional journalistic explanation of ethnic violence in Africa and elsewhere. But I would make the opposite argument. As Philip Gourevitch observes in his book on the Rwanda genocide, getting people to kill their neighbors is hard work; in a remarkable phrase, he writes of the strenuous efforts that were required "to prevent Rwanda from slipping toward moderation."[140] Studies of European genocide have made similar observations of the high degree of organization needed to overcome the human tendency *not* to kill. Pervasive as dehumanizing racial rhetoric was in 1960s Zanzibar, the violence there was perpetrated by a small minority. And as we shall see in the next chapter, even the most brutal mobs contained members who could not fully accept that their Arab neighbors, no matter how distasteful, were subhuman vermin.

Yet despite such hesitancy, those crowds *did* kill. Gourevitch is but one of several authors who have observed that individual acts of violence were themselves tools for accomplishing the hard work of getting people to accept the logic of mass murder. An armed crowd could compel a reluctant individual to join the killing, and such forced complicity could subsequently breed commitment. As we will see, then, far from being an expression of innate racial community, the act of collective killing was a key part of the process by which that sense of community was constructed, in part around a consciousness of having collectively violated the old moral community by stripping some its members of their humanity. The transgressive behavior of the pogrom figured centrally in the logic by which ordinary, law-abiding citizens joined mobs that raped, looted, and killed. This logic gave rise to the acts of excessive brutality that have so puzzled students of communal conflict: repeated wounds inflicted on bodies already dead, dismemberment, sexual assault. Paradoxically, Hobbesian interpretations are most powerfully refuted by such behavior—that is, behavior that results not simply in the death of one's enemies or the seizure of their property but goes out of its way to signal theatrical messages of transgression. Far from being primordial or natural, those messages were shaped by discourses that had been constructed through the historically precise processes that are the subject of this book.

We will look at instances of such behavior in the pages that follow. But I would like to close this chapter by offering an example that resonated clearly with the discourses that have been my subject here. On the third day of the June riots, an ASP mob surrounded the house of a Manga shopkeeper and copra cleaner in the hamlet of Mitikawani in central Unguja. After pelting the house with basketfuls of stones, they broke down the doors, ransacked the shop, and attacked the terrified shopkeeper and his wife with clubs and machetes. Some in the crowd then passed a spear from hand to hand, each stabbing the already fallen couple.

Similar use of a spear was recorded in several of the June killings for which we have reliable descriptions. I have already alluded to one aspect of such quasi-ritualized behavior: by forcing each of its members to plunge the blade in the victims' bodies, the crowd ensured that all its members were complicit in the murder. But why a spear? Virtually every member of the crowd carried a machete, a common agricultural implement and the weapon that in most cases had inflicted the fatal blow. Spears, in contrast, were relatively rare, and their ritualized use in this context calls attention to two meanings they may have conveyed. We have seen that they were regarded as emblematic of the Wamakonde, who in turn were emblematic of mainlanders in general: at home in the bush, as addicted to hunting bushmeat as they were to stealing coconuts, adroit and cruel in their use of such weaponry. What better instrument to sound the warning that "pure black Africans" would no longer endure being ruled and exploited by "alien races"?

Spears were also used to hunt bush pigs: destructive farm pests and a potent symbol of impurity in any Muslim society. One of the first signs of trouble at Mitikawani had come early in the day, when the victims' house servant saw a man carrying the very spear that would later be used on his employers. "When I saw him going with a spear," the servant later testified, "I asked . . . if he was going hunting pigs. He replied that they did not want to be ruled by Mmangas in their country." Admittedly, we must speculate to make all the connections in this laconic testimony. But two points about the spear-carrier's rhetoric seem obvious. First: as a weapon for hunting pigs, he regarded the spear as appropriate also for eradicating Wamanga. As the Swahili proverb puts it, "A spear is for a pig; for a human it's painful." And second: the years of racialized political rhetoric had rendered the criminalized Mmanga the very emblem of Arab rule that the mob at Mitikawani hoped to eradicate.[141]

7

Violence as Racial Discourse

Statements which were originally interpreted to be jokes are now
treated as threats even if the statements were exchanged between
people who have been friends for years and have practiced such jokes
for ages.
—Khamis Hassan Ameir, March 1962

Those innocent women and children—particularly the children—who
were killed and maimed, suffered in atonement of the sins of their fathers, grand-fathers and great-grand-fathers.
—Letter to the editor, *Tanganyika Standard,* June 1961

How had the ideologically driven historical debates discussed in earlier
chapters come to constitute inherited guilt that, in the minds of some, justified spilling even the blood of otherwise "innocent women and children" in
expiation? How had attitudes toward neighbors that had once been as lightly
regarded as folktales taken on such deadly seriousness? By examining the tensions of the sultanate's final thirty months, the next two chapters will continue
the inquiry begun in chapter 6 about the connection between racial thought
and popular violence. This chapter will focus in particular on the violence of
June 1961 and how such violence served to reproduce racial discourse and make
racialized group subjectivities salient.

At first glance this approach may seem counterintuitive: the natural assumption, after all, is that riots and pogroms are the end product of ethnic discourse, the "surface expression" of deeply rooted exterminationist beliefs.[1] Such
assertions, however, have been the subject of heated debate, particularly in a
rich literature on "communal violence" in South Asia and elsewhere. Contributors to this literature raise two central objections. First, they observe that far

from being "spontaneous," most incidents of large-scale ethnic or religious violence show evidence of coordination and planning, often by state officials or other political actors whose interests are served by the riot. Second, what may seem like a single spasm of mass communal violence often reveals itself, on closer inspection, to have been in fact a disparate series of incidents prompted by a variety of motives having little if anything to do with communal sentiment, such as theft, class tension, or personal revenge.

Thus, to try to explain communal riots as the expression of underlying mass sentiments, or indeed to explain them in terms of any single set of underlying "causes," is at best chimerical and at worst serves as a "smokescreen" that obscures the culpability of specific political actors.[2] Gyanendra Pandey and others, in fact, caution that the "communal riot narrative" originated as a form of "colonialist knowledge," a way by which colonial rulers sought to understand and control the wild array of local disputes that threatened state stability by reducing them to recurrent expressions of a fundamental, pre-political division; given the power of the colonial state (and its postcolonial heirs) to allocate resources and shape political discourse, those forms of knowledge were ultimately self-fulfilling.[3] Such critiques sometimes tend toward an arch-instrumentalism that seems prompted by a determination to exonerate the subaltern crowd of any charge of having been "really" motivated by ethnic hatred; those authors prefer instead to see communal violence as the masked expression of more "rational" struggles for economic or political advantage.[4] This last position flies in the face of the facts, as does the more common argument that ethnic thought is a colonial invention. But more measured scholarship like Pandey's is indispensable, for it forces us to recognize that the link between ethnic discourse and popular ethnic violence is not simple or straightforward.

Still, the arch-instrumentalist assumption that at a deeper level communal violence is really about something else points to an unresolved contradiction pervading much of this literature. Instructive examples can be found in debates over anti-Jewish pogroms in late imperial Russia. A conventional approach emphasizes the degree to which the pogroms were organized and directed by agents of the tsarist state; indeed, some scholars include official planning as part of their generic definition of the term "pogrom." Other scholars, in contrast, inspired by the revisionist work of Hans Rogger, discount the significance of official planning and instead stress the "spontaneity" of the pogroms and the deep-seated nature of the anti-Semitism that prompted them.[5] In an exemplary study of the 1905 Odessa pogroms, Robert Weinberg takes a persuasive middle course: the pogroms were neither an official plot, despite the benefits the autocracy derived from them, nor were they purely spontaneous. Rather, they "occupied a middle ground between premeditated violence and a spontaneous riot." The elements of spontaneity consisted of the proclivities of certain categories of "marginal" Odessans, who tended to use violence to vent their frustrations over joblessness, economic competition, and other material grievances. During the revolutionary crisis of 1905 those proclivities were exploited by reactionary and anti-Semitic "riot specialists" (Weinberg adopts this useful term from Paul Brass), some of whom enjoyed official patronage, who channeled this violence against Jews. So although the violence was generated "spontaneously," he concludes, its direction toward Jews was largely calculated.[6]

In its approach, if not its conclusions, Weinberg's analysis resembles others that reject the easy assumption that large-scale ethnic violence was expressive of preexisting mass exterminationist sentiments. Such analyses proceed by weighing the evidence to discover the extent to which the urge to communal violence was "spontaneous" rather than "planned." They usually draw one of two conclusions (Weinberg, in fact, draws both). In some cases, although the crowd may have shared "spontaneous" communal sentiments, close inspection shows that those sentiments had not been murderous but were made so only by the machinations of political agents. (This is a common observation in the literature on the Rwanda genocide.) Or, conversely, while some crowds showed a "spontaneous" proclivity toward violence, that violence was "not inherently ethnic in nature, but . . . acquired ethnic coloration because of social and political circumstances."[7]

Convincing as such analyses are, they fail to address a central conceptual question: How does one distinguish "spontaneous" motives from motives that are introduced from "outside" or "above"—introduced, that is, by "social and political circumstances"? The relevance of the question becomes clear when these authors write of the specific techniques "riot specialists" used to stir up ethnic violence. Most commonly observed is the deliberate spreading of inflammatory rumors. Yet rumors cannot be fed to a crowd as one force-feeds a goose; as several authors recognize, deliberately spread rumors will take hold only if they echo fears and convictions already in place. In other words, the effectiveness of professional rumormongers depends on the ambiguity of the distinction between "spontaneity" and its opposite. Speaking more generally, Paul Brass notes that "much of the organization and planning" that goes into ethnic riots "is designed both to give the appearance of spontaneity and to induce spontaneous actions on the part of the populace."[8] The first of these strategies is straightforward enough, a deliberate attempt to mask the distinction between spontaneous and planned violence, as when Nazi Party officials hid their involvement in plotting Kristallnacht. But the second calls the distinction itself into question. Brass's very wording leaves one perplexed: how can "spontaneity" be "designed" or "induced"?

In taking pains to determine the extent to which ethnic violence was planned or "spontaneous," then, even scholars as subtle as Brass or Weinberg share with the arch-instrumentalists an assumption that one might distinguish between discourses that are expressive of the authentic perceptions and experiences of the subaltern crowd (and hence likely to result in "spontaneous" bouts of popular violence) and others that are either imposed on the crowd or borrowed by it from others.[9] Building on that assumption, one would have to conclude that the racial thought that informed the June violence was borrowed, not spontaneous. The proximate cause of the riots was a conflict over electoral politics, and party activists plainly played a role in mobilizing the crowds (though the exact nature of their role is not clear). More to the point, the racial categories that informed the tensions of the Time of Politics had been elaborated largely by intellectuals, not by the squatters and urban poor who did most of the killing. This all implies, then, that the latter merely mimicked the racial discourse of intellectuals and activists who prodded them on and that their true passions were borne of other, more immediate experiences, such as class resentments or personal grudges.

But other facts make those conclusions untenable. The crowds' choice of targets roots their actions unambiguously in a deeply held racial discourse, as do, more pointedly, their non-instrumental or non-utilitarian modes of killing and maiming (*violenza inutile,* in Primo Levi's phrase). As in other instances, such "stylized" and "expressive" modes did more than simply kill; they were used to inflict dishonor and degradation. They indicate the "moral framework" that informed the killings and are impossible to reconcile with an image of the crowd espousing borrowed convictions that it wore lightly or insincerely.[10] Indeed, they were wholly of the crowds' own invention: although many political propagandists had spread messages of hate, they had never called for mass killing, let alone suggest (to paraphrase José Kagabo) how to go about it.[11]

The precise connection between popular violence and elite-generated communal discourse remains a key problem in even some of the richest literatures on the subject.[12] In earlier chapters we saw that it is not persuasive to think of racial identities simply as doctrines that are handed down by intellectuals to be internalized by others who learn about them in classrooms or political debates. Rather, subalterns reproduce racial identities in daily practices that make those identities seem rooted in personal experience. This is especially apparent when one is trying to trace what motivated ordinary people to commit acts as transgressive of moral norms as those touched upon at the close of the preceding chapter. Communal identities can achieve such power only when they become the stuff of *violent subjectivities*—that is, when they shape a sense of self based on experiences of violence, real or imagined, that can seem to justify counterviolence as either revenge or preemption.[13] Such subjectivities differ from the ethnic identities that were (and remain) most common in Zanzibar. As we have seen, a person might feel different from his Manga neighbor without wanting to forcibly exclude him from the moral community. But by June 1961 for significant numbers of Zanzibaris, and by January 1964 for even more, such a sense of self and otherness had come to the point that it might justify or impel subjecting one's Manga neighbor to the acts of dehumanizing violence that are the mark of a pogrom.

To uncover the processes that gave rise to such a situation, it is not sufficient to examine, as we have been doing in most of the preceding pages, questions of context and historical precedent. One must also examine the moment of violence itself: how the killing was done and how it was talked about afterward.[14] In this chapter and the next I will focus on two processes that often have been observed to contribute to the creation of violent group subjectivities: the actions of the racial mob[15] and the circulation of rumor.

Using mob violence to explain the emergence of violent racial subjectivities ceases to be a conundrum once we consider the observation, stressed in the South Asian literature, that most communal riots have a heterogeneity of motives and often become "communal" only after the fact, as they are talked about and remembered as such in political discourse.[16] What that literature often overlooks, however, is that communal discourse is generated not only by intellectuals and political elites but also by non-elites, including direct participants in the events discussed, and that the discursive formation of the communal mob often takes place in the course of the riot itself, not just afterward. In their actions as well as their words, the most powerful voices in the creation of the communal riot narrative are often those of the rioters, eyewitnesses, and victims themselves.

Scholars who have had the opportunity (and courage) to study contemporary ethnic violence up close have demonstrated that the dynamics of the mob can be especially powerful mechanisms by which individual subjectivities are submerged to that of the group. Psychologists have noted that the experience of being in a crowd, especially in situations of heightened emotion such as fear or religious devotion, can weaken the individual ego and render individuals more likely than usual to suspend personal judgment and instead model their behavior on that of others around them. This should not be taken to imply a Hobbesian notion "that, as personal identity disappears in a crowd, the residue is . . . some regressed, primitive state where the violent side of human nature is unleashed." Rather, as Sudhir Kakar emphasizes, in a crowd personal identity "gets refocused" so that "individuals act in terms of the crowd's identity." Taking his cue from Natalie Davis, Kakar likens the rampaging mob to participants in the liminal stage of group rituals, in which the individual experiences the "self-transcending" state that V. W. Turner called *communitas.* The shape such a group identity assumes in any given instance—whether it is imbued with hatred of an outgroup or a sense of truly transcendent universalism—depends on a variety of factors that are constructed by history, not by nature: for example, the values and identities people learned as children; the institutionalized structures of religion or politics; or the more informal leadership of crowd members who for whatever reason are well positioned to manipulate cultural capital to steer the crowd's actions in particular directions.[17]

To be sure, a mob can coerce an individual to kill (as we shall see). But even if coerced, participation in a racial killing renders the individual ego vulnerable to intense questioning that can result in identification with the new community of killers. Such questioning is almost ensured by the very form of mob violence, which, going beyond simple killing, renders its perpetrators complicit in dramatic transgressions of moral codes that had previously supported ties of community (and humanity) between racial self and racial other, no matter how prevalent the discourse of racial categorization may have already become. The violence of the racial mob, in short, is itself a discursive act that signals powerful messages about those involved: about the dehumanization of the victims and the transformative force of the killings.[18] Participants and eyewitnesses to mob violence, no matter how heterogeneous their motives in killing or watching, encounter powerful incentives to recast their experience in communal terms.

But acts of collective violence also have the potential to forge subjectivities far beyond this relatively limited circle. This occurs when they are related and embellished (and even invented) within circuits of rumor. Rumors are unattributed narratives about current events that can be defined in part by their mythic power—their ability to dramatize and substantiate general truths—and hence by their power to compel belief. This same quality contributes to their well-known infectiousness, the "almost uncontrollable impulse to pass [the rumor] on to another person."[19] Scholars have long observed that the circulation of rumors helps cement bonds of community among those who tell, believe, and retell them. In part this is a function of the aura of complicity involved. The very concept of rumor assumes a contrast with "authoritative" or "substantiated" forms of discourse that are controlled by the powerful, such as the government or the press. (That in matters of *content* this contrast can be illusory is a point I will take up in chapter 8.) Rumors assume their greatest power among people who feel cut off from control of such authoritative discourses or feel that their interests are not addressed in them. Among such people rumor often contributes to a rebellious subjectivity, a sense that in sharing rumors they are uncovering truths that those in power want suppressed.[20]

To observe that rumors of ethnic violence have the power to reshape subjectivities is to describe their peculiar power to generate motive and action. Through such rumors, Veena Das observes, "words come to be transformed from a medium of communication to an instrument of force."[21] Tales of massacres are particularly powerful in this regard. They are almost always told from the perspective of the victims; indeed, when circulated among members of the category that provided the killers, they portray the latter as the real victims, people who killed only to prevent worse outrages by their oppressors. They make especially compelling fare in contexts of ethnic political tension because they forcefully confirm the innocence of the ethnic self and the barbarism and inhumanity of the ethnic other. The circulation of such rumors often creates a sense that an individual's primary obligations are to a community defined by its need to act violently, either to avenge past acts of violent victimhood or to preempt future ones. In the worst cases, as in Burundi since 1972 or South Asia since 1947, tales of communal massacre pass from the realm of rumor into that of historical myth, contributing to decades-long spirals of violence, retelling, and retaliation.

So through the simple acts of telling and hearing (and believing), rumors of racial violence can remake ordinary people into witnesses and victims, even if they have never actually been anywhere near a riot. Ethnic nationalists and their academic commentators often invoke "memories" of massacres. In a literal sense, such memories are nothing of the sort. But the ideological fiction points to the central role that rumors of massacres play in reshaping images of the self; they replace the subjectivity of personal experience with false memories of victimhood.[22] Rumors of racial violence, in other words, often serve to transform racial political ideologies into what seem like reflections of "authentic" experience, which can then make ordinarily peaceful individuals willing to countenance or even perpetrate acts of racial vengeance. And to those who suffer or witness them, those acts, in turn, bestow a material "reality" on what had previously been merely the rhetoric of racial victimhood.

This understanding of the role of rumor is incompatible with a prevalent strain in the social sciences, usually associated with James Scott, that assumes that rumor and other "offstage" utterances are expressions of unmediated subaltern experience, forms of counterhegemonic discourse that not only are untainted by elite ideologies but also convey pointed challenges to them.[23] Such analyses, which are akin to those that seek to distinguish between spontaneous and engineered racial violence, rest on the assumption that discourses are discrete and internally consistent, each reflective of experiences peculiar to a particular social class.[24] The latter assumption is refuted by a consideration of the many rumors that roiled Zanzibar between the June riots and the 1964 revolution. In chapter 8 we will see that those rumors often reproduced hegemonic ideologies—not just of race and civilization but also of the Cold War. Rumor was an especially powerful mechanism in this regard because of its appearance of uttering truths based on the "authentic" experiences (or "memories") of the oppressed. The rebellious quality of "offstage speech," in other words, which according to Scott and his followers reveals the subaltern's ability to demystify dominant ideologies, in fact served quite the opposite function.

The Election Riots of June 1961

One implication of the above is to restore the importance of the precipitating incident to explanations of racial riots. Though perhaps less "glamorous" than "the search for 'ultimate' causes," the reconstruction of such incidents is nonetheless essential to understanding the processes that give rise to murderous group subjectivities. Writing of contemporary India, Kakar observes that the precipitating event—or more precisely its meaning as constructed via rumor—is what induces individuals to act and speak *as* Hindus or *as* Muslims. In the resulting spiral of perceived threats and counterthreats, he writes, "group salience" intensifies as "an individual thinks and behaves in conformity with the stereotypical characteristics of the category 'Hindu' (or 'Muslim') rather than according to his or her individual personality." Social identity displaces personal identity "as individuals perceive members of the Other group purely in terms of the former."[25] Thus it becomes possible for ordinarily peaceful individuals to countenance killing their neighbors in the cause of communal justice.

This might be expressed differently. The period after 1957 witnessed no dramatic changes in the socioeconomic factors that instrumentalists usually regard as the underlying causes of ethnicity in Zanzibar. What *had* changed were the conditions of electoral politics, which, though less sociologically profound, had actually mobilized people to act as ethnic collectivities. It is therefore not surprising that ethnic violence was precipitated by tensions over electoral politics. By June 1961 those tensions had been rendered especially acute by the rapid succession of two bitterly contested elections in the space of just six months. And as we saw in chapter 5, party propagandists sought to mobilize voters by appealing to racial and religious loyalties and fears.

The uncertainty that followed the January 1961 stalemate further sharpened the ASP's frustrations and raised the heat of the rhetoric on both sides. (The contest for the support of the ZPPP's three elected Legco members produced a particularly inflammatory cycle of rumored and threatened violence, replete with charges of kidnapping and images of scimitar-wielding Manga assassins.)[26] On election day, 1 June, watchful crowds in the overwhelmingly ASP neighborhoods of Ng'ambo queued to vote well before the polls opened, their attitudes shaped not only by the general tone of racial discourse but also by the specific conflicts over electoral procedures, in which the goal had been for "Afro to prevent Hizbu" from voting and vice versa. In the earliest incidents, Youth Leaguers assaulted ZNP poll watchers they presented their credentials. Within an hour after the polls opened, known or suspected ZNP members were being expelled from voting queues throughout Ng'ambo and beaten bloody. Soon pickup trucks with gangs of armed "Arab" toughs were seen cruising throughout Ng'ambo, shouting abuse, waving swords, and challenging their "African" counterparts with sticks and clubs. Attempts by party leaders to calm the crowds proved fruitless.[27]

At midday, ASP and ZNP toughs fought a pitched battle at Darajani, a commercial neighborhood that bridges Ng'ambo and the elite quarter of Stone Town. The police managed to disperse the combatants, but as the latter melted into the streets and alleyways of Ng'ambo, they continued to attack not only one another but also bystanders. Individuals suspected of supporting one side or the other were hauled out of shops and dragged off bicycles. Widespread rioting and looting continued in town late into the night; it was finally brought under control with the arrival of troops flown in from Kenya. Ten people were killed in town on the first day of the riots. All but one of the dead were identified as "Arabs," but the scores of wounded treated in hospital were evenly divided between "Arabs" and "Africans." Over the next five days, the distribution of casualties was similar.

Although much of the initial violence on the morning of 1 June had been prompted by considerations of electoral advantage—preventing the opponents' voters from going to the polls or defending one's own voters—few rioters were able to separate such calculations from the racial thought that had come to imbue every aspect of political culture. The ASP mob at Darajani turned on any would-be voter "who was a light-coloured Arab or Indian."[28] Even members of the Youth's Own Union, the disciplined cadre of ZNP youth loyal to Babu and other Marxist leaders, used racial markers to identify their political opponents, harassing Wamakonde (or people believed to be such) and abusing street sweepers as they did their jobs. (Street-sweeping was regarded as an especially degraded occupation that was emblematic of prisoners, mainlanders, and slaves.)[29] Of course, by the close of election day, when the outcome was clear, calculations of electoral advantage ceased to have any relevance, even in events planned by party operatives.[30] The most prominent motive was revenge: revenge for the attacks on ZNP voters and revenge for yet another election that ASP members believed had been stolen from them. And revenge prompted another motive: fear of retaliation. Soon after the first violence, rumors began to fly that the Arabs were making a concerted effort to kill Africans. Initially fed by the YOU's threatening response to the attacks on ZNP voters (and perhaps further nourished by memories of campaign speeches in which ASP politicians asserted that Hizbu had been planning such massacres), the rumors were later intensified by the arrival of vehicles bringing armed ZNP loyalists from the countryside. By midday on 2 June, Ng'ambo was gripped by fears that the Arabs' savage Manga retainers were descending on town.

On that same day, these rumors reached the countryside, which had remained quiet on election day, and they evidently had much to do with instigating the first violence there. The sight of ZNP supporters being ferried to town helped mobilize ASP crowds, who attacked them as they passed. Conversely, there may have been rumors that carloads of Makonde and other mainlanders were being brought from town to terrorize the countryside with their spears and arrows.[31] The first killings in the countryside took place at midday at Kitope Ndani, near Mahonda about thirteen miles north of town, where three Manga Arabs (one an eight-year-old boy) were killed by an ASP mob. Similar gangs continued to roam the countryside for several days, looting properties owned mostly by Wamanga, assaulting and sometimes killing their owners.

Onlookers often described these gangs as "mainlanders" and "squatters," but indigenous islanders were also prominent in many of the cases for which we have reliable evidence.

The geography of the violence, especially in the countryside, speaks to the particular wellsprings of racial tension that fed it. Most of the killings took place in the central plantation zone north and east of town, which had witnessed the most intense conflicts over squatter evictions and bus and shop boycotts. But few of the victims were large estate owners, who tended to live in town. Rather, most were Wamanga, the small leaseholders and rural shopkeepers who specialized in the copra trade. Because each of these entrepreneurs needed an adequate radius of estates on which to draw for their supply of coconuts, they tended to live isolated from one another, with squatters as virtually their only neighbors. This left them especially vulnerable once rumors about the election-day violence revived fears of Wamanga. For rural mobs looking to kill Arabs, Wamanga made convenient victims; they were highly visible by dint of their obvious somatic markers (when compared with members of the local-born Waarabu elite) and were already tainted with their own particular opprobrium.[32]

While violence in town was largely suppressed by 4 June, the killing continued for several more days in the north-central parts of Zanzibar Island, ending only with the deployment of four companies of troops flown in from the mainland. The final death toll was sixty-eight, only three of whom were identified as "African," and several hundred wounded were treated in hospital. Some 1,400 were arrested, 270 in connection with murder.[33]

The Search for Causes

Though the killing was over, the riot was just entering its second phase, which in many ways is the most significant: the post facto "struggle for representation and meaning" by which riots become fixed in public discourse as instantiations of communal or racial conflict.[34] In the present case an explicit record of these struggles is available in the transcripts of the Foster-Sutton Commission hearings. The commission advertised its hearings in advance and invited the public to submit evidence. Both parties responded by assembling teams of lawyers who, together with the government's attorneys, called witnesses and cross-examined them, often quite aggressively, for a period of almost three weeks in September and October 1961. The result was very much like a trial, held in the Legco chambers and open to the public. Witnesses included the islands' best-known political figures, who were called by their party's respective lawyers, as well as senior civilian and police officials.

In this acutely adversarial setting, each party did its best to implicate the other, and police witnesses found themselves on the defensive against allegations of dereliction and partiality (leveled mostly by the ZNP). But most understood that more than simple culpability was at stake. The lawyers and witnesses were all aware that the commission's report would be a key political and historical document that would have the power to influence subsequent events, and they did what they could to shape it. The opportunity to do so was all the greater inasmuch as the three commissioners had virtually no East African experience.[35] In seeking to reconstruct the underlying "causes" of the riots (a key word in the commission's terms of reference), the commissioners were particularly dependent on the testimony presented. Each side, then, strove to impress on the commissioners not only its version of the June events but also its understanding of Zanzibari society and history. In the exchanges between witnesses and lawyers, most of whom were aware of playing to a diverse audience of partisan Zanzibaris as well as the Britons who would write the report, we can see each side honing its repertoire of interpretations three months after the riots.

Although they disagreed vehemently about most issues, ASP and ZNP spokesmen were united in their conviction that the riots could be explained by a single set of "causes" and that the central question to ask was whether the violence had been calculated or spontaneous. Those most insistent on explaining the riots as the product of spontaneous mass sentiment were witnesses for the ASP. While this is not what one would expect from reading Pandey on the colonial origins of the "communal riot narrative" (government witnesses, in fact, were leery of such explanations), it is not inconsistent with the South Asian literature's finding that political actors often use such rhetoric to mask their own culpability for spreading ethnic hatred. The ASP's lawyers recognized that the evidence was against them: the precipitating incidents at the polls implicated ASP activists and virtually all the killing was done by mobs sympathetic to the ASP. Rather than refute those facts, they steered attention to Hizbu provocations. As for the killings themselves, ASP spokesmen explained them as a natural response to centuries of Arab abuse, committed by oppressed people who because of their backwardness and denial of opportunity were incapable of responding more rationally or with greater self-control.[36]

ZNP spokesmen, on the other hand, insisted that racial enmity was totally foreign to Zanzibar and was characteristic only of mainlanders. When testifying on these matters, the party's two star witnesses, Babu and Muhsin, were remarkably disingenuous. Each denied even an awareness of his own ethnic identity; when pressed, Muhsin admitted that he "used to be called an Arab" but had never believed it, even as a child. (His cross-examiner easily exposed the pretense by getting him to admit that he had served on the executive committee of the Arab Association.)[37] The ZNP never engaged in ethnic rhetoric, they insisted, and Babu pretended not to know the meaning of some of the routine anti-mainlander invective used by ZNP speechmakers. But unfortunately for the impression party leaders were trying to convey, Muhsin saw no contradiction in serenely voicing from the stand his assumption that all mainlanders were disloyal aliens and that Zanzibaris were justified in hating them. Most Zanzibaris, he added, could tell a mainlander by sight. Moments later, when an ASP lawyer pressed him to agree that Wamanga were inherently violent, Muhsin suddenly regained his antiracialist principles.[38]

The ZNP lawyers and spokesmen did their cause few favors by holding so tenaciously to the party line. Against the weight of the evidence, they were adamant that all the violence was plotted by the ASP leadership, that the victims were targeted solely because of their party membership, and that race was irrelevant to the June events because it was irrelevant to the thinking of all true islanders. At the same time, they wanted to demonize the ASP as the party of racialism. ZNP ideologues had been working out this line for months. Within a week of the violence, party organs were declaring that the riots were neither "racial" nor "riots." "There has been no fighting," *Mwongozi* declared on 9 June, only a one-sided political massacre organized by the "reactionaries" of the ASP in an attempt to throw the election. The ASP found such tactics necessary because its racial appeals had "failed to arouse any response" from the Zanzibar electorate. (The latter assertion overlooked the fact that the ASP won the popular vote.) That is why the ASP had to import its thugs from Tanganyika, *Mwongozi* claimed.[39]

The ZNP interpretation implicated not only the ASP's Tanganyikan backers but also Britain. The riots were the culmination of a broad imperialist scheme to forestall "genuine freedom" by dividing Zanzibaris by race. That is what prompted the imperialists to set them against one another in the conflicts over voter registration, according to ZNP propaganda; it is also why Britain allegedly created the ASP in the first place. Now, having failed to bring the ASP to power through the "barbaric thuggery of their allies," the imperialists had begun a campaign to misrepresent the massacre as a racial conflict. For obvious reasons, ZNP witnesses downplayed such anti-British rhetoric when they appeared before the Foster-Sutton Commission. Yet elements of it surfaced in their allegations against the police—allegations that, shorn of overt anti-imperialism, revealed more plainly the nativism that lay beneath, disdainful of the mainlanders who dominated the police force.

If I have devoted more space to the ZNP's understanding of events than to the ASP's cruder racial version, it is primarily because the former, being more in line with international currents of anticolonial nationalism, resonates more with the latter-day scholarship fed by those currents. (Indeed, there is reason to believe that the party line had a direct impact on East African scholars via the later influence of the brilliant and charismatic Babu.)[40] The nationalist propagandists anticipated later scholars most obviously by blaming Zanzibar's ethnic ills on the colonial state; their charge that colonialist discourse was responsible for misrepresenting the June events as a manifestation of racial conflict accords particularly well with the South Asian literature on "communal riot narratives." They also anticipated the scholarly fashion of explaining away racial resentments as irrelevant or as really about something else. Hence the ZNP's lawyer, Kanji, told the commission that the tensions over squatter evictions had nothing to do with race or even politics; rather, they were the result of impersonal economic forces that were causing "the squatter system" to wither away.[41] Much of the violence, they asserted, was the product of simple criminal lusts that had been harnessed by ASP activists to serve their political interests. But as we have seen, the discourse of criminality was intimately bound up with the discourse of race. For all their posing, then, even these ideologues could not escape the logic of their own racial thought. Most fundamentally, in asserting that racial sentiments were "unnatural and alien to this country"[42] and seductive only to false nationals, the spokesmen for the ostensibly antiracial ZNP gave voice to their own racial prejudices. A susceptibility to "racism," apparently, was an inborn quality that marked the mainland barbarian. No one seemed to notice the irony.

As I have indicated, neither the commissioners nor most of the British officials who appeared before them make good examples of Pandey's model of the colonial post hoc construction of mass communal hatred. In fact, although the commissioners refused to characterize the violence as one-sided and found no evidence that the ASP leadership had planned it, they more or less endorsed the ZNP's interpretation of the place of racial thought in Zanzibar society. Like the ZNP, they asserted that racial antagonism had been unheard of before 1957 and that the riots were the product of political mobilization by racial and religious demagogues. As to why most of the fatalities were Wamanga rather than elite Arabs, the commissioners concluded that that could best be explained not as a racial phenomenon but as the settling of "old scores" against rural shop-keepers.[43]

So the commissioners can be held no more responsible than any nation-alist (and a good deal less responsible than some) for portraying the riots as the product of primordial racial hatreds. In fact, like the interpretation in this book and like much of the critical literature on South Asian communal vio-lence, the commissioners stressed the role of political speech: what they called the "bombardment of words" to which Zanzibaris had been subjected during the Time of Politics. Where we differ, however, is that they and all the parties involved—nationalist and colonialist, ASP and ZNP—assumed there was a fundamental distinction between those words and the spontaneous motives of the crowd and understood race only as an expression of such spontaneity. If ra-cial concepts were introduced from outside the crowd by political speech (the "bombardment of words") or if a crowd's spontaneous motives seemed to flow from other concerns (criminal cupidity, an urge to "settle old scores"), then the crowd's motives could *not* be understood as "racial." Racial motives, being pri-mal and spontaneous, were not the product of political authority; they were nei-ther rational nor organized. Hence the ASP's excuse: because the killings were racial, no political party can be blamed for them. Conversely, if the crowd's mo-tives could be shown to have been connected with the inducements of politi-cal speech, then they could not be said to have been spontaneous. Hence the ZNP's refrain, which the commissioners more or less endorsed: the killings weren't "racial," they were "political."

All these attempts to determine whether the riots were spontaneous or politically calculated reflected a common assumption, shared by party ideo-logues and British officials alike, that the natural state of political leadership involved either nationalism or its counterimage, colonialism. Accordingly, if the riots were "racial," then they were by definition apolitical, the product of unconscious inherited subjectivities—perhaps those resulting from a long his-tory of oppression by Arab "settlers"—that had prompted "spontaneous" be-havior that ran counter to nationalist unity and nationalist mobilization. If, on the other hand, the riots were the product of conscious planning, it would have been by partisan operatives acting according to some ulterior motive or, most logically, by colonialists or other enemies of nationalism. Yet the evi-dence plainly refutes both positions. Restricting our example to the ASP mobs that did most of the killing, the ZNP's charge that they were commanded by party leadership is simplistic, and the suggestion that the British connived at their assaults is a fantasy. At the same time, the ASP's depiction of the killings as purely "spontaneous" outbursts of popular anger is also wide of the mark. Though Karume and other top party leadership cannot be connected directly to the violence, there is unmistakable evidence that some mobs were led by local-level ASP activists.

When we examine that evidence below, we will see that it accords with other studies that have found that while racial mobs often have ties to political or social forces outside themselves, those forces rarely command the mob in a straightforward way.[44] But the precise nature of the ASP's involvement was clouded by the political postures both parties took in the immediate aftermath of the riots. The behavior of the ASP itself gave the impression that it had played a central organizing role. It provided high-profile legal assistance to many of those charged in the riots, and in the months and years that followed, some of the more militant party propagandists threatened a repeat of the violence. As in similar cases elsewhere, they couched those threats vaguely so as not to openly contradict the leadership's contention that the riots had been spontaneous outbursts of popular feeling.[45] Yet the net impression, doubtlessly intended, was that the party could control the mobs and channel their anger as it wished.

The ASP's enemies, of course, were less circumspect in their efforts to create this impression. Particularly potent in this regard were rumors that the pogroms in the squatter districts were fomented by mainlanders who had been sent there by the busload after having been smuggled into Unguja. There is no evidence that such rumors were true or even that they had been circulating at the time of the riots. Their first mention appears a month later, in reports written by mudirs with pronounced ZNP sympathies that were forwarded to the Provincial Administration by their superior, Abdullah Said Kharusi, the DC whom the ASP had long vilified for his persecution of squatters. Thus these rumors entered the official records—couched, in the case of Kharusi's reports, in rhetoric he lifted directly from the pages of *Mwongozi*.[46] Of course ZNP journalists themselves did all they could to spread such rumors, skillfully hinting that information was being suppressed by mysterious parties who favored the ASP.[47]

In contrast to the impression given by the combined effects of rumor and propaganda, reliable eyewitness accounts make clear that the ASP's control of the mobs was at best tenuous. Each crowd seemed to generate its own leaders. In the countryside, those leaders were often described as members of the "hooligan element," apparently meaning that they were disreputable-looking young men with no previously known political commitment. Others were local, lower-level activists, most with ties to the ASYL or the Human Rights League—that is, precisely the young militants the party leadership had been struggling to control. In town things looked much the same.[48]

Though they thought of themselves as ASP loyalists, these crowds were far more responsive to their own informal leaders than to party spokesmen, whom they did not seem to fully trust. When Karume appeared before them with pleas for calm, they listened and made gestures of compliance but often acted up again as soon as he was gone.[49] A telling incident occurred in town late in the afternoon of 1 June as Karume, escorted by Mervyn Smithyman, tried to disperse a large and particularly refractory mob. Smithyman did not recognize any of the crowd's leaders; they were not regular political activists, he testified, but seemed more of the "hooligan element." Karume's pleading proved fruitless ("these people won't listen to me," he told Smithyman in frustration), and the crowd refused to move. "I was expecting any moment for them to start a riot on us," testified Smithyman,

> but suddenly one particular leader jumped out in front all in rags and said "Hip Hip," and everybody said "Hurray"; he said "Hip Hip" again and everybody said "Hurray," and then he said "Hip Hip, we are all going home," and they said, "We are all going home." I am quite convinced if he had said "Hip, Hip, we are all going to attack them," they would have attacked . . . just like that.

Karume's relative powerlessness is clear in this incident. "He did not know quite what to do," recalled Smithyman, "till this leader jumped up and took them away."[50]

Smithyman's tale suggests the ambiguities of the crowds' relationship to political authority. He interpreted it as an indication of the unthinking "feeling" that motivated such mobs, which "had got to the stage where they were hardly responsible for their actions," refusing deference to their political champion and responding instead to the impulses of anonymous rabble-rousers. Yet this crowd cannot be described as "spontaneous," if by that we mean that its actions were the result of unreflective impulses immanent to itself: it did not ignore Karume altogether, and Smithyman's own description indicates that it had a leadership structure, even if that structure seemed improvised on the spot and dominated by unknown leaders "all in rags." Still, what if we take seriously Smithyman's sense (apparently shared by Karume) that the crowd might have turned either way at that moment? As we shall see below, there is plentiful evidence that this was a distinct possibility—that had one of the ragged leaders invoked emotionally charged images of Arab depravity, some of the crowd might have been induced to defy Karume and indulge in politically counter-productive racial violence.

Scholars are often reluctant to entertain such possibilities, warned away by the classic arguments of George Rudé and E. P. Thompson against depicting crowds as disconnected from all social and political context or motivated by mindless passion. But to observe that some crowds behave inconsistently or that their violence transgresses "rational" behavior (the latter usually defined as the pursuit of material or political interests) is not to say that they are unthinking or unaware of their common objectives. Veena Das urges us to acknowledge the "painful" fact that racial mobs are usually as disciplined and conscious of fighting for a moral order as are bread rioters demanding food for their children.[51] Nor is it always possible to distinguish avenging mobs from organized crowds that gather to engage in (conventionally) "rational" behavior: in the present case, many of the mobs that took to looting and murder began as orderly voting queues, disciplined by party instructions not to allow "vote thieves" to enter the polling place.[52] In the following section I will examine some of the processes by which crowds of party loyalists, initially mobilized by the aim of prevailing in electoral politics, became transformed into mobs motivated by a desire to reconstitute or purify a transcendent racial community.

Through those processes, members of the crowd forged violent racial subjectivities: that is, a sense that they were bound together by a common obligation to exact racial vengeance. In using the word "pogrom" to describe their actions, my intention is to emphasize that these were "organized massacres" for the destruction or intimidation of a particular body or class—in this case, Arabs.[53] Such an emphasis places racial thought back at the center of the crowds' motives, contradicting the instrumentalist position that the killings were prompted by some other kind of subjectivity. At the same time, one should note that the word is usually understood to refer to *organized* massacres: most scholars recognize that pogroms are never the product of spontaneous, unthinking instinct. Yet the present case does not sustain the common assumption that behind every massacre stand state or party officials: contrary to ZNP allegations, there is no evidence that the killings were planned and supervised by the ASP leadership, let alone by colonial agents. While neighborhood party structures were indeed significant to the mobilization of many of the mobs, we shall see that the processes by which crowds were induced to direct their energies toward racial violence were premised on the ability of individual crowd members to command the disciplining power of discourse—to command, that is, what Das calls repositories of "organizing images, including rumours, that crowds use to define themselves and their victims."[54]

If we accept that racial mobs are as purposive in their actions as are more "rational" crowds, then we must also recognize that the aims of such mobs can differ dramatically. As we have seen, the overall casualty figures indicate that no one side had a monopoly on mob violence. But the one-sided fatalities indicate just as clearly that the violence of the ASP mobs was of a distinctive quality. This conclusion is further driven home when we consider the nature of the killings themselves. Donald Horowitz argues that even when ethnic killing falls short of genocide or ethnic cleansing, its discursive nature reveals the exterminationist logic behind it: while eliminating the target population may not be possible, degrading and dehumanizing them "is a good second-best" and may (and often does) prompt timidity and flight.[55] Hizbu propagandists, for all their reliance on racial categories and their demeaning language toward mainlanders, never envisioned an African-free Zanzibar; indeed, for them such a vision would have made no sense. ASP propaganda, in contrast, had often threatened expulsion and extermination. As we shall now see, a close examination of individual incidents from the June riots can suggest the intellectual processes by which many ordinary Zanzibaris became convinced of the need to act collectively to kill their Arab neighbors.

Racial Violence as Discourse

Details about individual pogroms are difficult to secure. Their emotion-laden symbolism, the very aspect that makes racial killings so different from other forms of political violence, also plays havoc with memories. Our most reliable contemporary sources, the trial records that resulted from the riots, have their own peculiar problems. As at the Foster-Sutton Commission hearings, the adversarial setting meant that many witnesses did their utmost to craft their testimony in ways they hoped would enhance its credibility. At the same time, many harbored deep partisan motives, often compounded by personal feelings of anger, grief, and shame. (Feelings of guilt or impugned innocence, on the other hand, were rarely relevant, because the accused usually made no statement other than a laconic denial—another limitation in the evidence.) These factors all contributed to shaping the testimony on which we must rely.

Such problems of evidence constituted the central reason that of all the murder trials arising from the riots, only one resulted in a conviction. The main obstacle, common in the prosecution of mob violence, lay in securing reliable identification of individual culprits. Of the many faces that flashed by in the brief span of a riot, victims and other witnesses usually identified only those they already knew by name—and, often, whom they associated with the ASP. In addition, many prosecution witnesses were coached by ZNP advisers, whose aggression in going after known ASP activists often undermined the credibility of their witnesses, obliging judges to acquit or prosecutors to drop charges altogether.[56] Nevertheless, if read critically, the trial records yield reliable (if anecdotal)[57] evidence about what motivated the killers and how their actions were understood at the time.

The basic shape of the pogroms and some of the problems involved in their interpretation can be seen in the first one recorded in the countryside. The incident occurred at Kitope Ndani, in the heart of an area that had endured particularly intense conflicts over squatter evictions and was racked by some of the fiercest clashes of the June riots. The mob at Kitope apparently intended to attack the family of Nassor bin Seif, a middle-aged Mmanga who had lived in the area for only nine months, leasing a farm and trading in coconuts. Early on the afternoon of 2 June, Nassor was visiting on the verandah of his neighbor, Amarsi Hansraji Raja, an Indian shopkeeper who had lived in the village since 1948. Amarsi's verandah was at the rear of his shop and house, facing Nassor bin Seif's own compound. Also present were two "other Arabs" (as Nassor put it), Abeid Suweid and Said Nassor, and a man identified as an "African," Simba Khatibu, who had come to buy oil from Amarsi's shop and had stopped to chat. Such relaxed social interaction is typical of Zanzibari rural life, especially given the place and time: the local *duka* just before or after *adhuhuri* prayers. We do not know what was being discussed on the verandah, but likely topics included the previous day's elections and the disturbances in town.

At around noon or one o'clock, Nassor bin Seif's eight-year-old son, Seif, came over to summon his father for lunch. Just then three men appeared, carrying clubs and *pangas* (machetes). Those sitting on the verandah were acquainted with the spokesman of the three, Miraji Selem, a 25-year-old squatter who managed the local ASP cooperative shop and coffeehouse. Upon his arrest Miraji identified himself ethnically as Zigua—that is, a mainlander from Tanganyika. But he had apparently grown up in Kitope; Amarsi had known him since he moved there, when Miraji was a boy of twelve. Significantly, neither Amarsi nor Nassor bin Seif knew Miraji's patronym; they knew only his given name. They knew Miraji, then, but not well—certainly far less than one would expect in such a small rural community. This might be taken as an indication of the unusually strained texture of social relations in Kitope after years of conflict over squatter rights and racial politics.

Miraji announced his intention to transgress all civil ties by refusing to respond properly to Nassor bin Seif's greeting. Greetings in Swahili society are famously formalized, a central mechanism by which civility is maintained in daily interactions; failure to offer a genial reply is considered the height of rudeness. Because the trial transcripts are in English only and Amarsi and Nassor differed slightly in their testimony, there is some uncertainty concerning the exact terms of Miraji's insult. Nassor evidently used the standard *salama aleikum*, "peace be upon us," to which Miraji, instead of echoing Nassor with the customary *wa-aleiku salaam*, countered *hakuna salama*, "there is no peace."[58]

During this encounter, a large crowd surrounded Amarsi's and Nassor's houses, which some began to pelt with stones. At a signal from Miraji or another of the three intruders already in the compound, the mob attacked, some shouting "Kill them! Strike them!" as they pursued the men who fled from the verandah. Abeid Suweid and Said Nassor were killed within moments; Nassor bin Seif testified that he saw the latter struck to the ground with a club and surrounded by men who then hacked at him repeatedly with *pangas*. This accords with the coroner's report. (As no charges were brought in Abeid's death, we know nothing of his wounds.) Nassor bin Seif, wounded on the shoulder by a *panga*, fled toward his house. Looking back, he saw his young son prostrate on Amarsi's verandah, Miraji's foot planted on his back. Miraji held the boy's head with one hand, a *panga* with the other. At that moment Nassor was struck in the belly with an arrow, and he scrambled into his house to get a gun.

Amarsi, meanwhile, had bolted himself in his shop. When the mob broke down the doors and shutters, Amarsi, wounded with a *panga* blow, pled for his life, offering the intruders money in exchange. They accepted; Amarsi gave them 300 shillings. Amarsi then heard the report of a gun, which the wounded Nassor bin Seif had managed to fire through the window of his house, and the intruders dispersed. The entire incident took no more than twenty or twenty-five minutes. Simba Khatibu, who was chased by the mob but not struck, ran off to Mahonda to inform the police, who arrived about an hour later and found the three bodies lying in the compound where they fell. The coroner later reported that the eight-year-old Seif was killed by a single slashing blow to the back of the neck.[59]

It is unclear who this crowd was, how it had been mobilized, and why it attacked these particular houses. The ten originally charged in the death of Said Nassor were all mainlanders. One should be cautious about accepting these ten as representative of the entire mob.[60] As in most riot situations, those who faced charges consisted solely of people known personally to the key witnesses,

Amarsi and Nassor bin Seif, who possibly harbored anti-mainlander prejudices. In other parts of the island, the mobs had a greater mix of indigenous islanders. But given what we know of the Kitope area, which was heavily settled
by squatter labor, the witnesses' characterization of this crowd as composed
primarily of mainlanders seems plausible. It was accepted by the police, who
in other instances showed no prejudices in that direction and refused to characterize mobs ethnically.

The tensions over evictions undoubtedly had sharpened the resentments
of the squatters who participated in the Kitope riot and in the many other incidents that plagued this corner of the sultanate. But such attacks cannot be interpreted simply as manifestations of a socioeconomic conflict between landlords and squatter labor. The Kitope mob did not attack Nassor bin Seif because
he was a landlord; in fact, he was himself a tenant and had not even been in the
neighborhood at the height of the eviction crisis in 1958–1959. Most victims in
the rural areas, as we have seen, were Wamanga rather than members of elite
landholding families. If squatter subjectivities entered the mob's motivations
at all, they had become subsumed to racialized group subjectivities: in oppress-
ing squatters, Arabs were perceived to be acting as members of a racial category (rather than a socioeconomic one) who had it in for Africans (rather than
for laborers). (As we have seen, the history of the squatter crisis comes closer
to this interpretation than to simple economistic ones.) And many perceived
Wamanga such as Nassor bin Seif and his family as a metonym for the entire
category—a category that in the preceding years had been described and re-
defined in the mutually reinforcing rhetoric of racial politics.

At the Foster-Sutton hearings Police Superintendant Wright vaguely suggested that the Kitope mob may have been connected with a criminal gang,
comprised mostly of squatters and mainlanders, that had been committing offenses against "Arab property" in the area since early that day.[61] If this were
true, the implication would be that pecuniary objectives were as important to
the Kitope mob as racialized ones—an implication that seems borne out by
their acceptance of Amarsi's payoff. Still, the police never offered anything specific about the criminal gang's link with the Kitope mob, and their suspicions of
a connection seem to have been based on rumor or hearsay. That does not necessarily render those suspicions inaccurate, but one must ask whether Wright
and others had allowed images of racial-political transgression, like those of the
Kitope mob, to become melded with images of criminal transgression, especially when the transgressors in both cases were mainlanders and the property
looted or robbed was owned by Arabs. As we saw in chapter 6, the riots encour-

aged popular perceptions that habitual criminals were motivated by racial politics or racial terror—perceptions that some of those criminals no doubt welcomed. On 1 June in the Ng'ambo neighborhood of Mikunguni, for example, a
petty thug mugged his Arab neighbor at knifepoint, demanding money as she
fled from a mob. This thug, however, was also an ASP activist, who earlier that
day had served as a poll watcher and participated in the battle at Darajani. Acts
like his blurred the distinction between political and criminal violence.[62]

Caught up in the atmosphere of the riots, even criminals with no previous
history of political involvement might find considerations of racial vengeance
creeping into how they thought of their transgressions. At the southern village
of Kichungwani on 3 June, at the height of the pogroms in the countryside, a
small band of about eight local men, none of whom had ever shown an interest
in politics, besieged a *duka* where the Arab shopkeeper and his family had bar-
ricaded themselves. In the course of the attack the shopkeeper was stoned to
death. Though the police were certain that this gang's motives were purely
criminal, the robbers' debates as they ransacked the shop over whether to kill
the shopkeeper's wife and children (a phenomenon to which we will return)
suggest that some confused notions of racial extermination had become mixed
in. In any case, this criminal attack, like the 1963 Vitongoji murder whose victim was conflated by rumor with the victim of a shark attack (see chapter 6),
entered the raging popular discourse about racial terror.[63]

The processes by which a criminal act might develop into an act of racial
terror are suggested in an incident that took place at Mgambo, not far from Kitope Ndani. All the principals in this incident were squatters on two adjacent
estates and all were Wamakonde, with the exception of Suzana Kisandi and
her immediate neighbor Bakari Ali, who were from north-central and northeastern Tanganyika, respectively. At 9:30 PM on 4 June, Suzana was visited by
the father and uncle of a child who lived with her. They and a third man who accompanied them were armed with spears, *pangas,* and bows and arrows. They
had come to make a demand concerning the child and an argument ensued, the
exact nature of which is unclear. After they departed, Suzana, Bakari Ali, and
a third neighbor took the precaution of leaving their wattle-and-thatch homes
to spend the night in the empty stone house that belonged to the landlord,
Abdallah Said. (That the house was empty is not surprising: Abdallah Said may
have fled to town for safety, as had many Arabs after violence erupted, or his
primary residence may have been in town, as was common among the landholding elite.) In court there was disagreement about why Suzana and the others had taken refuge in the landlord's house. The child's uncle claimed Suzana

had expressed fears that Arabs were plotting to slaughter mainlanders. But Suzana insisted it was the uncle and his companions who had frightened her.

At about 1 AM, Suzana and the others were awakened by a torrent of stones being rained on the house. Bakari shone a flashlight on the attackers, who were revealed to be a gang of about fifteen men, armed, again, with the emblematic spears, *pangas*, and bows and arrows. Bakari and Suzana recognized five of them as their neighbors, including the child's father and uncle, and when they called out to them by name, the whole gang disappeared into the night. The next day Bakari filed a complaint with the police. Summarizing the evidence, the magistrate who tried the case, A. S. Mohammed, said he had "no doubt" that the gang's intent had been not to attack Suzana but to burglarize what they thought was an empty house. When they instead encountered people who knew them by name, they fled.[64]

None of the factors that gave rise to this incident—the personal quarrel about the child, the criminal intent of the gang that stoned the landlord's country house—had anything to do with racial politics, and in the end no one was harmed. But it is easy to imagine how it might have developed into a pogrom had Abdallah Said been home. The fears that gripped Suzana and the others, whether of Arab threats or armed Wamakonde, were informed by the general atmosphere of the ongoing riots. (That Suzana and Bakari were themselves mainlanders does not contradict this. As we have seen, stereotypes about Makonde violence were pervasive and could prompt fears even among mainlanders.) That same atmosphere, in all probability, also informed the decision to burglarize Abdallah Said's house. In going about armed, the would-be burglars gave Suzana the impression, as they must give us, that they were at least anticipating violence, if not planning it. One must wonder, then, what might have happened if, instead of being surprised by people whom they knew intimately, they had been confronted by the landlord himself.

The evidence linking the Kitope mob to ASP party politics is much more reliable than that linking it to criminal gangs, though the exact nature of the link is difficult to determine. The mob's political sympathies are plainly indicated by the timing of its rampage, which stemmed from an awareness of the political conflict in town the day before, and, as in other instances, the ASP became involved in the legal defense of those charged in the murders. Most pointedly, the evidence highlights the role played by Miraji, the local ASP organizer. Again, one should be wary of the testimony against him, especially given the limited range of witnesses in the Kitope trials. We know nothing of Nassor bin Seif's political sympathies or of his brother's, who testified that he saw armed crowds gathered at the ASP cooperative an hour or two before the attack. (The latter detail, however, conforms with what we know of other incidents from the riots, in which party hangouts served as staging posts.) Amarsi Hansraji was probably a ZNP sympathizer.[65] Such doubts are exactly what made the courts mistrust testimony that identified specific participants in mob actions. Yet the overall evidence against Miraji, including his self-incriminating behavior after arrest, seems strong, and it convinced the otherwise skeptical court to sentence him to hang for the murder of Nassor bin Seif's child—the sole murder conviction resulting from the June riots.[66]

So there is little reason to doubt that Miraji played a key role. But the trial witnesses may well have embellished it, thus clouding our ability to understand how the Kitope mob was organized. We have seen that in general, political authority over the crowds was ambiguous and improvised. Yet Nassor, in particular, made Miraji's authority seem relatively straightforward, perhaps in an attempt to reinforce Miraji's guilt in his boy's death.[67] We must wonder if the mob really was so disciplined as to withhold its attack until receiving Miraji's signal (a tap with his stick) or if Miraji's "lieutenant" struck Nassor only upon being ordered to do so. That this crowd showed elements of coordination is indisputable. The same was true of other mobs during the June riots. But it was not simply an arm of the local party apparatus.

In sum, then, the evidence points to the racial motivations of the Kitope mob. Resentments borne of their experiences as squatters no doubt played a role in prompting many to participate in the mob's depredations, as did simple greed. But the most common unifying factor was the racialized political rhetoric that had been intensifying steadily over the previous decade. In this sense, the crowd's loyalty to the ASP made it more likely to heed the leadership of party activists such as Miraji, but there is no evidence that it was a disciplined party cadre. Rather, what unified the members of the mob was their common response to discursive practices that invoked images of favored and reviled racial categories. Whatever other aims may have prompted individuals to join the mob, during the course of the pogrom those aims became subordinated to the common purpose of harming or intimidating Arabs—not simply in order to seize Arab assets or deprive Arabs of political power but to dehumanize them and thus purge them from the moral community. The June riots, in other words, were acts of consciously dehumanizing transgression; they were not instrumental but purposively discursive.

The most straightforward example of discursive violence during the riots was the display of blood. The political journalists were already well practiced in using the language of blood to sharpen readers' fears and resentments. The metaphor of "bloodsucking" was common in descriptions of Arab oppression, and ASP journalists used lurid language to accuse their rivals (including those within the party) of plotting bloody massacres.[68] During the riots this discursive technique took more literal forms, which, given the context, were capable of eliciting more visceral responses.

Beginning on the morning of 2 June, observers noted the decapitated bodies of chickens, cats, and bushbabies strewn about in major thoroughfares, including the central town market.[69] (For perhaps obvious reasons, all that remained of the chickens were the heads.) This unnerving spectacle may have had a simple explanation. In the weeks leading up to the riots, politicians on both sides alleged that their opponents were planning to spread panic on election day by smearing themselves with animal blood. The specifics of the allegations varied. Some claimed that ASP activists planned to bloody their hands to make it appear that they themselves had been on the warpath. But the more common claim by both sides was that their opponents planned to use the sight of blood-soaked clothes to feign having been attacked. While it is difficult to ascertain the veracity of these allegations, there is evidence that "riot specialists" were not above using such deceptions to incite crowds to violence. On 1 June, as Karume was being ferried about town in attempts to calm the situation, a boy with a bloodied leg was paraded before one crowd as the victim of Arab brutality. Smithyman and Karume revealed the falsehood (the boy had cut the sole of his foot on broken glass), thus preventing a riot.[70]

But this relatively prosaic explanation cannot account for why the animal bodies were strewn about in public places. (Indeed, one would expect the perpetrators to have concealed their deception.) British witnesses at the Foster-Sutton hearings, noting that such behavior was common during ethnic clashes in other parts of the world, interpreted it as an example of the "blood lust" that had overtaken the combatants.[71] Though it would be mistaken to accept the implication that such acts were signs of atavistic madness, we must recognize that they could have had the effect, probably intended, of inducing fears of such madness.[72] Writing of similar behavior during the Troubles in Northern Ireland, Allen Feldman notes that massacring animals as substitutes for human victims or in anticipation of human victims can signal profoundly unsettling messages about the impending transgression of all civil ties with one's enemies. By suggesting that certain categories of people can be slaughtered with as little difficulty, moral or physical, as animals, such massacres convey potent threats linked to the dehumanizing logic of racial politics.[73]

Blood and wounds, then, were not simply rhetorical devices used to spread messages about the victimization of the racial self and the need to seek revenge; they were also used to reinforce the dehumanization of the racial other. This observation applies with particular force to the specifics of the human killings themselves. At the end of the last chapter I referred to some of the ways the killers demonstrated an awareness of the discursive power of their acts: the repeated wounding of an already-dead body and the quasi-ritualized use of emblematic weapons such as spears. Another indication that the mobs were motivated by more than a simple desire to end their victims' lives was the prevalence of particular kinds of wounds. Head wounds were especially common (in the Kitope case the coroner testified that the already-prostrate Said Nassor had sustained multiple wounds to his head), as were semi-decapitations like that of eight-year-old Seif.[74] This suggests an attempt to destroy the essence of what made victims distinct human individuals: their faces, their intellects, their ability to speak.

The disembowelment of women was a wound that attained a particularly high profile, becoming the stuff of much rumor, propaganda, and fantasy. It appears frequently in the global annals of racial and ethnic violence. It is usually understood to signal an attack on the enemy's ability to reproduce; that is, it is a discursive act shaped by the idiom of descent that underlies all racial thought.[75] (Given a context in which combatants and political actors are assumed to be male, it also signals, like the widespread use of rape, an assault on the enemy's manhood; that is, on his ability to fulfill the masculine function of protecting and controlling his women.)[76] In Zanzibar, it echoed historical narratives about the cruelties of "Arab" slavery: Titi Muhammad's speeches about the disembowelment of pregnant slaves were evidently taken as threats, at least by the ASP's opponents.[77]

Rumors about such wounds, amplified after the fact by the political press, were no doubt far more common than the wounds themselves.[78] But the discrepancy only emphasizes their discursive power. The most pointed demonstration of that power, in fact, was a case in which no disembowelment occurred. On 3 June in the Ng'ambo neighborhood of Mwembemimba, a mob stoned and ransacked the home and *duka* of an Arab shopkeeper, killing his pregnant wife. (The place name lent the incident some mythic aura: "Mwembemimba" means mango tree of the fetus or pregnancy.) The evidence of this attack's savagery was indisputable, including the brutality with which the woman was murdered: the coroner testified that she was killed by a heavy blow by *panga* or axe to the base of the neck, which severed her spinal cord. Yet although the coroner found no other wounds, the victim's husband and two teenage sons insisted that they also saw her disemboweled by one of the two men they accused of leading the mob. The husband was particularly adamant, stressing the nature of the wound and his wife's pregnant condition. Given such testimony, the bewildered judge felt compelled to acquit.[79]

The shopkeeper and his sons admitted that the two men they accused were the only members of the mob they recognized: both were regular customers, and at least one was a well-known ASP activist. (In fact, he was the same activist who was convicted of trying to rob his neighbor in Mikunguni on the first day of the riots.) So they may have felt prompted to level these specific charges by a sense of personal betrayal and/or political loyalty. Or they may have noticed or imagined the accused at the head of the mob simply because the two men were well known in the neighborhood for their ASP associations. But there remains the puzzling question of why the witnesses insisted on the one detail that undermined their credibility. Having had to endure watching their wife and mother murdered (and having been brutalized themselves), they may well have sincerely imagined her disembowelment. If so, this would be a remarkable instance of the ability of racial discourse to shape the perceptions of people caught up in racial violence. Alternately, or in addition, their testimony may have been an especially egregious instance of ZNP witness tampering. Either way, the case points to a peculiarly circular discourse, an instance of what Comaroff describes as the reciprocal dehumanization characteristic of ethnic thought. ASP rhetoric about Arabs' inhumanity toward their slaves inspired similar acts against Arab women in revenge or threats and rumors of such acts; victims of the June mobs imagined those same acts as evidence of the inhumanity of their African attackers.

The intentional killing of children can also be understood as expressive of an assault on the reproduction of the racial other. The statistics do not break down the June casualties by age, so we do not know how common such assaults were. But they were numerous enough to constitute pointed evidence that the June pogroms were shaped by racial discourse: no matter what form they took, such murders can have had nothing to do with efforts to loot property or prevent the ZNP from winning power. Like the other acts I've been describing, the killing of children was not the product of blind thoughtlessness but had understood meaning. It was considered the ultimate act of dehumanizing transgression—so much so that even in the most brutal mobs, many thought it beyond the pale. Nassor bin Seif's son Seif, for example, had a younger brother, five-year-old Suleiman, who was seized in the earliest moments of the Kitope pogrom but sustained only minor scrapes. Though Miraji (or whoever killed Seif) was clearly gripped by a profound sense that Arabs, including Arab children, were less than human, those who manhandled little Suleiman, though undoubtedly sharing the same general hatreds, were evidently unable to overcome humanizing inhibitions.

Nassor bin Seif's image of Miraji pausing before he struck Seif, then, has the ring of truth; one wants to believe Miraji was hesitating. In fact, there are at least three documented cases in which mobs paused to debate whether to kill children and decided to spare them. I have already mentioned one, at Kichungwani, although racial motives were apparently secondary in that case. More striking was the behavior of the mob at Mitikawani, described at the close of the last chapter. As we saw, that assault had all the hallmarks of a classic racial pogrom, shaped by the discourses of dehumanization; it also showed signs of planning and leadership, including the coordinated provision of stones with which to terrorize the family before attacking. The victims' four daughters had to watch as their parents were killed and their bodies mutilated. But when one of the mob called on his comrades to kill the girls too, an argument ensued and they were spared.[80]

It is in this regard that some of the darkest tales from June also yield a few glimmers of light. Among the most revealing was a pogrom that took place on 3 June at the village of Pangeni, in the north of the island. We have unusually fine-grained evidence of this incident, and perhaps for that reason it supplies some details that are extraordinarily compelling. As a whole this mob showed itself as determined as any to hunt down Arabs. Its first victim was Ali bin Swed, a Manga immigrant resident at Pangeni for only a month, whose wife, Salima binti Abdulla, had given birth the night before to their third child. (The other children were aged three and five.) The mob killed Ali bin Swed in a cassava field behind his house. Some then pursued Salima and her Arab midwife, Amina binti Hemed, who at the first sounds of trouble had hurried the older children into the house. The mob broke down the doors and windows and ransacked room after room, shouting to each other as they searched for the women. Three finally burst into the inner room where Salima and Amina had taken refuge. They did not notice the midwife and toddlers, hidden under a bed, but they slashed at Salima with *pangas* and a spear. One of the intruders then did something remarkable. He placed a bedstead on top of the fallen Salima, placed a large box on top of that, and announced, as Salima later testified, that "they should leave me as I was already dead." The three then left the room. A few moments later Salima heard someone in the hallway recall that there was a second woman. Two men then reentered the room, dragged Amina from under the bed and killed her with *pangas* and the spear.[81]

Salima recognized the man who had hidden her as John Alikumbeya, who had once worked for her and her husband, but she offered no explanation of his behavior. One suspects that, looking down at the prostrate Salima, he saw that she was in fact alive, saw the newborn in her arms, and placed the bedstead and box over her to hide both sights from his comrades. But someone in the mob remembered that Salima had been carrying an infant, and out in the hallway an argument ensued over whether they ought to kill it too. No need, said another (could it have been John Alikumbeya?); now that its parents are dead it would not survive. The exchange is revealing. It suggests a common assumption that the infant ought to die along with its parents, an assumption that could stem only from racial reasoning about the need to exterminate the entire family. But it also suggests that the assumption was not deeply felt—at least, not deeply enough to persuade the killers to overcome their scruples about taking the life of an infant.[82]

The disparity between the murder of Seif bin Nassor at Kitope and the sparing of his brother Suleiman and all three of Salima's children reminds us how misleading it can be to characterize a mob by a single mentality. In the Pangeni case, even the mob's murderous vanguard, the handful who stormed into the house hunting for Salima and Amina, were compromised by people whom Gourevitch might call backsliders into moderation (moderation being defined in relative terms, of course). We must also consider those members of the mobs, perhaps the majority, who merely stoned the houses of Nassor bin Seif and Ali bin Swed and went on their way. The significance of their behavior depends in part on how large the mob was. Yet even if the Kitope mob (for example) was not as large as Nassor claimed, it clearly had the physical capacity to inflict far greater harm than it did. If most of the Kitope mob were gripped by the same murderous rage as Miraji, why then were Nassor's two wives, like little Suleiman, relatively unscathed?[83]

When writing of communal riots, there is a danger of failing to note the significance of a phenomenon more common than murder: the *refusal* to kill. In an essay describing his struggle to find a way to write about what he observed during the anti-Sikh pogroms of 1984, the novelist Amitav Ghosh notes that the story of neighbors turning on one another was not the only or even the most compelling drama. Neighbors—and strangers—also reached across communal divides to protect one another, often at risk to their lives.[84] Unfortunately, criminal trials and official commissions of inquiry are geared not toward documenting such human goodness but toward ascertaining guilt (and, for the prosecutors, dramatizing it). Yet stories of Africans protecting their Arab neighbors in June 1961 even find their way into the trial records, if only in the margins. At Pangeni, for example, the mob's second target was the home and shop of Ali bin Swed's neighbor, Said Abdulla. After allowing Said's wife, Raya, to leave with her children, they set fire to the house, cutting down the fleeing Said as Raya watched from nearby. But some in the mob then changed their mind and started toward Raya. An African stranger grabbed Raya's hand and rushed her and the children to the wattle-and-thatch "hut" of a certain Binti Juma, an elderly African woman. Salima and her children were already hiding there, as was a prominent local Arab, Rashid Athuman. The refugees remained in the cramped dwelling until morning.

Such behavior required considerable courage—mobs were known to threaten servants or guests for being loyal to "their Arabs"—and its frequency is testimony to the limited depth of dehumanizing discourse in the minds of many or most Zanzibaris.[85] But its effectiveness was muted by the overall atmosphere in which individuals were intimidated into behaving as members of a racial category. This could be seen at the trial of the knife-wielding ASP thug who tried to rob his neighbor at Mikunguni, Ng'ambo. His would-be victim was a 22-year-old mother of three, who, panic-stricken, had tried to flee a mob that was breaking into her family's small shop and home. After being struck to the ground in a nearby alleyway, she was rescued by a middle-aged stranger who helped her to her feet, found one of the children who had run off, and escorted all four back to the courtyard of her house. There they encountered the ASP activist, Muhammad Chum, who, evidently having just helped ransack the house, demanded the young woman give him money. She and her oldest daughter testified that the unarmed stranger defied Chum and browbeat him into leaving.[86]

The evidence against Muhammad Chum was substantial; in his own testimony, which was otherwise contradictory and wildly improbable, he admitted having been present. But the Samaritan himself, a Shirazi named Sleyum bin Ramadhan, surprisingly denied having seen or spoken to Chum that day. In voting nevertheless to convict, the judges explained that on this point they had chosen not to believe Sleyum, who had not wanted to identify Chum in open court "for reasons best known to himself." Those reasons are not hard to guess. Muhammad Chum was a well-known neighborhood activist and ASP enforcer;[87] at his trial he boasted of his martial skills and his experience (perhaps feigned) as a professional soldier, which he had put to the party's service on voting day. In the heat of the riot, Sleyum's first impulse had been to ignore racial boundaries and help a stranger in trouble. But upon reflection, he evidently felt it would be prudent to do nothing on the witness stand that might draw attention to himself as the enemy of a party activist and with it the charge of race betrayal.

The significance of stories like Sleyum's and Binti Juma's is not that some Zanzibaris were unaffected by racial discourse. Such people may have existed, but they were undoubtedly less common than others who, though they deemed their neighbors different for belonging to another racial category and perhaps even mistrusted them for that, nevertheless considered them still their neighbors, still members of the same moral (or human) community. In many ways, the greatest tragedy concerned the processes by which such people were compelled into complicity in racial killing despite their better impulses. We have mentioned how an entire mob could be made directly complicit by the mutual insistence that each member inflict a wound on the victim's already-fallen body. Individuals could also be coerced into joining a mob in the first place. Such complicity could be especially powerful in lending material reality to the discourses of race by providing a powerful psychological incentive for the reluctant killers to accept the logic of exterminationist hatred. The resulting behavior in turn confirmed the belief among the victimized category that "they" are all the same, all killers, none to be trusted.

These and several of the other themes we've been examining are illustrated by another story from Pangeni, one that captures much of the horror and pathos of the race riot. Its central character was the assistant *sheha* for the neighborhood, Juma Ambari, who spent the hours before the pogrom warning local Arabs of the impending trouble and urging them to take precautions. A government physician later described Juma as sickly and feeble. He was 71 years old and identified himself ethnically as Nyasa; in other words, he had probably been born a slave. As assistant *sheha,* Juma Ambari's standing in the community was particularly delicate. Unlike mudirs, who were recruited from the educated Arab elite and appointed by the central administration, *masheha* were elected locally by public acclaim (though appointed only with the approval of the mudir and the DC). But at the same time, *masheha* and assistant *masheha* were expected to serve as village-level representatives of the administration and conduits for official orders. Thus they had to oblige two opposed sets of constituents. By the interwar years, the heads of locally powerful families had learned to nominate weak men for the posts to ensure that the *masheha* remained under their influence.[88]

During the Time of Politics many *masheha* found their position increasingly precarious: whereas the government forbade any public official from participating in politics, the local populace often demanded that the *sheha* take a side.[89] Many mudirs found it easy to ignore the ban on partisanship, since their Hizbu sympathies were shared by most of the elite Arabs who supervised them, and during the 1957 election campaign mudirs often leaned on their *masheha* to support the ZNP.[90] But in heavily ASP areas such as Pangeni, popular pressures worked the other way, especially once the political parties began actively contesting the selection of *masheha*. In the early 1960s many *masheha* were accused of actively supporting the ASP.[91]

As he paid private visits to Pangeni's Arab families late in the morning of 3 June, Juma Ambari appeared to be trying to negotiate a middle course between a genuine concern for his neighbors' safety and a fear of the angry crowd that was gathering outside the ASP cooperative on the main road. Among those he visited was Rashid Athuman, who because of his age (60) and length of residence was regarded as a senior figure in the local Arab community. He and Juma Ambari had long known and trusted one another; when Rashid first arrived in Pangeni in 1949 he had stayed as Juma's guest. Juma now appeared at his old friend's home to tell of his fears, and he urged Rashid to gather the local Arabs together to defend themselves.

A few hours later, Rashid's neighbor Ali bin Swed received a different kind of visitor. Mtumwa Hassan was a 27-year-old agricultural laborer who identified himself ethnically as Hadimu; several witnesses had seen him earlier that day among the growing crowd at the ASP cooperative. He now appeared at Ali bin Swed's, angrily demanding wages he said were owed him for work he had done on cassava fields behind Ali's house. A quarrel ensued, the central issue being the amount of work Mtumwa had performed. Ali suggested that Mtumwa go find Juma Ambari to mediate.

When the aged assistant *sheha* arrived, he was uneasy. Another visitor at Ali bin Swed's that day (a local African) had seen the crowd assembling on the main road and, knowing that Juma Ambari shared his concern, urged him to send for help from the police at Mkokotoni. But Juma said it couldn't be done; the crowds would attack anyone who tried to pass. He then accompanied Mtumwa and Ali bin Swed into the disputed cassava field to measure the rows that Mtumwa had cultivated. The argument was now loud enough to be heard from the house. Meanwhile, Amina binti Hemed, the midwife, who had been out, saw the armed crowd coming down the road. She ran to alert Rashid Athuman, begging him to investigate. The two headed into the cassava field, where they saw the three men arguing. (By this time the men in the field may have been joined by a fourth, John Alikumbeya.) At the same moment the approaching mob also turned toward the cassava field, its attention apparently drawn by the sound of the argument. The midwife, alarmed, rushed back to the house to warn Salima and the children.

As the mob caught sight of the men arguing in the cassava field—two or three Africans and one Arab (the latter readily recognizable as such)—some reportedly shouted, "What are you waiting for? Hit him! Kill him!" Rashid, the sole eyewitness to testify in court about this moment, stated that Juma Ambari struck the first blow, with a *panga*. There was no reason for Rashid to invent this detail about his old friend, who that very morning had gone out of his way to alert him and Pangeni's other Arabs. It is easy to imagine what transpired at that moment. Although he was a mainlander, Juma knew he was already compromised in the eyes of the mob because of his service as an assistant *sheha* and his friendship with prominent Arabs such as Rashid. He may also have feared that the mob knew of his activities that morning. And with the belligerent Mtumwa standing beside him, he would have felt triply threatened by the shouts of the mob, shouts that challenged him to demonstrate his racial loyalty. Thus, consumed with fear, he struck Ali bin Swed. But the weak old man could not have struck the fatal blow, which was so forceful it severed Ali's spinal chord.[92]

This scene does more than illustrate how fundamentally decent people could be turned into racial killers. It also encapsulates some of the broader themes with which I began this chapter. From close up the argument that culminated in Ali bin Swed's murder looked like a personal, private matter—a dispute about labor and wages and, perhaps, grievances between a patron and his client about gratitude and loyalty. That is probably how the dispute seemed to Ali bin Swed. But from a distance—from the perspective of the crowd moving down the road—it appeared as a conflict rooted in race. Such perceptions are not simply those of the colonial elite, as is suggested by some of the literature on South Asia. Few in the crowd could have known anything specific about Ali bin Swed: he was evidently not a landlord,[93] and he had not been in the area long enough to have developed a reputation for any activities specific to himself. The crowd saw him simply as an Arab shopkeeper who was arguing with one or several Africans. (They voiced that perception concisely as they pursued Rashid: "Here's one!" they cried.) This chapter's central story, and its central tragedy, concerns how the mob's perceptions were transformed into reality at the moment that Juma Ambari, trembling, lifted his *panga*.

8

"June" as Chosen Trauma

Indeed, what was the Great Fear if not one gigantic rumour?
—Georges Lefebvre, *The Great Fear of 1789*

By the time the sultanate celebrated its newly won independence in December 1963, countless Zanzibaris on both sides of the political divide had come to harbor "memories" of violent racial victimization that seemed to confirm the worst of what was being said by the ideologues of ethnic nationalism. Two mechanisms produced this effect. One was the experience of mob violence, chiefly the pogroms of June 1961 but also the countless smaller incidents that punctuated the closing years of the Time of Politics. As I have argued, such incidents were discursive acts, intended to convey threats of exclusion from the moral community whose contours were concurrently being debated by the nationalists. The other mechanism was the circulation of rumors, particularly rumors about past and anticipated violence. Rumors were notable for their ability to render ideology or fantasy in the form of remembered experience, which in turn could prompt individuals to take up arms or act in other ways that gave such fantasies material form.

In the months following June 1961, rumors and political speech from all sides transformed the riots into a "chosen trauma," an event invested with mythic meanings of victimization, dogged survival, and deferred revenge.[1] Hizbu propaganda highlighted the barbarism of the killers by emphasizing the helplessness of their victims, describing them as the elderly and infirm, as children and expectant mothers.[2] Such massacre motifs are common in the ethnonationalist rhetoric of historical "memory." But it is also common for the aggressors to recast their own experience as that of victims, pushed to kill by their enemies' provocations. Accordingly, ASP ideologues focused on the election itself, which they characterized as the second one that had been stolen from them. While Hizbu described the riots with the language of massacre, the ASP used the language of war and warned of a repeat if Hizbu didn't stop acting as if their ill-gained election victory gave them the right to abuse Africans.[3] Although during the heat of the riots party leaders had attempted to rein in their followers, in the riots' aftermath propagandists on both sides did what they could to keep alive memories of the violence and all the fears and anger they aroused.

Much discussion focused on the trials themselves, especially the failures to win murder convictions. ASP activists trumpeted the acquittals as an indication that the Hizbu-controlled government was harassing "black people" with false charges while the Arab "vote thieves" roamed free, brandishing daggers and scimitars.[4] *Agozi* assured its readers that British justice would prevail. (As we will see, the growing ASP conviction that Britain stood on their side played into ZNP propaganda.) All this encouraged the militants of the Afro-Shirazi Youth League to continue their threatening poses.[5] Hizbu's journalists also followed the trials. They too were at first confident in the courts, but that did not soften their language: some party leaders demanded public hangings. And by 1963 they were outraged that only a single murder conviction had been obtained.[6]

Memories of the riots kept the sultanate jittery throughout its remaining months. Fears focused especially on the next round of elections, slated for July 1963, and on the shape of the postcolonial government those elections would create. But in the generally tense atmosphere, even the most minor scuffle— a traffic accident, for example—could become infused with racial tensions prompted by memories of "June."[7] Many of those "memories," of course, were imagined, just as much of the "racial" violence that was their subject matter became construed as such only after the fact, by rumor and propaganda. But that did not diminish their power to shape the attitudes and actions people took in subsequent crises.

This chapter will explore the fears and rumors that circulated after June 1961 and ask how they served to give racial and other hegemonic discourses the power of lived experience. The post-June period provides us with rich sources for those processes, partly because the riots jolted the government into keeping close tabs on popular rumor via the newly formed district intelligence committees. But the main reason to concentrate on this period is the extent to which memories (and "memories") of the riots transformed Zanzibari political discourse, making it more violent than before. "June" became a simple byword that was capable of conjuring up conflicting fears and violent fantasies. (Its power can be gauged in the mythopoeic role it continued to play even after the revolution. Among Zanzibaris with long political memories, "June" retains these connotations today; although they sometimes mistake the year, they never mistake the month.)[8] Thus, an examination of rumor during these months can serve as a vital background to understanding the far vaster killings of January 1964.

By the closing years of the Time of Politics, administrators as well as party activists had come to appreciate the degree to which rumors could mobilize crowds or at least shape crowd action. They had also become keenly aware of the dense links between rumor and political propaganda. This latter understanding should warn us against treating rumor as if it were capable of expressing some pristine, authentic subaltern subjectivity. Such an unsullied subaltern subjectivity is as much a chimera as is a purely "spontaneous" crowd. In fact, we will see that some of the most compelling rumors from this period reproduced the globally hegemonic ideologies associated with the Cold War, in which events at the most local level were understood to have been determined by forces wholly external to Zanzibar and East Africa. These ideologies were gaining increasing prominence in how intellectuals imagined their projects of constructing political modernity. But they also played central roles in reproducing the discourses of racial fear.

The 1963 Election and Fears of Self-Government

During the 1963 election campaign, propagandists from both sides drew on memories of June in ways that seemed calculated to spark rumors of warning and threat. Hizbu and ZPPP speakers urged audiences to remember the barbarism of June, promising that upon independence they would put the perpetrators to death.[9] ASP speakers, warning that Hizbu was back to its old habit of "stealing votes," vaguely threatened another June.[10] Hizbu spread its rival's threats and amplified them, telling audiences that the ASP was advocating mass murder. The senior DC, Yahya Alawi, observed that whether or not such allegations were true, "The mention of the words 'kill' and 'blood' if repeated so often . . . could have an adverse effect in the minds of certain people in both camps." The bombardment of words continued thick and fast, as politicians became enmeshed in cycles of accusation and counteraccusation.[11]

Open political speech fed into and off of rumors that circulated among followers of both parties, rendering the rumors more credible. Throughout late 1962 and the first half of 1963, reports spread that ASP cells were plotting a repeat of the June election-day riots in an effort to intimidate Hizbu supporters from going to the polls.[12] A variant held that the Youth League was plotting massacres and even revolution should the ASP lose the July election. (Hindsight suggests the latter rumors had some basis in fact.) Saud Ahmed Busaidi, a longtime officer in the Provincial Administration—and a royalist who was notorious for his enmity toward squatters—added that mainlanders in the squatter districts planned to don *kanzu,* the flowing white robes characteristic of Muslim gentility, to conceal their weapons.[13] These false nationals thus would disguise their barbarism beneath what had become virtually a Zanzibari national dress, the emblem of male *ustaarabu.*

Such fantasies about mainlanders are a pointed indicator of the fears that circulated throughout the months in question. There was a resurgence of rumors about Makonde bogeymen; at Machui, the sight of Wamakonde sharpening a spear induced fears of an impending riot. Such fears were especially prominent in Pemba, where widespread anti-mainlander sentiments were encouraged by ZNP-ZPPP political speech.[14] Memories of June also contributed to an intensification of the discourse of mainlander criminality. In chapter 6, we saw how rumors about disparate crimes became elaborated into mythic narratives of racial-political terror. Such anxieties were understandably acute immediately following the June riots, but they continued throughout the period. In July 1962, for example, the ZPPP newssheet *Sauti ya Wananchi* used the story of a robbery and triple murder in a village not far from Kitope Ndani to hammer home messages about its political opponents. The paper described the killings as an act of racial terror and a revival of the events of June 1961. The code words used to describe the killers—barbarians, irreligious beasts—echoed the paper's overall rhetoric about mainlanders.[15]

Sauti ya Wananchi's strident anti-mainlander rhetoric was part of a broad ZNP-ZPPP campaign to impose tougher restrictions on immigration from the mainland, a campaign that, in turn, heightened anxieties among mainlanders about the intentions of the ZNP-dominated government. The ZNP's actions were partly inspired by renewed concern that the ASP was bringing immigrants from Tanganyika to register for the 1963 elections. But to mainlanders already resident in the islands, Hizbu behavior looked like indiscriminate harassment. In March 1963, ZNP-ZPPP vigilantes in Pemba were arresting mainlanders whom they accused of being illegal immigrants. That gave rise to heated exchanges between the political parties that each was imposing a "reign of terror" in Pemba, mainlanders being either the victims or the culprits.[16]

These conflicts fed into mounting fears that the ZNP-ZPPP government planned to sack all mainlanders from government jobs and deport them. Such fears were not unreasonable, given the numerous public pronouncements in which party spokesmen proposed doing exactly that.[17] Mainlanders' fears were further exacerbated by campaign rhetoric on the issue of "Zanzibarization," the policies by which Britons in administrative positions were gradually being replaced by Zanzibaris in anticipation of independence. ASP propagandists charged that those policies really amounted to "Arabization" and they demanded an aggressive form of affirmative action for Africans. Youth League militants promised that under an ASP government all African clerks and office boys would be promoted to responsible ranks.[18] Given bitter memories of the evictions and "boycotts" of the recent years, both sides had cause to fear racial retaliation in the sphere of employment. But the fears of ASP members were most immediate, both because ZNP sympathizers occupied the most powerful positions in the bureaucracy and economy and because the June elections had put the government in ZNP hands. Immediately after the riots, it was rumored that the government was rounding up mainlanders in Pemba and forcibly deporting them; the rumors had some basis in fact and were reported as such in the mainland press.[19] There were also allegations that Africans who stayed home from work during the riots found their jobs filled by Hizbu sympathizers upon their return, allegations that metastasized into rumors of wholesale sackings.[20]

A rumor that would later have an explosive impact alleged that the ZNP planned to sack all mainlanders from the police.[21] The rumor stemmed from charges of police disloyalty that ZNP spokesmen leveled in the aftermath of the June riots. Most outspoken in this regard was Ali Muhsin, who depicted mainlander police as a potential fifth column.[22] Muhsin's fears would soon become self-justifying. They played into a Youth League campaign that protested the relative lack of Africans in the upper ranks (compared to Arabs and Indians) and sought to drive a wedge between officers and the rank and file. By 1963 police administrators had recognized the problem and had begun rectifying it by recruiting Kenyan noncommissioned officers. But that only intensified Muhsin's determination to halt the promotion of mainlanders and purge them from the force altogether when, after the July elections, he became minister of home affairs. The combined effects of his policies and the Youth League's agitation bore fruit in January 1964, when disaffected and recently dismissed police were prominent in the forces that overthrew the sultanate.[23]

The return of the ZNP-ZPPP alliance in the July elections, this time to form the government slated to assume sovereignty in December, ensured that mainlanders' fears would remain acute during the last five months of the colonial era, especially as the new government launched an aggressive campaign to restrict civil and political liberties. The elections themselves had gone off peacefully, thanks in part to the presence of a battalion of Scots Guards flown in for the occasion and also, apparently, to a decision on the part of the militants that a resort to violence would stand a greater chance of success after the British were gone. But the frustration of having lost yet another election despite winning the popular vote—following months of confident predictions of an ASP sweep and repeated allegations of ZNP vote fraud—ensured that the moment would be tense.

The ASP leadership's particular anxieties about its growing inability to control the party's militant wing were plainly displayed on the front pages of the party organ. The first issue of *Afrika Kwetu* after the July election carried an official-sounding "Announcement" calling on people not to gather in the streets sharing "tobacco," slang for rumor. It is perhaps indicative of the genuine fear such rumors aroused that their particulars were never revealed in the many articles that *Afrika Kwetu* devoted to them. But it is clear that most alarming to ASP leaders were rumors that undermined their authority and the relevance of electoral party politics. The Honorable A. A. Karume still commands Africans' loyalty, the paper insisted, and the ASP is still strong. The irresponsible "youth" who spread rumors only pretend to know party secrets; if there is anything you need to know we will announce it at party offices or in official party publications.[24] Such pleas indicated the leaders' awareness of the power of rumor, a power that threatened their own.

Rumor and Geopolitics

Fears on both sides were fed by propagandists who emphasized the threats posed by extranational forces allied to each of the political blocs. Most immediately visible were pan-Africanists, whose leading voices emanated from Dar es Salaam, Nairobi, and Accra, and pan-Arabists, whose leading voices were based in Cairo. Significantly, both of these geopolitical discourses defined global interests in diasporic or racial terms, in what might be seen as a logical response to the racial paradigms of colonial rule. So both played into Zanzibar's local politics of race. More indirectly and from a greater distance, Zanzibar's political contests were also colored by the discourses of the Cold War. Cold War rhetoric ostensibly had nothing to do with race, but local thinkers nevertheless made effective use of it to further racial fears.

The ASP had advertised its ties to mainland nationalists since its inception, lionizing them in the party press and conducting its 1961 election campaigns beneath TANU flags and portraits of Julius Nyerere and Jomo Kenyatta. The ASP's close ties to Tanganyika and Ghana were much discussed in official circles and in the streets in 1962 and 1963. Nyerere was said to be especially influential. ASP propagandists and activists trumpeted these ties not only as emblems of their pan-Africanist credentials but also as threats: if the ZNP stole the next election, they warned, Tanganyika and Uganda would send troops to put Africans in power. The ASP's opponents, in contrast, used the ties as evidence that the party was merely a tool of alien forces.[25]

Just as insistently, the ZNP highlighted its ties to Nasser, who since the Suez crisis had emerged as a globally prominent anticolonial champion. And by 1963 the party had abandoned its earlier postures of pan-Africanist solidarity and instead portrayed the newly or soon-to-be-independent mainland governments as imperialist "hirelings" and enemies of Islam. Several factors lay behind the shift. During the PAFMECA crisis, ASP militants focused a stream of racial invective against Nasserism, which they described as a force that was using Hizbu to reenslave Africans.[26] With the collapse of the PAFMECA alliance, the region's pan-Africanist leaders seemed more solidly on the ASP's side. And in the years that followed, as Babu and the other secular leftists became marginalized within the party, ZNP propaganda became more aggressive in painting all mainlanders (and by extension the governments they controlled) as threats to *ustaarabu* and Islam.

The dangers of "foreign interference or domination" in postcolonial Zanzibar—Egyptian on one side, Tanganyikan and Kenyan on the other—shaped the parties' electioneering rhetoric for or against membership in the East African Federation that Nyerere and Kenyatta were discussing.[27] Parallel to this debate was a revival of monarchist agitation in right-wing ZNP and Arab Association circles that advocated the sultan's sovereignty over the coast of Kenya (see chapter 4). This evinced some impassioned anti-Arab rhetoric from ASP journalists, who demanded respect for Kenya and for "the grandfather of the nation, our beloved . . . Jomo Kenyatta." By the time of the 1963 elections ZNP had dropped the issue, but members of the party's right flank continued to harp on it as a way of voicing concerns about the threats posed by mainland barbarians.[28]

In themselves, these policy debates could have been of but remote significance to most Zanzibaris. Their importance lay in how they lent credence to the alarms spread by propagandists and rumormongers about racial outsiders. In the months before independence, ASP polemics about Hizbu's ties to Nasser gave rise to scares that the ZNP-ZPPP government would inundate the islands with Egyptian police and schoolteachers to replace Africans and eradicate "African culture."[29] These scares complemented the anti-intellectualism that imbued much ASP invective: Arab medical staff were particularly suspect, and rumors spread that people should not take any pills they prescribed. In March 1963 a scare over a new antimalarial pill prompted talk that Hizbu doctors were poisoning would-be ASP voters. According to one newssheet, such stratagems were typical of the foreign lands where Hizbu doctors were trained. Likewise, rhetoric about ASP's ties to mainland governments evoked images of Mau Mau and fears that TANU was arranging to send toughs to instigate a renewed bout of riots. (ASP propagandists, in fact, helped spread the latter rumors.) Another rumor alleged that Karume was planning to amalgamate Zanzibar with Tanganyika. This rumor apparently originated as an antimainlander scare tactic. But in March 1963 ASP speakers were, in fact, openly advocating union.[30]

Rumors also reproduced more distant extranational threats, those of the Cold War superpowers. ZNP propagandists led the way in introducing Zanzibar to this novel postwar geopolitical discourse. By and large, they embraced the form of nonalignment championed by Nasser, one that, having been shaped by anticolonial first principles, was less distrustful of the Eastern Bloc than of the Western powers allied to Britain. So long as Babu remained influential in the party, this position was reinforced by his genuine interest in Marxism, to say nothing of the support he received from China and Cuba. Thus Babu's wing took the lead in warning of U.S. neocolonialism. In 1960 they found a useful issue when the U.S. space agency installed a tracking station for the Mercury manned flight project in the village of Tunguu. ZNP leftists characterized it as a "rocket station" and a threat to Zanzibar's security, staging protests against it. In 1961 the United States opened a consulate at Zanzibar, which Babu's paper *ZaNews* denounced as a nest of spies.[31] This heated rhetoric was a useful cudgel with which to beat political rivals. Hizbu speakers mocked Othman Sharif as "Bald-Headed Tshombe," referring to the Western client widely held responsible for the murder of Patrice Lumumba in Congo.[32]

The ASP reacted by taking an opposite stand. Right up to the eve of the revolution, *Afrika Kwetu* published a steady stream of pro-American, anticommunist propaganda, apparently press releases supplied by the U.S. Department of State.

To be sure, the ASP, like the ZNP, was internally divided on Cold War issues. Some of the militants, for example, were attracted to the anti-Americanism then becoming fashionable in Third World political discourse, and their own speeches about the Katanga crisis inspired one Human Rights League militant to adopt "Lumumba" as his nom de guerre.[33] But anti-Western rhetoric remained rare in the ASP. Red-baiting, in contrast, was common. Propagandists depicted the ZNP's anti-American rhetoric and its ties to the Eastern Bloc as evidence that it was infested with communists eager to sell the country to Russia and China. The most strident red-baiting came from the Youth League militants, despite their occasional revolutionary poses. Yet their positions had a peculiar consistency. The common denominator was racial nativism: when the MaHizbu accept aid from the Russians and Chinese, the militants argued, just as when they turn to the Egyptians, they betray Africa to "white people." Such demagoguery comfortably melded anti-Arab rhetoric with the anticommunism prevalent in Western vilification of Nasser.[34]

Cold War rhetoric about Cuba and Katanga might have remained obscure to most islanders had it not resonated with their anxieties about violence. During the tense months leading up to the July elections and independence, rumors swirled that each side was stockpiling weapons (whether to attack or defend depended on the source of the rumor).[35] And the most powerful weapons, everyone understood, came from abroad. Zanzibaris were as transfixed as anyone by the image of the atom bomb, which figured both in their political rhetoric and their more extravagant fantasies.[36] On a less cataclysmic level, ZNP speakers encouraged rumors that they had received arms from Russia and Cuba and were prepared to use them. Similarly, it was rumored that the ASP was receiving arms from the United States and Israel and was stashing them at the Tunguu tracking station. The latter rumor circulated at the time of the Cuban missile crisis, along with others alleging that upon independence ZNP would allow the Soviets to install missiles aimed at the mainland.[37]

These rumors were not pure fantasy; the superpower rivals and their clients were giving the parties some assistance (mostly Chinese and Eastern Bloc support to ZNP leftists and some Israeli support to the ASP). But that support was minimal and the rumors greatly exaggerated it.[38] At about the time of the Cuban missile crisis, some were rumoring that Russia was about to force Britain to accede to the ZNP's demand for immediate independence. Others rumored that British and American support for the ASP was so total that party members could act however they wished. Propagandists for both sides encouraged the latter belief. It created some difficulty for ASP leaders when in January 1963 they tried to raise much-needed funds by selling a party clubhouse: their followers balked, believing that party coffers were already overflowing with money secured from foreign allies.[39]

Fears of violence thus helped reproduce globally dominant ideologies that imagined the Cold War rivals as possessing an overwhelming power to shape events. That assumption is recognizable as a variant of an older colonialist paradigm in which the major forces of historical change in Africa all originated outside the continent. But whereas at the start of the colonial era such understandings of power had been ambiguous among Africans (at most),[40] they were now complemented by a barrage of political rhetoric that encouraged Zanzibaris to regard themselves as the pawns of external powers. The most seductive of those illusions, certainly in the long run, was the contention that the suffering of the Time of Politics was caused not by local political actors but was the outcome of a Western master plan to keep Zanzibaris divided and subordinate. This belief appealed particularly to followers of the ZNP, who repeatedly charged that the racialist ASP was the creation and tool of colonial administrators. But militants in both camps were attracted by the suggestion that the British had engineered 1961's electoral stalemates. This interpretation fit perfectly with Cold War discourse; its chief purveyors included Radio Moscow. (Among those who explained Zanzibar's racial tensions this way was the Yugoslav News Agency; hindsight allows us to appreciate the irony.)[41]

The nationalists' exaggerated focus on geopolitical players fed into undercurrents of anxiety concerning foreign threats to morality. In all these cases morality was defined according to prevailing interpretations of Islam. Thus the charge that the ASP was merely a front for Tanganyikans and Kenyans evoked old notions of the barbarism of mainlanders and their uncertain devotion to Islam. After the June riots, Hizbu Christian-baiting intensified. Should the ASP take power, Hizbu audiences were told, it would convert all the islands' mosques to churches. Throughout 1963, *Mwongozi* became ever more strident in denouncing the ASP as enemies of Islam who were agents of Christian mainland governments and of Zionism.[42] During that year's election campaign, the Israelis were rumored to have provided the ASP with special pins that "when pushed into someone, will make him giddy and hence unable to register to vote." Othman Sharif was believed to have hosted a woman visitor from Israel who gave him money to distribute to thugs to instigate another round of riots; more such "Jewesses" were coming from Israel to help.[43]

For their part, ASP propagandists and rumormongers parlayed the well-known secularism of Babu and his YOU allies into charges of moral degeneracy, drunkenness, and sexual profligacy.[44] ZNP partisans took up this rhetoric after Babu left the party in June 1963, and the man whose name had once been a ZNP-ZPPP rallying cry[45] suddenly became anathema, the very emblem of godless dissoluteness. Rumors swirled that Babu's new Umma party received large amounts of money from abroad (for some time, in fact, Babu had drawn pay as a correspondent for the Chinese news agency), which it spent on wild parties at Babu's home on the outskirts of town. The parties enticed young people to join Umma with the lure of drink, "religious abuse," and lascivious dancing.[46] As *Mwongozi* marched to the right, it baited Babu and the members of his "Alcohol Party" as agents of foreign communists and enemies of Islam, followers of "their Jew prophet Carl Marx" and the "legendary Nine Tribes of Israel."[47]

Rumors from Pemba

The riot in October 1962 at the tiny Pemba village of Wingwi yielded the compelling spectacle of the incumbent head of government fleeing with his entourage from a rock-throwing ASP crowd (see chapter 5). This spectacle gave rise to months'-long cycles of rumor that illustrate several of the themes I have been addressing. The Wingwi riot itself was caused and shaped by rumors that revolved around the near-simultaneous visits of two party leaders: Muhammad Shamte, head of the ZPPP, who was to make a brief formal visit in his capacity as chief minister, and Ali Sharif, a leading ASP figure and the local Legco representative, who happened to be in Wingwi the night before to confer with colleagues about campaign strategies for the July elections. In a village closely split between the two parties, the appearance of these individuals had particular resonance. Ali Sharif was the former ZPPP leader who after the January 1961 elections had abandoned Shamte to rejoin the ASP, an act that sparked charges and countercharges of betrayal, political kidnapping, and attempted assassination that in turn had galvanized some angry crowds.[48] The day after the Wingwi riot, Sharif's house was set on fire, presumably in retaliation for the riot he was rumored to have organized. In subsequent weeks two more arson attacks were directed at ASP supporters in Pemba.[49]

The arson, together with the ongoing trials of those charged in the riot, ensured that Wingwi would remain the focus of widespread and often extravagant rumors. In Zanzibar Town rumor had it that the Wingwi riot had been ordered at the very highest levels of the ASP leadership, the goal having been to kill the chief minister. ASP rumor defended the rioters, saying that the disturbances had been caused by officials' attempts to humiliate them. ASP chapters in Pemba organized boycotts and ZNP-ZPPP landlords evicted ASP tenants. The rumor mill multiplied the three arson attacks, and soon all Pemba was said to be ablaze, the victims coming from both political camps. Pemba's Wamakonde were rumored to be sharpening their knives. For the first several months of 1963, both sides traded accusations about alleged outrages in the Pemba countryside. Ali Sharif's brother Othman threatened that incidents such as Wingwi could bring a return of the June massacres.[50]

As we have seen in other instances, it was not unusual for Pemba to be the source of such fanciful rumors. Yahya Alawi explained that Pemba's remoteness from the protectorate's main centers of population meant that reports from there, "heard by people who are far from the scene, . . . can easily be exaggerated in coffee shops."[51] This geographical remoteness served a function similar to that served by the darkness of night in many other rumors. In mid-1963 the two tropes converged in recurrent rumors that the various parties were conducting "night campaigns" in Pemba, driving through the countryside under the cover of dark to distribute arms and money. These rumors were infused with fears of violence and witchcraft. One claimed that ZNP-ZPPP activists planned to bury a goat near a registration station in a rural area as part of a rite that would blind any ASP supporter who came near. The rumor mobilized small ASP crowds who gathered at the spot for two nights prior to the opening of voter registration, gatherings that in turn prompted counter-rumors and threats of violence.[52]

Rumors inspired by the Wingwi riot, like those inspired by "June," continued to circulate up to the time of the revolution and are likely to have continued playing a role in mobilizing crowds.[53] In this regard, it is significant that rumormongers on both sides contended that the rioters enjoyed impunity because they were protected by the British and by the Western powers in general. Gossipers at ASP coffee shops took comfort from the aftermath of "the last riot" (i.e. June 1961), "when nothing happened": they were certain the Wingwi rioters would be released when their appeal reached the Zanzibar High Court. Particular emphasis was placed on the defendants' London lawyer, whom the ASP had hired with the assistance of an Israeli businessman. According to ASP rumor, the lawyer enjoyed official British backing. He was also said to be an Israeli agent who traveled about Pemba disguised in a *kanzu* and Islamic prayer cap.[54]

Uhuru, Revolution, and the Mobilizing Power of Rumor

The approach of the formal date of independence, 10 December, brought widespread fears that trouble would erupt during the festivities. Spokesmen for the ZNP-ZPPP government warned that the sultanate's internal enemies were plotting sabotage and they began a harsh crackdown on political opposition. On the radio and through other media, they threatened to deal harshly with anyone suspected of subversion. Their warnings seemed confirmed by some of the statements coming from ASP militants; Lumumba of the Human Rights League, for example, was making threatening references to June 1961. The long-smoldering tensions between the Youth League and the ASP leadership, now reportedly egged on by Babu's Umma group, flared over the question of whether to celebrate what the dissidents called "dummy" or "Arab" independence. ASP elders urged "all Africans" to participate in the festivities, but it was whispered that Youth Leaguers were planning to disrupt them. Meanwhile, Youth League vigilantes patrolled Ng'ambo, ostensibly to keep order during the celebrations, and youth groups from both sides intimidated their rivals with paramilitary drills. In Ng'ambo and the squatter districts, fears circulated that the Wamanga, armed by the government, were plotting wholesale massacres in retaliation for June as soon as the British departed. Those fears were reinforced by belligerent statements made by Hizbu sympathizers as well as by the sight of Manga groups rehearsing *raz'ha* sword dances for performance at the *uhuru* celebrations.[55]

The celebrations were in fact peaceful, if subdued. But that did nothing to dissipate the "atmosphere of impending crisis" or staunch the circulation of alarming rumors.[56] The vulnerability of the newly independent state was dramatized at the most local level by a spate of incidents in which the national flag—the red banner of the sultan that the ZNP had appropriated as its own—was removed from the homes of *masheha*, where it flew as a symbol of government presence. This was the culmination of a dispute that had been simmering for at least a year. In some cases the flag had been forcibly pulled down by militants without the *sheha*'s involvement. But in others the *sheha* himself refused to fly the flag, and by late December district officers were expressing alarm over the "disloyalty" of pro-ASP *masheha* and recommending their dismissal. Such incidents complemented open statements in which ASP speakers denounced the flag and the sultan himself as but symbols of "Manga rule."[57]

With hindsight it is difficult to fathom why the revolution took so many officials, British and Zanzibari, by surprise. They knew that militants had been talking of revolution since at least 1962 (indeed, some Youth Leaguers were hinting of the need to overthrow the sultanate as early as the days of the PAF-MECA crisis), and at the time of the 1963 elections Youth League and Human Rights League activists were rumored to be forming "suicide squads" to overthrow the government in case the ASP lost at the polls.[58] In a sense, however, it is understandable that officials failed to take such talk seriously: figures like Jamal Ramadhan Nasibu might one day talk of overthrowing the sultanate and the next day denounce their rivals as dangerous Bolsheviks. The militants had never spoken with one voice, and most officials seemed to think their threat would be neutralized so long as they remained locked in conflict with the ASP's senior leadership. Official fears focused more on Babu, especially after his break with the ZNP and the formation of his explicitly Marxist Umma party. Such myopia was but one example of how the Cold War discourse of communist subversion distorted perceptions of real political dangers.

Yet even though officials kept fairly well apprised of the activities of Youth League militants, they were unable to anticipate the precise nature of the threat the militants posed. Security officers had received reports that members of Umma and the Youth League had been meeting in the countryside at night to coordinate activities, but their sources told them that armed action was being planned for months later. Those sources were apparently correct. As it happened, events were forced by actors who had only marginal connections with any party structure. The story of how an obscure Ugandan immigrant, John Okello, mobilized the ragtag group that took the first decisive actions toward overthrowing the regime naturally strains belief. (Okello had been a bricklayer and Youth League member in Pemba until shortly before the revolution.) Yet the most substantial and disinterested studies of the revolution accept its basics, if for little other reason than that they comport with the documented facts better than any other account. In September or October, Lumumba set up contacts between the Youth League militants and Okello's group, which included many dismissed policemen, and together they began preparing for an uprising without the knowledge of the ASP leadership. District-level administrative officers knew vaguely of their activities at Kiboje, located in the central plantation district, but attached little significance to them.[59]

Preparations for the coup escaped most officials' attention in part because so much of the recruitment and mobilization was conducted through informal channels. The constant rumors of nighttime *ngomas* at which subversion was plotted, for example, contained at least a kernel of truth. Officials knew enough about festive ritual to be aware of its potential dangers (though they probably did not imagine anything more dangerous than what had ensued at Wingwi in 1962); hence their anxieties about the December *uhuru* ceremonies.[60] But they could not possibly have kept tabs on all the dances and feasts that were conducted throughout the weeks that followed. Those were the final weeks before Ramadan, always a time of multiple festivities, when people take the opportunity to celebrate weddings and other rites that are frowned upon during the austerities of the Holy Month. On the night of Saturday, 11 January, five days before the start of the fast, the rebels assembled for their assault on the main police barracks under the cover of an ASP-organized fête. It had been rumored that something was afoot for that night, but the worst that anyone in power imagined were June-like riots.[61]

Much of the violence of January 1964, like that of June 1961, appears to have been mobilized on the spot, including via the networks of mutual understanding forged by rumor.[62] Among the most effective was the rumor that the Wamanga were massing for an attack on Africans and had already begun to dig mass graves in which to bury their victims; as in June 1961, Wamanga would constitute a disproportionate share of those killed in the revolutionary pogroms.[63] The revolutionaries themselves later acknowledged that they propagated false rumors both to mislead the police and to mobilize popular support. The latter included rumors that Mau Mau guerillas had arrived from Kenya to help Zanzibar Africans overthrow the sultanate and would murder anyone who betrayed their plans. These rumors built on ASP rhetoric from the previous year that had alleged that Hizbu planned to introduce to Zanzibar the hated *vipande,* the identity cards worn around the neck that had sparked much bitterness in colonial Kenya.[64]

In the final weeks before the revolution the militants were spreading even more alarmist rumors about Hizbu's secret plans for postcolonial Zanzibar. Those rumors were reinforced by the threatening statements issuing from some Hizbu supporters and government spokespeople. But they also built on the more lurid rhetoric that had been circulated by ASP racial nationalists throughout the Time of Politics. John Okello later wrote that his revolutionary zeal was fired by what he had learned of the government's plans; those fantasies help explain the nature of the violence that ensued. After expropriating Africans of all their wealth, Okello believed, the Hizbu regime planned to expel the mainlanders and enslave the rest. "Retribution" would then be exacted for the killings of June 1961, at the rate of 60 Africans for each of the Arabs who had died then. (This assertion in fact built on some of the Hizbu rhetoric that had been common since the June riots.)[65] Perhaps most chillingly, Okello and his followers believed that

> All male African babies would be killed, and African girls would be forced to marry or submit to Arabs so that within a few years there would be no pure black skin on the Island, and there would be no Africans to remember the vile treatment of their ancestors.

The revolutionaries imagined they were acting to preempt such outrages, a belief that no doubt helped justify in their own minds the use of rape as a tool of terror.[66] And although Okello and the Youth League militants allied with him acted without the knowledge or support of the ASP leadership, their fantasies displayed clear links to the propaganda about slavery and intermarriage that had appeared in party organs years before the revolutionary moment.

––––––––––

Rumor was central to the creation of fears that mobilized people to commit acts of racial violence in the wake of the coup. I do not mean to suggest that the events of January 1964 can be understood simply as the product of rumor. In contrast to the June riots, the revolution involved coordination and forethought on the part of organized political cadres, both Okello's fringe group and the Youth League dissidents who joined up with him, some at the last moment.[67] But as Okello's memoirs indicate, the rebels' success in winning popular support depended in part on the circulation of rumors such as those we have examined in the preceding three chapters. The organizing force of rumor, while perhaps not responsible for the concerted attacks on government installations that brought down the sultanate, nevertheless helped forge the pogroms that terrorized the loyalist countryside once the assault on the state had created a crisis.

The ability of rumors to generate collective behavior has long been observed by historians and social scientists, at least since Georges Lefebvre's classic study of the rural panics of revolutionary France. Scholars often note the heightened effect of rumors in times of extreme anxiety. In Zanzibar, the thirty months following the June riots were just such a time, characterized by mounting uncertainties on every front and pervasive social tensions shot through with barely suppressed violence. At such moments, rumors, and especially rumors of violence, can become especially potent in shaping perceptions of social reality, to the point of actually "blurring the boundaries between events 'witnessed' and those envisioned," as Ann Stoler writes, "between performed brutality and the potentiality for it."[68] In some cases the resulting visions take on an apocalyptic quality, as the whole world seems to be in alignment with local conflicts. This helps explain the appeal of rumors based in geopolitics.[69] Such rumors further accentuate the sense of crisis, of a world collapsing, ready to be turned upside down. By signaling the potentialities of achieving a transcendent, purified society and the grave dangers of inaction, they enhance the ability of propagandists and riot specialists to persuade significant numbers of people to countenance drastic acts. (Although the killers themselves, as we saw in chapter 7, were a small minority.)[70]

Lefebvre emphasized the relative autonomy of the realm of rumor; responding to then-prevalent currents in the study of crowd behavior, he stressed that the revolutionary crowds and the discourse of rumor that did so much to shape their subjectivity could not be seen merely as tools of Jacobin or aristocratic conspirators. And most subsequent scholars, in one way or another, have followed his example. They have substantiated for other times and places Lefebvre's observation that rumors were not simply spread by individuals for their own utilitarian purposes (though they could sometimes originate that way) but had "an identity of their own."[71] By its nature, rumor is improvisational, meaning that it can quickly adapt to the circumstances or imaginations of particular tellers and their audience. This quality makes rumors more believable. It also makes them more likely to elude the control of any one person or party. Although Okello's group and his ASYL allies were no doubt important purveyors of rumor and racial fear, they were hardly the only ones.

But some scholars working in the tradition of Lefebvre have gone one step further, writing of rumors as if they were part of a discrete "offstage" realm of discourse: a peasant realm (in agrarian societies) entirely autonomous of the discourse of political elites. These scholars approach rumor and other forms of nonliterate "transmission" as wholly distinct from the written communications upon which the elite rely. In their less guarded moments, they depict rumor as inherently insurrectionary and counterhegemonic.[72] Such conclusions rest on a foundation of nested dichotomies, including the presumed disjunctures between official and unofficial speech, written and oral communication, hegemonic and counterhegemonic discourses, mimicry and spontaneous authenticity.

The material presented in the last three chapters should suggest the instability of such a foundation, at least in the present case. They have shown how infections and reinfections were constantly passed between elite and subaltern discourse, between the written communications of political activists and the oral communications of rumor; how the intelligentsia's historical narratives of *ustaarabu* and *ushenzi* were adapted and transformed into "memories" of racial violence; and how the activists' talk of international solidarity and communist subversion became the stuff of the darkest of fears. As a result, the vivid anxieties about past or anticipated violence that informed the killings were imbued with the influence of political speech and reproduced its prevailing categories, including those of race, civilization, and geopolitics. For these reasons, although the resulting upheaval was insurrectionary and its outcome transformed Zanzibari society in many ways, it did not transform dominant modes of thinking about race.

Conclusion and Epilogue: Remaking Race

The coup d'etat of January 1964 was immediately followed by a "terror," as Anthony Clayton has described it, that dwarfed the pogroms of June 1961. Urged on by Okello's radio broadcasts (for all his mental instability, he had the shrewdness to seize the radio station in the first hours of the coup), revolutionaries hunted down Arab families. Probably thousands were slaughtered, although precise numbers are unknown. Others were herded into squalid camps, and later in the year many were forcibly deported. By the end of 1964, Zanzibar had lost a quarter or more of its Arab population to expulsion, flight, or mass murder.[1]

In the years since, the revolution has taken its place in historical mythology as either the inevitable outcome of centuries of racial oppression at the hands of Arab "feudalists" and slaveholders or the culmination of an imperialist campaign to divide and cripple the Zanzibar nation. The contestants in this rhetorical battle have adjusted their narratives to fit the nationalist paradigm that since the 1960s has become the prevailing mode of explaining the modern history of the former colonial world. Accordingly, both the defenders of the 1964 revolution and its opponents present their protagonists (or themselves) as steadfast anticolonialists and their rivals as the tools of colonialism and neocolonialism. For the ASP, this was an especially dramatic turnaround.

But as we have seen, the spirals of rumor and panic that gripped Zanzibar had arisen from the confluence of a wide range of factors. As in most cases of large-scale communal violence, many of those factors had been constructed by actors who, if they did not consciously aim at mass killings, at least had an eye for the political advantages they might derive from sustained levels of racial fear. Although the killings were one-sided, the construction of racial fear was not; directly or indirectly, virtually all of political Zanzibar contributed to making men such as Jamal Ramadhan Nasibu—and even to making men such as John Okello, who, though he had been raised in Uganda, nevertheless partook of the poisonous atmosphere of Zanzibar's Time of Politics before he ever set foot on the islands.[2] Contrary to conventional interpretations that understand "racism" as the pathological propensity of one particular political camp—abetted by colonial agents, from whom it was learned—this book has argued that it grew from more pervasive discourses of racial thought.

Of course, British educators and administrative policies shaped those discourses in significant ways. But there are three reasons why colonial influence was not as straightforward as is usually assumed. First, the most profound Western influences on racial thought in Zanzibar were not those that arose from any consciously divisive British policies. Far more significant in the long run were Western discourses that encouraged African thinkers to locate political "modernity" in the project of nativist territorial nationalism and racial pan-Africanism. Although after 1964 nationalist intellectuals liked to present those discourses as having arisen in opposition to British rule, before independence they were more willing to recognize their debt to the colonial project itself. Second, colonial influences did not operate alone; other imported influences that shaped racial thought included pan-Arab and pan-Islamist discourses emanating from the Middle East and pan-Africanist influences emanating from the Afro-Atlantic world. Third, and most important, none of these influences worked as unmediated doctrines. Rather, their impact was felt in how they shaped the conversations and debates that were being conducted by Zanzibari intellectuals, elite and subaltern, who creatively combined them with inherited intellectual resources, including ancient ideas of *ustaarabu* and *ushenzi*, to arrive at discourses of nativist nationalism that were compelling to local people in ways that imported doctrines could never be. As we have seen in the last three chapters, those conversations included rumors and "memories" that mythologized particular acts of violence as the formative traumas of violent racial subjectivities.

Yet despite the pervasiveness of racial fears, the killings stopped almost as quickly as they began; despite the many parallels, Zanzibar did not become a Rwanda or a Burundi. That difference, however, has nothing to do with any categorical difference in the nature of ethnic thought in these regions; the numbing horrors of places that suffered genocide do not bespeak histories of race that are in some way more deeply rooted than in Zanzibar.[3] The explanation is far simpler: after early 1964, there was simply no political will in Zanzibar to continue violent racial fear. The degree to which the January pogroms were organized remains unclear; in this as in other matters the full story of the revolution has yet to be written. But in any case, no matter how heavily invested they were in the rhetoric of racial fear, the ASP leaders who took power after the coup had no interest in genocide. Once Karume and his allies had removed Okello from the scene in early March and neutralized the forces loyal to him, few elements remained in the revolutionary government that had any taste for large-scale ethnic violence.[4]

This prosaic explanation of why the killing ended highlights a more fundamental point: the urge to kill the racial "other," no matter how seemingly spontaneous and unorganized, does not arise inevitably from the existence of dehumanizing racial rhetoric any more than it arises from primordial wellsprings.[5] Throughout this book, I have emphasized the racializing *potential* inherent in the logic of ethnic or national categorization, and, in part 3, I emphasized that the rhetoric of racial dehumanization had the *potential* to make exterminationist violence imaginable. But there was nothing inevitable about either process. Given the evanescence of murderous racial hatreds and the "hard work" that government or party agents must sustain to keep them alive, the question of why no genocide occurred in this particular case is far less puzzling than the question of why genocide or large-scale ethnic cleansing ever happens at all. Without the commitment of a state or other substantially autonomous political entity, the killing fields of Rwanda or the ovens of Nazi Europe are unthinkable.

And yet racial identities have persisted in postcolonial Zanzibar and still seem to command the ability to shape political behavior. In 1992, multiparty democracy was reintroduced to Tanzania; the first multiparty elections were held in 1995 and multiparty elections were held again in 2000 and 2005. On the mainland, the governing party—the Chama cha Mapinduzi (CCM), or Party of the Revolution, formed in 1977 by the merger of TANU and the ASP—has retained broad electoral support. But in the islands it has faced formidable opposition. Most observers declared Zanzibar's 1995 and 2000 elections fraudulent; even so, the CCM was able to claim only the slimmest of margins against the opposition Civic United Front (CUF). Opinion was divided about the fairness of the 2005 election, which the CCM also claimed by a narrow margin. Throughout the past fifteen years the political atmosphere has been marked by bitterness reminiscent of the first Time of Politics, with legislative boycotts, intimidation, and sporadic outbursts of low-grade violence.

To the surprise and chagrin of observers who expected that three decades of single-party rule would have put an end to ethnic politics, voters' behavior during this stalemate has seemed to reflect many of the same divisions that preoccupied their parents and grandparents. In terms of policy there are few clear distinctions between the parties (with the exception of the status of the union between Zanzibar and the mainland, discussed below). But there is a widespread perception among both researchers and ordinary citizens that current tensions are undergirded by ethnicity. In a substantial study of Zanzibar's current period of multiparty politics, Mohammed Ali Bakari describes voters as being polarized along two axes. One axis is ethnic, with "Zanzibaris of Arab origin" overwhelmingly voting for CUF while Zanzibaris of mainland origin favor the CCM. The other axis is regional, dividing Shirazi in Pemba, who give strong support to CUF, from Shirazi in Unguja, who lean toward the CCM.[6] Whatever the causes of these patterns (and Bakari believes they may be misleading in terms of motivation), political actors clearly think there is something to them. So, for example, during the fraught registration process for the 2005 election, CCM thugs intimidated Pembans living in Unguja; in Pemba, their CUF counterparts targeted mainlanders. CCM speakers have repeatedly accused their opponents of representing the interests of "Arabs" who want to restore the sultanate, institute an Islamic republic, and expel all mainlanders. They depict the opposition's Pemba supporters as particularly tainted in that regard. CUF speakers respond by characterizing CCM politicians as the agents of mainland Christians.[7]

Such patterns and the rhetoric that sustains them will be familiar to my readers, as they are to all Zanzibaris who know the basic history of the first Time of Politics, when Arab voters supported one side, mainlanders the other, and the Shirazi were split between those in Pemba who leaned toward the ZNP-ZPPP alliance and those in Unguja who favored the ASP. Their reappearance is puzzling. Zanzibar society has been radically remade since the revolution: the estates were broken up and redistributed to those who cultivate them, including the squatters; the state solidified its control of the clove and copra trade; and the property of the islands' wealthiest Indian and Arab families was expropriated and most of those families emigrated. For most of the postrevolutionary period, political discourse was tightly controlled; before 1985 there were no electoral politics, not even the single-party kind that flourished in mainland Tanzania.

In such contexts, prevailing explanations of the persistence of racial or ethnic politics tend to reflect one of two familiar assumptions. On the one hand is the common conception that ethnic political loyalties grow from deeply rooted urges and modes of thought that are hardwired into a given culture or indeed into all cultures. Single-party rule may suppress the resulting tensions for a while, but once political pluralism is introduced, they break out with renewed force. Although old-school primordialism is out of fashion in academic circles, certain forms of constructivist scholarship tend to make a fetish of ethnic discourse, discerning in it the power to produce violent behavior almost autonomously, virtually unmediated by political actors.[8] Outside the academy, but still well within respectable intellectual circles, the troubles of the post–Cold War era in places such as Sierra Leone, Rwanda, and the Congo have encouraged the revival of interpretations that one critic describes as the "new barbarism."[9] But such Hobbesian understandings had never really faded from view.

On the other hand is the frequent assertion, especially concerning the former colonial world, that racial violence or other forms of communal conflict are epiphenomena that are really about something else: class or property theft or the machinations of colonial administrators. We have examined such possibilities in the case of the June riots. Similar interpretations abound concerning the 1964 pogroms. Most common are assertions that what looked like racial resentments were in fact about class; that what looked like pogroms were in fact jacqueries. Such assertions rest on the false distinction between what is racial and what is social or political, a distinction that appeared in statements made before (and by) the Foster-Sutton Commission. Thus, authors frequently insist that the events of January 1964 constituted not a racial but a social revolution.[10] This interpretation is often combined with an emphasis on the degree to which Arab privileges were supported or even created by British rule. It is not difficult to understand and indeed sympathize with the ASP's quick turn away from their old primordialism once they came to power; proclamations that racial divisions had been the products of colonialism created a comforting illusion that, if widely accepted, might help persuade Zanzibaris put their old hatreds aside. Now that the revolutionary regime no longer recognized racial privilege, proclaimed party ideologues, racial animus and even racial identities would wither away.[11] Still, it is bewildering to see scholars declaring Zanzibar's present-day racial politics "a British creation" close to a half-century after colonialism's demise.[12]

This book has argued that both views oversimplify matters. Certainly perceptions of race are not beyond history, and to understand the processes by which they have been created and rendered socially and politically significant one must look at a wide range of factors, including economic production and the policies of governing elites. But racial rhetoric is unlikely to exert a grip on significant numbers of ordinary people unless it resonates with some of the deeply rooted grammars of thought that pervade their cultural environment, such as (in our case) the discourses of civilization and barbarism. At the same time, it must also resonate with the concerns that arise in everyday life, concerns that change more quickly than broad cultural concepts. In other words, one cannot explain the workings of racial discourse simply by positing a point in time when it originated—be that point in the mists of antiquity or in the more recent colonial past—and then assuming its persistence. Race endures not by persisting but by being constantly made anew. In postwar Zanzibar, racial categories were reimagined in the course of conversations about how to realize the modernist dream of building a nation-state. And although open political debate was muted during most of the decades since the revolution, those conversations nevertheless continued, as the following brief narrative will show.

Remaking Nativist Discourse in Postrevolutionary Zanzibar

Zanzibar's present political polarization is often simply explained as a continuation of old loyalties from the 1960s that were driven underground during the period of single-party rule and have now been brought again into the open. "There are ostensibly new parties in Zanzibar," writes one political scientist, but they are more or less the same as the old ones. Another writes that the ZNP and ZPPP "bequeathed their membership to the CUF—even though the great majority of today's members had not even been born yet." He continues: "The split in beliefs and commitments must have remained throughout the 30-year period of single-party rule exactly as it evidenced itself in polls of the early 1960s." These are not just the views of scholars; they also reflect perceptions that are expressed in public opinion surveys and are encouraged by some political actors, particularly within CCM.[13]

Yet as Bakari and others have noted, this explanation is unlikely. For starters, it cannot explain the CCM's sharp decline in support, particularly in Pemba, relative to the support the ASP enjoyed in the 1960s.[14] Further, the opposition's core leaders are too young ever to have belonged to the ZNP or ZPPP, and rather than having been "born into [their] parents' politics as people are born into parents' religion,"[15] most in fact were the children of ASP members or had been ASP members themselves. Moreover, despite the picture painted by their CCM rivals, CUF members are ideologically diverse. Although some indeed sympathize with the ZNP government that was overthrown in 1964, others defend the revolution, which they believe the CCM has betrayed. Bakari writes that voters on both sides are motivated by a variety of factors. What unites the disparate opposition is not a shared racial animus or any other single ideological position but simply dissatisfaction with the ruling party's record of mismanagement, corruption, and civil rights abuses.[16]

It is nevertheless indisputable that Zanzibaris have proven susceptible to political manipulation on the grounds of ethnic or racial claims and that in the eyes of many the results seem to mirror the alignments of the 1950s and 1960s.[17] But the fact that so many understand current divisions in terms of the old conflicts indicates less the persistence of fixed ideas than it indicates the role that historical memories play in Zanzibaris' current projects of imagining the political sphere. Today's discourses of ethnicized politics are not simple holdovers but new creations crafted by political thinkers who draw, in part, from a repertoire of images and fears recalled from the first Time of Politics. They are the products of ongoing political discussions that do not replay old tensions so much as they seek to address newer ones.

The most obvious of the newer tensions are those generated by the postrevolutionary regime's systematic privileging of "African" racial identity and its simultaneous denigration of Middle Eastern racial markers. The crux of the matter is neatly expressed in memoirs by the educator Ali Saleh. Saleh belonged to a community that traced its descent to immigrants from the Comoro Islands and maintained family connections there. Comorians had long provided a disproportionate share of Zanzibar's intellectuals and were distrusted by the ASP racial nationalists. Many cherished putative Arab ancestry, and during the colonial period their most prominent political spokesmen claimed Arab status. Somatically, however, they could pass as African, and most of them probably preferred to negotiate their way between racial identities, resisting, like so many other Zanzibaris, the polarizing pressures of the Time of Politics. But a few days after the revolution, finding himself face to face with some of the toughs who had taken over as government officials, Saleh discovered what he calls, with bitter self-mockery, "the magic word." Asked his *kabila* (race or tribe), he responded "African."[18]

For uttering this "magic word," Saleh reproaches himself for cowardice and for abandoning the cosmopolitan values of coastal culture. But like Juma Ambari, the assistant *sheha* whose story concluded chapter 7, the choice had been imposed on him, this time not by a mob but by the more routinized violence of the revolutionary regime. Despite Karume's high-minded published speeches about the need to set aside racial animosity, he and his colleagues continued to vent the kind of race-baiting that had been their forte before the revolution, and his government pursued policies that penalized and persecuted members of the Arab, Indian, and Comorian minorities.[19] From time to time he also indulged in utopian projects of racial leveling that amounted to programs of intense, if sporadic, intimidation. In 1970 he revived the African Association's old campaign against Shirazi identity, undeterred by the fact that the ethnonym was enshrined in his party's name. As many as 18,000 people, mostly from the ASP strongholds of southern Unguja, were persuaded to sign documents denying that they were Shirazi or even that they knew the meaning of the word.[20] The same year saw the culmination of the forced marriages scandal, built upon the ruling party's rhetoric demanding the sexual empowerment of African men vis-à-vis Arab women (see chapter 4). The scandal had been brewing for years, prompted by threatening speeches, legislation to back up the threats, and rumors of specific outrages by members of the ruling Revolutionary Council.[21]

Central to the regime's racial rhetoric was the way it became invested with the language of class. This process was part of the ASP's ideological somersault following the revolution, when it suddenly switched from red-baiting its opponents and praising colonial paternalism to spouting quasi-Marxist slogans and warning of neocolonialist subversion. To some extent, this shift was connected to the geopolitical reorientation the party was induced to make after China and the Eastern Bloc rushed to recognize the revolutionary regime and lavish it with material aid while the West dithered. Western diplomats and the Western press furthered the pressure by raising scares that Zanzibar was about to become "Africa's Cuba" (although more level-headed diplomats realized that that was unlikely). This all enhanced the influence the Umma and Youth League Marxists exerted within the new government, particularly Babu and Abdalla Kassim Hanga, the latter a leader of the ASP's left wing.[22]

Yet despite the posturing of some of its adherents, Marxism never became deeply embedded in Zanzibar. (Karume remained wary of Babu and the other leftists and quickly sidelined or eliminated them.)[23] Its chief contribution was language that enabled the ruling party to recast its long-standing racial rhetoric in terms of class. Hence party propaganda reviled Arabs as "feudalists" and Indians as merchant capitalists, the running dogs of Omani-British colonialism. The stereotypes about Indians were especially revealing of the new racial logic at work. Although before the revolution ASP propagandists had not been above indulging in occasional anti-Indianism, they had never given it much emphasis, and Indian businesspeople had been among the party's financial supporters. But the "revolutionary racial essentialism" that became ascendant after 1964 thrived on just such rhetoric. This variant of the socialism of fools (as August Bebel described anti-Semitism) had long been a refrain among the Arab intelligentsia; it is ironic that it was under ASP rule that it came to full flower.[24]

Most of this discourse of class-inflected racial essentialism has taken the form of historical narratives. Despite Karume's ban on history as a formal subject in Zanzibar schools, historical discourse was propagated in other ways, including through literature and political speech. Textbooks in politics and popular Swahili novels depict Zanzibar's history as one in which classes and races coincided, with Arab landlords, Indian businessmen, and the colonial state joined in the oppression of Africans. "Arab slavery" is said to have continued throughout the colonial period, abolished only by the revolution itself. (This is still widely believed, including by youth born well after the Karume era.)[25] Though less crude and more factually accurate, similar interpretations of Zanzibar's racial history are standard fare among respected guild historians, Tanzanian and foreign: hence the common assumption that "racial differences went parallel with class divisions" and that the revolution was a "classic" revolt of "the landless peasantry and the labouring classes against the landed aristocracy."[26]

The prevalence of such racial language has colored citizens' attitudes toward the revolutionary regime, including Pemba's and Unguja's diverging responses to land reform. Land reform was undertaken chiefly during the period 1965 to 1974, as the government carved up clove and coconut estates and redistributed them in three-acre plots. Far more acreage was expropriated in Unguja—especially in the plantation districts, where it was redistributed to squatters—and far more families benefited. But more landlords had property expropriated in Pemba. This discrepancy can be explained by the landholding patterns described in chapter 2, where we saw that clove estates in Pemba were both smaller and more evenly distributed among the population. The benefits of land reform therefore were not as obvious in Pemba as in Unguja, and in fact many Pembans resented it as an intrusion. The same landholding patterns had also contributed to the greater affinity that Pemba's Shirazi felt toward their Arab neighbors and their lesser sympathy for the ASP's project of African racial nationalism. (Throughout the postwar years, the proportion of islanders who considered themselves Arabs was significantly higher in Pemba than Unguja.) Those factors, plus memories of Pemba's loyalty to the ZPPP during the Time of Politics, led Karume to subject the island to exceptionally gratuitous administrative abuse. Furthermore, as the main clove producer, Pemba has suffered disproportionately from the government's clove marketing policies, in which a state purchasing monopoly has offered producers only a fraction of the crop's market value. The heavy-handedness of the state's paramilitary anti-smuggling forces—which were deployed to stifle dissent in the recent political period—has aroused particular resentment.[27]

Thus, when the ruling party sought to justify its policies of land reform and state-controlled clove marketing in terms of racialized class equity—protecting the islands' indigenous Africans from the depredations of alien feudalists and merchant capitalists—people in Pemba were especially resistant. In contrast, since the reintroduction of multiparty politics, the CCM has been able to bolster its support in rural Unguja by invoking defense of the revolution's land reforms. Its speakers have warned that the opposition plans to reappropriate the three-acre plots and restore them to their pre-revolutionary owners. (Such fears have proven especially potent in the times of uncertainty that have come in the wake of the economic liberalization begun in the late 1980s.) CUF speakers, for their part, deride the revolution for having led to economic decline, although their position on the revolution has wavered over the years. Voters in Pemba, remembering their mistreatment under the previous ASP-CCM governments, have proven most responsive to such rhetoric. Many in the opposition attribute that mistreatment to the alien mainlanders who allegedly dominate the ruling party, thus using nativism to turn the CCM's rhetoric of African racial nationalism against itself.[28]

In other words, four decades of single-party rule in the name of African racial nationalism have reinforced nativist hostility toward mainlanders. The old discourses of civilization and barbarism—reinforced and reimagined in the nineteenth century by the intensified practices of slavery, in the nineteenth and early twentieth centuries by the hegemony of the Busaidi state, and during the colonial period by Western-inspired teachings about progress and modernity—have since the 1960s been reimagined once more, this time in oppositional terms. Casual antimainlander sentiments are ubiquitous in Zanzibar; even the most hospitable and open-minded people, for example, routinely attribute all the islands' crime to mainlanders. In politics, such nativism imbues the speech of both sides. Thus, any politician of whom a speaker disapproves is likely to be branded a mainlander, not a true islander, much as Ali Muhsin tried to have Abeid Karume disenfranchised on the grounds that he was allegedly born on the mainland.[29] But antimainlander sentiments are most pronounced in the politics of the opposition. People of mainlander background are assumed to be uniformly sympathetic to the CCM, and in opposition strongholds such as Pemba even those who have been living in the islands for years have been intimidated from registering or voting. Many regard the government as an instrument of mainlander domination and the 1964 revolution as nothing but an "invasion" of foreigners, abetted if not actually planned by Nyerere himself. Opposition supporters often characterize government officials with the same ethnonyms, emblematic of mainlander barbarism, that had circulated in the 1950s and 1960s: Makonde, Ndengereko, Nyamwezi.[30]

These themes help explain the political resonance of the endless debates over the status of the union between Zanzibar and Tanganyika. On the surface, these debates can seem relentlessly legalistic, focusing on the particularities of the constitutional arrangement.[31] But at their core are broad questions of historical interpretation, which invest the debates with vitriol. Champions of the union in its current form like to depict it as a singular triumph of pan-African solidarity, the only lasting instance in which two sovereign African states have joined to form a common polity. Its critics, in contrast, deny the significance of pan-Africanist ideals and instead regard it as the product of a cynical power play imposed by mainland politicians. The protocols creating the union were negotiated by Karume and Nyerere in secret, and their announcement in April 1964 took both sides of the Zanzibar Channel by surprise. The history of the union, then, has proven fertile ground for myth-making, and for many in the opposition it occupies a place alongside the revolution itself as a kind of chosen trauma, one that figures prominently in their accounts of the history of mainland domination. Such interpretations are often built around motifs of civilization, barbarism, and religious chauvinism. Their strongest iterations, which betray the influence of the exiled hard-line supporters of the old ZNP-ZPPP regime, attribute the revolution itself to a Christian project to contain Islam.

Ironically, such chauvinistic and antirevolutionary arguments build on an interpretation pioneered by the secular internationalist Babu, who, after losing his contest with Karume and going into exile after 1978, portrayed the union as a betrayal of the revolution and even of the pan-Africanist ideals by which it had been justified. The Babuist perspective accords overriding significance to geopolitical factors, above all Western fears that Zanzibar might become a communist beachhead in the region. Thus the union was engineered by the

United States and its clients, Nyerere in particular, to neutralize the communists. This interpretation is sometimes repeated in the scholarly literature. Yet it is seriously overargued, exaggerating the extent of Western fears (not incidentally, it rests on Babu's self-aggrandizing assertion that the January coup set off a "revolutionary tide" that threatened Western interests throughout the region), Western intervention, and the ability of such intervention to determine events.[32] Babu and Hanga, the islands' leading Marxists, in fact had supported the union, the immediate effect of which was to bring them into the federal government.[33] That removed them from the islands—no doubt Karume's intention—but their presence in Dar es Salaam contributed to an eastern shift in Tanzania's foreign policy and a near-rupture with the West.

In short, there is simply no credible evidence that Nyerere and Karume were CIA tools or the union a Western plot. Yet the geopolitical interpretation is useful to latter-day critics of the union in that it lends their arguments a nationalist gloss: that is, it enables them to cast their critique in accord with the nationalist paradigm, so ubiquitous in African political thought, by which anything unsavory is attributed to outsiders. But whereas Babu and his colleagues, steeped in the traditions of revolutionary internationalism, described Karume's and Nyerere's betrayals solely in terms of neocolonialism, many in Zanzibar's current opposition emphasize the traitors' ethnic and religious status as mainlanders and as (in Nyerere's case) Christian. The geopolitical interpretation has also proven helpful to the opposition insofar as it casts doubts on the pan-Africanism by which union is typically justified. Critics frequently assert, incorrectly, that the idea of union had never been broached before April 1964, when Karume and Nyerere used pan-Africanist ideals to mask the plan's CIA origins.[34] They often extend this assertion to a disavowal of pan-Africanism in general, insinuating that it was merely a ploy to secure the islands' subjugation to the mainland.

The narrow islands' nativism on which critics of union often rely had not been a constant feature of Zanzibar's political life, let alone a natural component of islanders' thought that would have persisted without political manipulation. Nor was union with Tanganyika as unpopular as latter-day polemics make it seem. Even the two actions that effected the union's final consolidation—the merger of the ASP and TANU in 1977 and of the security apparatus in 1984–1985—were widely welcomed in the islands as moves away from the abuses of the old ASP regime.[35] Still, the union was never without tensions. Karume and his successors all, from time to time, resisted fuller integration into the United Republic. Their main motivation, no doubt, was to guard their autonomy

294 / War of Words, War of Stones

against incursions from Dar es Salaam. But they were also willing to generate domestic support by cultivating islanders' old suspicion of anything or anybody connected to the mainland.[36] Hence, despite their official dedication to the principles of transterritorial unity, ASP and CCM politicians periodically played upon currents of islands' nativism throughout the era of single-party rule. Even today, when the opposition aggressively voices dissatisfaction with the union, members of the government often do the same, creating tensions with their CCM comrades on the mainland.[37]

But opposition politicians are more likely than their CCM counterparts to deploy the rhetoric of overt coastal chauvinism. Themes of religion have the most potential to be divisive. Many in the opposition assert that the union represents a threat to Zanzibar's historic role as a center of Islamic culture and learning. Some, voicing themes that can be traced back to rumors remembered from the 1960s, allege that Nyerere, a former seminarian, plotted the union and even the revolution as part of a broader Catholic scheme against Islam. Such rhetoric came to the fore early in the multiparty period, when in 1993 the Zanzibar government revealed that it had joined the Organization of the Islamic Conference (OIC), an international association of Muslim-majority states. Pressure from the federal capital, on the grounds that Zanzibar did not have the constitutional authority to make international alliances, forced a withdrawal from the OIC within months. It is likely that Salmin Amour, the islands' president at the time, purposely stirred the controversy in part to garner popular support; islanders widely resented the verbal attacks on him by mainland politicians. The sense that Zanzibar should be oriented diplomatically toward the Islamic world is widespread across parties, felt by all but the most ideological of CCM members. Members of Amour's government shared with other intellectuals a romantic nostalgia for the days when Zanzibar, according to the historical myths, commanded an empire reaching to the lakes and was Central Africa's prevailing center of civilization.[38] But in the end the OIC affair only furthered the impression that the CCM, like the union itself, was part of a plot against Islam.[39]

The CCM, in turn, has repeatedly attempted to characterize the opposition as animated by pan-Arabism and even by a wish to restore Arab rule and Omani feudalism. CUF is thus tagged with the Arab race-baiting that has long been a staple of certain CCM elements, even on the mainland.[40] The ruling party also accuses CUF of pursuing the politics of radical Islamism; since 2001, the United States' so-called war on terror has provided CCM propagandists with a ready-made geopolitical discourse on which to draw. (Conversely,

U.S. wooing of the Tanzanian government and the prominence of Western Islamophobia have enabled opposition figures to claim that their advocacy of religious issues gives them anti-imperialist credentials.) More subtly but probably more insidiously, government speakers have alleged that the opposition regards all CCM members as infidels or dubious Muslims. CUF leaders plausibly deny such allegations. But casual disparagement of mainlanders' religion occurs frequently in private conversations, and CCM supporters no doubt hear reverberations of that in CUF politicians' public statements about restoring Zanzibar's once-glorious history of Islamic civilization.

Bakari writes that few Zanzibaris put much stock in the CCM's misrepresentations, although, even allowing for fraud, the CCM continues to draw substantial electoral support in the islands. In any case, the CCM's calumnies have served to reinforce many islanders' conviction that the ruling party is animated by hostility to Islam; a popular joke asserts that CCM really stands for "Christian Church of the Mainland." And that, in turn, has further contributed to growing spirals of mutual suspicion and vituperation in which political tensions are reproduced in terms of religious and national betrayal. Fifteen years on, the OIC affair remains a sore point, and statistics pointing to the marginalization of Tanzania's Muslims in education and employment are interpreted as evidence of the union government's animus toward Islam. Agitation over such issues, the appearance of fringe groups that advocate reconstituting the caliphate, and the global prevalence of rhetoric vilifying "Islamic terrorism" have in turn encouraged some CCM supporters on the mainland to voice naked Islamophobia.

As during Zanzibar's first Time of Politics, these spirals of reciprocal vilification risk becoming transformed into violent communal subjectivities. So far, most incidents of violence have been sporadic and relatively minor, one significant exception being a January 2001 police rampage that killed dozens in Pemba and Zanzibar Town. But particular danger inheres in how those acts are reproduced in a more sustained manner through rumor and political speech. The most common forms of violence arise from the so-called *maskani*, a word that in its original usage describes street-corner hangouts where men gather to drink coffee, play cards or other games, and gossip. Since the 1990s *maskani* have become polarized along party lines, as they were during the original Time of Politics. In contemporary Zanzibar, this is the most visible example of the politicization of civil society, although it affects only a masculine realm.[41] The *maskani* are also sites where political activists, often operating through their parties' youth wings, mobilize young men to take violent action directly against their rivals. Party toughs have attacked rivals' *maskani,* disrupted rivals' political rallies, and intimidated would-be voters. Both sides have engaged in such violence, but CCM squads act with impunity, knowing the police are unlikely to interfere with them. Much of the worst violence, in fact, has been inflicted by the security forces themselves. Such activities have injected explicit references to violence into political speech. Each side portrays itself as the party of peace and its rival as the party of violence, and talk of victimhood is accompanied by threats of retaliation.[42]

When threats of violence are not explicit, they are implied by constant references to the 1964 revolution, and it is these historical references that have proven most polarizing. Of course, among Zanzibaris who are old enough, there are some for whom actual lived memories of revolutionary violence have created literal psychological trauma that shapes their responses to visual markers of ethnic difference.[43] But equally if not more significant is how political actors have reproduced and manipulated "memories" of 1964 as a way to reconstitute the revolution as a "chosen trauma" in the current political drama. The ruling party is most direct in its references to the revolution, building on a discourse that has been hegemonic since 1964. It uses such references both to rally its supporters (warning that CUF plans to reverse land reform and restore the rule of the sultans) and to intimidate the opposition. In January 2001, for example, in an effort to intimidate people and thus prevent them from participating in opposition demonstrations, government television ran footage of the revolution along with scenes of the massacres in Rwanda and Tiananmen Square. During the 2005 campaigns, CCM candidates, including the incumbent president, Amani Karume (son of Abeid), warned the opposition not to forget the violence that had brought the ASP to power. "This country has been created through bloodshed using knives, pangas and stones," one government speaker proclaimed. "What about today when we have modern weapons like guns? We shall never let this country go."[44]

Threats like these encourage opposition members, too, to shape their image of the ruling party along the contours of prevailing historical memories of the revolution. Ironically, although the regime's misrule has discredited its ideology of revolutionary essentialism, it has at the same time enhanced that ideology's significance in the minds of its opponents. As a result, the revolution has become a central "reference point" in political discourse. And that, in turn, has furthered the reproduction of essentialized categories parallel to those by which the revolution is conventionally narrated, placing an emphasis on "ethnic categorization rather than citizenship" in political discourse. "It is not that these historical versions have suddenly reappeared," writes Kjersti Larsen, "but rather that they have been intensified and reformulated."[45] Discourse that uses the revolution as a reference point encourages CCM members to emphasize their identities as Africans and vilify their enemies as Arabs who would re-enslave them; it encourages the opposition to imagine themselves as islanders rather than Africans, defenders of the islands' Islamic civilization against the threat of barbarism. Political tensions are imagined not simply in terms of partisan difference but in terms of the inherent incompatibilities of self and other.

The reformulated categories figure most potently in representations of present-day violence. This appears vividly in the accounts of the January 2001 massacres, which have begun to take on the role of a chosen trauma. The government blames CUF for instigating the violence, reshaping old discourses of Arab-baiting with newer language invoking al-Qaeda and "terrorism." The opposition, more plausibly, blames the ruling party. But opposition narratives represent the aggressors in similarly mythopoeic form: as mainlanders, Christians, and barbarians who are animated by a hatred of Islam. Some of the latter motifs are based on documented fact, such as the government's heavy-handed attempts to prevent gatherings at mosques, or, if unsubstantiated, are sadly believable, such as the beatings and other humiliations of Arabs, which in their details recall similar outrages from 1964. Others, however, strain credibility, especially motifs about insults to Islam. People are said to have been killed simply for praying or to have been forbidden to utter the name of Allah because "there is no god but Benjamin Mkapa," the union president at the time. (Visitors are often reminded that Mkapa, who congratulated the police after the massacres, is ethnically Makua, a group closely related to the Makonde.) Yet despite their fantastic nature, such tales are retold with the conviction conveyed by rumor.[46]

The most ubiquitous motifs in these narratives are those that represent the government and CCM aggressors as uniformly mainlander and Christian and the opposition as uniformly Muslim. Those statements fly in the face of the facts. Of the culprits named in the careful Human Rights Watch report on the 2001 massacres, for example, only one, the commander of the riot police, has a Christian name.[47] Virtually everyone in Zanzibar is Muslim, and government officials play prominent roles in major religious events. In such a state, it is simply implausible that a politician of any party would declare that "all Muslims" are terrorists. But these and similar assertions are made with such

straightforward simplicity that they have misled even some well-informed observers. Their most telling impact is how they have distorted perceptions of the
religious makeup of the mainland and islands. Mainland Tanzania contains
roughly equal numbers of Muslims and Christians; the peaceful coexistence
of these two groups has long been celebrated. Yet many Zanzibaris routinely
describe the mainland as "largely Christian," a description that heightens their
self-image as a threatened minority within the United Republic. Though apparently a simple statement of fact, often spoken without the slightest hint of chauvinism, this is in many ways more disturbing than even the many harrowing
details of police brutality reported by Human Rights Watch. If it is accepted by
Tanzanians as readily as it is accepted by many sympathetic outsiders, it could
provide a paradigm by which Zanzibaris' chosen traumas of ethnicized violence might be carried throughout the United Republic, encouraging Muslims
on the mainland to nurse grievances about violent victimization and Christians to think of the mainland as their privileged preserve. That would constitute a tragic parody of the old proverb about *ustaarabu:* When the piper plays
at Zanzibar, they dance at the lakes.[48]

The Shared Discourse of Race

Zanzibar's current political tensions have not yet been racialized to the
degree that they were during the first Time of Politics; most Zanzibaris seem
to have resisted the voices trying to stir up racial fears. But to the extent that
such voices still have some purchase, racial fears have not simply "persisted"
from the early 1960s. Rather, as I have tried to show in the preceding narrative,
they were remade during the intervening years, in part through the habits of
everyday life, but also by the willed actions of new generations of intellectuals and politicians. This is an example, in miniature, of the kind of processes
that have been my subject throughout this book. Racial thinking is remade not
simply by recirculating old ideas but by supplementing and reshaping them
with added elements, including, in our case, debates over the union and the
legitimacy of a state based on claims of African racial nationalism; the quasi-
Marxist rhetorics of class and of neocolonial domination; historical debates
about the events of 1964; and, most recently, the global discourse of the "war"
on "Islamic terrorism."

Of all these elements, the regime's racial nationalism has had the most profound effect. Although African racial nationalism has played a liberating role
in many parts of the world, in Zanzibar it has run a perverse course, shaping

opposition to the ASP-CCM government in ways that have reinforced nativist hostility toward mainlanders. The opposition's narrow nativism, in fact, demonstrates that the discourse of African racial nationalism has become hegemonic in the precise sense: not in how it supposedly stifles resistance or opposition to the regime—which clearly has not happened—but in how it shapes the resistance it arouses. For over a generation, Zanzibar's rulers have justified themselves with the language of racial nativism, claiming that their authority stemmed from having overthrown an alien regime and kept new alien threats at bay. Their opponents all too often respond with a limited negation, not by challenging the terms of nativist discourse but by merely transmuting them, redefining who the aliens are.

This tragic logic has beset nationalism elsewhere on the continent, as political elites cling to power by refashioning the nativist rhetoric of belonging that had once posed such a potent challenge to colonial domination.[49] That should not surprise us. All nationalisms are built on a nativist logic, one that allocates rights of citizenship according to reckonings of place and belonging. Of course, Africa's founding nationalists aimed for unity, not division. Pan-Africanism, the prevailing form of nativism they championed, promised to transcend the more local nativisms that threatened the stability of the new nation-states. And as Basil Davidson has observed, the very form of those new states, inherited from the arbitrary units drawn by the colonial powers, did not at first seem to lend themselves to being interpreted in the terms of blood and soil that have made the history of the modern European nation-state one of recurring brutality. But pan-Africanism's failure to contain local nativisms— to prevent them from being reconstructed and revived—is well known. And even the solidarities of the postcolonial nation-states themselves, despite the shallow political traditions from which they were crafted, have proven susceptible to manipulation by demagogues. In Ivory Coast, Zambia, South Africa, and elsewhere, entirely new nativisms that are no older than the young nation-states target immigrants from elsewhere in Africa as aliens to be purged.[50]

But racial nativism is far more ubiquitous in African political thought than are any of these narrower forms; it is unquestioned and, indeed, celebrated. Ironically, it is perhaps the most persistent inheritance, in intellectual terms, of the colonial order it was so central to overthrowing.[51] And its influence extends well beyond African politics, pervading much of how the world thinks of Africa, including scholars whose interests and sympathies are focused on the continent. The continental boundaries that delineate the taken-for-granted categories of conventional racial thought also determine our topics of study; even recent scholarship that seeks to transcend continental boundaries does so, by and large, by focusing on "diasporas" of Africans that are racially defined.

In focusing on African racial nationalism I by no means intend to minimize the importance that the practice of white supremacy had in shaping the modern world, including how it influenced the thinking of those oppressed by it: for colonial subjects hoping to end European rule, racial nationalism seemed the most logical response. But difficulties arise when we allow the essentializing paradigms of race to shape our own understandings of the African past—when, instead of investigating how those paradigms came to prominence in the thought of specific historical actors, we take them for granted. In many ways, the study of the Swahili coast has become emblematic of these difficulties. For much of the past fifty years, students of Swahili culture, African and foreign alike, have been enmeshed in what the anthropologist Deborah Amory calls the "Nani Debate," a label she coins from the Swahili interrogative for "who," as in the perennial question, "Who are the Swahili?" (*Waswahili ni Nani?*). The debate, Amory notes, had its origin early in the colonial period, when Western scholars struggled to characterize the inhabitants of the coastal towns according to the racial categories they had brought with them. On the one hand, the townspeople spoke a Bantu language and were, for the most part, African in appearance. On the other hand, their culture was cosmopolitan rather than tribal, oriented culturally and commercially toward the Indian Ocean. The colonial scholars defined Swahili culture as neither African nor Arab, or as both African *and* Arab. But in either case, writes Amory, their understanding of Swahili culture was structured by the essential racial binary of African versus Arab.[52]

With the rising hegemony of African nationalism in the 1960s and later, it was no longer acceptable to define the African essence in Hegelian terms as inward looking and unchanging. But, though valuated differently, the racial binary remained firmly in place, its influence on African thinkers much greater than it had been early in the century. And champions of the nationalist paradigm of race, perhaps more than advocates of the colonial version, felt threatened by contaminating cosmopolitanisms that fit into none of the binary's pristine categories. Given the obvious cosmopolitanism of Swahili culture (by which I mean—since authenticity and purity are everywhere a fiction—the ease with which its cosmopolitan origins can be discerned by minds for which continental divisions are paramount), it was virtually inevitable that the Nani Debate would be revived. Nationalist champions of Swahili culture in Tanzania and

Kenya focused their energies on sweeping the cosmopolitanism away, portraying Swahili culture as indisputably "African" in origin, not Arab.

But such positions have encountered difficulties of their own, inasmuch as they attempt to minimize the significance of Indian Ocean cultural influences that have long been cherished by coastal intellectuals, including Arabic and Islam. My point here is to emphasize the hazards of searching for the racial essence of a culture. Those hazards are not to be taken lightly; they have trapped the most powerful and worldly intellects. One well-known example involves a vitriolic exchange between two of Africa's most prominent public intellectuals: Wole Soyinka, the Nobel laureate, and Ali Mazrui, political scientist and author of an internationally circulated television series, *Africans: A Triple Heritage.* Mazrui is a Swahili-speaker and a scion of an eminent family that ruled Mombasa and Pemba centuries ago, before the advent of the Busaids. Soyinka, in his critiques of *A Triple Heritage,* accused not simply Mazrui but the entire Swahili language and culture of being inauthentically African, insufficiently black. Soyinka was particularly exercised by what he regarded as Mazrui's apologies for the Arab slave trade (a phrase both authors used). His charges are particularly ironic given that for many African Americans, Swahili is the chosen language of pan-Africanism. The irony was also noted by the eminent novelist and essayist Ishmael Reed, who prefers to study Soyinka's mother tongue, Yoruba. Swahili, said Reed, is "the Arab slave trader language. It has a Bantu syntax but an Arab vocabulary."[53]

Arab slave traders, African slaves: it seems that pan-Africanism cannot shake these baleful images, thrust into pan-Africanist consciousness by the Zanzibar Revolution.[54] Henry Louis Gates, another prominent African American public intellectual and probably today's best-known interpreter of Africa in the English-speaking West, directly confronts these images in his own television series, *Wonders of the African World.* (A close colleague of Soyinka, Gates was responsible for publishing his debate with Mazrui in the journal *Transition.*) In his episode on the Swahili coast, Gates focuses on Zanzibaris' racial identity, aggressively challenging interviewees who identify themselves as Shirazi by telling them they look as African as he. Gates also devotes much time to Zanzibar's "slave market church," a monument to the slave trade built by missionaries in the 1870s. In the years since the revolution, the monument has become a central site for the reproduction of racialized fictions about the brutalities of "Arab slavery," including tales that Bibi Titi Muhammad repeated on the eve of the 1961 pogroms and others that have been newly invented. Gates allows the keepers of this shrine to repeat those myths as fact.

Gates represents his series as an intellectual autobiography, an attempt to bring to the screen typically American responses to African realities. But in doing so, he inadvertently shows us the perils of approaching race in other parts of the world with categories derived from our own peculiar history. Perhaps the only solution would be to strive to abandon race altogether as a category of analysis and limit it instead to a topic of study—born, perhaps, of a universal propensity to categorize, but a propensity that is realized everywhere in patterns that are contingent and historically unique. Such diversity of experience makes humanity infinitely more complex than any paradigm of racial or national order can hope to capture. Though the ubiquity of such thinking divides us, the challenge of breaking with it is a burden we share.

Glossary

asili: origins, source, ancestry; nature, essence

Busaid: the ruling dynasty of the Zanzibar sultanate

duka: small general shop

gozi: colloquial for "Black," term of self-reference among ASP racial nationalists

Hizbu: the ZNP (from Hizbu l'Watan, Arabic for the National Party)

madarasa: Koranic schools

magozi: pl. of *gozi*

Mahizbu: pl. of Hizbu, ZNP members or loyalists

masheha: pl. of *sheha*

mchukuzi: carter or porter, a worker who specializes in hauling and packing commodities

mshenzi: barbarian

mstaarabu: civilized person (n. and adj.)

mudir: colonial official, usually an Arab, who reported to a district commissioner

mwinyi mkuu: Shirazi ruler who dominated Unguja before the advent of Busaid rule

mwungwana: gentleman/woman, civilized person

ngoma: drumming and dance

panga: machete

seyyid: lord or prince: honorific used to denote the Busaid sultans and males belonging to the royal family

sheha: lowest-level colonial official, usually an African; reported to a mudir

Shirazi: one of several terms of self-reference adopted by people who considered themselves indigenous to the islands; referred to distant ancestry in the Islamic Middle East

uhuru: independence, freedom

ulamaa: Islamic scholars

Unguja: the island of Zanzibar

ushenzi: barbarism

ustaarabu: civilization

uungwana: the state of gentility; the state of being civilized *wachukuzi*: pl. of *mchukuzi*

washenzi: pl. of *mshenzi*

Yarubi: Omani dynasty preceding the Busaids

Zanj: black (Farsi and Arabic); root of "Zanzibar," "Land of the Blacks"

Notes

Abbreviations

AfrKw:	*Afrika Kwetu*
Cah. d'ét. afr.:	*Cahiers d'études africaines*
CO	Colonial Office
F-S:	Foster-Sutton Commission hearing transcripts (in the Clarence Buxton Papers, MSS Brit. Emp. s. 390, RH)
IJAHS:	International Journal of African Historical Studies
JAH:	*Journal of African History*
Maz.:	*Mazungumzo ya Walimu wa Unguja*
PRO:	Public Record Office (National Archives), Kew, UK
RH:	Bodleian Library of Commonwealth and African Studies at Rhodes House
ZHCA:	Zanzibar High Court Archives
ZNA:	Zanzibar National Archives

Preface and Acknowledgments

1. *Africa Addio,* dir. Gualtiero Jacopetti and Franco Prosperi, Cineriz, 1966. Cf. Paul Johnson, "Colonialism's Back—and Not a Moment Too Soon," *New York Times,* magazine section, 18 April 1993.

2. M. Crawford Young, "Nationalism, Ethnicity, and Class in Africa: A Retrospective," *Cah. d'ét. afr.* 26 (1986): 425.

3. Particularly revealing in this regard is the furore roused early this decade by the sociologist Gavin Kitching. See Danny Postel, "Out of Africa," *Chronicle of Higher Education,* 28 March 2003; and the forum "Responding to 'Why I Left African Studies,'" in *African Studies Quarterly* 7, nos. 2/3 (online journal), available at http://www.africa.ufl.edu/asq/v7/v7i2.htm, especially the contribution by Timothy Burke.

4. Jan Vansina, "The Politics of History and the Crisis in the Great Lakes," *Africa Today* 45, no. 1 (1998): 42.

5. See Abdulrazak Gurnah, *Admiring Silence* (New York, 1996), for a poignant evocation of such memory-making set in the aftermath of the events recounted in this book. I paraphrase a passage on 62–63.

1. Rethinking Race in the Colonial World

1. The quotes are from a classic statement by Clifford Geertz: "The Integrative Revolution: Primordial Sentiments and Civil Politics in the New States," in *Old Societies and New States,* ed.

Clifford Geertz (New York, 1963); he attributed much of his language to the sociologist Edward Shils.

2. "False Identity," *Chicago Defender*, 16 January 1964, p. 15.

3. "Zanzibar Long Divided by Arab African Rivalry—Tensions of 25 Centuries Brought to a Critical Point in New Independence," *New York Times*, 13 January 1964, p. 9. Much Western attention was animated by fears that Zanzibar would become a base for communist subversion. But even the right-wing pundits who spun fantasies of Chinese and Cuban meddling agreed that the latter had merely been fishing in long-troubled waters. And the U.S. State Department responded to charges that it had "lost" Zanzibar by minimizing the role of communist infiltration and stressing the significance of local racial resentments. "Two Lessons from Zanzibar," *Chicago Tribune*, 16 January 1964 (editorial); "Zanzibar Coup Role of Cuba Called Small" (UPI wire), *Chicago Tribune*, 24 January 1964.

4. A. H. J. Prins, *Swahili-Speaking Peoples of Zanzibar and the East African Coast*, 2nd ed. (London, 1967). This theme appears throughout the literature on Swahili society: e.g., David Parkin, "Swahili Mijikenda: Facing Both Ways in Kenya," *Africa* 59 (1989): 161–175. For a useful review of other authors, see Roman Loimeier and Rüdiger Seesemann, "Introduction: Interfaces of Islam, Identity and Space in 19th and 20th Century East Africa," in *The Global Worlds of the Swahili*, ed. Loimeier and Seeseman (Berlin, 2006).

5. Alamin Mazrui and Ibrahim Noor Shariff, *The Swahili: Idiom and Identity of an African People* (Trenton, 1994).

6. [Abeid Amani Karume], *Baadhi ya Hotuba Zilizotolewa na Makamo wa Kwanza wa Rais* (Zanzibar, 1965), 7, 25, and passim. ASP rhetoric particularly stressed the government's alleged role in fomenting divisions between African mainlanders and the islands' indigenous "Shirazi" majority: e.g. ASP, *The History of Zanzibar Africans and the Formation of the Afro-Shirazi Party* (Zanzibar, 1965).

7. History was banished from the schools immediately after the revolution. It was not formally reintroduced until the late 1990s. Omar Ramadhan Mapuri, "Historia Kufundishwa Tena Zanzibar," *An-Nuur* (Dar es Salaam), 9–16 May 1997.

8. Ali Muhsin al-Barwani, *Conflicts and Harmony in Zanzibar: Memoirs* (Dubai, 1997), 45. Ironically, Muhsin derived the phrase "mixture of mixtures" from a classic colonial source on which his writings often drew: Reginald Coupland, *East Africa and Its Invaders* (Oxford, 1938), 11, who in turn quoted C. G. Seligman's description of the Swahili population in *Races of Africa* (London, 1930). Elsewhere in the memoirs, Muhsin went so far as to describe, contrary to his assertions to the contrary, how Arab families in Zanzibar strove to preserve their distinctiveness through carefully arranged marriages; he used his own marriage, which he described with pride, as an example. In the same vein, Juma Aley, a minister in Muhsin's government, wrote in the 1980s that "colonial administrators corroded the racial atmosphere for their own ends" and were personally responsible for the most inflammatory of ASP journalism. Yet when in power in the early 1960s, Aley openly expressed contempt for Africans. Juma Aley, *Zanzibar: In the Context* (New Delhi, 1988); Anthony Clayton, *The Zanzibar Revolution and Its Aftermath* (London, 1981), 63; Don Petterson, *Revolution in Zanzibar* (Boulder, 2002), 41, 69.

9. Quoted by E. J. Hobsbawm in *Nations and Nationalism since 1780* (Cambridge, 1992), 12.

10. I will consider the African literature below. The classic argument for South Asia is Gyanendra Pandey, *The Construction of Communalism in Colonial North India* (Delhi, 1990). For broad critiques see Sudhir Kakar, *The Colors of Violence* (Chicago, 1996), 12–24; C. A. Bayly, *Origins of Nationality in South Asia* (Delhi, 1998); and Rosalind O'Hanlon, "Historical Approaches to Communalism: Perspectives from Western India," in *Society and Ideology: Essays in South Asian History*, ed. Peter Robb (Delhi, 1993), 247–266.

11. Crawford Young observed this of the literature on African nationalism itself over twenty years ago, and the point remains valid; see "Nationalism, Ethnicity, and Class in Africa." For the literature on South Asia, see Gyanendra Pandey, *Remembering Partition* (Cambridge, 2001).

12. Ann Laura Stoler, "Racial Histories and Their Regimes of Truth," *Political Power and Social Theory* 11 (1997): 185; Loïc Wacquant, "For an Analytic of Racial Domination," *Political Power and Social Theory* 11 (1997): 222.

13. The parallel was pointed out long ago by René Lemarchand in "Revolutionary Phenomena in Stratified Societies: Rwanda and Zanzibar," *Civilisations* 5, no. 1 (1968); and Catharine Newbury, "Colonialism, Ethnicity and Rural Political Protest: Rwanda and Zanzibar in Comparative Perspective," *Comparative Politics* 15 (1983): 253–280.

14. The concept is often associated with the sociologist Michael Banton, *The Idea of Race* (London, 1977).

15. Mahmood Mamdani, *When Victims Become Killers* (Princeton, 2001). Villia Jefremovas observes that many authors neglect the role of indigenous Rwandan intellectuals in "Treacherous Waters: The Politics of History and the Politics of Genocide in Rwanda and Burundi," *Africa* 70 (2000): 298–308. Mamdani's interpretation is particularly egregious, since it contradicts his avowed determination to go beyond analyses that focus on state agency. In contrast, much of the literature that Mamdani claims to transcend in fact demonstrates the important role Rwandan intellectuals played in crafting racial myths. Examples include Jan Vansina, *L'évolution du royaume Rwanda à 1900* (1962; repr., Brussels, 2000); Claudine Vidal, *Sociologie des passions* (Paris, 1991), 45–61; and Jean-Pierre Chrétien, "Hutu et Tutsi au Rwanda et au Burundi," in *Au coeur de l'ethnie*, ed. Jean-Loup Amselle and Elikia M'bokolo (Paris, 1985), esp. 146–150. This literature renders implausible any suggestion that such intellectuals merely parroted their European teachers. Though racialization was indeed largely a product of the colonial era, the historical record prompts a leading authority to "summarily reject" the views of authors who attribute the distinction between Hutu and Tutsi (and their mutual hostility) to colonial masters. Jan Vansina, *Antecedents to Modern Rwanda* (Madison, 2004), 138.

16. Robert Miles, *Racism* (London, 2003). For critiques of the continued tendency to inflate race into a sociological category, see Mara Loveman, "Is 'Race' Essential?" *American Sociological Review* 64 (1999): 861–898; and Rogers Brubaker, Mara Loveman, and Peter Stamatov, "Ethnicity as Cognition," *Theory and Society* 33 (2004): 31–64. Understanding race as a mode of thought has become all the more prevalent as scientists have demolished lingering notions that racial boundaries have any biological significance, yet it long predates those advances. It informed Hannah Arendt's influential concept of "race-thinking" (*The Origins of Totalitarianism* [1951; repr., New York, 1973]), and in fact can be found in Weber, who did not consider race or ethnicity to be sociological categories. See Max Weber, *Economy and Society,* ed. Guenther Roth and Claus Wittich, vol. 1 (New York, 1968), 385–398; and Ernst Moritz Manasse, "Max Weber on Race," *Social Research* 14 (1947): 191–221.

17. Rogers Brubaker, *Ethnicity without Groups* (Cambridge, Mass., 2004), 3–4, 19.

18. For a consensus that race be regarded as "doctrine," see Michael Banton, "The Concept of Racism," in *Race and Racialism*, ed. Sami Zubaida (London, 1970), 17–34. Miles, *Racism,* prefers the word "ideology." Arendt's idea of "race-thinking" is more flexible, but she, too, treated it as specific to Western thought.

19. Nevertheless, folk racisms are usually regarded as distinct from the real thing—some authors simply refusing to consider them manifestations of racial thought, others assuming that popular notions arose as pale reflections of ideas whose origins lay in more erudite circles. Examples of the first approach include Banton, "The Concept of Racism"; of the second, Eric Wolf, "Perilous Ideas: Race, Culture, People," *Current Anthropology* 35 (1994): 1–12; and K. Anthony

Appiah, "Race, Culture, Identity: Misunderstood Connections," in Appiah and Amy Gutmann, *Color Conscious: The Political Morality of Race* (Princeton, 1996), 30–105. For an incisive discussion of "the continual barter between folk and analytical notions," see Wacquant, "For an Analytic of Racial Domination."

20. Etienne Balibar, "Is There a 'Neo-Racism'?" in Balibar and Immanuel Wallerstein, *Race, Nation, Class* (London, 1991), 21. This literature first arose in response to the arguments of Banton and other British sociologists that the anti-immigrant rhetoric of Tory politicians in the postcolonial U.K. could not properly be deemed "racism." Banton, *The Idea of Race*, chapter 9; Martin Barker, *The New Racism: Conservatives and the Ideology of the Tribe* (London, 1981).

21. Stoler, "Racial Histories."

22. Raciology was more about explaining difference than about ranking, and some raciologists considered themselves anti-racists—that is, politically opposed to ranking. For examples, see E. W. Count, ed., *This Is Race* (New York, 1950); Benoit Massin, "From Virchow to Fischer: Physical Anthropology and 'Modern Race Theories' in Wilhelmine Germany," in *Volksgeist as Method and Ethic*, ed. George W. Stocking (Madison, 1996), 79–154.

23. Balibar, "Is There a 'Neo-Racism'?" 23. The term "cultural monads" is from Wolf, "Perilous Ideas." For the marginal significance of raciology among British colonial policy makers, see Helen Tilley, *Africa as a Living Laboratory: Empire, Development and the Problem of Scientific Knowledge* (Chicago, forthcoming).

24. Classic accounts include Philip D. Curtin, *The Image of Africa* (Madison, 1964); and George W. Stocking, *Race, Culture, and Evolution* (Chicago, 1982).

25. Friedrich Nietzsche, *Toward a Genealogy of Morals*, section 13. In *The Portable Nietzsche*, ed. and trans. Walter Kaufmann (New York, 1954), 453

26. Stoler, "Racial Histories." An example is Ivan Hannaford, *Race: The History of an Idea in the West* (Baltimore, 1996). Compare to Benjamin Isaac, *The Invention of Racism in Classical Antiquity* (Princeton, 2004), which provides a thorough refutation of the modernist consensus. (The first half of Hannaford's book is an erudite exercise in correcting for the opposite error—that is, the assumption through backward induction that an act of apparent racism from the premodern past was the product of raciological doctrines.)

27. John Rex, "The Concept of Race in Sociological Theory," in Zubaida, *Race and Racialism*, 39. For similar arguments, see Immanuel Wallerstein, "The Construction of Peoplehood," in Balibar and Wallerstein, *Race, Nation, Class*, 71–85; Roger Sanjek, "The Enduring Inequalities of Race," in *Race*, ed. Steven Gregory and R. Sanjek (New Brunswick, 1994), 1–17; Eduardo Bonilla-Silva, "The Essential Social Fact of Race," *American Sociological Review* 64, no. 6 (1999): 899–906; and Howard Winant, *The World Is a Ghetto: Race and Democracy since World War II* (New York, 2001).

28. Banton, *The Idea of Race*. Much of Banton's argument draws on Leon Poliakov, *The Aryan Myth: A History of Racist and Nationalist Ideas in Europe* (New York, 1974).

29. These distinctions are developed further by Anthony Appiah, from whom I have derived some of my language: *In My Father's House* (Oxford, 1992), and "Racisms," in *Anatomy of Racism*, ed. David Theo Goldberg (Minneapolis, 1990), 3–17. Appiah writes of "racialism" rather than "racial thought."

30. Appiah calls the first of these "extrinsic racism," the second "intrinsic racism"; *In My Father's House*, 13–15. Parallel observations by social psychologists are described by Brubaker, Loveman, and Stamatov in "Ethnicity as Cognition," 40–41.

31. These comments of course do not refer to the French Enlightenment concept of *civilisation*, which, strictly speaking, included the embrace of universal (i.e., Western) reason. But the eighteenth-century French neologism was coined to express more general concepts that

long predated (and outlived) it, few of which were peculiar to the modern West. Lucien Febvre, "*Civilisation:* Evolution of a Word and a Group of Ideas," in Febvre, *A New Kind of History* (London, 1973), 219–257.

32. The best-known examples are China and Japan, for which see Frank Dikötter, "Group Definition and the Idea of Race in Modern China," *Ethnic and Racial Studies* 13, no. 3 (1990); Dikötter, "Introduction" and "Racial Discourse in China: Continuities and Permutations," in *The Construction of Racial Identities in China and Japan,* ed. Frank Dikötter (London, 1997), 1–11 and 12–33, respectively; and Kosaku Yoshino, "The Discourse on Blood and Racial Identity in Contemporary Japan," in Dikötter, *The Construction of Racial Identities in China and Japan,* 199–211. Many of the concepts that were to become racialized in colonial Rwanda had their origins in earlier distinctions between boorishness and urbanity; see Vansina, *Antecedents to Modern Rwanda,* 134–135; and David Newbury, "'Bunyabungo': The Western Rwandan Frontier, c. 1750–1850," in *The African Frontier,* ed. Igor Kopytoff (Bloomington, 1987), 164–192. For other African examples, many quite ancient, see J. Glassman, "Slower Than a Massacre: The Multiple Sources of Racial Thought in Colonial Africa," *American Historical Review* 109 (2004): 726n30.

33. Igor Kopytoff, "The Internal African Frontier: The Making of African Political Culture," in Kopytoff, *The African Frontier,* esp. 49–50, 56–57. Kopytoff notes that discourses of civilization and barbarism shaped the competing claims of peoples who met at the continent's many internal frontiers.

34. John Szwed, "Race and the Embodiment of Culture," *Ethnicity* 2 (1975): 19–33; Appiah, "Race, Culture, Identity"; Donald Horowitz, *Ethnic Groups in Conflict* (Berkeley, 1985). Again, these views were anticipated by Weber, who stressed the degree to which perceptions of group physical differences are culturally determined and therefore as subjective as other perceptions of common ethnic descent. *Economy and Society,* 2: 392.

35. Miles, *Racism,* 42–44; Saul Dubow, "Ethnic Euphemisms and Racial Echoes," *Journal of Southern African Studies* 20 (1994): 355–370; Elazar Barkan, *The Retreat of Scientific Racism* (Cambridge, 1992), esp. 296–302. As Barkan observes, the trend began between the wars. Similar trends can be found in the history of the French word *ethnie,* which, for example, was first applied to Rwanda only in the early 1960s. Dominique Franche, "Généalogie du génocide rwandais: Hutu et Tutsi: Gaulois et Francs?" *Les temps modernes* 582 (1995): 10; Claudine Vidal, "Le génocide des Rwandais tutsi et l'usage public de l'histoire," *Cah. d'ét. afr.* 38 (1998): 660.

36. Brubaker, *Ethnicity without Groups.* Sociologists appear to have been slower to problematize this notion than anthropologists, who nowadays tend to associate a belief in such "cultural monads" with functionalist anthropology and criticize it as such. But it also formed a central component of classic racial thought and was among the targets of Franz Boas's famous critiques of the latter.

37. An explicit emphasis on the blood relationship is not incompatible with an awareness that the relationship is a metaphor for something else. Sati al-Husri, a nationalist active in Baghdad and Cairo and a major influence throughout the Arab world, including among the Zanzibari intellectuals discussed below, recognized that common descent is merely a metaphor, yet he insisted that it is a useful metaphor for forging national unity. Sati al-Husri, "The Historical Factor in the Formation of Nationalism," in *Political and Social Thought in the Contemporary Middle East,* rev. ed., ed. Kemal Karpat (New York, 1982), 39–43. Similar complexities could be found in the attitudes toward biological concepts of race among many of the Volkish thinkers described in George Mosse, *The Crisis of German Ideology* (New York, 1964).

38. This discussion describes views held by a variety of authors, many of which were anticipated by Weber. The phrase "aura of descent" is from Ronald Cohen, "Ethnicity: Problem

and Focus in Anthropology," *Annual Review of Anthropology* 7 (1978): 379–403. Discussions relevant to the metaphor of descent also include Charles Keyes, "Towards a New Formulation of the Concept of Ethnic Group," *Ethnicity* 3 (1976): 202–213; Eric Voegelin, "The Growth of the Race Idea," *Review of Politics* 2 (1940): 283–317; and various sources already cited. For insightful discussions of the ambiguity of distinctions between race, nation, and ethnicity, see Elizabeth Tonkin, Maryon McDonald, and Malcolm Chapman, *History and Ethnicity* (London, 1989), 1–21; and Brubaker, *Ethnicity without Groups*. Religious ethnicities would seem at first glance to be an exception to this argument. Yet the notion of religious identity as an act of choice was "a delayed result of the Reformation and a direct result of the Enlightenment. . . . Outside the West, religion remained an ascriptive affiliation"; Horowitz, *Ethnic Groups in Conflict*, 50.

39. For a discussion of the neoconservative position, see Sanjek, "The Enduring Inequalities of Race," 8–9.

40. Horowitz, *Ethnic Groups in Conflict*, uses this phrase to describe similarities between idioms of kinship and ethnicity.

41. As Benedict Anderson has described them, nations are political communities that are "imagined as both inherently limited and sovereign"; see *Imagined Communities*, rev. ed. (London, 1991), 6. But my gloss is derived chiefly from Weber, "The Nation," in *From Max Weber*, ed. H. Gerth and C. Wright Mills (London, 1948). Anderson's justly influential study has prompted many authors to reduce his definition to the phrase used as its title and to suggest a contrast between "imagined" national communities and other communities that are rooted in more "real" social phenomena. But in doing so, they neglect Anderson's own observation that *all* communities are "imagined" and that being imagined makes them no less real. The contrast between Anderson's "modernist" position and that of scholars, such as Anthony D. Smith, who insist that nations have deeper roots in older ethnic discourses is often overstated; Smith himself strikes a useful balance when he notes that although nationalisms are generally recent historical phenomena, those who imagined them often built on preexisting ethnic discourses; see *The Nation in History* (Hanover, N.H., 2000), chapter 3. As Tonkin, McDonald, and Chapman observe, "it is no more than a tautology to say that nations have ethnic origins" (*History and Ethnicity*, 18)—provided that one remembers that ethnic communities are no less "imagined" than nations.

42. Anderson, *Imagined Communities*; Liisa Malkki, *Purity and Exile* (Chicago, 1995); A. M. Alonso, "The Politics of Space, Time and Substance: State Formation, Nationalism and Ethnicity," *Annual Review of Anthropology* 23 (1994): 379–405; Basil Davidson, *Black Man's Burden* (New York, 1992).

43. Historians of popular politics in Africa, Latin America, and South Asia have reconstructed with particular subtlety the uneven historical processes by which national thought became hegemonic. Examples include Steven Feierman, *Peasant Intellectuals* (Madison, 1990); Florencia Mallon, *Peasant and Nation: The Making of Postcolonial Mexico and Peru* (Berkeley, 1995); Gyanendra Pandey, "Peasant Revolt and Indian Nationalism," in *Subaltern Studies*, vol. 1, ed. R. Guha (Delhi, 1982); and Shahid Amin, *Event, Metaphor, Memory* (Berkeley, 1995).

44. As Hobsbawm has written, the criteria are "fuzzy"; see *Nations and Nationalism*, 6. For an unusually strong rejection of the search for a consistent definition, see Valery Tishkov, "Forget the 'Nation': Post-Nationalist Understandings of Nationalism," *Ethnic and Racial Studies* 23 (2000): 625–650.

45. Authors who have emphasized the ambiguity of the distinction between race and nation include Etienne Balibar, "Racism and Nationalism," in Balibar and Wallerstein, *Race, Nation, Class*, 37–67; Zygmunt Bauman, "Soil, Blood and Identity," *Sociological Review* 40

(1992): 675–701; Carole Nagengast, "Violence, Terror and the Crisis of the State," *Annual Review of Anthropology* 23 (1994): 109–136; and George Frederickson, *The Comparative Imagination* (Berkeley, 1997), 77–97. See also Brubaker's critique of the distinction between "civic" and "ethnic" nationalisms in *Ethnicity without Groups*, 132–146.

46. My thinking on these matters, which will be taken up again in chapter 4, has been much influenced by Davidson, *Black Man's Burden*; Frederick Cooper, *Colonialism in Question* (Berkeley, 2005); and Cooper, "Possibility and Constraint: African Independence in Historical Perspective," *JAH* 49 (2008): 167–196.

47. In contrast, see the intriguing studies of intellectuals from the French empire who struggled to craft a politics of postcolonialism within a continuing framework of the French Community. Examples include Gary Wilder, "Untimely Vision: Aimé Césaire, Decolonization, Utopia," *Public Culture* 21 (2009): 101–140; Gregory Mann, *Native Sons: West African Veterans and France in the Twentieth Century* (Durham, 2006); and the works of Cooper cited in the preceding note.

48. For the African diaspora as a product of the imaginative work of pan-Africanism, see Tiffany Patterson and Robin D. G. Kelley, "Unfinished Migrations: Reflections on the African Diaspora and the Making of the Modern World," *African Studies Review* 43 (2000): 11–45.

49. Kenneth James King, *Pan-Africanism and Education* (Oxford, 1971); James R. Brennan, "Realizing Civilization through Patrilineal Descent: The Intellectual Making of an African Racial Nationalism in Tanzania, 1920–50," *Social Identities* 12 (2006): 405–423.

50. For a critique of anticolonial politics as nationalist romance, see David Scott, *Conscripts of Modernity: The Tragedy of Colonial Enlightenment* (Durham, 2004).

51. See the literature on Rwanda discussed in note 15 above. Other examples include Patrick Harries, "Exclusion, Classification and Internal Colonialism: The Emergence of Ethnicity among the Tsonga-Speakers of South Africa," in *The Creation of Tribalism in Southern Africa*, ed. Leroy Vail (Berkeley, 1991), 82–117; Colin Leys, *Underdevelopment in Kenya* (Berkeley, 1974), 198–206; and Archie Mafeje, "The Ideology of 'Tribalism,'" *Journal of Modern African Studies* 9, no. 2 (1971): 253–261 (the latter is an influential statement that explicitly dismissed ethnic thought as "false consciousness"). For an "internal critique" of this position, see Terence Ranger, "The Invention of Tradition Revisited: The Case of Colonial Africa," in *Legitimacy and the State in Twentieth Century Africa*, ed. T. Ranger and Olufemi Vaughan (London, 1993).

52. Mazrui and Shariff, *The Swahili*; for Zanzibar, 132–135.

53. Leroy Vail, "Introduction: Ethnicity in Southern African History," in Vail, *Creation of Tribalism*, 1–19. Vail's essay has been taken as something of a manifesto by many scholars: see Paris Yeros, "Introduction: On the Uses and Implications of Constructivism," in *Ethnicity and Nationalism in Africa*, ed. Paris Yeros (London, 1999), 1–14.

54. Alongside the constructivists can be placed scholars who, without disavowing the latter's concern with intellectual matters, have carefully focused on the material networks of kinship and clientele that undergird many ethnic networks. The latter include Justin Willis, *Mombasa, the Swahili, and the Making of the Mijikenda* (Oxford, 1992); Sara Berry, *No Condition Is Permanent* (Madison, 1993); Peter Ekeh, "Social Anthropology and Two Contrasting Uses of Tribalism in Africa," *Comparative Studies in Society and History* 32 (1990): 660–700; and the analysis of colonial Zanzibar's racial politics in the final pages of Frederick Cooper, *From Slaves to Squatters* (New Haven, Conn., 1980). The constructivists owe much to groundbreaking earlier studies of East Africa such as John Iliffe's chapter "The Creation of Tribes," in *A Modern History of Tanganyika* (Cambridge, 1979); John Lonsdale, "When Did the Gusii or Any Other Group Become a 'Tribe'?" *Kenya Historical Review* 5, no. 1 (1977): 123–133; and Aidan Southall, "The Illusion of Tribe," *Journal of Asian and African Studies* 5, nos. 1–2 (1970).

55. Among Africa scholars, the best-known modern statement of this position was Hugh Trevor-Roper's dismissive comment about "the unrewarding gyrations of barbarous tribes," made infamous by the critique in J. D. Fage's inaugural lecture, *On the Nature of African History* (University of Birmingham, 1965).

56. Walker Connor, "Beyond Reason: The Nature of the Ethnonational Bond," *Ethnic and Racial Studies* 16 (1993): 373–388.

57. In this regard, the interpretive claim that the constructivists hold to be central to their project—that ethnic identities are historically constructed—is no more than what ought to be axiomatic to any historian and is relevant only in contrast to the ahistorical views they impute, often unfairly, to other scholars. Representative "neo-primordialist" studies include Carter Bentley, "Ethnicity and Practice," *Comparative Studies in Society and History* 29 (1987): 24–55; Horowitz, *Ethnic Groups in Conflict*; Kakar, *The Colors of Violence*; and Katherine Hoffman, *We Share Walls: Language, Land, and Gender in Berber Morocco* (Malden, 2008). All of these are richly aware of the historical dimensions of ethnic discourses; the same, in fact, can be said of Geertz's classic statement, "The Integrative Revolution."

58. Brubaker, Loveman, and Stamatov, "Ethnicity as Cognition," 51.

59. See the critiques of universal history in Gyan Prakash, "Writing Post-Orientalist Histories of the Third World: Perspectives from Indian Historiography," *Comparative Studies in Society and History* 32, no. 2 (1990); Steven Feierman, "African Histories and the Dissolution of World History," in *Africa and the Disciplines*, ed. Robert H. Bates, V. Y. Mudimbe, and J. O'Barr (Chicago, 1993); and Dipesh Chakrabarty, *Provincializing Europe* (Princeton, 2000).

60. Some of my language (and much of my argument) is derived from Young, "Nationalism, Ethnicity, and Class in Africa." Young's comments were directed specifically toward literature on nationalist intellectuals, but they are applicable more generally. Also see Timothy Burke's comments on the historiography of nationalism in "Eyes Wide Shut: Africanists and the Moral Problematics of Postcolonial Societies," *African Studies Quarterly* 7, no. 2&3 (2009), available at http://web.africa.ufl.edu/asq/v7/v7i2a12.htm.

61. Perhaps the most probing examples are Feierman, *Peasant Intellectuals*; and John Lonsdale, "The Moral Economy of Mau Mau," in Lonsdale and Bruce Berman, *Unhappy Valley: Conflict in Kenya and Africa*, book 2 (London, 1992), 265–504. Others include Paul La Hausse, *Restless Identities* (Pietermaritzburg, 2000); J. D. Y. Peel, *Religious Encounter and the Making of the Yoruba* (Bloomington, 2000); and Derek Peterson, *Creative Writing* (Portsmouth, 2004). Also see the discussion in Ranger, "The Invention of Tradition Revisited."

62. The phrase was coined by Carolyn Hamilton in *Terrific Majesty: The Powers of Shaka Zulu and the Limits of Historical Invention* (Cambridge, Mass., 1998). For critiques along these lines, see Ronald Atkinson, "The (Re)construction of Ethnicity in Africa: Extending the Chronology, Conceptualization and Discourse," in Yeros, *Ethnicity and Nationalism*, 15–44; and Thomas Spear, "Neo-Traditionalism and the Limits of Invention in British Colonial Africa," *Journal of African History* 44 (2003): 3–27.

63. Despite Young's plea of twenty years ago, this cliché has been abandoned less readily in studies of ethnic and nationalist politics than in studies of social history. See Nancy Rose Hunt, *A Colonial Lexicon* (Durham, 1999); and Frederick Cooper and Ann Stoler, "Between Metropole and Colony: Rethinking a Research Agenda," in *Tensions of Empire*, ed. Frederick Cooper and Ann Stoler (Berkeley, 1997), 1–56.

64. Horowitz is among those who have discussed the contrast between these two ways of imagining ethnic divisions: see *Ethnic Groups in Conflict*, chapter 1. He usefully refers to them as "unranked" and "ranked" ethnicities; the phrase "incipient whole societies" is also his. Similar distinctions are made by John Comaroff, "Of Totemism and Ethnicity," in John

and Jean Comaroff, *Ethnography and the Historical Imagination* (Boulder, Colo., 1992), and Lemarchand, "Revolutionary Phenomena in Stratified Societies."

65. See Banton, *The Idea of Race*; Banton, "The Concept of Racism"; Rex, "The Concept of Race in Sociological Theory"; Wallerstein, *Race, Nation, Class*; Wallerstein, "The Construction of Peoplehood"; and Sanjek, "The Enduring Inequalities of Race." A critique of such an approach is implicit in my earlier discussion of literature that approaches race as social structure and fails to distinguish between racism and racial thought.

66. As observed by Mamdani (*When Victims Become Killers*, 15), although, as we have seen, he does little better.

67. See Michael Chege, "Africa's Murderous Professors," *The National Interest* 46 (Winter 1996), for suggestive comments.

68. Hence the leading authority on Zanzibari history, in language similar to that used by many authors, explains ethnic divisions by invoking British "preferences" informed by policies of "divide and rule"; see Abdul Sheriff, "Race and Class in the Politics of Zanzibar," *Afrika Spectrum* 36, no. 3 (2001): 307–308.

69. For examples of the first interpretation, see Mazrui and Shariff, *The Swahili*, and Amrit Wilson, *US Foreign Policy and Revolution* (London, 1989); for the second, see B. D. Bowles, "The Struggle for Independence," in *Zanzibar under Colonial Rule*, ed. Abdul Sheriff and Ed Ferguson (London, 1991), esp. 86, 92; B. F. Mrina and W. T. Mattoke, *Mapambano ya Ukombozi Zanzibar* (Dar es Salaam, 1980); and various contributors to T. Maliyamkono, ed., *The Political Plight of Zanzibar* (Dar es Salaam, 2000).

70. Non-Zanzibari examples of similar practices are described in René Lemarchand, *Burundi: Ethnic Conflict and Genocide* (Cambridge, 1994). The official and oppositional Zanzibari histories differ in which groups are identified as British stooges. Official versions include Omar Mapuri, *Zanzibar: The 1964 Revolution: Achievements and Prospects* (Dar es Salaam, 1996); and R. K. Mwanjisi, *Abeid Amani Karume* (Nairobi, 1967). Opposition versions include Muhsin al-Barwani, *Conflicts and Harmony in Zanzibar*; and Zanzibar Center of Human and Democratic Rights, *Zanzibar Dola Taifa na Nchi Huru* (Copenhagen, 1994).

71. Appiah, *In My Father's House*, 7. Appiah's comment stands in contrast to much of the literature on colonial education: see the critical reviews in Sybille Küster, *Neither Cultural Imperialism nor Precious Gift of Civilization: African Education in Colonial Zimbabwe* (Münster, 1994); and Philip Zachernuk, "African History and Imperial Culture in Colonial Nigerian Schools," *Africa* 68, no. 4 (1998). For a rich example of the kind of intellectual history advocated here, see Zachernuk, *Colonial Subjects: An African Intelligentsia and Atlantic Ideas* (Charlottesville, 2000).

72. The concept of subaltern intellectuals received its classic elaboration in Antonio Gramsci, *Selections from the Prison Notebooks*, ed. and trans. by Q. Hoare and G. N. Smith (New York, 1971) and has been fruitfully developed by Feierman, *Peasant Intellectuals*. A rich literature on rural communities in colonial and postcolonial Africa focuses on the innovations of subaltern intellectuals (without necessarily calling them that). Classics include T. O. Ranger, *Revolt in Southern Rhodesia* (Evanston, 1967); John Janzen, *Lemba, 1650–1930* (New York, 1982); David Lan, *Guns and Rain* (Berkeley, 1985); J. B. Peires, *The Dead Will Arise* (Johannesburg, 1989); and David Anderson and Douglas H. Johnson, eds., *Revealing Prophets: Prophecy in Eastern African History* (London, 1995). These studies stand in contrast to the elitist focus of many of the instrumentalist or constructivist studies of ethnic politics.

73. The 1990s saw the rise of a journalistic literature on Africa that Paul Richards criticized acerbically as the "new barbarism" in *Fighting for the Rainforest* (Oxford, 1996). Well-known examples include Robert D. Kaplan, "The Coming Anarchy," *Atlantic Monthly*, February

1994, 44–76; and Keith Richburg, *Out of America: A Black Man Confronts Africa* (New York, 1997).

74. Excellent examples, both of which have reached popular audiences, are Davidson, *Black Man's Burden*; and Bill Berkeley, *The Graves Are Not Yet Full: Race, Tribe, and Power in the Heart of Africa* (New York, 2001).

75. The latter approaches can be found in several of the essays in Vail, *Creation of Tribalism*. Also see Shula Marks, "'The Dog That Did Not Bark, or Why Natal Did Not Take Off': Ethnicity and Democratization in South Africa–KwaZulu Natal," in *Ethnicity and Democracy in Africa*, ed. Bruce Berman, D. Eyoh, and W. Kymlicka (Oxford, 2004).

76. These points are argued in Rogers Brubaker and David Laitin, "Ethnic and Nationalist Violence," in Brubaker, *Ethnicity without Groups*, 88–92.

77. Brubaker and Laitin, "Ethnic and Nationalist Violence,"109–110; also see Mark Levene and Penny Roberts, eds., *The Massacre in History* (New York, 1999). I will return to these arguments in chapter 7.

78. Such scholars include Jonathan Spencer, "On Not Becoming a 'Terrorist': Problems of Memory, Agency, and Community in the Sri Lankan Conflict," in *Violence and Subjectivity*, ed. Veena Das, Arthur Kleinman, Mamphela Ramphele, and Pamela Reynolds (Berkeley, 2000), 120–140; Veena Das, ed., *Mirrors of Violence: Communities, Riots and Survivors in South Asia* (Delhi, 1990); Veena Das, *Life and Words* (Berkeley, 2007); Kakar, *The Colors of Violence*; Allen Feldman, *Formations of Violence* (Chicago, 1991); and Scott Straus, *The Order of Genocide* (Ithaca, 2006).

79. In addition to Malkki, *Purity and Exile*; Pandey, *The Construction of Communalism in Colonial North India*; Pandey, *Remembering Partition*; and Pandey, "Peasant Revolt and Indian Nationalism"; see Alison Des Forges, *Leave None to Tell the Story: Genocide in Rwanda* (New York, 1999); and Norman Naimark, *Fires of Hatred: Ethnic Cleansing in Twentieth-Century Europe* (Cambridge, Mass., 2001).

2. The Creation of a Racial State

1. Though some details on the earliest phases of Swahili prehistory are still in debate, this paragraph represents a consensus view. Useful summaries include Thomas Spear, "Early Swahili History Reconsidered," *IJAHS* 33 (2000): 257–290; Mark Horton and John Middleton, *The Swahili: The Social Landscape of a Mercantile Society* (Oxford, 2000); and Randall Pouwels, "Eastern Africa and the Indian Ocean to 1800: Reviewing Relations in Historical Perspective," *IJAHS* 35 (2002): 385–425. For the rise of Indian Ocean trade systems; see K. N. Chaudhuri, *Trade and Civilisation in the Indian Ocean* (Cambridge, 1985); and Michael N. Pearson, *Port Cities and Intruders* (Baltimore, 1998)

2. In addition to sources already cited, see Randall Pouwels, *Horn and Crescent* (Cambridge, 1987).

3. Horton and Middleton, *The Swahili*, 56. Some scholars suggest that the Shirazi myths contain a kernel of truth: e.g., Abdul Sheriff, "The Historicity of the Shirazi Tradition along the East African Coast," in *Papers Presented during the First Conference on the Historical Role of Iranians (Shirazis) in the East African Coast* (Nairobi, 2001). Yet even they acknowledge that the Persian settlers, if they existed, had disappeared or been absorbed long before the close of the classic period of the city-states.

4. A palimpsest of pre- or non-Islamic foundation myths can possibly be discerned in the Swahili Liongo epic, according to James de Vere Allen; see "Swahili Culture and the Nature of East Coast Settlement," *IJAHS* 14 (1981): 332–333; and Joseph Mbele, "The Identity of the Hero in the Liongo Epic," *Research in African Literatures* 17, no. 4 (1986): 470; but cf. Ibrahim

Noor Shariff, "The Liyongo Conundrum: Reexamining the Historicity of Swahilis' National Poet-Hero," *Research in African Literatures* 22, no. 2 (1991): 153–167. Examples of the non-Swahili traditions can be found in Jan Vansina, *The Children of Woot* (Madison, 1978); David Schoenbrun, *A Green Place, a Good Place* (Portsmouth, 1998); and David Newbury, *Kings and Clans* (Madison, 1991). Kopytoff, "The Internal African Frontier," discusses the common claim of external origins, which, he argues, is a component of many African cultures.

5. Examples of such colonial scholarship include W. H. Ingrams, *Zanzibar: Its History and Its People* (London, 1931), 131–135; and F. B. Pearce, *Zanzibar: The Island Metropolis of Eastern Africa* (London, 1920).

6. The archaeological record shows conclusively that the coast towns grew from indigenous roots and contains none of the cultural discontinuities that would have been attendant on alien conquest.

7. For the Portuguese and early Omani periods, see John Gray, *History of Zanzibar, from the Middle Ages to 1856* (London, 1962); Pearson, *Port Cities and Intruders*; Horton and Middleton, *The Swahili*; Pouwels, "Eastern Africa and the Indian Ocean to 1800"; and Pouwels, *Horn and Crescent*.

8. To avoid confusion, I will use the term "Zanzibar" to refer only to the polity that since 1890 has comprised the islands of Unguja and Pemba.

9. Though the *wenye wakuu* were conventionally described as the quintessential "Shirazi" rulers and often boasted of Shirazi ancestry, the incumbent in 1729 in fact claimed paternal descent from a Yemeni clan, the al-Alawi. This inconsistency was common: "Shirazi" was often used not as a specific place name, but merely as a vague reference to ancestry in the Islamic Middle East.

10. Derek Nurse and Thomas Spear, *The Swahili: Reconstructing the History and Language of an African Society* (Philadelphia, 1985).

11. Abdulla Saleh Farsy, *Seyyid Said bin Sultan* (Zanzibar, 1942), 27–28. Said initially held the throne jointly with his brother, Salim.

12. Essential sources for nineteenth-century economic history include Abdul Sheriff, *Slaves, Spices and Ivory in Zanzibar* (London, 1987); Edward Alpers, *Ivory and Slaves in East Central Africa* (London, 1975); Frederick Cooper, *Plantation Slavery on the East Coast of Africa* (New Haven, 1977); and J. S. Mangat, *A History of the Asians in East Africa* (Oxford, 1969).

13. Cloves were introduced shortly before Said came to the throne; see W. W. A. Fitzgerald, *Travels in the Coastlands of British East Africa and the Islands of Zanzibar and Pemba* (London, 1898), 553–554. Oman's demand for slaves (who worked, inter alia, on date plantations) had been an important factor in the steady rise of East African slave exports after ca. 1700; see Thomas Vernet, "Le commerce des esclaves sur la côte swahili, 1500–1750," *Azania* 38 (2003): 69–97.

14. Cooper, *Plantation Slavery on the East Coast of Africa*.

15. For the tenor of Zanzibari influence along the trade routes, see Jonathon Glassman, *Feasts and Riot* (Portsmouth, N.H., 1995); and Feierman, *Peasant Intellectuals*, chapter 4.

16. See the illuminating comments in Clayton, *The Zanzibar Revolution and Its Aftermath*, 2–4. The interwar political thought of the sultanate's elite intelligentsia will be the focus of the next chapter.

17. Richard Burton, *Zanzibar: City, Island, and Coast*, vol. 1 (London, 1872), 412–413.

18. Gray, *History of Zanzibar*, 156–169, from which much of this account is taken. But cf. Burton, *Zanzibar*, 1:411.

19. The literature on these events has been clouded by a twentieth-century intellectual tradition that is apologetic for Arab domination and that in the 1950s and 1960s gave rise to a "se-

rious debate" over the extent and nature of Hadimu dispossession. This apologetic tradition is the subject of the next chapter; for the debate see Michael Lofchie, *Zanzibar· Background to Revolution* (Princeton, 1965), 44–46. In the scholarly literature the key proponent of the apologists' view has been John Middleton, whose informants included some of the Arab intellectuals I will discuss in chapter 3; the opposite position has been taken by Gray, Cooper, and Lofchie. Nineteenth-century evidence supports the latter view: see, e.g., the memories recorded in the 1890s and published in Charles Sacleux, *Dictionnaire Swahili-Français* (Paris, 1939), 621–622; and Oscar Baumann, *Der Sansibar-Archipel*, vol. 2, *Die Insel Sansibar und Ihre Kleineren Nachbarinseln* (Leipzig, 1897), 19.

20. Compare with the 1865 letter in which Seyyid Majid bin Said (r. 1856–1870) ordered "the [Wa]Hadimu of Tumbatu" to obey the ruler he had appointed over them (quoted in Gray, *History of Zanzibar*, 169–170). This suggests that in 1865 the term was still understood in its strictly political sense, encompassing the categories, Tumbatu and Hadimu, that a century later were considered ethnically distinct. Still, all the references stress that Wahadimu shared descent from Unguja's earliest inhabitants.

21. Indispensable for such matters is John Middleton, *Land Tenure in Zanzibar* (London, 1961).

22. For the earlier figure; see Fitzgerald, *Travels in the Coastlands of British East Africa and the Islands of Zanzibar and Pemba*, 554, 559–561.

23. In addition to sources already cited, see Norman Bennett, *A History of the Arab State of Zanzibar* (London, 1978), 199, for differences in landholding patterns on the two islands.

24. Sacleux, *Dictionnaire Swahili-Français*, 621.

25. Ingrams, *Zanzibar: Its History and Its People*, 129–130; Oscar Baumann, *Der Sansibar-Archipel*, vol. 3, *Die Insel Pemba und Ihre Kleineren Nachbarinseln* (Leipzig, 1899), 9–10. The 1948 census found that of self-identified "Arabs" who were native-born rather than immigrants on both islands, three-quarters had been born and lived in Pemba: Edward Batson, "The Social Survey of Zanzibar," 1958, BA 28, ZNA.

26. What follows is informed by the discussions of coastal slavery in Cooper, *Plantation Slavery on the East Coast of Africa*; and Glassman, *Feasts and Riot*. Also see my review of the comparative literature in Glassman, "No Words of Their Own," *Slavery & Abolition* 16, no. 1 (1995): 131–145.

27. For this etymology, see Sacleux, *Dictionnaire Swahili-Français*, 577.

28. The sultanate's most violently exploitative slave regimes were not on the islands but on grain and sugar estates on the mainland coast; see Cooper, *Plantation Slavery on the East Coast of Africa*; and Glassman, *Feasts and Riot*.

29. These struggles are described in Glassman, *Feasts and Riot*, chapters 2–5. For "civilized slave," see Sacleux, *Dictionnaire Swahili-Français*, 598; and Ludwig Krapf, *A Dictionary of the Suahili Language* (London, 1882), 257.

30. Suzanne Miers and Igor Kopytoff, "African 'Slavery' as an Institution of Marginality," in *Slavery in Africa*, ed. Suzanne Miers and Igor Kopytoff (Madison, 1977); and the critiques in Frederick Cooper, "The Problem of Slavery in African Studies," *JAH* 20 (1979): 103–125; and Glassman, "No Words of Their Own."

31. The 1890s, in fact, witnessed particularly acute master-slave conflicts on the island; see Cooper, *From Slaves to Squatters*, 53–54. For slave smuggling, see Fitzgerald, *Travels in the Coastlands of British East Africa and the Islands of Zanzibar and Pemba*, 609–610. In 1911, J. E. Craster recorded pronounced mainlander cultural practices among the former slaves and vivid memories of the harshness of slavery; see *Pemba, the Spice Island of Zanzibar* (London, 1913), 39–40, 82–94, 212–213.

32. Abdul Sheriff, "An Outline History of Zanzibar Stone Town," and Garth Myers, "The Early History of the 'Other Side' of Zanzibar Town," both in *The History and Conservation of Zanzibar Stone Town*, ed. A. Sheriff (London, 1995), 8–29, 30–45; and Laura Fair, *Pastimes and Politics* (Athens, Ohio, 2001). Sheriff warns against overemphasizing this geographical division, especially before the late nineteenth century. Still, little evidence justifies Bissell's claim that it was "the colonial legal context that shaped the city as a zone of inequality in the first place"; see William Bissell, "Conservation and the Colonial Past: Urban Planning, Space and Power in Zanzibar," in *Africa's Urban Past*, ed. David Anderson and Richard Rathbone (Oxford, 2000), 246.

33. For a critique of this tendency in the literature, see Sheriff, "Race and Class in the Politics of Zanzibar."

34. Lofchie, *Zanzibar*, 14; also see 83. In offering this description, Lofchie invoked the influential models of M. G. Smith and J. S. Furnivall.

35. Unless otherwise indicated, I will use "India" and "Indians" throughout this book to refer to India before partition, including present-day Pakistan. In the censuses of 1924, 1931, and 1948, Indians constituted approximately 6 percent of the islands' population; in earlier decades, the proportion was probably smaller.

36. These figures are from 1875; see Mangat, *A History of the Asians in East Africa*, 13. About 100 (less than 3 percent) were Sunni Muslims, and a few dozen were Catholics from Goa.

37. Sheriff, "Race and Class in the Politics of Zanzibar"; Sheriff, "An Outline History of Zanzibar Stone Town," 19–21; Bissell, "Conservation and the Colonial Past," 249. For Indian tenement dwellers, see documents in "Increase of Rent (Restriction) Decree, 1922," AB 36/5, ZNA.

38. For the rise of *ustaarabu*, see Pouwels, "Eastern Africa and the Indian Ocean to 1800," 413; and Fair, *Pastimes and Politics*, 43. The word's usage and etymology will be discussed in chapter 3.

39. Members of elite families distinguished between "true" Arabs who could trace membership in an Arab clan (*"waarabu wa ukoo hasa"*) and people of local descent who identified as Arabs but lacked such a pedigree (*"wasiokuwa na ukoo"*). Muhammad Othman, "Asili ya neno 'ustaarabu na mstaarabu,'" *Maz.* 12, no. 4 (April 1938): 59–61.

40. A. N. Doorly, B. C. Johnstone, and H. Allen, "Report on Native Administration," 9 September 1932, AB 8/87, ZNA.

41. J. E. Flint, "Zanzibar, 1890–1950," in *History of East Africa*, vol. 2, ed. Vincent Harlow and E. M. Chilver (Oxford, 1965), 651. Also see Clayton, *The Zanzibar Revolution and Its Aftermath*, 2.

42. Cooper, *From Slaves to Squatters*, 158–172. Cooper offers a brief account of such mobilization on 279–288, where he assumes more about class consciousness than I believe the evidence warrants.

43. Robert Gregory, *Quest for Equality: Asian Politics in East Africa, 1900–1967* (New Delhi, 1993), 32; Mangat, *A History of the Asians in East Africa*, 114.

44. For the founding of the Arab Association, see "Mafveraky: Who Is Who?" *Al-Falaq*, 21 December 1946.

45. Bennett, *A History of the Arab State of Zanzibar*, 167–174.

46. Lofchie, *Zanzibar*, 62–63.

47. For reasons explicated in chapter 7, the *masheha* were typically men of low social standing. The racial categorization of the administrative structure appears, inter alia, in J. O'Brien, "Annual Report of the Provincial Administration 1940," BA 30/7, ZNA.

48. W. R. McGeagh, "District Annual Report, 1934," BA 30/4, ZNA. Also see annual re-

ports by G. E. Noad for 1936 and 1937, BA 30/5, ZNA. Among British territories the closest analogy was Fulani dominance in northern Nigeria; see Flint, "Zanzibar," 652.

49. Lofchie, *Zanzibar*, 65. The following account of the Legislative Council is based chiefly on Lofchie. Also useful is R. H. Crofton, *Zanzibar Affairs, 1914–1933* (London, 1953), 75–82.

50. Iliffe, *A Modern History of Tanganyika*, 375.

51. W. H. Ingrams, *Memorandum on Native Organization and Administration in Zanzibar* (Zanzibar, 1926), 5. As was common in informal English, Ingrams used the term "natives" to distinguish Africans from Arabs. But contrary to the assumptions of some latter-day scholars, the distinction had no legal standing in Zanzibar.

52. Doorly, Johnstone, and Allen, "Report on Native Administration," 9 September 1932.

53. The figures cited here are from 1928–1929. Bennett, *A History of the Arab State of Zanzibar*, 205; Crofton, *Zanzibar Affairs*, 85. The initial increase in clove prices was due in part to newly discovered industrial uses; from the 1920s on clove prices depended largely on the Indonesian demand for flavoring for cigarettes.

54. This analysis of early twentieth-century economic policy is based on Cooper, *From Slaves to Squatters*; and Lofchie, *Zanzibar*, who quotes an official statement that the justification for rescuing the Arab planters from their chronic indebtedness "rests on grounds which are not economic" (113–114). Other details are from Bennett, *A History of the Arab State of Zanzibar*, 200–205; and Abdul Sheriff, "The Peasantry under Imperialism," in *Zanzibar under Colonial Rule*, ed. A. Sheriff and Ed Ferguson (London, 1991), 132.

55. The best source for the debt reduction schemes of the 1930s and the ensuing political crisis is Lofchie, *Zanzibar*, 104ff.; the quote on preserving the Arab is from 113. For an example of official attitudes toward Indians, see those quoted in Timothy Welliver, "The Clove Factor in Colonial Zanzibar, 1890–1950" (Ph.D. diss., Northwestern University, 1990), 195–196.

56. Lofchie, *Zanzibar*, 121.

57. J. T. Last, "Report from the Collector of Zanzibar," 1906, BA 18/1, ZNA.

58. This and the next several paragraphs are based mostly on Cooper, *From Slaves to Squatters*.

59. Fitzgerald, *Travels in the Coastlands of British East Africa and the Islands of Zanzibar and Pemba*, 549, 558; Welliver, "The Clove Factor in Colonial Zanzibar," 92–100; Fair, *Pastimes and Politics*.

60. For squatters and tree crops, see Middleton, *Land Tenure in Zanzibar*, 43.

61. In addition to Cooper, *From Slaves to Squatters*, see Sheriff, "Race and Class in the Politics of Zanzibar"; Anthony Clayton, *The 1948 Zanzibar General Strike* (Uppsala, 1976), 16 ff.; and Fair, *Pastimes and Politics*, 29 ff.

62. For this and the next paragraph, I have relied on R. N. Lyne, "Report from the Director of Agriculture," 1909, BA 18/2, ZNA; B. C. Johnstone, "Memorandum on Labour in Zanzibar," 14 August 1930 and R. H. Crofton, "History of Labour in the Zanzibar Sultanate" [1927], both in AB 4/224, ZNA; and Clayton, *The 1948 Zanzibar General Strike*, 13 ff. Mainlanders also settled on estates in Pemba, but to a lesser extent, both in absolute numbers and in proportion to each island's overall population: see figures in Edward Batson, *Report on Proposals for a Social Survey of Zanzibar* (Zanzibar, 1946), 20.

63. After a boom in the 1920s, net immigration was erratic during the Depression and declined during World War II before booming again in the 1950s. Batson, *Report on Proposals for a Social Survey of Zanzibar*; Clayton, *The 1948 Zanzibar General Strike*, 14; Clayton, *The Zanzibar Revolution and Its Aftermath*, 11, 38.

64. Cf. Sheriff, "Race and Class in the Politics of Zanzibar," 308.

65. Among the most recent is Fair, *Pastimes and Politics*, 28–55; also valuable are Cooper, *From Slaves to Squatters*; and Deborah Peters Amory, "The Politics of Identity on Zanzibar" (Ph.D. diss., Stanford University, 1994).

66. E.g., Bowles, "The Struggle for Independence," 93.

67. Examples of the former approach by Fair and others will be discussed below. Cooper's illuminating analysis of late-colonial Zanzibar on the closing pages of *From Slaves to Squatters* might be taken as a variant of the latter approach, which emphasizes the class background of the networks so constructed. But more typical are the interpretations exemplified by Willis, *Mombasa, the Swahili, and the Making of the Mijikenda.* See also Carol Eastman, "Swahili Ethnicity: A Myth Becomes Reality in Kenya," in *Continuity and Autonomy in Swahili Communities*, ed. David Parkin (Vienna, 1994), 83–97.

68. Census figures are drawn chiefly from Batson, *Report on Proposals for a Social Survey of Zanzibar*; and Batson, "The Social Survey of Zanzibar"; plus works by Lofchie, Cooper, Fair, and Clayton.

69. Fair, *Pastimes and Politics*, 44. The literature Fair cites to support this assertion fails to substantiate the point or even argue it, and her own subsequent discussion focuses primarily on the shift to Shirazi rather than Arab identity. Her proposition that the two identities were equivalent has no basis outside the ideologically driven memories of her oral informants, especially Jamal Ramadhan Nasibu, whose own prominent role in the racialization of ethnic politics will be examined in later chapters.

70. These attempts were in part inspired by the privileges Arabs in colonial Mombasa enjoyed; many of the Pemba petitioners were connected to this group. See "Status of Bajunis and Members of Thelatha Taif," AB 26/63, ZNA. For the situation in Mombasa, see Ahmed Idha Salim, *The Swahili-Speaking Peoples of Kenya's Coast, 1895–1965* (Nairobi, 1973). Forced labor continued, sporadically, into the early 1920s; see Sheriff, "The Peasantry under Imperialism," 120.

71. Middleton, *Land Tenure in Zanzibar*, 53.

72. The concept of *uraia*, or subjecthood, was by no means a colonial invention: see Krapf, *A Dictionary of the Suahili Language*, 315. Fair contends (*Pastimes and Politics*, 42, 55) that only Arabs were allowed the status of "citizen" and that Africans in contrast were relegated to a distinct and inferior status as "subjects." Fair derives this distinction from Mahmood Mamdani, *Citizen and Subject* (Princeton, 1996). But it is entirely without basis and obscures the core conception by which citizenship was defined, both in law and common political rhetoric, as the status of being a "subject of His Highness." Such rhetoric is ubiquitous throughout the records, primary and secondary, official and unofficial.

73. Examples include the prison riot and Ng'ambo ground-rent strikes of the late 1920s, both of which will be discussed in chapter 6. Such behavior was also observed of rebels in precolonial times; see Glassman, *Feasts and Riot*, 111–113, 267–268. The myth of the just monarch is a familiar occurrence in the historical literature: e.g., Daniel Field, *Rebels in the Name of the Tsar* (Boston, 1976); Ranajit Guha, *Elementary Aspects of Peasant Insurgency in Colonial India* (Durham, N.C., 1999), 271–273; and Georges Lefebvre, *The Great Fear of 1789: Rural Panic in Revolutionary France*, trans. Joan White (New York, 1973), 39–40, 94–97.

74. See Fair's account of the conflict over waqf properties that resulted in popular resentment of Sultan Hamed Thuweni, whose sudden death in 1896 was widely greeted as divine justice. *Pastimes and Politics*, 134–136.

75. Exceptions from between the wars will be discussed in later chapters. But Khalifa's general popularity among all classes and communities was widely observed throughout his

reign. The question why overtly antimonarchical politics emerged so late remains one of the key puzzles of the 1964 revolution. For heated debates within the ASP, see *Afrika Kwetu*, 26 November 1959.

76. Fair, *Pastimes and Politics*, 30–31; Abdul Sheriff and Chizuko Tominaga, "The Shirazi in the History and Politics of Zanzibar," paper presented at the International Conference on the History and Culture of Zanzibar, Zanzibar, December 1992. Among census takers in 1931 and 1948, there was widespread understanding that "Shirazi" and these other ethnic categories were not mutually exclusive; see Batson, *Report on Proposals for a Social Survey of Zanzibar*, 17–19. Shirazi Association activists of the 1940s and 1950s took a similar attitude.

77. The most prominent recent example is Fair, *Pastimes and Politics*, 46–52; also see Mrina and Mattoke, *Mapambano ya Ukombozi Zanzibar*, 49–50. The political uses of this argument have been transparent and prominent, both in the polemics of the Times of Politics and in subsequent official and quasi-official texts. For the latter, see ASP, *The History of Zanzibar Africans*, 2–3; and Mapuri, *Zanzibar*, 13–14.

78. Shirazi in Pemba were briefly issued Asiatic rations, but the practice was stopped as soon as administrators in Zanzibar Town heard about it in April 1944; they deemed it "ridiculous" and "unsupportable" to draw a distinction between Shirazi and other Africans. See Provincial Commissioner to Chief Secretary, 30 June 1944, AK 17/70, ZNA. None of the other documentary sources cited by Fair support her interpretation of the link between rationing and claims to Shirazi identity; see *Pastimes and Politics*, 51 and 287nn120–121. Her most explicit evidence comes from an interview with Jamal Ramadhan Nasibu, a virulently racial ASP activist who was behind much of the anti-Shirazi propaganda that first voiced this interpretation during the Time of Politics. The Unguja branch of the Shirazi Association did seem to promise that the government would provide rations for it to distribute to its members, but this was the association's own invention. See R. H. W. Pakenham, District Report, December 1943, BA 30/7, ZNA.

79. Attorney-General, "Memorandum on the Status of Half-Castes in Zanzibar," 30 August 1933, AB 26/65, plus other documents in this file and in AB 26/63, ZNA. The distinction between Africans and Arabs was retained after 1925, but Shirazi were legally defined as belonging to the former category. The Zanzibar literature has imported its focus on the "native/non-native" distinction from a very different situation in Kenya. But a similar overemphasis is pervasive throughout the literature on colonial Africa. For a critique, see Christopher Joon-Hai Lee, "The 'Native' Undefined: Colonial Categories, Anglo-African Status and the Politics of Kinship in British Central Africa," *JAH* 46 (2005): 455–478.

80. "Memorandum III" [Pemba, September 1943], AB 12/2, ZNA. In fact, some of the most common expressions of resentment concerning rationing were not about racial privilege but about towns being privileged over the countryside. District Monthly Reports, 1943, BA 30/7, ZNA.

81. These protests most commonly focused on official appointments. Secretary, Shirazi Association, to Resident, Wete, 22 April 1948, AB 12/2, ZNA. See also other documents in this file.

82. Ali Sharifu, Secretary, Shirazi Association, to DC Pemba, Wete, 29 August 1940, AB 12/2, ZNA. For "persons of note," see G. E. Noad, DC, to Provincial Commissioner, 2 September 1940, in the same file.

83. At least one official noted the paradox: R. H. W. Pakenham, 10 May 1948, AB 12/2, ZNA.

84. O'Brien to Chief Secretary, 1 October 1940, AB 12/2, ZNA, and other documents in the same file.

85. For a description of how "Swahili" was used as a pejorative epithet of reference, see Aboud Jumbe, "Ah! Waswahili Bwana!" *Mazungumzo ya Walimu wa Unguja* 12, no. 1 (January 1938): 13.

86. This increase is documented for the years 1931 to 1948. We have no relevant post-1948 census figures, but the political history recounted in the following chapters speaks eloquently to the point. Sources for the 1950s spike include Clayton, *The Zanzibar Revolution and Its Aftermath,* 38.

87. This is Clayton's assessment (*The 1948 Zanzibar General Strike*), though the figures do not allow any precise estimation of the relative proportions. Cooper, in contrast, writing of the earliest decades of the century, assumes that most mainlanders were descendants of slaves, including virtually all who identified themselves as Yao, Nyasa, and Manyema—that is, from the regions that had supplied most of Zanzibar's slaves. This may have been true early in the century (supporting evidence includes Ingrams, *Zanzibar: Its History and Its People,* 28–29), although there is ample evidence from the 1930s of voluntary immigrants who identified themselves by such ethnonyms as well. See the discussion of Manyema in chapter 4.

88. Clayton, *The 1948 Zanzibar General Strike,* 44.

89. The figures in Batson, *Report on Proposals for a Social Survey of Zanzibar,* are unequivocal on this point.

90. Some of these points are outlined in Fair, *Pastimes and Politics,* 54–55. We will return to these themes in chapter 6.

91. Clayton, *The Zanzibar Revolution and Its Aftermath,* 24–35.

92. The latter were the terms most commonly used in the Arab Association's weekly paper, *Al-Falaq.* Terms in Swahili usage were similarly neutral (e.g. *wakulima,* cultivators), although the common term *mgeni* (guest) referred explicitly to the patronage relationship. For Kenyan usages of "squatter," which had been imported early in the century from South Africa, see Tabitha Kanogo, *Squatters and the Roots of Mau Mau* (Athens, Ohio, 1987). The earliest non-European use I have encountered in Zanzibar comes in *Al-Falaq,* 23 September 1939. Like many articles in *Al-Falaq,* this one expressed the interests of the best-capitalized planters and argued for rationalizing production by restricting "squatters'" rights. The author put the word in quotation marks, indicating its novelty, and it did not reappear in political rhetoric until well after the war. The word had appeared earlier among British officials: e.g. the useful description of squatting in W. R. McGeagh, diaries, vol. 2 (1933–1935), pp. 90, 102–103, MSS. Afr. r. 89(2), RH. But McGeagh had previously served for many years in Western Kenya. For the word's use in later anti-squatter invective, see "Thousands of Zanzibaris Lodge Their Protest," *Mwongozi,* 6 December 1957.

93. E.g., Fair, *Pastimes and Politics,* 42, 99; Sheriff, "Race and Class in the Politics of Zanzibar," 308–309; William C. Bissell, "Colonial Constructions: Historicizing Debates on Civil Society in Africa," in *Civil Society and the Political Imagination in Africa,* ed. John and Jean Comaroff (Chicago, 1999), 125, 127–128.

94. E.g., W. Addis, Monthly Report, October 1943, BA 30/7, ZNA.

95. "Unjustifiable," *Al-Falaq,* 17 March 1945, in AB 12/28, ZNA. For the empire-wide move away from policies of explicit racial paternalism, see Michael Crowder, "The Second World War: Prelude to Decolonization in Africa," in *The Cambridge History of Africa,* vol. 8, ed. M. Crowder (Cambridge, 1984), 22–24.

96. Bennett, *A History of the Arab State of Zanzibar,* 246, 248–249 (the quote is from Provincial Commissioner J. O'Brien, 1946); Mrina and Mattoke, *Mapambano ya Ukombozi Zanzibar,* 51–52. For Tajo's vilification of the labor unionists, see chapter 4, below.

97. The main source for the account on these pages is Lofchie, *Zanzibar*. Also see Bennett, *A History of the Arab State of Zanzibar*; and Clayton, *The Zanzibar Revolution and Its Aftermath*.

98. E.g., see the negotiations over reforming the Town Council recounted in E. A. Vasey, *Report on Local Government Advancement in Zanzibar Township* (1954), BA 31/3, ZNA.

99. Lofchie, *Zanzibar*, 157.

100. I draw this assessment from Lofchie's careful account, which observes that the political parties "were not separated in the final analysis by disparate attitudes toward foreign or domestic policies; they were separated by elemental and irreducible racial fears" (*Zanzibar*, 269). Of course, by describing such fears as "elemental," Lofchie begs questions of how they came to be constructed over time and how Zanzibaris came to regard them as elemental—the questions addressed in the following chapters.

3. A Secular Intelligentsia and the Origins of Exclusionary Ethnic Nationalism

The first epigraph is from "Pride of Race," *Normal Magazine* 4, no. 4 (April 1930): 30–33. In 1932 the magazine was renamed *Mazungumzo ya Walimu*. The second epigraph is from *Mazungumzo ya Walimu*, n.s. 1, no. 3 (May 1957): 14.

1. Allowing for the oversimplification necessary in summing up a complex work, this stands as a fair representation of the argument in Lofchie, *Zanzibar*. Clayton criticizes Lofchie for underestimating the divisiveness of ZNP rhetoric; his own account of the Time of Politics serves as a useful corrective. See *The Zanzibar Revolution and Its Aftermath*, 37–49.

2. Partha Chatterjee, *The Nation and Its Fragments* (Princeton, 1993), 5.

3. The intelligentsia linked the transmission of religious expertise to the inheritance of Arab status; see José Kagabo, "Réseaux d'*ulama* 'swahili' et liens de parenté," in *Les Swahili entre Afrique et Arabie*, ed. Françoise le Guennec-Coppens and Pat Caplan (Paris, 1991), 59–72. For descriptions of intellectual life in nineteenth and early twentieth-century Zanzibar, see Abdallah Salih Farsy, *The Shaf'i Ulama of East Africa*, trans. and ed. Randall Pouwels (Madison, 1989); Anne K. Bang, *Sufis and Scholars of the Sea* (London, 2003); Randall Pouwels, "Sh. Al-Amin b. Ali Mazrui and Islamic Modernism in East Africa, 1875–1947," *International Journal of Middle East Studies* 13 (1981): 329–345; and Amal Nadim Ghazal, "Islam and Arabism in Zanzibar: The Omani Elite, the Arab World and the Making of an Identity" (Ph.D. diss., University of Alberta, 2005). Also see Aley, *Zanzibar: In the Context*, 58; Muhsin al-Barwani, *Conflicts*; Shaaban Saleh Farsi, *Zanzibar: Historical Accounts* (n.p., 1995: first publ. 1955). The thorough study by Roman Loimeier, *Between Social Skills and Marketable Skills: The Politics of Islamic Education in 20th Century Zanzibar* (Leiden, 2009), came to my attention too late for me to make full use of it in this book.

4. E.g., Ingrams, *Zanzibar: Its History and Its People*, 125, 189–190. Another colonial historian, L. W. Hollingsworth, will figure prominently below.

5. The mudirs' reports are discussed explicitly in I. H. D. Rolleston, Annual District Report 1935, BA 30/5, ZNA; the same file contains examples of them. These and similar reports continued to be written, and British officials often referred to them.

6. I take the phrase "intimate enemies" from Heather Sharkey, *Living with Colonialism: Nationalism and Culture in the Anglo-Egyptian Sudan* (Berkeley, 2003); she in turn adapted it from Ashis Nandy.

7. E.g., Lofchie, *Zanzibar*; cf. Fair, *Pastimes and Politics*.

8. For European nationalism, see Smith, *The Nation in History*, 8–10. Similar themes in pan-Arab nationalism will be discussed below.

9. J. D. Y. Peel, "Social and Cultural Change," in *The Cambridge History of Africa*, vol. 8, ed. Michael Crowder (Cambridge, 1984), 178. For a suggestive account of the role of Kenyan schoolteachers in crafting a local cultural nationalism, see David Sandgren, *Christianity and the Kikuyu* (New York, 1989).

10. For an explicit statement, see the comments by W. Hendry, the director of education, on agricultural education, 21 July 1924 and 8 June 1925, AB 1/365, ZNA. Also see Hendry, "Some Aspects of Education in Zanzibar," *Journal of the African Association* 27, no. 108 (1928): 351.

11. For a firsthand explanation of the discrepancy between town and country, see Zam Ali Abbas, "Yaliopita huzungumzwa (maendeleo ya skuli)," *Maz.*, n.s. 1, no. 2 (January 1957): 15–18. Indians were also disproportionately represented in the islands' classrooms. General sources for education include Bennett, *A History of the Arab State of Zanzibar*, 194–196, 222–234, 245; Farsi, *Zanzibar: Historical Accounts*, 20; Loimeier, *Between Social Skills and Marketable Skills*; and O. W. Furley and T. Watson, *A History of Education in East Africa* (New York, 1978), chapters 6 and 10.

12. For reforms inspired by the Tuskegeeist Phelps-Stokes Commission, see King, *Pan-Africanism and Education*; and Lene Buchert, *Education in the Development of Tanzania* (London, 1994).

13. Zanzibar Protectorate, *Annual Report of the Education Department for the Year 1927* (Zanzibar, 1928), esp. 6–7; W. Hendry, "Memorandum by the Director of Education," 27 February 1934, and "Memorandum of the Arab Association," 5 February 1934, both in CO618/60/15, PRO. Figures from 1937 indicate that teaching school was the most likely salaried post available in the administration for "African" and "Arab" school-leavers; see folder AB 1/184, ZNA.

14. Abbas, "Yaliopita huzungumzwa (maendeleo ya skuli)"; Muhsin al-Barwani, *Conflicts and Harmony in Zanzibar*; Aley, *Zanzibar: In the Context*; and Farsi, *Zanzibar: Historical Accounts* explicitly acknowledge how the experience of classroom teaching helped foster a sense of belonging to a leading intelligentsia; the latter three discuss Hollingsworth. Also see Acting Director of Education to Treasurer, 12 June 1933, AB 1/76, ZNA; "Dr. Hollingsworth and Uhuru," *Mwongozi*, 20 September 1963; and Roman Loimeier, "Coming to Terms with 'Popular Culture': The *Ulama* and the State in Zanzibar," in Loimeier and Seesemann, *The Global Worlds of the Swahili*, 118n10.

15. Most of these details are culled from the magazine itself and from Hollingsworth's appendix to Zanzibar Protectorate, *Annual Report of the Education Department for the Year 1927*.

16. They include Abdulla Saleh Farsy, one of East Africa's most prominent Islamic scholars and public intellectuals; Yahya Alawi, who would become one of the highest-ranking Zanzibaris in the colonial administration (among his posts he served as information officer in charge of broadcasting); Zam Ali Abbas, founder of the Zanzibar Association, the islands' first explicitly nationalist organization; Ahmed Seif Kharusi, founder of the influential weekly *Mwongozi*; Juma Aley and Muhammad Salim Hilal Barwani, leading figures in the ZNP; Muhammad Shamte, chief minister of the ZNP-ZPPP government that would be overthrown in 1964; and Aboud Jumbe, second president of the Revolutionary Government.

17. Given Hollingsworth's encouragement of discussion of topical issues as a way of honing expressive skills (and his sympathy for the goals of Arab-led cultural nationalism), there is little doubt that the schoolteachers inculcated some of their ideas in the classroom. Muhsin al-Barwani describes the classroom influence of A. M. al-Hadhrami, the leading figure on *Mazungumzo*'s editorial board in the 1930s, in *Conflicts and Harmony in Zanzibar*, 64.

18. Contrary to their later claims, journalists of the *Mazungumzo* circle used the term routinely, with all its pejorative implications. There was eventually a small debate over its appropriateness, in which Arab Association journalists defended the usage against the objections,

ironically, of a British educator. See *Al-Falaq*, 8 November 1941; and Aley, *Zanzibar: In the Context*, 40.

19. The version of Tuskegeeism adopted by educators in East Africa in the 1920s stressed schoolteachers' roles as community leaders in "community development"; see King, *Pan-Africanism and Education*. Zanzibar's longtime acting director of education, G. B. Johnson, was an internationally prominent advocate of Tuskegeeism, and his Swahili-language adaptation of *Up from Slavery* was a standard reader in Zanzibar schools. See G. B. Johnson, *Maisha ya Booker T. Washington, Mtu Mweusi Maarufu* (London, 1937). Parts of the latter first appeared in *Mazungumzo*; see Ousseina Alidou, "Booker T. Washington in Africa: Between Education and (Re)Colonization," in *A Thousand Flowers: Social Struggles against Structural Adjustment in African Universities*, ed. Silvia Federici, George Caffentzis, and O. Alidou (Trenton, 2000), 27–28.

20. See "Mafveraky: Who Is Who?" *Al-Falaq*, 21 December 1946, for the founding of the Arab Association. Its founding coincided with aroused local sentiments of pan-Islamism; see the descriptions in Edward Clarke to Foreign Office, 29 November 1911, and appended Police Inspector's Report, AC 1/151, ZNA. For a full discussion of pan-Arabism and pan-Islamism among the elite, see Ghazal, "Islam and Arabism in Zanzibar."

21. Such themes can be found in the writings of pan-Arabists and Islamic modernists at least as early as Jamal al-Din Afghani and the Egyptian nationalist Rifa'a Badawi al-Tahtawi. See Albert Hourani, *Arabic Thought in the Liberal Age* (Cambridge, 1983). For interwar currents, see Reeva Simon, "The Teaching of History in Iraq before the Rashid Ali Coup of 1941," *Middle Eastern Studies* 22 (1986): 37–51. See also Reeva Simon, "The Imposition of Nationalism on a Non-Nation State: The Case of Iraq during the Interwar Period, 1921–41," and Israel Gershoni, "Rethinking the Formation of Arab Nationalism in the Middle East, 1920–1945," in *Rethinking Nationalism in the Arab Middle East*, ed. J. Jankowski and I. Gershoni (New York, 1997), 3–25 and 87–104, respectively; I. Gershoni, "The Emergence of Pan-Nationalism in Egypt: Pan-Islamism and Pan-Arabism in the 1930s," *Asian and African Studies* 16 (1982): 59–94; and C. Ernest Dawn, "The Origins of Arab Nationalism," in *The Origins of Arab Nationalism*, ed. Rashid Khalidi, Lisa Anderson, Muhammad Muslih, and Reeva Simon (New York, 1991), 3–30.

22. Evidence of the schoolteachers' image of themselves as members of an Arab elite is ubiquitous and usually unintentional, making it all the more powerful. Examples can be found throughout the pages of *Mazungumzo*.

23. Administrators' concerns appear, for example, in a message from the director of education in the earliest issue that I have been able to locate: *Normal Magazine* 3, no. 1 (January 1929); also see Furley and Watson, *A History of Education in East Africa*, 130–131. For teachers' perspectives, see "Mwunguja," "Maneno mazuri humtoa nyoka pangoni," *Maz.* 6, no. 9 (October 1932): 118–119.

24. See esp. Hollingsworth's monthly "Barua ya mtengenezaji" ("Letter from the Editor"), *Maz.* 6, no. 7 (August 1932): 85–86; also *Normal Magazine* 5, no. 7 (August 1931): 93–94.

25. A. A. Seif, "Nasiha (Shauri Njema)," *Normal Magazine* 3, no. 4 (May 1929); "Editor's Letter," *Normal Magazine* 4, no. 10 (October 1930): 117. For Seif, see Zanzibar Protectorate, *Annual Report of the Education Department for the Year 1927*, 17–20.

26. Arab nationalists had often stressed explicitly racial themes in their definitions of the Arab nation: see the passages quoted from Rifa'a al-Tahtawi and Lutfi al-Sayyid in Hourani, *Arabic Thought in the Liberal Age*, 79, 173. See also Eve Troutt Powell, *A Different Shade of Colonialism* (Berkeley, 2003); and Eve Troutt Powell, "Brothers along the Nile: Egyptian Con-

cepts of Race and Ethnicity, 1895–1910," in *The Nile: Histories, Cultures, Myths,* ed. H. Erlich and I. Gershoni (Boulder, 2000), 171–181.

27. Simon, "The Teaching of History in Iraq before the Rashid Ali Coup of 1941"; Simon, "The Imposition of Nationalism on a Non-Nation State"; C. Ernest Dawn, "The Formation of Pan-Arab Ideology in the Interwar Years," *International Journal of Middle East Studies* 20 (1988): 67–91. Omnia el Shakry recounts the interplay of universal history and concepts of race in Egyptian nationalism; see *The Great Social Laboratory: Subjects of Knowledge in Colonial and Postcolonial Egypt* (Stanford, 2007), 55–86. The basic assumptions of universal history, which can be traced to Schiller, Hegel, and Ranke, were until recently ubiquitous in Western historical writing. For an exploration of their implications, see Dipesh Chakrabarty, *Provincializing Europe* (Princeton, 2000).

28. L. W. Hollingsworth, *Milango ya Historia,* 3 vols. (London, 1925–1931). *Milango ya Historia* was promoted in *Mazungumzo* and reprinted many times over four decades; the 1965 edition was approved for classroom use by the Tanzania Department of Education. Hollingsworth acknowledges the assistance of A. A. Seif, A. M. al-Hadhrami, and Muhammad Salim Hilal al-Barwani; Seif apparently prepared the Swahili text from an English original. See Glassman, "Slower Than a Massacre," 740–741n87.

29. Explicit statements of these themes can be found in *Milango ya Historia* 1:15–27 and 42–48. Given the importance of the Greeks as examples in volume 1, Hollingsworth could hardly insist on monotheism as part of his definition of civilization (as he does the other attributes), but the entire work, particularly the last two volumes, emphasizes the civilizing power of Judeo-Christian-Muslim values. A widely used geography primer was less equivocal about proclaiming religion "the foundation of all true civilization"; see G. W. Broomfield and D. V. Perrott, *Habari za Walimwengu,* Book 3, *Masimulizi ya Juma juu ya Waingereza* (London, 1954), 101. Similar views of "civilization" were common in mainstream social science at the time; see Charles Ellwood, *The Psychology of Human Society: An Introduction to Sociological Theory* (New York, 1925).

30. Hollingsworth, *Milango ya Historia,* 3: 87–94. Also see Hollingsworth, *Short History of the East Coast of Africa* (London, 1929), which was assigned in the upper standards. These aspects of East African history figured prominently in the middle school exams in 1933 and the Teachers Training School exams in 1957; see AB 1/184 and AD 1/213, ZNA. Geography primers told similar stories of civilization and barbarism, often in explicitly racial terms. See B. M. Hart, *Bara Afrika: Chanzo cha Jiografia ya Afrika* (Nairobi, 1948); E. C. Francis, *Afrika* (London, 1952); and Broomfield and Perrott, *Habari za Walimwengu,* Book 3. E. C. Francis's *Afrika* was first published in English in 1933.

31. "Pride of Race," *Normal Magazine* 4, no. 4 (April 1930): 30–33. Seif explained the circumstances of the essay's publication in an editorial note introducing it. It had originally appeared in October 1929 in the Accra *Teacher's Journal,* which was inaugurated one year later than *Mazungumzo.*

32. For these contradictions in classic British indirect rule, see Karen Fields, *Revival and Rebellion in Colonial Central Africa* (Princeton, 1985). For the Gold Coast, see Cati Coe, "Educating an African Leadership: Achimota and the Teaching of African Culture in the Gold Coast," *Africa Today* 49, no. 3 (2002): 23–44.

33. M. Abdurrahaman [M. Abdulrahman], "Maisha ya Watu Wengine," *Maz.* 12, no. 11 (November 1938): 162–163; *Maz.* 12, no. 12 (December 1938); and following issues. Examples of similar essays include M. Abdulrahman, "Safari ya Kilwa," in six parts, beginning in *Maz.* 12, no. 2 (February 1938): 24–26; Muhammad Othman, "Siku Kuu ya Mwaka," *Normal Magazine*

4, no. 9 (September 1930): 112–115. Compare to the biographical sketch of Tippu Tip written by one of the founders of the Arab Association and published in a Cairo journal in 1906: Ghazal, "Islam and Arabism in Zanzibar," 140–141.

34. Muhammad Othman, "Asili ya Neno 'Ustaarabu na Mstaarabu,'" *Maz.* 12, no. 4 (April 1938): 59–61. In this concern for whether *ustaarabu* can refer to Eurocentered as well as Arab-centered forms of civilization, the debate in *Mazungumzo* resembles a debate from a decade earlier in the journal *Mambo Leo*, published by the Tanganyikan Department of Education; see Katrin Bromber, "*Ustaarabu:* A Conceptual Change in Tanganyikan Newspaper Discourse in the 1920s," in Loimeier and Seesemann, *The Global Worlds of the Swahili*, 67–81.

35. Ali Said al-Kharusy, "Asili ya Waarabu," *Maz.* 12, nos. 6 and 7 (June–July 1938): 81–83, 99–101. For al-Kharusy, whose brothers included other distinguished businessmen, educators, and government officials, see his personal file, AK 33/97, ZNA; and *Afrika Kwetu*, 20 March 1952.

36. For example: "*Mshenzi, n. wa-* a barbarian, savage, one of the aborigines, a person untouched by civilization. Often used contemptuously by the coast native of those who come from the interior, although they are frequently more cultured and refined than the coast native!" Frederick Johnson, *Standard Swahili-English Dictionary* (Oxford, 1939), 419.

37. "'Ustaarabu,'" *Maz.* 12, no. 4 (April 1938): 61–62. In a later intervention, al-Hadhrami amplified some of these ideas in ways that seem to owe much to concepts from universal history that attribute "civilization" everywhere on the globe to a small handful of original sources—in Africa's case, Europe (specifically Rome) and the Arabs: "Tamaduni," *Maz.* 12, no. 8 (August 1938). Despite his youth, al-Hadhrami was already an influential teacher, fluent in Arabic and conversant in the history and politics of the Islamic Middle East. In addition to his many essays in *Maz.*, see Muhsin al-Barwani, *Conflicts and Harmony*, 64; and "Swahili Teaching and Arabs," *Al-Falaq*, 24 February 1934.

38. The importance of the descent metaphor should be clear from chapter 2's discussion of Arab and Shirazi identity and the taint of slave descent. For an explicit statement, see the careful consideration of how best to reckon ethnic identity in Mohammed Shamte, "Mpemba," *Maz.* 11, no. 4 (April 1937): 52–54; Shamte opts for a strict reckoning based on descent.

39. The literature still suffers from embarrassed silence about the degree to which Arab-centered notions of skin color as a status marker were and remain widespread on the Swahili coast. A good indication of this is the furor raised among Lamu intellectuals by the publication of A. H. M. el Zein, *The Sacred Meadows* (Evanston, 1974), which describes such notions. Also see Fair, *Pastimes and Politics*, 94–96; and for nineteenth-century material, Fred Morton, *Children of Ham* (Boulder, 1990). For the Arab and Islamic world more generally, see John Hunwick, "Islamic Law and Polemics over Race and Slavery in North and West Africa," *Princeton Papers: Interdisciplinary Journal of Middle Eastern Studies* 7 (1999): 43–68; Bernard Lewis, *Race and Slavery in the Middle East* (New York, 1990); and Powell, *A Different Shade of Colonialism*.

40. Muhammad Othman, "Asili ya neno 'ustaarabu na mstaarabu,'" *Maz.* 12, no. 4 (April 1938). Othman reminds readers of the standard etymology, which traces *mshenzi* to the Persian word *zinj*, meaning black. And the Swahili word he uses to describe coast peoples' supposedly lighter skin color is far from neutral: the color is cleaner, purified, brightened (*takata*). Othman cites a book entitled *History of Zanzibar*, presumably Ingrams and Hollingsworth's 1925 school text. But his essay reflects a variety of influences, including local understandings of Islam.

41. Hollingsworth, "Editor's Letter," and G. W. Broomfield, "The Development of the Swahili Language," both in *Normal Magazine* 5, no. 2 (March 1931): 17–18 and 19–21, respectively. Broomfield served on the Interterritorial Language Committee; his article originally appeared in *Africa*, the journal of the International African Institute.

42. Muhammad Othman, "Tumbatu Island," *Normal Magazine* 4, no. 3 (March 1930): 20–23; Said Ali, "Kijiji cha Mangapwani," *Normal Magazine* 5, no. 8 (September 1931): 118–119. The latter author noted the paradox that descendants of slaves often spoke "purer" Swahili than indigenous villagers, the reason being that the slaves had learned Swahili from their Arab masters. For the interterritorial conference, see Wilfred Whiteley, *Swahili: The Rise of a National Language* (London, 1969), chapter 5; and Ali A. Mazrui and Alamin M. Mazrui, *Swahili State and Society* (Nairobi, 1995), 45.

43. Hollingsworth, "Barua ya mtengenezaji" and Uledi Jabu, "Watu wa mjini kwa watu wa shamba," both in *Maz.* 6, no. 7 (August 1932): 85–86 and 95–96, respectively.

44. Documents from 1926 to 1938 in "Teaching of Koran and Arab [*sic*] in Govt Schools," AB 1/390, ZNA; the quotes are from translations of articles from the Arab Association weekly *Al-Falaq*, 23 July and 27 August 1930. In its Arabic pages, *Al-Falaq* dismissed Swahili with the pejorative adjective *zanji*, connoting both blackness and barbarism. It warned that the Education Department's language policies threatened to barbarize or, literally, "zanjify" Zanzibar, whereas the goal should be to Arabize and thus civilize it; see Ghazal, "Islam and Arabism in Zanzibar," 231–234.

45. This is more elegant in the original, owing to the peculiarities of Swahili's Bantu (not Semitic) grammar: "*Kiswahili kilichovuliwa na Kiarabu si Kiswahili tena bali ni Kishenzi.*" See A. M. al-Hadhrami, "Kiswahili," *Maz.* 11, no. 10 (Oct 1937): 145–146. For a more general description of such attitudes, see G. B. Johnson, "Report on Text-Books in the Swahili Language," appendix to Zanzibar Protectorate, *Annual Report of the Education Department for the Year 1927*, 54.

46. So, for example, whereas in 1930 the author of a fierce critique of female initiation felt compelled to take a swipe at "thoughtless people" who argued that such backward customs ought to be tolerated out of misplaced respect for one's ancestors (Saleh Muhammad, "Ubaya wa somo juu ya mwari wake," *Normal Magazine* 5, no. 12 [December 1930]: 147–148), by 1932 the magazine was replete with essays enjoining not simply courteous behavior toward the uneducated but also respect for their language and customs. For Tuskegeeism as the source of British educators' interest in the nation-building potential of "tribal customs," see King, *Pan-Africanism and Education*, 167–170, 263.

47. Odile Racine, "The *Mwaka* of Makunduchi, Zanzibar," in *Continuity and Autonomy in Swahili Communities: Inland Influences and Strategies of Self-Determination*, ed. David Parkin (Vienna, 1994), 167–175. As early as the 1930s, Makunduchi's annual Mwaka drew spectators from throughout the island, who expected to see mock battles that sometimes became real. W. R. McGeagh, District Report, 12 October 1935, BA 30/6, ZNA; K. H. Clarke, Monthly Report, August 1939, BA 30/7, ZNA.

48. Examples of such rhetoric can be found in Abdul Rahman Muhammad, "Sikukuu ya Mwaka," *Normal Magazine* 3, nos. 10–11 (November/December 1929): 148–149, 162–163; Zam Ali Abbas, "Kwenda kwingi kuona mambo," *Normal Magazine* 3, no. 6 (July 1929); Saleh Muhammad, "Ubaya wa somo." For dance and other festive rites in the previous century, see Glassman, *Feasts and Riot*.

49. Scholars often used the Swahili terms *uzushi* and *ushirikina*. For these concerns among East African *ulamaa*, see Pouwels, *Horn and Crescent*; and Farsy, *The Shaf'i Ulama of East Africa*. They were shared by the influential reformer Rashid Rida, whose Cairo paper *al-Manar* was read in Zanzibar.

50. See the monthly and annual district reports in BA 30/5–7, ZNA; and the documents from 1935 to 1936 in AB 30/22, ZNA. The *ulamaa*'s independent theological motivations were well established, as they had been criticizing such feasts long before British rule. And they continued to condemn them well after the British campaigns; see, for example, Muhammad Saleh

Abdulla Farsy, *Ada za Harusi katika Unguja* (Nairobi, 1956). For the *ulamaa*'s leadership in similar campaigns in Mombasa and coastal Tanganyika, see Sarah Mirza and Margaret Strobel, *Three Swahili Women* (Bloomington, 1989); and Ali bin Hemedi al-Buhuriy, "Habari za Mrima," *Mambo Leo* 141–147 (1934–1935).

51. The Arab Association endorsed Sheikh Tahir's position; see Sheikh Tahir [Abubakr al-Amawi], 21 March 1936 (with a postscript by the Ibadi qadi, Sh. Said bin Nassor, expressing his agreement), AB 30/22, ZNA; and Loimeier, "Coming to Terms with 'Popular Culture,'" 115. For other *ulamaa* who took similarly puritanical views, see Saidi Musa, *Maisha ya al-Imam Sheikh Abdulla Saleh Farsy katika Ulimwengu wa Kiislamu* (Dar es Salaam, 1986), esp. 65ff. (although this source, written by a latter-day proponent of similar reform, must be treated with caution). The tensions produced by such teachings were revealed in 1949 when Sheikh Abdulla Saleh Farsy published an article criticizing rural practices of the Sufi ritual *dhikr* and the Makunduchi Sufi leader Mahmoud Kombo brought an angry demonstration of his followers to town in protest. See AB 70/7, ZNA.

52. Bennett, *A History of the Arab State of Zanzibar*, 228–229; Furley and Watson, *A History of Education in East Africa*, 122–123; Teaching of Koran and Arabic in Government Schools, 1924–1957, AB 1/390, ZNA. The analogy to parrots was made by one of the qadis on the commission; see Ingrams, *Zanzibar: Its History and Its People*, 230. For the *ulamaa*'s contribution to colonial educational projects, see Bang, *Sufis and Scholars of the Sea*, 173–187.

53. M. A. al-Haj (Mudir, Koani), "The Koran Schools," 1936, AK 33/294, ZNA. For the report's circulation within the Education Department, see AB 1/82 and AB 1/390, ZNA. Al-Haj worked as a teacher for four years before being appointed mudir in 1933. Over the next three decades he steadily climbed the administrative ladder, becoming one of the most decorated and highly paid Zanzibaris in the colonial bureaucracy. His reports on diverse subjects were widely praised and circulated by his administrative superiors. Personal files, AK 33/294 and AK 33/185, ZNA; and staff lists for 1962–1963, BA 82/44–45, ZNA.

54. Louis Brenner, "Muslim Representations of Unity and Difference in African Discourse," in *Muslim Identity and Social Change in Sub-Saharan Africa*, ed. Louis Brenner (Bloomington, 1993), 1–20.

55. Hourani, *Arabic Thought in the Liberal Age*, 299–301; Gershoni, "The Emergence of Pan-Nationalism," 76–77. For echoes of such teachings among the Zanzibar elite, see Ghazal, "Islam and Arabism in Zanzibar," 204ff.

56. *Mazungumzo*'s authors often appeared in *Al-Falaq*, sometimes as attributed authors (although most pieces in *Al-Falaq* were unsigned) and more commonly in glowing notices about Zanzibar's leading scholars and teachers, including comments on pieces published in *Mazungumzo*. The publications carried much similar material, including Arab-centered historical narratives intended to illustrate the concept of *ustaarabu*.

57. "Zanzibar Must Appeal," *Al-Falaq*, 29 June 46. *Al-Falaq*'s writers often conflated Arab influence with the Persians who supposedly had created the "Great Zenj Empire"; see the narrative by "Mtambuzi," *Al-Falaq*, 15 June 1940. The Portuguese theme may have informed the choice of the paper's title, which means "the dawn," but in Koranic rather than spoken Arabic. *Al-Falaq* was also the name of the flagship of the seventeenth- and eighteenth-century Omani prince Seif bin Sultan; at the time of the paper's founding (1929), Seif and his ship were vividly remembered in oral tradition for their role in liberating the coast from Portugal (Ingrams, *Zanzibar: Its History and Its People*, 118–121). This is yet another important theme in nationalist discourse that was the product of a convergence of locally preserved historical traditions and narratives composed by colonial writers such as Hollingsworth and Coupland.

58. "Our New Educational Chief," *Al-Falaq*, 20 May 1939; "Native Trusteeship (1)," *Al-Falaq*, 29 July 1939; "Memorandum by the Arab Association," 5 February 1934, CO618/60/15, PRO; "Report on Zanzibar Education (II)," *Al-Falaq*, 1 October 1938. Also see "Budget Session," *Al-Falaq*, 24 December 1938.

59. M. A. al-Haj, "Hadimu Land Tenure," May 1940, AK 33/294, ZNA; also see the long letter by "Mtambuzi" in *Al-Falaq*, 15 June 1940.

60. For such discourse in the wider Islamic world, see Powell, *A Different Shade of Colonialism*, esp. 145–146; and Ehud Toledano, *Slavery and Abolition in the Ottoman Middle East* (Seattle, 1998), 112–134. For a recent Zanzibari example, see Issa bin Nasser al-Ismaily, *Zanzibar: Kinyang'anyiro na Utumwa* (Ruwi, Oman, 1999).

61. A. Muhsin [al-Barwani], "Slavery As It Used to Be Practised in Zanzibar," *Makerere College Magazine* 1, no. 4 (August 1937): 111. Muhsin al-Barwani acknowledged his intellectual debt to Hollingsworth to the end of his life: see *Conflicts and Harmony in Zanzibar*, 66–68. Slavery's place in the universal history of human progress is stressed in the most influential historical texts of the time, including those by Coupland. For a similar apology for Zanzibar slavery (though not for the trade that brought slaves to the islands), see Hollingsworth, *Short History of the East Coast of Africa*, 128–129.

62. Sceptic's reply originally appeared in *Makerere College Magazine* 1, no. 5 (December 1937); it was reprinted, with a rejoinder from Muhsin, under the headline "An Undoubted Infamy and the Retort," *Al-Falaq*, 23 April 1938. For more on Sceptic, see chapter 4.

63. "The So-Called Native Lethargy," *Al-Falaq*, 3 September 1938; emphasis added.

64. See Cooper, *From Slaves to Squatters*, for British efforts to convince Zanzibari planters of the merits of industrial work discipline.

65. Cooper's chapters on Malindi in *Plantation Slavery on the East Coast of Africa* and my own discussion of Pangani sugar slavery in *Feasts and Riot*, 79–114, show how plantation-gang slavery grew out of the "benign" forms usually taken as typical of "African slavery."

66. "What Is Wrong to the Question?" *Al-Falaq*, 20 August 1938. For a rich account of *Al-Falaq*'s Arabism, see Ghazal, "Islam and Arabism in Zanzibar," 209–253.

67. "Itihad-el-Watani," *Al-Falaq*, 11 February 39. The subject of this notice (the Homeland Union) was an explicitly chauvinist bus owners' cooperative that was set up to drive Indian bus owners out of business. Al-Falaq's glowing notice is a distortion; the Homeland Union was in considerable disarray at the time. See District Reports, 1936–1938, BA 30/5–7, ZNA.

68. R. H. W. Pakenham, *Land Tenure among the Wahadimu at Chwaka, Zanzibar Island* (Zanzibar, 1947); Middleton, *Land Tenure in Zanzibar*; and Sheriff, "The Peasantry under Imperialism."

69. The standard narrative told how the islanders, grateful to the Omanis for the blood they had sacrificed in liberating them from the Portuguese, invited them to be their rulers. A particularly explicit statement is in "Mtambuzi," *Al-Falaq*, 15 June 1940.

70. Al-Haj, "Hadimu Land Tenure," AK 33/294, ZNA.

71. G. E. Noad, Annual Report 1941, BA 30/5, ZNA. For the system of harvest labor that was in place by the 1930s, see Cooper, *From Slaves to Squatters*, 92–104.

72. Report by Hamis Musa [al-Timamy], Mudir Makunduchi, 29 September 1944, AB 4/39, ZNA. There is ample documentation of often unruly competitive feasting in rural Zanzibar in the 1930s and 1940s, especially in the Hadimu fringe; see the documents in AB 30/22, ZNA; Pakenham, *Land Tenure among the Wahadimu at Chwaka, Zanzibar Island*; and numerous entries in the district commissioners' monthly and annual reports, BA 30/5–7, ZNA. For the prestatory moral economy of the Hadimu communities, see Pascal Bacuez, *De Zanzibar à*

Kilwa: relations conflictuelles en pays swahili (Louvain, 2001); and more generally for the Swahili coast, Glassman, *Feasts and Riot.*

73. G. E. Noad, Annual Report 1941, BA 30/5, ZNA; G. E. Noad, Monthly Reports, July–October 1937 and December 1937, BA 30/6, ZNA.

74. "Subira," "Karafuu," *Maz.* 12, no. 11 (November 1938): 163–165. The pseudonym means "Patience" or "Resignation." During these years, all of *Mazungumzo*'s signed articles were by men, and women were not represented in the postprimary institutions that trained government teachers: therefore my assumption that the pseudonymous author was a man. The essay's literary sophistication, especially in its use of rural idiom, dissuades me from the possibility that its author was a European.

75. Specifically, as if their wives were "our *maboi,*" the Swahili version of the colonial English "boys." The archival record confirms that the 1937 crop was a good one that enabled pickers to abuse the contract system and left them with much ready cash to spend on *ngoma*; see, e.g., G. E. Noad, Monthly Reports, September–December 1937, BA 30/6, ZNA; K. H. Clarke, Annual Report 1938, p. 11, BA 30/5, ZNA.

76. The narrator's description of such expenditures places particular emphasis on the purchase of cloth, which was demanded as a customary gift, as for bridewealth, in many Hadimu festive rituals. This aspect of cloth consumption is present throughout the archival record in the 1930s and 1940s.

77. G. E. Noad, Monthly Reports, July–August and September–October 1937, BA 30/6, ZNA; G. E. Noad, Annual Report 1941, BA 30/5, ZNA.

78. "Our Hope and the Government," *Al-Falaq,* 21 January 1939, translated passage in AB 5/36, ZNA. Much more of such rhetoric appeared in subsequent years of *Al-Falaq* and continued to echo in Ali Muhsin al-Barwani's memoirs (*Conflicts and Harmony in Zanzibar,* 167).

79. See the reports by J. O'Brien and others in Clove Labour (1943–50), AB 4/39, ZNA. A preliminary salvo had been fired in 1940, when penal sanctions were lifted from all violations of the Masters and Servants Decree except, notably, in the case of clove-picking contracts. G. E. Noad, Annual Report 1941, BA 30/5, ZNA.

80. Specifically, pickers complained that planters had hired greater numbers of workers than was usual for any one estate. Because of the peculiar wage structure for piecework, that meant that each picker earned less than he had anticipated. The timing of this complaint, if there were any grounds to it, indicates the planters' newfound ability to hold laborers to their contracts.

81. The basic sources for the clove-picking boycotts of 1944 and 1946 are AB 4/39, ZNA, passim; and the following documents, all in BA 30/8, ZNA: District Report, September 1944; W. Addis to Chief Secretary, 25 October 1944; and District Report, July/Sept 1946. Also see Welliver, "The Clove Factor in Colonial Zanzibar," 380–384; and Sheriff and Tominaga, "The Shirazi in the History and Politics of Zanzibar." For conflicts engendered by the planters' demand that pickers pay for the food they consumed, see "End of Clove Harvest," *Al-Falaq,* 15 January 1944.

82. Lofchie, *Zanzibar,* 169. For Tajo's lack of English, see CO822/1376, PRO; and Ali Saleh, *Zanzibar 1870–1972, le drame de l'indépendance* (Paris, 2007), 57. For the Shirazi Association generally, see AB 12/2, ZNA; and for its headquarters in Ng'ambo, W. Addis, Annual Report 1943, BA 30/7, ZNA.

83. Report by Provincial Commissioner J. O'Brien, 4 October 1944, and other documents, AB 4/39, ZNA. For the Shirazi Association's advocacy of rationing issues, see R. H. W. Pakenham, Monthly Report December 1943, and other documents, BA 30/7, ZNA; "Shirazi Association," AB 12/2, ZNA.

84. Colonial officials overestimated the Shirazi Association's role in instigating the boycott; O'Brien, for example, assumed that the association's circulation of the *Al-Falaq* article discussed below was instrumental in sparking the boycott, whereas in fact the article originally was written in *response* to the boycott. Nevertheless, the association's influence in shaping the boycott's rhetoric is unmistakable.

85. Cooper, *From Slaves to Squatters*, 84 ff.

86. "Whisperings," *Al-Falaq*, 26 August 1944. "Mafveraky" was the pen name of Harith bin Suleiman bin Nasser al-Lemki (1888–1946), scion of a prominent family of planters and politicians and one of the founders of the Arab Association. See "Mafveraky: Who Is Who?" *Al-Falaq*, 21 December 1946; and James F. Scotton, "Growth of the Vernacular Press in Colonial East Africa" (Ph.D. diss., University of Wisconsin, 1971), 69. For his father, see John Iliffe, *Tanganyika under German Rule* (Cambridge, 1965).

87. A point argued forcefully in Comaroff, "Of Totemism and Ethnicity."

88. Although his published report states that he undertook the research in 1944, Pakenham's research notes are dated 1943; see Pascal Bacuez, "Une ethnographie dans son contexte: administration coloniale et formation identitaire," *Cah. d'ét. afr.* 38 (1998): 103–133. He had served in the Provincial Administration since at least 1933; see BA 30/3, ZNA.

89. Although Pakenham states that Chwaka had probably experienced a greater degree of disruption during the preceding quarter-century than had most other Hadimu villages, he explicitly includes the main southern centers of Makunduchi and Kizimkazi among the villages that "to some extent" shared the disruptive processes he describes; see *Land Tenure among the Wahadimu at Chwaka, Zanzibar Island*, 33. It is therefore reasonable to extrapolate, particularly since the tensions described by Pakenham closely parallel those that produced the clove-picking boycott at Makunduchi.

90. Ibid., 4.

91. This analysis is implicit in much of Pakenham, *Land Tenure among the Wahadimu at Chwaka, Zanzibar Island*; also suggestive is the incisive reading of Pakenham's unpublished research notes by Bacuez in "Une ethnographie dans son contexte." On all these points Pakenham's Chwaka data are clearly relevant to the south.

92. Reports by Hamis Musa [al-Timamy], 29 September 1944, and J. O'Brien, 4 October 1944, both in AB 4/39, ZNA. Musa was a longtime resident with good knowledge of the area.

4. Subaltern Intellectuals and the Rise of Racial Nationalism

The first epigraph is quoted in Febvre, "Civilisation," 233. The second epigraph is from S. S. Farsy, *Swahili Sayings from Zanzibar*, vol. 1, *Proverbs* (Nairobi, 1958). I have modified Farsy's translation.

1. E.g., "Leaders do not create a new nation nor do they resuscitate a dead one, but it is the nation that creates the leaders": "To the Young Generation," *Al-Falaq*, 26 January 1946.

2. "Babu Mkiwa na mjukuu wake," *Afrika Kwetu*, 7 February 1952. Cf. Ecclesiastes 7:13: "Consider the work of God: for who can make that straight, which he hath made crooked?"

3. They include Jamal Ramadhan Nasibu, whom we will meet below; he learned his first lessons in nationalist politics from Ahmed Lemke, editor of *Al-Falaq*. For other examples, see Lofchie, *Zanzibar*, 141; and Muhsin al-Barwani, *Conflicts and Harmony in Zanzibar*, 5, 199–201.

4. "Risala ya Unguja," *Al-Falaq*, 26 January 1946.

5. The series began by inveighing against unnamed troublemakers who had tried to sow ethnic tension between planters and their workers: "Risala ya Unguja," *Al-Falaq*, 19 January 1946.

6. "Warning," *Al-Falaq*, 19 January 1946.

7. E.g., Abul Barakat, "The Maimed Road," *Al-Falaq,* 7 September 1940, translation (from Arabic) in AB 5/36, ZNA.

8. Muhsin had written articles for the paper since its inception. He remained its chief editor until entering government in 1961. See Muhsin al-Barwani, *Conflicts and Harmony in Zanzibar,* 171–172, 202–204.

9. Mtoro Reihan was born around the turn of the century and came to the islands in the 1920s as a musician. Information about Mtoro is derived from Mariam Hamdani, "Zanzibar Newspapers, 1902 to 1974" (Diploma thesis, Tanzania School of Journalism, 1981); Senior Commissioner, minutes on list of local journalists, 3 March 1954, AB 1/309, ZNA; and conversations with older Zanzibaris.

10. Cooper, *Colonialism in Question,* 18; also see Frederick Cooper, *Africa since 1940: The Past of the Present* (Cambridge, 2002). For an exploration of the resonances of racial ideas in pan-Africanist thought, see Appiah, *In My Father's House.*

11. N. J. Westcott, "An East African Radical: The Life of Erica Fiah," *JAH* 22 (1981): 85–101.

12. King, *Pan-Africanism and Education;* J. Ayodele Langley, *Pan-Africanism and Nationalism in West Africa, 1900–1945* (Oxford, 1973); Zachernuk, *Colonial Subjects.*

13. Fair, *Pastimes and Politics,* shows that although "thick and extensive" political myths color the memories of many former footballers, for most club members football was first and foremost a game and an arena for the performance and contestation of their masculinity. Also see Laura Fair, "Kickin' It: Leisure, Politics and Football in Colonial Zanzibar, 1900s–1950s," *Africa* 67 (1997): 224–251.

14. Fair, *Pastimes and Politics,* 249 ff.; Mrina and Mattoke, *Mapambano ya Ukombozi Zanzibar,* 43–44. It is unclear whether African Sports disbanded immediately upon formation of the new association. It had certainly ceased to exist by 1937, if not earlier; see Provincial Commissioner, "The African Association," 17 May 1937, AB 12/180, ZNA.

15. Mtoro bin Abu Reihan to Chief Secretary, 30 March 1937, AB 12/180, ZNA. Mtoro's letter sought the government's intervention in the leadership dispute discussed below; thus, its cooperative pose might be discounted. But a similar tone would continue to characterize the association's most open political rhetoric well into the 1950s.

16. These ideals were enshrined, inter alia, in a constitution published at Zanzibar in 1935; Iliffe, *A Modern History of Tanganyika,* 406. Anthony Clayton writes that the Zanzibar association initially called itself the African Association for Immigrant Workers, although he offers no source; see Clayton, "The General Strike in Zanzibar, 1948," *JAH* 17 (1976): 422.

17. Mrina and Mattoke, *Mapambano ya Ukombozi Zanzibar,* 51–52; see chapter 2, above.

18. Iliffe, *A Modern History of Tanganyika,* 416–417; Mrina and Mattoke, *Mapambano ya Ukombozi Zanzibar,* 44–49; Provincial Commissioner to DC, 26 April 1937, AB 12/180, ZNA. For the Kiungani teachers, see also Anne Marie Stoner-Eby, "African Leaders Engage Mission Christianity: Anglicans in Tanzania" (Ph.D. diss., Univ. of Pennsylvania, 2003). Ramadhani was the son-in-law of Cecil Majaliwa, a *mateka* who became the first African priest ordained by the Universities' Mission to Central Africa. His son later became an Anglican archbishop.

19. Although Karume was often associated with Manyema immigrants from eastern Congo, his official biography states that his father was born west of Lake Nyasa, also a major catchment zone for the slave trade. His mother came from Rwanda as a child. Mwanjisi, *Abeid Amani Karume,* 9–10 (this account also includes curiously gratuitous comments denying any slave background); Karume's testimony in F-S; biographical sketch in G. Mooring, "Biographical Notes of Zanzibar Personalities," 11 September 1963, no. 4 and enclosures, CO822/3232, PRO.

20. Mwanjisi's hagiography, published after the revolution when the ASP had adopted a left-wing official line, depicts this position as an activist one in which Karume battled un-

scrupulous Indian exploiters to defend the rights of African labor. But before that ideological turnaround, when the African Association was allied with Indian business interests, *Afrika Kwetu* praised Karume simply for having strengthened the boatmen's pension plan. In fact, the syndicate had been established in cooperation with the (Indian) motor-launch owners themselves. Mwanjisi, *Abeid Amani Karume*, 18–19; "G. President the African Association Zanzibar and Pemba Bwana Abeid Amani Karume," *Afrika Kwetu*, 20 June 1957 (copy in AB 5/21, ZNA); Mooring, 11 September 1963, no. 4 and enclosures.

21. C. B. Norman, District Report, October 1936, BA 30/6, ZNA; G. E. Noad, District Reports, April and June 1937, BA 30/6, ZNA; various documents, AB 12/180, ZNA. The religious aspects of these divisions are recalled in the memoirs recorded in Minael-Hosanna O. Mdundo, *Masimulizi ya Sheikh Thabit Kombo Jecha* (Dar es Salaam, 1999), 43–45.

22. This abbreviated account is based on Mrina and Mattoke, *Mapambano ya Ukombozi Zanzibar*, 54; issues of *Al-Falaq* and *Mwongozi* for 1944; Zanzibar District Report, June 1947, and appended memo, DC Zanzibar to Provincial Commissioner, 25 August 1947, BA 30/8, ZNA; K. G. S. Smith, District Reports, January and March 1948, BA 30/8, ZNA; and "The African Association," *Samachar*, 11 January 1948.

23. Lofchie, *Zanzibar*. For more on Barnabas, see Clayton, *The 1948 Zanzibar General Strike*, 38, 64.

24. The Dancing Club was formed in 1940; it changed its name in 1949–1950. Karume to Chief Secretary, 21 January 1949; Committee of the African Youth Union to Chief Secretary, 5 December 1950; *African Youth Union Zanzibar, Sheria* (rules book), 1951 and other documents, all in AB 12/33, ZNA. Also Mwanjisi, *Abeid Amani Karume*, 19–20.

25. In addition to the examples discussed below, see the general description of mutual aid societies, including savings clubs, in Clayton, *The 1948 Zanzibar General Strike*, 23.

26. British officials estimated that roughly 3,000 Manyema were living in Unguja in the 1930s, with one-third or one-half living in town. The "disaffected Manyema" who objected to being subjects of the sultan were concentrated in town, they believed, but the overall number grew, in both town and country, throughout the 1930s. See B. C. Johnstone, 16 August and 1 September 1933, and DC Zanzibar to Provincial Commissioner, 24 September 1937, AB 12/30, ZNA; G. E. Noad, District Report, November 1937, BA 30/6, ZNA. These conflicts may have originated in Ujiji, on the eastern shore of Lake Tanganyika; see Sheryl McCurdy, "The 1932 'War' between Rival Ujiji (Tanganyika) Associations: Understanding Women's Motivations for Inciting Political Unrest," *Canadian Journal of African Studies* 30 (1996): 10–31.

27. The government had begun appointing tribal headmen soon after World War I in response to the demands of the immigrants themselves, who had complained of the existing arrangements, which had been handled by the area headman, an urban version of the *sheha*. (The properties involved were not necessarily trivial: disputed cases often involved the auctioning of a house and all its effects.) Documents in AB 12/30, ZNA; and Clayton, *The 1948 Zanzibar General Strike*, 55–56. In the late 1940s the government phased out the position of tribal headman; see R. H. W. Pakenham, Minute on Agreement with Basukuma Union, 8 June 1953, AB 12/134, ZNA.

28. This paragraph is based on documents in a file titled "Manyema Union (1933–40)," AB 12/30, ZNA; the quotes are from Fuigela bin Kalembwa, Yusufu bin Makwenzo [*sic* for Makuluzo?], and Seif bin Idi, Manyema Union, to DC, 12 July 1937. Also see G. E. Noad, District Report, November 1937, BA 30/6, ZNA.

29. Although the pace of Nyamwezi migration to Zanzibar slowed during the 1930s, in 1948 they still constituted the single largest source of mainland immigrants; see Clayton, *The 1948 Zanzibar General Strike*, 15.

30. Paul Kondemzigo, "Sifa ya Wanyamwezi," *Rafiki Yangu*, October 1912, quoted in Iliffe, *A Modern History of Tanganyika*, 162–163 (also see 389); Peeps [pseud.], "Serikali Bado Imeziba Macho," *Kwetu*, 3 May 1939.

31. This discussion of the Nyamwezi Association is based on documents in "Basukuma Union," AB 12/134, ZNA. Also see G. E. Noad, District Reports, June–September 1946–January 1947, BA 30/8, ZNA. The founding of Zanzibar's Nyamwezi Association was no doubt connected to the founding of a similar organization in Dar es Salaam in 1936; see Iliffe, *A Modern History of Tanganyika*, 389–390. In both cases the association was formally headed by a "tribal headman" named Juma Sultani, probably the same man.

32. W. Addis to Chief Secretary, 25 October 1944, BA 30/8, ZNA.

33. The district commissioner, though otherwise hostile to the dissidents, found substance to the latter accusation. G. E. Noad, Report January 1947; [author illeg.], Report May 1947; Salim M. Barwani, Report February 1947; all in BA 30/8, ZNA. Something of the gulf between these elders and the typical Nyamwezi squatter is revealed in the details about the personal accumulation of Abdulla Katutwa, president of the Baraza Kuu in 1950. Likewise, Juma Sultani, who had been tribal headman in the 1930s, left an estate substantial enough to become the subject of prolonged disputes. Reports by R. H. W. Pakenham, 13 November 1950, and D. B. Barber, 30 September 1950, AB 12/134, ZNA.

34. The dissidents sometimes called their organization the Agreement Basukuma Union, and they had previously constituted themselves as the Wanyamwezi Community (1946).

35. These doubts arise when one compares the district commissioner's monthly reports from the mid- and late 1940s (BA 30/8) with the senior commissioner's general assessments of the union (AB 12/134); both in ZNA. Unlike the latter, the district commissioner's reports were written on a variety of issues with no specific agenda shaping them from month to month. The senior commissioner's memos, on the other hand, were aimed at justifying the administration's hostility to the Agreement Union and its favoring of the Baraza Kuu.

36. Quotes are from Agreement Wanyamwezi and Basukuma Union to Resident, 28 January 1954, and Agreement Basukuma Union to Chief Secretary, 7 October 1952, AB 12/134, ZNA. Also see the petitions on behalf of the union, signed by Honorary President Mohamed Mtunda and directed to the senior commissioner, dated 25 August 1950 and 23 November 1950, in same file.

37. Clayton, *The Zanzibar Revolution and Its Aftermath*, 34.

38. Such approaches were especially pronounced in Tanzanian studies. A notable example is George Hadjivayanis and Ed Ferguson, "The Development of a Colonial Working Class," in Sheriff and Ferguson, *Zanzibar under Colonial Rule*, 188–219. For a critique of these trends, see William H. Sewell, "Toward a Post-Materialist Rhetoric for Labor History," in *Rethinking Labor History*, ed. Lenard R. Berlanstein (Urbana, 1993). Such ideological overdetermination also distorts the depiction of dock labor in Adam Shafi Adam's popular novel about the general strike, *Kuli* (Dar es Salaam, 1979), a book that was part of the canon of leftists at the University of Dar es Salaam at the time the essays in Sheriff and Ferguson's volume were written. See Issa Shivji, "The Life and Times of Babu: The Age of Revolution and Liberation," *Law, Social Justice & Global Development*, 2001(2), available at http://www2.warwick.ac.uk/fac/soc/law/elj/lgd/2001_2/shivji/ (accessed 5 June 2010).

39. See esp. Frederick Cooper, *Decolonization and African Society* (Cambridge, 1996); and Lisa Lindsay, "Domesticity and Difference: Male Breadwinners, Working Women, and Colonial Citizenship in the 1945 Nigerian General Strike," *American Historical Review* 104 (1999): 783–812.

40. The latter interpretation shapes the memories of many of Laura Fair's oral informants in "Pastimes and Politics: A Social History of Zanzibar's Ng'ambo Community, 1890–1950" (Ph.D. diss., Univ. of Minnesota, 1994), chapter 8; and appears most strikingly in Said A. Mohamed's widely read novel, *Dunia Mti Mkavu* (Nairobi, 1980).

41. Clayton, *The 1948 Zanzibar General Strike*, 21–22 and appendices; Batson, *Report on Proposals for a Social Survey of Zanzibar*, 19–20. Mainlanders constituted just under a third of the population within the town proper (15,000, overwhelmingly in Ng'ambo), but an additional 10,000 lived in the town's immediate suburbs. Mainlanders constituted 27 percent of Unguja's overall population and 22 percent of the population of the protectorate as a whole. Although a handful of these self-identified mainlanders were former slaves or descendants of slaves, most were immigrants or their children.

42. Clayton, *The 1948 Zanzibar General Strike*, is invaluable for these matters. For shuttling between town and countryside, see also K. G. S. Smith, Annual Report 1947, BA 30/5, ZNA; and Middleton, *Land Tenure in Zanzibar*. The evidence that urban workers' wives maintained plots in the countryside is anecdotal; see personal details about Abbas Othman, a leader of the 1948 strike, later in this chapter.

43. The government workers were employed in two departments in town, public works and public health. The Agriculture Department employed an additional 1,100 workers on government plantations in the countryside. See R. H. W. Pakenham, *Labour Report for the Year 1948*, BA19/3, ZNA.

44. For the second figure, see J. O'Brien, *Labour Report for the Year 1946*, BA 19/1, ZNA.

45. For work conditions among *wachukuzi* laborers, see Hadjivayanis and Ferguson, "The Development of a Colonial Working Class," 189–190; O'Brien, *Report on Labour for the Year 1945* and *Labour Report for the Year 1946*, BA 9/14 and BA 19/1, ZNA; J. M. Gray, "Wachukuzi and Produce Shippers Association," 9 October 1948, AK 20/1, ZNA. Additional details are from Ian Parkin, "Report on Inquiry into Labour Conditions in the Port of Zanzibar, May 1959," BA 38/3, ZNA.

46. For an explicit statement, see Hardinge to Kimberley, 13 March 1895, quoted in Arthur Hardinge, *A Diplomatist in the East* (London, 1928), 389.

47. In addition to the sources already cited, see lists of office holders from the 1950s, in the documents filed in "Labour (Wachukuzi) Association," AB 12/145, ZNA; and biographical details about some of that association's founding members and longtime leaders in John Gray, *Report of the Arbitrator to Enquire into a Trade Dispute at the Wharf Area at Zanzibar* (Zanzibar, 1958), 5–6. For political rhetoric likening such labor and the disdain suffered by *wachukuzi* to slavery, see "Watende Wao el-Harara," *Agozi*, 20 July 1959. The parallels are striking. Like their twentieth-century counterparts, slave *wachukuzi* were often bonded to low-status masters, including fellow slaves and impoverished Yemeni immigrants; see Glassman, *Feasts and Riot*, 87–88.

48. Details in this and the next two paragraphs are drawn from J. O'Brien, *Report on Labour for the Year 1945*, BA 9/14; J. M. Gray, "Wachukuzi and Produce Shippers Association," 9 October 1948; and documents in "Labourers (Wachukuzi) Association 1946–51," AB 12/20, ZNA.

49. O'Brien, *Report on Labour for the Year 1945*, BA 9/14, ZNA; J. O'Brien to D. Barber, 26 February 1946, AB 12/20, ZNA.

50. Although its ranks were decimated by the strike, the union quickly rebuilt in the years that followed. It survived in part because government officials remained convinced of its value to them. In addition to the sources already noted, see O'Brien, *Labour Report for the Year 1946*, BA 19/1; and "Labour Wachukuzi Association, 1942–65," AB 12/144–145, ZNA.

51. The petition from Abdulrahman Hija, secretary of the association, was penned by Ibuni Saleh, a "licenced writer"; see the petition, dated 10 July 1946, in AB 12/20, ZNA. Saleh went go on to a political career within the Arab Association in which he, like Tajo, vilified mainlanders.

52. Government-employed carpenters, who struck at the same time, formed Zanzibar's second union after having first expressed a desire to join the Wachukuzi Association. O'Brien, *Labour Report for the Year 1946*; O'Brien, "Labour Disputes," 25 March 1946, AB 12/20, ZNA. As in many African cities, labor activities at the time were no doubt encouraged by the declining real wages of the war years.

53. District reports for January, September, and October 1947 and for April, May and June 1948, BA 30/8, ZNA. Also see K. G. S. Smith, District Annual Report 1947, BA 30/5, ZNA.

54. Fair advances this interpretation most fully in her dissertation, which has chapters on both the rent strike and the 1948 general strike. See "Pastimes and Politics: A Social History of Zanzibar's Ng'ambo Community, 1890–1950." In *The 1948 Zanzibar General Strike*, Clayton concurs that such concerns were a major source of solidarity among the 1948 strikers.

55. Hadjivayanis and Ferguson, "The Development of a Colonial Working Class," 202–203.

56. The pay terms won by the dockworkers were only 1 shilling per month above the earlier offer, with 5 cents more in hourly overtime. Except where noted, all details about the 1948 strike are derived from Clayton, *The 1948 Zanzibar General Strike*; and Clayton, *The Zanzibar Revolution and Its Aftermath*, 24–35. For details regarding casual labor, also see R. H. W. Pakenham, *Labour Report for the Year 1948*, BA 19/3, ZNA; and "Report of the Labour Conciliation Committee," 2 September 1948, AK 20/1, ZNA. Similar tensions over casual versus contract labor had informed the Mombasa dockworkers' strike of the previous year; see Cooper, *Decolonization and African Society*, 236.

57. Salim M. Barwani, District Report for August 1948 (20 September 1948), BA 30/8, ZNA.

58. In addition to Clayton, see Pakenham, *Labour Report for the Year 1948*; Glenday and Ameri Tajo, speeches in Legco, 6 September 1948, BA 16/59, ZNA; Fair, "Pastimes and Politics," 373–374.

59. Barwani, District Report for August 1948. In contrast, strike organizers who sought food support in Pemba, where anti-mainlander sentiment was marked, were brusquely turned away.

60. Such assertions, made after the strike was over, may have been the disingenuous attempts of officials to absolve themselves of blame for having failed to anticipate the disturbance. R. H. W. Pakenham, the senior commissioner, was most explicit, adding that such racial instigation was alien to local traditions; see *Labour Report for the Year 1948*, BA 19/3, ZNA.

61. A. H. M. Dryden, "Strike Rumours," 24 January 1949, and "Labour Unrest," 1, 2 and 5 February 1949, all in AK 20/1, ZNA. Fair's informants also remembered Abbas Othman as having lived in Zanzibar for years; see "Pastimes and Politics," 370–371. Despite this evidence, several colonial officers told Clayton (decades later) that they believed that Abbas Othman was a newcomer who had moved from Dar es Salaam shortly before the strike, using that conjecture to support their "outside agitator" interpretation; see *The 1948 Zanzibar General Strike*, 31–32.

62. Legislative Council Debates, 6 September 1948, BA 16/59, ZNA; Clayton, *The 1948 Zanzibar General Strike*, 25.

63. Busaidi belonged to the ruling family and had close ties to the royal court. His role in recruiting the Tumbatu strikebreakers is suggested by his detailed knowledge of the arrangements, which he conveyed to Clayton.

64. See Dryden, "Strike Rumours," and "Labour Unrest." Having temporarily departed for Dar es Salaam (in bad odor over allegations of having misappropriated some strike relief funds), Othman returned quietly to Zanzibar in January 1949 with no political aims save perhaps organizing a branch of the Zaramo Union.

65. Mtoro Abur-Reihan Mzigua to Chief Secretary, 11 October 1948, AB 5/21, ZNA.

66. Lofchie, *Zanzibar*, 133–134; Lofchie quotes Seif Hamoud, vice-president of the Arab Association, writing in the newspaper *Al Nahadha*, 26 April 1951.

67. Francisco A. Scarano, "The *Jíbaro* Masquerade and the Subaltern Politics of Creole Identity Formation in Puerto Rico, 1745–1823," *American Historical Review* 101 (1996): 1398–1431; Rebecca Earle, "Creole Patriotism and the Myth of the 'Loyal Indian,'" *Past & Present* 172 (2001): 125–145. Cf. Mamdani, *When Victims Become Killers*, which attributes Zanzibar's politics of nativism, like Rwanda's, to the colonial state and especially to colonial law.

68. Lofchie, *Zanzibar*, 132. Those Indians who did take an interest in politics would work with one of the established political parties. Some, like the journalist Ruti Bulsara (from the small Parsi community), were drawn ideologically to the ZNP's multiracial and progressive left wing; others, especially among the businessmen who supported the ASP, were prompted by enmity for their old rivals among the Arab planter class.

69. Literally "war," although "Cattle Riot" is the usual rendering. At the time, the word *ghasia*, which more closely approaches the meaning of "riot," was heard.

70. The fullest account remains the careful report compiled by John M. Gray, *Report on the Civil Disturbances in Zanzibar on July 30th, 1951* (Zanzibar, 1951); also see Abdurahman M. Juma, "Cattle Riot (Vita vya Ng'ombe): A Case Study of Peasant Rising" (M.A. diss., Department of History, University of Dar es Salaam, 1982). I also rely on the following files in ZNA: Salim M. Barwani, District Monthly Reports, April–July 1951, in AB 8/3; "Anthrax Trouble, 1951," AK 1/59; "Compulsory Cattle Dipping 1949–50," AU 11/9; "Compulsory Cattle Dipping 1951," AU 11/10; Yahya Alawi, District Annual Report 1949, BA 30/5; and District Reports, March 1948–December 1949, BA 30/8.

71. This appears in the villagers' behavior in the months after the riot, when much community activity and all cooperation with government came to a halt in resentment over the arrest of their "leaders." Yahya Alawi, District Report March 1952, AB 8/3, ZNA; District Reports for September and November 1953 and March 1954, AB 8/4, ZNA.

72. Particularly useful for such details, including verbatim statements by participants and witnesses, is R. E. Middleton, "Report on Police Action during Disturbances 30th July 1951" and attachments, CO822/620, PRO. Middleton recorded that the crowds chanted "Allah, Allah"; it is more likely that they were chanting "Allahu Akbar," which is how Ali Muhsin remembered it; see Muhsin al-Barwani, *Conflicts and Harmony in Zanzibar*, 88–89. The calls to jihad are attested to in several additional sources.

73. "Result Obtain from CATTLE," *Afrika Kwetu*, 9 August 1951; "An Unhappy Event," *Al-Falaq*, 8 August 1951; Ruti Bulsara, "All Quiet," *Adal Insaf*, 4 August 1951.

74. "Regrettable," *Mwongozi*, 3 August 1951.

75. Babu, "Tulitokea Wapi?" *Mwongozi*, 29 May and 12 June 1959 (the last two installments of a three-part essay); Zanzibar National Party [Ali Muhsin], *Whither Zanzibar? Growth and Policy of Zanzibar Nationalism* (Zanzibar, 1960).

76. Babu dates the riot to 1954, erroneously linking *Al-Falaq's* imagined defense of the rioters to its editors' indictment for sedition in that year; Muhsin, in his memoirs, repeatedly dates it to 1955, the year ZNP was founded. Babu, "Appendix I: The Background to the Zanzibar Revolution," in Wilson, *US Foreign Policy*, 141–144; Muhsin al-Barwani, *Conflicts and Harmony*

in Zanzibar, 88–89. In both cases the intent behind the error may well have been unconscious. The importance Muhsin lays on the supposed chronological convergence is suggested by his failure to notice the contradictions the error introduces into his broader narrative.

77. A. R. Mohamed [Babu], "Book Review—'Isle of Cloves,'" *Mwongozi*, 20 July 1956; A. M. Babu, "The 1964 Revolution: Lumpen or Vanguard?" in Sheriff and Ferguson, *Zanzibar under Colonial Rule*, 221. The latter essay was written in 1976.

78. In this regard, the ZNP propagandists' use of the Cattle Riot resembled a compressed version of the process by which Congress nationalists rewrote the history of the Chauri Chaura riot of 1922; see the subtle analysis in Amin, *Event, Metaphor, Memory*.

79. Middleton, "Report on Police Action"; and P. Pullicino, "Administrative Secretary's Report," 9 August 1951, both in CO822/620, PRO. As to the lack of monarchist sentiments, it is, of course, always difficult to marshal evidence of absence. However, none of the rioters whose verbatim statements appear in the police report make any reference to the sultan—and a statement to the police would seem the ideal occasion to profess such loyalty. In advance of the riot there were rumors that the protestors would make a representation to the sultan, who instructed his gatekeepers to allow a delegation into the palace. But a delegation never appeared.

80. For example, His Highness's Subjects National Association, set up to rival the then anti-Arab Shirazi Association, which had a brief existence in Pemba in 1946. G. E. Noad, Monthly Reports, November and December 1946, BA 30/8, ZNA.

81. When read critically, Muhsin's sprawling memoirs are a rich source on these organizations. Although at some points he repeats the official line attributing the party's origins to the NPSS and the peasants of Kiembe Samaki, at others he relates more convincing details about at least half a dozen other organizations that he describes as direct forerunners of the ZNP. For these particular details, see Muhsin al-Barwani, *Conflicts and Harmony in Zanzibar*, 90–91, 130.

82. Ibid., 79–83; G. E. Noad, Annual Report 1936, BA 30/5, ZNA; and District Reports for May through October 1936, July/August 1937, and October 1938, BA 30/6–7, ZNA. For other examples of such movements, also organized by kinsmen of Muhsin who would later become important ZNP functionaries, see "Boycott of Indians," police bulletin, 4 July 1938, AB 12/114, ZNA.

83. See *Conflicts and Harmony in Zanzibar*, 167, for Muhsin's description of the clove-buying crisis. In a similar vein, he portrayed Badr Muhammad and other elite men of honor, who later became ZNP stalwarts, as representative of the "children of the soil, the peasant farmers, the country folk, the genuine Zanzibaris" (80). Although these words were written decades later, such rhetoric was amply in evidence in the Arab Association journalism at the time. Muhsin fudged the class nature of Itihad in his memoirs, and Babu described it as a "peasant movement" ("The Background to the Zanzibar Revolution," 142). But at the time *Al-Falaq*, which was not imbued with Babu's and Muhsin's latter-day populism, was frank: Itihad was a success, it stated plainly, because it was organized and led by Arabs, not "natives"; see "Itihad-el-Watani," *Al-Falaq*, 11 February 1939.

84. Muhsin al-Barwani, *Conflicts and Harmony in Zanzibar*, 199–201. Muhsin mentions Lemki but not his National Union, for which see Lofchie, *Zanzibar*, 140–141.

85. Balibar makes this point more generally in "Racism and Nationalism," 60.

86. *Al-Falaq*'s anti-Indian rhetoric continued sporadically into the 1950s, although it never returned to the level of the 1930s clove-buying crisis. Both major political parties of the Time of Politics included Indians among their leading journalists. Still, neither lacked propagandists who were willing to stoop to occasional Indian-bashing.

87. "Nionavyo Mimi Bingwa," *AfrKw*, 15 November 1956. Monarchist sentiments can be found throughout *Afrika Kwetu* from the early and mid-1950s, often combined, as here, with expressions of racial resentment. During the ZNP's first year, *Afrika Kwetu* frequently accused it of republicanism, pointing to the known Nasserite and socialist sympathies of some of its leaders.

88. Rai Samha, "Correspondence," *Mwongozi*, 4 December 1953; "Wananchi Wameungana— Hizbul Watan Imesimama," *Mwongozi*, 20 January 1956.

89. For a pointed example see "National Manifesto (x)," *Mwongozi*, 18 March 1955. With Kenya's impending independence in the early 1960s, the cause of Mwambao was again taken up, this time with the covert support of white settlers and some anti-federalist African politicians, two groups that were united in their hostility to KANU. In this campaign for complete separation of the coast from Kenya, the rhetoric about the threat to coastal Islamic civilization from upcountry barbarism became quite sharp. See Clarence Buxton Papers, Box 3, file 1 and Box 3, file 3, MSS. Brit. Emp. s. 390, RH. For the Mwambao controversy generally, see Salim, *The Swahili-Speaking Peoples*; and James R. Brennan, "Lowering the Sultan's Flag: Sovereignty and Decolonization in Coastal Kenya," *Comparative Studies in Society and History* 50 (2008): 831–861.

90. Such rhetoric could be found throughout the pages of *Mwongozi* in late 1956 and early 1957.

91. Or so claimed *Afrika Kwetu*; see "Kwa Nini Waafrika Wanachukiwa na Wageni Wao?" *AfrKw*, 3 January 1957; and "Mwafrika Vyengine Hawi Ila ni Mwafrika tu," *AfrKw*, 15 November 1956. The epithet *wamishin*, which carries derogatory connotations, was observed in the 1920s and may well have dated to the earliest days of missionary activity among *mateka*, former slaves; see Ingrams, *Zanzibar: Its History and Its People*, 223–226.

92. "Sensational Speech at the Budget Session," *Mwongozi*, 21 December 1956.

93. The quotes from Samha are in "Correspondence," *Mwongozi*, 4 December 1953.

94. *Mwongozi*, 1 February, 8 February, 5 April, and 14 June 1957. Such accusations continued and indeed intensified after the ZNP lost the July 1957 elections. *Mwongozi's* arguments that the government was soft on ASP racialism were specious, sophist, and anti-democratic (see esp. "Stop This Double-Talk," 14 June 1957) and seem to support the chief secretary's comment that the ZNP would have been satisfied only if government had actively opposed the ASP. See P. A. P. Robertson to J. Stringer, 20 October 1958, in AB 70/11, ZNA. The latter file documents the government's efforts to combat racial politicking in the wake of the 1957 elections. In fact, "the government," insofar as it consisted of its civil servants, was largely sympathetic to Hizbu.

95. "Waafrika wa visiwani sio wa barani," *AfrKw*, 16 September 1954.

96. "Maulizo yenyi faida kwa Waafrika," *AfrKw*, 26 August 1954. The first page of Hollingsworth, *Milango ya Historia*, asserts that the islands were once connected to the mainland but says nothing of people having crossed.

97. As Martin Lewis and Kären Wigen observe, Western concepts of race are "inescapably geographical"; see *The Myth of Continents* (Berkeley, 1997), 120.

98. "Messing about with Politics (II)," *AfrKw*, 11 September 1952; "Nani anaedai Africa kuliko Muafrika mwenyewe," *AfrKw*, 12 July 1956.

99. "Wrong Move Is Eclipse of the Mind," *AfrKw*, 5 August 1954. The adjective describing African hair is unreadable in the copy I consulted; I derive "kinky" from the article's Swahili version, published 12 August. For more on this article, see J. Glassman, "Sorting out the Tribes: The Creation of Racial Identities in Colonial Zanzibar's Newspaper Wars," *JAH* 41 (2000): 409.

100. "Mkutano mkuu Makunduchi," *AfrKw*, 14 February 1957. Karume's geography lesson was replicated in poetic form in "Sharazi [*sic*] na Afrika," by "Shirazi African-Zbar," *AfrKw*, 2 May 1957.

101. Karume's logic and language on this point echoes arguments that had appeared in *Afrika Kwetu* for several months, and echoes of the Koranic gloss would continue to appear. The verse in question is Surat al-Hujurat, v. 13. Abdullah Saleh Farsy's famous Swahili translation, which was serialized in *Mwongozi*, contains no commentary on this verse, but other commentaries by Farsy, then Zanzibar's most widely respected Islamic scholar, leave no doubt that he would have objected to Karume's interpretation. Although Islamic scholars had long debated the significance of race, most held that skin color is irrelevant in the eyes of God and that the community of the faithful transcends all other distinctions. But the scholars also recognized that those ideals were not always observed in practice. Lewis, *Race and Slavery in the Middle East*.

102. The quotes are from "Waafrika wa visiwani," *AfrKw*, 16 September 1954; see also "Maulizo yenyi faida kwa Waafrika," *AfrKw*, 26 August 1954. This argument was repeated often in *AfrKw*. In its more combative moments, the paper asserted that islanders' origins lay not merely on the mainland but in the interior as opposed to the coast; see "Waafrika na makabila ya kiafrika," *AfrKw*, 1 September 1955. The paper published many articles extolling pan-Africanist virtues, including paeans to pan-Africanist icons such as Marcus Garvey and Paul Robeson.

103. Glassman, "Sorting Out the Tribes," 411.

104. Sources for the preceding two paragraphs are discussed in ibid., 412–414.

105. "Waafrika wa pwani," *AfrKw*, 27 January 1955.

106. "Mkataa asili yake dhalimu wa kweli kweli," *AfrKw*, 3 February 1955. The poem, its language, and its author are discussed at greater length in Glassman, "Sorting Out the Tribes," 414–417.

107. See the discussion in Glassman, "Sorting Out the Tribes," 414–415. A similar range of meanings appears in Sacleux's magisterial *Dictionnaire Swahili-Français*, which was compiled around the turn of the century. Also see Carl Velten, *Suaheli-Wörterbuch*, vol. 1, *Teil Suaheli-Deutsch* (Berlin, 1910).

108. See the account of Ameri Tajo's speech at the February 1957 ASP rally at Makunduchi in "Mkutano mkuu Makunduchi," *AfrKw*, 14 February 1957; see also Ng'weng'we, "Fitina zisio na maana," *AfrKw*, 28 March 1957. For an explicit argument that Shirazi share the same black skin as other *magozi*, see "Wanachama wa Afro-Shirazi—Magozi na Mapakacha," *AfrKw*, 22 October 1959.

109. "Kwa nini Waafrika wanachukiwa na wageni wao?" *AfrKw*, 3 January 1957; "Mwafrika vyengine hawi ila ni Mwafrika tu," *AfrKw*, 15 November 1956. The logic of this second article resembles that of Karume's Koranic gloss.

110. Mapuri, *Zanzibar*, 17. The phrase used was "*Hizbu matope.*" Jamal Ramadhan's racial propaganda is remembered by Zanzibari informants, and he left plentiful published evidence, including "Uafrika wa Kununuwa si wa Kuzaliwa," *Agozi*, 14 September 1959. Others will be examined below.

111. E.g., "National Manifesto (IV): The Racial Question," *Mwongozi*, 4 February 1955, in which appears the phrase "mixture of blood."

112. "Nionavyo mimi Bingwa," *AfrKw*, 15 November 1956. ("Citizens": *wenyeji*; "pure African": *Mwafrika safi*.)

113. "Furnish Us with the Zanzibar History," *AfrKw*, 27 January and 3 February 1955 (the Swahili version begins in the latter issue); "The Aims and Objects of 'Sauti ya Cairo,'" *AfrKw*, 16 February 1956 (with a Swahili version in the following week).

114. For the contradictions this introduced to the paper's polemics, see Glassman, "Sorting Out the Tribes," 419.

115. "Native or African?" *Al-Falaq*, 8 November 1941.

116. In fact, Muhsin was still issuing such apologies forty years later; see Muhsin al-Barwani, *Conflicts and Harmony in Zanzibar*, 177–186.

117. Such rhetoric appeared throughout the 1950s; see Glassman, "Sorting Out the Tribes," 421n101. In speeches after the revolution, Karume continued to describe the sultans as "Manga"; see Abeid A. Karume, *Karume na Siasa, Uchumi na Maendeleo ya Kimapinduzi* (Zanzibar, 1973).

118. A. Muhsin, "Slavery as It Used to be Practiced in Zanzibar," *Makerere College Magazine* 1, no. 4 (August 1937): 111; "An Undoubted Infamy and the Retort," *Al-Falaq*, 23 April 1938. (See the discussion of this exchange in chapter 3.) Of the four Zanzibari students then at Makerere (Muhsin al-Barwani, *Conflicts and Harmony in Zanzibar*, 69), Shariff was most likely to have written such remarks. But we cannot be sure whether "Sceptic" was in fact a Zanzibari.

119. Older single women, including divorcees and widows, would have been most ready to shed concerns over status in order to secure the protection that came with marriage; see Glassman, *Feasts and Riot*, 120–133.

120. The egalitarian emphasis was greatest in the teachings of the modernist reformers—although, as we have seen, many made exceptions for Arab distinctiveness. For debates on *kafa'a*, see Mandana Limbert, "Marriage, Status and the Politics of Nationality in Oman," in *The Gulf Family: Kinship Policies and Modernity*, ed. Alanoud Alsharekh (London, 2007), 167–179; and Abdalla Bujra, *The Politics of Stratification: A Study of Political Change in a South Arabian Town* (Oxford, 1971), 93–94, 130–132.

121. For an illustrative case and a review of how these issues were debated by Islamic jurists, see John Gray's ruling in Civil Appeal No. 8 of 1949, Zanzibar High Court, *Law Reports, Containing Cases Determined by the High Court for Zanzibar*, vol. 7 (Zanzibar, 1954), 117–121. Also see Ali bin Hemedi el Buhriy, *Nikahi, a Handbook of the Law of Marriage in Islam*, translated by J. W. T. Allen (Dar es Salaam, 1959). This influential text, originally published in Swahili in 1934, assumes the centrality of racial/ethnic categories in the calculation of *kafa'a* (3). The principle of hypergyny, however, appears only implicitly, and, like the precedents cited by Gray, Buhriy allows for ample leeway.

122. "Majibu yenu," *AfrKw*, 28 January 1954.

123. Ali Muhsin Barwani, "Usawa upo kama haupo," *AfrKw*, 18 and 25 March 1954. For a comparison with the standard commentaries on these verses (Surat al-Ahzab, v. 36–37), see Glassman, "Sorting Out the Tribes," 422n105. Muhsin's idiosyncratic reading was shared by Abdullah Saleh al-Farsy, whose Koranic translation and commentary first appeared in *Mwongozi* in the 1950s; see *Qurani Takatifu* (Nairobi, 1984), 527–528.

124. Despite al-Farsy's close collaboration with Muhsin and *Mwongozi*, even *Afrika Kwetu* saw fit to sing his praises, and he survived the revolution in his position as Chief Kadhi. See "Khadithi ndogo Sh. Abdalla Salehe Farsi," *AfrKw*, 31 January and 7 February 1963; and Musa, *Maisha ya al-Imam Sheikh Abdulla Saleh Farsy*, 59.

125. For sources on the forced marriages, see note 21 of the Epilogue and Conclusion, below. The ideologies that motivated them and the rhetoric with which they were officially justified (including the 1966 Marriage Code that made them legal) are easily traced to the racial rhetoric of 1950s ASP journalism.

126. Contributors to *Agozi* possibly included Othman Sharif and Abdulla Kassim Hanga, both of whom became prominent ASP figures and members of the Revolutionary Council. The paper was banned in August 1962. See Glassman, "Sorting Out the Tribes," 423–424.

127. "Vipi uwe ndugu yangu" [How You Can Become My Brother], *Agozi*, 3 August 1959. For an extended discussion of this piece, see Glassman, "Sorting Out the Tribes," 424.

128. The issue of intermarriage would continue to provoke some of *Agozi*'s most heated language. See "Ati fedheha—wasema l'harara—Mwarabu kuolewa na Mwafrika" [It's a Disgrace!— Say the Exalted Ones—for an Arab Woman to be Married by an African], *Agozi*, 7 March 1960.

129. Emblematic was the exchange between Ali Muhsin and "Sceptic": the former relied on colonialist literature to make his point; the latter cited no sources whatsoever. A recent example of the phenomenon is the apologetic account of Zanzibar slavery in al-Ismaily, *Zanzibar: Kinyang'anyiro*.

130. Examples include "Waafrika na makabila ya kiafrika," *AfrKw*, 1 September 1955; "Kale hata leo," *AfrKw*, 13 January 1955.

131. "Makunduchi," *AfrKw*, 29 October 1959, and "Mtumwa mwenye ari si mungwana asiekuwa na ari," *AfrKw*, 5 November 1959; Security Report, July–August 1961, CO822/2046, PRO; "Umma Hay!" *Mwongozi*, 21 April 1961. The new party, ZPPP, will be discussed in chapter 5; its political rhetoric abounded with anti-mainlander sentiments. The political events of the Time of Politics are best recounted by Lofchie, *Zanzibar*, though his assertion that ZPPP never posed a threat in Makunduchi is belied by his own data, which show that in 1963 the party lost to ASP there by a mere sixteen votes.

5. Politics and Civil Society during the Newspaper Wars

1. S. M. Khamis, "Utenzi," *Mwongozi*, 17 February 1961. Many of Zanzibar's most respected poets were women, but we do not know this poet's gender.

2. S. A. Busaidi, DC, Reports on Urban District, June–July 1957, AB 8/7, ZNA. Busaidi was well known for his monarchist sentiments and hostility to the ASP (and thus probably was a target of such abuse himself). Yet he noted that the abuse was heard from both sides.

3. The comments were made in a symposium of former colonial officers convened by historian Alison Smith; the other officers concurred with Robertson's description. Zanzibar Symposium, 16 October 1971, MSS. Afr. s. 2250, Item 2, p. 24, RH. In 1961 Robertson had twenty-five years' experience in the colonial service, most of it in East Africa.

4. S. S. Foster-Sutton, V. Tewson, and C. A. Grossmith, *Report of a Commission of Inquiry into Disturbances in Zanzibar during June 1961* (London, 1961), 15. The commission's hearings will be discussed in Chapter 7. Its transcripts, which are in the Clarence Buxton Papers, Boxes 4 and 5, Mss. Brit. Emp. s. 390, RH, will henceforth be cited as F-S, followed by number of the day of the hearing and, when appropriate, the page number(s) (e.g., day 7:24 would mean day seven of the hearing, page 24).

5. As Lofchie observed in *Zanzibar*, 210–211.

6. Mark Knights, *Representation and Misrepresentation in Later Stuart Britain: Partisanship and Political Culture* (Oxford, 2005), 224–225. Knights describes a situation in which the sudden introduction of frequent elections and the expanded availability of cheap political pamphlets combined to give rise to a national public sphere. He reminds us that "since the press interacted with other forms of popular expression," a focus on the one should not be taken to mean that the others were unimportant; rather, print allows us a way to study public discourse (222).

7. The campaign was launched in "Waafrika Hawapendi Ugima," *AfrKw*, 25 April 1957. For "Hyena," see *AfrKw*, 30 May 1957. This general description of newspaper culture is derived from Hamdani, "Zanzibar Newspapers," and conversations with informants who witnessed it.

8. "Afrika Kwetu," *AfrKw*, 4 June 1959. Such a linkage has been explored at length in Anderson, *Imagined Communities*.

9. In many of the papers, punctuation and grammar are rough, with frequent elisions of verbs and prepositions: in other words, they were written according to the conventions of informal *spoken* Swahili. Significantly, when Zanzibari friends helped me with particularly difficult passages, they often worked them out by reading them aloud, a technique I adopted as my own.

10. In British law, sedition includes the charge of creating "ill will" between different classes of people. Colonial law was notoriously broad in its prosecution of sedition and related offenses; unlike in English common law, for instance, it was not necessary to prove the use or advocacy of violence. In East Africa, the *Al-Falaq* sedition convictions of 1954 had a particularly chilling effect. See James S. Read, "Criminal Law in the Africa of Today and Tomorrow," *Journal of African Law* 7 (1963): 5–17; and Scotton, "Growth of the Vernacular Press in Colonial East Africa," 15 ff., 237–248. Also see James Scotton, "Tanganyika's African Press, 1937–1960," *African Studies Review* 21, no. 1 (1978): 1–18; and Stanley Shaloff, "Press Controls and Sedition Proceedings in the Gold Coast, 1933–39," *African Affairs* 71 (1972): 241–263.

11. "Makhaini Wanazidi Kujitokeza," *Mwongozi*, 24 March 1961.

12. Letters by "Mzanzibari," *Mwongozi*, 3 May 1957; and Khamis Akida, *AfrKw*, 16 May 1957.

13. The words are Ali Muhsin's; see Visit of Secretary of State for the Colonies, Notes on Informal Discussions, 30 October 1957, CO822/1376, no. 11, PRO.

14. Among those who entertained these thoughts was Muhsin himself. But most party leaders opposed this kind of thinking. See "Nationalist Party, Zanzibar, 1957–1959," CO822/1378, PRO, esp. documents from June to July 1959.

15. "Mkutano Mkubwa Uliokuwa Mnazi Mmoja, Freedom Day," *AfrKw*, 16 April 1959. For the Freedom Committee alliance, see Lofchie, *Zanzibar*, 189 ff.; and Joseph Nye, *Pan-Africanism and East African Integration* (Cambridge, Mass., 1967).

16. "Racial Discrimination," *AfrKw*, 16 July 1959.

17. In addition to Lofchie, *Zanzibar*, see documents in CO822/1376, PRO, esp. the extracts from the Intelligence Committee Monthly Reports.

18. "Vitimbi vya Hizbu na Uchaguzi 1960," *Agozi*, 28 September 1959. The untranslatable vulgarity is used to accentuate the Arab's lack of respect for his newfound allies. For a century and a half of Arab rule, *Agozi* asserts, your Arab neighbor has never come to inquire "*hata NYOKO*": literally, he has never even come to ask after "your mother. . . ."

19. "Queer Way of Baying the Moon," *Agozi*, 27 July 1959; Lofchie, *Zanzibar*, 193. *Afrika Kwetu* of 14 May 1959 contains a detailed report of a dissidents' meeting.

20. For colonial conceptions of "hooligans," or what the British and many of their East African subjects called *"wahuni,"* see Andrew Burton, *African Underclass* (London, 2005). For Othman Sharif on educational qualifications, see Mrina and Mattoke, *Mapambano ya Ukombozi Zanzibar*, 69; Zanzibar Intelligence, January 1960, CO822/2132, PRO.

21. Karume and Mtoro were, indeed, older than most of the dissidents, but not by much: Karume was born in 1905, Othman Sharif in 1914. Jamal Ramadhan was of the same generation. Among dissidents in both parties, the language of "youth" served two purposes: it enabled the dissidents to mount serious challenges without seeming to question the established party hierarchy, and it harnessed the continent-wide discourse that linked nationalist aspirations to youth and modernity. See Thomas Burgess, "Remembering Youth: Generation in Revolutionary Zanzibar," *Africa Today* 46, no. 2 (1999): 29–50. For the rhetoric of "youth" in the previous century's politics, see Glassman, *Feasts and Riot*.

22. Jamal Ramadhan based his activities in the Zanzibar African Youth Movement (ZAYM), which he founded expressly to contest the ASP's participation in the Freedom Alliance. Othman

Sharif was based in the Young African Social Union (YASU), which Jamal Ramadhan had established in 1954. See Hamdani, "Zanzibar Newspapers," 42–47.

23. For sympathetic intellectual biographies of Babu, see the essays by Haroub Othman, Samir Amin, and Issa Shivji in H. Othman, ed., *Babu: I Saw the Future and It Worked* (Dar es Salaam, 2001).

24. Sources on these matters are copious, especially during the years after the June riots. See Mooring, Intelligence Summary for January 1963 and enclosures, CO822/3063, PRO. For earlier sources, see R. H. V. Biles testimony, F-S, days 3–4; Intelligence Report, January 1960, CO822/2132, PRO; G. Mooring, Security Report, 26 June 1961, CO822/2046, PRO; Intelligence Report March 1960, CO822/2134. For the ASYL and the revolution, see Burgess, "Remembering Youth"; and Burgess, "Youth and the Revolution: Mobility and Discipline in Zanzibar, 1950–1980" (Ph.D. diss., Indiana University, 2001). Jamal Ramadhan's role in the ASYL is muted in official histories published after the revolution; this might be attributable to continuing bitterness engendered by his rivalry with Karume and his allies.

25. Lofchie, *Zanzibar*, is an indispensable guide to the electoral politics of these years. Also see Intelligence Committee reports for 1959–1960, CO822/2137, PRO.

26. The comparison was made by many observers, including John F. Hill, interview with John Tawney (n.d.), MSS. Afr. s. 1429, RH. For property and literacy qualifications, see Lofchie, *Zanzibar*, 239.

27. Hill interview; also J. R. Naish, interview with John Tawney, 16 October 1971, MSS. Afr. s. 2249, RH.

28. "Mashal na Uchaguzi," *Agozi*, 16 November 1959.

29. So complained *Afrika Kwetu*, and there is ample evidence to substantiate the accusation, including Timothy Mayhew, "Zanzibar Elections, 1957" and "Zanzibar Elections: Propaganda," August 1957, both in T. Mayhew, MSS. Afr. s. 1361, RH.

30. "Lipi Liliozidi?" *AfrKw*, 5 February 1959; R. H. V. Biles testimony, F-S, day 3; P. A. P. Robertson testimony, F-S, day 2; "Ubaya wa Mahizb [*sic*] na Uchaguzi Kasikazini," *Agozi*, 26 October 1959.

31. E.g., "Nationalization of Africans in Africa," *AfrKw*, 29 January 1959; this article was also published in Swahili. Other examples of such rhetoric can be found in *AfrKw* as early as 1957. *Agozi* expressed its concerns over these matters in typically harsh rhetoric. An example is "Unjuga na Utawala," *Agozi*, 2 November 1959, where the arguments about who is and is not a "foreigner" appear to be based on the experiences of the Manyema and Basukuma unions of previous years.

32. Mervyn Smithyman, evidence given to the Delimitation Commission, 11 August 1962, in Clarence Buxton Papers, Box 3, file 3.

33. Ibid. Smithyman was working with the Shamte government at the time and was no friend of pan-African nationalism.

34. Naish interview.

35. Mayhew, "Zanzibar Elections, 1957"; *AfrKw*, May–June 1957 and later issues. Ali Muhsin never stopped pushing the issue: he emphasized it in his testimony before the Foster-Sutton Commission (F-S, day 11:22) and came up with new details in his 1997 memoirs. For Karume's version of events, see F-S, day 12:52–53. His official biography strikes a defensive note when recounting his birth in Zanzibar; see Mwanjisi, *Abeid Amani Karume*, 9–10. The life of the issue is indicated by the diverse uses ASP dissidents made of it during the PAFMECA crisis, some to remind Karume of the perfidy of his newfound ZNP allies and others, more opportunistically, to themselves cast aspersions on Karume's "doubtful citizenship" (see Cleopa F. K. Seme in *Agozi*, 26 October 1959). Many Zanzibaris still insist, as a way of delegitimizing his rule and that of his political successors, that Karume was born on the mainland.

36. E.g., "Makunduchi Haitaki Chama cha Wageni," *Mwongozi*, 26 August 1960; "Kiziwi Hasikii na Bubu Hasemi," *AfrKw*, 6 April 1961.

37. Examples of such rhetoric include Muhsin to Blood, 27 April 1960, Clarence Buxton Papers, Box 3, file 1; "Yepi Yaliyowaleta Pamoja Wananchi na Wazalendo," *Mwongozi*, 3 March 1961; "The Writing on the Wall," *Mwongozi*, 26 August 1960; and "Makhaini Wanazidi Kujitokeza," *Mwongozi*, 24 March 1961. For ZPPP speeches, see Extract from Intelligence Report, February 1960, CO822/2137, PRO. The ZPPP and its precursors in the Pemba Shirazi Association and Ithadi el Umma had long demanded that immigration from the mainland be curtailed; see "Imposing of Immigration Restrictions" (1956), AB 26/79, ZNA.

38. See articles in English and Swahili in 10 February 1961, *Mwongozi*, and the general coverage of electoral issues in the *Tanganyika Standard* of 1961. The scorn heaped on mainland politicians became especially strident during the run-up to independence in 1963.

39. A telling example is the party pamphlet *Whither Zanzibar?* which, although it reproduces standard pan-Africanist phrases, opens with a frontispiece of Muhsin shaking hands with Nasser. Nasser's attempts to reconcile pan-Arabism with pan-Africanism were often tripped up by his assumptions that Africa was the "Dark Continent" in need of Arab enlightenment. In this he was echoed by Muhsin and many other ZNP intellectuals. Gamal Abdul Nasser, *Egypt's Liberation: The Philosophy of the Revolution* (Washington, 1955), esp. 109–111.

40. The line about leaves and hides appeared in a speech by Mahmoud Kombo, reported in "Makunduchi Haitaki Chama cha Wageni," *Mwongozi*, 26 August 1960. It contains sly references to two ASP emblems: *mapakacha*, items made of thatched green coconut leaves, and the language of *gozi*, which was echoed in the phrase Kombo used for hides, *mapande ya magozi*. For Katanga and Rufji, see G. B. Mohamed, "Uhuru wa Visiwa vya Unguja na Pemba," *Mwongozi*, 26 May 1961.

41. See the paper he and Jamal Ramadhan published in 1956, *Voice of Workers*, 15 December 1956.

42. Mmanga Said and the Human Rights League took positions that were populist and elitist, pro-ASP and pro-ZPPP, and anti-Arab, anti-Indian, and anti-mainlander. They also were proponents of anti-communist international trade unionism, narrow nativism, and racial nationalism; secular socialism and political Islamism; loyalist moderation; and radical social leveling. Jamal Ramadhan's positions were as protean as those of his friend, as demonstrated throughout *Agozi* and his checkered political career as an international trade unionist, an Islamist (for which see "Young Muumin Society," AB 12/84, ZNA), a populist, an elitist (see his diatribes against Karume and other rivals for their lack of education), a ZPPP nativist, a pan-Africanist, a racialist, and, after the revolution, a secular socialist.

43. The police and other officials described Human Rights League members as "hooligans," an overused epithet that however seems to have some justification in this case, given the ages of league members and their social marginality and political irresponsibility. The league was banned after the June riots, and several of its leading members were detained. But by 1963 they were again at the fringes of Zanzibar's political arena, forming similar organizations with names such as the African Democratic Union. Sources for Mmanga Said and the Human Rights League include "Human Rights League," CO822/2139, PRO; testimony by R. H. V. Biles, F-S, days 3–4, and W. Wright, F-S, day 7; "Security Situation, 1962," CO822/2047, PRO; Mudirs Central and North to DC, 1 July 1961, Clarence Buxton Papers, Box 3, file 2; "Haki Yamkaribisha Bwana Balozi Mpya," *Agozi*, 1 February 1960; "Simu," *Agozi*, 28 December 1959; and "Haki za Binadamu Husema Kweli," *AfrKw*, 9 March 1961.

44. "Kibarua," *AfrKw*, 2 April 1959. Other examples abound. *Masetla* was more commonly used in ASYL discourse, including *Agozi*. *Afrika Kwetu* displayed a slight preference for *walowezi*, a synonym that was perhaps considered more neutral because it did not share the En-

glish root of *masetla*. When speaking of these issues, even the most militant of racial nativists invoked Harold Macmillan's rhetoric about the "winds of change," first directed at the South African Parliament. See the account of a speech by the Human Rights League activist Othman Bapa, whose rhetoric apparently had earned him the nickname "Setla": "Haki za Binadamu," *AfrKw*, 9 March 1961.

45. A much-discussed incident disrupted an ASP rally at Makunduchi; see "Makunduchi," *AfrKw*, 29 October 1959; and "Mtumwa Mwenye Ari Si Mungwana Asiekuwa na Ari," *AfrKw*, 5 November 1959. During the party crisis induced by the PAFMECA alliance, *Agozi* played a sly game, simultaneously reminding Karume how his newfound ZNP allies had castigated him as a slave and at the same time humiliating him by repeating the charge in untempered terms. See "Mungu Si Mzee Mkumba," *Agozi*, 20 July 1959.

46. "Utwana ni Kitu Thakili," *Agozi*, 1 June 1959.

47. This strategy is discussed in chapter 7 and in J. Glassman, "Racial Violence, Universal History, and Echoes of Abolition in Twentieth-Century Zanzibar," in *Abolitionism and Imperialism in Britain, Africa, and the Atlantic*, ed. Derek Peterson (Athens, Ohio, 2010). Pointed examples include two detailed accounts of a speech given by the religious scholar Said Ahmed Darwesh: "Wasia wa Bw Darwesh," *AfrKw*, 27 April 1961; and "Unaye Okota Naye Kuni Ndiye Wakuota Naye Moto," *Sauti ya Afro-Shirazi*, 28 April 1961. Also see "Aliepewa Kapewa," *AfrKw*, 23 March 1961; and extract from Intelligence Report February 1960, no. 2, CO822/2132, PRO. John Okello later recalled emphasizing slavery in speeches he made during the 1961 campaigns, when he was secretary of the ASYL branch in Vitongoji, Pemba; he also claimed that on the eve of the 1964 revolution his "intelligence" officers uncovered Hizbu plots to reenslave Africans. See Okello, *Revolution in Zanzibar* (Nairobi, 1967), 80–81, 119–120.

48. I have reconstructed details of Titi Muhammad's speech chiefly from three sources: "Afrika Inajitawala," *AfrKw*, 4 May 1961; extract from *Sauti ya Afro-Shirazi*, 5 May 1961, translation prepared for the Foster-Sutton Commission, Clarence Buxton Papers Box 3, file 2; and a summary of the same *Sauti ya Afro-Shirazi* item in Mrina and Mattoke, *Mapambano ya Ukombozi Zanzibar*, 80. For the vituperation the speech caused, see also "Kuondowa Adabu ni Njia ya Ujinga, Bibi Titi Sio Muhuni," *AfrKw*, 11 May 1961; "Hatutakuwa Watumwa," *Mwongozi*, 21 April 1961 (which shows that Bibi Titi's speech was much anticipated); and Mudir North to DC, 1 July 1961, Clarence Buxton Papers, Box 3, file 2. More detailed versions of the myths Bibi Titi recounted can be found in two postrevolution publications: Okello, *Revolution in Zanzibar*, 108; and Mwanjisi, *Abeid Amani Karume*, 50.

49. "Makosa ya Viongozi Wote Duniani," *Agozi*, 1 June 1959; "Appeal to the Government," *Agozi*, 8 June 1959 (adding layers of opportunism, in this piece *Agozi* poses as a pillar of moderation and a friend of the government); "Agozi Yauliza Sirikali," *Agozi*, 25 May 1959. ASP polemicists accused the ZNP of taking Mau Mau oaths in "Rabid Politics," *AfrKw*, 16 March 1961. Mervyn Smithyman recalled hearing conversations about Mau Mau at the time: F-S, day 8.

50. "Hapana Ushirika wa Ardhi," *Agozi*, 6 July 1959.

51. "Rabid Politics," *AfrKw*, 16 March 1961; "Mkutano wa ASP Raha Leo," *Sauti ya Afro-Shirazi*, 16 September 1960; "Weed Out the Stooges!" *Adal Insaf*, 10 September 1960.

52. Sources for Titi Muhammad's speech cited in note 48 above; extract from *Sauti ya Afro-Shirazi* in Clarence Buxton Papers, Box 3, file 2; "Afrika Inajitawala," *AfrKw*, 4 May 1961.

53. For a colorful example of the latter phenomenon, in which boycotters forced a shopkeeper to feast the village, see Smith, District Report 1947, p. 17, BA 30/5, ZNA. Other examples can be found in G. E. Noad, District Report 1937, BA 30/5, ZNA; and W. Addis, Monthly District Reports February and June 1944, BA 30/8, ZNA.

54. Saud Ahmed Busaid, DC Urban, District Reports, April and June 1957, AB 8/7, ZNA. Although the sources do not tell us why these particular establishments were targeted, they do suggest that the boycotters invoked racial politics.

55. "African/Shirazi Association," CO822/1376, PRO; al-Haj, Report for February 1958, AB 8/7, ZNA; Mervyn Smithyman testimony, F-S, day 8; Karume, quoted in *AfrKw*, 16 July 1959; "Siri: Squatter Traders" (1961), AK 18/1, ZNA; P. A. P. Robertson, "Security Zanzibar," 14 September 1958, CO822/1377, no. 62, PRO; Intelligence Committee Report, October 1957, CO822/1377, no. 13, PRO; "Nalitote Muligawe Mbao Viongozi," *Agozi*, 19 October 1959; "Kiroja Hiki" and "Agozi Aduwi wa Uhuru," *AfrKw*, 29 October 1959.

56. Intelligence Report, January 1960, CO822/2134, no. 4, PRO.

57. Clyde Sanger, "Zanzibar's New-Fangled Politics: A Legacy from Transport House," *Guardian*, 10 October 1960, reprinted in *Mwongozi*, 28 October 1960; Babu testimony, F-S, day 10. Also see the following PRO files: Minute by B. E. Rolfe, 26 June 1958, CO822/1377; Intelligence Report, February 1960, no. 5, CO822/2134; and Intelligence Report, June 1958, no. 52, CO822/1377.

58. "Confidence Pervades First Annual Conference of Hizbu Lwatan," *Mwongozi*, 22 February 1957. The elision of party membership and national status appears dramatically when one compares two versions of the ZNP's election manifesto that appeared in the same issue of *Mwongozi*. In the English version (which would be designed to appease British rulers and appeal to educated islanders, especially those, including Indians, for whom Swahili was not a primary language), the relevant clause reads: "nationals deserve priority in education and employment over aliens." But in the Swahili version the people who deserved priority, the people who stood in contrast to aliens, were described not as "nationals" but as "party members" (*wanachama*). The same discrepancy appeared in a ZNP party handbill: AKP 16/6, ZNA.

59. Lofchie, *Zanzibar*, is illuminating on these matters, esp. 224 and 261. This paragraph also draws on Intelligence Reports for October 1957, July 1958, and September 1958, in CO822/1377, PRO; and "Security Situation," 23 February 1962, CO822/2047, PRO. For "V2 bombs," see M. A. al-Haj to senior commissioner, 24 September 1958, AK 20/1, ZNA. (V2 bombs, among the earliest long-range ballistic missiles, had become infamous by terrorizing Londoners during the Blitz.) Former colonial officials later asserted that labor unions, the formation of which they themselves had encouraged, played a minimal role in Zanzibar's nationalist politics, and that politicians such as Babu tried but largely failed to harness them to the nationalist cause. Whether or not that assessment is valid, it is certain that the role of working-class consciousness has been overplayed in many accounts, especially those produced at the University of Dar es Salaam in the 1970s and 1980s. Just before Babu split with ZNP in mid-1963, he and some ASP counterparts attempted to forge a labor front uniting the unions affiliated with the two parties. To their frustration, however, they found that sentiments of narrow ethnic nationalism trumped those of class. See P. A. P. Robertson, A. H. Hawker, and J. S. Rumbold, interviewed by Alison Smith and A. H. M. Kirk-Greene, 16 October 1971, MSS. Afr. s. 2250/2, RH; and Yahya Alawi, District Intelligence Sub-Committee Report, 4–10 May 1963, AK 9/29, ZNA.

60. This paragraph is based on Gray, *Report of the Arbitrator*; and documents from AK 20/1, ZNA. Also see Zanzibar Protectorate, *Labour Report for the Year 1958*, in BA 19/13, ZNA; B. D. Bowles, "The Struggle for Independence," 97–98; Ali Muhsin testimony, F-S, day 10; and "Watende Wao El Harara," *Agozi*, 20 July 1959. One of the leaders of the ZNP operation, Abdulrahman Amur al-Barwani, was a driver and mechanic valued by his comrades for his skill in wielding canes and knives: see Muhsin al-Barwani, *Conflicts and Harmony in Zanzibar*, 82–83. Also involved in the dispute were the Dhow Captains' and Owners' Association, a ZNP affiliate, and the United Agriculturalists Organization (UAO), an estate owners' association

affiliated with the Arab Association. For the UAO connection see also R. H. V. Biles to chief secretary, 27 October 1960, AK 16/45, ZNA; and Jamal Ramadhan Nasib, "Maendeleo baada ya Mapinduzi ya Januari 1964," *Uhuru* (Dar es Salaam), 25 July 1987, p. 7.

61. Karume testimony, F-S, day 12; his role is attested to in several of the sources cited above. Similar examples of such language are preserved in a ZPPP leaflet commenting on the actions of Hizbu and ZPPP strikebreakers during a strike of government street sweepers in July 1962; see "Mgomo na Safari," *Sauti ya Wananchi*, 16 July 1962, AK 20/1, ZNA.

62. In such responses, landlords and party officials insisted that the evictions were economically motivated. These explanations became especially prevalent after the government issued a decree in January 1959 stipulating precise conditions under which a landlord could evict. They were offered, unconvincingly, before the Foster-Sutton Commission; they also were offered by the ZNP sympathizers who were Middleton's main informants on such matters in *Land Tenure in Zanzibar*. It is telling that Hizbu's eviction campaign was initially greeted with ambivalence by some of the estate owners in the Arab Association, who were concerned about the insecurity it would engender, including, no doubt, labor shortages. But they were pressured by party activists and the Manga shopkeepers who had been especially hurt by the ASP boycotts. See Intelligence Report, September 1958, no. 76, CO822/1377, PRO; *Labour Report for the Year 1958*, BA 19/13, ZNA; and testimony by R. H. V. Biles and Mervyn Smithyman in F-S, days 3 and 8, respectively.

63. "Serikali Inajidai Kufumba Macho," *AfrKw*, 26 March 1959; "Rabid Politics," *AfrKw*, 16 March 1961.

64. R. H. V. Biles testimony, F-S, day 3. Also for this paragraph see Resident, "Zanzibar Security Situation," 8 December 1962, CO822/2048; Intelligence Report, May 1960, CO822/2134; P. A. P. Robertson, "Security Zanzibar," 14 September 1958, CO822/1377; and Executive Council no.160, 8 November 1961, CO822/2139. All in PRO.

65. P. A. P. Robertson testimony, F-S, day 3:17; R. H. V. Biles testimony, F-S, days 3:88 and 5:30; and Khamis Mohamed Rajaby, Town Mudir, Coffee-House Gossip Report for October 1962, AK 13/11a, ZNA.

66. G. E. Noad, District Report, January 1937, BA 30/6, ZNA. For Indian "social boycotts," see Ranajit Guha, "Discipline and Mobilize," in *Subaltern Studies VII*, ed. Partha Chatterjee and G. Pandey (Delhi, 1992), 69–120.

67. J. E. E. Craster, *Pemba: The Spice Island of Zanzibar* (London, 1913), 184–187. In an incident from 1940, a man was shunned for having informed the police about a minor scuffle that others in the community believed should have been left to village authorities to mediate: District Report February 1940, BA 30/7, ZNA. In the 1937 incident described by G. E. Noad (in District Report, January 1937), the Indian whose bus was being boycotted was himself targeted for having refused to transport a body for burial.

68. A. S. Kharusi, DC Rural, 21 June 1961, AK 5/28, ZNA.

69. A well-documented example of such a search for consensus took place on Tumbatu Island in October 1962, when villagers argued bitterly over "the party [for] which we should vote." See documents about Sheha Ali Kombo of Gomani in "Siri: Masheha," pp. 53–62, AK 13/6, ZNA. John Middleton and Jane Campbell offered a functionalist interpretation of this particular dispute as arising from a traditional structural conflict between village "moieties" in *Zanzibar: Its Society and Its Politics* (London, 1965), 64. I do not find that explanation convincing; in any case, the archival evidence explicitly shows the participants advancing arguments that were very much shaped by the political discourses I have been exploring in this book.

70. R. H. V. Biles testimony, F-S, day 3:87–89; Mdundo, *Masimulizi ya Sheikh Thabit Kombo Jecha*, 78.

71. For examples of both in a set of villages divided by rivalries between ZPPP and ASP, see Abdulla Rashid, DC Pemba, Intelligence Summaries, February and March 1963, AK 31/15, ZNA.

72. For an example of the connection between personal boycott and arson, see Special Branch Intelligence Summary, encl. to Mooring, Intelligence Summary May 1963, CO822/3063, PRO.

73. The literal meaning of *pinga* is to block, bar, obstruct, oppose.

74. Yahya Alawi, Senior DC, Intelligence Sub-Committee report, 14–19 April 1963, AK 9/29, ZNA.

75. F-S, day 8:20–21; also see day 8:18–19.

76. M. A. al-Haj to senior commissioner, 24, 27, and 30 September 1958, AK 20/1, and various documents on the same dispute in AK 1/28, ZNA. In a similar instance, some *wachukuzi* attempted to mediate an end to a boycott of a tea shop near the wharf, only to be threatened with ostracism. When the boycott was eventually ended two months later, the shop owner served free tea to mark the occasion and, one supposes, to reestablish friendly relations. S. A. Busaid, District Reports for April, May, and June 1957, AB 8/7, ZNA.

77. "Watende Wao el Harara," *Agozi*, 20 July 1959. In standard usage, *harara* is an adjective denoting enthusiasm, hot-temperedness, rashness. I am grateful to the late Sheikh Salum Said of the Zanzibar Archives for my understanding of the term's connotations in the political rhetoric of the Time of Politics.

78. "Unguja Hayendi kwa Ukubeli," *Agozi*, 11 January 1960.

79. Swahili terms were often literal equivalents of the English; two that I have found are *maboy wa nyumba* and *mtoto wa nyumba*.

80. Such rhetoric appeared frequently in *Afrika Kwetu* in the early and mid-1950s. For its use during the political campaigns, see Mervyn Smithyman testimony, F-S, day 8:20–21; and *Labour Report for the Year 1958*, 8, BA 19/13, ZNA. The polemicists were rarely explicit when targeting Indians, whom they regarded as their enemy's enemy. Racial targeting of Arabs as the abusers of houseboys and housegirls became most explicit after the revolution, when the Karume government attempted to end the practice; see Afro-Shirazi Party, *Afro-Shirazi Party: A Liberation Movement*, Book 2 (Zanzibar, 1974), 1–2; and [Karume], *Baadhi ya Hotuba*, 16.

81. "Mama Yaya na Mr. Opel," *Agozi*, 2 November 1959.

82. "Mama Gozi Eshambuliwa kwa Faru Shangani," *Agozi*, 5 and 12 October 1959; "Magozi," *Agozi*, 19 October 1959. Elements of this story and the story of Mr. Opel and his nursemaid (including the use of animal epithets as *matusi*) are echoed in a widely read revolutionary novel by Adam Shafi Adam, *Kasri ya Mwinyi Fuad* (Dar es Salaam, 1978).

83. Glassman, *Feasts and Riot*. There is ample evidence that festive rituals remained fraught in colonial Zanzibar; particularly rich evidence can be found in the District Reports, ZNA.

84. After the June riots the government felt it prudent to restrict the festivities. See "'Battle' to be Restricted," *Tanganyika Standard*, 31 July 1961; and dispatches from July–August 1961, "Security Situation in Zanzibar, 1961–1962," CO822/2046, PRO.

85. "Konsel Isitiye Ulimi Puwani" and "[Ill.] Ya Wingwi—ga Ngoma" (part of the headline is torn away from the copy I consulted in ZNA), *Agozi*, 7 and 14 March 1960.

86. The Wingwi riot subsequently gave rise to widespread rumors, threats, boycotts, and arson; see chapter 8. For the riot itself, the main sources are C. E. V. Buxton and W. Wright, "Report on the Riot at Wingwi," and other documents in AK 17/85, ZNA; and Judgment in Criminal Case No. 875 of 1962, Resident Magistrate's Court, Pemba, copy in Clarence Buxton Papers, Box 8.

87. Intelligence and Special Branch Summaries for August 1962, CO822/2070, PRO; In-

telligence Report, July 1958, CO822/1377, PRO; Minutes, Security Council Meeting, 28 November 1962, AK 18/2, ZNA. ZNP was by no means the only party to sponsor *maulids*; the 1962 Wingwi riot, mentioned above, was sparked when ASP adherents insisted on performance of a *maulid* instead of the ZPPP's *ngoma*.

88. E.g., "Mungu Awalani Wanaopenda Kutawaliwa," *Kijumbe cha Kipanga*, 14 January 1962.

89. Al-Haj, Pemba Intelligence Sub-Committee Report, 7/13 July 1963, AK 31/16, ZNA.

90. "Kujitapa Amerudi" and "Njugu na Mimba za YOU," *Sauti ya Afro-Shirazi*, 28 April 1961.

91. "Wapo Wanawake Weupe Wameweka Nyumba za Danguro Ngambo," *AfrKw*, 12 September 1957; "Wakuu wa Jumuia za Siasa Msipite Njia moja ya Dunia," *AfrKw*, 19 September 1957.

92. This particular contretemps occurred soon after the Wingwi riot and in the same general part of Pemba; P. A. P. Robertson to resident, 29 March 1963, EB 10/11, ZNA. The same file contains a clipping on how the incident was used by political speakers: "'Terror' in Pemba—ASP," *Tanganyika Standard*, 23 March 1963. For a general statement on disputes over burials between 1958 and 1961, see P. A. P. Robertson testimony, F-S, day 2.

93. *Mwongozi*, 1 February 1957.

94. Letter by "Hydrogen Bomb," *Agozi*, 18 May 1959; also see the letter by "Atomic Bomb" in the same issue and another by "Hydrogen Bomb" in the issue of 4 May 1959.

95. R. H. V. Biles testimony, F-S, day 4. This is still remembered by elderly Zanzibaris, including some who were supporters of ZNP at the time.

96. Abdulla Rashid, Pemba Intelligence Summaries, February–March 1963, AK 31/15, ZNA. The well-documented dispute at Tumbatu mentioned at note 69, above, also involved access to water.

97. *Kijumbe cha Kipanga*, 14 January 1962. For an eyewitness account involving the heir to the throne, see R. H. V. Biles, interview with John Tawney, 11 December 1971, pp. 11–12, MSS. Afr. s. 1446, RH.

98. *Kijumbe cha Kipanga*, 9 February 1962; "Mchukuzi Katupiwa Kigari," *AfrKw*, 8 February 1962.

99. Mervyn Smithyman testimony, F-S, day 8. This conviction was reproduced in Mwanjisi's classroom text, *Abeid Amani Karume*, 31–36.

100. Mooring, Intelligence Summary, October 1963 (and enclosures), CO822/3063, PRO. This and the preceding paragraph are also based on other documents in this file; the intelligence reports in CO822/2045 through 2050 and 2070, PRO; and the Intelligence Sub-Committee Reports in AK 9/29, ZNA. Also see Clayton, *The Zanzibar Revolution and Its Aftermath*.

101. Guha, "Discipline and Mobilize."

102. Rosalind O'Hanlon, "Recovering the Subject: *Subaltern Studies* and Histories of Resistance in Colonial South Asia," in *Mapping Subaltern Studies and the Postcolonial*, ed. Vinayak Chaturvedi (London, 2000), 74. Under this conception, adds O'Hanlon, "Man . . . can be either free or he can be bound; but in either case, he himself looks very much the same" (87).

6. Rumor, Race, and Crime

The epigraph is from F-S, day 3:71–72.

1. "Record of a Meeting Held to Consider Measures to Counteract Rumours," 25 April 1962, AK 31/15, ZNA. Present were A. E. Forsyth-Thomson, Permanent Secretary to the Civil Secretary; Yahya Alawi, Senior DC; Yusuf Mohammed, Broadcasting Officer; and Ahmed Mohammed Yahya, Information Officer. For empire-wide rumor control measures, see Terry Ann Knopf, *Rumors, Race, and Riots* (New Brunswick, 1975); and Jean-Noel Kapferer, *Rumors: Uses, Interpretations, and Images* (New Brunswick, 1990).

2. Quote from A. L. Pennington, 2 October 1962, AK 31/15, ZNA. See also District Intelligence Report, 23 January 1963, AK 31/15, ZNA; and R. H. V. Biles, interviewed by John Tawney, 11 December 1971, MSS. Afr. s. 1446, RH.

3. Biles, who had good Swahili and over two decades of East African experience, added daggers to the list of weapons on the second day of his testimony; see F-S, day 4:34–35.

4. A sophisticated literature has traced how efforts to stiffen legal sanctions against such "customary appropriation" were central to the rise of industrial capitalism in early modern Europe. See Peter Linebaugh, *The London Hanged* (London, 2003); Douglas Hay, Peter Linebaugh, and E. P. Thompson, *Albion's Fatal Tree* (New York, 1975); and E. P. Thompson, *Whigs and Hunters* (London, 1975). Other works have traced similar processes in colonial Africa, including Cooper's analysis of the crime of vagrancy in early colonial Zanzibar in *From Slaves to Squatters*.

5. Much of this literature has been generated in response to the work of Eric Hobsbawm, especially *Bandits*, new ed. (New York, 2000). Yet despite Hobsbawm's teleological assumptions about the emergence of authentic class politics, the crux of his argument concerned the ambiguities that characterized attitudes toward "social crime" among the poor and among the criminals themselves. For sensitive appraisals of the literature, see Gilbert Joseph, "On the Trail of Latin American Bandits: A Reexamination of Peasant Resistance," *Latin American Research Review* 25, no. 3 (1990): 7–53; and Joanna Innes and John Styles, "The Crime Wave: Recent Writing on Crime and Criminal Justice in Eighteenth-Century England," *Journal of British Studies* 25 (1986): 395–399.

6. For a study that touches on these themes, see Clive Glaser, *Bo-Tsotsi: The Youth Gangs of Soweto, 1935–1976* (Portsmouth, 2000). Glaser, in turn, builds on a rich literature on crime and politics in urban South Africa.

7. Clayton, *The Zanzibar Revolution and Its Aftermath*, 38.

8. For an explicit statement, see Saud Busaidy, 20 November 1962, AK 16/45, ZNA.

9. The quoted phrase is from Magistrate J. E. R. Stephens, who blamed such individuals for most of the islands' crime; Appendix to the Administrative Report on HBM's Court and HH's Court, 1914, BA 18/6, ZNA.

10. Cooper, *From Slaves to Squatters*.

11. I. H. D. Rolleston, *Annual Report on the District of Zanzibar*, 1935, BA 30/5, ZNA; J. T. Last, *Administrative Report from the Collector of Zanzibar*, 1906, p. 21, BA 18/1, ZNA. Similar comments concerning the criminal propensities of freed slaves and mainlanders were made by Last's counterpart in Pemba, J. P. Farler, in *Administrative Report from the Collector of Zanzibar*, 1906, p. 27. For an extended study of colonial understandings of the links between rootlessness and crime, see Burton, *African Underclass*.

12. For the disorder caused by Hadimu harvest laborers, see Bennett, *A History of the Arab State of Zanzibar*, 219–222. For squatters building "substantial" houses, see *Labour Report for the Year 1958*, BA 19/13, ZNA. See also chapters 2 and 4, above.

13. Ingrams, *Zanzibar: Its History and Its People*, 32–33. Ingrams made these observations during the 1920s, when immigrant mainlanders were first becoming a marked presence in agricultural labor; see R. H. Crofton, "History of Labour in the Zanzibar Sultanate," 1927, AB 4/224, ZNA.

14. Crofton, "History of Labour," AB 4/224, ZNA; Bennett, *A History of the Arab State of Zanzibar*, 219. This process can still be observed.

15. B. C. Johnstone, "Memorandum on Labour in Zanzibar," 1930, AB 4/224, ZNA.

16. K. H. Clarke, Monthly Report, November 1939, BA 30/7, ZNA.

17. Reports on the Zanzibar Police for 1927 and 1928, BA 18/18 and BA 18/19, ZNA.

18. Administrative Reports, BA 18/1–3 (1906–1910), ZNA. In 1938 the DC for rural Unguja observed that the offense of drunkenness was concentrated among mainlanders, who, being permitted to drink under Tanganyika law, brought the practice with them to Zanzibar, thus becoming "potential law breakers at once." K. H. Clarke, District Report 1938, BA 30/7, ZNA.

19. See the poem by George Masudi, a founder of the Zanzibar African Association, published in *Kwetu* of June 1938, quoted in Iliffe, *A Modern History of Tanganyika*, 407; and the poem by Kesi Mtopa Salimini from *Afrika Kwetu* 1955, discussed above in chapter 4. Ndengereko immigrants were also commonly held up as emblematic of barbarism, as they still are today; this too was acknowledged in the ASP press.

20. In any case, the complexity of Ameir's analysis makes it doubtful that it was overly colored by political bias. The tense and complex texture of Ameir's relationship with his superior officer, M. A. al-Haj, and of the latter with Ameir's classmate Mohammed K. Abdulla, reveals much about the impact racial politics had within the Provincial Administration during these years. See AK 18/2, ZNA; and the personal files for the three men: AK 33/319, AK 33/185, AK 33/294, and AB 86/250, ZNA.

21. K. H. Ameir, "Wamakonde Activities," 24 March 1962, AK 18/2, ZNA.

22. A. Jorge Dias, *Portuguese Contribution to Cultural Anthropology* (Johannesburg, 1961); J. Gus Liebenow, *Colonial Rule and Political Development* (Evanston, 1971); Karl Weule, *Native Life in East Africa*, trans. Alice Werner (New York, 1909); Karl Weule, *Wissenschaftliche Ergebnisse meiner ethnographischen Forschungsreise in den Südosten Deutsch-Ostafrikas* (Berlin, 1908); Pekka Seppälä and Bertha Koda, eds., *The Making of a Periphery: Economic Development and Cultural Encounters in Southern Tanzania* (Uppsala, 1998); Harry G. West, *Kupilikula: Governance and the Invisible Realm in Mozambique* (Chicago, 2005). Similar reputations of ferocity toward outsiders were attributed to the Doe of eastern Tanganyika and the maroon communities of highland Jamaica and Surinam.

23. Clayton, *The Zanzibar Revolution and Its Aftermath*, 13. Marja-Liisa Swantz notes a similar preference in colonial Dar es Salaam; see "Notes on Research on Women and Their Strategies for Sustained Livelihood in Southern Tanzania," in Seppälä and Koda, *Making of a Periphery*, 171–172.

24. Bennett, *A History of the Arab State of Zanzibar*, 234–245; W. Murphy, "Report on Zanzibar Police," 1926, BA 18/16, ZNA.

25. A. H. M. Kirk-Greene, "'Damnosa Hereditas': Ethnic Ranking and the Martial Races Imperative in Africa," *Ethnic and Racial Studies* 3, no. 4 (1980): 393–414. See also Heather Streets, *Martial Races: The Military, Race and Masculinity in British Imperial Culture* (Manchester, 2004).

26. R. H. V. Biles, interview with John Tawney, 11 December 1971, MSS. Afr. s. 1446, RH. Biles describes conditions as he found them upon his arrival in the islands in 1956, before a set of reforms and improvements begun at that time. They conform to more fragmentary evidence in earlier sources. For police arms, also see F. H. Bustard, "Report on the Action Taken by the Police for the Suppression of the Riots of Feb. 7th 1936," MSS. Afr. s. 542, RH.

27. For representative statements, see the District Monthly Reports in ZNA, including G. E. Noad, July–August 1937, BA 30/6, and K. H. Clarke, August 1939, BA 30/7.

28. In 1961 Middleton (*Land Tenure in Zanzibar*, 77) wrote that the ASP slogan, "The trees are theirs, the land is ours," was contradicted by the fact that the planters' rights of freehold tenure were commonly acknowledged. If he was correct, it was a recent development. (One should note, however, that Middleton's main informants were members of planter families who were sympathetic to the ZNP.) Pearce wrote in 1920 that Zanzibaris, especially the poor, had little regard for the rights of land ownership; see *Zanzibar: The Island Metropolis of Eastern Africa*, 159–160.

29. Pearce, *Zanzibar: The Island Metropolis of Eastern Africa*, 160, 231. Early evidence for squatters' attitudes toward the use of tree crops is circumstantial, but it accords with the developments discussed below. Today such understandings are common on farms townspeople own that are cultivated by migrants. Significantly, some of the earliest and most persistent complaints about crop theft that appear in the archives concerned mainlander palm-wine tappers. The prominence of this complaint is significant because the loss incurred was not simply a portion of the crops, which Pearce states most landlords were willing to accept, but the coconut palm itself, which could be damaged irrevocably by careless tapping.

30. Welliver, "The Clove Factor in Colonial Zanzibar," 195–196, 202–203.

31. G. E. Noad (and marginalia by Hathorn-Hall), District Report, March 1938, BA 30/7, ZNA. For the debates surrounding these and similar measures, see G. E. Noad, District Annual Report 1936, BA 30/5; G. E. Noad, Monthly Report June 1937, BA 30/6; R. H. W. Pakenham, Annual Report Northern Dist., 1933, BA 30/3; and "Thieving Fraternity Active Again," *Al-Falaq*, 23 July 1938. All in ZNA.

32. G. E. Noad, Monthly Report, July/August 1937, BA 30/6, ZNA; G. E. Noad, November 1942, BA 30/7, ZNA; Smith, Annual Report 1947, BA 30/5, ZNA; Zanzibar Protectorate, *Report of the Commission of Enquiry Concerning the Riot in Zanzibar on the 7th of February 1936* (Zanzibar, 1936).

33. W. Murphy, Administrative Police Reports, 1926 and 1927, BA 18/16 and BA 18/18, ZNA; Brian Wardle, testimony to the Prisons Enquiry Committee, July 1929, AB 61/10, ZNA.

34. Report of the Prison Enquiry Committee: Third Term of Reference (April 1930), CO618/47/16, PRO; Prison Enquiry Committee, Minutes for July 1929, AB 61/10, ZNA.

35. Zanzibar "Watoto" Club: Annual Report, 1936, SA 1/50, ZNA; "Floggings, 1932," CO618/53/18, PRO. Conditions were marginally improved after passage of the Prisons Decree of 1932.

36. This and the following paragraphs on the 1928 prison break are based on documents in AB 61/10, ZNA; and documents in CO618/45/2 and CO618/47/16, PRO. Research by Melissa Graboyes suggests that access to outside food items was central to the prisoners' grievances. See Graboyes, "Chappati Complaints and Biriani Cravings: Food and Diet in Colonial Zanzibari Institutions," Working Paper in African Studies, Boston University, 2009.

37. Juma Aley, who remembered the prison break sixty years later, lists the neighborhoods in his colorful account, *Zanzibar: In the Context*, 76–77.

38. Some of the ringleaders of the prison break were deported to Tanganyika but others were not, and we lack precise information on their background. Yet the police described the rebel prisoners, and criminal gangs in general, as predominantly mainlanders. This perception may have been a distortion but even so was likely shared by the civilian population.

39. "The Responsibility for the Incidents which Occurred on the 29th and 30th of October," Committee of Enquiry statement (n.d.), AB 61/10, ZNA. Juma Aley specifies that the prisoners refrained from "molesting" anyone during their march to the Sultan's palace, although his account is no doubt colored by nostalgia (*Zanzibar: In the Context*).

40. Even some British officials had ambiguous attitudes toward smuggling; see the memo by the provincial commissioner, 11 November 1942, BA 30/8, ZNA. For "thieves' slang," see Ingrams, *Zanzibar: Its History and Its People*, 223.

41. Examples from South African urban history can be found in Glaser, *Bo-Tsotsi*; and A. W. Stadler, "Birds in the Cornfield: Squatter Movements in Johannesburg, 1944–1947," *Journal of Southern African Studies* 6, no. 1 (1979): 93–123.

42. The following account of the rent strikes is based largely on Fair, *Pastimes and Politics*, chapter 3. Additional details are from Fair's dissertation, "Pastimes and Politics," chapters 2 and 3.

43. The transformation from patron-client relationships was acknowledged in a statement by Ng'ambo's leading landlords; see Tharia Topan et al., 22 November 1928, AB 36/13, ZNA.

44. These tenants lived in squalid Stone Town tenements (the landlords were also Indians); see AB 36/5, ZNA.

45. The anti-Indian tone of the rent strikes is illustrated throughout Fair's accounts. The quoted passages are all from Silima bin Khamis, 14 January 1929 and L. E. Skinner, Police Report, 19 January 1929. See also Aredeshir Faredun Alamsha, 14 January 1929. All in AB 28/12, ZNA.

46. For the Sufi orders, see Felicitas Becker, *Becoming Muslim in Mainland Tanzania, 1890–2000* (Oxford, 2008), chapter 6; J. Glassman, "Stolen Knowledge: Struggles for Popular Islam on the Swahili Coast, 1870–1963," in *Islam in East Africa,* ed. Biancamaria Scarcia Amoretti (Rome, 2001), 209–225; and August Nimtz, *Islam and Politics in East Africa* (Minneapolis, 1980).

47. Fair, "Pastimes and Politics," 115–116; Juma Omar, sworn statement, 14 January 1929, AB 28/12, ZNA. British officials indicated that intimidation was a major tool in the enforcement of solidarity, although such sources must be treated with caution. Ahl-Badr would later figure in the Cattle Riot; see A. M. Juma, "Cattle Riot," 16–17. The oath is also known as *hal-badir.*

48. Khamis bin Ali, sworn statement, 14 January 1929, AB 28/12, ZNA.

49. Statements by Msellem bin Mohammed el Khalasi and Aredeshir Faredun Alamsha, 14 January 1929, and Skinner, 19 January 1929, AB 28/12, ZNA.

50. A newspaper report in fact suggested that the strikers had been inspired by the prisoners; see clipping from *East Africa,* 7 February 1929, in AB 28/12, ZNA.

51. Fair, *Pastimes and Politics;* Fair, "Pastimes and Politics," 127–130; statements by B. Wardle (superintendant of CID), P. Sheldon (senior commissioner), Gilbert (acting chief secretary), and Skinner, 14 and 19 January 1929, AB 28/12, ZNA. Officials believed the predominance of women was a calculated move based on the expectation that the police would exercise more restraint with women than they would if they were confronted by men. (At previous mass rallies, women had been in the minority.) But other factors may have been at work: on this occasion the women were more militant than the men, taunting them when they refused to fight the police. Women formed a significant and especially vulnerable portion of the "floating population" of town and were more likely to pin their hopes on living permanently in town than were the mostly male migrant laborers from the mainland.

52. Statement by Skinner, 19 January 1929, AB 28/12, ZNA.

53. Gray, *History of Zanzibar,* 137–141; Pearce, *Zanzibar: The Island Metropolis of Eastern Africa,* 190–193.

54. For this incident and its repercussions see the documents in AB 5/36, ZNA, especially K. H. Clarke to provincial commissioner, 7 February 1939, and clipping from *Zanzibar Voice,* 11 February 1939. Also see "Sensational Allegation," *Samachar,* 5 February 1939; and "A Figment of Imagination," *Al-Falaq,* 11 February 1939.

55. Said Ali, "Kijiji cha Mangapwani," *Normal Magazine* 5, no. 8 (September 1931): 118–119.

56. Harold Ingrams, *Arabia and the Isles* (London, 1942), 16; "Sartorial Significance," *Al-Falaq,* 11 March 1944; R. H. V. Biles testimony, F-S, day 5:7.

57. Johnson, *Standard Swahili-English Dictionary,* 258–259; J. G. Hava, *Al-Farâ-id Arabic English Dictionary* (Beirut, 1982), 794. Thanks to Bernard Haykel for help with the Arabic etymology.

58. Ingrams, *Arabia and the Isles,* 16, 38–39, 42–46. The contrast between rural Manga entrepreneurs and urban Shihiri shopkeepers is highlighted in "Arab Settlement," *Al-Falaq,* 4 March 1944; and Zanzibar Government, *A Guide to Zanzibar* (Zanzibar, 1952), 9. Rural Manga shopkeepers figure throughout the district reports in the BA 30 series, ZNA; especially useful is the

survey of all the merchants and traders of the Northern District in R. H. W. Pakenham's 1933 Annual Report, BA 30/3.

59. For Hadrami emigrants and their domination by the so-called *sadah* families who claimed perquisites and religious obligations as descendants of the Prophet, see Bujra, *The Politics of Stratification*; and Ulrike Freitag and William Clarence-Smith, eds., *Hadhrami Traders, Scholars and Statesmen in the Indian Ocean, 1750s–1950s* (Leiden, 1997), including the chapter by Françoise Le Guennec-Coppens, "Changing Patterns of Hadhrami Migration and Social Integration in East Africa," 157–174. For East Africa's Yemeni religious scholars, see Bang, *Sufis and Scholars of the Sea.*

60. Ingrams, *Zanzibar: Its History and Its People*, 205–206; Ingrams, *Arabia and the Isles*, 37–38; Marchant to chief secretary, 23 July 1936, AK 14/10, ZNA; "Disturbances by Shihiris, 1923–38," AB 70/1, ZNA. A reputation for martial skills and the readiness to use them was a carefully preserved aspect of masculine honor among some Hadramis (another aspect was their reputation for Islamic scholarship), and Hadrami emigrants were valued as mercenaries in many parts of the Indian Ocean. See Bujra, *The Politics of Stratification*; and Freitag and Clarence-Smith, *Hadhrami Traders.*

61. This resolved an ongoing conflict, perhaps shaped by doctrinal divisions, between the Hadhramis and the Shihiri proper, from Yemen's coastal plains."Disturbances by Shihiris, 1923–1938," AB 70/1, ZNA; G. H. Shelswell-White, "Notes on the Hadhrami and Shihiri Community in Zanzibar," BA 106/13, ZNA.

62. Ingrams, *Arabia and the Isles*, 287–288; Affidavit of W. Murphy, 20 March 1928, CO618/43/14, PRO. See also CO618/70/23, PRO.

63. Affidavits in CO618/43/14, PRO, including P. Sheldon, W. Murphy, and Sultan Ahmed, 20 March 1928. Also "Disturbances by Shihiris, 1923–38," AB 70/1, ZNA. In 1927 and again during the 1928 riot, Nasir bin Abdulla appealed to dhow crews from the Omani town of Sur, who were Sunnis, for solidarity against the apostate Ibadis from Muscat; see Seyyid Khalifa to Resident, 23 March 1928, CO618/43/14, PRO.

64. Except where noted, the following account of the March 1928 riots is derived from the affidavits in CO618/43/14, PRO. (The quote about the "Manga retainer" is from Frank Bustard, superintendent of the CID.) Also see AB 70/1, ZNA.

65. Officials who made such bald assessments included the resident, the senior commissioner, and the sultan himself. They were largely absent from the reports of the police, who, however, observed that Washihiri were the instigators of this particular spiral of violence. The quoted phrase is from the resident, A. C. Hollis.

66. Abdulla certainly had no anticolonial principles: within a decade he was loyally serving Britain and had dropped his enmity toward the sultan. Ingrams, *Arabia and the Isles*, 287–288.

67. Ibid.

68. Although the clove-buying crisis did not peak until early 1938, as early as 1935 Arab Association activists were voicing chauvinist rhetoric signaling their determination to challenge other social groups in asserting its right to rule.

69. The following account is based largely on Zanzibar Protectorate, *Report of the Commission of Enquiry Concerning the Riot in Zanzibar*, plus additional material from Welliver, "The Clove Factor in Colonial Zanzibar," 312–323; and F. H. Bustard, "Report on the Action Taken by the Police for the Suppression of the Riots on Feb. 7th 1936," Mss.Afr.s.542, RH. The compulsory inspections did not apply to licensed exporters, who included most of the large planters.

70. Zanzibar's small British community remembered the 1936 riot as a crucial moment; see the following memoirs in the Oxford Colonial Records Project, Bodleian Library of Commonwealth and African Studies at Rhodes House: Helen Haylett, "An Account of My Two

Tours as Office Assistant in the Secretariat, Zanzibar, 1935–42," typed ms., no date, Mss. Afr. s. 1946; and Margot Irving, "Manga Arab Riot, 7 February 1936, Personal Narrative," typed ms., no date, Mss. Afr. s. 816.

71. Bustard's records of what he was told by Swahili bystanders preserve contemporary perceptions that it was a Manga affair; see "Report on the Action Taken by the Police for the Suppression of the Riots on Feb. 7th 1936." He also mentions that upon his arrival at Malindi, after the rioters had already moved on to Darajani and the market, bystanders gave him "graphic accounts" of the Wamanga's "savage" assaults: this may indicate the ambivalent delight they took in narrating illustrative tales of Manga violence against the police.

72. A letter published in the Indian weekly *Samachar* as part of that paper's polemics against the Arab Association stated tendentiously that the term "Manga" had been "concocted" during the 1936 riot (22 January 1939, p. 4a). The statement is patently false, and it is difficult to understand what precise point was being aimed at. But it does suggest the power of the riot's image at the time.

73. "Seasonal Immigration," *Al-Falaq*, 10 February 1940; "Tightening Up of Immigration Laws," *Al-Falaq*, 29 June 1940.

74. "Control of Manga Arab Immigrants (1943–45)," AB 26/92, ZNA.

75. E.g., "Still on the Subject," *Al-Falaq*, 19 February 1944; "Arab Settlement," *Al-Falaq*, 4 March 1944. For the complex history of British attempts to control immigration from Yemen and the political rhetoric they aroused in the 1940s, see Friedhelm Hartwig, "The Segmentation of the Indian Ocean Region: Arabs and the Implementation of Immigration Regulations in Zanzibar and British East Africa," in *Space on the Move: Transformations of the Indian Ocean Seascape in the Nineteenth and Twentieth Centuries,* ed. Jan-Georg Deutsch and B. Reinwald (Berlin, 2002), 21–37.

76. These themes are apparent theoughout *Al-Falaq* from 1944 through the mid-1950s.

77. "Sartorial Significance," *Al-Falaq*, 11 March 1944.

78. *Al-Falaq*, 28 January 1939; "Comming [sic] of the Omani Arabs to East Africa," *Al-Falaq*, 28 January 1953; "Light on the Dark Continent," *Al-Falaq*, 9 December 1953.

79. W. Addis, District Reports, February and June 1944, BA 30/8, ZNA. On at least one occasion Manga shopkeepers objected to a ration officer because he was African; this is reminiscent of the copra sellers who in 1936 took offense at having to submit to African produce inspectors.

80. "The African Message of Welcome," *AfrKw*, 10 January 1952; "Messing about with Politics," *AfrKw*, 4 September 1952 (a Swahili translation appeared 18 September); "Philosoph of Love and Harted [sic]," *AfrKw*, 25 September 1952.

81. See the reports on speeches made by Aboud Jumbe during the week before the revolution in Abdulla Rashid, Pemba Intelligence Report, 2/10 January 1964, AK 31/16, ZNA. Such rhetoric appears more generally (although usually without the overt sedition) throughout *Afrika Kwetu* in the years 1955–1957.

82. F-S, day 14:11–12; F-S, day 2:79–81. Karume mistook the name of the man killed in 1936. The ASP lawyer was B. E. K. Swanzy, a Ghanaian, who could only have learned this version of local history from his clients. The witness was P. A. P. Robertson.

83. "Maintenance of Plantation," *Al-Falaq*, 22 April 1944; "Food Campaign," *Al-Falaq*, 23 February 1946; Welliver, "The Clove Factor in Colonial Zanzibar," 406–407. See also chapter 2.

84. Ghalib Barghash, DC Zanzibar, 12 April 1946, BA 30/8; K. G. S. Smith, District Report 1947, BA 30/5; District Monthly Reports for November 1942, May 1943, and September 1943, BA 30/7, and for 1951–1952, AB 8/3, ZNA. Coconut theft became especially prominent in 1947,

owing to an unusual price spike that left dealers scrambling to come up with supplies that they had already contracted to deliver to brokers at much lower prices. That consideration further implicated small-scale dealers in the eyes of officials and other rural elites.

85. District Monthly Reports for 1946, BA 30/8, ZNA. For an example of one such patrol and the gang it intercepted, see Sessions Case no. 13 of 1946, Zanzibar High Court, *Law Reports, Containing Cases Determined by the High Court for Zanzibar*, vol. 7 (Zanzibar, 1954), 93–94.

86. G. E. Noad, Monthly Report, December 1946, BA 30/8, ZNA.

87. "Imminent Tragedy," *Al-Falaq*, 16 March 1946; "Cassava or Life" and "Jumuiya ya Ziraa," *Al-Falaq*, 20 April 1946; "Mass Assembly," 27 April 1946; Welliver, "The Clove Factor in Colonial Zanzibar," 406–407. For the founding of the UAO, see 8 June 1946, *Al-Falaq*. The "loitering" provision of the 1949 Agricultural Produce Decree is described in DC Rural, 18 October 1960, AK 16/45, ZNA.

88. The earliest reference I have seen to the Rangers is from December 1958. But the UAO was active in the organization of landlord-led "vigilante committees" from at least a year after its inception. See R. H. V. Biles to Senior Commissioner, 18 December 1958, AK 19/3; R. H. V. Biles to Chief Secretary, 27 October 1960, AK 16/45; District Monthly Reports, 1947–1949, BA 30/8. All in ZNA.

89. These issues are discussed in "Trespass, Uprooting of Crops, etc. (Squatters and Landowners), 1958–63," AK 19/3, ZNA. For criminal trespass laws, see Abdulla Said Kharusi, DC Rural, 30 December 1958; and J. D. Stringer, Senior Commissioner, 8 January 1959. The former, of a prominent Arab family, recommended immediate enactment of such laws; the latter demurred.

90. These assessments can be read throughout AK 16/45, ZNA, including "Record of a Meeting between the Sr. Commissioner and Representatives of the UAO," 31 October 1960; R. H. V. Biles to Chief Secretary, 27 October 1960; DC (Rural), 18 October 1960.

91. Such assumptions were sometimes made explicit: e.g., "Maintenance of Plantation," *Al-Falaq*, 22 April 1944.

92. ZNP letter of welcome to the Secretary of State for the Colonies, October 1957, in CO822/1377, PRO; "Mzanzibari," "Barua," *Mwongozi*, 3 May 1957; "Yepi Yaliyowaleta Pamoja Wananchi na Wazalendo," *Mwongozi*, 3 March 1961.

93. Documents in AB 26/79, ZNA, including Secretary of Itihadi el Umma Party, Wete, to Chief Secretary, 24 October 1956; and Legco speech read by Rashid bin Hamadi Mshirazi, 21 November 1956. For more on this party, whose founders were mostly from Pemba, see Lofchie, *Zanzibar*, 172–173; and Ittihad al Umma Party 1956, AB 12/34, ZNA.

94. ZNA, AK 16/45, especially Yahya Alawi to Permanent Secretary, 25 October 1962; Saud Busaidy to Superintendent of Police, 27 August 1962; Saud Busaidy to Senior DC, 20 November 1962; and T. A. Sulemanji, "Factual Report on Praedial Larceny," 29 December 1962.

95. Not surprisingly, the village also developed an early reputation for political fractiousness. See District Reports (Urban), 1951–1958, AB 8/3–4 and 8/7, ZNA.

96. S. M. Mauly to DC Urban, 13 November 1962; and affidavits from Mohammed Saad al-Furkani, Abdulla Mohammed al-Busaidy, and Ramadhan Wakati, 18 October 1962, AK 16/45, ZNA. The names of the principals in this incident delineate their statuses. The Arabs who made the arrest belonged to prominent aristocratic clans, as did the mudir who took up their cause and the DC to whom he reported. Both George Cheusi and the police sergeant (whom we know only as "Philip") had Christian names, a sign of mainlander identity. (As if to underscore the squatter's status in the eyes of the elite, "Cheusi," fittingly, means "black.")

97. Saud Busaidy to Senior Commissioner, 20 November 1962, AK 16/45, ZNA.

98. R. Nassor (Mudir Magharib), "Squatter Cases," 3 April 1959, AK 18/26, ZNA.

99. See the cases involving Musa bin Mohammed's estate at Kiembe Samaki, August 1959, and Meya binti Salim Busaidia's estate at Mtoni, October 1962, in AK 18/26, ZNA. Also see S. M. Mauly (Mudir Magharib), 22 October 1962, AK 16/45, ZNA.

100. Stringer, "Record of a Meeting," 31 October 1960, AK 16/45, ZNA. UAO spokesmen denied that they had resolved to evict Wamakonde; they had only resolved not to allow Wamakonde to squat. The senior commissioner apparently accepted this distinction.

101. Mervyn Smithyman testimony, F-S, day 8:27–28. Like other witnesses before the Foster-Sutton Commission, Smithyman was cross-examined by attorneys for both parties, none of whom challenged this assessment.

102. Politics were denied when evictions became matters of adjudication: officials were known to be unsympathetic to landlords who acted out of political motivations. Hence when landlords did not accuse their squatters of theft, they claimed the evictions had been prompted by a decision to make commercial use of land that had previously been left to squatters.

103. This discussion of the eviction crisis is based largely on documents in "Trespass Uprooting of Crops etc.," 1958–1963, AK 19/3, ZNA. Also useful is "Squatters," AK 18/26, ZNA; P. A. P. Robertson testimony, F-S, day 2:18–19; and Welliver, "The Clove Factor in Colonial Zanzibar," 407–412.

104. Abdulla Said Kharusi, 19 November and 22 November 1958, and Stringer, 1 December 1958, AK 19/3, ZNA; Mervyn Smithyman testimony, F-S, 8:28–34. Kharusi describes all seventeen of the squatters involved as mainlanders. This was not the only such incident at Kitope at the time.

105. "Urithi wa Unguja," AfrKw, 6 October 1955; the slogan ends the article. Karume later denied having made such speeches; see F-S, days 5 and 12.

106. K. S. Talati, cross-examination of R. H. V. Biles, F-S, day 4:23–24. Older Zanzibaris, including some affiliated with ZNP at the time, still remember conflicts over the use of wells. This in fact is the issue that embroiled the family of George Cheusi's arrester with their Makonde squatters.

107. Jamal Ramadhan's speeches alleged that the evictions demonstrated the Arabs' intention to kill all Africans; see "Mkutano wa ASP Raha Leo," Sauti ya Afro-Shirazi, 16 September 1960.

108. "Z. F. C. Itengwe Tupiganie Voti," Agozi, 5 October 1959. The squatters are each identified with a mainland ethnic label.

109. Al-Kharusi's reports on the squatter crisis (AK 19/3, ZNA) are distinctly sympathetic to the landlords, urging, for example, that sanctions be imposed so that landlords could prosecute for criminal trespass. His report on the 1961 riots, which advocated ethnic targeting of mainlanders for selective surveillance, repeated ZNP rhetoric almost verbatim, suggesting that he was at least a reader of Mwongozi. See DC Rural to Senior DC, 6 July 1961, in Clarence Buxton Papers Box 3, file 2.

110. "Wazungu Chunguweni: Hizibu Inaanza Chuki Zake," Kijumbe cha Agozi, 21 July 1961.

111. "Jibu Uulizwavyo Mwongozi," Sauti ya Afro-Shirazi, 21 April 1961; the word "criminal" here is in English. Afrika Kwetu used similarly lurid language when covering the murderer's trial in 1956. The belief was widespread that the assassin was backed by men who later became prominent in the ZNP; see Clayton, The Zanzibar Revolution and Its Aftermath, 39. Rhetoric about a "Barwani Association" may have drawn on the existence of the "Board of the Barwanis," the only one of its kind in the islands; it was established in the 1940s to look after the affairs of the clan.

112. "Njugu na Mimba za YOU," Sauti ya Afro-Shirazi, 28 April 1961. In 1957, Afrika Kwetu

accused Hizbu of protecting an Arab-run prostitution ring operating in Ng'ambo: see "Wapo Wanawake Weupe Wameweka Nyumba za Danguro," *AfrKw*, 12 September 1957; and "Wakuu wa Jumuia za Siasa Msipite Njia Moja ya Dunia," *AfrKw*, 19 September 1957.

113. *Agozi*, 4 May 1959. I have corrected a few obvious typos for clarity. "The fringes of Mnazi Mmoja" presumably refers to Kikwajuni.

114. This account of the June riots is based on documents in Clarence Buxton Papers, Box 3, file 2; testimony before the Foster-Sutton Commission; and Foster-Sutton, Tewson, and Grossmith, *Report of a Commission of Inquiry into Disturbances in Zanzibar during June 1961*. A more detailed discussion will be found in chapter 7.

115. Thieves apprehended in this way are lucky if they escape with their lives. For descriptions of the practice from a century apart, see Ralph Tanner, "Crime and Punishment in East Africa," *Transition* 21 (1965): 35–38; and "Nasii," in Ludwig Krapf, *A Dictionary of the Suahili Language* (London, 1882), 273.

116. The groundwork for such expectations had been prepared by ASP propaganda that portrayed its members as loyalists and the ZNP as criminal subversives. Testimony of R. H. V. Biles and A. Derham, F-S, day 5. In addition, see copies of the following documents contained in Clarence Buxton Papers, Box 3, file 2: Hilal Muhammad al-Barwani, evidence to Foster-Sutton; Nuhu Pandu Yusuf, court evidence, October 1961; and Town Mudir to Senior DC, 27 September 1962. The latter source reported that when one crowd finally yielded its bloodied victim, a member of the crowd that had beaten him announced "*Bwana kafurahi [kuwa] kazi nzuri inafanywa*" (The *bwana* [in this case, the British police commissioner] is glad to see good work being done).

117. Lofchie, *Zanzibar*, 206; Karume testimony, F-S, day 14:11–12.

118. Saud A. Busaidy, "Security," 6 July 1963, AK 18/2, ZNA; Clyde Sanger, "Introduction," in Okello, *Revolution in Zanzibar*, 19–20; al-Haj, minutes of mudirial meeting, 9 December 1963, AK 9/29, ZNA.

119. Mudir Central to DC, 1 July 1961, Clarence Buxton Papers, Box 3, file 2. This mudir (the only legible part of his signature reads "Hamoud") made little effort to hide his biases.

120. F-S, day 7:17 ff.

121. F-S, day 5:42–44.

122. Mudir Central to DC, 1 July 1961 (the quote about "bush-knives" is from this source); S. H. M. Kanji testimony, F-S, day 5:18; K. H. Ameir, "Wamakonde Activities," AK 18/2, ZNA. For similar inflation during the course of the riots, see R. H. V. Biles testimony, F-S, day 3:73–74.

123. Saud A. Busaidy, "Rumours on Security," 28 June 1963, AK 18/2, ZNA.

124. F-S, day 4:19–20.

125. Ameir, "Wamakonde Activities." For an example of such panic, see Mudir Central, "The Wamakonde Movement Machuwi," 21 June 1963, AK 18/2, ZNA.

126. Okello, *Revolution in Zanzibar*, 73–79.

127. The rumors of crime during these months originated disproportionately in Pemba, but they circulated in both islands. These two paragraphs are based on the Intelligence Sub-committee Reports, May–July 1963, esp. the Pemba District Reports of DC Abdulla Rashid for 24–31 May 1963 and DC al-Haj for 1–7 June and 20–26 July 1963, AK 31/16, ZNA; and Yahya Alawi, Senior DC, Zanzibar District Report for 26–31 May 1963, AK 9/29, ZNA.

128. Similar behavior was observed during the Cattle Riots of 1951; see police constables' statements in CO822/620, PRO.

129. W. Addis, District Report, September 1943, BA 30/7, ZNA; High Court Criminal Appeals 1961, nos. 90–93, 97, ZHCC; High Court Sessions no. 16 of 1961, from Criminal Case 1135, ZHCA; High Court Inquest no. 19 of 1961, HC 21/18, ZNA.

130. K. H. Ameir, "Security," 24 March 1962; al-Haj to Senior DC, 23 March 1962; al-Haj, "Security," 27 March 1962. All in AK 18/2, ZNA.

131. Okello, *Revolution in Zanzibar*, 86. Some of these petty criminals will appear in the next chapter.

132. Welliver, "The Clove Factor in Colonial Zanzibar," 385.

133. Intelligence committee meeting report, 19 September 1962, AK 31/15, ZNA. The committee was chaired by Saud Busaidy, DC Urban.

134. Alawi to Police Superintendent Speight, 21 September 1962, AK 31/15, ZNA.

135. Alawi did not specify whether the gang used the English word "party" or whether he was translating. Given the international language of nationalism that the label "Ghana" evoked, one suspects they used the English word.

136. TANU did, in fact, provide the ASP with Land Rovers. There is no evidence that Ghana did so.

137. Yahya Alawi to permanent secretary, 25 September 1962, AK 31/15, ZNA.

138. Ibid.

139. This recurs throughout the examples offered in Hobsbawm, *Bandits*, as well as in the works of Hobsbawm's critics. For an excellent example from the South Africa literature see Gary Kynoch, *We Are Fighting the World: a History of the Marashea Gangs in South Africa, 1947–1999* (Athens, Ohio, 2005).

140. Philip Gourevitch, *We Wish to Inform You That Tomorrow We Will Be Killed with Our Families: Stories from Rwanda* (New York, 1998), 95.

141. High Court Sessions no. 16 of 1961, ZHCA. For the proverb, see Farsy, *Swahili Sayings*, 27 (I have modified Farsy's translation). There is a third possible dimension of meaning: according to Muhsin al-Barwani, *Conflicts and Harmony in Zanzibar*, elite Arabs deemed it a mark of masculine honor to lead pig-hunting parties. ASP propagandists, he reports, even mocked the ZNP as a "pig-hunters' association."

7. Violence as Racial Discourse

The first epigraph is from K. H. Ameir, "Security," 24 March 1962, AK 18/2, ZNA. The second epigraph is from H. R. Dharani, letter to the editor, *Tanganyika Standard*, 19 June 1961.

1. I adapt my wording from Feldman, *Formations of Violence*, 20.

2. Paul R. Brass, "Introduction: Discourses of Ethnicity, Communalism and Violence," in *Riots and Pogroms*, ed. Brass (New York, 1996), 46.

3. Pandey, *The Construction of Communalism in Colonial North India*.

4. Natalie Zemon Davis noted similar reductionist literature about religious mobs in the opening pages of her classic essay, "The Rites of Violence: Religious Riot in Sixteenth-Century France," *Past and Present* 59 (1973): 51–91. Despite Pandey's critiques of the arch-instrumentalists (e.g., *The Construction of Communalism in Colonial North India*, 14–21), he comes under similar criticism, including in Kakar, *The Colors of Violence*, 13–24. I discussed similar debates in the Africa literature in chapter 1.

5. Brass, "Introduction"; Hans Rogger, "Conclusion and Overview," in *Pogroms: Anti-Jewish Violence in Modern Russian History*, ed. John D. Klier and Shlomo Lambroza (Cambridge, 1992). See also chapters by Klier and Lambroza in the latter volume. Contrary to Brass's misleading critique, Rogger does not reject any consideration of official collusion.

6. Robert Weinberg, "Anti-Jewish Violence and Revolution in Late Imperial Russia: Odessa, 1905," in Brass, *Riots and Pogroms*, 56–88.

7. Ibid., 81. Additional examples of this approach can be found in other contributions to Brass, *Riots and Pogroms*; and Klier and Lambroza, *Pogroms*.

8. Brass, "Introduction," 33.

9. More broadly, such assumptions have featured in a rich debate about the relative autonomy of subaltern consciousness in the context of modern South Asian history. O'Hanlon, "Recovering the Subject"; Gyan Prakash, "Subaltern Studies as Postcolonial Criticism," *American Historical Review* 99 (1994): 1475–1490.

10. The quotes are from Spencer, "On Not Becoming a 'Terrorist,'" 122, 125. I also draw on Claudine Vidal, "Le génocide des Rwandais tutsi: cruauté délibérée et logiques de haine," in *De la Violence*, ed. Françoise Héritier (Paris, 1996), 325–366; and Donald Horowitz, *The Deadly Ethnic Riot* (Berkeley, 2001), 424–425, 430–433. Levi's translator renders his phrase "useless violence," a locution that evacuates such violence of the potent uses that Levi himself found in it; see *The Drowned and the Saved*, trans. Raymond Rosenthal (New York, 1988). Cf. Levi's original, *I Sommersi e i Salvati* (Turin, 1986).

11. Writing of Rwanda, where, in contrast to Zanzibar, right-wing politicians had urged the killing of Tutsi for several years prior to 1994 and had planned the Final Solution of that year, Kagabo notes that they had nevertheless provided no "directions for use"; see "Après le génocide: notes de voyage," *Les Temps Modernes* 583 (1995): 102–125.

12. Das, *Life and Words*; Claudine Vidal, "Questions sur le rôle des paysans durant le génocide des Rwandais tutsi," *Cah. d'ét. afr.* 38 (1998): 331–345.

13. Some of these issues are discussed in Veena Das and Arthur Kleinman, "Introduction," in Das, Kleinman, Ramphele, and Reynolds, *Violence and Subjectivity*, 1–18.

14. I paraphrase Gyanendra Pandey, "In Defense of the Fragment: Writing about Hindu-Muslim Riots in India Today," *Representations* 37 (1992): 41; and Vidal, "Le génocide des Rwandais tutsi et l'usage public de l'histoire," 658. Also see Straus, whose microlevel analysis refutes those in which history "overdetermines" the Rwanda genocide: *The Order of Genocide*, 18.

15. Fifty years ago, George Rudé and E. J. Hobsbawm taught us to avoid the word "mob" because of its connotations of unthinking passion. As my entire analysis emphasizes the intellectual history of the Zanzibar mob, I do not feel constrained by this consideration. Nor do I feel a compunction to protect the dignity of crowds that engaged in the acts described below.

16. Paul R. Brass, *Theft of an Idol: Text and Context in the Representation of Collective Violence* (Princeton, 1997).

17. This is a summary of arguments from Kakar, *The Colors of Violence* (quotes from 45–46); and Kakar, "Some Unconscious Aspects of Ethnic Violence in India," in Das, *Mirrors of Violence*, 135–145. Kakar does not cite Turner's concept of *communitas* (which influenced Davis); see Victor Turner, *Dramas, Fields, and Metaphors* (Ithaca, 1974). Kakar's discussion of the first of these factors, the values learned as a child, is informed by his expertise in the psychoanalytic formulations of social identity theory; they are discussed in more explicitly historical terms in some of the neo-primordialist literature I have cited in Chapter 1. The historical background of the third set of factors is explicated in a rich literature on crowds and subaltern intellectuals in Africa, South Asia, and early modern Europe: e.g., Davis, "The Rites of Violence"; Feierman, *Peasant Intellectuals*; Peires, *The Dead Will Arise*; and Sumit Sarkar, "The Kalki-Avatar of Bikrampur: A Village Scandal in Early Twentieth Century Bengal," in *Subaltern Studies*, vol. 4, ed. R. Guha (Delhi, 1985), 1–53.

18. Veena Das, "Introduction: Communities, Riots, Survivors—the South Asian Experience," in *Mirrors of Violence*, ed. V. Das (Delhi, 1990), 1–36; Feldman, *Formations of Violence*.

19. J. Prasad, "The Psychology of Rumour," *British Journal of Psychology* 26 (1935), quoted in Guha, *Elementary Aspects of Peasant Insurgency in Colonial India*, 257.

20. My neglect of the concept of "untruth" in the definition of rumor should not be taken as a postmodernist rejection of our ability to determine whether a particular rumor was true.

Rather, the concept of untruth simply does not suffice: many rumors, after all, turn out to be true. My thinking on rumor draws on, among others, Gyanendra Pandey, "The Long Life of Rumor," *Alternatives* 27 (2002): 165–191; Luise White, *Speaking with Vampires: Rumor and History in Colonial Africa* (Berkeley, 2000); Veena Das, "Specificities: Official Narratives, Rumour, and the Social Production of Hate," *Social Identities* 4, no. 1 (1998): 109–130; Susan Coppess Pendleton, "Rumor Research Revisited and Expanded," *Language and Communication* 18 (1998): 69–86; and Kapferer, *Rumors.*

21. Das, "Specificities." The argument in this and the following paragraph also draws on Kakar, *The Colors of Violence*; and Feldman, *Formations of Violence.*

22. Not surprisingly, one of the most insightful discussions of the process was written by a psychoanalyst: Kakar, *The Colors of Violence.* A different perspective on the same phenomenon is taken by Ann Laura Stoler: "'In Cold Blood': Hierarchies of Credibility and the Politics of Colonial Narratives," *Representations* 37 (1992): 151–189. See also Glen A. Perice, "Rumors and Politics in Haiti," *Anthropological Quarterly* 70 (1997): 1–10.

23. James C. Scott, *Weapons of the Weak* (New Haven, 1985); and Scott, *Domination and the Arts of Resistance* (New Haven, 1990). Other examples of such analysis in the realm of rumor include David Samper, "Cannibalizing Kids: Rumor and Resistance in Latin America," *Journal of Folklore Research* 39 (2002): 1–32; Homi Bhabha, "In a Spirit of Calm Violence," in *After Colonialism*, ed. Gyan Prakash (Princeton, 1995), 326–343.

24. See the critiques of "class-theoretical analysis" outlined in Glassman, *Feasts and Riot*, 15–25.

25. All quotes in this paragraph are from Kakar, *The Colors of Violence*, 41–42.

26. R. H. V. Biles testimony, F-S, day 4; "Rabid Politics," *AfrKw*, 16 March 1961; "Jibu uulizwavyo Mwongozi," *Sauti ya Afro-Shirazi*, 21 April 1961; "Dust in Their Eyes," *Mwongozi*, 26 May 1961.

27. The main sources for this narrative are Foster-Sutton, Tewson, and Grossmith, *Report of a Commission of Inquiry into Disturbances in Zanzibar during June 1961*; the testimony on which the *Report* is based (F-S); and the Police Diary of Events, 1 to 5 June 1961, Clarence Buxton Papers, Box 4, file 1. For the Youth League's role, see Mdundo, *Masimulizi ya Sheikh Thabit Kombo Jecha*, 113–114. My use of racial labels in this account reflects perceptions of witnesses from across the spectrum—ZNP and ASP, European and Zanzibari—who appeared before the Foster-Sutton Commission. We need not be detained by the ZNP witnesses' occasional denials, driven by party ideology, that such labels had any relevance: they repeatedly relied on those labels themselves.

28. Testimony of Police Superintendant Suleiman Said Kharusi, F-S, day 6.

29. For YOU harassment of street-sweepers, see R. H. V. Biles testimony, F-S, day 3:61; Police Diary of Events, 4–5 June. Harassment and vilification of street sweepers reached a peak when ASP-affiliated street sweepers went on strike in mid-1962; see Intelligence Committee Appreciation, July 1962, no. 56, CO822/2070, PRO; "Mgomo na Safari," *Sauti ya Wananchi*, 16 July 1962; and documents in AK 20/1 and AK 18/60, ZNA.

30. An example is the appearance of several hundred ZNP stalwarts outside the ASP's Ng'ambo headquarters early on the morning of 2 June; their aim was to threaten revenge. That the outcome of the election was known by the close of day was apparent in the next day's *Mwongozi.*

31. Mudir Central to DC, 1 July 1961, Clarence Buxton Papers, Box 3, file 2. Reports that such rumors were circulating are difficult to assess, for reasons discussed below.

32. Ali Muhsin, who had worked as an agricultural extension officer, made the observation about Manga settlement patterns and coconut supply in F-S, 11:92. Abeid Karume, on the other hand, explained the targeting of Wamanga in unselfconsciously racial terms, recalling

their alleged history of violent transgression and blaming them for the squatter evictions: F-S, day 14:11–12.

33. Casualty figures in Foster-Sutton, Tewson, and Grossmith, *Report of a Commission of Inquiry into Disturbances in Zanzibar during June 1961,* supplemented by the earlier figures in Mooring to Secretary of State, 11 June 1961, CO822/2045, PRO.

34. Brass, *Theft of an Idol,* 14; Stanley Tambiah, *Leveling Crowds: Ethnonationalist Conflicts and Collective Violence in South Asia* (Berkeley, 1996).

35. Though Foster-Sutton had served briefly on some advisory boards concerning the Kenyan civil service, most of his colonial experience had been in Cyprus, Malaya, and Nigeria; the other two commissioners had little or no colonial experience of any kind.

36. The shrewdest of the ASP lawyers, K. S. Talati, invoked the stereotype of Makonde barbarism, as we saw in the last chapter. His colleague B. E. Kwaw Swanzy, a Ghanaian less attuned to local conditions, argued more simply that because of their long oppression, Africans were "backward" compared to Arabs—an adjective that the government witness, Mervyn Smithyman, was reluctant to endorse (F-S, day 8:50ff.). For an example of ASP rhetoric blaming the violence on pent-up racial resentment, see *Kijumbe cha Agozi,* 21 July 1961.

37. F-S, days 10 (Fraser-Murray examination) and 11 (Swanzy cross-examination). Babu, more sensibly, argued that his ethnic background was so mixed that "I prefer to call myself Zanzibarian": F-S, day 10:62.

38. Babu testimony, F-S, day 10:42ff; Muhsin testimony, F-S, day 10:111–116, day 11:22ff.

39. This paragraph and the following quote from "The Truth, II," "Ukatili wa Kinyama," and "Cowardly Massacre," *Mwongozi,* 9 June 1961; and the official ZNP-ZPPP statement published in the *Tanganyika Standard,* 8 June 1961.

40. For Babu's influence, including among scholars at the University of Dar es Salaam, see Shivji, "The Life and Times of Babu"; and Othman, *Babu.*

41. F-S, day 5:11ff. Kanji then contradicted himself by saying that the squatters had been evicted not because their landlords wanted to reform labor relations along progressive lines but because they felt their tenants were neglecting their "traditional duties"; in other words, their landlords wanted not to abolish the old "squatter system" but to maintain it.

42. "Time for Action," *Mwongozi,* 28 July 1961.

43. Foster-Sutton, Tewson, and Grossmith, *Report of a Commission of Inquiry into Disturbances in Zanzibar during June 1961,* 13, 26, and passim. This passage also draws on the transcripts of the commission hearings.

44. Horowitz, *The Deadly Ethnic Riot,* 211–220. This was even the case in the Rwanda genocide, which had been planned by elements within the state: Vidal, "Questions sur le rôle des paysans durant le génocide des Rwandais tutsi."

45. Brass, *Theft of an Idol,* 14. I will return to these threats in chapter 8.

46. Mudir Central to DC, 1 July 1961; Mudir North to DC, 1 July 1961; and DC Rural to Senior DC, 6 July 1961, all in Clarence Buxton Papers, Box 3, file 2.

47. For the irresponsibility of ZNP journalists in this regard, see the exchange in the following sources: "A Timely Broadcast," *Mwongozi,* 23 June 1961; "Watu wa Bara au Watu Wabaya?" *Mwongozi,* 7 July 1961; and P. A. P. Robertson, letter to the editor, *AfrKw,* 29 June 1961. Many other examples might be cited.

48. W. Wright testimony, F-S, day 7:22–24; Mervyn Smithyman testimony, F-S, day 8:19–20. Smithyman observed that many in the crowds in town were young teens, barely out of childhood.

49. In addition to the evidence discussed below, see A. Derham testimony, F-S, day 5. In his official history, Mapuri reproduces a telling photograph of Karume "calming down youth

during the June 1961 riots." In fact, the youths in the photo have their backs to Karume and look none too calm.

50. Mervyn Smithyman testimony, F-S, days 7:85–87 and 8:12–13. Smithyman had long administrative experience in East Africa and spoke Swahili well.

51. Das, "Introduction" to *Mirrors*, 27.

52. See the instructions for voting day in "Alkhamisi 2 Furaha," *AfrKw*, 25 May 1961.

53. This definition loosely paraphrases that of *The Shorter Oxford English Dictionary*, third ed. (Oxford, 1973), 1615. See the discussion of etymology and usage in John Klier, "The Pogrom Paradigm in Russian History," in Klier and Lambroza, *Pogroms*, 34–35.

54. Das, "Introduction: Communities, Riots, Survivors," 28. In a similar vein, Horowitz describes ethnic riot leadership as a "pickup game" that "amateurs can play with ease" in *The Deadly Ethnic Riot*, 266.

55. Horowitz, *The Deadly Ethnic Riot*, 424–425, 433–443.

56. R. H. V. Biles, interview with John Tawney, 11 December 1971, MSS. Afr. s. 1446, RH. Biles's account is confirmed by a reading of the trial records. The transparent mendacity of one of the ZNP's professional witnesses was revealed when he appeared before the Foster-Sutton Commission; see F-S, day 9:42 ff.

57. I must stress that the size of my sample is small and thus what follows must be tentative. In addition to sketchier data on other incidents and a detailed account of an isolated pogrom from July 1962, the detailed trial records to which I have gained access cover only nine incidents from June 1961, which resulted in twelve deaths. This represents just over 17 percent of the total killings that month, though the sample is slightly more representative of the places where (the north-central plantation districts) and dates when (the first three days of June) most of the killings occurred.

58. This is a speculative reconstruction of Nassor's greeting; the depositions tell us only about Miraji's reply. Amarsi remembered the exchange slightly differently, in a way that suggests Nassor had used the standard *"Habari gani?"* (What's the news?), to which a positive reply is expected, no matter how dire one's personal problems; Miraji reportedly answered *"Habari mbaya"* (Bad news).

59. There were two trials for the deaths at Kitope Ndani (plus appeals): one for the death of Nassor bin Seif's son, Seif; the other for the death of Said Nassor. Records of these trials are contained in Court of Appeal, Criminal Appeal No. 176 of 1961, filed in HC 21/18, ZNA; and High Court Sessions Case no. 21 of 1961, from Criminal Case no. 1202, ZHCA. Additional details are in F-S, esp. W. Wright's testimony, day 7; Police Diary of Events, Clarence Buxton Papers, Box 4, file 1; G. Mooring to Secretary of State, 3 December 1961 and 8 December 1961; and other documents in CO822/2046, PRO.

60. Charges were eventually dropped against all but two (though a third, Miraji, was tried and convicted separately for the murder of the boy), for reasons like those described above. Nassor bin Seif initially identified forty-two participants in the riot by name. As that number dwindled with each subsequent hearing, the judge, G. M. Mahon, found it impossible to assign guilt for Said's death to the two who remained. Nevertheless Nassor's basic testimony about the shape of the attack was corroborated by other evidence, and Mahon believed it likely that the two accused had participated in the riot in some way.

61. F-S, day 7:18–20. The criminal gang reportedly included two "Arabs," a detail that not only serves as a salutary reminder of the limits of ethnic labels but also suggests that whatever politics may have been mixed in with the criminal gang's motives must have been limited and contradictory. (The two Arabs were not squatters.) Wright's testimony is in fact confused concerning whether there was one gang operating in the area or two.

62. Criminal appeals 1961, no. 110, from Resident Magistrate's Court, no. 771, ZHCA.

63. Thus Wright felt compelled to comment on it in his testimony before the Foster-Sutton Commission: day 7:24–26.

64. Criminal Appeals 1961, nos. 90–93, 97, ZHCA. The five whom Suzana and Bakari identified were convicted of being armed in public, assembling unlawfully, and carrying offensive weapons and received prison sentences. The judge also recommended that four of them, who were relatively recent immigrants, be deported to Mozambique upon their release. The records do not clarify the relationship between Suzana and the child.

65. ZNP lawyers called him as a witness before the Foster-Sutton Commission.

66. Documents in CO822/2046, PRO, including Mooring to Secretary of State, 3 December 1961. Miraji was hanged on 30 November 1961.

67. In this regard one might also question whether Nassor in fact saw Miraji about to strike the boy. Yet if he were to lie about it, one would expect him to have said that he actually saw Miraji do the deed. On the other hand, a sense of shame at having failed to protect his son may have prompted Nassor to tweak his testimony about the precise timing of his arrow wound (he could not have faked the wound itself) and how it prevented him from stopping Miraji.

68. In her infamous speech of 1 May 1961, Bibi Titi Muhammad reminded her audience that Arabs "suck the blood" of black people; see "Afrika Inajitawala," *AfrKw*, 4 May 1961. Other samples of such language include "PAFMECA Yadhulumu," *Agozi*, 21 September 1959; "Kusema Uwongo Kuna Maneno Yake," *Kipanga*, 15 January 1962; and "Hizbu waache Majisifu na Matishio," *AfrKw*, 20 April 1961. For a discussion of similar rhetoric in Tanganyika, see James R. Brennan, "Blood Enemies: Exploitation and Urban Citizenship in the Nationalist Political Thought of Tanzania," *JAH* 47 (2006): 389–413. For the more general metaphor in several parts of the continent, see White, *Speaking with Vampires*.

69. F-S, day 4:9–10; Police Diary of Events; R. H. V. Biles, interview with John Tawney, 11 December 1971, MSS. Afr. s. 1446, RH. Bushbabies, or galagos, are small arboreal primates. As their common English name suggests, their primate characteristics (including hands and monkeylike faces) and their piercing wail resembling that of a human infant might have rendered their slaughter all the more disturbing.

70. Both men claimed credit. F-S, days 7:44, 7:64–65, 7:85–86, 12:68.

71. Biles and Dalton, the attorney-general, referred to a report on the Kano riots of 1953; Foster-Sutton himself noted other instances. Careful readers may note that these implications of atavism contradict the overall description of British testimony I have offered above. But compared to party ideologues, British witnesses felt more constrained by the weight of evidence; thus their testimony was more inconsistent.

72. At the same time I would not want to discount the possibility that these animal massacres were done in the heat of passion; see the psychological interpretations discussed in Horowitz, *The Deadly Ethnic Riot*, 106, 116. John Okello reported that during the 1964 revolution, in a fit of rage at encountering some particularly stubborn Arab "resistance," he ordered his soldiers "to kill whatever came before them: men, women, children, disabled persons, even chickens and goats": Okello, *Revolution in Zanzibar*, 151. (Although the entire passage, like many in Okello's memoirs, might be dismissed as a fantasy born of his biblical delusions; cf. Joshua 6:21.)

73. Feldman, *Formations of Violence*, 81–82. Also see the suggestive comments in Mark Levene, "Introduction," in *The Massacre in History*, ed. Mark Levene and Penny Roberts (New York, 1999).

74. Examples include High Court Sessions 1961, no. 16, ZHCA; J. R. Naish interview (1971), 24–25, MSS. Afr. s. 2249, RH. Head wounds have been common in other racial massacres. Dur-

ing the 1972 Hutu massacres in Burundi, for example, most died by having their skulls crushed; see Leo Kuper, *The Pity of It All* (Minneapolis, 1977), 90.

75. Castration is another form of stylized violence that seems to signal meanings about reproduction. In Zanzibar, the practice was foreshadowed in the historical myths regarding slavery. Hard evidence of such wounds is scanty, however. In the only example I found in my limited sample of court records from June 1961, the victim sustained "an incised vertical wound of the penis and scrotum" that was inflicted by a spear, apparently after he had already fallen from the *panga* wounds that killed him. High Court Sessions 1961, no. 27, ZHCA. Also see the reminiscences in Petterson, *Revolution in Zanzibar*.

76. For a suggestive discussion of similar issues, see Das, *Life and Words*.

77. E.g., "Kwa Nini Hamuikabili Kweli?" *Mwongozi*, 15 September 1961.

78. E.g., "Time for Action," *Mwongozi*, 28 July 1961. But such wounds *did* occur. An example was the murder of Jokha binti Hamed at Jang'ombe on June 3. In addition to being disemboweled (perhaps with a spear), she sustained numerous wounds about the head; when police found her she was still alive. High Court Sessions 1961, no. 18, ZHCA.

79. *Crown v. Mohammad Chum and Khamis Baruti*, High Court Sessions 1961, no. 12, ZHCA. Laura Fair has kindly informed me that Mwembemimba was named for a maternity hospital.

80. High Court Sessions 1961, no. 16, incl. trial record from Criminal Case no. 1135 of 1961, ZHCA; W. Wright testimony, F-S, day 7:24–25. The children were the chief witnesses. Unfortunately we have no information on the precise content of the argument.

81. This mob also used the spear on another of its victims, Ali Swed's neighbor Said Abdulla, repeatedly stabbing his already-dead body. High Court Sessions 1961, no. 27, ZHCA.

82. The accounts of the incidents at Pangeni, both here and below, are reconstructed from a critical reading of three cases in ZHCA: High Court Sessions 1961, nos. 25, 26, and 27, which contain records from Criminal Cases nos. 1708, 1709, and 1710 of 1961. Salima's testimony about the arguments in the hallway was corroborated by two other witnesses, strangers who were hiding in the crawlspace beneath the roof.

83. One of Nassor's wives testified that when the mob descended on the house where the two of them were cooking, some of its members shouted "Kill them!" Nassor numbered the mob at Kitope at no fewer than 150, but Simba Khatibu, the African who was visiting at Amarsi's shop, thought it far smaller.

84. Amitav Ghosh, "The Ghosts of Mrs. Gandhi," *The New Yorker*, 17 July 1995, 35–41. Numerous instances of such heroism have been documented from the Rwanda genocide; Gourevitch, *We Wish to Inform You*, is chock-full of them, though, inconsistently, he discounts their significance. For more considered discussions, see Vidal, "Questions sur le rôle des paysans durant le génocide des Rwandais tutsi" and "Le génocide des Rwandais tutsi et l'usage public de l'histoire"; John Janzen, "Historical Consciousness and a 'Prise de Conscience' in Genocidal Rwanda," *Journal of African Cultural Studies* 13 (2000): 153–169; and Léonard Nduwayo, *Giti et le Génocide Rwandais* (Paris, 2002).

85. Many Zanzibaris remember such behavior. Such acts of kindness of course went both ways, including Arabs who protected Africans from Hizbu gangs. E.g., Idi Bakari testimony, F-S, day 14:38–50.

86. For this and the following paragraph, see Criminal Appeal no. 110 of 1961, from Case no. 771, Resident Magistrate's Court, ZHCA.

87. Defense lawyers at his trial for the Mwembemimba murder were prepared to call some of the party's heaviest hitters as witnesses, including Mtoro Reihan and J. R. Nasibu. Mtoro trumpeted Chum's acquittal in that case; see "Kesi ya Kuuwa Haikuthibiti," *AfrKw*, 20 July 1961.

88. This and the following paragraph are based on Annual and Monthly District Reports, 1934 and 1937, BA 30/4–6; and documents in AK 13/6, Masheha (1950–1964). All in ZNA.

89. Such pressures appeared as early as the 1951 cattle-dipping crisis, when at least one *sheha* found himself exposed to violent popular sanctions for cooperating with government, while another simply stopped reporting to his supervising mudir. DC to Senior Commissioner, 27 July 1951, AK 1/59, ZNA.

90. Mayhew, "Zanzibar Elections 1957," in T. Mayhew, August 1957, MSS. Afr. s. 1361, RH.

91. Most of these accusations were brought by mudirs and district commissioners with patent ZNP sympathies, but some at least appeared to be true. (One of the most contentious partisan conflicts took place in 1959 in the mudiria containing Pangeni.) ASP activists accused Hizbu-leaning officials of practicing a double standard on such matters; see "Rabid Politics," *AfrKw*, 16 March 1961. During the evictions crisis of 1958–1959, a *sheha* led an armed attack on a Muzariin ranger; see W. Wright to Commissioner of Police, 25 February 1959, AK 19/3, ZNA.

92. Sources for the Pangeni pogrom as cited in note 82, above. Despite the assessors' unanimous vote to convict Juma Ambari, Mtumwa Hassan, and John Alikumbeya in the death of Ali Swed, Judge Mahon acquitted them. The obstacle to a conviction, he ruled, was that the testimony of the sole eyewitness to Ali Swed's death, Rashid Athuman, was too inconsistent to be accepted without corroboration. The main inconsistency was that Rashid had failed to mention John Alikumbeya in his initial statement to the police. Nevertheless, a critical reading of all the testimony justifies the reconstruction I have offered. John Alikumbeya's participation in Ali Swed's murder is, indeed, not adequately proved in the evidence. But Mtumwa's account of the argument is consistent with that of the other witnesses. Juma Ambari simply denied having been present at all, despite the testimony of several witnesses in addition to that of Rashid that stated otherwise.

93. He probably leased the fields on which Mtumwa worked; the nature of the crop— a cheap staple, rather than permanent tree crops such as clove or coconut—suggests he was a short-term entrepreneur. His main business was apparently the *duka* he kept with Salima.

8. "June" as Chosen Trauma

The epigraph is from Lefebvre, *The Great Fear of 1789*, 74.

1. For "chosen trauma," a term coined by Vamik Volkan, see Kakar, *The Colors of Violence*, 50. Also see Levene, "Introduction" to Levene and Roberts, *Massacre*; and Das, *Life and Words*.

2. E.g., "Tuiunde Zanzibar Mpya," *Mwongozi*, 16 June 1961; "Time for Action," *Mwongozi*, 28 July 1961; Awena Nassor, "Utenzi," *Mwongozi*, 15 September 1961.

3. E.g., "Uchochezi unaanza," *Kijumbe cha Agozi*, 18 July 1961; "Wazungu chunguweni," *Kijumbe cha Agozi*, 21 July 1961; "Afro-Shirazi sio chama cha ukatili," *AfrKw*, 29 June 1961. The latter piece includes veiled threats against Arab women and children who were disrespectful to Africans.

4. *AfrKw*, July–August 1961.

5. "Kifungo na Uhuru Waafrika," *Kijumbe cha Agozi*, 18 July 1961; and Acting Resident to Secretary of State, 24 July 1961, G. Mooring to Secretary of State, 23 August 1961, and G. Mooring to Lord Perth, 9 September 1961, in CO822/2046, PRO.

6. "Hangings in Public Wanted," *Tanganyika Standard*, 19 June 1961; "Tuiunde Zanzibar Mpya," *Mwongozi*, 16 June 1961; "Washtakiwa Nani Aliyedhulumiwa?" *Mwongozi*, 7 July 1961; "ZNP on the General Security Situation," *Mwongozi*, 29 March 1963.

7. E.g., *Kijumbe cha Kipanga*, 9 February 1962.

8. Examples from the antirevolutionary opposition are numerous; they include the memoirs of Amani Thani in *Unser Leben vor der Revolution und Danach—Maisha Yetu Kabla ya Mapinduzi na Baadaye*, ed. Sauda A. Barwani, R. Feindt, L. Gerhardt, L. Harding, and L. Wimmelbücker (Cologne, 2003), 152–156. Examples from the revolutionary side include Karume, *Karume na Siasa*, 42–43; and ASP, *Afro-Shirazi Party: A Liberation Movement*, 158–197. The latter, an official history, devotes over twice as much space to the June riots and their aftermath as it does to the revolution itself, stressing ZNP provocations and the arrests and acquittals of ASP loyalists.

9. Special Branch Intelligence Summary, April 1963, CO822/3063, PRO.

10. Given what had happened in June, admonitions that citizens do whatever was needed to prevent a repeat of Hizbu vote fraud constituted intimidation in themselves; examples appear throughout ASP organs of the time, including *AfrKw* and *Tai*. But although ASP threats were sometimes oblique (speakers were aware of the sedition laws), they were clear enough. See the speeches recorded at a rally in September 1962, in which Karume threatened another June and Saleh Saadala threatened revolution; CO 822/2070, no. 61, PRO. Also see P. A. P. Robertson, Report, March 1963, no. 7, CO822/3063, PRO.

11. Alawi, "Security," 23 March 1963, AK 18/2, ZNA. Alawi was probably pro-ZNP, but his report criticized both parties. The thick webs of intertextuality in these cycles would numb the mind of even a postmodernist literary scholar. See, for example, Karume's speech in "Provocative Words Should Stop," *AfrKw*, 27 September 1962, translation in EB 10/11, ZNA.

12. Some versions rumored that ASP was merely planning "whispering campaigns" that such violence had broken out. Coffee-Shop Gossip Monthly Reports, September 1962–January 1963, AK 13/11a, and Intelligence Sub-Committee Reports, 1963–1964, AK 9/29, ZNA.

13. "Rumours on Security," 28 June 1963, and "Security," 6 July 1963, AK18/2, ZNA. Saud seemed to believe the rumors.

14. Nevertheless, as we have seen, both sides were willing to exploit such fears. [Mudir Central], "The Wamakonde Movement Machuwi," 21 June 1963, AK 18/2, ZNA; Special Branch Intelligence Summary, April 1963, CO822/3063, no. 8, PRO; Minutes of Meeting at DC's Office, Wete, 28 February 1962, AK5/28, ZNA.

15. "Makatili Wamefufuka," *Sauti ya Wananchi*, 16 July 1962, in AK 20/1, ZNA.

16. P. A. P. Robertson, Intelligence Summary for March 1963, CO822/3063, no. 7 and enclosures, PRO; "Zanzibar Nationalist Party on the General Security Situation," *Mwongozi*, 29 March 1963.

17. Examples include S. H. M. Kanji testimony, F-S, day 2:61–63; and Muhsin testimony, F-S, days 10 and 11. Numerous such ZNP pronouncements also appeared in the *Tanganyika Standard* and in *Mwongozi*.

18. Scotton, "Growth of the Vernacular Press in Colonial East Africa," 435–436; M. A. al-Haj, DC Pemba, Coffee-Shop Gossip Monthly Report, 31 October 1962, AK 13/11b, ZNA; "Bushes and Thorns Grow Underneath the Government," *AfrKw*, 15 March 1962. Khamis Hassan Ameir and Muhammad K. Abdulla, district officers whom ASP claimed had been unjustly denied promotion because of their race, figured largely in ASP propaganda. The main issues of the 1963 campaign are summarized in Lofchie, *Zanzibar*, 213ff., although his statement that the campaign had an "almost silent quality" underestimates the intensity of vituperation revealed in the political press and intelligence reports.

19. Vans circulating in Pemba announced over loudspeakers that the government would provide free passage to any mainlander who wished to leave; many who took up the offer said

they had been intimidated into doing so. Mooring to Secretary of State, 23 June 1961, CO822/ 2046, PRO. See also "Tanganyikans Repatriated from Pemba," *Tanganyika Standard*, 17 June 1961; and the follow-up on the story in *Tanganyika Standard*, 23 June 1961.

20. Rashid M. Mbarak, Labour Officer, to Permanent Secretary, 5 July 1961, AK 20/1, ZNA; "Ripoti ya watu wanaofukuzwa kazini bure kwa kuhusika na siasa," *AfrKw*, 22 June 1961.

21. Police Superintendant Pitcher to Senior DC, 27 July 1963, AK 31/16, ZNA; Mooring, Intelligence Summary October 1963, Zanzibar Intelligence Summaries, 1963, CO822/3063, PRO.

22. F-S, day 10:111–112. Also see *Mwongozi*, 29 September and 30 October 1961, for rhetoric about the preponderance of mainlanders in the police. ZNP allegations of police misconduct were endorsed by ZNP sympathizers within the Provincial Administration, some of them British, who had long harbored bureaucratic resentments against the police force; see R. H. V. Biles, interview with John Tawney, 11 December 1971, MSS. Afr. s. 1446, RH.

23. Biles interview, 20–24; testimony of R. H. V. Biles and K. S. Talati, F-S, day 4:35–36; Okello, *Revolution in Zanzibar*; Clayton, *The Zanzibar Revolution and Its Aftermath*. In the second half of 1963, Babu's Umma party was also rumored to be agitating among the police; see Intelligence Subcommittee Report, 10–16 August 1963, AK 9/29, ZNA.

24. "Tangazo," *AfrKw*, 18 July 1963; "Yasemwayo Sio ya Kweli—Uvumi Umetapakaa," and "Rejareja sio Mwendo," *AfrKw*, 25 July 1963; "Unatabua?" [*sic*], *AfrKw*, 1 August 1963; "Afro Shirazi Party Haikuunga Popote," *AfrKw*, 15 August 1963.

25. Coffee-Shop Gossip Reports, 1962–1963, AK 13/11a–b, and Intelligence Sub-Committee Reports, 1963, AK 9/29, ZNA; files in CO822/3063 and CO822/2070, PRO; also see *AfrKw* and *Mwongozi* from throughout these years. ASP propagandists also relied on media outlets in Kenya and (newly independent) Tanganyika, including Voice of Dar es Salaam: Y. Alawi to Permanent Secretary, 23 March 1963, AK 18/2, ZNA; "Extracts from Local Press," EB 10/11, ZNA.

26. *Agozi* even ran a regular "Cairo Page" devoted to polemicizing against the ZNP propaganda broadcast by the Swahili service of Radio Cairo. For Radio Cairo, see the memoirs of Amani Thani in Barwani, Feindt, Gerhardt, Harding, and Wimmelbücker, *Unser Leben*; and James Brennan, "Radio Cairo and the Decolonization of East Africa, 1953–1964," in *Making a World after Empire: The Bandung Moment and Its Political Afterlives*, ed. Christopher J. Lee (Athens, Ohio, 2010).

27. The quote is from an ASP statement reported in "Zanzibar Repaints the Red Cockerels for June Election," *Tanganyika Standard*, 12 May 1961; the same statement endorsed membership in the British Commonwealth. The ASP charged that Hizbu's opposition to the federation (and to the commonwealth) was prompted by a desire to bring Zanzibar into the Arab League: "ZNP Leader 'Changed His Mind,'" *Tanganyika Standard*, 17 June 1961.

28. For ASP rhetoric, see, e.g., "Hizbu wadanganya wa Mwambao," *Kipanga*, 16 January 1962; "Waarabu sahauni kudai Mombasa," *Agozi*, 21 July 1961; and "Yapo usoni: Unguja na Mwambao," *AfrKw*, 15 February 1962. Examples of irredentist rhetoric appear in *Mwongozi*, 15 March, 2 August, and 13 September 1963. Clarence Buxton, himself a Kenyan and passionately anti-KANU, was a conduit between Mombasa and the Zanzibar court, where the irredentists were concentrated; see Clarence Buxton Papers, Box 3, files 1 and 3.

29. Mooring, Intelligence Summary, 1 November 1963, no. 24, CO822/3063, PRO; al Haj, Intelligence Sub-Committee Reports, 11–18 October and 18 October–1 November 1963, AK 9/29, ZNA; Pemba Intelligence Report, 26 October–1 November 1963, AK 31/16, ZNA.

30. Invective against medical staff was part of ASP polemics against "Zanzibarization." Examples include "Mama Gozi eshambuliwa kwa faru Shangani," *Agozi*, 5 October 1959; and "Meno ya mbwa hayaumani," *Agozi*, 4 January 1960. This paragraph also relies on Coffee-Shop

Gossip Reports, October and November 1962, AK 13/11a, ZNA; *Ngao*, 30 March 1963, copy in EB 10/11, ZNA; Intelligence Reports, March 1963, nos. 6–7, CO822/3063, PRO; A. E. Forsyth-Thompson to Permanent Secretary, 13 April 1963, EB 10/11, ZNA.

31. When a mysterious fire bomb did some minor damage at the newly opened consulate in August 1961, Babu and his followers were instantly suspected; they retorted that it was the work of provocateurs. Petterson, *Revolution in Zanzibar*, 21–22; "Bombs Hurled at Zanzibar Consulate," *Tanganyika Standard*, 31 August 1961.

32. It took some time for the ZNP to recognize the station's symbolic value, and the party's conservative leadership remained uninterested. In addition to *Mwongozi*, see Mooring's dispatches for 1961, CO822/2050, PRO; Resident to Secretary of State, 29 November 1962, CO822/2135, PRO; and "Anti-American Posters Greet Williams in Zanzibar," *Tanganyika Standard*, 27 February 1961. For "Tshombe Mapara," see F-S, days 8:61–63, 12:56–57. "Tshombe" had become common street slang for a troublemaker.

33. For rhetoric of the Youth League militants about Congo, see "Waafrika wataipinga ZNP ndole mbili," *Kijumbe cha Afro-Shirazi*, 7 July 1961; and "Hizbu wadanganya wa Mwambao," *Kijumbe cha Kipanga*, 16 January 1962. (The first article red-baits its ZNP rivals even as it echoes their anti-Western discourse.) Anti-Western polemics did not become common among the ASP militants until late 1963, as they were forging their alliance with Babu's Umma Party. ASP leaders were angered and embarrassed when two party radicals, Kassim Hanga and Hasan Moyo, objected to a Legco resolution expressing sympathy with the United States on the assassination of President Kennedy; see al-Haj, Intelligence Report 23–30 November 1963, AK 9/29, ZNA.

34. Examples of red-baiting include "Jibu Uulizwavyo Mwongozi," *Sauti ya Afro-Shirazi*, 21 April 1961; and Joseph Khamis, Letter, *Tanganyika Standard*, 12 June 1961. Red-baiting came especially easily to J. R. Nasibu, who during the PAFMECA crisis had vilified Karume as the head of a "Kremlin regime." In a polemic against ZNP hypocrisy on Cold War issues, Nasibu lumped the United States and Russia together in the same category as treacherous white people; see "Marekani Ashukuriwa Katika Baraza Unguja," *Kijumbe cha Agozi*, 9 July 1961.

35. The rumors were further propelled by references in political speeches. Examples can be found in Mooring, Intelligence Report, 11 March 1963, CO822/3063, PRO; DC Urban, 6 July 1963, AK 18/2, ZNA; "Provocative Words Should Stop," *AfrKw*, 27 September 1962; P. A. P. Robertson, Intelligence Summary April 1963, PRO, CO822/3063.

36. Examples include the rhetoric in "Hotuba ya Bwana Khamis Masoud," *AfrKw*, 20 April 1961, and the noms de plume used by two correspondents to *Agozi* on 4 and 18 May 1959: "Hydrogen Bomb" and "Atomic Bomb." Already in the 1950s some were rumoring that Egypt possessed the bomb and would use it to assist anticolonial struggles throughout the continent: see the anecdote recounted by F. D. Ommanney in *Isle of Cloves: A View of Zanzibar* (London, 1955), 129–130. The latter story is not dated, but it appears to have occurred around the time of Nasser's 1952 army revolt.

37. Special Branch Intelligence Summary for April 1963, CO822/3063, PRO; Khamis Mohammed Rajaby, Coffee-Shop Gossip for October 1962, AK 13/11a, ZNA.

38. The level of superpower presence continued to be exaggerated in the years since the revolution by political actors who had cause to present themselves (or their enemies) as disciplined Marxist-Leninists beset by the powers of Western neocolonialism. In this regard, their self-presentation converged, ironically, with the fantasies of cold warriors in London and Washington who regarded China and the Eastern Bloc as the region's greatest threats to stability. Relatively measured assessments are contained in Mooring's intelligence reports for 1962 and 1963 in CO822/2070 and 3063, PRO. Reports in the same files by Mooring's deputy, Robertson,

are less reliable, as they are colored by his intemperate anticommunism. For a description of how Cold War ideologies distorted Western perceptions, see Petterson, *Revolution in Zanzibar*; cf. the accounts written or influenced by Babu, including Wilson, *US Foreign Policy*. A variant of Babu's perspective comes from former members of ZNP's right wing, including Amani Thani (in Barwani, Feindt, Gerhardt, Harding, and Wimmelbücker, *Unser Leben*) and Ali Muhsin, who depict themselves as defenders of Nasserism and/or Islam against the schemes of Zionism. For Israel and ASP, see Resident to Secretary of State, 29 November 1962, CO822/2135, PRO.

39. Al-Haj, Coffee-Shop Gossip Reports of 6 October 1962 and 16 January 1963, AK 13/11b, ZNA; Town Mudir, Coffee-House Gossip Report, 5 October 1962, AK 13/11a, ZNA; Intelligence Sub-Committee Report, 13 September 1963, AK 9/29, ZNA.

40. For the older understandings, see Glassman, *Feasts and Riot*, esp. 48–54, 260–261, and 264–265, and compare to the thinking described on 269–270.

41. "Appeal to Sanity," *Tanganyika Standard*, 7 June 1961; Morgan to FO, 12 July 1961, CO822/2046, PRO. This kind of rhetoric was especially ubiquitous in ZNP propaganda.

42. Supplement to Special Branch Intelligence Summary August 1962, CO822/2070, no. 60, encl., PRO; Alawi, Intelligence Sub-Committee Report, 17–23 August 1963, AK 9/29, ZNA; *Mwongozi* 1963, passim.

43. One wonders if the latter rumors were in any way inspired by gossip about the left-wing ASP leader Abdulla Kassim Hanga, who returned from study in the USSR with a Jewish wife. Intelligence Committee Appreciation, March 1963, CO822/3063, PRO; Saud Busaidy (DC Urban), 6 March 1963, AK 31/15, ZNA; Abdulla Rashid al-Mendhiry (DC Pemba), Coffee-Shop Gossip, 11 January 1963, AK 13/11b, ZNA.

44. The latter charges peaked just before the June riots, and on voting day ASP mobs alleged that "their women" had been abused as they waited to vote. "Njugu na mimba za YOU," *Sauti ya Afro-Shirazi*, 28 April 1961; Mudir North to DC Rural, 1 July 1961, Clarence Buxton Papers, Box 3, file 2.

45. During Babu's 1962 imprisonment a common ZNP-ZPPP chant was "Uhuru and Babu": Special Branch Intelligence Summary, August 1962, CO822/2070, PRO; "Mgomo na Safari," *Sauti ya Wananchi*, 16 July 1962. Also see Amani Thani's memoirs in Barwani, Feindt, Gerhardt, Harding, and Wimmelbücker, *Unser Leben*, 174–176.

46. Alawi, District Intelligence Report, 27 July/2 Aug 1963, AK 9/29, ZNA; Busaidy, District Intelligence Committee Meeting, 16 August 1963, AK 31/15, ZNA. Muhsin repeated the accusations of debauchery in a radio speech in August; see Petterson, *Revolution in Zanzibar*, 31.

47. *Mwongozi*, 16 August, 27 September, and 18 October 1963. "Their Jew prophet" is my rendering of the unusual locution "*Mtume wao Jahudi.*" The precise meaning of the "Nine Tribes" rhetoric, which is in English, is difficult to decipher. *Mwongozi* came easily to its anti-Semitism, averring an "age-old Islamic disapprobation of Jews and of things Jewish": "Disturbing Knowledge," 23 August 1963. Such sentiments can be traced back to the interwar Arab Association in *Al-Falaq*.

48. Pemba Intelligence Summary, October 1962, AK 31/15, ZNA; DC Pemba to Senior DC, 3 November 1962, AK 13/6, ZNA.

49. Two British investigators (at least one of whom was hostile to the ASP) found no basis to the rumor about Ali Sharif's involvement. Details of the Wingwi incident are recorded in C. E. V. Buxton and W. Wright, "Report on the Riot at Wingwi," 24 January 1963, AK 17/85, ZNA; and a draft of the same in the Clarence Buxton Papers, Box 3, file 1.

50. Rajaby, Town Mudir, Coffee-Shop Gossip October 1962, AK 13/11a, ZNA; Pemba Intelligence Summaries, October and November 1962, AK 31/15, ZNA; Mooring to Colonial Office, 4 December 1962, no. 66 plus enclosures, CO822/2070, PRO; Mooring, Intelligence Summary,

3 January 1963, CO822/3063, no.1, PRO; "ZNP on the General Security Situation," *Mwongozi*, 29 March 1963; Othman Shariff, "The Civil Service and Politics," *AfrKw*, 6/7 March 1963.

51. Alawi, Senior DC, "Security," 23 March 1963, AK 18/2, ZNA.

52. Al-Haj, Pemba Intelligence Subcommittee Reports, 8–14 June, 29 June–6 July and 7–13 July 1963, AK 31/16, ZNA; Pemba Intelligence Summary April 1963, AK 31/15, ZNA.

53. Over a decade later, Wingwi continued to figure in the official mythology of the revolution; as with ASP accounts of the June riots, the narrative emphasized Hizbu's legal persecution of the alleged rioters. See ASP, *Afro-Shirazi Party: A Liberation Movement*, 195–197.

54. Al-Haj and al-Mendhiry, Pemba Coffee-Shop Gossip Reports for October 1962 through February 1963, AK 13/11b, ZNA. In AK 31/15, ZNA: Busaidy, Urban District Intelligence Committee Meeting, 19 October 1962; al-Haj, Pemba Intelligence Summary, 22 November 1962; and Busaidy to Senior DC, 6 March 1963. For Israel's legal assistance, see Resident to CO, 29 November 1962, CO822/2135, PRO. For the Israeli businessman who also helped, see Clayton, *The Zanzibar Revolution and Its Aftermath*, 71; and Petterson, *Revolution in Zanzibar*, 30.

55. For the general picture, see Clayton, *The Zanzibar Revolution and Its Aftermath*; Petterson, *Revolution in Zanzibar*; Sanger, "Introduction," 19–20. Some details here are also drawn from District Intelligence Sub-Committee Reports, 14 September through 6 December 1963; and al-Haj, Minutes of Mudirial Meeting, 8 December 1963, in AK 9/29, ZNA. For ZNP's alarmist rhetoric during the four months prior to *uhuru*, see, e.g., "The Darkest Hour" and "Broadcast Talk" (the text of a radio speech by Muhsin), *Mwongozi*, 16 August 1963. ASP debates over whether to participate in the Uhuru celebrations appear in *AfrKw* throughout November and early December.

56. Sanger, "Introduction," in Okello, *Revolution in Zanzibar*. Also see District Intelligence Sub-Committee Weekly Reports, AK 9/29, ZNA.

57. "Siri: Masheha," AK 13/6, ZNA; also Intelligence Sub-Committee Weekly Reports, 6–27 December 1963, AK 9/29, ZNA. For the flag and "Manga rule," see the accounts of Aboud Jumbe's speeches in Pemba Intelligence Sub-Committee Weekly Reports, 27 December 1963–10 January 1964, AK 31/16, ZNA; and Sanger, "Introduction," in Okello, *Revolution in Zanzibar*, 21.

58. Nasibu risked sedition charges by printing a veiled challenge to the sultan's rule in "Hapana Ushirika na Ardhi," *Agozi*, 6 July 1959. Joseph Fikirini and Hasan Moyo did likewise in speeches in January 1960. See Extract from Intelligence Report, CO822/2132, no. 1, PRO. Later examples include speeches by Moyo described in "'Zanzibar Revolution' Threat," *Tanganyika Standard*, 11 October 1962; and speeches in October–November 1962 and March–May 1963 by Saleh Saadala, Aboud Jumbe, and others. These are described in the following PRO files: P. A. P. Robertson to Colonial Office, 6 October 1962, plus enclosures, and Mooring to Colonial Office, plus enclosures, CO822/2070, nos. 61 and 66; Robertson, Intelligence Summary for March 1963, plus enclosure, CO822/3063, no.7; and Special Branch summary, CO822/3063, no. 9, encl. For the "suicide squads," see DC Urban, "Rumours on Security," 28 June 1963, and DC Urban to Senior DC, 8 July 1963, AK 18/2, ZNA. By this time, the Human Rights League had changed its name to the African Democratic Union; I will retain the former name to reduce confusion.

59. District Intelligence Subcommittee Weekly Reports, 30 November 1963 through 4 January 1964; and al-Haj, Minutes of Mudirial Meeting, 9 December 1963, both in AK 9/29, ZNA. Okello's account is in *Revolution in Zanzibar*. Authors who have verified its basics include Clayton, Petterson, and Burgess, although the latter's ASP informants minimized Okello's autonomy from the Youth League. The authors of the official ASP account, who go to implausible lengths

to portray Karume as having planned and executed the revolution, feel compelled to devote a lengthy, detailed section to minimizing Okello's significance; see ASP, *Afro-Shirazi Party: A Liberation Movement*, 265–267.

60. The security schemes established in the wake of the June riots paid particular attention to the disruptive potential of dances and religious processions. See Central Intelligence Appreciation and Special Branch Intelligence Summary, August 1962, CO822/2070, PRO; and Minutes of Security Council Meeting, 28 November 1962, AK 18/2, ZNA.

61. Clayton, *The Zanzibar Revolution and Its Aftermath*, 57–58, 67, 71; Burgess, "Youth and the Revolution," chapter 5; Mwanjisi, *Abeid Amani Karume*, 53; the memoir of Amani Thani in Barwani, Feindt, Gerhardt, Harding, and Wimmelbücker, *Unser Leben*, 182.

62. That the violence was well out of control of party leaders is demonstrated not only by the difficulties the politicians had reining in Okello but also by the massive looting that accompanied the revolution. (For the latter, see ZNA: AK 17/10, AK 17/68, AK 17/69, and AK 17/72.) Petterson's eyewitness accounts of revolutionary cadres confirm the impression that they were lightly controlled, if at all; even Burgess's ASYL informants, who generally emphasized the role of party organization, remembered the improvisational nature of their own involvement.

63. In addition to sources already cited, see ASP, *Afro-Shirazi Party: A Liberation Movement*, 264, 267. Given the footage of mass graves recorded during the January upheaval in Gualtiero Jacopetti's film *Africa Addio*, their appearance in pre-revolutionary rumors may be an example of what those plotting genocide in 1990s Rwanda called "accusations in the mirror"; that is, accusing one's enemies of the very acts one was planning oneself. Des Forges, *Leave None to Tell the Story*.

64. This emerges in conversations with former revolutionaries and in Mwanjisi, *Abeid Amani Karume*, 53. For the earlier ASP rhetoric, see "Vipande Havitakiwi," *AfrKw*, 3 January 1963; District Intelligence Committee, 21 January 1963, AK 31/15, ZNA; "Re: Coffee Shop Gossip," 5 January 1963, AK 13/11a, ZNA.

65. Hizbu rhetoric had threatened to kill a number of Africans (typically ten) for each victim of the June pogroms. In general, Okello's memories of Hizbu threats are recognizable as exaggerated versions of what is preserved in the archival and printed record; see *Revolution in Zanzibar*, 94–95, 119–121. Rhetoric similar to Okello's concerning Hizbu plots also appears in official party accounts: e.g., ASP, *Afro-Shirazi Party: A Liberation Movement*, 247–248, 250–253.

66. Even in his self-serving memoir, Okello seems to acknowledge that he did not forbid rape outright, only under certain conditions; *Revolution in Zanzibar*, 126.

67. This is the picture that emerges from Burgess, "Youth and the Revolution," which is based on interviews with ASYL participants; Clayton, *The Zanzibar Revolution and Its Aftermath*; and my own reading of relevant documentary sources.

68. Stoler, "'In Cold Blood,'" 154. As in many aspects, this view was anticipated by Lefebvre, *The Great Fear of 1789*, 140.

69. Thus, on the eve of the Xhosa Cattle Killing of 1857, rumors flew that the Russians were a black nation who after defeating the British in the Crimea would arrive on the shores of the Cape Colony as liberators. Similarly, at the outset of World War I, Pakistani peasants learned that the kaiser and Germany had converted to Islam and declared jihad against Britain. Peires, *The Dead Will Arise*; Martin Sökefeld, "Rumours and Politics on the Northern Frontier: The British, Pakhtun Wali and Yaghestan," *Modern Asian Studies* 36 (2002): 299–340.

70. The most powerful recent instance is Rwanda in 1994. Yet even there, only a minority of Rwandans participated in the killing; see Straus, *The Order of Genocide*, 115–118.

71. I paraphrase George Rudé, in his "Introduction" to Lefebvre, *The Great Fear of 1789*, xi.

72. Scott is the best-known proponent of this approach and the most pointed in suggesting the counterhegemonic nature of what he calls "offstage" discourse. Influential essays by Spivak and Bhabha contrast the insurrectionary character of rumor with the exploitative character of writing. Both rely on Guha, who describes rumor as a "universal and necessary" form of "insurgent communication," distinct from the written forms of communication that constitute the "prose of counter-insurgency." Guha, however, is less romantic than Scott, recognizing that peasant rumors can be conservative in their effects or expressive of "false consciousness." Scott, *Weapons of the Weak*; Scott, *Domination and the Arts of Resistance*; Gayatri Chakravorty Spivak, "Subaltern Studies: Deconstructing Historiography," in *Selected Subaltern Studies*, ed. R. Guha and G. C. Spivak (New York, 1988); Bhabha, "In a Spirit of Calm Violence"; Guha, *Elementary Aspects of Peasant Insurgency in Colonial India*.

Conclusion and Epilogue

1. Clayton estimates that the pre-independence Arab population of 50,000 had been reduced by 12,000 to 15,000; Petterson that it was halved. Estimates of the number killed vary widely; most range between 3,000 and 10,000. Clayton offers a judicious review in *The Zanzibar Revolution and Its Aftermath*, 78–82, 97–100. Despite the uncertainties, numbers are often presented as if they were documented fact. The choice is often shaped by the author's attitude toward the revolution. Its opponents, including those sympathetic to the current political opposition, inflate the number; many like to quote Okello's boast that 13,000 Arabs were killed, a figure that almost certainly was one of the apocalyptic fantasies that run throughout his memoir. Its apologists, in contrast, minimize it.

2. Okello experienced a variant of Zanzibar's vituperative rhetoric of racial history while on the Kenya coast, where it accompanied the ongoing Mwambao movement for coastal autonomy; he emphasized its impact on his thinking in *Revolution in Zanzibar*, 59–64. Of course, this is not to deny the impact of Okello's experiences of racism in colonial Uganda and upcountry Kenya before coming to the coast.

3. See Straus, *The Order of Genocide*, esp. 224–231.

4. Burgess writes that the killings were "spontaneous" ("Youth and the Revolution"), and eyewitness accounts indeed suggest that they were relatively unorganized: e.g., Petterson, *Revolution in Zanzibar*; and Juli McGruder, "Madness in Zanzibar: 'Schizophrenia' in Three Families in the 'Developing' World" (Ph.D. diss., University of Washington, 1999). But one must be cautious of Burgess's ASYL sources, whose interest in emphasizing the spontaneity of the killings resembles the interest that shaped ASP testimony before the Foster-Sutton Commission. The sheer scope of the killings (especially if the higher numbers are accepted) suggests at least some level of organization, as does the disturbing footage in Gualtiero Jacopetti's film *Africa Addio*. In any case, Clayton and other sources concur that whatever formal elements were involved in the killings were those loyal to Okello. Karume and his allies were the most racialist factions left in the government after Okello's removal, yet most accounts suggest that they were appalled at the killings and could behave generously, if capriciously, toward those caught in the roundup of Arabs and political enemies.

5. These issues are lucidly discussed in James Fearon and David Laitin, "Violence and the Social Construction of Ethnic Identity," *International Organization* 54 (2000): 845–877.

6. He describes patterns from the 1995 election, but they have been repeated subsequently. Bakari, *The Democratisation Process in Zanzibar: A Retarded Transition* (Hamburg, 2001), 237. For survey data suggesting that Zanzibaris commonly perceive electoral politics in terms of

ethnic alignments, see D. Mukangara, "Race, Ethnicity, Religion, and Politics in Zanzibar," in Maliyamkono, *The Political Plight of Zanzibar*, 35–54.

7. Tanzania Election Monitoring Committee (TEMCO), *The 2005 Presidential and General Elections in Zanzibar* (n.p., n.d.); Mapuri, *Zanzibar*, 75 ff.

8. Fearon and Laitin, "Violence and the Social Construction of Ethnic Identity."

9. Richards, *Fighting for the Rainforest*.

10. For a particularly clear enunciation of this position, see L. Rey, "The Revolution in Zanzibar," in *Socialism in Tanzania*, ed. L. Cliffe and J. Saul (Dar es Salaam, 1972). Bakari takes a similar approach to the first Time of Politics and then draws an analogy to the present situation in *The Democratisation Process in Zanzibar*, 177–178.

11. Examples of such rhetoric abound in Karume's speeches in *Karume na Siasa*.

12. J. Mbwiliza, "The Birth of a Political Dilemma and the Challenges of the Quest for New Politics in Zanzibar," in Maliyamkono, *The Political Plight of Zanzibar*, 3, 5.

13. The quoted scholars are all associated with the Eastern and Southern African Universities' Research Programme (ESAURP), which has done invaluable research on the Zanzibar political stalemate. See Mukangara, "Race, Ethnicity," 43–44; and T. L. Maliyamkono, "What Next?" in Maliyamkono, *The Political Plight of Zanzibar*, 246. During the 1995 election campaign, CCM supporters identified themselves as the heirs to the ASP and their rivals as the heirs of the ZNP; see C.A. Rugalabamu, "Electoral Administration during the 1995 General Elections in Zanzibar," in Maliyamkono, *The Political Plight of Zanzibar*, 118.

14. Greg Cameron, "Political Violence, Ethnicity and the Agrarian Question in Zanzibar," in *Swahili Modernities*, ed. Pat Caplan and Farouk Topan (Trenton, 2004), 107–108.

15. ESAURP, *Muafaka: The Roots of Peace in Zanzibar* (Dar es Salaam, 2004), 6.

16. At the same time, Bakari observes, many CUF members have no evident dedication to democratic principles. His observations accord with what I have heard in many conversations with Zanzibaris over the past fifteen years.

17. Bakari, *The Democratisation Process in Zanzibar*, passim. His assessment of the latter point is stated most clearly on 300.

18. Saleh, *Zanzibar 1870–1972*, 73–75. For Comorians' claims to Arab status, see Ibuni Saleh, *A Short History of the Comorians in Zanzibar* (Dar es Salaam, 1936).

19. Bakari, *The Democratisation Process in Zanzibar*, 71–72, 76–77; Esmond Bradley Martin, *Zanzibar: Tradition and Revolution* (London, 1978), 68–69 and passim. For Karume's anti-Comorian campaigns, see also Saleh, *Zanzibar 1870–1972*, 98–101.

20. Amory, "The Politics of Identity on Zanzibar," 115–123; Bakari, *The Democratisation Process in Zanzibar*, 71–72.

21. Amory, "The Politics of Identity on Zanzibar," chapter 5; George Triplett, "Zanzibar: The Politics of Revolutionary Inequality," *Journal of Modern African Studies* 9 (1971): 612–617; and documents from Amnesty International and others, in Papers of the Anti-Slavery Society, MSS. Brit. Emp. s. 22, G.932b, RH. (The latter source implicates figures at the party's highest levels.) Saleh believes the issue was blown out of proportion by the Western press, though he was already in exile at the time; see *Zanzibar*, 104–107. In any case, the intimidating rhetoric from government spokesmen was real enough, as were the rumors. For rumors that predated the scandal, see Ahmed Seif Kharusi, *Letters Smuggled out of Zanzibar* (Southsea, 1971), 8, 22, 29–30. The forced marriages still figure prominently in memories of the Karume era; see Kjersti Larsen, "Change, Continuity and Contestation: The Politics of Modern Identities in Zanzibar," in Caplan and Topan, *Swahili Modernities*, 126; and McGruder, "Madness in Zanzibar," 100.

22. When not otherwise referenced, the narrative in these pages is based on Clayton, *The Zanzibar Revolution and Its Aftermath*; Petterson, *Revolution in Zanzibar*; and Michael Lofchie,

"The Zanzibari Revolution: African Protest in a Racially Plural Society," in *Protest and Power in Black Africa*, ed. Robert Rotberg and Ali Mazrui (New York, 1970), 924–967. For the international dimension, see also Ian Speller, "An African Cuba? Britain and the Zanzibar Revolution," *Journal Imperial and Commonwealth History* 35 (2007): 1–35.

23. Though Karume was curious about some of the Marxists' collectivist policy ideas, Marxism nevertheless had a marginal influence on the islands' political culture. See the candid memoirs of Ali Sultan Issa, one of the Karume government's most committed communists, in G. Thomas Burgess, *Race, Revolution, and the Struggle for Human Rights in Zanzibar* (Athens, 2009).

24. The quoted phrase is adapted from Cameron, "Political Violence, Ethnicity and the Agrarian Question in Zanzibar." For examples of such anti-Indian rhetoric, see ASP, *Afro-Shirazi Party: A Liberation Movement*; and Adam Shafi Adam's revolutionary novels.

25. Jan-Georg Deutsch, "Imaginaries of the Past: Nostalgia and Social Conflict in Zanzibar," paper presented at the conference Celebrating Memories and Visual Cultures, Zanzibar International Film Festival, Zanzibar, 2–3 July 2007. Deutsch attributes this misconception about slavery to the vagaries of oral historical tradition, but it is conveyed in such widely read texts as Adam, *Kasri*; and Mwanjisi, *Abeid Amani Karume*, 49.

26. Haroub Othman, "The Union with Zanzibar," in *Mwalimu: the Influence of Nyerere*, ed. Colin Legum and Geoffrey Mmari (London, 1995), 172–173.

27. K. I. Tambila, "Aspects of the Political Economy of Unguja and Pemba," in Maliyamkono, *The Political Plight of Zanzibar*, 71–103; Ibrahim F. Shao, *The Political Economy of Land Reform in Zanzibar* (Dar es Salaam, 1992); Deutsch, "Imaginaries of the Past"; Cameron, "Political Violence, Ethnicity and the Agrarian Question in Zanzibar," 111. For abuse during the 1960s and 1970s, see also Petterson, *Revolution in Zanzibar*, 219–220; Clayton, *The Zanzibar Revolution and Its Aftermath*; and Martin, *Zanzibar*, 80, 116–118, 130.

28. TEMCO, *The 2005 Presidential and General Elections*; Tambila, "Aspects of the Political Economy of Unguja and Pemba"; William Bissell, "Engaging Colonial Nostalgia," *Cultural Anthropology* 20 (2005): 215–248.

29. E.g., Tambila, "Aspects of the Political Economy of Unguja and Pemba," 78. Such a person might be described, jokingly, as "Mzanzi*bara*," that is, a Zanzibari from *bara*, the mainland. Contrary to some authors, I have heard this epithet used by CCM loyalists as well as by members of the opposition—and, most tellingly, by people who are resolutely apolitical.

30. I have heard such narratives repeatedly over the years. Published examples include Amani Thani's memoir in Barwani, Feindt, Gerhardt, Harding, and Wimmelbücker, *Unser Leben*; al-Ismaily, *Zanzibar*; Seif Sharif Hamad's memoir in Burgess, *Race, Revolution and the Struggle for Human Rights in Zanzibar*, 190–191; and Khatib M. Rajab, "Nyerere against Islam in Zanzibar and Tanganyika," available at victorian.fortunecity.com/portfolio/543/nyerere_and_islam.htm (accessed 29 October 2009).

31. The dispute mainly concerns proposals to reform the union; contrary to CCM allegations, few in the opposition demand its outright dissolution. See Chris Maina Peter and Haroub Othman, eds., *Zanzibar and the Union Question* (Zanzibar, 2006).

32. The most frequently cited of the geopolitical accounts is Wilson, *US Foreign Policy and Revolution*, which was written in collaboration with Babu and includes an introduction by him (whence the phrase "revolutionary tide"). Although Wilson documents American concerns, she fails to substantiate her central argument. Also sometimes cited is Susan C. Crouch, *Western Responses to Tanzanian Socialism, 1967–83* (Aldershot, 1987), which offers no documentation at all for the assertions that are relevant here. A less distorted account would be complex, complicated by the momentary convergence of Western interests with those of Karume and

Nyerere, the latter two motivated as much by realpolitik as by pan-Africanist ideals. See Cranford Pratt's review of Wilson's book in *Journal Modern African Studies* 28 (1990): 164–166; Petterson, *Revolution in Zanzibar*; Clayton, *The Zanzibar Revolution and Its Aftermath*; Othman, "The Union with Zanzibar"; and Othman, "Tanzania: The Withering Away of the Union?" in Peter and Othman, *Zanzibar and the Union Question*, 35–72 (although the latter reproduces a few of Crouch's and Wilson's unsubstantiated assertions).

33. In Dar es Salaam, both men eventually fell out with Nyerere. Hanga was arrested on Karume's insistence in 1969 and sent back to Zanzibar, where he was executed. Babu was arrested in a sweep following Karume's assassination in 1972; he was released in 1978 and spent the rest of his life in the United States and Britain, teaching, writing, and mentoring another generation of progressive internationalists.

34. E.g., Cameron, "Political Violence, Ethnicity and the Agrarian Question in Zanzibar," 106. Similar statements can be heard from opposition supporters (who are Cameron's main informants). Unlike most other critics of the union, Aboud Jumbe, in his polemic *The Partner-Ship: Tanganyika-Zanzibar Union: 30 Turbulent Years* (Dar es Salaam, 1994), fully acknowledges the ideological role of pan-Africanism in its formation. He writes from first-hand knowledge.

35. Othman, "Tanzania: The Withering Away of the Union?" 56–57. The second of these actions was credited to Ali Hassan Mwinyi and Seif Shariff Hamad, two of the most popular politicians in Zanzibar's postrevolutionary history. (Hamad now leads the opposition.)

36. Ariel Crozon, "The Influence of Zanzibaris in Tanzanian Political Life, 1964–1992," in *Continuity and Autonomy in Swahili Communities*, ed. David Parkin (Vienna, 1994), 111–122.

37. Othman, "The Union with Zanzibar," 173; Othman, "Tanzania: The Withering Away of the Union?" In a debate in the Tanzanian parliament in July and August 2008, Zanzibar's CUF and CCM representatives united in their demands for the union's reform.

38. Zanzibar's officially backed romantic nostalgia is described in Bissell, "Engaging Colonial Nostalgia." Such sentiments are widespread among Zanzibar intellectuals, even among revolutionary internationalists such as the late Babu. By the end of Amour's last term in 2000, he and his allies had been pushed aside in an internal party conflict that was won by Amani Karume, Abeid Karume's son, who was perceived to have had more secure mainland backing.

39. That is how the events are interpreted in Jumbe, *Partner-Ship*, one of the most influential polemics against the union. Jumbe was a founding member of the ASP and succeeded Abeid Karume as president, facts that make his argument all the more credible to many readers. His chapter on religion draws on a study published in Swahili by an American Maryknoll Father that charts the efforts of the Catholic hierarchy to influence and moderate TANU's policies. Quoting passages from the book out of context, Jumbe suggests that it documents a TANU conspiracy to battle Islam. See John C. Sivalon, *Kanisa Katoliki na Siasa ya Tanzania Bara 1953 hadi 1985* (Peramiho, 1992).

40. Mazrui and Shariff, *The Swahili*, 160–162, for such rhetoric early in the multiparty period. For Arab race-baiting in mainland politics, see James R. Brennan, "Nation, Race and Urbanization in Dar es Salaam, Tanzania, 1916–1976" (Ph.D. diss., Northwestern University, 2002), and Brennan, "The Short History of Political Opposition and Multi-Party Democracy in Tanganyika, 1958–1964," in *In Search of a Nation: Histories of Authority and Dissidence in Tanzania*, ed. Gregory Maddox and James Giblin (Oxford, 2005). In 2005 such race-baiting came to the fore when Salim Ahmed Salim, a prominent diplomat and CCM figure, unsuccessfully sought the party's nomination for the union presidency.

41. For other examples, which bear striking resemblance to the matters discussed in chapter 5, see TEMCO, *The 2005 Presidential and General Elections*, 214–215.

42. Bakari explicates the *maskani* phenomenon in *The Democratisation Process in Zanzi-*

bar, 179–184. Other sources for violence include Commonwealth Observer Group, *The Elections in Zanzibar, United Republic of Tanzania, 29 October 2000* (London, 2001); and Human Rights Watch, *Tanzania: "The Bullets Were Raining": The January 2001 Attack on Peaceful Demonstrators in Zanzibar* (New York, 2002), available at www.hrw.org/reports/2002/tanzania/.

43. Larsen, "Change, Continuity and Contestation," 124–125; McGruder, "Madness in Zanzibar." Memories (and "memories") of the revolution led many to have misgivings about the reintroduction of multiparty politics in the 1990s.

44. TEMCO, *The 2005 Presidential and General Elections*, 61–62. For the 2001 broadcasts, see Human Rights Watch, *Tanzania: "The Bullets Were Raining."*

45. Larsen, "Change, Continuity and Contestation," 121–122, 124. Cameron, "Political Violence, Ethnicity and the Agrarian Question in Zanzibar," supports this interpretation, as does Rugalabamu, "Electoral Administration during the 1995 General Elections in Zanzibar." For a subtle reading of literary narratives of the revolution, see Garth Myers, "Narrative Representations of Revolutionary Zanzibar," *Journal of Historical Geography* 26 (2000): 429–448.

46. The details in this paragraph are taken mostly from Human Rights Watch, *Tanzania: "The Bullets Were Raining."* That valuable report notes that the government's interpretation of "terrorism" and al-Qaeda became prominent only months later, after September 11. But I heard such apologies from CCM apparatchiks as early as March.

47. Of course this observation cannot be taken as indicative of the overall makeup of the government forces; during a police riot, as during any other kind, the culprits most likely to be identified will be those already known to the victims.

48. Paradoxically, CUF supporters sometimes make such claims to mask the degree to which their party has a Muslim base: since CUF also enjoys support on the mainland, which, they assert, is "largely Christian," the charge that the party's appeal is based on religious solidarities presumably cannot be true. This and similar arguments are repeated uncritically by the authors of the Human Rights Watch report, who have close sympathies and connections to CUF. Echoes of Zanzibari myth-inflected narratives about Muslim victimization already circulate on the mainland.

49. The most prominent current example is Robert Mugabe, whose populist demagogy has won silent endorsement from other political leaders in Africa's southern cone. See Ian Phimister and Brian Raftopoulos, "Mugabe, Mbeki and the Politics of Anti-Imperialism," *Review of African Political Economy* 31 (2004): 385–400.

50. The literature on these new nativisms, especially in South Africa, is growing. Examples include Peter Geschiere, *The Perils of Belonging: Autochthony, Citizenship, and Exclusion in Africa and Europe* (Chicago, 2009); Francis Nyamnjoh, *Insiders and Outsiders: Citizenship and Xenophobia in Contemporary Southern Africa* (Dakar, 2006); Beth Elise Whitaker, "Citizens and Foreigners: Democratization and the Politics of Exclusion in Africa," *African Studies Review* 48, no. 1 (2005): 109–126; Martin J. Murray, "Alien Strangers in Our Midst: The Dreaded Foreign Invasion and 'Fortress South Africa,'" *Canadian Journal of African Studies* 37 (2003): 440–466; Jonathan Crush and David McDonald, eds., *Transnationalism, African Immigration, and New Migrant Spaces in South Africa*, special issue of *Canadian Journal of African Studies* 34, no. 1 (2000).

51. Appiah, *In My Father's House*—which, however, stresses the prism of New World pan-Africanist thought through which most African intellectuals were introduced to Western notions of race.

52. Amory, "The Politics of Identity on Zanzibar," 53.

53. Soyinka, "Triple Tropes of Trickery," *Transition* 54 (1991): 178–183; Ishmael Reed and Michael Franti, "Hiphoprisy," *Transition* 56 (1992): 158. For the rest of the Soyinka-Mazrui de-

bate, see Ali Mazrui, "Wole Soyinka as a Television Critic: A Parable of Deception," *Transition* 54 (1991): 165–177; Ali Mazrui, "The Dual Memory: Genetic and Factual," *Transition* 57 (1992): 134–146; and Soyinka, "Footnote to a Satanic Trilogy," *Transition* 57 (1992): 148–149.

54. For an account of broader debates within pan-African circles about "Arab slavery," see Hishaam D. Aidi, "Slavery, Genocide and the Politics of Outrage: Understanding the New Racial Olympics," *Middle East Report* 234 (2005): 40–56.

References

Archival Sources (cited more than once)

Colonial Office, Public Record Office (National Archives), Kew, UK
    618 East Africa Correspondence, Zanzibar
    822 East Africa Correspondence, Zanzibar Intelligence Summaries, 1963
Bodleian Library of Commonwealth and African Studies at Rhodes House, Oxford
    MSS. Afr. r. 89, W. R. McGeagh, Diaries, vol. 2, 1933–1935
    MSS. Afr. s. 542, F. H. Bustard, Acting Commissioner of Police, "Report on the Action Taken by the Police for the Suppression of the Riots on February 7th 1936," manscript, 16 February 1936
    MSS. Afr. s. 1361, T. Mayhew, August 1957
    MSS. Afr. s. 1429, John Frederick Hill, interview with John Tawney (no date)
    MSS. Afr. s. 1446, R. H. V. Biles, interview with John Tawney, 11 December 1971
    MSS. Afr. s. 2249, J. R. Naish, interview with John Tawney, 16 October 1971
    MSS. Afr. s. 2250/2, Zanzibar Symposium, 16 October 1971
    MSS. Brit. Emp. s. 22, G.932b, Papers of the Anti-Slavery Society
    MSS. Brit. Emp. s. 390, Clarence Buxton Papers
Zanzibar High Court Archives
Zanzibar National Archives

Newspapers and Magazines Consulted

Adal Insaf
Afrika Kwetu
Agozi
Al-Falaq
Kipanga
Kwetu
Mambo Leo
Mazungumzo ya Walimu wa Unguja
Mwangaza
Mwongozi
Sauti ya Afro-Shirazi
Sauti ya Wananchi
Tai

Tanganyika Standard (Dar es Salaam)
Voice of Workers
Zanzibar Voice

Published Sources (cited more than once)

Adam, Adam Shafi. *Kasri ya Mwinyi Fuad.* Dar es Salaam, 1978.
———. *Kuli.* Dar es Salaam, 1979.
Afro-Shirazi Party (ASP). *Afro-Shirazi Party: A Liberation Movement.* Book 2. Zanzibar, 1974.
———. *The History of Zanzibar Africans and the Formation of the Afro-Shirazi Party.* Zanzibar, 1965.
Aley, Juma. *Zanzibar: In the Context.* New Delhi, 1988.
Alonso, A. M. "The Politics of Space, Time and Substance: State Formation, Nationalism and Ethnicity." *Annual Review of Anthropology* 23 (1994): 379–405.
Alpers, Edward. *Ivory and Slaves in East Central Africa.* London, 1975.
Amin, Shahid. *Event, Metaphor, Memory: Chauri Chaura, 1922–1992.* Berkeley, 1995.
Amory, Deborah Peters. "The Politics of Identity on Zanzibar." Ph.D. diss., Stanford University, 1994.
Anderson, Benedict. *Imagined Communities.* Rev. ed. London, 1991.
Appiah, K. Anthony. *In My Father's House.* Oxford, 1992.
———. "Race, Culture, Identity: Misunderstood Connections." In Appiah and Amy Gutmann, *Color Conscious: The Political Morality of Race.* Princeton, N.J., 1996.
———. "Racisms." In *Anatomy of Racism,* ed. David Theo Goldberg. Minneapolis, 1990.
Babu, A. M. "The Background to the Zanzibar Revolution." In Amrit Wilson, *US Foreign Policy and Revolution: The Creation of Tanzania.* London, 1989.
———. "The 1964 Revolution: Lumpen or Vanguard?" In *Zanzibar under Colonial Rule,* ed. Abdul Sheriff and Ed Ferguson. London, 1991.
Bacuez, Pascal. "Une ethnographie dans son contexte: administration coloniale et formation identitaire." *Cah. d'ét. afr.* 38 (1998): 103–133.
Bakari, Mohammed Ali. *The Democratisation Process in Zanzibar: A Retarded Transition.* Hamburg, 2001.
Balibar, Etienne. "Is There a 'Neo-Racism'?" In Etienne Balibar and Immanuel Wallerstein, *Race, Nation, Class: Ambiguous Identities.* London, 1991.
———. "Racism and Nationalism." In Etienne Balibar and Immanuel Wallerstein, *Race, Nation, Class: Ambiguous Identities.* London, 1991.
Bang, Anne K. *Sufis and Scholars of the Sea: Family Networks in East Africa, 1860–1925.* London, 2003.
Banton, Michael. "The Concept of Racism." In *Race and Racialism,* ed. Sami Zubaida. London, 1970.
———. *The Idea of Race.* London, 1977.
Barwani, Sauda A., R. Feindt, L. Gerhardt, L. Harding, and L. Wimmelbücker, eds. *Unser Leben vor der Revolution und Danach B Maisha Yetu Kabla ya Mapinduzi na Baadaye.* Köln, 2003.
Batson, Edward. *Report on Proposals for a Social Survey of Zanzibar.* Zanzibar, 1946.
Baumann, Oscar. *Der Sansibar-Archipel.* Vol. 2, *Die Insel Sansibar und Ihre Kleineren Nachbarinseln.* Leipzig, 1897.
———. *Der Sansibar-Archipel.* Vol. 3, *Die Insel Pemba und Ihre Kleineren Nachbarinseln.* Leipzig, 1899.

Bennett, Norman. *A History of the Arab State of Zanzibar.* London, 1978.

Berry, Sara. *No Condition Is Permanent.* Madison, 1993.

Bhabha, Homi. "In a Spirit of Calm Violence." In *After Colonialism: Imperial Histories and Postcolonial Displacements,* ed. Gyan Prakash. Princeton, N.J., 1995.

Bissell, William C. "Conservation and the Colonial Past: Urban Planning, Space and Power in Zanzibar." In *Africa's Urban Past,* ed. David Anderson and Richard Rathbone. Oxford, 2000.

———. "Engaging Colonial Nostalgia." *Cultural Anthropology* 20 (2005): 215–248.

Bowles, B. D. "The Struggle for Independence." In *Zanzibar under Colonial Rule,* ed. Abdul Sheriff and Ed Ferguson. London, 1991.

Brass, Paul R. "Introduction: Discourses of Ethnicity, Communalism and Violence." In *Riots and Pogroms,* ed. P. Brass. New York, 1996.

———. *Theft of an Idol: Text and Context in the Representation of Collective Violence.* Princeton, N.J., 1997.

———, ed. *Riots and Pogroms.* New York, 1996.

Broomfield, G. W., and D. V. Perrott. *Habari za Walimwengu.* Book 3, *Masimulizi ya Juma juu ya Waingereza.* London, 1954.

Brubaker, Rogers. *Ethnicity without Groups.* Cambridge, Mass., 2004.

Brubaker, Rogers, and David Laitin. "Ethnic and Nationalist Violence." In Brubaker, *Ethnicity without Groups.*

Brubaker, Rogers, Mara Loveman, and Peter Stamatov. "Ethnicity as Cognition." *Theory and Society* 33 (2004): 31–64.

Bujra, Abdalla S. *The Politics of Stratification:A Study of Political Change in a South Arabian Town.* Oxford, 1971.

Burgess, G. Thomas. *Race, Revolution, and the Struggle for Human Rights in Zanzibar: The Memoirs of Ali Sultan Issa and Seif Sharif Hamad.* Athens, 2009.

———. "Remembering Youth: Generation in Revolutionary Zanzibar." *Africa Today* 46, no. 2 (1999): 29–50.

———. "Youth and the Revolution: Mobility and Discipline in Zanzibar, 1950–1980." Ph.D. diss., Indiana University, 2001.

Burton, Andrew. *African Underclass: Urbanisation, Crime and Colonial Order in Dar es Salaam.* Oxford, 2005.

Burton, Richard. *Zanzibar: City, Island, and Coast.* London, 1872.

Cameron, Greg. "Political Violence, Ethnicity and the Agrarian Question in Zanzibar." In *Swahili Modernities,* ed. Pat Caplan and Farouk Topan. Trenton, N.J., 2004.

Chakrabarty, Dipesh. *Provincializing Europe.* Princeton, N.J., 2000.

Chatterjee, Partha. *The Nation and Its Fragments.* Princeton, N.J., 1993.

Clayton, Anthony. *The 1948 Zanzibar General Strike.* Uppsala, 1976.

———. "The General Strike in Zanzibar, 1948." *JAH* 17 (1976): 417–434.

———. *The Zanzibar Revolution and Its Aftermath.* London, 1981.

Comaroff, John. "Of Totemism and Ethnicity." In John and Jean Comaroff, *Ethnography and the Historical Imagination.* Boulder, Colo., 1992.

Cooper, Frederick. *Africa since 1940: The Past of the Present.* Cambridge, 2002.

———. *Colonialism in Question.* Berkeley, 2005.

———. *Decolonization and African Society.* Cambridge, 1996.

———. *From Slaves to Squatters.* New Haven, Conn., 1980.

———. *Plantation Slavery on the East Coast of Africa.* New Haven, Conn., 1977.

Coupland, Reginald. *East Africa and Its Invaders.* Oxford, 1938.

Craster, J. E. E. *Pemba: The Spice Island of Zanzibar.* London, 1913.

Crofton, R. H. *Zanzibar Affairs, 1914–1933.* London, 1953.

Das, Veena. "Introduction: Communities, Riots, Survivors—the South Asian Experience." In *Mirrors of Violence,* ed. V. Das. Delhi, 1990.

———. *Life and Words: Violence and the Descent into the Ordinary.* Berkeley, 2007.

———. "Specificities: Official Narratives, Rumour, and the Social Production of Hate." *Social Identities* 4, no. 1 (February 1998): 109–130.

Das, Veena, and Arthur Kleinman. "Introduction." In *Violence and Subjectivity,* ed. Veena Das, Arthur Kleinman, Mamphele Ramphele, and Pamela Reynolds, 1–18. Berkeley, 2000.

Davidson, Basil. *Black Man's Burden: Africa and the Curse of the Nation-State.* New York, 1992.

Davis, Natalie Zemon. "The Rites of Violence: Religious Riot in Sixteenth-Century France." *Past and Present* 59 (1973): 51–91.

Des Forges, Alison. *Leave None to Tell the Story: Genocide in Rwanda.* New York, 1999.

Deutsch, Jan-Georg. "Imaginaries of the Past: Nostalgia and Social Conflict in Zanzibar, c.1950–2000." Paper presented at the conference Celebrating Memories and Visual Cultures, Zanzibar International Film Festival, Zanzibar, July 2–3, 2007.

Dikötter, Frank. "Group Definition and the Idea of Race in Modern China." *Ethnic and Racial Studies* 13, no. 3 (1990).

———, ed. *The Construction of Racial Identities in China and Japan.* London, 1997.

Fair, Laura. "Pastimes and Politics: A Social History of Zanzibar's Ng'ambo Community, 1890–1950." Ph.D. diss., University of Minnesota, 1994.

———. *Pastimes and Politics: Culture, Community, and Identity in Post-Abolition Urban Zanzibar.* Athens, Ohio, 2001.

Farsi, Shaaban Saleh. *Zanzibar: Historical Accounts.* n.p., 1995: first publ. 1955.

Farsy, Abdallah Salih. *The Shaf'i Ulama of East Africa,* trans. and ed. Randall Pouwels. Madison, 1989.

Farsy, S. S. *Swahili Sayings from Zanzibar.* Vol. 1, *Proverbs.* Nairobi, 1958.

Fearon, James, and David Laitin. "Violence and the Social Construction of Ethnic Identity." *International Organization* 54 (2000): 845–877.

Febvre, Lucien. "Civilisation: Evolution of a Word and a Group of Ideas." In *A New Kind of History: From the Writings of Lucien Febvre,* ed. Peter Burke. London, 1973.

Feierman, Steven. *Peasant Intellectuals.* Madison, 1990.

Feldman, Allen. *Formations of Violence.* Chicago, 1991.

Fitzgerald, W. W. A. *Travels in the Coastlands of British East Africa and the Islands of Zanzibar and Pemba.* London, 1898.

Flint, J. E. "Zanzibar, 1890–1950." In *History of East Africa,* vol. 2, ed. Vincent Harlow and E. M. Chilver. Oxford, 1965.

Foster-Sutton, S., V. Tewson, and C. A. Grossmith. *Report of a Commission of Inquiry into Disturbances in Zanzibar during June 1961.* Colonial No. 353. London, 1961.

Freitag, Ulrike, and William Clarence-Smith, eds. *Hadhrami Traders, Scholars, and Statesmen in the Indian Ocean, 1750s–1960s.* Leiden, 1997.

Furley, O. W., and T. Watson. *A History of Education in East Africa.* New York, 1978.

Geertz, Clifford. "The Integrative Revolution: Primordial Sentiments and Civil Politics in the New States." In *Old Societies and New States,* ed. Clifford Geertz. New York, 1963.

Gershoni, Israel. "The Emergence of Pan-Nationalism in Egypt: Pan-Islamism and Pan-Arabism in the 1930s." *Asian and African Studies* 16 (1982): 59–94.

Ghazal, Amal Nadim. "Islam and Arabism in Zanzibar: The Omani Elite, the Arab World and the Making of an Identity." Ph.D. diss., University of Alberta, 2005.

Glaser, Clive. *Bo-Tsotsi: The Youth Gangs of Soweto, 1935–1976.* Portsmouth, N.H., 2000.

Glassman, Jonathon. *Feasts and Riot: Revelry, Rebellion, and Popular Consciousness on the Swahili Coast, 1856–1888.* Portsmouth, N.H., 1995.

———. "No Words of Their Own." *Slavery and Abolition* 16, no. 1 (1995): 131–145.

———. "Slower than a Massacre: The Multiple Sources of Racial Thought in Colonial Africa." *American Historical Review* 109 (2004): 720–754.

———. "Sorting Out the Tribes: The Creation of Racial Identities in Colonial Zanzibar's Newspaper Wars." *JAH* 41 (2000): 395–428.

Gourevitch, Philip. *We Wish to Inform You That Tomorrow We Will Be Killed with Our Families: Stories from Rwanda.* New York, 1998.

Gray, John. *History of Zanzibar, from the Middle Ages to 1856.* London, 1962.

———. *Report of the Arbitrator to Enquire into a Trade Dispute at the Wharf Area at Zanzibar.* Zanzibar, 1958.

Guha, Ranajit. "Discipline and Mobilize." In *Subaltern Studies VII: Writings on South Asian History and Society,* ed. P. Chatterjee and G. Pandey. Delhi, 1992.

———. *Elementary Aspects of Peasant Insurgency in Colonial India.* Durham, N.C., 1999.

Gurnah, Abdulrazak. *Admiring Silence.* New York, 1996.

Hadjivayanis, George, and Ed Ferguson. "The Development of a Colonial Working Class." In *Zanzibar under Colonial Rule,* ed. A. Sheriff and E. Ferguson. London, 1991.

Hamdani, Mariam. "Zanzibar Newspapers, 1902 to 1974." Diploma thesis, Tanzania School of Journalism, 1981.

Hobsbawm, E. J. *Nations and Nationalism since 1780: Programme, Myth, Reality.* Cambridge, 1992.

Hollingsworth, L. W. *Milango ya Historia.* 3 vols. London, 1925–1931.

———. *A Short History of the East Coast of Africa.* London, 1929.

Horowitz, Donald. *The Deadly Ethnic Riot.* Berkeley, 2001.

———. *Ethnic Groups in Conflict.* Berkeley, 1985.

Horton, Mark, and John Middleton. *The Swahili: The Social Landscape of a Mercantile Society.* Oxford, 2000.

Hourani, Albert. *Arabic Thought in the Liberal Age.* Cambridge, 1983.

Human Rights Watch. *Tanzania: "The Bullets Were Raining": The January 2001 Attack on Peaceful Demonstrators in Zanzibar.* New York, 2002. Available at www.hrw.org/reports/2002/tanzania/.

Hunt, Nancy Rose. *A Colonial Lexicon: Of Birth Ritual, Medicalization, and Mobility in the Congo.* Durham, N.C., 1999.

Iliffe, John. *A Modern History of Tanganyika.* Cambridge, 1979.

Ingrams, W. H. *Arabia and the Isles.* London, 1942.

———. *Zanzibar: Its History and Its People.* London, 1931.

al-Ismaily, Issa bin Nasser. *Zanzibar: Kinyang'anyiro na Utumwa.* Ruwi [Oman], 1999.

Jefremovas, Villia. "Treacherous Waters: The Politics of History and the Politics of Genocide in Rwanda and Burundi." *Africa* 70 (2000): 298–308.

Johnson, Frederick. *Standard Swahili-English Dictionary.* Oxford, 1939.

Juma, A. M. "Cattle Riot (Vita vya Ng'ombe): A Case Study of Peasant Rising, Zanzibar." M.A. diss., Department of History, University of Dar es Salaam, 1982.

Jumbe, Aboud. *The Partner-Ship: Tanganyika-Zanzibar Union: 30 Turbulent Years.* Dar es Salaam, 1994.

Kakar, Sudhir. *The Colors of Violence.* Chicago, 1996.

Kapferer, Jean-Noel. *Rumors: Uses, Interpretations, and Images.* New Brunswick, N.J., 1990.

[Karume, Abeid Amani.] *Baadhi ya Hotuba Zilizotolewa na Makamo wa Kwanza wa Rais.* Zanzibar, 1965.

———. *Karume na Siasa, Uchumi na Maendeleo ya Kimapinduzi.* Zanzibar, 1973.

King, Kenneth James. *Pan-Africanism and Education: A Study of Race Philanthropy and Education in the Southern States of America and East Africa.* Oxford, 1971.

Klier, John D., and Shlomo Lambroza, eds. *Pogroms: Anti-Jewish Violence in Modern Russian History.* Cambridge, 1992.

Kopytoff, Igor. "The Internal African Frontier: The Making of African Political Culture." In *The African Frontier,* ed. I. Kopytoff. Bloomington, Ind., 1987.

Krapf, Ludwig. *A Dictionary of the Suahili Language.* London, 1882.

Larsen, Kjersti. "Change, Continuity and Contestation: The Politics of Modern Identities in Zanzibar." In *Swahili Modernities,* ed. Pat Caplan and Farouk Topan. Trenton, N.J., 2004.

Lefebvre, Georges. *The Great Fear of 1789: Rural Panic in Revolutionary France.* Trans. Joan White. New York, 1973.

Lemarchand, René. *Burundi: Ethnic Conflict and Genocide.* Cambridge, 1994.

———. "Revolutionary Phenomena in Stratified Societies: Rwanda and Zanzibar." *Civilisations* 5, no. 1 (1968).

Levene, Mark, and Penny Roberts, eds. *The Massacre in History.* New York, 1999.

Lewis, Bernard. *Race and Slavery in the Middle East.* New York, 1990.

Lofchie, Michael. *Zanzibar: Background to Revolution.* Princeton, N.J., 1965.

Loimeier, Roman. *Between Social Skills and Marketable Skills: The Politics of Islamic Education in 20th Century Zanzibar.* Leiden, 2009.

———. "Coming to Terms with 'Popular Culture': The Ulama and the State in Zanzibar." In Loimeier and Seesemann, *The Global Worlds of the Swahili.* Berlin, 2006.

Loimeier, Roman, and Rüdiger Seesemann, eds. *The Global Worlds of the Swahili.* Berlin, 2006.

Lonsdale, John. "The Moral Economy of Mau Mau." In Lonsdale and Bruce Berman, *Unhappy Valley: Conflict in Kenya & Africa.* Book Two, *Violence & Ethnicity.* London, 1992.

Loveman, Mara. "Is 'Race' Essential?" *American Sociological Review* 64, no. 6 (1999): 861–898.

Maliyamkono, T. L., ed. *The Political Plight of Zanzibar.* Dar es Salaam, 2000.

Malkki, Liisa. *Purity and Exile.* Chicago, 1995.

Mamdani, Mahmood. *When Victims become Killers.* Princeton, N.J., 2001.

Mangat, J. S. *A History of the Asians in East Africa.* Oxford, 1969.

Mapuri, Omar. *Zanzibar: The 1964 Revolution: Achievements and Prospects.* Dar es Salaam, 1996.

Martin, Esmond Bradley. *Zanzibar: Tradition and Revolution.* London, 1978.

Mazrui, Alamin, and Ibrahim Noor Shariff. *The Swahili: Idiom and Identity of an African People.* Trenton, N.J., 1994.

McGruder, Juli. "Madness in Zanzibar: 'Schizophrenia' in Three Families in the 'Developing' World." Ph.D. diss., University of Washington, 1999.

Mdundo, Minael-Hosanna O. *Masimulizi ya Sheikh Thabit Kombo Jecha.* Dar es Salaam, 1999.

Middleton, John. *Land Tenure in Zanzibar.* London, 1961.

Middleton, John, and Jane Campbell. *Zanzibar: Its Society and Its Politics.* London, 1965.

Miles, Robert. *Racism.* London, 2003.

Mrina, B. F., and W. T. Mattoke. *Mapambano ya Ukombozi Zanzibar.* Dar es Salaam, n.d. [1980].

Muhsin, A. "Slavery as It Used to Be Practised in Zanzibar." *Makerere College Magazine* 1, no. 4 (August 1937): 111.

Muhsin al-Barwani, Ali. *Conflicts and Harmony in Zanzibar: Memoirs.* Dubai, 1997.

Mukangara, D. "Race, Ethnicity, Religion, and Politics in Zanzibar." In *The Political Plight of Zanzibar,* ed. T. Maliyamkono. Dar es Salaam, 2000.

Musa, Saidi. *Maisha ya al-Imam Sheikh Abdulla Saleh Farsy katika Ulimwengu wa Kiislamu.* Part 1. Dar es Salaam, 1986.

Mwanjisi, Rungwe Kasanda. *Abeid Amani Karume.* Nairobi, 1967.

Nurse, Derek, and Thomas Spear. *The Swahili: Reconstructing the History and Language of an African Society.* Philadelphia, 1985.

O'Hanlon, Rosalind. "Recovering the Subject: Subaltern Studies and Histories of Resistance in Colonial South Asia." In *Mapping Subaltern Studies and the Postcolonial,* ed. Vinayak Chaturvedi. London, 2000.

Okello, John. *Revolution in Zanzibar.* Nairobi, 1967.

Othman, Haroub. "Tanzania: The Withering Away of the Union?" In *Zanzibar and the Union Question,* ed. C. M. Peter and H. Othman. Zanzibar, 2006.

———. "The Union with Zanzibar." In *Mwalimu: The Influence of Nyerere,* ed. Colin Legum and Geoffrey Mmari. London, 1995.

———, ed. *Babu: I Saw the Future and It Worked.* Dar es Salaam, 2001.

Pakenham, R. H. W. *Land Tenure among the Wahadimu at Chwaka, Zanzibar Island.* Zanzibar, 1947.

Pandey, Gyanendra. *The Construction of Communalism in Colonial North India.* Delhi, 1990.

———. "Peasant Revolt and Indian Nationalism." In *Subaltern Studies,* vol. 1, ed. R. Guha. Delhi, 1982.

———. *Remembering Partition.* Cambridge, 2001.

Parkin, David. "Swahili Mijikenda: Facing Both Ways in Kenya." *Africa* 59 (1989): 161–175.

Pearce, F. B. *Zanzibar: The Island Metropolis of Eastern Africa.* London, 1920.

Pearson, Michael N. *Port Cities and Intruders.* Baltimore, Md., 1998.

Peires, J. B. *The Dead Will Arise.* Johannesburg, 1989.

Peter, Chris Maina, and Haroub Othman, eds. *Zanzibar and the Union Question.* Zanzibar, 2006.

Petterson, Don. *Revolution in Zanzibar: An American's Cold War Tale.* Boulder, Colo., 2002.

Pouwels, Randall. "Eastern Africa and the Indian Ocean to 1800: Reviewing Relations in Historical Perspective." *IJAHS* 35 (2002): 385–425.

———. *Horn and Crescent: Cultural Change and Traditional Islam on the East African Coast, 800–1900.* Cambridge, 1987.

Powell, Eve Troutt. *A Different Shade of Colonialism: Egypt, Great Britain, and the Mastery of the Sudan.* Berkeley, 2003.

Prins, A. H. J. *Swahili-Speaking Peoples of Zanzibar and the East African Coast,* 2nd ed. London, 1967.

Ranger, Terence. "The Invention of Tradition Revisited: The Case of Colonial Africa." In *Legitimacy and the State in Twentieth Century Africa,* ed. T. Ranger and Olufemi Vaughan. London, 1993.

Rex, John. "The Concept of Race in Sociological Theory." In *Race and Racialism,* ed. Sami Zubaida. London, 1970.

Richards, Paul. *Fighting for the Rainforest: War, Youth, & Resources in Sierra Leone.* Oxford, 1996.

Rugalabamu, C. A. "Electoral Administration during the 1995 General Elections in Zanzibar." In *The Political Plight of Zanzibar,* ed. T. Maliyamkono. Dar es Salaam, 2000.

Sacleux, Charles. *Dictionnaire Swahili-Français.* Paris, 1939.

Saleh, Ali. *Zanzibar 1870–1972, le drame de l'indépendance.* Paris, 2007.

Salim, Ahmed Idha. *The Swahili-Speaking Peoples of Kenya's Coast, 1895–1965.* Nairobi, 1973.

Sanger, Clyde. "Introduction." In John Okello, *Revolution in Zanzibar.* Nairobi, 1967.

Sanjek, Roger. "The Enduring Inequalities of Race." In *Race,* ed. Steven Gregory and Roger Sanjek. New Brunswick, N.J., 1994.

Scott, James C. *Domination and the Arts of Resistance.* New Haven, Conn., 1990.
———. *Weapons of the Weak.* New Haven, Conn., 1985.
Scotton, James. "Growth of the Vernacular Press in Colonial East Africa: Patterns of Government Control." Ph.D. diss., University of Wisconsin, 1971.
Seppälä, Pekka, and Bertha Koda, eds. *The Making of a Periphery.* Uppsala, 1998.
Sheriff, Abdul. "An Outline History of Zanzibar Stone Town." In *The History and Conservation of Zanzibar Stone Town,* ed. A. Sheriff. London, 1995.
———. "The Peasantry under Imperialism." In *Zanzibar under Colonial Rule,* ed. A. Sheriff and E. Ferguson. London, 1991.
———. "Race and Class in the Politics of Zanzibar." *Afrika Spectrum* 36, no. 3 (2001).
———. *Slaves, Spices, & Ivory in Zanzibar: Integration of an East African Commercial Empire into the World Economy, 1770–1873.* London, 1987.
Sheriff, Abdul, and Chizuko Tominaga. "The Shirazi in the History and Politics of Zanzibar." Paper presented at the International Conference on the History and Culture of Zanzibar, Zanzibar, December 1992.
Sheriff, Abdul, and Ed Ferguson, eds. *Zanzibar under Colonial Rule.* London, 1991.
Shivji, Issa. "The Life and Times of Babu: The Age of Revolution and Liberation." *Law, Social Justice & Global Development,* 2001(2). Available at http://www2.warwick.ac.uk/fac/soc/law/elj/lgd/2001_2/shivji/ (accessed 5 June 2010).
Simon, Reeva. "The Imposition of Nationalism on a Non-Nation State: The Case of Iraq during the Interwar Period, 1921–41." In *Rethinking Nationalism in the Arab Middle East,* ed. James Jankowski and Israel Gershoni. New York, 1997.
———. "The Teaching of History in Iraq before the Rashid Ali Coup of 1941." *Middle Eastern Studies* 22 (1986): 37–51.
Smith, Anthony D. *The Nation in History: Historical Debates about Ethnicity and Nationalism.* Hanover, N.H., 2000.
Spear, Thomas. "Early Swahili History Reconsidered." *IJAHS* 33 (2000): 257–290.
———. "Neo-Traditionalism and the Limits of Invention in British Colonial Africa." *JAH* 44 (2003): 3–27.
Spencer, Jonathan. "On Not Becoming a 'Terrorist': Problems of Memory, Agency, and Community in the Sri Lankan Conflict." In *Violence and Subjectivity,* ed. Veena Das, Arthur Kleinman, Mamphele Ramphele, and Pamela Reynolds. Berkeley, 2000.
Stocking, George W. *Race, Culture, and Evolution: Essays in the History of Anthropology.* Chicago, 1982.
———, ed. *Volksgeist as Method and Ethic: Essays on Boasian Ethnography and the German Anthropological Tradition.* Madison, 1996.
Stoler, Ann Laura. "'In Cold Blood': Hierarchies of Credibility and the Politics of Colonial Narratives." *Representations* 37 (1992): 151–189.
———. "Racial Histories and Their Regimes of Truth." *Political Power and Social Theory* 11 (1997): 183–206.
Straus, Scott. *The Order of Genocide: Race, Power, and War in Rwanda.* Ithaca, N.Y., 2006.
Tambila, K. I. "Aspects of the Political Economy of Unguja and Pemba." In *The Political Plight of Zanzibar,* ed. T. Maliyamkono. Dar es Salaam, 2000.
TEMCO (Tanzania Election Monitoring Committee). *The 2005 Presidential and General Elections in Zanzibar.* n.p., n.d.
Tonkin, Elizabeth, Maryon McDonald, and Malcolm Chapman, eds. *History and Ethnicity.* London, 1989.

Vail, Leroy. "Introduction: Ethnicity in Southern African History." In *The Creation of Tribalism in Southern Africa*, ed. Leroy Vail. Berkeley, 1991.

Vansina, Jan. *Antecedents to Modern Rwanda: The Nyiginya Kingdom*. Madison, 2004.

Vidal, Claudine. "Le génocide des Rwandais tutsi et l'usage public de l'histoire." *Cah. d'ét. afr.* 38 (1998): 653–663.

———. "Questions sur le rôle des paysans durant le génocide des Rwandais tutsi." *Cah. d'ét. afr.* 38 (1998): 331–345.

———. *Sociologie des passions*. Paris, 1991.

Wacquant, Loïc. "For an Analytic of Racial Domination." *Political Power and Social Theory* 11 (1997): 221–234.

Wallerstein, Immanuel. "The Construction of Peoplehood." In Etienne Balibar and I. Wallerstein, *Race, Nation, Class*. London, 1991.

Weber, Max. *Economy and Society: An Outline of Interpretive Society*. Ed. Guenther Roth and Claus Wittich. New York, 1968.

Weinberg, Robert. "Anti-Jewish Violence and Revolution in Late Imperial Russia: Odessa, 1905." In *Riots and Pogroms*, ed. Paul Brass. New York, 1996.

Welliver, Timothy. "The Clove Factor in Colonial Zanzibar, 1890–1950." Ph.D. diss., Northwestern University, 1990.

White, Luise. *Speaking with Vampires: Rumor and History in Colonial Africa*. Berkeley, 2000.

Willis, Justin. *Mombasa, the Swahili, and the Making of the Mijikenda*. Oxford, 1992.

Wilson, Amrit. *US Foreign Policy and Revolution: The Creation of Tanzania*. London, 1989.

Wolf, Eric. "Perilous Ideas: Race, Culture, People." *Current Anthropology* 35 (1994): 1–12.

Yeros, Paris. "Introduction: On the Uses and Implications of Constructivism." In *Ethnicity and Nationalism in Africa*, ed. Paris Yeros. London, 1999.

Young, M. Crawford. "Nationalism, Ethnicity, and Class in Africa: A Retrospective." *Cah. d'ét. afr.* 26 (1986): 421–95.

Zachernuk, Philip S. *Colonial Subjects: An African Intelligentsia and Atlantic Ideas*. Charlottesville, 2000.

Zanzibar Center of Human and Democratic Rights. *Zanzibar Dola Taifa na Nchi Huru*. Copenhagen, 1994.

Zanzibar High Court. *Law Reports, Containing Cases Determined by the High Court for Zanzibar*. Vol. 7, *1939 to 1950*. Zanzibar, 1954.

Zanzibar National Party. *Whither Zanzibar? Growth and Policy of Zanzibar Nationalism*. Zanzibar, 1960.

Zanzibar Protectorate. *Annual Report of the Education Department for the Year 1927*. Zanzibar, 1928.

———. *Report of the Commission of Enquiry Concerning the Riot in Zanzibar on the 7th of February 1936*. Zanzibar, 1936.

Index

Page numbers in italics refer to illustrations.

Abdulla, Mohammed K., 352n20, 368n18

Abdulrahman, M., 85–86

Abeid Suweid, 249–50

abolitionism, 3, 6, 17, 30, 46, 49, 92, 111, 130, 140, 144

Africa, Western images of, ix

Africa Addio, ix

African, as racial or ethnic identity, 57–58, 59, 62, 111, 117, 132–39; after 1964, 288, 291. *See also* African Association; pan-Africanism

African Association, 6, 53–54, 57, 59–63, 76, 77, 108, 122–23, 138; early history of, 110–13; and tribal associations, 115, 116; and vilification of Manga, 203–204. *See also Afrika Kwetu; Afro-Shirazi Party (ASP)*

African Democratic Union, 345n43, 372n58. *See also* Human Rights League

African Sports Club. *See* football

Afrika Kwetu, 106, 108, 110, 122, 126, 144–45, 158–59, 203; and racial essentialism, 132–42

Afro-Shirazi Party (ASP), 4, 7, 17, 76, 106, 113, 116, 143, 151–54, 284, 293; cooperative shops, 161–62; establishment of, 63, 133, 138; and geopolitics, 269–74; on Makonde, 216; after revolution, 282, 286, 289–90; and revolution, 276–77, 373n62; and squatter evictions, 209–10; and War of Stones riots, 244–48, 252, 253–54, 257, 260–61. *See also* African Association; *Afrika Kwetu;* Afro-Shirazi Youth League (ASYL); *Agozi;* Chama cha Mapinduzi (CCM); elections

Afro-Shirazi Youth League (ASYL), 153–54, 158, 174, 265, 268, 272, 289; and revolution, 64, 154, 174, 214, 216, 219, 267, 276–77, 279; and War of Stones riots, 158, 238, 246

Agozi, 143–44, 151, 152–53, 168–69, 210–11, 212–13. *See also* Jamal Ramadhan Nasibu

Ahl-Badr, 192–93

Alawi, Yahya, 220, 221, 266, 275, 323n16

Aley, Juma, 162, 323n16

Al-Falaq, 60, 91–95, 99, 106–107, 126, 139, 144, 202–203, 204, 328n57, 343n10

Ali bin Swed, 258, 262–63

Alikumbeya, John, 259, 263

Amarsi Hansraji Raja, 249–51, 254

Ameir, Khamis Hassan, 185–86, 216–17, 219, 230, 352n20, 368n18

Amory, Deborah, 300

Amour, Salmin, 294

animal slaughter, 255

anti-communism, 271–72, 274. *See also* Cold War

anti-intellectualism, 271

anti-Semitism, 45, 128, 231–32, 274, 371n47

Appiah, K. Anthony, 18

Arab: ethnic identity, 34, 38–39, 50–53, 69, 91, 94, 107; ethnonym, 39, 98. *See also* Arabocentrism; Manga; Omani Arabs; Shihiri

Arab Association, 41, 44, 45, 58, 59–61, 76, 94–95, 98, 107, 123–24, 126, 127, 183; and debates on immigration, 202–203; and education, 81, 89; and Manga riot, 200, 203. *See also Al-Falaq*

Arab nationalism, 78, 82, 83–84, 86, 88, 131, 157, 269–71. *See also* Arab Association; Arabic; Egypt

Arabic, 4, 78, 84, 86, 89, 90–91, 107, 157, 301

Arabocentrism, 6, 23–39, 52

arson, 274–75

Asiatic, 53, 59, 132

asili, 136, 159

ASP. *See* Afro-Shirazi Party (ASP)

ASYL. *See* Afro-Shirazi Youth League (ASYL)

uto.

automobiles, as symbols of power, 168, 172, 220–21

Babu, Abdulrahman, 127, 128, 146, 153, 162, 174, 270, 274, 277; and Cold War rhetoric, 271; influence on later scholars, 243, 292–93, 377n33; after revolution, 289, 292–93, 377n33; testimony to Foster-Sutton Commission 241–42. *See also* Umma (political party)
Badr Muhammad, 128
Baghdad, 82
Bakari, Mohammed Ali, 285
Balibar, Etienne, 9
Bamanga. *See* Mmanga Said Kharusi
barbarism. *See* civilization and barbarism
Barghash bin Said, 32
Barnabas, Herbert, 112
Barwani, clan, 211–12
al-Barwani, Ali Muhsin. *See* Muhsin, Ali (Ali Muhsin al-Barwani)
al-Barwani, Hilal Muhammad, 209, 211, 213–14
al-Barwani, Muhammad Salim Hilal, 323n16
Barwani, Salim M., 121, 122
Batson, Edward, 55
Bibi Titi Muhammad. *See* Titi Muhammad
Biles, R. H. V., 179–80, 215–16
blood, 254–56
boycotts, 121, 128, 161–66, 171–72, 175, 207, 275. *See also* labor unions and strikes
Brass, Paul, 232–33
British colonialism: conquest, 23, 39–40; governing policies, 39–49, 59–61, 63, 144, 183, 186, 231, 283, 286. *See also* education
Brubaker, Rogers, 8, 11
Burundi, 21, 236
Busaid dynasty, 27–39, 40. *See also* Omani Arabs; sultans of Zanzibar
Busaidi, Saud A., 122, 208, 267
butchers, 167
Buxton, Clarence, 369n28

cannibalism, 85
caravan trade, 29
castration, 160, 366n75
Cattle Riot (1951), 125–27
Chama cha Mapinduzi (CCM), 284–85, 287–88, 291, 294–97
chepe, 118
children: criminalization of, 189; killing of, 230, 252, 257–59, 264, 279
China, 271, 272, 274
chosen traumas, 264, 292, 296–97, 298
Christianity and Christians, 3, 54, 111, 130, 131,

184, 297–98; and denigration of mainlanders, 6, 131, 273, 292, 294, 295, 297–98 (*see also under* Islam)
Chuini, 209
Chum, Muhammad, 260
citizenship, 52, 113, 129–30, 138–39, 144, 155–56, 174, 297. *See also* voter registration
Civic United Front (CUF), 285, 287–88, 291, 294–97
civil society, politicization of, 63, 147–49, 160–76
civilization and barbarism, 3, 6, 9, 10–11, 26, 34–35, 38, 48, 49, 291, 292; in electoral rhetoric, 157–58; in the interwar writings of the intelligentsia, 82–104. *See also* ushenzi; ustaarabu
class: 117; and race, 37, 120, 172, 286, 289–90, 291. *See also* labor unions and strikes
Clayton, Anthony, 40, 117, 182
Clove Growers Association (CGA), 44–46, 199
clove-buying crisis, 45–46, 94–95
cloves and clove production, 30, 31–34, 44–45, 291; clove picking labor, 95–102; Makunduchi clove-picking boycott, 98–102. *See also* crop theft; plantation production; reception of stolen goods
coconuts, 30, 44. *See also* crop theft; Manga riot (1936); reception of stolen goods
Cold War, 237, 266, 270, 271–74, 277, 289, 292–93. *See also* geopolitics
Comoros Islands and Comorians, 24, 288
Congo, 158, 271, 272. *See also* Manyema
constructivism, 14–15, 286
Cooper, Frederick, 41, 47, 108
cooperative shops, 128, 161–62
court records. *See* trials and trial records
crime and criminalization, 21, 172–73, 179–229, 243, 267, 291; criminal gangs, 189–91, 205, 215, 218–21; criminals and the War of Stones riots, 251–53; criminals as community leaders, 191–94, 217–20; "social" crime, 180–82, 198, 227. *See also* crop theft; looting; police; rape; reception of stolen goods; vigilantes; violence
crop theft, 185, 187–88, 191, 204–208, 210–11
crowd behavior, 217–20, 221–29, 234–35, 245–48, 250, 254, 261–63. *See also* violence
Cuba, 271, 272
CUF. *See* Civic United Front (CUF)

dacoits, 189. *See also* crime and criminalization
Damascus, 82
dance. *See* festive ritual

Dar es Salaam, 109, 120
Darajani, 67, 200, 238–39
Das, Veena, 236, 247, 248
Davidson, Basil, 299
disembowelment, 19, 160, 169, 256–57
district intelligence committees, 179, 220, 265
dockworkers, 117, 118, 120–22. *See also wachukuzi*
domestic service, 168–69

East African federation, 157, 270. *See also*
   union, Zanzibar and Tanganyika
education, 13, 17–18, 42, 75–91, 157
Egypt, 60, 78, 82, 91, 162, 269–71, 272. *See also*
   Nasser, Gamal Abdel; Suez crisis
elections, 59, 60–61, 63–64, 150–57, 166, 206,
   238; of 1957, 151; of January 1961, 154–55, 173;
   of June 1961, 155, 173; of July 1963, 173, 217,
   265, 266–69; after 1992, 284–86, 292. *See
   also* Legco (Legislative Council); Time of
   Politics; voter registration; War of Stones
   riots (1961)
ethnic divisions in Zanzibar: and British rule,
   40–44, 49–58; emergence before 1890,
   31–39; after 1964, 284–98. *See also* racial
   thought; tribe; *and individual ethnonyms*
ethnicity, 8, 11–16, 49–50; and class, 37

Fair, Laura, 110, 192, 319nn69,72
al-Farsy, Abdulla Saleh, 142, 146, 323n16,
   340n101
Feldman, Allen, 255
Feraji Mpira, 192–94
festive ritual, 89–90, 96, 97, 100–102, 149, 169–
   71, 277–78
Fiah, Erica, 109
football, 110
Foster-Sutton, Stafford, 148
Foster-Sutton Commission, 148, 203–204,
   215–16, 240–44, 286, 342n4
Freedom Committee alliance, 143, 151–54
funerals, 170–71
Fuoni, 207–208, 211

Gandhi, Mohandas, 175
Garvey, Marcus, 109
Gates, Henry Louis, 301–302
generation. *See* youth
genocide, 227–28, 248, 284. *See also* Rwanda
geopolitics, 113–14, 294–95; and rumor, 269–
   74, 280, 281. *See also* Cold War
Ghana, 220–21, 269–70. *See also* Gold Coast
Ghosh, Amitav, 259
Gold Coast, 75, 85. *See also* Ghana

Gourevitch, Philip, 227–28, 259
Government Secondary School, 81
gozi, 133–34, 138, 143
Guha, Ranajit, 175, 374n72
Gurnah, Abdulrazak, xi

al-Hadhrami, Abdullah Muhammad, 87, 89,
   323n17
Hadimu, 31–32, 34, 37, 48, 52, 57, 89–90, 95–
   102, 135, 183, 226; Hadimu fringe, 32
Hadramis, 196–97. *See also* Shihiri
al-Haj, Muhammad Abeid, 91, 95–96, 167, 217,
   219, 328n53, 352n20
Hanga, Abdulla Kassim, 289, 293, 371n43,
   377n33
al-Harara, 168
head wounds, 256
Hilal Muhammad al-Barwani. *See* al-Barwani,
   Hilal Muhammad
history: historical memory and personal subjectivities, 20–22, 236, 264–66, 281; intelligentsia's writings on, 62, 76–77, 83–94, 95,
   104, 144, 203; as myth and memory, x–xi,
   5–6, 19, 58, 62, 159, 282–83, 288, 290, 292,
   294, 296–97; subaltern intellectuals on, 77,
   99, 132, 145; universal, 83–84, 92. *See also
   under* June, as trope of memory; marriage;
   slavery
Hollingsworth, L. W., 81, 83–85, 88–89, 92
hooligans, 153, 154, 218, 245
Horowitz, Donald, 248
Human Rights League, 158, 164, 174, 246, 272,
   276, 277, 372n58

Ibadi, 38–39
immigration, debates on, 131, 174, 198, 201–
   203, 206, 215, 267–68
independence, 59, 64, 214, 264, 269, 276
India, 29, 30. *See also* Indians; South Asia,
   communal violence in
Indian National Association, 41, 45
Indians: and British rule, 40, 41, 43, 45; before
   1890, 29, 37–38; after 1964, 285–86; vilification of, 45–46, 97–98, 121, 123–24, 128, 129,
   161, 192, 194, 197, 205, 289–90, 338n86
Ingrams, W. H., 43
instrumentalism, 14–16, 19, 22, 23, 40–41, 50,
   59, 231, 238
intellectuals, x, 6–7, 12, 13, 14, 17–18, 61–62,
   144–46; elite intelligentsia, 18, 61–62, 75–
   104, 105–107, 123–32; subaltern intellectuals, 18, 61, 62, 76–77, 79–80, 99, 102–104,
   105–23, 125, 132–44

Ireland, Northern, 255
Islam, 6, 24–26, 30, 34, 36, 38–39, 62, 78, 81–82,
    84, 146, 301; and Cattle Riot, 125, 126; and
    denigration of mainlanders, 35, 88, 184, 186,
    270, 273, 293, 294, 295, 297 (see also under
    Christianity and Christians); and geo-
    politics, 273–74, 292, 294–95; intelligen-
    tsia's critiques of popular, 90–91; and race,
    88, 133, 139, 141–44, 340n101; and "terror-
    ism," 294, 297; and Washihiri, 39, 196–98;
    and ZNP, 130–31, 157, 170
Islamophobia, 295
Israel, 272–74, 275. See also Zionism
Itihad al-Watan, 128, 329n67

Jamal Ramadhan Nasibu, 138, 143, 152–53, 158,
    210, 277, 283, 344n24, 345n42. See also Agozi
Juma Ambari, 261–63, 289
Jumbe, Aboud, 323n16
June, as trope of memory, 174, 264–81. See also
    War of Stones riots (1961)

kafa'a, 141. See also marriage
Kakar, Sudhir, 235, 237
Kanji, S. H. M., 215, 243
Karume, Abeid Amani, 5–6, 112–13, 133–34,
    152–53, 156–57, 203–204, 209, 269, 344n35,
    362–63n32; after revolution, 284, 289, 290,
    291, 292, 293; during War of Stones riots,
    246–47, 255
Karume, Amani, 296
Kenya, 58, 269–70, 278. See also Kenyatta,
    Jomo; Mau Mau; Mwambao
Kenyatta, Jomo, 121, 122, 270
Kesi Mtopa Salimini, 136–37
Khalifa bin Haroub (sultan), 52, 69, 192
Khamis, S. M., 147–48, 149
al-Kharusi, Abdullah Said, 211, 245
al-Kharusi, Ahmed Seif, 107, 323n16
Kharusi, clan, 211
al-Kharusy, Ali Said, 86–87
Kichungwani, 252
Kiembe Samaki, 125–27
Kilimani Prison. See prison and prisoners
Kilwa, 24, 26
Kipanga, 172
Kitope, 209, 210, 220. See also Kitope Ndani
Kitope Ndani, 239, 249–51, 253–54, 257–58,
    259. See also Kitope
Kwetu, 109, 110

labor migration, 19, 48–49, 56–57, 101; and
    pan-Africanism, 109. See also immigration,

debates on; mainlanders; squatters (labor
    tenants)
labor tenants. See squatters (labor tenants)
labor unions and strikes, 57–58, 60, 116–23,
    162–63, 165, 207. See also boycotts; cloves
    and clove production
land reform, 285–86, 290–91
language. See Arabic; and under Swahili
Last, J. T., 46
Lefebvre, Georges, 279–80
Legco (Legislative Council), 43, 59–61. See
    also elections
Lemke, Ahmed, 60, 128
al-Lemki, Harith bin Suleiman bin Nasser,
    331n86. See also Mafveraky
Levi, Primo, 19, 233
Lofchie, Michael, 43, 61, 123, 125, 322n100
looting, 180, 194, 197, 214–15, 217
Lumumba (Human Rights League militant),
    272, 276, 277
Lumumba, Patrice, 271
Lyne, R. N., 48

machetes. See pangas
maduka, 188
Mafveraky, 99
Mahiwa. See Makonde
mainlanders, 6, 17, 48–49, 55–58, 91–92, 222–
    23, 225; and pan-African racial identity,
    108–23; stereotyped as criminals, 182–91,
    206–11, 214–17, 267, 291; and War of Words
    riots, 250–51. See also immigration, debates
    on; labor migration; Makonde; Manyema;
    nativism; Nyamwezi; squatters (labor ten-
    ants); tribe
Makerere College, 81, 92
Makonde, 137, 179–80, 208, 221, 239, 275, 297;
    stereotyped as violent criminals, 179–80,
    184–86, 207, 215–17, 253, 267, 292
Makunduchi, 90, 98, 133, 138, 145, 170. See also
    cloves and clove production
Mamdani, Mahmood, 7–8
Manga, 39, 118, 119, 161, 163, 188, 225; etymology,
    195; feared as racial avengers, 170, 214, 239,
    276, 278; as representative of all Arabs, 140,
    198, 202–204, 221, 228–29; stereotyped as
    criminals, 179–80, 188, 191, 194–201, 203–
    204, 212–14, 216; as victims of pogroms,
    39, 160, 203, 228–29, 234, 239–40, 243–44,
    251, 278
Manga riot (1936), 194–95, 198–201, 203
Manga-Shihiri riot (1928), 194–95, 197–98
Manyema, 113–14, 192, 222–23

marriage: debates over, 137–44; forced, 142, 279, 289; politicization of, 170–71

Marxism, 162, 239, 271, 289–90. *See also* Babu, Abdulrahman; Cold War; Hanga, Abdulla Kassim; Umma (political party)

masheha, 42, 166, 261–62, 276

maskani, 295–96

matusi, 147, 150

Mau Mau, 160, 271, 278

al-Mauli, S. M., 207

maulid, 170

Mavia, 185. *See also* Makonde

Mazrui, Alamin, 5, 14

Mazrui, Ali, 301

Mazrui clan, 28, 301

Mazungumzo ya Walimu, 75–76, 81–91, 97–98

memory. *See* June, as trope of memory; rumor; subjectivities; *and under* history

Mercury space project. *See* Tunguu

Mikunguni, 252, 257, 260

Milango ya Historia, 84

Miles, Robert, 8, 10

Miraji Selem, 249–50, 253–54, 258, 259

Mitikawani, 228–29, 258

Mkapa, Benjamin, 297

Mmanga Said Kharusi, 158

mob, usage, 361n15

modernity, discourses of, 12, 13, 80, 81–82, 84, 85, 88, 111, 115, 266, 283, 287; and newspapers, 150

Mombasa, 24, 26, 27, 28, 120

monarchism, 43, 124–25, 127, 129–30; anti-monarchism, 52, 113–14, 116, 160. *See also* Mwambao; National Party of the Sultan's Subjects; sultans

Mooring, George, 174

Mtoro Reihan, 108, 110, 112–13, 126, 134, 152–53. *See also Afrika Kwetu*

mudirs, 42, 262

Mugheiry, Ali Sultan, 60, 211–12

Muhammad bin Ahmed (*mwinyi mkuu*), 31

Muhammad Chum. *See* Chum, Muhammad

Muhsin, Ali (Ali Muhsin al-Barwani), 6, 107, 130, 156–57, 162, 174, 211, 268–69; and origins of ZNP, 126–29; on slavery, 92, 139–42; testimony to Foster-Sutton Commission, 241–42

multiracialism, 6, 87, 105, 106–107, 123, 124, 138, 140–41, 144, 159

Musa, Ali Sharif. *See* Sharif, Ali (Ali Sharif Musa)

Musa, Othman Sharif. *See* Sharif, Othman (Othman Sharif Musa)

Muyuni, 184

Muzariin Rangers. *See* United Agricultural-ists Organization (UAO)

Mwaka Koga, 90, 170

Mwambao, 130, 270

Mwembemimba, 256–57

mwinyi mkuu, 27, 28, 31–32, 34

Mwongozi, 107, 126, 128–29, 130–32, 138–39, 144, 147–48, 151, 206–207, 242, 245

mwungwana, 35

Naipaul, V. S., ix

Nasibu, Jamal Ramadhan. *See* Jamal Rama-dhan Nasibu

Nasir bin Abdulla al-Kathiri, 197–98

Nasser, Gamal Abdel, 157, 270–71, 345n39

Nassor bin Seif, 249–51, 253–54, 257–58

National Party of the Sultan's Subjects, 126–29

nationalism, x, 3–4, 6–7, 8, 12–13, 15, 61, 76–77, 80, 94, 105–107, 108, 166; and nativism, 123–24; racial, 61, 77, 105–106, 132–46, 298–302

nationalist orthodoxy, 7, 17, 131–32, 243, 273, 282–83, 286–87

native, 81, 323n18

nativism: African racial, 57–58, 59, 111, 124, 132–37, 288–90, 294, 299 (*see also* Afri-can, as racial or ethnic identity; pan-Africanism); anti-mainlander, 53–54, 60, 90, 122, 123–32, 174, 241–42, 243, 291–95, 299 (*see also* civilization and barbarism; *and under* Christianity and Christians; Islam); and electoral rhetoric, 157–59, 206. *See also* citizenship; immigration, debates on; voter registration

Ndengereko, stereotypes of, 292, 352n19

newspapers, Zanzibari, 150–51. *See also names of individual newspapers*

Ng'ambo, 37, 48, 66–67, 68, 110, 121. *See also* rent strikes

ngoma, 170, 277–78. *See also* festive ritual

Ng'weng'we, 138

Nkrumah, Kwame, 109

Norris, A. W., 75, 85

Nyamwezi, 114–16, 202, 292

Nyasa, 56, 136

Nyerere, Julius, 63, 109, 152, 157, 270, 292–94

Okello, John, 219, 277, 278–79, 282, 283

Omani Arabs: and British rule, 41–45; before 1890, 23, 27–39. *See also* Arab; Busaid dy-nasty; Manga; Yarubi dynasty

oral history, x–xi, 7

Organization of the Islamic Conference (OIC), 294, 295
ostracism, 164–66. See also boycotts
Othman, Abbas, 121, 122. See also Kenyatta, Jomo
Othman, Muhammad, 86, 87–88

PAFMECA. See Freedom Committee alliance
Pakenham, R. H. W., 100–101
pan-Africanism, 13, 57–58, 108–23, 132–37, 145, 269–71, 292, 293, 299–300. See also Ghana; Kenyatta, Jomo; Tuskegeeism
pan-Arab nationalism. See Arab nationalism
Pandey, Gyanendra, 231, 241, 243
pangas, 249
Pangeni, 258–63
paternalism during Time of Politics, 166–69
Pemba: and Arab identity, 34, 52; as ethnonym, 34, 52, 135; in nineteenth century, 32–34; rumors about, 217, 218–19, 267–68, 274–75, 359n127; before Seyyid Said, 27, 28; and Shirazi identity, 53, 102–103; and Unguja compared, 32–34, 36–37, 63, 102–103, 285, 290–91
Persia, 25–26, 85. See also Shirazi
plantation production, 44–49, 93. See also cloves and clove production; coconuts; slavery; squatters (labor tenants)
pogroms: definitions of, 231, 247; Russian, 231–32. See also violence
police, 172, 175, 186–87, 190, 198, 200, 207–208, 213–14, 241, 242–43, 268–69; and revolution, 64, 175, 269, 277
Portugal, 26–27, 92, 328n57
praedial larceny. See crop theft
primordialism, ix, 4–5, 14–15, 20, 286
Prins, A. H. J., 5
prison and prisoners, 189–91, 193, 226. See also crime and criminalization
Provincial Administration, 42, 78, 214

racial thought, 7–12, 16–18, 244; and color, 11, 87–88, 133–34, 135, 138; distinct from racism, 10; "new racism," 8–9; racial science, 8–10, 11, 44, 103; remaking, 284–302
raciology, 8
raia, 52
Ramadhani, Augustine, 111
Rankine, John, 60
rape, 19, 141, 142, 212, 218, 256, 279. See also marriage
Rashid Athuman, 260, 262–63
rationing, 53, 99
reception of stolen goods, 188, 191, 194, 199

rent strikes, 110, 191–94
resident (British official), 40
revolution, January 1964, ix, xi, 3–4, 64, 174–75, 219, 234, 269, 276–79, 282–84, 285–86; and historical memory, 296–97; and rumor, 170, 212, 216, 266, 275, 276–81, 283
riots. See Cattle Riot (1951); Manga riot (1936); Manga-Shihiri riot (1928); War of Stones riots (1961)
riot specialists, 232. See also crowd behavior
Robertson, P. A. P., 148
Rogger, Hans, 231
Rolleston, Ian, 200
Rudé, George, 247
rumor, 21, 169, 173, 179, 232, 234, 235–37, 264–81, 283; and crime, 179–80, 212–21; and geopolitics, 269–74, 280; during War of Stones riots, 245, 256. See also under revolution, January 1964
Rural Middle School, 81, 85
Russia, 272
Rwanda, 7–8, 16, 21, 40, 43, 50, 80, 227–28, 232, 296, 361n11, 366n84

Said bin Sultan al-Busaid. See Seyyid Said (Said bin Sultan al-Busaid)
Said Nassor, 249–50
Saleh, Ali, 288–89
Saleh, Ibuni, 336n51
Salima binti Abdulla, 258–59, 263
Sauti ya Wananchi, 267
"Sceptic" (pseudonym), 92, 141
Scott, James C., 237, 374n72
sedition laws, 151, 343n10
Seif, Abdulla Ahmed, 83, 84, 85, 88
"settler," in nativist rhetoric, 151, 157, 158–59, 169
sex scandals, 171. See also marriage, rape
Seyyid Said (Said bin Sultan al-Busaid), 29–30, 31
Shamte, Muhammad, 152, 154, 170, 173, 274, 323n16
Sharif, Ali (Ali Sharif Musa), 60, 152, 154, 274
Sharif, Othman (Othman Sharif Musa), 141, 152, 153, 271, 273, 275
Shariff, Ibrahim Noor, 5, 14
sheha. See masheha
Shihiri, 39, 118, 161, 163, 194, 196–98, 202, 212, 224
Shirazi, 25–26, 31, 32, 38, 39, 48, 52–56, 59–60, 63, 315n9; as African, 138; and electoral politics, 154, 285; as "non-native," 59, 135–36, 289, 319n69; Shirazi ethnic nationalism, 94–103, 145

Shirazi Association, 53–54, 60, 63, 77, 98–103, 138, 152. *See also* Afro-Shirazi Party (ASP); Shirazi

slavery, 3, 30, 34–37, 46–48, 55–57, 70–71, 182; "Arab," 3–4, 92–94, 290, 301; in debates about history, 92–94, 130–31, 135, 139–44, 156, 159–60, 256, 257, 301; in political rhetoric, 99–100, 112, 116, 156–57, 159–60; and squatter labor, 47–48, 182–83, 184. *See also* abolitionism

Smithyman, Mervyn, 166–67, 246

South Asia, communal violence in, 21, 230–31, 234, 236. *See also* Brass, Paul; Das, Veena; Kakar, Sudhir

Soyinka, Wole, 301

spears, 177, 225, 226, 228–29, 256, 258, 267

squatter evictions, 58–59, 163, 167, 205–11, 214, 215, 243, 251, 275

squatters (labor tenants), 47–48, 56, 57, 58, 70–71, 182–84, 187–88, 204–11, 285. *See also* squatter evictions

stevedores. *See wachukuzi*

Stoler, Ann, 7, 9, 279

Stone Town, 37, 65, 66–68, 110, 121, 224

stones, as instruments of discursive violence, 218–19, 228, 250, 258, 296

strikes. *See* labor unions and strikes

subaltern intellectuals. *See under* intellectuals

subjectivities, 20, 21, 59, 175, 230, 234–37, 247, 251

Suez crisis, 131, 158, 270

Sukuma, 114, 116. *See also* Nyamwezi

sultans of Zanzibar, 29; and British rule, 40, 43, 69; overthrow of, 3 (*see also* revolution, January 1964); as symbol, 52, 62–63, 76, 105, 190–91, 193–94; and ZNP, 129, 155. *See also* Busaid dynasty; monarchism; *names of individual sultans*

Swahili: culture, 4–5, 23–27, 300–301; as ethnonym, 24–25, 36, 46, 48–49, 55–56; language, 4, 24, 26, 27, 107, 131, 171, 300, 301; linguistic reform, 88–89

taifa, 116

Tajo, Ameri, 60, 99, 119, 122, 138, 145, 152, 154

Talati, K. S., 216

Tanganyika, 22, 42, 48, 57, 64, 111, 152, 154, 200, 220, 242, 267, 269–70. *See also* East African federation; mainlanders; Nyerere, Julius; TANU (Tanganyika African National Union); union, Zanzibar and Tanganyika

TANU (Tanganyika African National Union), 159, 270, 284, 293

Tanzania. *See* Tanganyika; union, Zanzibar and Tanganyika

teachers, 80–91, 128. *See also* education

Teachers Training School, 80–81, 83

Thompson, E. P., 247

Time of Politics, 59–64

Titi Muhammad, 159–60, 256

trials and trial records, 248–49, 250–51, 253–54, 259–60, 260–61, 265, 275

tribal headmen, 114, 115–16, 333n27

tribe: tribal associations, 113–16; tribal identities, 109, 134–37. *See also* ethnicity

Tumbatu, 31, 32, 37, 48, 52, 122, 135, 163

Tunguu, 271, 272

Turner, V. W., 235

Tuskegeeism, 80, 82, 89, 109

Uganda, 270

Umma (political party), 174, 274, 276, 277, 289

Unguja: in nineteenth century, 30, 31–32; and Pemba compared, 32–34, 36–37, 63, 290–91; before Seyyid Said, 27, 28–29

union, Zanzibar and Tanganyika, 64, 271, 285, 292–94. *See also* East African federation

United Agriculturalists Organization (UAO), 205–206, 208, 347n60; Rangers, 206, 209, 210, 214

United States, 271–72, 294–95. *See also* Cold War

ushenzi, 34–35. *See also* civilization and barbarism

ustaarabu, 38–39, 86–88. *See also* civilization and barbarism

vagrancy, 183

Vail, Leroy, 14

vigilantes, 205–206, 207–208, 213–14, 267, 276. *See also* United Agriculturalists Organization (UAO)

violence: criminal, 21, 180–81, 182–87, 189, 190–91, 192–93, 194–98, 205, 211–21, 214–29; as discourse, 19–20, 210, 218, 228–29, 230, 233–35, 254–63; ethnic and racial, ix, 16, 18–22, 64, 179–263, 264; since 1995, 285, 295–96, 297; and Omani rule, 31–32, 34; and political speech, 148–49, 160, 174–76, 233–34, 244, 254, 264–65, 266–67, 283, 295–98; and spontaneity, 175–76, 230–37, 241, 244–47, 284, 286. *See also* crowd behavior; disembowelment; genocide; rape; revolution, January 1964; squatter evictions; stones, as instruments of discursive violence; vigilantes; War of Stones riots (1961); *and names of other riots*

Vitongoji, 217
voter registration, 155–57, 206. *See also* citizenship; elections

wachukuzi, 117–20, 163, 172, 224. *See also* dockworkers
Wacquant, Loïc, 7
wahuni, 154. *See also* hooligans; youth
waqf, 191–92
War of Stones riots (1961), 21, 63–64, 148, 173, 207, 208, 210, 212, 213–20, 230–63; memories of, 264–81. *See also* June, as trope of memory; stones, as instruments of discursive violence
Washington, Booker T. *See* Tuskegeeism
Weinberg, Robert, 231–33
white supremacy, ix, 10, 11, 17, 300
Wingwi, 170, 274–75
witchcraft, 275
women: in informal economy, 117, 354n51. *See also* marriage; rape
World War I, 40
World War II, 53, 58, 119
Wright, W., 215, 217, 251

xenophobia, 11, 299. *See also* nativism

Yao, 56
Yarubi dynasty, 27–28
Yemenis. *See* Shihiri
Young, M. Crawford, x
youth, 113, 153–54, 174, 269, 343n21. *See also* Afro-Shirazi Youth League (ASYL); Youth's Own Union (YOU)
Youth's Own Union (YOU), 153, 219, 239, 274

Zahor Muhammad al-Barawa, 192–93
Zam Ali Abbas, 128, 323n16
ZaNews, 271
Zanj, 24, 26, 27
Zanzibar and Pemba People's Party (ZPPP), 154, 173, 174, 206–207, 266, 267, 274
Zanzibar National Party (ZNP), 4, 6, 58, 63, 76, 123–32, 174, 206–207, 270; cooperative shops, 162; electoral rhetoric, 157–58; formation of, 61, 107, 124–28; and geopolitics, 270–74; and labor unions, 162–63, 174; organization during Time of Politics, 162; and squatter evictions, 209, 210; on War of Stones, 214–15, 241–44; and War of Stones trials, 249, 257. *See also* *Mwongozi*; Youth's Own Union (YOU)
Zanzibarization, 174, 175, 268
Zionism, 131, 273. *See also* Israel

JONATHON GLASSMAN is Associate Professor of History at Northwestern University. He is author of *Feasts and Riot: Revelry, Rebellion, and Popular Consciousness on the Swahili Coast, 1856–1888*, which was awarded the Herskovits Prize in African Studies.